BOOKS BY STEFAN HEYM

Hostages

Of Smiling Peace

The Crusaders

The Crusaders

STEFAN HEYM

THE
Crusaders

1948

LITTLE, BROWN AND COMPANY · BOSTON

To Gertrude

NOTE

THIS is a historical novel despite the fact that to many of my generation the events portrayed here are not history in the sense of retrospect but part of their lives — and possibly a very important part. But books are not written for the current year alone; and those about this war will in time assume the color of history.

Certain events described in this book took place. There was a Fourth of July leaflet; the American Army helped to liberate Paris, and it operated a radio station in Luxemburg. It fought the Battle of the Bulge and it encircled the Ruhr area. There were Germans penetrating our lines in American uniforms, and some of them were executed. There is a mining village called Ensdorf, and the tragedy of the Woman of Ensdorf, by and large, happened as I wrote it. And there was also a man named Kavalov. The stories of these two people I took from life. I think they are worth it.

All other characters and their connection with events, actual or fictional, are purely my own invention. Should anyone find that he has done similar things or expressed himself in a similar way, under circumstances similar to those related in this book, he may feel pleased, or perhaps peeved, imagining that he has ended up in the printed word. But it isn't he at all. It is somebody else who came out of my typewriter.

S.H.

CONTENTS

CONTENTS

The Crusaders

Book One

FORTY-EIGHT ROUNDS
FROM FORTY-EIGHT GUNS

I

THE GRASS, this good, soft, lush grass. You could lie in it, and if you stretched out flat, the grass about you would be as high as your body. It would sway in the wind which came from the Channel, from the beach-heads still strewn with the remnants of invasion, the gear thrown off in battle, the fragments of German guns, the vehicles smashed and twisted. At moments, it seemed to Bing that this wind still carried a trace of the heavy, sweet odor of the dead. But that could not be — the dead had been buried in the dunes of Omaha and Utah. He himself had seen the parties of German prisoners dig the graves; and now the graves were filled up with bodies and sand, and the wind caressing the grass around him had caressed the crosses in the dunes.

He turned his head sideways. Between the leaves of grass he could see the Château, Château Vallères, with its round tower, its dilapidated roofs, its small, half-blind windows. At a distance, from the shed near the brook flowing into the still moat which closed like a dark green belt around the Château, sounded an unceasing, steady flap-flap-flap; the tenant's two daughters, fat and strong, with crude red faces which made it difficult to distinguish which one was Manon and which Pauline, were beating clean the wash — the shirts and pants and drawers and socks and undershirts of the Detachment.

It was a fine day for washing, Bing thought. In a little while, Manon and Pauline would emerge from the shed and hang the wash. Stretching themselves, they would try to reach the line suspended between the trees of the copse near the brook, their skirts would slide up, and between the hems of their skirts and the tops of their black wool stockings, a strip of the red flesh of their thighs would show.

Bing folded his hands behind his head and turned his eyes toward the sky. The sky was blue. It didn't have the depth of the English sky he had

3

seen before he went into the invasion; it was different. It was Continental sky, the sky he remembered from his boyhood. Not a cloud in this light-flooded sky. Insectlike, an observation plane crawled across, its thin drone swallowed by the height. Except for the plane, there was peace.

The girls came out of the shed, the wet wash in their plump arms. Bing got up and slowly walked toward them.

"*Bon jour, mes petites,*" he said.

"*Bon jour, M'sieur le Sergent,*" said Manon, and the sisters giggled.

"When will you have my laundry? And I want my shirt pressed, this time — you won't forget?"

"Will you have *du chocolat* for us?" asked Pauline, closing her eyes as if she were tasting the melting chocolate on her tongue.

"We will see, we will see. You're round enough as is."

"Tomorrow evening, maybe," said Manon, "we will have finished. The sun is good, everything will dry fast. But there is no hurry. You are not going to move out."

"You are very clever," said Bing. "How do you know?"

They giggled again. "*Le Capitaine* Loomis, he has had two soldiers carry the big bed of the Comtesse into his room. It has a canopy, this bed has, a light green canopy full of dust, and the soldiers were sneezing and cursing, you should have heard them. And *Monsieur le Commandant* Willoughby, he has ordered two geese killed for tomorrow night, and he has sent the *Sergent* Dondolo to Isigny to buy cheeses."

Pauline broke in. "This Dondolo! He is the one! He trades your cigarettes for Calvados, and then he sells the Calvados to the soldiers. A very shrewd man. He will be rich."

Bing laughed. "You don't think I will be rich?"

Pauline and Manon both studied him. Then Manon said, "You? You are too serious. You always think."

He did not answer. The girls began to hang the wash.

The drawbridge over the moat had not been raised for generations. Its hinges and chains were corroded by rust; its aged wooden planks groaned each time one of the heavy American trucks drove over it into the court-yard of Château Vallères.

Lieutenant David Yates stood on the bridge, his back against the railing, his feet nervously crushing and breaking the fine splinters which formed the top layer of the wood. The sun beat down on him from the sky; under his helmet, his head felt like a piece of dough shoved into the oven and about to rise. From the moat, a second, reflected, wave of heat was coming at him, carrying with it the foul smell of decaying water plants.

Yates wiped away a drop of sweat that was trickling from behind his ear

4

and making its itching way down the side of his neck. He felt sticky and dirty and uncomfortable. Added to everything else was the acute misery of being unable to make up his mind. The dark, cavernous shade of the Château's interior, the possibility of going to the pump to splash his face and hands, lured him; but he didn't dare leave the bridge for fear of missing Bing and having to delay the start of his mission. It was the same as standing at a street corner, back home, to hail a taxi. No chance. The few that came by would be filled up. But step off the curb to walk or catch the streetcar, and not only would the long-awaited taxi arrive, but somebody else would take it.

Where was Bing keeping himself?

"Abramovici!" Yates called sharply.

The little Corporal, who was marching along in the shade of the Château's main building, stopped. Under his helmet, he looked to Yates like a turtle whose predetermined route had been disturbed by some insurmountable obstacle. Then Abramovici discovered Yates and, moving his short legs faster, he crossed the yard and came onto the bridge.

"Pull up your pants!" said Yates, wearily. "Try to look like a soldier."

This pained Abramovici, who had been trying to look like a soldier ever since he got into the Army and who believed that he was moderately successful. And he was all the more pained because the reproach came from Yates, whom he liked and who usually didn't care if anyone looked like a soldier or not.

"I can't help it," he protested, "if the Government issues me pants that don't fit."

Yates concealed a smile. "It isn't the Government, it's your stomach."

Abramovici looked at his stomach. His freckled lids covered his pale blue eyes as he glanced downwards. His pants had slid from his midriff, and his shirt was split open over his bulge. Then he glanced up and compared his own squatness with the well-knit physique of Yates who even in the sweated shirt that stuck to his chest maintained a certain distinction.

"You see what I mean?" said Yates. "If Captain Loomis caught you, you'd have your behind in a sling. Now go and fetch Bing. And tell him to hurry. No," he added, noticing Abramovici's questioning expression, "I have no idea where he is. Show some initiative, man! Find him!"

"Yes, sir."

Yates watched Abramovici trot off and disappear beyond the drawbridge, the butt of his rifle kicking against his calves. Abramovici was a good man, invaluable. He knew both German and English shorthand. But at times he was annoying.

What didn't annoy him? Yates asked himself. The little things that connived to throw him seemed to accumulate. They nagged at his sense of

5

well-being. And his dependence on his sense of well-being was what annoyed Yates most.

It had been difficult enough to adjust himself to the idea that David Yates, Ph.D., Assistant Professor of Germanic Languages at Coulter College, was being changed into a soldier, for reasons and purposes which he could clearly perceive, but which did not blot out his belief that war was vicious, a throwback, a degrading attempt at solutions for problems that never should have been allowed to arise. Nevertheless, once he became part of it, he followed the patterns and did what he was supposed to do without rancor and even with a show of pleasantness, expecting that the small things would cease cluttering up his life.

Yates caught himself; for the last few minutes his damp palm had been rubbing the wart on his left index finger. He had several warts and he was self-conscious about them. The first one had appeared on his hand shortly after he had been inducted, and the closer he had come to where the war became serious, the more warts he had grown. They appeared at identical spots on his fingers. The Army medics had treated them with chemicals, they had burned them out with electricity, they had tried x-rays. The warts had come back. They were embarrassing and offensive to him. Then one doctor had told him, "Let them be. They'll go away sometime. They're psychosomatic."

"Psychosomatic," Yates had said. "I see."

"No, you don't," the doctor had said. "But don't let it bother you. They'll go away."

So it wasn't really his body that grew the warts, thought Yates, it was his soul. Uncanny. It intrigued him for a while, the Why of it. But he never really dared to answer the Why. He still tried the chemicals, and blamed the dirt, the food, the cold, the heat. The people with whom he was thrown, the war into which he had been pushed, had left little ambassadors on his skin.

Abramovici finally returned, trailing Bing. By this time, Yates's anger had petered out. Resignedly he asked, "Where have you been keeping yourself? Damn it! You knew you were to report to me!"

Bing's high spirits had vanished upon seeing the stocky figure of the Corporal cut across the field and leave a broad trail of broken blades in the high grass. Whatever it was Yates wanted, Bing was determined to try to talk him out of it.

"Nobody told me anything," Bing stated matter-of-factly.

Loomis screwed that one up, thought Yates. Loomis always did. The Captain was mostly concerned about himself, his own comfort, his own safety. He made the men stay out in the fields, while the officers slept in the beds of the Château. Yates knew that Bing and Preston Thorpe and some

6

other men had found themselves a dry spot in the attic of the Château's tower; but he kept that fact from Loomis.

"We've had a call from Matador," Yates said. "They want a special leaflet. Get your equipment and let's go."

Under other circumstances, Bing would have welcomed the trip to General Farrish's Armored Division, which had been given the code name Matador. The trip was a change of routine and atmosphere. But Bing felt too tired.

He said, "I've just returned from the prisoners' cage. I was there two days. I talked to dozens of them, and my brain is crapped up. I wouldn't be of any use to you."

Yates saw the shadows of fatigue under the Sergeant's eyes. The boy *was* worn out. He hesitated.

Bing continued, "If you bring all the information from G–2 at Matador, I'll get out the leaflet for you. I won't let you down. But I must get some sleep."

Yates snorted. "That's just it! We don't want to write the leaflet!"

"You don't?" Bing searched the face of his lieutenant, trying to find some sense in the apparent contradiction. From the wings of Yates's sharp nose two lines ran down to the corners of his full, sensitive mouth; Bing saw the dust lodged in them. He realized that Yates, too, must be frightfully tired; Major Willoughby, in charge of the Detachment, was sending Yates everywhere because the Lieutenant was one of the unit's few officers with intelligent judgment; and Yates, like a good shnook, always went and came through. "Well," said Bing, "if there's going to be no leaflet for Matador, why the hell do we have to go?"

Yates grew impatient. "I'd like to see any other outfit in this Army where so many people ask so many dumb questions. Get your stuff and get going — it's not my decision, it's Mr. Crerar's and Major Willoughby's."

Bing shrugged. He left, disappearing through the small, arched door to the Château's aged, round tower. Yates studied the fissures in the tower. It seemed to him they had become deeper and wider — the bombings at night made the old walls shake to their foundations. He liked the Château; he had a sense for tradition and romance. Not that there was much of that left around, after the Germans had taken over. One day Mademoiselle Vaucamps, the chatelaine, *petite,* ruffles and lace and parchment face, had noticed his interest and shown him, in return for some cigarettes, what remained of the treasures.

In front of the delicate Sèvres clock, Mademoiselle Vaucamps had stopped and told him of the big Bavarian officer who had commanded the Germans at Vallères and warned her to keep an eye on the clock. The Germans would return soon, he had said, and he planned to send the clock to his home in Bayreuth.

"Don't you worry," Yates had assured the little old woman. "He won't come back." But underneath, he was not at all sure that the officer from Bavaria wouldn't get his second chance at the clock.

Dust covered the dense, high hedges along the road. Dust hung over the road, thrown up by the vehicles whose heavy wheels bit and ground into it, tore holes in it from which new dust constantly arose. So fine was this dust that it would sink back only slowly, if at all. It powdered the faces of drivers and passengers, it penetrated the uniforms, it parched the throat and inflamed eyes and nostrils.

Sheaves of wire, equally white with dust, ran alongside the hedges. Behind the hedges, Yates knew, were other hedges. All of Normandy seemed to be divided into small squares, and each square was hedged in. The men who had planted and raised the hedges must have had a strong sense of property rights, he thought. The solid green walls prevented the cattle from straying; they kept your neighbor from looking into your own field.

Now, troops were lying in most of these fields. Seeking what little concealment could be found, they huddled close to the hedges, dug holes into the root-veined soil; or, if they were lucky enough to find an orchard, they settled underneath the fruit trees.

"If the Germans could get more stuff up in the air, they could blast the whole Army to bits." Yates pointed vaguely ahead.

Bing looked up. Convoys of trucks, half-tracks, cars, crept along the narrow road in both directions. A snarl seemed to develop at a crossing.

Yates went on, "All they need do is strafe along the hedges and bomb the fields. Everybody sitting on everybody else's neck." He took off his helmet and let the breeze touch his wet hair.

Bing leaned back, his eyes resting on the gray at Yates's temples, the only gray on an otherwise perfect head of brown, wavy hair. He saw the frown on Yates's well-formed forehead.

"The Kraut prisoners tell me their air force is going to be back in strength any day," Bing said slowly. "I remember the first days here, when we had to hop out of the cars and make for the ditches. And then they came down and — you feel so God-damned naked when the dirt flies up around you. Naked and scared, and your head is heavy, and you want to pretend to yourself that you're very small, and all the time you know that you're as big as life. . . ."

Yates had come in on D plus Two; he had had his share of hopping into ditches and being swooped down at by the Messerschmitts. His mind still retained the image of the brush into which he had retched, every leaf of it.

He forced a laugh.

"Cigarette?" Bing offered.

"Thanks." Yates had trouble lighting the cigarette against the wind. He

8

used the pause to find a safer subject. "Poor slobs, the German prisoners. Just look at their faces! They've gone through the same thing. Only they got it worse."

Bing glanced sideways at his lieutenant. Was he kidding? "I hate 'em," he stated categorically. He made the Krauts sweat. He got out of them all he wanted to know — and more. They opened up under him like budding stinkweeds under the sun.

"Hate . . ." Yates said doubtfully, and added in his lecturing way: "This is a scientific war. You want to understand the Germans, don't you? If you have to gauge their state of mind, you have to put yourself in their place. How can you, if you hate them?"

"I can," said Bing, sarcastically.

"Maybe I'd feel that way, too, if I'd been driven out of Germany, out of my own country. But you must be able to detach yourself from the work we're doing."

"I don't want to," said Bing.

"You're very young!" Yates said. "Look at things as they are. At all sides of the question. The man over there's been doing the same thing you've been forced to do: He's followed orders. He's got the same trouble: Protecting his own posterior. He's the victim of his politicians as we're the victims of ours. That's what determines his mind, and that's what we want to get at — don't we?"

"You talk like the German prisoners," said Bing.

Yates's hand shot up, but he controlled himself and adjusted the sweat-soaked collar of his shirt.

"I can shut up . . ." offered Bing.

"You've got a right to your opinions," Yates said sourly.

Bing wanted to make amends. After all, Yates was a decent guy. "When you talk to them," he asked, "what line do you take?"

Yates said, "Yesterday, I had a paratrooper. He told me he wasn't a Nazi. He asked me what we were doing over here. We Germans and Americans had the same kind of *Kultur*. Neither the Germans nor Hitler had planned to attack the United States, he said. A man of education, too."

"And what did you answer?"

"I asked him whether concentration camps were his conception of culture. And then he turned around and said the British had invented the concentration camps in the first place."

"Of course he was a Nazi!"

"Of course!" Irritated, Yates challenged, *"You* try to answer them."

"Too many sides to the question," said Bing.

Yates got the quip. And he couldn't answer Bing, either.

Bing was suddenly serious. "They believe they know what they're fighting for. And they think we don't."

9

"They don't know either. Nobody knows. You start out into the war equipped with newspaper headlines. Flimsy stuff."

Bing said, "In one part of the cage at Omaha Beach, they're keeping Americans — deserters. I talked to one. He was from Farrish's Division. They'd been in the line since they hit the beach. Of his whole platoon, three men were left. Three men. He said he wanted to live, just live. He didn't give a damn how and under whom."

Yates felt for the deserter.

"If that's so," he said uncertainly, "then what are you going to feed these guys?" And *these guys* meant himself, too. "And what're you going to tell a German to compel him to leave his own kind, his own organization, to surrender at the risk of death? Show me an idea that strong!"

Bing couldn't. He felt it, but he couldn't express it.

Yates spit on the road. "Farrish wants us to produce a leaflet along that line, with all the sauce about justice, democracy, freedom."

"Farrish?" asked Bing. "Of all people . . ."

"Yes, Farrish." Yates smiled. "He isn't going to get it. And we'll have to tell him so."

"Nice job they picked for us," said Bing.

"For me," corrected Yates. "You probably won't have to say anything. You're just a demonstration of good will."

"But why?" Something in Bing resisted the supercilious refusal, the inconsistency. "Why shouldn't he get that kind of leaflet?"

Yates stared at his hand, at the confounded warts. "People like you and me are inclined to exaggerate the importance of the word. In the end, what counts are guns and more guns, planes and more planes. And — this is the Army. Why should Major Willoughby or Mr. Crerar go out on a limb? All our Detachment is supposed to do is to inform the Germans they're in a tough spot, and if they raise their hands they'll be treated right and get corned beef hash and Nescafé."

"Maybe that's why we're still bottled up on a little patch of land called Normandy?"

It's a fresh viewpoint, at least, Yates reasoned. The kid has his wits about him. But he's just a kid. At his age, I saw my father lose his shirt in the crash, and from then on, until I landed the job at Coulter, it was always touch-and-go. . . . There was no sure thing. There were far too many questions and not enough answers and none of them clear. And that's why the only credible appeal to the Germans was corned beef hash, Nescafé, and the beauties of the Geneva Convention. . . .

Farrish liked to have his Command Post near the front. This one was set up in the sprawling park belonging to the château of a French merchant — a château quite different from crumbling Vallères.

Yates, not without envy, admired the rococo statuettes, the spacious windows, the high arch of the door to the manor house. Out of this door came two anemic-looking children, their bony little legs sticking out from neat little overcoats. The children were followed by an old man in a black frock coat with silver buttons. He took them by the hand and led them off into the park, for their afternoon walk.

Yates and Bing stared after the children and the old man. It was all so incongruous. The three could have stepped right out of a Maupassant novel onto the ground which shook from the fire of the near-by mobile heavy artillery.

A soldier came toward Yates. "Captain Carruthers will see you now, sir," he said.

"Can you fix up the Sergeant?" asked Yates. "He's had no chow. . . ." Then, turning to Bing, "No reason for both of us to starve. Meet me at G–2."

Bing went with the soldier, who had the serious face of a child thrown into the world too soon. "Can you beat it?" the soldier said. "I sleep in a hole in the ground, and I've got good reason for it. Those kids and the old man, they stay in the house, all alone. We've told them to move into the cellar. The old man says he's worried the kids would catch cold. At night, the Jerries start firing, and you can hear their big stuff come over — *huiiit, huiiit.* The kids stay on the upper floor, in the dark, naturally. Crazy. . . ."

He pointed to an alley. "See this road? Take it for about three hundred yards, then turn left, and you'll find a clump of trees. That's where the mess tent is set up. We ate about an hour ago; so you'll have to argue with the Sergeant."

Bing found the kitchen. He didn't have to argue. He was given what was left — heated C-ration which had grown cold again, crackers, lukewarm coffee. He sat down on the ground, his back against a tree trunk, and began to eat listlessly. Three black sows, their teats caked with mud, made their way toward him, pushed their snouts against his feet and legs, and grunted furiously when he pulled up his knees and tried to defend his food.

A voice behind him said, "Don't mind them now — you should have seen them when it was raining here. They ran around like mad, splashing everybody."

"Why don't you shoot them?"

"We kind of like them," said the voice, "they're friendly. They belong to the farmer down the road. He's got two daughters. The girls say, if you kill the pigs, no *coucher avec vous.* You see how it is."

Bing kicked the sow who had come closest to his food. The animal retreated a few steps and lay down, shaking its head.

"All we have to do is to keep the officers away from the pigs," the voice continued, "and the other way round. The other day, one of them got killed, stepped on a mine or something. We had pork chops."

"You don't think anyone — the big one over there, for instance — would step on a mine this afternoon? I could make it my business to be here for supper, you know . . . !"

The soldier who belonged to the voice stepped around the tree and placed himself protectingly before the pigs. He was a tall fellow with twinkling eyes and with hands which looked as if they could kill any pig with one blow. "You're a killer, aren't you?" he said to Bing.

Bing got up and threw the rest of his hash to the animals. "I like pork chops," he said; "can I help it?"

"I like the girl down the road," said the man, "see?"

Bing resolutely closed his mess kit. "I won't interfere." He smiled. "So long!"

"So long!"

Bing entered the G–2 dugout as Yates was explaining to another officer why it was impossible to supply a special leaflet for Matador. Bing could hear Yates, but all he could see was the brawny back of the other man outlined against the dim light of a suspended bulb.

Yates was saying, "And there you have it, Captain — a statement of this kind amounts to pronouncing our war aims. That involves decisions on policy which neither you nor we are entitled to make."

Bing's eyes became accustomed to the light in the dugout. It was a fine, solid dugout. Only a full hit would affect it. It was well dug into the earth, and the walls were hung with maps and empty flour bags. The roof was made of a continuous layer of wooden beams, and the dirt excavated had been thrown on top of it.

Yates saw him and called him over. "Captain Carruthers — this is Sergeant Bing. He's one of our specialists. He would have to do the job if we were to get clearance from SHAEF."

For his broad shoulders, Captain Carruthers had a small head. This smallness was accentuated by a handle-bar mustache. During Yates's argument, Carruthers had been twirling it uncomfortably. Now he stopped twirling and triumphed, "You see, Yates — you brought your man along! All that's left is to discuss the contents. Now, as I was saying — there will be this barrage in the morning. Something unprecedented. Something we otherwise would do only before a large-scale attack. It'll scare the bejeezus out of them. And then — "

"But I'm telling you, Captain — we'll never get the approval of SHAEF. And even if we got their O.K., it would be much too late for your show. Why don't you take something we have in stock?"

Yates was not so happy in the part Crerar and Willoughby had wished on him. Carruthers had by no means persuaded him that such a leaflet would have any effect; but he believed that it would do no harm.

"I have the samples here. For instance this one — it covers the situation after the surrender of Cherbourg. It has a map on it. Everybody likes maps, even if they don't want to read the text. . . ."

Carruthers rose. Bing expected him to hit his head against the beamed ceiling, but there was a comfortable margin between Carruthers's pate and the roof.

"We have millions of these," Yates continued, his voice carrying less and less conviction. "We can deliver them, ready for loading, to your ammunition supply points day after tomorrow."

He was lucky, he thought, that Farrish was not around. Carruthers had to accept his excuses and to argue; the General would have taken none of that.

Carruthers pleaded, "But we don't want that old stuff! It hasn't been getting us anywhere. We might as well fire toilet paper or save the ammunition."

And why shouldn't they get the leaflet, Yates asked himself. Was he against it, was he for it? Certainly, he didn't care about a question of competency in the Army — about who made policy — all these competing echelons stressed their own importance only to justify their jobs.

"Then fire safe-conduct passes, Captain!" he said absent-mindedly. "The Germans hang on to them! You've found them on plenty of prisoners. You've reported so yourself! Besides, they're signed by Eisenhower; that's always impressive."

No, he *was* against it. The leaflet imposed on him the necessity of facing questions he was not prepared to answer. Well, Bing would have to write it, not he. . . . But what was the difference? He had a sense of duty; and even if no word, no single idea, were asked of him, he would have to reject it, or approve it, for himself.

"Lieutenant Yates!" Carruthers's voice rang with so much refusal that a man who had been sleeping behind a switchboard at the far end of the dugout woke up and jumped from his chair. "This is the General's idea. I told you that! And it's a damned good one, and I'm for it. The Fourth of July —"

Yates, tired, broke in. "I know. The Fourth of July is the Birthday of the Nation and the nation is at war. . . . Why don't you see my position? You're afraid of your general."

"I most certainly am not!"

"All right! All right!" Yates conceded. "You want to follow your general's orders. We've got to follow ours."

13

"God damn it! It's still the same Army!"

"That's just the point. General Farrish is in this Army, too. Unfortunately, it will be you who will have to explain that to him."

"Explain what?" a full, throaty voice said from the doorway.

Everybody turned.

" 'Ten-shun!" the man behind the switchboard shouted, secretly thanking his patron saint that he had awakened in time for the great moment.

Farrish, his head bent, stooping to avoid the roof, strode toward the field desk. He wore riding boots and carried a crop. He placed it on the desk and sat down on Carruthers's chair, which creaked under his weight.

"At ease, carry on," said Farrish. "Explain what? Who are these people, Carruthers?"

"This is Lieutenant Yates, sir, from Propaganda Intelligence. . . . And this is Sergeant — "

"Bing, sir."

Yates was not afraid of Farrish, though he knew the General's reputation for irascibility. Yates was too sophisticated for that. But he was impressed by the man's personality, toward which everything immediately gravitated, and would have gravitated even if Farrish had worn no stars on his broad, erect shoulders.

Carruthers explained, "They're here to discuss the Fourth of July operation."

"Wonderful!" beamed Farrish.

He was a powerful man — more, he was conscious of it. Everything he did expressed this consciousness. His voice, manner, gestures — even his appearance — were bent to it; so that now, over the course of years, the studied effect had lost all affectation and had become part of him.

"Do you know the situation?" said Farrish.

Yates said he did. Carruthers had explained it to him.

That is, he knew the situation in the field. The situation here, in the little game he had been ordered to play, had been altered thoroughly by Farrish's entrance. Yates asked himself whether sticking to his orders, saving Crerar and Willoughby personal embarrassment, was worth all the trouble he now would have.

Farrish outlined the plan, disregarding all Carruthers might have said. He liked to hear himself talk. "I have more artillery than as per Table of Equipment. I have forty-eight guns in the Division. I have saved up enough ammunition to blast St.-Lô to shambles — or Coutances, or Avranches, or any of these towns. At five o'clock on the morning of July Fourth, I am going to fire forty-eight rounds from each of the pieces. Forty-eight rounds from forty-eight guns. There are forty-eight states, forty-eight stars in the flag. This is the voice of America, in this year of our Lord, 1944. Great, huh?"

"Yes, sir," said Yates, in spite of himself. He thought, The man is cracked. But he had to admit there was significance in his madness.

Bing began to see the idea. It intrigued him.

Farrish reached for his crop. Softly, he knocked its handle against his chin. "You can imagine the total effect of such bombardment on the German positions. It will soften up the Fritzes, it will unnerve them. After the forty-eighth round, there will be silence. You can hear that silence, can't you?"

"Yes, sir," said Yates. Remarkably enough, he could. He was carried away by Farrish's folly.

"They will wait — what is left of them. They will wait for the infantry and the tanks to attack. But instead, we will fire the leaflets."

Some anticlimax, thought Yates.

"We will tell them why we gave them this hell. We will tell them why we can afford to waste the shells. We will tell them what this Fourth of July means, and why we are fighting, and why they don't have a chance, and that they'd better give up."

The last was said with dangerously raised voice. The General's sharp blue eyes had grown small; the short, white, cropped hair seemed to bristle; and the ruddy face had become uncompromisingly hard.

Carruthers pulled at his mustache. He was not vicious, but he felt that Yates had it coming to him. Yates should have been more co-operative.

"The Lieutenant thinks," he said, choosing his words, "he won't be able to supply the leaflet. It is a matter of policy and SHAEF would have to decide."

Farrish's eyes grew even smaller, but he said nothing.

Yates searched frantically for an explanation. He could not argue against Farrish. He could not say that what we are fighting for was a maze of motives, some clear, some hidden, some idealistic, some selfish, some political, some economic, and that one would have to write a book instead of a leaflet; and that even then, the issue would be anything but straight. Farrish wanted to commandeer thought; and believed he could, as readily as he ordered ammunition, or food, or air support.

"You mean to tell me that your superiors would refuse this perfectly legitimate, sensible request of mine?" The General's voice was flat. "That they would stand in the way of an operation decided on by the Commander in the field?"

No, they wouldn't — Yates knew that. Play along with Farrish, Willoughby had said to him before he went on his mission to Matador. Farrish is important. He has a reputation from North Africa. He has caught the imagination of the people. You've got to handle this discreetly.

"We are most anxious to co-operate," Yates defended himself. Then it occurred to him that the General would understand technical limitations.

"The Sergeant, here, is our specialist. He will bear me out. It is impossible to produce the required leaflet in time. If you permit me, sir, I will explain the technical procedure. A draft must be prepared and agreed on. Then the text must be set up in type, proofread and corrected. Plates must be made. Thousands of sheets must be printed, dried, cut. The leaflets must be bundled and rolled for insertion in the shells. They must be carried to your ammunition supply points. The shells must be loaded. All this takes time. We don't have enough time. Isn't that so, Sergeant Bing?"

Farrish's whip beat the desk. "Time! Time!" he shouted. Then, moderating his voice almost down to a whisper, he said, "Do you know what time means, Lieutenant? Lives, that's what it means! The lives of my men! I want to break out of this trap in which every hedgerow is a fortification. I want to deploy armor where it can operate. Did you ever try to attack a hedgerow? Try it, sometime! You've got to go across an open field, you can't see the Germans, you can only hear their bullets. And when you finally clean them out, and count your own men, you have lost half of them."

Farrish's casualty lists were longer than anybody else's. Yates was only too well aware of that. Was Farrish sincere, now? Yates, had it depended on him alone, was inclined to believe him and support him. But the casualties and the hedgerows had little to do with a statement of policy. Yates looked at Bing, almost imploringly. The Sergeant's technical advice must clinch the case. Or was it that he was simply pushing the decision away from himself and onto Bing's shoulders?

Carruthers was at the point of saying that Yates's original objections had been quite different — that policy and Supreme Headquarters had figured largely in them — when Bing spoke up.

"Sir, I believe it will be possible to produce your leaflet in time for the Fourth of July."

"You see!" said Carruthers.

Yates said nothing. He had beaten his argument out of his own hand. He had relied on an oracle, and the oracle had spoken against him. It was funny, and he could imagine what Willoughby's face was going to look like. Willoughby would have to take the rap. The pyramidal system of the Army had its advantages.

Farrish nodded approvingly. "When you write this thing, Sergeant, you must keep in mind what I would say, had I the chance to speak to these Germans. I am an American. That's a hell of a great thing, Sergeant. Remember that."

Bing stood stiffly. He did not feel the need to answer. He was suddenly taken aback by the size of the job he had cut out for himself. What had made him contradict Yates? He must think this through. In truth, it was the temptation to play a joke on history. He, Sergeant Walter Bing, a nobody, a boy who had come to America without roots and ties, banished from home and school, was about to state the aims of this war. Because this would be the essence of the leaflet. Once fired, it could not be disavowed. They would have to stick to it, all these big operators who hated to commit themselves. Farrish didn't know what he had started. Bing hadn't known either when he jumped into the breach. But now he knew. Was he conscious of his responsibility? Yes. And he was frightened, too.

Somebody stumbled over the roughhewn stairs into the dugout. The newcomer seemed little impressed by the General, who sat, a great block of man, under the light.

"Hello, Jack!" said the newcomer. "Those stairs are a menace. You wouldn't want anything to happen to me?"

It was a woman. Even the General turned around.

Her face was not beautiful, it was rather plain; and the helmet, hiding her hair, was not too helpful; and whatever her figure, it was swallowed up in coveralls. Yet, her presence transformed everybody. The man behind the switchboard began to clean his nails.

The woman was accustomed to this stir. It happened every time she met men in uniform at or behind the front lines. The first few times she had felt self-conscious because she had not yet decided what it was that upset them. Then she recognized it was neither beauty nor homeliness, neither charm nor dullness, on her part. It was the singularity of being a woman who spoke their own language, among so many men who lived with men only. That, in turn, she found disappointing, then funny, then pathetic. It was sad, not flattering, when men, who at home or in any surroundings where women were plentiful would not have given her a second look, came slinking after her, begging for the favor of a few words from her, or the touch of her hand.

The General half rose and bowed slightly. Carruthers, proud and at the same time embarrassed by the familiarity of her greeting, introduced her.

"This is Miss Karen Wallace."

Yates remembered her name. He had read some of her human-interest stories on the Italian campaign — the kind of stories that hit him the wrong way because they spoke of "our boys" with that mixture of affability and intimacy which made the soldiers appear naïve. Apparently, the American public wanted its Army like that. Wallace's stories were widely read and she was well paid. Perhaps she was courageous, too. She had gone fairly close to the line — but one never knew how much was courage and how much the craving for sensation.

"I've heard a lot about you, General," she said in a deep, surprisingly warm voice. "I didn't expect to meet you here — I dropped in to say Hello to Captain Carruthers and to find out about things."

Farrish became cordial. "You've been keeping her to yourself, Jack!" And then, beaming, "I can understand why!"

She laughed.

It's a real laugh, thought Yates. Thank God, she isn't coy. But she should make her excuses sound more probable. Carruthers was not the Press Relations Officer from whom one found out about things; he was Assistant G-2. Well, he was a good-looking man, if you went in for mustaches.

Carruthers introduced Yates and Bing. She took off her helmet. It dropped to the floor. Bing handed it to her. She had thick reddish hair, cut short. The strap of the helmet liner had left a red mark across her forehead. Their eyes met. Her eyes were gray; quiet eyes. Bing's mouth went dry.

"Thank you," she said.

Farrish broke in. Perhaps he had noticed the interlude, Karen was not sure. Perhaps he simply couldn't bear not being the center of attention.

"I have a story for you!" he announced. "Wonderful title: 'Forty-eight Rounds from Forty-eight Guns'! How do you like it?"

Carruthers whispered to the General.

"Let her have the story!" Farrish waved his captain's objections aside. "Women know more about how men think than we do ourselves — right?"

She smiled. "About certain things, maybe . . ."

"This is a story about the mind of men, German men!" said Farrish. Once more he developed his plan. It grew in significance as he embellished the details. "The boy here — Bing, right? — he's going to put my thoughts into German. First-rate writer!" It was natural that anyone working for Farrish would be a first-rate man. "Can't you see the Germans after the pasting they'll get, digging themselves out of their holes, trembling, fearing what comes next? And then those papers come fluttering down. The relief! They read. We're talking to them, man to man, we're telling them! This Fourth of July isn't ancient history, it has meaning, today! Talk about history, Miss Wallace! We're making history!"

He leaned back, pleased.

As pleased as a boy who has shot off his firecrackers, she thought.

Yates hid a grin. The big man was showing off.

But Karen saw the story. It wasn't the story of the great General and his new and exciting gimcrack; it was the story of this man Bing who would have to sit down and write why our ideals were better than the Germans'; who would have to convince a tenacious enemy that, because of this, he should fight less hard, or cease fighting altogether. It was a fascinating story — something new. It required, first of all, that you be absolutely clear in your own mind, sure of yourself; that you believed in the justice of your cause. It meant believing in the principle of Good and Evil. To convince

18

"Welcome!" he said. "These women are so nervous. *C'est la guerre.* Come in!"

Through the hallway that smelled of fish and cider, they entered his shop. Glodin squeezed his magnifying glass under his eyebrow, opened Karen's watch and studied its works.

"You wore it in the water?"

Karen laughed. "I had to jump, Monsieur Glodin. Something hit the ship I was on."

Glodin pushed up his magnifying glass. It sat on his forehead like a horn, and he looked like a satyr. "You are lucky, Mademoiselle, it is only the watch. The watch I can repair in a few days."

He suddenly remembered something. "You will visit with us, won't you, please? A young American woman coming over here, and taking such risks! My wife has gone to the cellar for the red wine, the good one. I've always said to my wife, we must save this wine for a celebration. . . ."

Yates looked at his own watch. He felt someone pushing against his legs. It was a child, a girl. She stepped back and, in embarrassment, began to twist her skirt around her wrist. Yates saw her thin little thighs.

"Cute kid," said Bing.

Yates ruffled her hair. She purred. Then she asked, "*Chocolat?*"

"*Chocolat!*" Yates said to Karen. "*Liberté* and *chocolat.*" But he fished through his pockets.

"Don't you like children?"

"Love 'em!" he said.

"Do you have any?"

"No." He hesitated. Then he said quickly, "Ruth and I — Ruth's my wife — well, I felt we couldn't afford them."

Karen noticed his reticence and said, "To tell you the truth, Lieutenant, you don't look married."

Yates smiled to himself. *Touché!* he thought.

Glodin came from behind the counter and lifted the child on his arm. "She is the baby. We never thought we would have another one — but we are a hardy race. The older one is a boy. He is sick. But he is getting up."

"Don't let him get up!" said Yates. "We're leaving soon."

Glodin protested, "But it is nothing!"

"Half an hour," said Yates, resignedly. "Not more. We have to be back before dark."

Glodin led his guests into what was, obviously, the parlor. He seated them at a shaky, oval-shaped table, while his crinkled wife set out the wine and the glasses. Then a tall, ungainly woman with a slight mustache, dressed in pants and an old sweater, helped in a pale boy whose shoulders were hunched over homemade crutches.

"This is Mademoiselle Godefroy, the teacher," Glodin introduced the

21

gaunt woman. "She lives with us for the time being." He pointed with pride at the boy. "My son Pierre — he was lamed when the Germans moved out."

"How did it happen?" asked Karen.

The teacher of Isigny assisted the boy into a chair.

Pierre smiled at Karen. "We were standing on the roofs," he said, "my little sister, my whole family, all the neighbors. We heard the fighting from the church. Then the fighting stopped. On the street, the Germans were assembling. They were in great haste. They had to leave most of the things they had packed up beforehand. They saw us. One of their officers said something. The Germans aimed at us and fired. Then they turned and ran. My father and mother say they ran. I could not see them, I could only see a dark green veil before my eyes. It was really dark green, I don't know why."

Gently patting the boy's hand, Mademoiselle Godefroy said, "I can understand why the Germans shot at us, but it is not reasonable."

As if to support her point, the watchmaker added, "Mademoiselle Godefroy's house was burned down completely, in an American air raid. All her clothes were destroyed."

Yates cast a doubtful glance at his colleague from Isigny. "Of course it isn't reasonable," he said. "Neither is war."

The woman's face was stern. Yates felt that his words, well-meant as they were, had been repelled. He tried to imagine what he would feel if the buff little house back at Coulter, which he and Ruth hadn't yet fully paid for, were bombed out and burned — his books, his desk, everything gone.

His tone was conciliatory. "It was we who destroyed your house — that wasn't reasonable, either. . . ."

The woman looked straight at Yates. Karen, too, turned her expectant face to him.

"You imply," said Mademoiselle Godefroy, "that I am welcoming you, and all of us are welcoming you, because now it is you who are here, and you who have the guns?"

"No," answered Yates, uncomfortably. He hadn't wanted to go that far.

The woman continued gravely, "It is true that a Frenchman loves his house and what he owns, loves it perhaps more than other people do. But I tell you it was worth while to lose my house, my furniture, my clothes, and all the souvenirs of my life, just to see the Boches run."

"Bravo!" said Karen.

Yates sipped his wine. He had been trying to be rational, to get at the bottom of this thing in a rational manner; the schoolteacher of Isigny seemed to hold that against him.

"Please understand!" she said. "It was like this: They were so strong, and they had been here so long, that we had lost count of the years. We had almost come to believe that it was forever, that they were the kind of men who could not be made to turn their backs. And then they ran."

"You Americans made them run," Glodin said, because he was the host.

The teacher's hand described a small circle in the air. "It re-established the laws of life as we had been taught them when we were young, and as I have been teaching them."

Yates could see that, for the people of Isigny, the moment when the Germans turned heel must have been of terrific impact. Had he been one of them, he might have felt it, too. But he wasn't. He was like the doctor whose fingers, lightly touching the patient's burning forehead, could feel the fever, but was not, himself, shaken by it.

He gave another piece of chocolate to the little girl. He couldn't think of an answer to Mademoiselle Godefroy.

The Glodins and their neighbors in the street waved after them as they left Isigny.

Yates was thoughtful. Something in him had received a jolt.

"When the war's over — " he said — "and it is going to be over someday! — how will they ever live together? So much hate! A schoolteacher talking that fanatically!"

Karen glanced at her booted, legging-encased, shapeless legs. She had a few nylons in her bag, and she hadn't had a chance to wear them. She wanted to, very much.

"Has it ever occurred to you, Lieutenant, that it would do you good to have a little of her spirit?" she said.

"I respect the woman!" protested Yates. "I have all the sympathy in the world for her!"

"Yes," she said, "that's cheap enough."

Yates saw he would have to change his line with Karen. What could you expect from a girl whose business it was to glorify this dirty, stinking, senseless, costly war? He smiled wryly. Women were that way. They wanted their warriors not only handsome but also positive.

"Let's not fight about it, shall we?" he suggested.

Bing kept his face discreetly neutral.

They arrived at Château Vallères toward sundown. They stopped at the main gate: two stone pillars, set centuries ago, where the road came out of the woods. The Château lay before them, across the expanse of a meadow and the moat, its towers and chimneys and roofs etched blackly against a blazing orange and red sky.

As the immediate sound of the motor subsided, the ominous rumbling of the evening cannonade asserted itself. The air was already cooling. Karen shivered slightly.

23

Yates felt her tremble. "Let's get out of here and walk, Karen. The driver can take the car to the pool." Helping her to step down, he suggested, "I'll take you to Mr. Crerar first; he usually has some Scotch."

"While you drink up your ration as soon as you get it?" She smiled.

"Mr. Crerar has Scotch because he's a civilian whom the OWI has wished on us, and because he's a simulated lieutenant colonel, and because he's our Operations Chief who welcomes Very Important Personages."

Yates led her to the slope at the right of the road where the Operations tent was set up. In front of it stood Abramovici, leaning on his rifle, his short legs spread. A kitten jumped forward as if trying to catch something. Then it decided otherwise, snuggled against Abramovici's leg, and raised its tail.

"The kitten's name is Plotz," said Yates. "Mr. Crerar brought it from England."

Abramovici came down the slope, setting his large feet carefully. Reaching Yates and his little group, he stared vaguely at Karen, then flushed all over his round cheeks, and said lamely, "The Major's waiting for you, sir. . . ."

"I know," said Yates. He had seen Willoughby's heavy-set figure step out of the tent, followed by the taller, loose-limbed, thin-shouldered Crerar.

Willoughby rushed down the slope and, still a few paces away, stretched out his pudgy hands and said, "A lady! What an unexpected pleasure!"

He meant it. His heavy jowls were lifted in a beatific smile; his small, sharp eyes sparkled above their pouches.

"This is Major Willoughby," said Yates, "the Boss. Miss Karen Wallace has come to do a story on the Fourth of July operation."

"On what?" Willoughby looked up at him, in surprise. But he caught himself immediately. "We'll talk about that later," he said, and resumed smiling at Karen. He put his arm under hers. Karen could feel his stubby fingers against the inside of her wrist, pressing it lightly.

Staking his claim, thought Yates. But he noticed the slight pursing of Karen's lips — she was up to that kind of game. Maybe he had been too obvious, too; had underestimated her when she had come along so easily, leaving Carruthers to his maps, his dugout, and Farrish. Leading the way to the Operations tent, Yates announced, "You must meet Mr. Crerar. He'll tell you all you want to know, Miss Wallace."

Crerar held out his hand. The kitten Plotz had returned to him and was sitting on his shoulder, rubbing its side against his ear.

"By all means," said Willoughby, "let's meet Mr. Crerar. He knows everything."

Crerar's long, fleshy nose overhung his thin lips. The deep lines next to his eyes were those of a cynic. "Willoughby always exaggerates," he said;

"you'll find out. Don't trust him, my girl. He's much too interested in himself."

Willoughby laughed. "He's jealous. Men get that way when women are scarce." He slapped Crerar's back. The kitten, scared, jumped to the ground, miaowed, stretched itself, and slunk toward the tent.

"She has her milk in there," explained Crerar.

"We'll have a party for Miss Wallace!" said Willoughby. "Nothing big — just the fellows. Yates! Would you tell the French in the kitchen to roast those geese for tonight? Miss Wallace, do you know the story of the man who unexpectedly dropped in on his relatives?"

He not only slaps people's backs, he tells stories, too, thought Karen.

Yates had no desire to go to the kitchen. He passed the buck to Bing; and Bing, seeing the brass vie with each other, obeyed unhesitantly and went off to tell Manon and Pauline, the tenant's ruddy daughters.

"Do you know the story?" insisted Willoughby.

"No," said Karen.

"Well, it's really too long," said Willoughby, "but I'll give you the punch line."

"Don't!" said Crerar. "It stinks."

"Jealous!" repeated Willoughby. "Crerar must get drunk before he can have a good time. Me, I'm just one of the fellows. I like to work hard, and to live hard, and to have fun. We'll get along, Miss Wallace, we'll get along."

"I always get along," said Karen, disengaging herself from him. She looked at Yates, who was intently studying the colors of the sunset.

A car approached. Somebody shouted, "Here we come!" — the rest was unintelligible.

"I thought they had closed down that joint in the village," said Crerar.

"They have," said Willoughby. "I must have a word with Loomis. He must stop the men from drinking. This Calvados — " He laughed.

Crerar watched an officer stumble out of the car.

"It's Loomis," he said. "What a coincidence!"

Loomis was preceded by a waddling civilian with a hangdog look. Loomis was cursing loudly, his Midwestern drawl taking some of the terror out of his words. He gave the civilian a vicious shove.

As the two reached Willoughby and the others, they stopped. Loomis, swaying slightly, saluted. "Captain Loomis reporting," he said. "I've made an arrest." He held his pistol against the back of the sweating civilian. "Name!" he shouted. "What's your name? Name!"

The civilian did not dare to move, except for his eyes, which darted about like lizards. "Léon Poulet," he whispered.

"Loomis, you're drunk," said Crerar.

25

"He's a collaborationist," said Loomis. "I've arrested him. Nice and fat," he poked the man in the stomach, "a collaborationist."

Then he noticed Karen. "A woman!" he mumbled. "Jesus — a woman!"

He came to her, his right hand still brandishing the pistol. "Lady, you're a pleasure to my sore eyes!" His drawl was accentuated by his difficulties in controlling his tongue. "Don't mind this guy, this Poulet. I'll take care of him, don't you be afraid of him. . . ."

He paused. Then a new thought entered his mind. "We'll have an execution. Regular execution!" He aimed his pistol at Poulet, who held his trembling hands before his face. "Bang! Bang!" said Loomis.

Willoughby took the pistol out of Loomis's hand. "Take it easy, fellow!" he said. "Get yourself to bed."

"I won't go to bed!"

"This lady is a correspondent," Willoughby warned. "I don't want you to show yourself in this shape."

"Newspapers?" asked Loomis. "Writes?" He considered the situation. Then he shook his head. "I'm a gentleman, Willoughby!"

"Of course you are! Now go!"

"You!" gestured Loomis to his prisoner. "Come over here, you! We're going to get our names in the papers, me and you — what the hell is your name? Name!" he shouted at Poulet.

The unfortunate Poulet stood before Karen. His checkered waistcoat had slipped up from his ample stomach, the knees of his baggy pants shook, the thin black curls around his bald, rosy pate drooped limply.

Yates watched for Karen's reaction. The whole thing was offensively ludicrous. Loomis, even when sober, didn't know a collaborationist from a hole in the wall.

"How did you arrest this guy?" asked Willoughby.

Loomis waved his hand. "Aw, it was nothing — really. All in a day's work!"

"Good man!" said Crerar. "To keep his head with all that booze inside . . ."

"Calvados!" Loomis said proudly. "I always say a man that can't hold the stuff shouldn't drink it. Loosens your tongue. Stands at the bar and talks and talks and gets nasty. Very nasty. Dead giveaway."

"What bar? Where?" asked Willoughby.

"Vallères! Vallères village!" Loomis was still high. He turned on Poulet. "Confess!"

Poulet drew a deep breath. Then he fell on his knees before Karen. He began to talk in a fast patois, stroking her boots timidly, imploringly.

"Get up, you!" Loomis was furious. He sensed that his story was a bust.

Poulet didn't get up. He was sobbing. Karen tried to step back, but he held on to her.

Yates felt a kind of shame. Not at the spectacle of the man on his knees, not at Loomis — human dignity was trampled on every day in war, and nobody gave it a second thought; and as for the drunk, he wasn't a bad sort. What made Yates squirm and want to get away was the fact that all this took place before an outsider, before Karen. He realized suddenly that he, himself, had become like the men with whom he associated. Since they had nobody but themselves to check on themselves, they had stopped checking altogether. But for Karen, he would have thought Loomis's antics with Poulet funny and pushed them out of his mind with a laugh.

Roughly, he grasped Poulet's shoulders and pulled the heavy man to his feet. "Stop sniveling," he said in French; "we're not going to hurt you."

Poulet squinted and blew his nose through his fingers. Had he not smelled so strongly of fear and bad soap, Yates would have felt almost kindly toward him.

Loomis had lost some of his aggressiveness and was sulking. Willoughby seemed undecided.

"What do you want me to do with this guy?" Yates asked angrily. "He isn't my responsibility!"

A soldier and a woman came from the road. The woman began to run, her wooden sabots flattening the grass. Yates recognized the soldier behind her. The soldier saluted and said, "I've come to pick up the Mayor of Vallères."

"Tolachian," Yates called out to him, "you know this man?"

"Yes, sir!" Tolachian took off his helmet and wiped his forehead. His dense white hair, despite the half-light, stood out in sharp contrast to his deep-set eyes that were like dark cherries.

Through the fog in his mind, Loomis guessed that Tolachian's arrival meant a critical turn. "And who ordered you here?" he said heavily. "You've got no business here. Get back to the village!"

"Now wait a minute! Wait a minute!" said Willoughby. "Let's straighten this out, first!"

Before anyone was able to begin straightening it out, the woman lashed into Poulet who, at the sight of her, tried to throw himself once more at Karen's feet.

"*Cochon!*" she screamed. Her beady eyes pierced Poulet. "Getting drunk with the *Américain!*" She smoothed her apron, which was tied so firmly around her middle that her angular hips bulged. She looked around for the person in authority and fixed her attention on Willoughby.

"Monsieur! My husband, he is innocent! He has never done anything wrong. . . . Oh, I wish you were home, you! . . . He is the Mayor of Vallères, and the owner of the café, and his license has been confirmed by the American authorities. . . ."

27

She shook her head wildly. Karen expected her little knot of hair to fly off her flat skull.

"Poulet!" the woman whined. "Ah, you miserable one — why did you have to let him in? Him — there!"

And she turned on Loomis. "You and your Calvados! You come in and you coax my poor innocent into selling you a glass — just a little glass — and then another, and then another. . . ."

Madame Poulet paused for breath. Loomis was beginning to sober up under her fury. Willoughby grinned. He saw no reason for stepping between Loomis and the rage that was pouring over the Captain.

"Monsieur, he has the *Légion d'Honneur*," the woman resumed; "he is a law-abiding citizen — all he wants is to oblige this captain! I say to him, you must close down, the police will be around, you are forbidden to sell strong liqueur to the *Américains* because, God bless them, they cannot hold it. . . ."

"Woman!" Loomis was collecting himself. "You're talking to an American officer!"

"*Fou!* You bring shame over my house! You abduct my man! Kidnap!"

Her bony nose was being turned from one to the other of the group, searching out support and sympathy. She addressed Yates, "*Mon Lieutenant!* Poulet, he says to this drunk, Get out! He pleads with him, leads him to the door, as the peasant leads the sick lamb. Poulet, he wouldn't hurt anybody. . . . But then!"

She moved in on Loomis.

"You — you have no understanding for the heart! You fight and fall on my poor innocent. . . . Drunk? My husband, the Mayor, never gets drunk! You force him out on the street, you lower him in the eyes of the peasants — him, the authority! How will he ever enforce the orders of the *Américains* after you beat him and kick him and threaten him with your pistol? How? How? How?"

Loomis's hands shot up to his ears. He stared glassily at the thin face of Madame Poulet, the waving arms, the yellow brooch which imprisoned her neck in her blouse.

Then he saw Tolachian, whose business it was to stay in Vallères village with the mobile presses set up there. Loomis dimly perceived that there was a connection between Tolachian's presence and the predicament in which he found himself.

"How did this whole thing happen, Tolachian?" he demanded, trying to steady his voice.

"It seems you arrested the Mayor, sir!" Tolachian said dryly. "Then she came to the shop. . . ."

He pointed at Madame Poulet, who was grasping her husband's collar and struggling to shake the paunchy man.

28

"She screamed at me. . . ." Tolachian spread his hands helplessly. Then he added, "I'd seen you leave the café, sir."

Yates said to Crerar, who had been enjoying the rumpus, "Don't you think it's time we break up this thing?"

Crerar nodded. "Go ahead!"

Yates went over to Loomis and whispered to him, "You'd better go to the Château. We'll settle it with the Poulets."

But Loomis, realizing that his reputation had been badly dented, shouted, "I will not budge an inch! You keep out of my affairs!"

He pushed Yates aside and, carefully avoiding Madame Poulet, made for Tolachian. "So you had to stick your God-damned nose into this, too? I don't like people who do that! I don't like 'em!"

Tolachian stood rigidly. He was almost twice as old as the Captain. He had volunteered for the war. He knew when to stand rigidly.

Loomis hated Tolachian; it seemed to him he had hated the man ever since Tolachian had reported himself to the Detachment, back in the States. A man with white hair coming in, a sturdy man, with the quiet certainty of his years.

"It's time you learned you're in the Army, soldier! You'll report to me later, tonight!"

Yates tried to mediate. "I don't think Captain Loomis really arrested the Mayor. They both were in high spirits and decided to take a trip to the Château — isn't that it?"

"I did so arrest him!" insisted Loomis. "He made treasonous remarks!"

Willoughby, who had been quipping to Karen, finally noticed that she did not relish the incident. "Captain Loomis," he said sharply, "you won't mind releasing your prisoner in the custody of Madame Poulet and Private Tolachian?"

He motioned off the Mayor's wife, who was about to break into a fresh stream of words.

"All right, all right! Take them back to Vallères village, Tolachian. And next time, don't bring any local wives around unless you're sure they're welcome."

He laughed at his own joke. To Karen he said, "If you will follow me, I'll show you your room in the Château. It isn't much, but it's the best we have. . . . Captain Loomis, you will let Miss Wallace have your canopied bed, and you will move in with Lieutenant Yates for the night!"

"Anything for the ladies!" said Loomis, pocketing the pistol Willoughby had handed back to him.

"I don't see how we can get out of it," Yates concluded his report. "Farrish wants the leaflet, and he wants it his way. He wants us to tell the Germans what we're fighting for. He had me cornered. You've been around

29

the Army long enough, Mr. Crerar, you know how it is. I'm a lieutenant, and he's a general. So, I suppose it will be up to you or the Major to tell him."

Crerar, his legs crossed, was sitting on his cot, the kitten Plotz nestling on his lap.

Willoughby seemed to be only half-listening. "That's one of the best stories of the campaign," he said cheerfully, "Loomis and the collaborationist. We'd better think up something good for the girl, or we'll get some writeup! . . . DeWitt won't like it."

"Won't like what?"

"The leaflet business," said Willoughby. "In any case I am not going to stick my neck out. What *are* we fighting for? Do you know?"

Crerar nodded. "I'm fighting for a very beautiful place. A farm. It's about fifty miles north of Paris. I had cows there, and some riding horses. There was an orchard, and a small woods. It used to be mine. Now the Nazis have it. I wonder what they did with the cattle."

"Probably killed them," said Yates.

Crerar continued, "I had some of the best years of my life on that farm, with Eve. She was like a child about it. She loved it. Now she's cooped up in a New York apartment. . . . It worries me."

Yates looked at the shaggy hair of the old man. He wants the Army to recapture his youth, he thought. Oh my God, aren't we all crazy?

"But Farrish wants his leaflet," he repeated.

"He can't have it," said Willoughby. "If we do it, SHAEF is going to raise the biggest stink ever."

"And if we don't do it, Farrish will send a complaint through channels," said Crerar. "I can see it all: Corps will get excited, and Army will scream, and finally SHAEF will take it up, and it will all end in the same big stink."

"Can't we get in touch with DeWitt?" suggested Yates. "He's a reasonable man, at least that was my impression of him."

"He's an Army man!" Willoughby paused reminiscently. "West Point, in fact. Conscious of his prerogatives. Besides, he can't do a thing either. War aims! That means policy — War Department, State Department, the President, Churchill, Stalin . . . "

Loomis came into the tent. He was completely sobered and contrite. "I have spoken to Bing," he offered. "I don't like him, personally. He thinks he knows a lot. But he will turn out an A Number One job. This is the biggest break we ever got — producing a thing like that for Farrish!"

Sure, thought Yates, a break for him! As long as the Detachment justified its existence and remained intact, Loomis could keep himself at a comfortable distance from the line. Much better than being transferred to the Infantry.

Crerar stroked the kitten.

Willoughby said, "I am against it."

Loomis was perplexed. He rumpled his sparse hair. Then he said, "Naturally, there are other considerations, too. This kind of leaflet can't be done in a hurry. I'm sure Yates explained all that at Matador."

Yates's annoyance gradually reached the saturation point. "I did," he said, "but the situation is all screwed up."

"Well — do we or don't we?" asked Crerar.

Nobody spoke.

"And if we don't, what are we going to say to Farrish? And if we do, what are we going to say to DeWitt?"

Christ Almighty, Yates asked himself, what are we trying to dope out here? Whether it's better to antagonize a man named Farrish, or a man named DeWitt? What did these guys concern themselves with — principles? Poor Mademoiselle Godefroy, who thought her little house had been blown to smithereens for a principle — *to re-establish the laws of life,* she'd said. Shenanigans and personal politics, that's what they were after. He didn't condemn them. He had nothing better to offer with which to replace the shenanigans and politics. And they weren't particularly vicious. Willoughby was an immensely able person, shrewd, imaginative, and even kind if it didn't cost him anything. Loomis was stupid and self-centered, but not much more so than the average man back home or over here; and he was, at least, aggressive only when he felt his own precious corns trod upon. And Crerar? Yates liked Crerar. In another twenty years, he himself, probably, would be like Crerar, capable, as always, of seeing the rot but unwilling to get into a stew about it because there was too much that smelled.

On the other hand — if it was possible for a schoolteacher to say, *It is worth while to lose all I have to see the Boches run* — if a boy could put up with a lame leg for the rest of his life — there must be something more to it than he, himself, knew or cared to admit. Karen had said it would do him good to have some of that spirit. These women! Ruth would be the same way. She would analyze it and lecture him on it until he itched with impatience and wanted to get away from facing it: That something new had entered the lives of these people — through us, Americans; through the freedom we brought them; and that we don't know the consequences of our own gifts, of the war we're waging.

Yates realized he had been rubbing his wart again.

The hell with all of it! It was conjecture. It had nothing to do with the case.

Willoughby slapped his thigh.

"Yates," he cried, "tell me again: What exactly did Farrish say? *'Forty-eight Rounds from Forty-eight Guns'?* Was that it?"

31

"Yes."

Willoughby gave himself an air of finality, superiority, and secrecy. "The thing is settled," he announced. "I'll handle it my way."

"How?" asked Crerar.

But he didn't seem any too curious. Crerar was tired. The experience of his long life had taught him that blind-alley situations mostly solve themselves, somehow. He was content to leave the problem to Willoughby.

Willoughby wanted to keep his secret. It was so simple, so obvious that he couldn't resist the pleasure of savoring it. "War," he said, "is the same as everything else in life. You rub elbows with people, you meet them, shake hands, make friends. Someday, it all comes in handy. This is one of those days."

He stretched.

"In any case, we'll have Bing prepare a draft. That will be our second line of defense. But I don't think we'll have to use it."

3

PETE DONDOLO had a nice voice. Miss Walker, back in his public-school days, had said, "Pete, if we only could find someone to give you singing lessons!" She used to look at the boy, her head cocked, like a bird undecided whether to fly off or not. Young Dondolo stared right back at her and said nothing. Singing lessons!

Dondolo never cultivated his voice. But he was secretly proud of it. By breathing a certain way, by forcing the tone against the roof of his mouth, he could make it sound loud and clear, and it could be heard farther than anyone else's. He could give it a sharp overtone which would make his wife Lina grow pale and want to hide in the kitchen. After the second baby arrived, she became fat and old and he talked to her only in this manner.

Then he discovered a new talent. He could imitate other people's speech, their accent, their mannerisms, their tone. He could sound so exactly like his oldest boy, Larry, that Lina didn't know whether the kid was in the room or not, and no longer dared to call him. When they had the opposition candidate in the Tenth Ward Association — the Association controlled a lot of things, and Marcelli, the boss, didn't like opposition — Dondolo took the floor after the unfortunate candidate, and gave such a perfect take-off of the man, perverting the meaning of everything he had said, that the candidate was laughed out of the hall. Even Marcelli had had trouble keeping a straight face, and had said to him, "You're a regular actor, Pete, regular!"

The war had interrupted Dondolo's career with the Tenth Ward Association. He had tried to keep out of it. Marcelli had said, "Is no good, this war. Is like I fight against Shea. . . ." Shea ran the Fourteenth Ward. "Would I fight against Shea when I can get together with him peaceful?"

Marcelli had promised to look after Larry and Saverio, the little one. But that wasn't enough. Dondolo worried. He sent half his pay and half of all the money he made on the side, into a special bank account for the kids. Lina was not allowed to touch it, didn't even know of it. Only Marcelli knew; he had power of attorney.

And then the Army stuck Dondolo as Mess Sergeant into this outfit. The outfit was full of people not at all his kind. It was hard to operate and be comfortable, to feel good about a bad deal, when you had to watch yourself all the time. He was not alone, though. There were quite a few who felt as he did — Lord, the Motor Sergeant, and Vaydanek, the Second Cook, for instance. They formed a clique. They discovered that it was easy to keep the others in check. Most of the others were men who wanted to do their job, to be left in peace — which showed their weakness.

Again, Dondolo's gift as an actor came in handy. He had a sharp eye and a sharp ear, and he was merciless. He would imitate and exaggerate and put his victim to a ridicule against which there was no defense. It was all good, clean fun; they had to take it. Dondolo could always retreat and say: Why, it was just a joke. And Loomis would protect him. Loomis was afraid of him. Loomis had a fine nose for where real power lay.

This evening, Dondolo picked on Abramovici. After the conference in the Operations tent had ended, Crerar had called Abramovici to take down a message to DeWitt — the message had to be typed and sent off to Message Center. This made Abramovici late for chow.

"Vot eees it?" Dondolo opened the scuffle.

This "Vot eees it?" had become his battle cry. Some of the more unworldly men in the organization, when roughly brought back to the realities of life and the war, in surprise would say: "What is it?" To Dondolo, who never in his life had asked: *What is it?* about anything, but who had assumed its existence and immediately tried to eat it or appropriate it, or at least to put it to use for himself, the question seemed utterly funny.

"Vot eees it?" he repeated, and Lord and Vaydanek, upon hearing the battle cry, came over to watch the fun before the mess tent.

"I want chow," said Abramovici, holding out his mess kit.

"You want chow!" repeated Dondolo. "Chow he wants!" this was directed to an imaginary large audience. Lord and Vaydanek laughed. "He comes after chow time, and he wants chow!" His tone changed, became sharp. He stemmed his fists into his hips, leaned forward, the thin lower lip of his long mouth jutting out, accentuating the sinews of his thick neck. "This ain't no restaurant, see? You come late, you wait for breakfast. Vot eees it?"

Abramovici still held out his mess kit. He was hungry. He was always hungry. His small, compact body could consume vast amounts of food, he chewed thoroughly, ate slowly, thinking of the old adage he had heard in his native Rumania: *Well chewed, half-digested.* Abramovici lovingly cared for his digestion and all other functions of his body.

Dondolo grabbed a big ladle and smashed the mess kit from Abramovici's outstretched hand. It clattered to the ground. Abramovici picked it up patiently.

Then, with the absoluteness of the law which he knew, and which was on his side, he said, "A soldier who has worked all day has got a right to eat."

"A soldier has got a right to eat!" Dondolo sounded exactly like Abramovici. "And a sergeant hasn't got no rights at all, has he? Perhaps me, I don't work? I don't get up at four in the morning? I don't stand over the hot stoves all day? I don't have no right to quit at quitting time? *I* don't get overtime pay, time and a half! *I'm* in the Army! *You're* in the Army. Chow time is over!"

Had Abramovici lost his temper, had he shouted back, had he complained aloud, giving Dondolo and Lord and Vaydanek the fun they provoked and wanted, the Sergeant would quite willingly have given the little Jew some food. But Abramovici remained quiet. He held out his mess kit, demanding. His big feet were rooted to the ground, his eyes, which seemed to have almost no pupils, betrayed no emotion. It disappointed and angered Dondolo.

All this was nothing new in Abramovici's life. As a child, he had seen pogroms. Dondolo, to him, was just another official in power. Such officials could be humored. But if they were in an ugly mood, you could do only one thing: Accept it, let it run off your back, like water off a duck's.

But Dondolo believed he had invented something new. And his invention did not work.

Vaydanek said, "Give him something to eat. What the hell."

This unexpected weakness in his own ranks increased the fury into which Dondolo had worked himself. Perhaps Vaydanek intended that.

Dondolo came from behind the table on which the remains of the evening's servings still stood, and pushed Abramovici. He didn't push him hard, just enough to make him stumble backwards and lose his mess kit once more.

"You can't do that!" said Abramovici. "A soldier has got the right . . ."

"I can't! I'll show you — "

His outbreak was interrupted.

"Give him something to eat," someone said. "You've got the food!"

Quietly, his steps swallowed by the grass, Preston Thorpe had joined the group. He had been watching the scene for quite a while, and everything in him was hurt. He did not like the strong ganging up on the weak;

34

it was not just. He didn't like Dondolo's provocations — they smacked of bigotry and all the things he had been brought up to despise.

Dondolo turned to the new enemy. Thorpe was taller than he, and seemed wiry, too. Dondolo had never dared to attack Thorpe — Thorpe was the only man in the Detachment who had been in the war before they landed in Normandy. Thorpe had been in North Africa, with the Infantry.

"You'd throw it away anyhow," said Thorpe. "And he's got a right —"

It was Thorpe's mention of *right* which made Dondolo lose all control. In his world, nobody had a right; everything was favors.

In the big GI can, standing next to the table, what was left of the evening's coffee blinked blackly. The mess cup with which the coffee had been served, hung on the rim of the can. Dondolo took it, dipped it fast, and swung it at Thorpe. The gush of warm brew hit Thorpe's face. It blinded him momentarily.

It blinded him and stunned him and made him defenseless. He felt it run down his neck, under his shirt, down his chest and back. It stuck to him like — like blood.

Yes, that's what it was.

He screamed, wounded again. All he had tried to forget came back, rushed at him, overthrew him. . . . The dull pain and the life slowly dripping out of him, the fear of the eternal blackness, the nothing around you, the great, great, great unending emptiness. There it was again, and he could not lift his arms, nor move, nor speak.

A thin thread in his brain was the thought: Throw yourself forward, beat this man, kill him. But he was terrified, terrified of having to touch something; and even more, of being touched. His muscles, his skin, everything was fleeing, running away, retreating into itself, shrinking.

Thorpe was a coward, he knew it. And he knew that Dondolo now knew it, too. It was like a chain, it went on and on, and he was enmeshed in it.

He came to, feeling somebody wipe his face.

Bing, even later than Abramovici, had come to get his supper.

"Vot eees it?" crowed Dondolo.

"I ought to turn you in, you sonofabitch," said Bing.

"Come on here," said Dondolo, "come on here and fight!" He was fairly sure Bing wouldn't fight. If Bing did, he would lay himself wide open for court-martial, at least in an outfit whose men were subject to Loomis. And Bing was too shrewd for that.

"Fight!" Dondolo challenged again.

"Wouldn't you like that!" Bing hesitated. He probably would be beaten. And then there was the matter of a court-martial. And then, there was the leaflet, the war. It was more important to fight the Germans than Dondolo.

Germany, the German Army, the Nazi Party — they were millions of Dondolos. But how could you fight them if you had Dondolos in your own ranks, unchallenged and unchallengeable?

"Yellow bastard!" Dondolo spit. "Yellow bastards, all of them. Jews! Foreigners! Vot eees it!"

Dondolo stopped. The silence was oppressive. Then the ground seemed to give off waves, hollow rumbling. American artillery opening up, answering the Germans.

"Let's go," said Abramovici. "I've lost my appetite."

"Vaydanek!" Dondolo called. "Might as well give 'em something to eat."

"All right, you guys!" shouted Vaydanek. "Over here — come and get it!"

"Thank you, no," said Abramovici, "it'll be too cold by now."

Dondolo shrugged. "Your own fault. Come in time, you get your chow."

"I'd like to ask you something, Dondolo." Bing closed his mess kit and approached the Mess Sergeant. Dondolo involuntarily stepped back. He had gone too far. There were things that one thought, or spoke of among friends — but one did not blurt them out, at least not yet. What was Bing up to? Bing was sly, he wanted to trap him.

"What the hell do you think this war is being fought for?" said Bing. "And why are *you* in it?"

Dondolo tried to think. After the excitement, it was an effort. Where Dondolo came from, people didn't hold discussions after a fight. They called the police, or they ran. But maybe these guys were such cowards that they wanted to talk, to make up, to act as if nothing had happened. If this was an olive branch, Dondolo was tempted to take it, just because he had gone too far.

Carefully, he said, "Me? I've got nothing to do with it. I was drafted!"

"So was I. There was a law. But you could have refused!"

"What! And get myself in trouble?"

"You're in trouble right now. You're over here — listen to the guns! Can hit you just like that!" Bing snapped his fingers.

There was no answer.

"You've got to have some idea about why you're going to die, maybe!"

"I'm not going to die."

"I hope you don't," Bing said quietly, "but you have a damned good chance."

Lord, the Motor Sergeant, who had kept quiet, lit a cigarette and said, "That's a lot of crap."

"Vot eees it?" Vaydanek tried to laugh.

The Germans resumed their fire. It seemed to be coming closer. The still evening air carried the sound clearly.

"A lot of crap!" repeated Lord, but without fervor.

"You're afraid of dying," said Bing. "You don't like to talk about it. It would be tough on those two kids of yours."

"You leave my kids alone! They're none of your God-damned business!"

"They're yours! Are you fighting for them?"

Dondolo was getting mad again, but in a different way. Bing was hitting below the belt. Larry and Saverio, the little one — not even their names should be mentioned here. It was like putting the Evil Eye on them, and on him, too.

."Shut up!" he said. "Sure I'm fighting for my kids. I'm going to get back to 'em, too! It's because of people like you I had to leave 'em. If anything happens to them, I'll kill you. Bunch of Jews get themselves into trouble, and the whole American Army swims across the ocean. This fellow Hitler, he knew what he was doing, and Mussolini, he, too. Everything is wrong. We should be fighting with them, against the Communists. They're against the family, against everything . . ." His voice trailed off.

"Come on!" said Lord. "Come on!"

"I fix a cup of coffee for everybody!" said Vaydanek.

"No, thank you," said Bing.

They were leaning over the railing of the drawbridge. The moat was very black, interspersed with white splotches where the light of the moon broke on islands of pond leaves. From the tenant's kitchen came the subdued voices of Manon and Pauline.

Thorpe threw a pebble and listened to the splash. For the fraction of a second, the frogs ceased croaking.

Abramovici slapped his cheek. "Mosquitoes," he explained.

"Got it?" asked Bing.

"No." Abramovici coughed. "Mosquitoes are the carriers of many diseases. Malaria, for instance."

"Not here."

"How do you know?" Abramovici had a morbid interest in diseases. He read manuals and handbooks on prevention. He tried to follow their rules. "In the armies, there are men who've had malaria in the tropics. The mosquitoes go after them, then they sting a healthy person. That's how malaria can come to Normandy."

"Well, smoke a cigarette. It will drive them away."

"I don't smoke," said Abramovici. "I'm not going to poison my body of my own free will. Besides I wouldn't light a cigarette in the dark. The light of a match can be seen for several miles, at night. The Army has made tests on that. You might give away your position to a German plane."

Bing drew away from Abramovici. Ordinarily, he did not relish his company. Abramovici washed himself entirely too often, he had the faint smell of cleanliness. He slept regularly and deeply, with a slight, hiccuping snore. Whenever he could, Abramovici took off his shoes and socks and exposed his feet to the air. His pink toes were spread apart — in his youth, he must have worn square-toed orthopedic shoes.

Now, Abramovici had attached himself to Bing and Thorpe, grateful because they had allied themselves with him against Dondolo. Bing wished the man would stop being grateful.

But Abramovici felt secure and pleased. "My father," he told them, "was in the first war. When I went overseas, he said to me: Leopold, you must listen to me. War is a dangerous business unless you take care of yourself. Be careful what you eat and drink and where you go. Don't fight unless you have to. I have given you an education, you've learned many things you can use. Anybody can fight, but what the Army really needs is brains. And remember — a war is absolutely no good for you unless you get through alive."

Thorpe threw another pebble. "Damned frogs!"

"If they would only pour oil on this moat," said Abramovici, "the larvae of the mosquitoes would choke and there would be no more mosquitoes."

"So your primary war aim is to get through alive," said Bing.

"No," said Abramovici, surprised, "I didn't say that."

"Yes, you did — what else is it?"

Abramovici frowned. "America — " he said. Then he laughed and took on a confidential air. "Sure. I am honest. I want to live, don't you? All these guys taking chances . . . I don't. I sleep in a foxhole. I know you sleep in the Château, on the top floor of the tower. What if the Château is hit? It will collapse, it will burn, and then where will you be?" He paused to pull up his pants. "I am doing my duty, I am essential. Mr. Crerar says so, too."

Thorpe said, "Go to your bed, Soldier, it's time."

Abramovici felt the touch of irony. "Soldiers, after a day's work, have got to rest!" he defended himself with conviction.

"Sleep," said Thorpe. "Sleep! Maybe the Germans will forget to come over tonight."

"Do you think so?" Abramovici asked hopefully.

"Aw, why don't you go away?"

As Abramovici marched off, Thorpe turned to Bing. "Disgustingly healthy creature!" He lit two cigarettes and held out one to Bing.

"Lights out!" someone shouted.

"Jumpy," said Thorpe. "Everybody is jumpy. Except me. It's not because I've been in this before. They say the more you've been through, the more scared you get. Probably true, too. And I am scared, I don't say I am not. But there are other things I am even more scared of. This Dondolo — and that I stood there, not able to move. As if my feet were sealed to the ground, my arms to my sides. Have you ever felt that way? Now I have a headache. I can't look down at the water for long, those light spots, those leaves, begin to turn and turn."

"Maybe you need sleep, too. I can give you some aspirin. The kind of sleep we get!"

"I can't sleep," said Thorpe. "I even sort of like the German planes. They come, and the noise starts, and they drop those bunches of red, green, yellow lights. I like to see them float down. I see them and I forget about the other thing. . . ."

"What other thing?"

"I can't describe it. I'm trying to explain it to myself. This Dondolo, he's helped me. . . . Yes, he has. He's made it a little clearer."

"You have a headache — why do you talk so much?"

"Why did you ask Abramovici what he's in the war for?"

"I asked Dondolo, too."

"Why?"

"Because I don't know, myself," said Bing. "I have some ideas, but none of them cover it entirely. And I must write a leaflet about it — tell it to the Germans. Farrish wants it."

"Farrish?"

"Odd, isn't it? So God-damned tough that you get the feeling he's got leather for brain tissue. Yet he thinks, thinks up there in his brain, and worries. . . ."

"But you *must* know! How can you tell the Germans if you don't know, yourself?"

"There are dozens of slogans."

"They're no good." Thorpe beat his fist on the railing. "I tried them all. I told them to myself when I lay in the hospital, when I saw the men, suffering. Suffering, that's a slogan in itself. And they're all so brave about it. I thought I was the only one who wasn't brave — but then I found out that they all were putting up a show, including myself. If you ask me, we're constantly putting up this show, every one of us, even if we're not hit. If you were all alone, if nobody, no man, no officer, were looking at you — wouldn't you run? Run as fast as you could? We keep going simply because we're never alone. That's the whole secret. Organization. Clever, such organization. In a group, you don't dare to admit that you're scared stiff and that you want to go home."

Out of the shadow stepped Tolachian. "I've seen Loomis," he said.

"What did he want?" asked Thorpe.

"He said he didn't like my attitude. It implied insubordination." The big words came hesitantly from Tolachian's heavy lips. "And he said he'd personally see to it that I had no more chance of interfering."

"Interfering with his relations with the French?" The story of Madame Poulet's clash with Loomis had made the rounds of the Detachment.

"I suppose so." Tolachian scratched his wrist. "They're biting tonight."

Bing shook his head. "You'd better watch out. You've made him ridiculous. People don't forgive that. Especially Loomis."

"They're all bastards," said Thorpe, with conviction, "all of them."

Tolachian, elbows on the railing, folded his hands. They were big hands with thick, strong fingers. In the darkness, he tried to read Bing's face. "I am not worried," he said.

"Well — think a little bit of yourself! You've got a wife at home, you tell me. She works hard. You want to come back to her, one day, and make it easier for her. . . ."

"I want to," said Tolachian, "I want to very much."

For a while, everything was still. Thorpe, unable to pay more than passing attention to anything outside himself, reverted to his pet compulsion. "All right, you go through with it," he said; "you stick it out, you don't run. And then you feel that the same things you've been fighting against crop up behind your back. . . ."

"For instance?"

"It's catch phrases again — and words don't give the full meaning of it. Injustice. Intolerance. Cruelty. Narrow-mindedness. Egotism. Vanity. What have you."

"Dondolo," said Bing.

"Yes, he too."

"What's Dondolo been up to?" asked Tolachian, trying to get the drift of what was on the other two men's minds.

"What's he been up to?" said Bing. "His old tricks. Him and his bunch, ganging up on Abramovici. Then they went after Thorpe."

"Somebody should beat his brains out," Tolachian said, with feeling.

"I should have done it," Thorpe said miserably.

"You keep out of it," said Tolachian. "You got enough scars."

But Thorpe didn't accept the excuse for himself. "Dondolo!" he said. "He's just one of them! It goes up all the way. Loomis, Willoughby, Farrish! I've seen Farrish come through our hospital in North Africa. There was a guy with shock, crazy. The guy stands before his bed, at attention, and has to listen to Farrish calling him names. Afterwards, they had to take the guy to the other ward where they don't allow visitors. I tell you, I was grateful I at least had a couple of honest-to-goodness shrapnel holes in my body to show."

He took a deep breath.

"So I fight for democracy, against fascism. Wonderful idea, you know? Government of the people, by the people, for the people. Then I think about it, and I see: Everybody free to cut everybody else's throat."

40

The frogs' croaking swelled.

Tolachian's voice cut through it.

"Once I had a friend," he said; "Tony was his name. He was a great big man with the heart of a child. You could tell him that there was an angel who cut slices off the moon every month, and gave the silver to the widows and orphans; and he would believe it because he liked to believe nice stories.

"One day, Tony got himself into a fight. That was in Chicago, and there was a strike. You know how it is, you want to give your wife something to wear, and your kids something to eat and an education. . . .

"It was a Sunday, and the workers with their wives and kids were walking near the plant, on the South Side of Chicago. The sun was shining, and the strike began to look like a holiday, almost. Suddenly, police were all over the place, and they began clubbing the people and beating them up, and some were even shooting.

"Tony saw all that. He didn't belong to those workers, he worked somewhere else, a printer, like me. But he went in, and with his strong arms, he grabbed the nearest cop and tore him away from a woman. And he did more. He was like — what was his name? — like Paul Bunyan; and where he stood, the people had some air.

"So they shot him. I saw him in the hospital. His round face was very thin, and all the blood had gone out of it. I want to cough, he said to me, but I can't, it hurts too much. . . . That's how bad it was, he couldn't even cough.

"I asked him: Tony, I said, what for did you get yourself mixed up in that? You were very stupid, Tony.

"Tony said nothing for a while. And then he said: Sarkis — he called me by my first name — Sarkis, I did right.

"Sure you did right, I said. I didn't want him to get excited.

"No, you don't understand, he said. When men with guns beat up men without guns, and women and children, that is not right. But me, I know this: When a thing like that happens somewhere, it will happen all over. When it happened to those people on the South Side of Chicago, it happened to me. And I would do it all over again. Yes, I would. When you see a bad weed, you tear it out, roots and all. Otherwise, it will swallow the whole field. If you see a bad weed, Sarkis, he said to me, and you will see them. . . . Then he coughed."

Bing's mind was working rapidly. In a voice that seemed not to come from him, he repeated, "*If it happens somewhere, it happens to me. . . .*"

That was America!

"What became of Tony?" asked Thorpe.

Tolachian unclasped his hands. "He died."

41

4

KAREN WALLACE was looking for Bing.

She told herself that she wanted to ask him how he was making out with the leaflet. But as she walked around the Château, its shadows sharply marked by an immense moon — as she met men who stared at her and involuntarily took a few steps toward her, only to stop and sheepishly say, "Hello!" or "Good evening," or just whistle — as she finally turned into the driveway that led to the drawbridge and recognized Bing and felt the slight constriction of her heart, ever so slight — she knew that the leaflet was a pretense. She laughed at herself. A chance meeting in a dugout, a car ride through a part of Normandy, and I must be older than he is — be sensible, girl, don't overdo it!

She was too well aware of her own chemistry. She could say in advance what she was going to do, if she let herself do it — every step in the game: Approach, allure, take — and then, the same thing all over again — break away without too much emotion.

Yet, there was the chemistry.

Bing noticed her coming toward him. He was glad that Thorpe was still around — Tolachian had taken off, back to his quarters in Vallères village. He was glad for two reasons: He was afraid of being alone with her because he would probably try to make her, and she would repulse him, or scream, and there would be a scene, unpleasant and disappointing. Also, he knew that she was being followed by dozens of eyes, longing, envious, greedy, lonely. If they saw her talk to the two of them, Thorpe and himself, that was all right. But he and the woman alone . . . The men would slap his shoulder, tomorrow, and ask him how it had been, with jealous intimacy, and yet boastful over his having done it — through him, they all would have had her. And the men expressing this good-natured, bawdy solidarity were the better ones — there were others who would feel: If this guy, why not me? She does it with him; probably she does it with everybody. And they would look at her, all hours of the day, and look right through her clothes with shameless directness, look at her breasts and her thighs and the between-her-legs.

Hiya, babe! Raucously.

He wanted to spare her that. "This is Preston Thorpe," he said. "Thorpe was in North Africa before he got into this."

Thorpe felt her eyes on him. He raised his hand. "North Africa! I want to forget about it. I want — "

Bing heard the panic in Thorpe's voice. He saw the mistake he had made. He had thought, if I were Thorpe and here was this girl, coming out of the night — I'd grab at the chance and gab and show myself off for all North Africa and I were worth.

"I've got a splitting headache," said Thorpe. He looked at Bing and at Karen and managed a smile.

Karen placed her hand on Thorpe's forehead. Thorpe shivered. "Maybe you'd better lie down," she said.

There was much compassion in her voice, and much understanding. Bing wished he were alone with her, somewhere, anywhere except here, among these men.

"There's nothing the matter with him," he said for Thorpe's benefit.

Thorpe squirmed. He was afraid of the woman, just because she seemed kind, just because he wanted her as everyone around here wanted her. If he didn't get away soon, something in him would give, he would either stand as he had stood before Dondolo, coffee and blood running down his neck and his shoulders, or a worse thing would happen, he didn't know what.

She must have sensed it. She was casting about for a neutral subject.

"The leaflet!" she said to Bing. "I can't find out a thing about it from Willoughby or any of the other officers." She wanted to know everything — the viewpoint from which Bing approached the problem, the method by which he was going to treat it, and what were the arguments to which the Germans might listen?

"Well, Miss Wallace," said Bing, "if only someone could state definitely what we're supposed to be fighting for, I would have something to go on." He nudged Thorpe.

Thorpe said nothing. He had turned halfway and was staring at the leaves of the water lilies that swam on the moat — quiet, whitish patches.

"I've been spending the last few hours," Bing continued, "kind of polling people . . ."

"Well — take the Four Freedoms," Karen suggested, hesitantly. "They ought to be good enough."

"And pretty hazy, too. Ask the average man: Is he in the war to fight for freedom of speech and religion — other people's speech, other people's religion? For freedom from want and fear — other people's want, other people's fear? The Germans aren't going to accept that baloney."

Abruptly, Thorpe faced Karen and Bing. "What about the flag," he sneered, "what about our tradition?"

Bing felt it better to treat this straight. "You know," he said, "the Krauts have got more tradition and a hell of a lot more flags."

"O.K., O.K.," said Thorpe, "why do you go around asking people if you don't take their suggestions? The flag is plenty good enough for me! Good night, Miss Wallace!" He began to laugh to himself, a soft, oblique laugh, and went off, almost at a run.

43

There was an oppressive minute of quiet. Then Karen asked, "What's wrong with your friend?"

"I don't know. He's never been that bad before."

"Do you think it's — because I came?"

"No," Bing said uncertainly. "Maybe I'd better go after him and see . . ."

But he didn't go. "He'll be all right," he said finally. "A little too much war, and this crazy moon, I guess. What have you been doing with yourself?"

"I've been gathering impressions."

"I can imagine what kind."

She looked at him. He saw the tiny reflections of the moon in her eyes. He was very conscious that he was alone with her, though he could hear the constant going and coming of men on the other side of the bridge, in the yard of the Château. He had tried not to be alone with her. He had tried to hold Thorpe. It hadn't worked.

"Karen!" he said.

"Huh-uh!"

He withdrew his hand.

"So — what kind of impressions did you gather?"

"I've met only the brass. You must have a tough time of it, Sergeant Bing. But then, in the Army you all seem to be drilled to the point where you accept the authority of anything that carries a piece of metal on its shoulders."

"Yes, I accept it. But between us," he added, "I do pretty much as I see fit. The difference between good and bad officers is simply that the good ones let you do it, while the bad ones try to make it more difficult."

"And you get away with it?" She smiled.

"Well," he said — and then paused. He was not sure whether he should tell the story of St.-Sulpice. She might feel that he was trying to put in his own oar, and by God, he did want to — but he didn't want her to know it. How could a man be casual, on a Normandy night, in summer, in the war where nobody knew what was going to come tomorrow, with a woman at his side?

"What were you going to tell me?" she urged. "I'm a good listener."

He *would* try to bring it in casually. "Take Major Willoughby," he said. "With all his faults, he's a good officer. When we went into St.-Sulpice to get the fort, Willoughby had enough sense to park himself in a café and get drunk, and to leave the operation to Sergeant Clements and myself."

"I've heard rumors of the story — what really happened?" she asked, the woman in her giving way to the reporter.

"The Germans were cut off inside the fort, hundreds of them — we didn't know how many. But we knew that they had ammunition and food to last for a long while. It would have meant trouble, and the generals said

44

they needed the road for the approach to Cherbourg. Willoughby must have offered them the loudspeaker truck — I can show it to you later, it's parked right across the bridge. We were to tickle the Germans out of the fort."

"And Willoughby, meanwhile, went to the café?"

Bing laughed. "Maybe he had confidence in us. . . . Clements and I doped out the situation. So we gave the Germans an ultimatum. We told them over the loudspeaker that we had enough artillery and tanks outside to blast the whole fort to dust, and we gave them ten minutes to make up their minds and come out. And ten minutes only.

"And then — that was the main trick — we counted off the minutes. It must have made them nervous, that counting: Nine minutes to go — eight minutes — seven minutes . . . but they couldn't possibly have been as nervous as we were."

"How far did you have to count?" she asked.

"Well, when we were down to three minutes, the first Germans came out, hands raised. More and more came, they seemed to gush out; there was no end to them. They surrounded us. And instead of the guns and tanks we had promised, they found this loudspeaker truck and a measly platoon of MP's — maybe not even that many. They felt like fools, and we felt pretty silly, too, with the MP Lieutenant running around trying to corral reinforcements. Then the Germans got mad. They said we had lied to them — which was true enough — and they couldn't surrender that way."

She laughed.

"It was against their honor. We didn't know what to do — honor is an important proposition with the Germans, their kind of honor, I mean. Anyhow, we couldn't let them go back into the fort — and I don't think they wanted to, much. Their bundles were packed so neatly, they were ready to quit."

"They could have rushed you and killed you. . . ."

"They weren't in that mood. They were just sore that the tanks weren't there. And one of their officers came and demanded that we get the tanks, and that the tanks fire some rounds so that they could claim they had surrendered to superior force. They must have a myth to hang on to — funny, isn't it?"

"What did you do?"

"I sent Clements to the café to get Willoughby. Willoughby was to get us the tanks. Willoughby wasn't there. Somebody said he had gone off with some girl and that he was not to be disturbed. But Yates and Laborde were there — Laborde is another one of our lieutenants, you'll probably meet him. He was supposed to be in on that operation, but thank God, he had come too late. Laborde probably would have opened fire on the Germans, if he had been around. Well, Yates got us the tanks, about half a dozen of

45

them, and they fired at the fort, and then the Germans were marched off."

"And you tell all this so lightly!" she said.

"Intentionally," he laughed. "I want you to admire me. Nobody else does."

"Did you get a medal?"

"Hell — nothing."

"I'd like to write up this whole story."

"Please — don't. Just be glad that maybe some of our guys are alive today because Clements and I got those Germans to give up. But if the facts of the story get out, Willoughby will get sore, and Loomis, and the others — and they'll take away the little freedom I have. . . ."

She wished she could say something that would express how much she liked him.

He asked, "You won't stay at Vallères too long, will you?"

"No, I won't."

"Let's go somewhere," he said. "This place has all the privacy of a short arm inspection."

"I must get back soon," she pleaded, against herself. "They're throwing a party for me, I can't disappoint them."

They walked away from the drawbridge. Somebody whistled after them. Bing winced.

Karen took his arm.

"If *you* don't mind . . . !" He shrugged.

They walked on, without talking. Under a group of trees, one of the loudspeaker trucks was parked. A camouflage net was hung over it, and before the net someone had placed a toolbox. They sat down on the box.

"That leaflet," said Bing — "it's beginning to worry me. And I'm partly the cause of it. Just before you arrived at Carruthers's dugout, I stabbed Yates in the back — I really did, out of pure insolence. Yates had come to Farrish's Division for the express purpose of telling them it was impossible to produce the leaflet. I don't know what bit me — I said it could be done. No, I do know: I wanted to write this thing. I wanted to write what we are fighting for — because I wanted to get clear about it myself, and because I believe that this is a war of ideas as much as a war of guns and tanks and airplanes. Don't you think so?"

"Oh yes."

She was becoming impatient. She was giving him this chance, she was leaning toward him, he must feel her — and he talked and talked. It was his excessive seriousness. It was sort of pathetic.

"That's one side of it," she agreed. "But there are people who make millions in profits, and who are in it for that. And there are soldiers who are in it because they have been drafted, and what else could they do? And

46

there are men who fight for their very right to live. But in fighting for this right, they also fight for the profits of the first group. That's how it seems to me. It's all mixed up, and I don't know that you can find a common denominator."

"You talk strange. . . ."

"How should I talk?"

"Oh, I suppose more like a woman — more with love — compassion for the oppressed — love for the people who are struggling . . ."

"Listen," she said, "I've been around."

"I know."

"I've lost the grand ideals. When it comes down to facts, you reckon in numbers — numbers of men, machines, money. Without that, all your ideals would remain hanging in the air, and the men believing in them hanging by their necks."

"I'd like to kiss you," he said gruffly. He stroked her hand, felt the texture of her skin, the life pulsating underneath.

"No. It's too late for that, tonight. I've talked too much. You've made me come out with a lot of disillusioning things. You don't want to kiss me, really. You think, Here's this woman, and we're alone. You just see the opportunity and you feel obliged to use it. Now, be good."

Her hand touched the back of his neck.

"Angry?"

"No, of course not."

They walked back to the yard and encountered Yates.

Yates's pace quickened as he saw her. "I've been looking for you everywhere, Miss Wallace. But I see you've found company. . . ."

She believed she detected a note of sarcasm in his voice, but his next words belied this impression.

"I've come to apologize. I've been a bad host. I'm glad that Major Willoughby got you a decent dinner — but when I came to pick you up, he said you'd gone out. Thank you, Bing, for taking such good care of Miss Wallace."

"We were talking of the leaflet," said Bing.

"An interview . . ." confirmed Karen.

"Thank you, Bing," Yates repeated, pointedly. He felt he had certain rights. It was he who had discovered the girl and taken her away from Carruthers. True, she had fenced with him all afternoon, on the long ride through Isigny. But her heckling probably was her way of saying: *I don't make love that easily and that readily.*

Bing appreciated Yates's feelings. Yates might have as liberal an outlook as possible — he was still an officer. It was a question of supply and demand. If sufficient beds were available, the men would get them, too. If

47

not, they were given to officers only. With women it was the same. Karen might have played with him, Bing thought, because his having to write the leaflet made him a little more interesting to her than he actually was — but when it had come to the point, she had said No.

Bing decided to withdraw.

"It was a great pleasure," he said to Karen. "You have been very helpful."

Yates took Bing's retreat as a matter of course. "Good night, Sergeant," he said.

Karen looked from one to the other of the two men. A silent agreement, a code, seemed to be in force.

"What kind of people are you?" she burst out. "Don't you ever stop being lieutenants and sergeants, colonels and corporals?"

"Pardon?" said Yates, unprepared for her outbreak.

Bing said, "Well, Miss Wallace — there is this party for you. I don't want to hold you up."

Something personal *was* going on between Bing and the woman. Yates didn't like it. Not counting the Norman peasant wenches, she was the first real woman he had seen since England. Life having been given to him anew each invasion day he had survived, she was, in a sense, *the* first woman.

"I decide where I go," she said, "and when and with whom." This was said for the benefit of both Yates and Bing; she would have the boy know that he could not hand her over whenever he felt it was time.

She turned to go.

She was almost swallowed by the darkness; Yates was about to hurry after her, when she and the world were doused in a bright new light. Like gigantic chandeliers, the German parachute flares hung in the air. A deep whirring closed in on the three of them with breath-taking speed.

The ack-ack guns opened up. Whether they were big ones, or the light caliber which spattered their shells in haste, the guns always sounded as if their crews had been asleep and had started too late and were trying to make up for lost time. The arcs of their tracer bullets converged on their targets.

The woman, the Sergeant, the Lieutenant, were shaken back into the reality of war.

Karen made a move toward the Château. Yates dashed after her and grabbed her arms.

"Stand still!" he hissed.

"I don't think they can spot us," said Bing. But he, too, remained fixed.

Not too far away, the German bombs began falling. Yates could feel the tremor of the earth as they exploded. There was an empty drawing in his stomach, from his chest down to his groin.

48

"Nothing to be afraid of," he said to Karen. "They're falling quite a ways off."

"But it's beautiful!" said Karen. "There's another flare — a whole bunch of them! Right on top of us!"

Their faces were white and seemed overly big in the reflection of the flares; the natural shadows came out deeper, sharper, black.

Yates said, "Yes, it has its own beauty!" If she could think it beautiful, so could he, damn it.

"I hate to have these ack-ack fragments come down near me," said Bing. "They're the real nuisance." He sounded cool.

"Aren't you afraid?" asked Karen. She was ready to drop her aloofness; she wanted to be in his arms, to close her eyes.

"Sure I am. . . . Hey, look at that! They've got him!"

The planes had been invisible, hidden behind the flares they had dropped. Now, one of them was lit up. It floundered. It became a star, a comet, a glistening, burning, plummeting star.

Bing reached out. Before Karen knew what was going on, she lay on the hard ground, bruised, aching, thrown down by Bing, who lay next to her, close, very close.

A wave of warm air rolled over them, the air pressure released by the explosion.

Karen huddled up to Bing. He felt her breath against his ear, she was breathing fast.

"That was close, whew!" She heard Yates's voice, very thin, as if from a great distance. "It went down over there, across the field. You can see it burn."

She felt Bing's arms let go of her. She felt Yates take her by her elbows and lift her up. "You aren't hurt, are you?" he asked. He sounded genuinely concerned, and his hands were considerate as he brushed the dirt off her jacket. She let him lead her. She was defenseless, and liked it — was it because she had been in Bing's arms, or because of the force of the explosion? She didn't know.

"I think I was very foolish," she said, "very scared. Not when it came down — I didn't realize what it meant. But after the crash. . . ."

"Must have had a couple of his bombs left," Yates said. His relief made him talkative; he felt that she had softened up, that her barriers were down. "The bombs blew up. There won't be much left of the plane. Do you want to go there?"

"I don't feel much like walking."

"I'm glad you hugged the ground so fast," said Bing. He was standing a little to the side, but he seemed farther away, much farther.

Everything was quiet now, except for the crackling of the flames that came through the still air.

49

"Oh, nuts!" said Bing.

"Miss Wallace!" Yates said with artificial cheerfulness. "The party is still waiting for us. Let's go!"

She followed him.

Bing lay on his sleeping bag in the attic of the Château's tower, trying frantically to recapture the spirit of what Tolachian had said. What had he said? If it happens somewhere, it happens to me. . . . What? Injustice, suffering, probably. Bing had been so sure the solution lay in Tolachian's tale of Tony, of Paul Bunyan, of the giant with the child's heart. Now, he wasn't sure of anything. He should have taken the woman. It would have done him good. She wasn't even pretty, but her voice was in his blood. And she had a good body, he could see that from the way she walked. Coveralls and boots — what a combination. For all he knew, she might have scrawny legs underneath. But her breasts were firm, he had felt them when the Nazi plane had come down. Women — you had to protect them; it was nice protecting her. The cracks in the wall had become bigger again. Plaster was falling down, all the time, all the time — but now, there was much more plaster. Tomorrow, I must shake out this sleeping bag, full of dirt and dust. Tomorrow, I must think of Tony the child's heart, and Karen, the woman's heart — Aw, what the hell, why don't you forget about it all and sleep? No, I can't, they will start again with their planes, and the ack-ack — Karen, a nice name. But she is honest, she tells you what she's thinking — that's the trouble, destroys illusions. I've never had a woman like that. . . .

Aw, God damn it to hell. This war.

5

THE BOTTLES, lined up in a row, were exceedingly decorative. There were sherry and Benedictine found in a cellar in Isigny, Scotch and gin which were saved-up rations from England, and the clear, sharp Calvados, bartered by Dondolo from the peasants for cigarettes. Mademoiselle Vaucamps, approached by Yates, had agreed to let them have some of the glasses belonging to the Comte in Paris — his best Venetian set, especially cut to show his heraldic design: a unicorn over two lions grappling with one another.

"Ah!" exclaimed Willoughby, "this is the life!" He looked at Karen's legs.

Karen had changed to a skirt. She sat in a corner of the Comte's blue Louis Quatorze sofa, its worn upholstery comfortably giving to her body. The light bulbs in the glittering chandelier were turned on full and gave the room a semblance of its onetime splendor. The windows were blacked out with cardboard from ration boxes and with posters showing an American tank driver emerging from his turret, and shaking the hands of a grateful, liberated family.

"Say something, Miss Wallace!" urged Willoughby. "Isn't this cozy? We try to shut out the war." He began to sing, swinging his glass in rhythm, "*Malbrough s'en va-t-en guerre! Rataplom! Rataplom!*" With each *plom* his arm came down and the liquor spilled over.

Yates sat on the armrest of the sofa, one of his legs dangling. With one hand, he held a glass, with the other, he tried to edge up on Karen's shoulder.

"*Rataplom! Rataplom!*"

Yates said, "What do you think made Madame Poulet say we can't hold liquor?"

Willoughby gave up singing and looked at Karen and Yates from under drooping eyelids.

The radio officer, who was a captain, and three lieutenants had settled on the floor in a corner of the room. A blanket was spread between them; they were playing poker. Piles of invasion francs were shifted around. One of the lieutenants, a middle-aged, yellow-haired, pasty-faced man, got up and said, "I quit. I'm broke."

The others berated him. "I'll stake you!" shouted the captain. "You'll be around. This is going to be a long war!"

"That's a perpetual game," said Yates. "It started on the LST coming across the Channel. If they have liquor, the money rolls faster. No, Miss Wallace —" his voice sank low — "we drink because we're lonely."

His hand now lay on her shoulder. She took it off, but in a way that prevented his feeling offended.

"Oh, Karen," he said, "it's good to have you around."

"Thank you," she said softly. She was beginning to like him; he was becoming more human as he gave up some of his pretenses — or perhaps he only shone in comparison to the others here.

Willoughby was coming closer.

Yates saw him and wanted to tip off Karen; but she was asking who was the officer over there?

Lieutenant Laborde, his ascetic face screwed up in wrinkles, sat alone, studying his hands. He desperately wanted to attract the woman's attention; now that he had it, he didn't know it, and he would have been unable to think of anything to say which would interest her. Could he tell her that he was a hero? That he was willing to sacrifice his life at the slightest provocation? The others would have laughed him out of the room. They had made up their minds to avoid being heroes if they could help it. But he had always been that way — from the time when, working for the great chemical trust, he had gone into the gas chamber not sure at all whether he would come out alive. And then the thousands of times he had been spun around in the dummy cockpit so they could find out what the human stomach could stand — his stomach could stand it. But who the hell was interested in his stomach?

"That's Lieutenant Laborde," Yates said to Karen, and he said it in such a way that the drink he took immediately afterwards seemed very necessary. "Shall I call him over? You would make him very happy."

Willoughby sat down at Karen's other side. That precluded an invitation to Laborde. Willoughby said, "It's really cozy!"

Loomis opened another bottle. The cork made a *pop!* and Loomis stared at it. "Remember how we came up from Carentan?" he said as if he expected an answer. "Doesn't anybody remember how we came up from Carentan? With the road under fire? Hey, Crabtrees!"

He was appealing to a lieutenant who had draped his slender body on a chair. Crabtrees giggled. "I sure do! Never forget it in my life. Not as long as I live. That was the time when it was still dangerous," he added. "Over the bridge — I've forgotten the name of the darned river — "

"MP's were killed there every day, Miss Wallace. They couldn't show their heads!" confirmed Loomis. "The Germans were right across the hill, and they had the road under observation. You ever been under mortar fire? I don't know what I prefer — artillery or bombs from the air — but certainly not mortars. They're the worst."

"Decidedly!" said Crabtrees. He tightened his belt around his too slim waist.

Finally, Loomis succeeded in eliciting a question from Karen. "So what happened, Captain?"

Loomis leaned forward, ready to launch the great story. "Well — we had to go over this road — there just wasn't any other. And it was the time of the day when the Germans would start their shelling — "

"Five o'clock in the afternoon!" said Crabtrees. "Every afternoon! Precise as clockwork, these Germans!"

"All right! All right!" Loomis waved. "I say to the driver, We're taking our lives in our hands, but it's got to be done! O.K., sir, says the driver. Good men we have in this Detachment, very good men. And we start out — "

Willoughby said, "So you got shot at."

"Shot at? My God, it was a regular barrage. Bang bang bang! Behind us, in front of us! I say to the driver: Put your foot down, all the way! It's down all the way, sir, he says. We're flying along, sixty, seventy miles . . ."

"At least seventy!" Crabtrees released his belt. He was breathing heavily, to show his excitement.

"And then?" asked Karen.

52

"Then we were through! We had made it! Saved!"

"Thank God," said Crerar, picking up the kitten Plotz.

Yates bent back and let out a genteel guffaw.

"You don't know how risky it was!" remonstrated Loomis. "These roads! And under fire! But we had no choice."

Willoughby stood up. He emptied his glass and set it down, heavily, on the table. "Miss Wallace," he said, "don't let them tell you stories. Of course, everybody does his duty. That's what we're here for. But this is what's known as rear echelon. Sometimes, we get shot at, or bombed, or shelled — but that's all in a day's work. We can't compare ourselves to those boys up front, in their foxholes, fighting it out eye to eye with the Krauts. They're the real heroes, those fellows. . . ."

Some modesty! thought Yates. He went and poured himself another drink and returned to Karen's side. What the hell does he take the girl for? — A starry-eyed débutante?

Willoughby went into his jowly smile. "Not that I want to belittle you, Loomis . . ."

"Oh, no!" said Loomis. He knew he was beaten. He knew his inferiority — to Willoughby, to any lousy man in a foxhole.

"Sometimes we do little tricks," said Willoughby. He came over to Karen, bottle in hand, and filled her glass and his own. "If you don't mind, Yates . . ." He sat down close to her, he was moving in, taking possession.

"Little tricks — they may not mean much, but then — what is much, or little, in the grand total of the war effort? Only doing our duty!"

Yates left the armrest of the sofa. He faced Willoughby and Karen. He gulped down his drink, he felt the liquor burn down his gullet, his head became light, very pleasantly light. He said, "Ha, ha!"

Willoughby said to Karen, "He's drunk, our friend." Then he turned to Yates, "Go ahead! There's plenty — only don't come to me with a headache, tomorrow!"

Yates did not answer him. He walked up to Loomis and said, loudly, "You're a poor specimen, Loomis, one of the poorest I've ever seen."

"Why?" inquired Loomis, still much too depressed to fight back. But Yates dropped the subject.

Willoughby continued. "St.-Sulpice, for instance, Miss Wallace, was strictly our show. More than a thousand prisoners, immense amount of food, supplies, and ammunitions — all goes to our credit. You don't mind if I brag just a little?"

"Brag," she said, "why not?" The Benedictine was beginning to take hold. Willoughby's sallow face swam before her eyes.

"And it was really simple!" he said. "I came up there, I surveyed the situation. It would have taken the troops days to take the fort. So I said, Let's give them an ultimatum. An ultimatum with teeth in it — ten minutes to

53

come out of their holes. We told the Nazis, There are tanks and artillery waiting to blast you to bits. And then I had the minutes counted off to them — you realize the psychological effect, Miss Wallace! Eight minutes to live — five — three!"

"Very clever," said Karen. She felt Willoughby's hand on her thigh. "And you worked it all out, yourself?"

"Oh, shucks!" he said with the candor of the little man on the Alka-Seltzer ads. "It's part of the game — really nothing."

"You're lying," said Yates. His voice was calm, sharp, and angry. The conversation of the others died. Even the poker players stopped shuffling. Only Crerar could be heard saying, "Plotz! Plotz! Come here! Come to Poppa!"

Yates was stuck in his own track. He had been driven into the attack — driven by Willoughby's brazenness, Willoughby's being all over Karen; and by a certain loyalty to his own men, to Bing or anyone else who was doing an honest day's work.

Karen removed Willoughby's hand. She rose and crossed over to Yates and whispered to him, "Don't argue. Please don't. It isn't necessary. I know the whole story, I know the truth."

From Bing, of course, thought Yates.

"But it's such a God-damned big lie!" he said.

Willoughby smiled thinly. "Miss Wallace!" he said. "Come, sit down again. No reason in the world to get upset. Lieutenant Yates is right, to an extent. The actual job was done by two sergeants. His name-calling, we'll agree, is in bad taste. But we will say he is under the influence of liquor. The fact is that I, as Commanding Officer of that mission, bore the responsibility and therefore have a certain right to claim credit for it. If anything had gone wrong, I would have had to take the blame — that's the Army, Miss Wallace."

"Absolutely correct," said Loomis. "Major Willoughby is most broad-minded, so to speak, to drop the matter in which Lieutenant Yates, unfortunately . . ." He became entangled in his own words, and could not finish. "Anyhow . . ."

"Shut up!" said Willoughby.

Crerar tickled the kitten. It lay on its back, its white belly stretched taut, and fought back with its soft paws. "Atcha, atcha, atcha," said Crerar, "you don't know from nothing, Plotz — atcha, atcha, atcha — you're just a civilian cat!"

"I resent that!" said Laborde.

"Pardon?" Crerar let go of the kitten.

"We're soldiers! Your remarks were not directed at the cat, obviously."

"Quiet!" shouted Willoughby. "If you fellows can't behave in front of a lady, I'll break up the whole party, now!"

54

One of the poker-playing lieutenants came from their corner. "You wouldn't let all this liquor go to waste, Major?"

"Well . . ." Willoughby seemed mollified. He closed his eyes meditatively. He could imagine what the girl was thinking — about him, about the whole lot of them.

He poured himself another drink. "You see, Miss Wallace, I had to give you some story about our work so you wouldn't feel you had come here for nothing."

He expected a question from her, but she sipped her Benedictine in silence.

"For nothing!" he repeated. "Because that leaflet story you wanted to do — well, there won't be any."

Crerar whistled softly.

"There won't be any leaflet," Willoughby continued. "There won't be any 'Forty-eight Rounds from Forty-eight Guns.' "

"Why?" she asked.

"I've stopped all that."

"Why?"

This was his scoop. He only needed to look at the faces of the men to know that it was. The group he headed might be small, at the beck and call of any G-2, buffeted about between the big boys at SHAEF and the echelons in the field — still, it was he who made the generals conform. Let her know that!

"Why?" he said. "I stopped it because the whole plan was preposterous. Farrish knows something of armored warfare, of pincers and stuff like that — but he has no idea of how the human mind functions."

"I thought his plan was pretty good."

"Do you seriously think, Miss Wallace, that the German soldier gives a damn about what we're fighting for? Why should that touch his heart? Is he a politician, a philosopher, an analyst? I ask you!"

"I wouldn't know," she said. She was dead sober, now. She fixed her eyes on Willoughby's jowls. "But how do you propose to stop it? My impression of General Farrish is that what he says goes."

Crerar listened closely. He wondered if Willoughby would now spill the secret he had refused to divulge at their conference. If he did, he was a damned fool, a reckless braggart. However, if Willoughby wanted to stick his neck out — it was *his* neck.

Willoughby himself hesitated. Yates had called his bluff on the St.-Sulpice surrender. If he backed out now, it would look as if he were calling his own bluff. And it was too beautiful a story.

He turned full face to Karen. "I trust you, kid," he said. "This is off the record?"

"Off the record," she said.

55

"Besides," he added thoughtfully, "if it got out, I'd deny it. . . . It is one of my pet theories that war distinguishes itself from ordinary everyday life merely by the added risk some of us take. Otherwise, relations between people are just the same. Ambition, jealousy, politics — you know. I can't say I'm particularly clever, really not . . ."

"But you are, sir!" said Crabtrees. He was very drunk and kept himself upright by hanging on to Loomis.

"Farrish's plan included the waste of a lot of ammunition. So I called up Corps Artillery — General Dore. General Dore is an old friend of mine, I know him socially; he calls me Clarence, I call him Charlie. I say: Charlie, listen, old boy — Farrish has this wonderful plan, firing forty-eight rounds from forty-eight guns on July Fourth — a great big fireworks to celebrate the day. Isn't it wonderful, Farrish going all out for Old Glory and so on? You should have heard Dore. What! he says. Does Farrish know how much ammunition that is? How much time it takes us to get it across the Channel? A regular blow-up . . . Well, Miss Wallace, and gentlemen — that call went through at nine, tonight. I expect, by this time, General Farrish has given up his project."

Willoughby sat down. He was pleased with himself. The girl looked at him, and her eyes were big. Wonderful eyes, full of admiration. She was a modern girl, she appreciated brains and power.

Yates tried to be objective, but the alcohol interfered. This operating behind scenes made history! In college, they had taught him that there were men of purpose who thought in terms of masses of people and trends of development, and who exerted their influence and power with the community in mind. But all he had ever encountered were the Willoughbys who pushed pawns over extremely limited fields. It was a frightening vista: today, Willoughby killed a leaflet; tomorrow, perhaps — Yates.

Karen did admire Willoughby. There was something colossal about the pettiness of his intrigue.

"Do you really believe, Major," she asked, "that there is so little difference between war and — well, and peace? Don't you overlook the fact that, in war much more than in peace, any decision involves the lives of men?"

"That is a difference in degree, not in character," Willoughby replied.

"Not to me!" Yates said sharply. "In war, my life happens to depend on you!"

"Plotz thinks it's a dirty trick," said Crerar, "but effective." He laughed and turned to Karen. "Don't worry about it. All these shrewd operators think a lot of themselves, they're very proud of their trade. But people and their actions are like molasses, they move very slowly, and the matter somehow remains the same."

Loomis, who only now had reached the point of evaluating Willoughby's story, grew voluble in his praise. "Great!" he said to the Major. "Great!" And, with envy, "Of course, one must have connections!"

Willoughby was about to use his re-established stature for moving in on Karen.

Yates thought, In another minute he'll be on her lap. Why doesn't she keep him off? Maybe she likes the idea. . . . But he didn't want to look at it. He'd had enough of this party. He got up to go.

The doorway was blocked.

The figure standing there was like a drunk's distorted vision: a white face, pale lips tautly drawn, the shirt torn open at the collar as if the stranger had been fighting for breath.

It was Thorpe.

"For Chris'sake, man!" Yates rushed to him, fearing Thorpe would collapse. But Thorpe didn't. He regained sufficient control over himself to enter the room and to speak in a voice ragged with the strain that was in him.

"I couldn't sleep," he said, "I am sorry, I couldn't sleep."

Karen poured a drink for him and approached him. She wished Bing were here; Bing would be able to handle his friend and to handle her.

Thorpe didn't seem to see her, he didn't see the offered glass. "I can't sleep!" It sounded like a cry for help.

"All right, Thorpe! Get hold of yourself!" said Yates.

Loomis asked, "Hasn't anyone some pills we can give him?"

Thorpe was oblivious to his surroundings and to the stir he had created. "Why can't you sleep?" asked Karen.

Without looking at her, and in a strangely impersonal way, Thorpe said, "It is so quiet. Far too quiet. They're all around us."

"Who is?" said Willoughby. "This is silly."

Thorpe's eyes became fixed on Yates.

"You're an honest man," he said monotonously. "You're in the same boat. Don't you see this war is being lost? We're losing it every day. The fascists are all over us. I'm not sick, Lieutenant, believe me, I'm not sick. I see it, with my own eyes I see it, creeping up on us. Right here, in this room, in this Château, in this Army, at home . . ."

Yates felt the attention of the officers shift from Thorpe to him.

Karen said, "He was in North Africa . . ."

"It was the bombing," said Crabtrees; "some people just can't take it."

Crerar said, "But he complained it was too quiet!"

Thorpe raised his hand. "Silence, all of you! What good is it to win battles, if we lose the war? The flag, that's just a piece of gaudy cloth. Isn't it so, Lieutenant? Tell me!"

Yates was tongue-tied. He did not fully understand what Thorpe was

57

saying and what was going on inside the man. He only sensed the man's misery and how torn his mind was. But he knew that this officers' party was not the place for an attack of nerves.

"One of your men, Yates?" said Willoughby. "Get him out of here, will you?"

Thorpe, though almost completely absorbed in his fears, grasped some part of Willoughby's order. "Don't!" he cried, "don't drive me out, Lieutenant! I must have an answer! Am I right? Am I wrong?" Without waiting for a reply, he continued, lowering his voice as if to take Yates into his confidence, "There won't be any place to go! Where can you go? It will be one all-consuming night, black, dense, choking us."

Yates said hesitantly, "Don't worry, I won't leave you alone."

Loomis went to the door and shouted, "Sergeant of the Guard! Sergeant of the Guard!"

Thorpe came closer to Yates. "As long as we have a chance, let's you and me, and all the honest people we can find — let's go somewhere."

"Drink this!" Karen urged Thorpe.

Thorpe seemed to recognize her. "You're from the press — I know, I know. . . . Will you wait a minute? I'll give you a statement that will shock everybody. But first, some urgent business, excuse me."

He grabbed Yates's sleeve. "They'll say something is wrong with me because I can see through them, all of them. I know what they want. You won't believe them, Lieutenant, promise me that you won't!"

"I won't."

Yates was deeply disturbed. Thorpe's mad pleading, this concoction of phantasy and fear and matters which Yates sometimes darkly sensed but never dared to examine, fell on his chest. He wanted nothing to do with the whole problem — and yet, he felt that from this moment on, he would never be rid of it, that Thorpe had branded him, before the others and before himself.

"We must do something for the man," he said to Loomis.

Loomis apologized to Willoughby and to Karen. "We'll put him on sick call, in the morning." Then he saw that Dondolo, fully armed, had entered.

"Sergeant Dondolo," said Loomis, "what do *you* want?"

"I'm pinch-hitting for the Sergeant of the Guard, sir. Sergeant Lord —"

"I see, I see. . . ." Loomis pieced the story together. Lord probably was paying Dondolo ten bucks or so to take over the detail for him. "Well," he said authoritatively, "if you're the Sergeant of the Guard, take this man out and put him to bed."

"Thorpe," said Dondolo, "well, Thorpe . . ."

Thorpe shrank back as if hit by a whip; he tried to say something but couldn't. His hands closed around Yates's arm, a drowning man's grip.

"Let go of the Lieutenant," said Dondolo. Addressing everybody, he added, "I know the man. He's a little peculiar, sometimes, but harmless. . . . Come along now, Thorpe, no sense in hanging around here." He spoke kindly, almost tenderly.

Thorpe's arms fell down weakly. He bowed his head and, slowly but obediently, walked toward the door, to Dondolo. Dondolo placed his arm around Thorpe's shoulder. "Don't worry, Captain Loomis — I'll take care of him. Sorry, folks, about the disturbance. Good night."

They went out.

Yates was relieved. For a moment he had felt the urge to follow Thorpe. There was something fishy about Dondolo's solicitude, something frightening. But it was bad enough that the whole incident had centered around himself. He didn't want to widen the gulf Thorpe had created between him and the other officers; he wanted to close it, smooth it over. And the incident had somehow separated Willoughby from Karen, and the night was only half gone. Tomorrow was another day; he would look after Thorpe tomorrow.

Karen asked Loomis, "Are you sure the Sergeant will understand the boy? I think he needs a psychiatrist."

Willoughby said, "Men sleep badly, sometimes. War is no fun. If we sent everybody who's had a nightmare to the psychiatrist, we'd have nobody left to fight the war. Forget about it."

"Thorpe will be well taken care of!" said Loomis. "Just leave the men to themselves — they understand one another."

One flight below, Dondolo was kicking Thorpe in the groin. As Thorpe bent forward, in pain, Dondolo hit his kidneys. With every blow, he was hissing a few words, "Going up to the officers — brown-nosing — telling on me — I'll show you — you sonofabitch. . . ."

Thorpe went down on his knees. Dondolo jerked him up.

Dondolo heard the singing of the officers: "*For she's a jolly good fellow! For she's a jolly good fellow!*"

They wouldn't give me a drink, he thought, not even one lousy drink. He kicked Thorpe once again.

It was the Germans who saved Thorpe from Dondolo's violence, from the overjoy at having the boy delivered into his hands.

The German planes came in low. Their bombs fell before the ack-ack batteries could open their fire.

Dondolo threw himself down. He pressed his sturdy body into the corner formed by stairs and wall. Thorpe staggered down the stairs, past the

59

huddled Dondolo, and into the courtyard. Dondolo let him escape. If the guy wanted to get himself killed, that was his affair.

Upstairs, Willoughby was giving a speech on the necessity of living a full life. "If there is anything that must be done, do it now!" he said. "And make up your mind to enjoy it."

Loomis approved of these sentiments. He nodded.

Willoughby went on, "The war teaches us how little there is to be expected from the Tomorrow —"

Then the first explosion, and complete darkness.

Anxious silence.

"Where is everybody?" asked Loomis.

Someone said, "The generator must be out."

"Light! Get some light!" shouted Crabtrees.

"The windows! Get away from the windows!"

The men scurried about, to find their flashlights, or candles, or to find a safe spot for themselves.

The second bomb exploded, closer than the first. Glass splintered and clattered on the floor.

Karen felt somebody take hold of her and pull her down. A body covered hers. She felt lips searching for hers, lips pressing hers. She slapped a face.

Then the lights went on.

Near the wall farthest from the windows lay the participants of the party. Willoughby was hiding his head under a chair. Crabtrees cowered behind Loomis. Crerar held the kitten Plotz close to his chest and was saying, "I suppose we've had enough noise now for Thorpe to go to sleep." Yates was kneeling before Karen, explaining, "I wanted to protect you, I'm sorry, don't you understand?"

Lieutenant Laborde sat on the table, his legs crossed like a tailor's, his arms around the remaining bottles. As everybody looked at him, he smiled, satisfied. He had finally managed to get the center of the stage.

6

ABRAMOVICI typed out the message which the code clerk had handed him. Abramovici typed slowly and methodically and prided himself on the neatness of his spacing and the cleanness of his copy. When anybody tried to hurry him, saying, "Let's get going, man! I don't need a fancy job — just type it off!" Abramovici would look up, hurt, and explain, "Modern war is conditioned on precision." You couldn't argue with Abramovici.

Nobody hurried him this morning. Mr. Crerar and most of the officers were suffering the after-effects of last night's party. Abramovici had all the

time in the world to read and re-read the message: First, a series of mysterious names, connected by *from,* several *through's,* and *to.* These were the
code names of the units through which the message had been channeled,
and of the sending as well as of the receiving unit.

Then the message proper: *Strongly advise against project Matador.
Policy decision will follow.*

Then the signature: *DeWitt.*

Abramovici nodded. That was that. General Farrish would have to give
up his idea. Abramovici approved of the contents of the message. What
would become of the Army if everybody decided to meddle in everybody
else's business?

Crerar came in, unshaved, his gray hair untidy. The stubbles of his beard
accentuated the flabbiness of his skin; he looked old and disheartened.
Plotz, the kitten, followed him and began pawing for a wad of paper
which protruded from the wastebasket.

Crerar threw himself on the cot. "What did you do last night?" he asked.

"I was awake most of the time," Abramovici informed him. "If I have to
die," he said gravely, "I don't want to die in my sleep."

"Nonsense!" Crerar was annoyed. "I'm not sure of much, these days —
but I am 100 per cent sure that you're going to live through this war, and
that you will flourish and grow fat on it."

"I hope so, Mr. Crerar. But one must be prepared. Preparedness is the
essence of victory."

If the guy didn't know shorthand, I would fire him right now, thought
Crerar. Too much is too much.

Abramovici went on happily. "It may interest you to know, Mr. Crerar,
that your position in regard to the proposed leaflet for General Farrish has
been completely vindicated by Colonel DeWitt."

"You don't say!"

"He fully supports you."

"Is there a message?"

"Yes — here." Abramovici picked up the sheet and, stretching his fat
arm as far as he could, handed it to Crerar.

Crerar sighed. "Don't you think you could have given me the message
the minute I came in? You knew it was marked urgent!"

"You must trust my judgment," said Abramovici. "When I saw you
come in, I knew you were not in the mood for business; besides, this is one
of those cases where the higher echelon agrees with the conclusions
reached in the field."

Crerar grimaced. He crumpled the sheet and threw it on the ground.
Abramovici stooped to pick it up and disposed of it in the wastebasket.

"Don't be so God-damned neat!" cried Crerar. "I'm sick and tired of
neatness. Mess up your desk! Go ahead, mess it up!"

"I can get you some aspirin," suggested Abramovici.

Crerar rolled off the cot. In one step, he reached Abramovici and began to rummage through his papers. Leaflet samples, blank sheets, carbons, flew in all directions. The floor was littered.

"There, now," said Crerar, falling back on his cot, "the place looks much better. Looks like work, activity."

Stubbornly, Abramovici picked up the papers, built little piles, arranged and rearranged them. Crerar kept his eyes closed. He was cursing the Army. Last night, after Willoughby had given away his big secret intrigue, Crerar had begun to wish that there were some power to stop all this — that people were human again, instead of being little officials with official minds and official considerations — that the God-damned leaflet would be fired just to spite Willoughby and his vested interests.

Crerar knew that DeWitt would veto the leaflet. If the Colonel were here, it would be different. DeWitt, though a soldier for God knows how long, was a man of imagination who would buck a higher headquarters, if the issue was sufficiently important. But since DeWitt, himself, represented the higher headquarters, the case was lost.

The more Crerar thought about it, the more he became interested in the possible merits of a political appeal. What if Farrish, the rumbling, ranting extrovert, had hit on something?

He thought of his farm and of the things he had lost because people lacked imagination, people couldn't see what was going on in the world. That one's own life should be indivisibly tied up with so much stupidity, so much cowardice! Eve, he thought, *ma petite Eve*. He saw her crossing the yard of the farm, stepping lightly, winged steps, her soft, soft hair moving to the rhythm of her steps. His young wife, his child wife, God bless her and bring her back to him. But first, the farm. A woman needs atmosphere, one must give her the atmosphere in which she can live and bloom.

He heard Abramovici's typewriter going, the steady staccato of sobriety. And then a voice, urging, "Mr. Crerar!"

"Yes?" He sat up with such suddenness that the blood rushed from his head, making him feel slightly dizzy.

"I want to show you the leaflet." Bing was holding out two heavily corrected sheets. "It's still a draft, but I think it is pretty much what we need."

Crerar rubbed his eyes. He blinked. "You've attached a translation? Good."

Bing watched Crerar as he read. He tried to explore the meaning of the slight changes on Crerar's face — a half-smile, a scowl. This wasn't just any job he had done, it was more, much more. If the words could influence Crerar, could wean him away from Willoughby, the thing would have a chance. Not for his own sake, Bing thought, not for the joke he had planned to put over on history — but for the others, for Tony, Tolachian, Thorpe, Karen, even for Yates, even for Farrish. . . .

Crerar read slowly:

Salute to the Fourth of July!

Our cannon have spoken. This is the language of America, this Fourth of July, 1944.

To us, the Fourth of July is a hallowed day. On July Fourth, 1776, the United States was born as a nation — a nation of free men, equal before the law, and determined to govern themselves.

For these rights and liberties, we went to war in 1776. For these rights and liberties, we are fighting today. For, wherever they are threatened, we are threatened. Wherever the dignity of Man is affronted, we feel that it happens to us. Wherever people are oppressed and suffering, we are affected. Because we are that kind of nation, we have come to Europe to stop a tyrant from imposing his will on a nation, on Europe, and on the whole world.

And you, Germans — what are you fighting for?

To prolong a war already lost, a war which, if it lasts, will destroy you.

You have fought, five long years. Millions of you have died in Russia — yet the Russians are closing in on Germany's borders. In Italy, you were forced to give up two thirds of the country — and your retreat continues. And here, in the West, the pressure on your front grows stronger every day. Meanwhile, your towns and cities are reduced to ruin and ashes under the blows of the Allied Air Forces.

If you want to save yourselves, if you want to save Germany, there is only one way out:

Stop the war!

"Cigarette?" Crerar offered his case to Bing. He folded the sheets and handed them to Abramovici. "Let's type off some clean copies."

Abramovici read the text. Then he screwed up his face. "What a shame that it never will be printed."

Bing lit a cigarette to hide his concern. He thought of Karen. Perhaps he could make her threaten this whole gang of opportunists with exposure in the press. Of course, there was the Army censorship — but he could try.

"The main question," Crerar said suddenly, "the main question is: Do you believe in it? And how strong is your belief?"

"My God, I would never have written it — " Bing was surprised by the sympathy in Crerar's voice. "Mr. Crerar, I started the whole thing! There was a moment, at Farrish's Command Post, when it could have been stopped cold. Lieutenant Yates claimed it was impossible to produce the leaflet in time; and I think the General was ready to accept the inevitable. Then I said it could be done."

Crerar looked at him; his sunken lips seemed to frown.

Bing thought, Now why have I given myself away? He'll resent it. I'm just a wise guy. Why can't I keep my mouth shut?

Crerar said lightly, "I admit the stuff sounds all right, but I can't judge whether it will carry conviction, especially with the Germans. You see, I don't believe in it."

"You don't . . ."

"Sergeant Bing, the Revolution is ancient history. Today, if you mention the word, people cry 'Red'! You've written a revolutionary leaflet. . . . Equality before the law! You know as well as I do that millions of men in our country don't even have the right to vote. . . . Determined to govern ourselves! I know something of who's governing our country — I used to be a Big Business executive myself. And the war hasn't changed it a bit. The same type of men run Europe, the same type of men run the show in Germany. And don't tell me the methods are so different. In America, we don't believe at the moment in concentration camps or in the mass extermination of minority groups. But if the men in power found them necessary, we would have them— " Crerar snapped his fingers — "just like that!"

"No," said Bing, "we won't. I grant you, I started this leaflet on the cuff. I didn't know what I was letting myself in for. I didn't even know what to put in it. But then I talked to some of the men. Some stink; they'd be the guards in your concentration camps. But there are others who'd say, *Who are you trying to push around?* And ask, *What are you trying to put over?* I think they'd even fight against it."

"But you aren't sure!" said Crerar. "I am telling you, if ever we have fascism in the States, the German form of it will seem like a pastorale. They won't do anything to me; I'd stand to gain by it. But they sure as hell would get you. You consider this war as a God-damned crusade. I know that was mimeographed in some order. I like your idealism, your naïve approach. In fact, it gives me some hope. But I'm inclined to be realistic."

"So you don't think the leaflet's any good?"

"It's very good. But it's a mouthful of hypocrisy."

"I'm sincere about it, Mr. Crerar."

"Yes, you are, Bing — and probably thousands of others are, too. But it isn't a man named Bing speaking to the Germans, this Fourth of July. America is speaking. America is trying to sell itself. But its goods have become shoddy."

Bing was now defending Tolachian and the dead man Tony whom he never had known. "That may be so, Mr. Crerar. But we're trying, now. This war — it's different. Yes, damn it, it's necessary and it's just."

Crerar buried his head in his hands. He was exhausted. Crerar, too, really wanted to believe in what Bing had said, but his experience denied it and depressed him.

64

"We won't come to an agreement," he said in a dull voice, "and the argument is futile, anyhow."

But Bing needed to win the argument, for himself even more than for the leaflet.

"I know we aren't crusaders," he said. "We're egotists, opportunists, cowards. That's O.K. There's something odd about this war, though. Some people have set their mind on their own ends, but they can't quite get through. In the middle of their shenanigans, things run away with them. When I see that bastard Dondolo warm up Spam, he warms it up for me, and I turn out this leaflet. And take a man you know better — any man — even Major Willoughby, Willoughby at St.-Sulpice. . . ."

Crerar laughed. "Yes, let's take him. He furnishes a wonderful example. It may interest you to know, Sergeant, that it was the personal and very smart effort of Major Willoughby which is preventing the leaflet from being printed and fired. I told you, the argument was futile. . . ."

Bing sat down. He felt spent.

Farrish came into the Operations tent like Judgment Day. He was the right man for the part.

"What about the leaflet? Do you have it ready?" he asked after a cursory glance at Crerar, who had introduced himself.

Captain Carruthers, his mustache drooping dejectedly, said under his breath, "This morning, he decided to check up on the thing himself. . . ."

"What are you saying?" shouted Farrish. "I can hear you! Of course I check up myself! Whatever I don't do myself doesn't get done!" He turned to Crerar. "Outside my own Division, I mean. God, if anything like this ever happened among my men!"

"Well — what happened, sir?" said Crerar.

Carruthers was about to explain, but the General cut him short.

"Let me see the thing. You must have done some work on it!"

In the narrow tent, Abramovici could not help brushing against the General as he came over to give a clean copy of the translation to Crerar. Farrish pulled the copy out of Crerar's hand.

Bing, who had made himself inconspicuous in the half-dark corner of the tent, watched the General scan the copy. He saw the incongruity of this man judging the fine points of a political and psychological appeal; yet he knew that if Farrish chanced to like the job, he would find in him an ally against Willoughby.

Farrish read slowly, moving his lips. Bing asked himself: Did the General really comprehend the text and all its implications? If Farrish expressed disapproval, it would be too late to re-do the job, and the whole matter would have to be dropped.

"A little weak, isn't it?" Farrish seemed not too sure of his opinion. "I

65

should say — you really ought to tell the bastards! Strong language!"

He saw Crerar getting ready to object.

"Hold it, Mister! I don't say we should call them names — just let them know we'll lick the bejeezus out of them if they don't see the light. We used to have a preacher where I come from — powerful speaker, he was. He gave us a damned good idea of hell and the devil and how you'd get your damned soul run through with red-hot pokers! It made you shiver, even on a Summer Sunday — and when he got through preaching, damn it, you really felt you wanted to start living right. That's what I mean. This is all very nice, very civilized. Makes you feel good to be an American — but with that line of talk, you're a kind of namby-pamby American, not exactly my brand. . . ."

Since nobody contradicted him, he coughed and drummed with his finger nails on his helmet. It sounded tinny.

"Well — I guess you people know better. I don't tell my medics how to sew up a man's gizzards — I won't tell you how to run your business. So — this is it!" With the back of his hand, he struck the sheet and turned it over to Crerar.

Bing wondered what Crerar would do now — act as if he had never heard of Willoughby's interference and of the fact that the leaflet would never be fired?

Farrish said, "Shells to be loaded by the evening of July Three at my ammunition supply points. Carruthers will give you the locations. You have loading crews?"

"Yes," answered Crerar; "yes, of course, sir." He was too accomplished a negotiator to ask questions or show doubts.

A dangerous light slowly brightened the General's eyes. "You're amazed, aren't you?"

"Amazed, sir?" Crerar shook his head, smiled. "We're happy about your co-operation, we're happy that you approve of our suggestion!"

"Smooth," said Farrish, "very smooth, indeed. . . . Well, perhaps you don't know. . . ."

Willoughby and Loomis trooped in and breathlessly saluted the guest.

Farrish ignored their salute, sat down, and stretched his long legs. The high polish on his boots shone even in the dimness of the tent. Carruthers saw the danger signals. Unhealthy red showed in spots on Farrish's cheeks and forehead. It would be some blow-up. Carruthers tried to say something — but it was too late; Farrish broke out: "Some sonofabitch tipped off Corps!" He slammed his helmet on the desk. "Some God-damned thirty-silver-pieces Judas! I'm telling you, Crerar, I'm going to find the guy, I'm going to break his back! And believe you me, I'm the man to do it."

Bing's lips pursed in a silent whistle. He's standing right there, Bud!

Fascinated, as if the man against whom Farrish had been railing were not he, Willoughby stared at the General. At first, upon learning that Farrish himself had come to the Detachment, he had hesitated — then he had decided that it was better to face the music and answer it on his own terms, if any music had to be faced; he and Loomis had rushed from their beds and hurried over from the Château to introduce themselves and to make a good impression.

Farrish was going strong. "This morning, I get a call from General Dore — gets me out of bed, too! . . . And he says, Farrish, he says, this Fourth of July firecracker business of yours, that's out. Ammunition is going to be used for tactical purposes, he says. Now, I ask you: Where does Dore get the dope?"

Crerar shrugged.

"Huh, where?"

"I assumed Corps was behind your plan, sir!" lied Crerar.

"They are, now!" triumphed Farrish.

Willoughby was upset — not so much over General Dore's failure to stand up under Farrish's barrage of words, not so much over the trouble with SHAEF and DeWitt which he had to anticipate, as over his own error. There was no question of choice between DeWitt and Farrish, between following a directive and following this man. One look at Farrish was enough.

Yates, that professor, didn't have the eye for it. Yates hadn't told him that here was a Man, a Leader, a Power! This was no ordinary brass hat — this was a man on whose side you had to be, who would go places, whom you had to follow as you'd followed and never questioned Old Man Coster back home in the office of Coster, Bruille, Reagan and Willoughby, Attorneys at Law.

"Yes, I got Corps lined up behind me!" Farrish shouted. "Solid! I said to Dore, Why, this is tactical! And damned good tactics at that! We'll lay it on, forty-eight rounds from forty-eight guns, and then we'll tell them — The strength of America! The voice of America!"

Both Bing and Willoughby were in the grip of the image. Only Crerar, his long nose drooping over his thin lips, remained unmoved; and Abramovici had his mind set on one thing — to keep out of the reach of Farrish's pumping arms.

"The idea of America! But Dore doesn't want to understand. Somebody's put a bug in his ear. Waste, he cries, pure waste! So you know what I did?"

Respectful silence. Carruthers leaned forward and whispered to his chief, "There are enlisted men around, sir!"

"I don't give a good God-damn! This is no secret! It was a secret, but it isn't any more! You know what I did? I made a compromise. I retreated

67

in one sector to break through all along the line. Now, gentlemen, the whole Army in Normandy is going to adopt my stunt! All right, it won't be half as spectacular. It'll be watered down. It won't be Farrish doing it — but what the hell. Every piece of artillery, along the entire front, simultaneously at five in the morning, is going to fire one round to salute the Day. . . . But I'm the only one who'll have the leaflets."

"Magnificent!" said Willoughby.

"Huh?"

"Magnificent, sir!"

Farrish discovered Willoughby. "Sure, it's magnificent. Who are you?"

"This is Major Willoughby, commanding," said Crerar, "and this is Captain Loomis, our Exec."

The two men saluted. Farrish gave them a perfunctory wave of the hand.

"Sir," said Willoughby modestly, "I was responsible for the drafting of the leaflet."

"*Willoughby?*" said Farrish. "Do you write German, Major Willoughby?"

"No, sir. I'm sorry I don't. But I gave the order."

"*I* gave the order, Major. To some Lieutenant."

"Yes, sir, to Lieutenant Yates," said Willoughby. He beckoned to Abramovici. "Go fetch Lieutenant Yates."

"I don't need any more people around here," said Farrish. "Captain Carruthers, can't you explain to this Major that I hate people butting into my business! . . . Now, what I need is this: I need some tangible success to the whole operation. I'll have Dore eat his own words. I'm not wasting men or material. What's the sense of putting on the show if nothing happens? I need some guarantee that some Fritzes will come over after we fire those little papers. What can you do about that?"

Loomis wanted to speak up. He wanted desperately to speak. But he didn't dare. He raised his hand and stood on his toes and made wheezing noises. Willoughby pulled down the Captain's arm. "What do you want?" he hissed.

"Loudspeakers!" Loomis said into Willoughby's ear. "Loudspeakers! Send out a team — right after the barrage!"

"Pipe down!" said Willoughby.

Crerar said, "I'm afraid, General, we have to rely on the appeal of the leaflet."

Willoughby came forward. "No, sir, we can do more — much more!"

Farrish glanced from Crerar to Willoughby and back. "Make up your minds!"

Willoughby saw his opportunity. "We can place a loudspeaker team at your disposal, sir. They'll go into the line, and they'll talk across to the

Germans. If you will select a spot where the unit confronting your troops has had losses, the combination of loudspeaker and leaflet ought to work. No doubt, sir, you've heard of the spectacular success our loudspeakers had at St.-Sulpice. We made the fort surrender. . . ."

"You did, huh?"

Loomis could not restrain himself. "Sir, if you permit me — we have just the right man for the job. Sergeant Bing here — he worked on the leaflet — he will be excellent to follow it up with a spoken appeal. . . ."

Oh my aching back! thought Bing.

Another brainstorm took hold of Loomis. He sweated with excitement. "And as his assistant, we have an experienced, quiet man, a technical expert who'll insure the success of the mission — Private Tolachian. The team to be led by Lieutenant Laborde, the best officer for the job — "

Farrish snapped, "What's the matter here? Everybody nuts? I'm not interested in your details. Bunch of Boy Scouts, huh? . . . Loudspeakers is a good idea. Let's have one."

Let's have one, echoed in Bing's mind. Tolachian, Laborde, and himself — some team!

His eyes tried to find Crerar's. But Crerar was busy ushering out the General.

The meeting over and Farrish gone, Loomis could neither find rest nor settle down to his daily routine. He paced up and down the yard of the Château, smiling happily to himself.

He had done so much this morning, and he had done it so well. He had brought himself to the General's attention with a sound suggestion — Willoughby had taken part of the credit, but Willoughby always did that. He had arranged matters so that Tolachian would get his lesson — next time, Tolachian would think twice before trying to make a fool of him. And Bing — wise guy, arrogant — would have a chance to show whether he was so God-damned clever when the bullets were whistling around his ears. You could rely on Laborde to go ahead without any consideration for the natural tendency of Messrs. Bing and Tolachian to keep themselves out of trouble.

Loomis saw Karen come out of the Château. Jovially, he called to her, "The General was here, you know — the General himself!"

Karen nodded. "What for? Did he find out about Willoughby?"

"Oh, no! The leaflet is going to go through! A big show, Miss Wallace — very big!"

"Is that so?" Bing would be so glad, she thought. He'd gloat a little and be very charming in his serious enthusiasm. "Excuse me, Captain," she said, "I'm busy," — and walked away to find Bing.

Her curtness didn't deflate Loomis. Exuberantly, he waved at Crerar who, the kitten Plotz on his arm, had entered the yard. As Crerar came within hearing distance, Loomis noticed that the Operations Chief was talking to his cat. In fact, he seemed to be telling it a story. The kitten was tilting its head as if it could understand.

Crerar reached Loomis, stopped, then circled around the Captain, talking all the while to his cat: "And David wrote in the letter, saying, Set ye Uriah in the forefront of the hottest battle, and retire ye from him, that he may be smitten, and die."

"What do you mean?" Loomis drew himself up to his full height.

Crerar, his face all wrinkles, looked up at him. "The shoe wouldn't fit you, Captain, would it?"

7

KAREN left Château Vallères the day of Farrish's visit. She went to the Army Press Camp and tried to write the story of the leaflet. She usually worked fast — she outlined her stories, and formulated her sentences in her mind before she put them on paper. She had a style of her own, and she was proud of it. She used a plain, sometimes even clipped language — though often she dealt less with events than with background. Recently, her editors had suggested that she stress what they called the "Woman's Angle." "We want you to put more heart in your stuff, Karen," they said; "like your writing in your *Portraits of GI's.* . . ."

"Sentiment?" she asked back.

"Well, yes — sentiment."

She had refused. "I've seen a lot of war since then. Maybe I've changed. The grammar is the same for women as for men, and so are the facts."

The editors didn't argue. She was successful in her own way. Her features continued to be widely syndicated, even though they now lacked the homey elements.

However, the leaflet story offered unusual difficulties. She stared at the typewriter, idly fingering the keys. She was not permitted to write of the fight over the leaflet, of Farrish's folly, Willoughby's chicanery, and Bing's search. No censor would pass it. Military security covered a big field, she thought; the boys protected one another, naturally, under the quite appropriate heading of *Security*. They were justified, perhaps — it was important to maintain the public's confidence in the Army. Wives and mothers were fearing for the lives of their beloved; they had to be made to feel that these lives were in the good and responsible hands of conscientious, far-seeing, and long-planning men. But that reduced her story to the fact that, on the morning of July Fourth, a great number of guns would bark once, and that the Germans would receive a leaflet which said the following. . . .

After the Fourth, the censors would probably agree to release the text. But by then, unless she added something striking of her own, the story would be Old Hat; every other correspondent could pick it up, too, if he felt like it. And if she gave an interpretation? She would inevitably get caught in the trap of What Are We Fighting For — she would have to give her own opinion on it; and she hated editorializing; and she knew that her own uncertainty would make her story heavy and lumbering. When she thought of Bing, she felt he was right, and she was tempted to endorse the leaflet — but only when she thought of him. Whenever she read the words he had written, they blurred and his face seemed to glide over the paper, shadowy, but insistent. But she had to distinguish between the Man and the Idea; and the Idea was subject to a great many doubts and to the experiences which had made her wary of politics, of war, and of the people who were in both. She could not endorse the leaflet, but neither could she afford to raise doubts in the public mind — there were, again, the wives and the mothers; and they had a hard time of it, anyhow.

When she had come to this point, she tabled the whole argument. Why, my girl, she asked herself, why aren't you frank with yourself? When you're tired, you must sleep; hungry, you must eat. There's nothing the matter with your story — except it isn't complete. Relax, go back there, complete it. Go back there, get your fill of life. You don't know either how long it's going to last, his life, or yours. . . .

She asked the Public Relations Officer to arrange for her to go along on the loudspeaker mission.

Yates learned of the composition of the loudspeaker team through Crerar. The matter was mentioned in passing; Crerar talked of it as an accomplished fact. "Laborde," said Crerar, "and Bing, and Tolachian — I wonder how that's going to work out."

"It's not going to be fun," said Yates, "and I doubt if it'll net us anything. Why don't you change it?"

"I can not and I will not meddle in the details of an operation," replied Crerar. "That's Willoughby's and Loomis's business."

"I don't understand you," Yates said angrily. "You see this messy situation, you know that Laborde should be kept on ice, if anywhere — and what do you do? You sit back."

"Yes," said Crerar, "I sit back. . . . Look at all the mental acrobatics we went through over that damned leaflet — and then it was taken out of our hands anyhow." He saw that Yates wasn't satisfied and asked pointedly, "How's your special friend, Thorpe?"

"All right, I guess," Yates said evasively. He had observed Thorpe. Thorpe was pale and thin-mouthed and was going about his jobs as if nothing had happened. Yates wanted to talk to him, but Thorpe seemed to

71

avoid him, slinking away as soon as he noticed that Yates was approaching him.

It bothered Yates. But he didn't have the drive to pursue Thorpe, to re-win his confidence — it would have been ridiculous to try; after all, they were soldiers, grown-up toughened men, both of them.

He had no right to blame Crerar for letting things ride. But things were riding along in an awkward way.

"Do you mind if I try to meddle?" he asked Crerar; since Crerar only shrugged, Yates went to Loomis.

Loomis was in his room, lying on the big bed of the Comtesse. The light reflected from the canopy gave the Captain's self-satisfied face a greenish tinge. Crabtrees and Laborde were with him; Crabtrees, sitting at the foot of the bed, showed through his posture that the world was wonderful; and Laborde's customary moroseness was dissolved in a kind of camaraderie which made Yates sick to his stomach.

"We were just talking about you," lisped Crabtrees. "We were admiring the way you have with the men, and I said it must be because you're a pedagogue. What do you think?"

Yates could imagine what they really had been saying. "I don't know that I have any particular method."

"Whatever your method," said Laborde, "you're undermining the authority of us all."

Loomis said, "I don't suppose you've come without a special purpose. What do you want?"

Yates would have preferred not to make his request in front of Laborde. He hesitated, but then considered that Laborde would get the story hot, anyhow. "I want to volunteer," he said.

"Volunteer?" asked Loomis.

"I missed most of the fun at St.-Sulpice; and I'd like to go out with a loudspeaker team."

"Something bitten you?" said Crabtrees.

"All right," said Loomis, "next time a job comes up, count yourself in."

Did Loomis intentionally misunderstand him? Yates glanced at the Captain stretched out on the lush bed. He looked guileless enough.

"No," said Yates, "I don't mean just any mission. I mean the Fourth of July operation."

Loomis sat up.

Crabtrees tapped his small foot against Yates's shin. "Because the girl is coming along, hmm?"

"I didn't even know she was coming along, Crabtrees." But he felt his pulse quicken. "I don't base my requests on personal reasons. I happen to be interested in the success of the mission." He stopped. Was he really? Had the leaflet begun to mean something to him?

"We all are interested in its success," corrected Loomis. "However, the team has been fixed, the orders have been cut. You should have spoken up sooner."

"You can easily substitute one name for another," pleaded Yates. "I would like to head this team."

"And why?" asked Laborde.

"Yes, sir," drawled Loomis, "why *are* you so eager to get in on just this operation?"

The question was justified, Yates found. What concern was it of his whether Bing and Tolachian got their heads shot off? And what guarantee was there that, with him in command, the enemy's fire would be less deadly? As Willoughby put it, in war you have to take added risks. . . .

"Well, I'll tell you. . . ." He faced Loomis. "Because I think you've chosen the wrong men for the job."

"Who d'you think *you* are?" asked Laborde.

"I wish you wouldn't take this personally," said Yates. "I just have the feeling — "

"Feeling!" Loomis interrupted him. "We don't decide on the basis of feelings. This is still the Army. I've noticed for the longest time that you've been trying to forget that."

I'd better drop this thing, Yates said to himself. But he saw the outrage on Loomis's face — there was more on Loomis's than on Laborde's — too much outrage for a simple discussion on who was to go where and with whom.

Loomis went on: "I've sent professors and doctors on KP, just like anybody else. In this Army, we're all equals. I used to have a little radio store, back home. Nothing wrong with that, is there? Or maybe you think it's wrong that I'm a captain and you're a lieutenant, and it should be the other way 'round? You think so, do you?"

"All right," said Yates, disregarding Loomis's demagogy, "I'll give it to you bluntly. Don't blame me; you're forcing me into it."

"We can take it!" laughed Crabtrees. "We're big boys."

"I don't like your choice of Tolachian. The man is too old, he doesn't belong in the line."

"Go on!" said Loomis.

"I don't like your choice of Laborde."

"Is that so!" Laborde said caustically.

"I'm not being personal, Laborde! You're as good as they come, you've got guts and all — why the hell don't you understand! — you're just not the man for this job with Tolachian along and with the front in an uproar after the barrage. . . ."

Loomis bit his lips. Crerar and Yates were in cahoots on this — Crerar with his dumb Biblical story, Yates with this open warning. But if he

73

back-tracked and gave Yates the team, it would be an admission of guilt.

"I'm afraid," said Loomis, "the team will go out as is. The Army sent Tolachian over here; I presume the medics are better judges of a man's capability than you or I. The selection of Lieutenant Laborde to head the team was approved by Major Willoughby and, for that matter, by General Farrish, who was informed of it. That's all."

"Why did you pick on Tolachian?" Yates insisted.

"Listen, Yates, I don't pick on anybody. In this outfit, every man gets his turn to prove himself."

"You'll get yours, too!" said Crabtrees.

What faces! It was futile, Yates knew it now; he had known it all along. He was isolated — not because Thorpe in his mania had picked on him, but because he was beginning to become the kind of man on whom Thorpe would pick.

The small truck which made its way to the front, that night before July Fourth, carried four people — Karen Wallace, Bing, Tolachian, and Lieutenant Laborde. Tolachian drove. Laborde, still plagued by the memory of Yates's insinuations, moved about uncomfortably on the front seat next to Tolachian. Yates had spurred Laborde into hectic mending of his ego's fences. This took its form in curt, sharp orders to Bing and Tolachian, in a significant, manly good-by to Loomis, in an exaggerated formality toward Karen, and in the firm resolve not to return at all, unless successful.

In the rear of the truck, the amplifier unit and a radio receiving set were mounted on the one side; on the other sat Karen and Bing.

They had left Vallères after dark. The plan was to drive part of the night and to arrive in the small hours of the morning at Battery F, one of the several batteries selected to fire the leaflets. There, Karen was to stay behind, while the truck went forward to Company C of Monitor, an armored infantry regiment in Farrish's Division. The loudspeaker operation was to take place in C Company's sector. Laborde carried a map on which the various locations were marked, and a compass in a pocket hanging importantly from his belt.

Laborde was supinely confident. "Miss Wallace," he advised before they took off, "it won't be a comfortable ride, but it will be safe. I've asked Bing to take along a few blankets so you can stretch out and sleep."

Bing wasn't so sanguine. From Crerar, who had received an overlay of Carruthers's situation map, he knew that the Germans opposite Monitor's Company C were by no means in a spot which would make surrender attractive to them. They were dug in as firmly as were the Americans; they were neither surrounded nor cut off; they seemed to have a perfectly coherent front with their neighboring units. The conditions which

74

had made the surrender at St.-Sulpice appetizing to the Germans did not apply. Bing thought that the Army, instead of having its own particular way of thinking, functioned not unlike the ordinary civilian mind — especially the female one. If it was fashionable to wear low heels, everybody wore them, whether or not a girl had the legs that went with low heels. If a loudspeaker was successful at St.-Sulpice, why should it not be successful opposite C Company, too? That's how they figured. Bing felt that the mental laziness which inclined to mechanical repetition, instead of the proper evaluation of each given case on its own merits, worked against him, personally. Had he failed at St.-Sulpice, they would have debated the question of whom to send out now; as it was, he made the fort surrender, and so he was in for it any time they needed a champion hog-caller. And all that, so Willoughby and Loomis could please Farrish, whom they had schemed against only a day before! It was cockeyed to assume that the leaflet was good if he could lure a few dead-tired Krauts across the line; bad, if he couldn't. The words he had written were designed to eat themselves into the brain and the blood of the enemy slowly — but neither Willoughby nor Farrish had any conception of that. . . .

What was even worse, to Bing, was the choice of Laborde to head the team. The operation required that the man who actually handled the mike act according to his own judgment, his own judgment only. Well, Bing concluded, if Laborde chose to interfere, he would simply ignore him. Bing knew his own strength in the outfit; they could not punish him much because they would have difficulties replacing him in his job.

More hazardous yet was the fact that Tolachian would handle the technical side. Tolachian had been trained for the job, but he had never worked the loudspeakers under combat conditions. He had been used on the mobile presses, which was natural enough since he was a printer in civilian life. Bing had no fears that the man who was the dead Tony's friend would ever leave him in the lurch; but there was the chance of technical failure which might mean that they would have to stay an unnecessarily long time under fire, or wouldn't be able to do their stunt at all. . . . Loomis must be out to get Tolachian.

They should have sent along Clements with whom he had worked at St.-Sulpice; they should have spared him Laborde and, if any brass was needed, given him Yates.

Better not worry about it too much. It was too late to change anything, and every revolution of the wheels brought him closer to the action.

He often had thought about the inescapable, the terrifying logic with which this machine called Army worked — how it took people and sucked them in like a maelstrom. You thrashed about, made frantic movements trying to escape the vortex — some succeeded, no doubt — but all in all, by degrees, you were processed through until, some beautiful night, you traveled to the spot where a mere accident would decide whether or not you were swallowed and drowned.

Looking back, you could see that everything pointed to this very moment — from the day when the first uniform was issued, through training of various kinds, through the trip across the ocean, through the assembly areas in Britain, through lying in the grass at Vallères — everything, everything. It was this feeling of being caught, helplessly, which made men resentful; especially since only at rare moments could you glimpse any good reason for being caught this way. And never, never, did anyone supply a valid answer for why just you should be caught, and others not. Millions of men could stay at home, with the wife and the kiddies. Other millions were permitted to stay safely in the rear, while you, Bud, went into the line. Why? Why? Who decided that *you* should have to take it and be among the chosen few to risk your life? And who decided that *you* were to be blown to bits and that *your* guts should be spattered and *your* blood fatten the soil?

No wonder that most of the soldier's waking and much of his sleeping time was spent in resenting — resenting the noncom, the officer, the chow, the wretched living conditions, the exhaustion, the demands, the hurrying, the waiting . . . and most frustrating: never a chance to express this resentment to anyone really responsible for the whole thing, for the great wrong that was done to you on the day you left your soft bed at home and knew you wouldn't see it again for a long time.

A soldier could be good-natured only if he was very stupid or very fatalistic — or, if he was very wise and could see the reason for it all. But even if he was very wise and saw the reason for the war and the good in it, he was confronted every day with finding the reason for many smaller events occurring in the process of the war, events which made no sense whatever. Best not to ask any questions. Best to take the opportunities as they came, reduce life to the minimum essentials: sleep, food, digestion, fornication — and the hell with the rest and the immortal soul.

"You haven't said a word since we started out," said Karen. "Do you mind that I came along?"

Bing was startled. He had almost forgotten that she was next to him. Here he was in the rear of a tarpaulin-covered truck, alone with an American woman who was washed in the places where a woman should be clean, who wore lipstick and plucked her eyebrows. Any hundred thousand men in Normandy, had they known of his incredible luck, would have said "Jesus Christ!" and wished to be in his place.

"Do I mind it?"

The back of the truck was open and let in just enough light for him to see the outline of her face, throat, shoulders, and breasts.

"I am frantic with joy, don't you see? I keep my mouth shut to keep it from saying things which would shock you. At Vallères, it was like this: Nobody could rape you because everybody watched everybody else. And here we are alone, all alone, you and me — nearly a whole night before us and, if Tolachian loses his way, it will be the entire night. And nobody to watch me but myself."

"You are rude."

"I am trying to be very, very reasonable, Karen — may I call you Karen?"

"I've noticed all along that everybody at Vallères who was watching everybody else never gave a second thought about me and about how I might be feeling."

"I haven't started a necking party, have I? But, for God's sake, understand that we're not whole human beings — we're men, men, only men — and we are frightened men. I am very much frightened. And it would do me a world of good to be able to bury my head at your breast."

She looked out of the truck. Outside, the road, a lighter gray, seemed to flow back underneath them into the night.

Karen said, "I want to go with you — all the way."

"All the way? What do you mean?"

"Up to the infantry, up to where you're going to speak to the Germans."

He took her hand. "No, Karen. I appreciate it. I think you're wonderful, and courageous, and all that. But I don't want you to do it."

She answered sharply, "This is quite impersonal. Your job is to talk to the Germans — mine to write a story. And I'll write it my way, I'll gather the material my way, and you keep your nose out of it."

"Karen!" he pleaded. There was just enough gentle reproach in his voice to make her grow all soft inside. She didn't want to become soft. Neither could she continue being harsh. She was annoyed with herself; whatever she did or said proved wrong because she insisted on complicating an issue which was primitive and simple. What did she want? She wanted to be with this man; and when he went into danger, she wanted to share this danger with him. He, on the other hand, wished to protect her, and to keep her out of danger. Why couldn't they speak openly to one another? Why did they have to argue and fight?

"If it's the story you want," he said, "I'll tell you all the details, after I am through. If it's the sensation — for God's sake! you'll be able to live out the rest of your life very well without having been a few yards from the German line. I can protect myself, to a certain extent. But you would be as helpless as a clay pigeon."

"I am perfectly capable of taking care of myself."

"If you persist," he said, "I will tell Laborde that you can't come along because you would hinder me in my work. And he would agree — you can't have a crowd of people up there. And if Laborde were afraid of stopping you, the guys up in the line wouldn't be — "

"That would be a lousy trick! But it fits in very neatly with the treatment I've been receiving all around: Respectful, but with that 'Come on, let's stop kidding and let's get down to business' look. Well, I let myself in for it, and I know what to do about it. Let's drop it."

He said, "I will do everything to keep you out of trouble. I don't care what you think of me or of what I do. I want you to stay alive and whole, because . . ."

The sentence remained unfinished.

"Because?" she asked.

But he passed up his cue. She wanted him to say, *Because you are dear to me,* or *Because I like you more than I can say,* or even *Because I love you.* And if he had said it, she would have known it to be a lie, a phrase out of the rule book.

Instead, he said, "Somehow, I think you are putting up a show — all this — being a newspaper woman and a traveler and hanging out with soldiers and wearing pants and a helmet. Karen, don't you think I want you to be with me when I go out there with the microphone, and can't even defend myself because I have to hang on to the damned thing and have to think up words to speak? I want it terribly much — but more than that, I want to come back to you, afterwards, and find you still there."

She came into his arms and laid her head on his shoulder.

"I am afraid for you," she said.

He caressed her hair. "You will stay at the Battery, and wait for me. It isn't going to take more than half or three quarters of an hour. Afterwards, we both will feel — "

"Tell me," she begged. "How will we feel?"

"Oh, well — " he smiled — "as if we had done something great together, you and me, the two of us."

She fell asleep. He covered her body with a blanket, and then sat back, bedding her head on his lap. He stroked her forehead, toward her temples, again and again, so as to deepen her sleep.

The night, which had been very dark, seemed to lighten somewhat. The clouds withdrew, and stars began to shine. He observed the road which swayed before his eyes with the swaying of the truck. The road had become very lonely. At first, they had encountered other vehicles which had come out of the night like solid, sliding shadows and had flown by. Driving under black-out conditions, the cats' eyes at the vehicles' rear were merely two tiny red slits which disappeared soon. But while they were there, they had aroused confidence. The Army was there, hidden in the dark, but watchful; the silent vehicles were witnesses.

Now, however, Bing had not seen a truck for what seemed ages. And it was impossible to overlook them — even the moon had come out and the road was clearly outlined. It seemed to Bing that he was riding, the girl entrusted to his arms, from nowhere to nowhere. And he began to worry. It couldn't be that the road was completely deserted, if it was the right road.

On and forward they drove. Bing felt the road change from macadam to cobblestones. He shouted for Tolachian to stop. As the truck came to a halt, Karen awoke. She had forgotten her surroundings and asked unintelligible questions.

Bing grabbed his carbine and went forward to the driver's seat. "Do you know where we are?" asked Bing.

"Certainly!" answered Laborde, defensively. He pulled out his map, and in the dim light showed Bing the road he had followed. "We must be about here — " he said. His bony finger pointed at a black spot.

"Well," Bing pushed the Lieutenant's finger aside, "if this is the town we're supposed to be in, we should have come by this crossroad here. But we didn't. I watched the road very closely."

"No," said Tolachian, "I didn't see a crossroad either."

Laborde pulled out his compass. He lay down on the ground, and pushed the little instrument around, squinting along the luminated lines of the dial. "North is there!" he pointed vaguely. "We're headed south all right. We'll get to this Battery — don't worry."

"As far as I'm concerned, I don't care whether we ever get there," Bing informed Laborde. "But I'd sort of hate to find ourselves suddenly in the German lines — we've got some equipment on the truck which the Heinies might like to get hold of."

This consideration made Laborde pensive. He returned to the study of his map and muttered hopefully, selecting several localities which might possibly be those in which they found themselves.

Karen left the truck and joined the men. "Lost your way?" she inquired.

Bing grinned. "We can't really lose our way," he explained. "If we keep on going south or southeast, we must come to the front, and we'll notice it all right when we get there. However, we aren't quite sure where we are." He turned to Laborde. "Lieutenant — I'd like to snoop around here and see whether we can't find some friendly natives or some G.I.'s to tell us where we are."

Laborde nodded and grudgingly let Bing take the initiative.

"May I come along?" asked Karen. And since none of the men answered, she made off after Bing, who was walking in the direction of the center of the town. He walked carefully, keeping close to the walls of the houses. But the nearer he came to the center of the town, the more difficult it was to walk — the road was strewn with stones and bricks and rubble; he had to pick his way and often stumbled.

Karen kept up with him well. It must be an effort for her, he thought, but he didn't cut down his speed. She had elected to follow him, let her sweat a bit.

Suddenly she touched him. "Look!"

"Where?"

Silently, she pointed. His eyes followed her outstretched hand. And then he saw. Concentrated as he had been on his task, he had been blind to everything else — and now it was as if a veil had been torn from his eyes.

They had arrived at a part of the town which was completely demolished. Only the burned-out walls of the houses were standing. Behind them, the phantasmally white moon was shedding its pale light. The empty windows of the ruins were filled with this light, with a life of their own. This life had a sharp, painful beauty; the jagged outlines of half-broken-down walls showed up with etched clarity, and the whole scene was immersed in the silence of absolute death.

"What a stage setting!" she said.

Bing nodded and whispered, "And what are they supposed to play here?"

"You don't think there can be people around?"

"People?" he tore himself away, "oh, people can be almost anywhere."

Somewhere, a stone fell and kept rolling for a second.

Bing motioned her to crouch.

Only an echo.

He waited for a while, then he lifted her up and moved forward. "Damn it," he said, "we'll never find anybody here."

"Just let's look back once more," she pleaded. She looked at the silver light, the enchanted, cruel landscape. She wanted to photograph it in her mind. It was part of Bing, too. "I wish I could paint," she said. "I would paint a picture of you — just your head underneath your helmet, and in the background the white light of the hollow windows."

"No," he said, "this isn't my kind of life. I didn't want it, I didn't ask for it. . . ."

"But you have grown into it," she said with determination.

They walked on. The moon and the ruins became an accustomed sight. And then, as suddenly as they had entered the field of destruction, they left it behind and once more reached the open road. Along this road, they heard the slowly increasing purr of an approaching car.

"Step aside," ordered Bing.

She followed his order implicitly. After the walk through the ruins, no thought of doubting him could enter her mind. She observed how he, too, stepped into the shadow and trained his eyes on the road.

As the vehicle was almost upon them, Bing advanced and waved it down. Screeching, it came to a halt. It was an American jeep, stripped-down for combat. Its windshield was down, and its floor was covered thickly with sandbags. In it sat three men, equally ready for combat. They were unshaved, and their uniforms showed the traces of prolonged stay in the ground. The man next to the driver carried a knife strapped to his leg.

"Funny," he said, his eyes, small with fatigue, trying to make out Karen. "You sure look funny. You ain't got no weapon either. Where you two guys from?"

"This is no guy, it's a girl," explained Bing, and as he saw the amazement of the three men and anticipated more questions, he talked on fast in order to get his own questions across first. "She's a newspaper woman. Our truck is at the other end of this God-damned town. What's its name anyhow?"

"Hell, I don't know!" said the man. "These French names all sound the same. What you doing here?"

"We sort of lost our way. I'm glad we met you. There doesn't seem to be a soul in this heap of shambles."

"There sure isn't. And you'd better get out of it, too. The Germans throw mortar fire over whenever they feel like it — and they feel like it too damned often for my comfort."

The three men in the jeep really did not look very comfortable. The driver's foot raced the motor impatiently.

"I still would like to know where we are," said Bing. "We have to get to Division artillery. Do you have any idea where they are located?"

"No," said the man. "Sometimes I wish I knew where they were. I'd like to go back there and give them a piece of my mind — they're asleep most of the time."

"Well — where the hell are you going?" asked Bing.

"To the Company," the man next to the driver answered carefully.

"And where are you coming from?"

"Company."

"You mean to tell me you are going from one Company to another Company?"

"Yeah — that's about it!"

"Then — we're at Company level?"

"Sure!" the man laughed, and the driver and the other man in back laughed, too. "You get up here so rarely that you're surprised?"

Bing did not react to the taunt. "And where, please, are the Germans?"

"Oh — down this road, about four hundred yards, I would say."

"Thanks a lot!" Bing wanted to laugh out loud, with relief.

"Don't drive down there," recommended the man, "the Germans keep that road pretty well covered. You must visit us sometime, with that lady, when we're not so busy!"

"Thanks!" said Karen.

The three men drove off.

The road which led into the German lines lay innocuously quiet and open.

"Let's turn around," said Bing, "Laborde will be waiting for us."

The night had spent its strength when they arrived at the Battery position. In the East, a slight gray haze prepared to blot out the waning stars, a haze so tender and young it was almost impossible to believe that it heralded a day in which men would die by the score.

And, in truth, nobody at the Battery thought of it that way. The men, just roused from sleep — with the exception of those on duty — sat around gimlet-eyed, yawned, and waited for the coffee to get ready. Some of them were preparing the guns for that odd round to be fired precisely at five o'clock.

None of them were conscious of the day's date and the significance of the single round about to be fired. If there was any comment at all, it ran along the line: What a hell of a nuisance to get up at this ungodly hour, for one round. But most of them didn't even go that far. The howitzers were complicated machines; and the men were skilled hands who had learned to work these machines and to care for them and to prepare them for the pregnant fraction of a moment when the shell left the muzzle and whined through its predetermined arc to the target — a target they did not know, represented by a set of figures hurriedly given over a field telephone.

Tolachian stood next to one of the howitzers and studied the breech mechanism. There was something final about the closing of the breech — as if a door were closed to a safe deposit box of death. A couple of men were carrying the shell to the gun; they looked more like workmen in a steel mill than soldiers, except that the mill lay under the open sky; and camouflage netting, supported by sticks, was the roof.

"Tough job you fellows have," said Tolachian.

One of them, his sleeves rolled up, his shirt open down to his belt, his face drawn with the effort of carrying the shell, said, "Aw — it isn't so bad." He and the other man deposited the shell next to the gun. Then he straightened, wiped his forehead, and looked at the sky. "Beautiful day it's going to be — hot again, I guess." As Karen approached the gun position, he asked Tolachian, "What's she doing here? You been driving her around?"

Before Tolachian could explain, Karen had joined them. The other artillery man, who had not spoken, turned to her, licked his parched lips, and suggested hoarsely, "Would you like a cup of coffee, Miss?"

She nodded and smiled. The boy was so incredibly young. A strand of yellow hair hung over his eye, and his small face appeared almost gray in the dim light of the morning.

"The sun is rising," he said, "look!"

Between a group of trees to the left an orange radiance sparkled. The branches and leaves were deepest black; they trembled. A slight wind came up, cool and clean. Then the sun seemed to spring up into the trees and hang there, a ball of heavenly fire. Everything attained different outlines and a new, more real perspective. The howitzer which had loomed up gigantically was reduced to its proper size. Men seemed to have cropped up out of the earth, busy and determined men with planned jobs, which they pursued with the silent bustle of ants who knew where to go and what to pick up without ever being told.

Bing came with a mess cup of black coffee. He offered it to Karen. She drank, feeling the warmth of it penetrate her body. She felt really awake now. She combed her hair and did her face while he looked on, smiling critically.

"Better?" she asked.

"Yes," he said. "The night was in your face."

"I wish I could wash up."

"I looked around," Bing said, "they have just a little drinking water here, and they'll need that for the day."

Tolachian took out his canteen. He offered Karen the bottle. "Take some water," he urged. "It is all filled up, and I won't need that much."

"Maybe you would like to wash yourself?"

Tolachian's face was broad with the pleasure of sharing what he had. She saw the grime of the road on it, and the dust in the corners of his red-rimmed eyes. "Oh no," he said, "it's all a matter of habit. I wouldn't feel good if I weren't just a little dirty."

Bing said, "It's almost five o'clock. H-hour, the Fourth of July. You want to come?"

Tolachian and Karen followed him back to the howitzer. The gun crew had assembled. They were loading the shell which was to announce the Day to the enemy. Lined up on the ground lay the leaflet shells, their fuses screwed on. They were to follow the first live death-bearing shell by a few minutes.

She marveled at the quiet efficiency of the workers behind the gun. What an industry had risen in these fields! Men turned wheels, and slowly, the howitzer changed the angle of its stubby nose. Its powerful trails rested firmly on the ground, like the legs of a sprinter dug in before the start. The men moved about the gun, threw the round into the chamber and slammed closed the breech. All this was done without effort. She heard one man tell a joke about a virgin who was riding a horse — halfway through the joke, the storyteller became conscious of her presence and stopped. The young boy with the yellow hair laughed in embarrassment. She observed the play of the muscles in his arms as he pulled one of the leaflet shells across the tarpaulin. Then he called to a sergeant who had come over — she could not understand what he was saying, but the Sergeant seemed satisfied. The Sergeant looked at her, grinned and waved. "Open your mouth when we fire!" he joshed. "It's going to be good and loud."

"Yes!" she shouted back. "Like this?"

She held her mouth wide open; it must have looked foolish to him, for he laughed.

"That's it, Miss! Watch the birdie!"

At this moment, the front broke open. It started far on the right, an angry *basso profundo*. It came closer in a matter of seconds, made the earth recoil in the simultaneous roar of hundreds of guns. She saw somebody raise an arm — a little man in a ridiculous gesture.

The Battery fired.

Karen stood, awed. The roar had become continuous because now, with the echo of the Battery's guns, mingled the sound of the detonations on the other side where the shells landed and exploded, tearing up the ground, throwing up soil and shedding fragments over the heads of the Germans and into their holes.

For another few seconds, the thunder continued. Then it ceased, as suddenly and surprisingly as it had begun. The silence was almost as overwhelming as the wave of fire had been. Somebody laughed, thinly, as the empty powder-case, still smoking, fell out of the opened breech and rolled over the trampled grass.

Bing was speaking to her. Was it the overpowering sound which had deafened her temporarily, was it her absorption in the magnitude of the concentrated barrage? She did not immediately grasp what he was saying. But then it became clear to her, and the words gained an impact they had not carried before.

"This is the language of America," Bing was saying to her, "this Fourth of July, 1944. . . . A nation of free men, equal before the law, and determined to govern themselves . . . For these rights and liberties, we are fighting today. . . . We are that kind of nation. . . . To stop a tyrant from imposing his will on a nation, on Europe, on the whole world . . ."

He has a sense for timing, Karen thought, he certainly has. But it was good so, very good. The words were now so strong, so pregnant with meaning that she gave herself completely to their sound. She trembled. She had witnessed the birth of something new, a new epoch, perhaps — an epoch born in blood and in the thunder of hundreds of guns. Oh God, she was all carried away, and she loved it, and she felt as if purged after a tremendous cataclysm of her heart.

84

The Germans, overcoming their surprise, opened a desultory counter-battery fire. Somewhere, near by, a shell whistled and crashed.

"I knew it," said the Artillery Sergeant, "they'll get nasty about this."

Bing took Karen's hand, pressed it, and felt her answering pressure. "I'll go now," he said, "it's time." He saw that her eyes were swimming.

"Take care of yourself," she said.

"I'll see you later."

8

THE TRUCK lumbered forward. There were no more roads, only lanes between hedges. Bing was grateful for the hedges, they offered concealment. He was thoroughly shaken up, he hung on to the seat and swore. Even for the misery of the ride he was grateful. You can't think of women if you have to concentrate on keeping yourself from falling and being bruised. He had to make himself forget Karen. You can't nurse your own fears and speculate on what the next hours will hold in store for you, if you are constantly exposed to the ridiculous risk of being thrown to the hard floor of the truck and of bumping your head against the edge of a tool chest. And he had to forget his fear if he wanted to formulate sentences that carried sufficient conviction to make the Germans consider them.

The ride had lasted about ten minutes, when the truck suddenly swerved to a halt. Bing climbed off. He found Laborde talking to a captain who said his name was Troy, and that he commanded Company C.

Troy leaned against the fender of the truck. His huge frame was relaxed. He seemed happy compared to Laborde's tenseness, although his words gave no reason for happiness, either to himself or to anyone else.

"You want to bring this big thing up?" he asked, pointing to the truck.

"Of course!" confirmed Laborde. "We will dismount the loudspeakers, but we can't place them at too great a distance from the truck. The longer the wires between the amplifying unit in the truck and the loudspeakers, the bigger the resistance and the less the carrying power of the loudspeakers."

"How far do they carry?" Troy asked doubtfully. Bing saw that, as easily as the man's face fell into a smile, so it fell out of it, too.

"If you want the Germans to understand what we're saying," explained Laborde, "the distance shouldn't be more than sixty to a hundred yards. These loudspeakers are very weak. Originally, we were supposed to have loudspeakers with ten times their power — but somehow, they never materialized. You know the Army. However, it doesn't make much difference. It just means that we have to go closer to the Germans."

"Closer to the Germans . . ." Troy said thoughtfully. "We aren't as close as all that. We don't like to be close to them."

"Well," said Laborde, "we like it."

"You're crazy!" Troy had made up his mind about this visitor. "You're either crazy or you don't know how things are, here. I won't risk the lives of my men because you haven't got the right kind of equipment. This big truck of yours is going to draw fire as sure as hell. And the fire is going to hit my men."

Laborde's ascetic cheeks became even thinner. His eyes assumed the expression of a Christian martyr about to be thrown to the lions. "To be shot at is one of the risks you run in war; it can't be helped."

"Listen, Bud," said Troy very quietly. The dimple in his cheek had disappeared, and the line of his chin was set. "I don't know where you've kept yourself all this time. But this Company has been in the fight since we hit the beach, and there hasn't been a day when I haven't been losing men. I'm responsible for these men. Every morning I must give an accounting on whether or not the men who died, or were wounded, were lost for nothing."

"Now, don't get excited!" said Laborde. He could not afford to antagonize Troy, though he had disliked the man from the moment the Captain stepped out between two hedgerows and stopped the truck, and announced that he couldn't permit it to go any farther. Troy evidently had his own ideas and intended to stand by them. And since the Captain was commanding the sector of this Company, he could make Laborde's job difficult, if not impossible; Laborde had to swallow his pride and dislike.

"I haven't come for my own fun," Laborde continued. "I was ordered here to do a job, and the job will be worth it to you as well as to us. If we get any Germans to come over here, they will count as your prisoners."

Troy wasn't taking the bait. He said, "You can't guarantee that the Germans will give up, can you? But I can guarantee that the truck and the loudspeakers and the whole commotion will bring us very much to their attention, and considering the shape of my outfit and the importance of the sector we hold, I'd like to keep out of that."

Laborde pulled a sheet of paper out of his pocket. On it were the orders signed by General Farrish. The orders said that the loudspeaker team commanded by Lieutenant Laborde was to be assigned for a tactical mission to C Company, and that C Company was to give all co-operation needed.

As Troy glanced through the orders, Laborde said, "For the past few minutes, our artillery has been firing thousands of leaflets to the Germans. The Germans will be reading them now. They are prepared for the appeal we are going to broadcast."

"I don't know . . ." Troy left the fender against which he had been leaning and walked to the rear of the truck. He inspected the equipment —

looked at the dials and wires and gleaming instrument boards. "I'll give you all the co-operation as long as it doesn't endanger my men and our position."

Bing felt that Laborde would never get anywhere with this Captain Troy. He liked Troy's stand, his feeling of responsibility toward his men. If Troy were able to dissuade Laborde from the undertaking, it would be very much all right with him. But the best Troy could achieve would be Laborde's going ahead on his own and making a complete mess of the mission.

"Captain," Bing said, "do you think I could come with you and sort of survey the situation? We'll leave the truck here, meanwhile. Perhaps we can find a location from where the job can be pulled off without hurting your men and without exposing ourselves too much."

Troy's face lightened. "Sergeant, that's the first reasonable suggestion I've heard. Let's go!"

Laborde's expression was all vinegar; but he did not object.

Troy walked ahead with long steps, Bing had to jog in order to keep up with him. Troy's head, shoulders and chest were hunched forward — this way of walking had become a habit with him, it reduced him as a target.

They were still clinging to the hedges. In the field to the right, a few cows were grazing peacefully between dark spots of humid earth. "Craters," said Troy as if he had noticed Bing's questioning glance, "nice pattern bombing. Except that the bombs came from our own planes."

He stopped where the hedge ended and spoke to a man who had appeared as suddenly as if he had sprung from the ground — and he had. Bing could not understand what they were saying to one another, but he saw the man pointing ahead, and Troy nodding.

There were no more hedges for the next two hundred yards. Before them lay a hilly field, scarred by shellholes and by much smaller dark spots — foxholes in which, occasionally, something moved. An intense, sweet smell filled the air, and a dark, persistent humming.

Troy had come back to him; the man to whom he had talked had vanished completely.

"Dead cow," said Troy, "very dead. Lies on the other side of the hedge. I can't have it buried because the Germans have that side under observation. Funny thing about the smell of the dead — you never get accustomed to it."

"Flies humming?"

"Yes — great big ones. They come from all over, green ones and blue ones."

"Where are the Germans?"

"Well — look across the field. You see that hedge running almost at a ninety-degree angle to this one? That's where they have their outposts.

They have a machine-gun emplacement, too — several, in fact, but only one gun. They switch emplacements quite often. I've tried to have my mortars knock out that gun, but no luck."

"Should we go farther forward?" asked Bing.

"I wouldn't, now," said Troy. "The Germans keep themselves very quiet, and so do we. If they see someone running around, they'll get suspicious. You can see the position well enough from here. The Germans can see it, too — with the exception of a few spots where you have cover behind these elevations.

"There — " he pointed ahead — "next to that clump of bushes, we've had three of our boys killed. We couldn't bury them for a whole day because each time someone went out to pull back the bodies, the Germans would lay it on. Being dead in that heat — I'm telling you — they swelled up in no time. They looked terribly big and alive, and they moved . . . the gas in them moved them. They stretched their arms and their legs. Their clothes kept them from bursting; they were like balloons. . . . You don't want to look at that, but you can't help it. It has a sort of fascination. . . ." He moved his hand across his forehead as if to wipe out the memory.

A sharp sound like a whip cracking.

"Somebody didn't keep his head down," Troy said. "The barrage of this morning, and then all those little papers fluttering down on the Germans — they're excited, I guess."

Bing said, "I don't like it."

"Neither do I." Troy pulled out a pair of field glasses and scanned the German hedge. "This Lieutenant of yours — the valor of ignorance, I call it, the valor of ignorance. A good line, isn't it?"

"Yes, it covers it, I guess."

"Well — have you found a spot from where you can operate, you think?"

"What about that elevation — almost in the center of the field? We could run up the truck behind it; it could serve as a kind of defilade. We could place loudspeakers in the brush to the right and to the left of it, and I could speak from a place fairly close to the truck, still behind the hill."

Troy trained his glasses on the elevation and the brush on either side. "We have some men dug in fairly close to the thing — I suppose that can't be helped. Yes, I guess it's the best place for that damned vehicle of yours. What you going to tell the Germans?"

"Well — I haven't thought about it much."

"You mean you speak just what comes into your mind?"

"More or less, Captain. Of course, there is a certain line of approach which we usually take. . . ."

"Does it work — usually?"

They turned back, carefully following the course of the hedge.

88

"Sometimes it does." Another thought struck Bing. "Tell me, Captain — do you know whether the field is mined?"

"Not on our side. But you can never tell what goes on, at night, on the German side. We'll probably find out when we attack their position — if we ever get around to attacking it, and if they don't attack first."

"You see — if there are mines in front of their position, they'll think twice before they come out and over to us. No fun being blown up by your own mines, when all you want is to enjoy the comforts of an American PW camp."

"Yeah — I don't suppose it is." Troy smiled at the idea of comforts in a PW camp. "You have to think about a lot of things in your work, Sergeant?"

"I don't think. Lieutenant Laborde does my thinking."

They were approaching the waiting truck. Troy turned to Bing and looked at him as if he were seeing him now for the first time. "Don't mind the guy," he said mildly, "give him a chance."

The truck was in position. Tolachian had made it dash across the field, narrowly skirting the shellholes, and had brought it to a quick stop behind the elevation. There had been some rifle shots from the Germans — less, however, than Bing had expected. Apparently, the Germans were surprised by the impertinence of the men in the truck. They couldn't see much sense in a truck riding about so close to their lines, and awaited further developments. Or they were bringing up mortars to get at the truck now covered by the hill — and that would take some time.

Tolachian was detaching the loudspeakers from the truck. There were four of them. Bing suggested that they place two on the right, and two on the left of the hill.

"What's going on here?" Someone, who remained invisible, shouted at them. "Get the hell away from here — do you want to kill us all?"

Tolachian looked around for the caller. He could not find him. "Aw, shut up!" he said. "This is all for your benefit."

"Benefit — hell!"

"Going to have movies?" another one shouted. "We haven't had the Articles of War for a long time!"

Bing had to laugh in spite of his tension. "No movies," he shouted back — "hog-calling!"

"That's dangerous, Bud! You'll get shot at!"

"Yeah — and us, too!" said the first voice.

A series of sharp, short explosions — as if somebody beat a metal ruler on a wooden board.

"Hear that?" shouted the first voice. "That's only the beginning!"

89

Bing felt at least as badly as the man who owned that voice. Something went wrong with his knees, he seemed to be wading through water. The water had a strong current which beat against his shins.

He noticed again the sweet smell of the dead, though he knew that he was far away from the hedge behind which the killed cow was disintegrating, and oozing into the earth, and feeding the blue and green flies with her matter. It seemed that particles of the smell had remained in his nostrils, and continued to choke his nerves. And the loudspeakers were heavier than they looked. He hugged one to his body and huddled over it and tried to run, crouching, from behind the knoll to the shrubs on the right. The smaller he made himself, the more conspicuous he felt. Something whistled — a strange bird. He fell down. He couldn't make himself get up. This isn't my job, he thought. What the hell am I doing with these things?

Tolachian crawled to him and took the loudspeaker out of his arms. Tolachian's face glistened with sweat. He licked his upper lip and Bing thought, What a big tongue he has, a big fat animal tongue! Tolachian crawled back to the brush where he already had installed one speaker, pulling Bing's behind him. He plugged in the wires and waved to Bing, "Okay! Get back!"

Tolachian was wonderful. Taking the loudspeaker out of Bing's hands had been more than a gesture of help — it indicated that he was taking over. Bing relaxed a little. He was breathing deeply. As he reached the truck, he found Laborde standing behind it, stamping his foot impatiently. "It's getting late!" Laborde complained. "Hurry up! Hurry up!"

Bing noticed that the Lieutenant was grinding his teeth. His brows were drawn high, his lips open. With the lucidity of such moments, Bing saw the empty space between Laborde's two upper front teeth, and he felt the temptation to smash his fist right into this spot.

"Why don't you help with the loudspeakers instead of standing there like a dummy!" he said.

"What?" said Laborde.

"Do something!" shouted Bing.

Then he went to the truck and pulled out the microphone and found a place for himself, ten steps or so away from the truck — a slight hollow into which he could fit his body. He lay down there and closed his eyes. As he opened them again, he saw Laborde obediently carrying a loudspeaker, dragging it along as he followed Tolachian to the brush on the left.

But Bing had no time to enjoy this sight. The Germans had decided, whatever the intentions of the Americans and their truck, they were bad. The Germans were firing away at anything that moved on the American side. The whip cracked more and more often, and regularly.

Bing wished that Troy were with him. As long as he had been with Troy, he had been calm in the confidence this man instilled through his big body, his measured movements, and his matter-of-fact tone. Now, Tolachian was taking Troy's place; but only partially, since Tolachian was busy with tasks of his own. How Tolachian could carry on at all, was a miracle to Bing. He, himself, would not be able to move — he was not able to move, he was soldered to the ground by his sweat and the humidity of the earth, which mingled.

And he must think. It was high time he detached himself from his fears, from the desire to shrink each time the Germans resumed firing. He had no idea of what he was going to say to them. His mind was barren, and all he could think of was that he wanted to get away from here. Another fear gripped him and settled in his stomach: What if he were not able to speak? What if all he produced were disconnected stammerings? What then? All the agony for that?

Somebody tapped his shoulder. Tolachian lay next to him. Tolachian smiled. "All set," he said. "You ready?"

"No," said Bing, "not yet."

"What's the matter?"

"Nothing."

Tolachian turned over. He pulled out a soiled pack of cigarettes. Through a flip of his hand, the cigarettes shot out. "We've got time for a smoke."

Bing, too, turned over, and they lay on their backs, smoking, looking at the sky.

"This is beautiful," Tolachian stretched himself. "Some time after the war, I'm going to come back here with my wife, for a visit. They sure picked a nice place to make war in. Did you notice the apple trees where we had parked the truck — when we were waiting for you, I mean? I tried the apples, they aren't ripe yet, but they will be, soon." He picked up a handful of dirt, rubbed it between his fingers, and let the finely ground earth rain down. "Good soil," he said, "everything grows here, and it'll be even better after the fighting is over. So much iron going into the soil . . ."

"So much blood."

"Well — that, too."

A detonation, off to the side.

"Mortars," said Bing.

"Yes." Tolachian pressed the stub of his cigarette into the ground. "You can't hear them when they come in. That's good, too. Sort of sudden, painless — right?"

"I wonder what they're thinking, over there?" Bing pointed his thumb toward the German positions.

"Aw — I don't know. I've got to go now, turn on the machine. Blow into the mike when you're ready."

"Right."

Bing watched Tolachian as he climbed heavily into the truck. For his age and build, Tolachian was agile enough.

Another mortar shell fell and exploded, as far off the target as the first one. Bing picked up the microphone. A little black bug, disturbed by the sudden move, hastily scampered down a blade of grass and hid behind a crumb of earth.

Very sensible little bug, thought Bing.

He began to speak.

"Achtung! Achtung!"

His voice came surprisingly strong over the amplifiers.

"Achtung! Deutsche Soldaten!"

It wasn't his voice at all. It sounded strangely sure and confident, almost cocky. He smiled. The tension had gone from his body. He felt more comfortable and slightly shifted his position to give better support to the elbow of the arm holding the microphone. His mind was clear.

"Deutsche Soldaten — a little while ago, you received a sample of American strength. We fired only one round from each of our guns — you know enough to realize what effect a sustained barrage would have on you in your positions."

That's right, he said to himself. Keep it light, it's a form of conversation. Treat them like a bunch of kids who have gone astray; you are the voice of reason, you don't much care whether they listen to you, but you want them to know, anyhow, so that afterwards, when things get tough for them, they can't blame you.

"Then we sent you some leaflets explaining why all our guns were fired this morning, all along the front. It was because of the date — the Fourth of July. Today is our American national holiday, the day on which the United States was founded. Several of you may have read the leaflet — I don't think your officers could stop you."

The machine gun on the other side opened up, chattering excitedly. On the right, one of the loudspeakers was hit. Bing could hear the bullets tear into the metal.

"Stop that!" he shouted. "Stop that God-damned shooting! Are you so much afraid of the truth that you can't afford to listen?"

They were listening all right. The machine gun ceased firing. Bing, now, almost enjoyed the job. He knew he had established contact with his audience. He wished he could see their faces — curious faces, anxious faces, faces which wanted to know what was going to follow. Furious faces, frustrated faces, faces which wanted to shut him up but couldn't, because that would concede weakness.

"This morning's barrage confirmed what you have experienced yourselves. For every gun of yours, we have six; for every shell of yours, a dozen. During the day, your Air Force doesn't dare show itself. Ours can afford to bomb every foxhole of yours."

These are facts, Bing thought. Make a little pause. Give the facts a chance to sink in.

"Your leaders promised that the Atlantic Wall would be impenetrable. We have broken through it and destroyed it. Your Führer said we would not stay more than twelve hours on European soil. Today, it is almost a month since our landings, and we have pressed you back farther and farther. At Cherbourg, generals and admirals surrendered gladly. They and their men saw the meaning of events."

Another pause. Give them time to get the meaning, too. Don't hurry the conclusion, let them come to it themselves; you only confirm it.

"These officers and men — they were Germans like you — these officers and men knew that as American prisoners they would get fair treatment and survive the war. We will now give you your chance. For ten minutes, starting now, we will cease fire. Come out of your positions, unarmed, hands raised. We will receive you and take you immediately out of the zone of fighting. This is your chance — take it. It may be your last."

Bing stopped. He waved to Tolachian. He switched off the microphone. Thank God, he thought, this is over. He was wringing wet. Let's get out of here, for Chris'sake, let's get out. Over there, they can't take a thing like that without doing something about it. They just can't.

For a time which seemed to stretch interminably, everything remained quiet. Even the desultory rifle fire which had lasted through most of Bing's appeal had ceased.

Near the hedge on the American side, from where Bing had selected the location for the loudspeaker truck, someone was waving — Bing thought it was probably Troy, waving them back. But Laborde had crawled around the hill to the side facing the Germans. Bing crawled forward himself to let Laborde know that Troy wanted them back.

As he rounded the hill and the German positions came into view, he saw the unexpected. A figure detached itself from the enemy's hedge, hesitated a moment, and then began to run toward him. It ran with a peculiarly stiff gait, as if its arms and legs were attached to wires manipulated by an invisible hand. After half a minute it was followed by a second figure, then a third, then more. Bing counted fourteen in all, breaking from the hedges and lumbering across the field, their hands raised. The field was now flooded by the light of the morning sun, the little figures cast sharp shadows. To Bing, the whole scene looked incredible, as if it were artificially posed. Because of this, he failed to get excited, and failed equally to make preparations for the moment the deserters would reach the hill.

Bing saw Laborde rise. Laborde lit a cigarette, pasted it to the corner of his mouth, folded his hands behind his back, and began to strut about in front of the hill in Napoleonic grandeur.

On the German side, the long silent machine gun opened up again. Bing saw the dirt thrown up by its bullets; it was aiming at its own men.

Laborde was unconcerned. He continued walking up and down, and Bing knew there would be a studied smile of contempt about his lips.

One of the deserters fell and remained prone. Another stopped in his tracks, turned slowly around as if in amazement over what went on behind his back, fell on his knees, screamed a long thin scream, and then tumbled forward. The rest of the deserters ran faster, whipped on by the machine gun. Apparently, they perceived the lonely figure of Laborde. While the direction of their course at first had been indefinite, they now converged on the American, in the hope that he who was strong enough to face the machine gun, standing, smoking a cigarette, could give them protection.

They reached their goal. They crowded about Laborde, miserably frightened, their hands still raised. They had done something superhuman: they had torn themselves away from the security of their own organization in order to find a greater and lasting one. But that new security had not yet received them; on their gray faces, in their fear-filled eyes, stood the bewilderment over their own decision, the exhaustion of the effort, the question unanswered: What have I done? What is going to happen now?

Laborde eyed them disparagingly. He pointed at the blouse of one of them — the man, grinning apologetically, buttoned it and stood at attention.

The thing was utterly improbable, Bing could not understand it, it was out of this world. Laborde considered the twelve precious prisoners — each of whom held valuable information — as his personal property and was holding a dress parade with them, while those Germans who had remained in their positions, and possibly some hurriedly called up reinforcements, were taking pot shots at the group in front of the hill.

Yet Laborde's act was impressive. From the sides of the hill came a kind of cheering. Four of Troy's men scrambled out of their holes to get a close-up look at the show, forgetting that they were in full sight of the enemy. They were recent replacements, not seasoned at all.

Another detonation, close by.

That damned mortar again, thought Bing.

The four Americans hastily made for their holes. But Bing, half raising himself, stopped them. The prisoners had to be taken to the rear. Neither he nor Tolachian could escort them, and Laborde could not be trusted — the Lieutenant would have paraded them along a considerable sector of the front, just to prove that he was untouchable.

"Hey, you!" shouted Bing. "Take those guys back!"

The four soldiers looked around, saw the Sergeant, dimly understood the meaning of his order. More explosions followed, even nearer. The mortar had found its bearings. The German deserters, helpless in the face of Laborde, waiting for orders, pressed in on one another like sheep under a thunderstorm.

"Okay, Sarge!" one of the Americans said, with a show of bravery.

They went to the wretched group of deserters, their rifles leveled. They gestured at them to move ahead. The deserters started out.

Bing sighed. That was done. He sank to the ground, ready to crawl back behind the hill where there was at least some cover. If Laborde wanted to pose some more, let him. Nuts were happiest by themselves. The German fire had assumed a steady character, punctuated by the periodic explosions of mortar shells. Small clouds of earth were rising about the hill.

One last look.

Bing thought the world was upside down. It couldn't be true. It couldn't. He was too upset himself — first the speech into the mike, the concentration on words, and then the sudden result, so tangible, so clear.

He looked again.

The four American soldiers were marching the German deserters straight back to the German lines.

They, too, were shell-shocked. They, too, had forgotten right and left, front and rear, in the dizziness of constant death around the holes in which they had huddled, in the daze of constant apprehension and watchfulness.

Laborde stood in front of the hill. Now, his arms were crossed before his chest, one foot was set forward, and he was very conscious of his profile.

Bing wanted to laugh. Only the laugh stuck in his throat. He could let things ride. He had done all that could be expected of him. And more.

God-damned fool, he said to himself. You God-damned fool.

Then he jumped up and forward, ran like mad, ran to catch up with the four American soldiers and their twelve wards. They weren't under fire, at the moment. The Germans were holding their fire as deserters and guards approached their lines. What they were thinking, God only knew. Perhaps they figured that the deserters had convinced the Americans to switch roles.

Bing reached the group.

"Back!" he shouted. "Back! Back!"

The four soldiers looked at him. Their eyes were blank. Their faces were like the faces of the German deserters — the same vagueness, the same: *What do you want of us? Leave us be! Why doesn't anyone say it's all over?*

"Back!" Bing pointed toward the American positions.

One of the soldiers slowly shook his head.

The idea came to Bing quite unsummoned. He grinned. The drill ground. The hours of up and down, mechanically, until you were like a machine. He was the Sergeant.

He roared, "Ten — shun! 'Bout — Face! Forward — March!"

And it worked. It worked with the four Americans; and as they turned, the deserters turned.

Bing waved them on. He ran. They ran, following him.

Laborde remembered his functions of command.

Pursued by ever denser mortar and small-arms fire, the prisoners and their guards had reached the comparative safety of the hedges on the American side. Near the hill in the open field, only the truck with Tolachian and Bing, and the loudspeakers in the shrubbery, were left to Laborde's authority.

Bing urged that they get away immediately, as fast as they could. They were now the only remaining target. The Germans could concentrate everything they had on them — and would, frustrated as they were because the deserters had slipped their hands.

"What!" said Laborde, "and leave the loudspeakers?"

Tolachian sat on the driver's seat, ready to take off.

"They're expendable," said Bing.

"Only in an emergency!" Laborde was dogmatic. "Besides, there is the wire. I'm not going to lose Government property."

"Now, Lieutenant!" said Bing. "We've done a lot today. We don't have to stretch our luck." He pleaded, "Be reasonable!"

"Afraid?" said Laborde.

"All right," said Bing, "so I'm afraid. Let's get out of here! . . . Tolachian, we're going!" He took a few steps toward the truck. Tolachian raced the motor.

"Stop!" shouted Laborde. "I'll have you court-martialed! Refusing an order! Cowardice in the face of the enemy!" Laborde was going full blast.

He had found something to get his teeth into. He had not contributed to

96

the operation. The location from which the appeal was made had been found without him. Somebody else had made the speech. The deserters had come over of their own will. They had been taken to the rear by four strange soldiers. But he would bring back the loudspeakers.

"Aw, shut up . . ." said Bing.

"You don't have to go out!" Laborde's voice failed him. "Tolachian!"

"Yes, sir!" Tolachian stuck his head out of the truck.

"The loudspeakers — go get the loudspeakers!"

Tolachian climbed from the truck. He glanced at Bing — a kind of help-less look. It was Tolachian's job to bring in the loudspeakers. He went off.

Bing saw the fire close in on them. Laborde lit another cigarette. Laborde was mad — power-mad, glory-mad.

Then Bing left the little protection the hill afforded. He went after Tolachian, who was crawling ahead slowly and had just about reached the first brush on the right where one loudspeaker was hidden.

Only much later could Bing pluck apart the pack of sensations which followed: the earth's upheaval, the deafening blow of the explosion, the hammering on his back as clumps of ground and stone fell on it, the acrid smell, the black blindness before his eyes. His body was one great pain, which quickly subsided. Wet, sticky warmth was on his cheek. He felt his face. There was a cut, nothing deep. He was able to move. He could see again — the first thing he saw, the broken wad of grass into which he had buried his head.

He looked up.

Before him lay Tolachian — Tolachian on his back as he had lain, when? — ages ago — when they smoked a cigarette behind the hill, before Bing began to speak to the Germans. Tolachian lay quiet. He is dead, thought Bing.

The thought entered his head so readily. Had Bing expected him to die? Had he known all along that he would find Tolachian one day, stretched out like this, dead?

Frantically, Bing crawled the short distance between himself and the body. He touched Tolachian's hand. It was heavy. He grabbed Tolachian's shirt, trying to turn him over. The shirt slipped from his grip. It was wet through and through.

Bing crawled to the other side of Tolachian. That he was able to see this side of a man's body, take in the detail, the torn flesh, the bone splinters, the mess of brown cloth, skin, and organs which could be anything: lungs, kidneys, liver, intestines — formless, shapeless, pulpy, slippery . . . But he saw it, took it all in, and remained with all his faculties, with his mind functioning.

Not far from Tolachian stood Laborde's loudspeaker, unharmed.

Bing carried the dead Tolachian back to the truck. He grabbed Tolachian's good arm and, using it as a handle, hoisted the body on his own shoulders. His back was drenched. The dead man weighed heavily. Bing feared Tolachian would come apart, simply split open at the side, and that he would be choked in the body's embrace. But Tolachian held together.

Bing loaded the dead friend on the rear of the truck, next to the tool chest which had been his. He found Laborde's trench coat and folded it as a pillow and placed Tolachian's head on it.

Then he went forward and got behind the wheel and started the motor. Next to the truck, he saw Laborde. Laborde lay on the ground. He had begun to dig a hole, but had not got very far with it. The cigarette was still in his mouth. It had gone out. Its paper was drenched in the saliva which had dribbled from the Lieutenant's mouth.

"Hold it!" cried Laborde as Bing started the truck. Bing did not stop. Laborde had to jump on the running board and hang on for dear life as Bing raced across the field, the German fire still pursuing them.

Troy received them quietly. He ordered some of his men to unload the body of Tolachian.

Then he took Bing aside and led him to his own dugout. Troy lived in a hole burrowed into a hedge — a deep hole in which he could stretch out. A shelter-half before it served as an awning and offered some shade.

"Sit down," he said.

Bing took off his helmet and sat down. Troy reached into his hole and took out a bottle.

"Calvados," he said, "help yourself."

Bing drank and felt the stuff burn down his throat, into his stomach.

"More!" said Troy, "drink more!"

Bing did.

"Feel better?"

"Yes, sir."

But he didn't feel better. His stomach came up into his throat, his mouth was forced open.

"Let go!" said Troy.

Bing gave himself to the convulsions of his body. It felt good to stop hanging on to himself. Again and again. His head felt lighter.

After a while, Troy came with a shovel full of dirt and covered the mess which lay between Bing's knees.

"Get out of your clothes," ordered Troy. "You can have a shirt and a pair of my pants."

"Thank you, sir," said Bing.

The shovel hung from Troy's relaxed hand, swinging lightly. "Death is always ugly," he said. "Don't let 'em tell you different. But you get accustomed to it."

98

"It's the wrong guys that die!" said Bing.

"No, the institution is rather impartial," said Troy. He smiled encouragingly. "We just notice it more when it happens to people whose job is living."

9

AT THE Battery, they picked up Karen. Laborde was driving the truck. Bing had refused to drive. He had told Laborde plainly that, if the Lieutenant wanted to get back to Vallères, he should get himself another driver. Laborde, seeing the Sergeant's disturbed face, did not insist; he had visions of ending up in a ditch, smashed; and he believed Bing would not care much if that should come to pass. But he, himself, cared.

Fear shot through Karen as she saw Laborde at the wheel, and the seat next to his empty, and nobody getting out. Laborde motioned her to sit in front.

"Where are the others?" she asked, forming her words with effort.

Laborde inclined his head toward the rear of the truck.

In Karen, relief mingled with the question: Why doesn't he show himself? Is he ill, wounded, exhausted? "Thank you," she said, "I'd rather sit back there."

"But this seat is empty, now!" urged Laborde. "It's much more comfortable!"

Then she saw Bing. He was leaning back, his eyes closed, his face drawn. He seemed to be asleep.

Suddenly he said, without moving, without opening his eyes, "Is that you, Karen? Come in. Be careful, the floor is slippery."

It was. The rust-colored, dull splotches, into which she couldn't help stepping, made her feel slightly squeamish. She knew what it was, without asking.

"Tolachian . . ." he said. "They didn't clean out the truck."

"Dead?"

"Yes."

The truck bounced forward.

Bing tumbled against her. "Pardon!" he said mechanically. Then he looked at her as if she had come to him from another world. "You won't be able to understand. I hate that sonofabitch. He killed Tolachian."

She felt that any word from her would break the mood; she was glad he was talking; whatever had happened, he must talk it out of himself. If she could help him by listening quietly and by understanding, that was what she wanted to do most of all in the world.

"Him, I mean!" Bing pointed with his thumb to the tarpaulin behind which Laborde was steering the vehicle. "We are like targets on the range, the Germans firing at us — small-arms, mortars, anything they had — and Laborde forcing Tolachian to pull in the loudspeakers."

"You — could have left?"

"Of course! We were all through. Fourteen Germans came over after the broadcast — two of them got killed — but we had twelve live ones."

"That's a lot?" she asked.

"I didn't expect any!"

"And then what happened?"

"I don't want to talk about it."

"You've got to."

"Karen! He made us stay out there! These loudspeakers are expendable, do you understand? We can get new ones whenever we need them! Why didn't I shoot him? Explain that to me! Why didn't I?"

"He can hear you!"

"So what! Let him. I could have killed him like that. Nobody would have known the difference. There was enough German stuff flying around. But with me — I get the right ideas too late. This man Tolachian, he would be alive, now, instead of that morbid bastard sitting in front."

Bing reached into his pocket, and pulled out a fistful of small articles. "This is what's left of him — look: Dog tags, pocket knife, a watch, wallet with — oh, about hundred and fifty francs, PX card, a photograph — wonder who that guy is in Armenian costume? Probably his father — then, this locket. . . ."

He opened the locket. "That's Tolachian, this must be his wife — a bad picture, they always carry around bad pictures, a picture is what you see in it. . . . And this letter, unmailed. I'll read it to you. I've been reading and reading it. *Dear Anja,* he says — I think her name is Anastasia — *you don't say so in your letters, but I can read between the lines, that you are very tired all the time. You must take care of yourself. Don't work so hard. I hate for you to have to work at all. Better quit and take four weeks off. Go to your uncle in Schenectady, he will be glad to have you. And don't you worry about me. I'm doing fine. The war will be over soon, I guess, and then I will come home and you won't have to work. I have a good job here and nothing can happen to me, so you can rest easy. I have been called out for a little trip, I must go now, I will finish this letter when I get back. . . .*"

"How did he die?"

"He didn't know what hit him, I don't think he did."

"That's good," she said, "sometimes they take a long time dying."

"You don't understand, Karen, you don't understand at all. He wanted to come home and see that this woman Anja stopped working. I suppose now she will have to work for the rest of her days — ".

"Unless she meets someone else."

"Don't say that!"

"Tolachian would find it right. Life goes on."

"Karen!" he said. "Have a heart."

The glistening splotches on the floor of the truck were drying out. Just the rust color remained, in odd shapes.

"I'm saying it for your sake," she insisted.

"You know what is driving me crazy?" he asked. "Just this, that life goes on. That there will be springs, many springs, after we are gone; that girls in light clothes are going to meet young men and that they will hold hands, long after our hands have rotted away — I'm so insatiable, I don't want it to end; what have I had? Nothing. And even if I'd had the fullest life, I would always want it to be more and fuller. There's something else, and maybe you'll think I'm no good: it isn't only Tolachian — oh, sure, he was the salt of the earth, and they don't come any better — it's myself. As I carried him on my back, I realized that it had reached for me. And once you've felt that, you can't be the same; you want to cram into every minute what others have in a year. . . ."

Karen gave up all pretense. This was her man, here and now, and he had come back, wounded. The terrible fear that had shot through her when she saw the truck arrive at the Battery, and did not see him — the wild joy in her breast as she found him — the disregard for everything, even the death of Tolachian, except as it concerned him!

Bing had sunk back into the stupor of exhaustion. His body swayed with the motion of the truck. She unbuttoned his shirt. The thin, white skin over his ribs filled her with uncontrollable pity.

Laborde drove straight through to Vallères. Loomis met them in the courtyard of the Château and received Laborde's report. Twelve German prisoners, one American casualty; in regard to the morning report which he would have to sign, everything was better than even.

Yet, Loomis felt anxious. He had not intended Tolachian to be killed, he assured himself immediately. He had wanted Tolachian to receive a lesson — that the man died in the course of the lesson was a freak, was definitely not his fault, and by no stretch of imagination could he admit to any blame for it.

Laborde remained hazy on the details of Tolachian's death; he did not mention the orders he had given, and merely announced that the loudspeakers could not be recovered. Bing was too numb to say anything.

Then Yates came. Yates had been waiting for the loudspeaker truck to return, he had counted the hours, he had delayed his own departure to the prisoner cage. When he heard the truck pull into the courtyard, he had rushed down from his room, relieved that the team had come back, and eager and elated to see Karen.

Loomis was the first to realize that Yates had joined the group, and he braced himself. He began to praise Bing extravagantly, calling him brave and an example for the men in the organization; lauding his presence of mind and his calmness under fire. He said he knew what a terrible shock the death of Tolachian must have been to Bing, how he sympathized with Bing and would do anything to help him get over it. Did Bing want a few days off? He could have them. Did Bing want the Bronze Star? He more than deserved it, what with twelve prisoners; and Loomis would push the matter personally.

"So Tolachian is dead. . . ." said Yates. "How did it happen?"

Laborde hastily stepped into Loomis's groove, forgetting he had threatened Bing with court-martial. "Sergeant Bing has distinguished himself," he said, his dour face flushing. "Anything Captain Loomis suggests will find my full approval and backing."

"They killed Tolachian," said Bing. He kept his head bowed.

Loomis began eulogizing again.

Yates stared at him. The Captain's performance, the drivel he was spilling, was such a miserable epilogue. Too late, Yates thought, too late. He felt enervated, down to the tips of his fingers. He felt the itching of his warts. He wanted to talk to Karen, to tell her that he had tried to prevent this; and that, after all, the leaflet *had* been fired. And he wanted to help Bing.

But before he could rouse himself, he heard Karen break into Loomis's self-defense, "Why don't you leave the man alone, Captain? Can't you see he doesn't care about this eyewash?"

Loomis stopped cold. He stammered something; his face became puffed up and red. "I beg your pardon!"

"I mean it," she said quietly. "A man has died; and if you ask Lieutenant Laborde he'll have to confirm that the man died unnecessarily. And all this yak-yak will not bring him back."

Loomis's expression tightened. "Sergeant Bing!"

"Yes, sir!"

"You've been handing out military information to the press — without your commanding officer's permission!"

Yates was not permitting Bing to be victimized as Tolachian had been. "You're too damned fast with your charges, Captain! Why don't you ask Laborde what happened?"

Laborde's lips came open. Spittle collected in the space between his upper front teeth; he hissed at Karen: "How do you know under what circumstances the man was killed? That's what I love about people like you

— you stay behind, but you promote the most outrageous stories about what happens up front. Do you want to blame me for the way the German shells were coming in? It could have hit me just as easily! I never ducked for cover — "

Yates said angrily: "The question is not whether you did or didn't duck — but whether you kept others from ducking in time. Furthermore, you'll apologize now to Miss Wallace — apologize! Or I'll take you behind the Château and beat your brains out!"

Laborde saw Yates's eyes. He saw the taut whiteness around Yates's mouth; and suddenly the man who'd been spun around at dizzying speed in the dummy cockpit, the man who had gone silently into the gas chamber, became small and shabby and said, "I apologize. Miss Wallace, I'm sorry — I'm sorry. . . ."

Karen ignored the apology. "I can handle any attacks on me, Lieutenant Yates!" she said cuttingly. "But what are you going to do about this thing?"

Yates had no answer.

"Now, now, now!" said Loomis, trying to appease everybody. He was glad Yates had made Laborde apologize — Willoughby would never stand for any offense to the press. But the woman had to be kept out of this, she was a troublemaker. "Miss Wallace — don't you see that you're interfering in strictly military matters? You have no complaints about accommodations, about lack of co-operation, have you? Well, if you have any reports to make, the Public Relations Officer at Army will be glad to discuss them with you. We're all doing our best — the same as Sergeant Bing here, the same as Private Tolachian, who was unfortunately killed in the line of duty. Won't you come along with us? . . . Sergeant Bing! Dismissed!"

Karen gave him no reply. She followed Bing out of the courtyard and over the drawbridge.

Yates made a move to go after her, to bring her back. But he checked himself. Maybe it was good so, he thought. Good for him, good for her who had made her choice, and good for Bing. He smiled ruefully: Big of me, isn't it! . . .

"Look at that!" he heard Loomis say. "The nerve of that bitch!"

"The men around here take too many liberties," said Laborde. "It's your business to stop them."

"You shut up!" Loomis replied sharply. "It's your business to bring back your men alive!"

"Why don't you give me men that can move faster?"

Loomis nudged Laborde. Laborde looked up and saw that Yates was listening. "Well!" Laborde said cheerfully, "we got twelve Heinies anyhow!"

"Tolachian was such a nice, quiet person, too!" said Loomis. "You know, I forgave him long ago for the trick with that Frenchwoman. . . . Everybody's entitled to make *some* mistake!"

"Twelve Heinies!" repeated Laborde.

Loomis forced a smile. "What d'you think Farrish is going to say?"

"You've got it all down pat, haven't you!" said Yates.

They went across the meadow behind the Château, past the laundry shed which lay empty in the heat of the afternoon sun, up the brook whose waters fed the moat, to a copse of trees.

They sat down in the shade.

"What did you do that for?" asked Bing. He maneuvered his body so that he could lay his head on her lap. He dropped back and looked at her chin and her nose, he saw the lines around her throat and, brought alive by the sun, the soft fuzz on her cheek. "Why not let them hush it up? The man is dead; I should know — very dead."

She caressed his forehead. "I was stupid. They will make even more trouble for you. . . ."

Of course they will, thought Bing. But he said: "Oh, no. What can they do to me? Don't worry. But you must go away from here. You know too much about that whole gang, and they won't feel comfortable as long as you are here. And if they don't feel comfortable, they'll be up to all sorts of nuisance."

She laughed softly. Then she said, "Do *you* want me to go?"

"No."

She said nothing and closed her eyes.

"How's your story coming along?" he asked.

"I will write it soon. Shall I send you a copy?"

"You look very pretty — from down here."

"Yes?"

"I remember my mother when she was young. She was very pretty, at least I thought so. Her hair was softer than yours, but you probably have little chance to take care of it, now."

She wanted to cradle him. She wanted to take him into her arms and make him small and hold him close to her breast and rock him. How out of character, she thought. I'm doing a man's job, I dress like a man, I'm in the middle of a man's war.

"Have you had many women in your life?" she asked.

"A few."

"Are you still in love with some of them — or one of them? . . ."

"I don't know."

I shouldn't ask him these questions. This isn't Central Park, I'm not his little girl.

"I will go away soon," she said. "We may never see one another again. I want to tell you how much I — I appreciated being with you. When I met you, I didn't much believe in anything — "

"And now you do?"

"In something — I can't clearly define what it is — integrity, perhaps — that a man must do what he believes in, regardless of what others may do, say, or think. . . ."

"Very nice," he said, "very nice."

"All right. Forget it. Forget I ever said it."

"No," he said. "No, I like it. Is that what one is supposed to say? Can't you be quiet? Listen to the water down there, it flows and flows — it makes no polite conversation — it just *is*."

"I thought I would help you . . ."

"But you do, Karen, you do. One day, I'm going to come to you, after the war, maybe . . ."

"Nonsense. You'll have forgotten me, I'll have forgotten you."

"Right," he said, "it was just a thought. . . ."

The conversation fizzled out. The crowns of the trees began to dance, the blood in his brain sang, a steady, high-pitched tone like a far-faraway chorus of crickets. I must stop looking up, he thought. Her hand caressed his face, again and again — her fingers had a life of their own, their soft tips taunting.

He raised his head. He turned over. His face was close to hers. He smelled her hair, a dry, warm smell like the sun, on a summer's afternoon, falling between the pines on needle-covered soil.

He opened her coveralls and the shirt underneath. She leaned back, limply, let her head rest on the ground. The skin beneath her collarbones was white and smooth. He kissed the hollow between her shoulders and breasts.

Almost unnoticeably, she helped him to undress her — a slight move of the shoulder here, a raising of the hips. "Your boots," he said with a short laugh, "we must take off your boots."

Then her clothes lay at her feet. Her body stretched in its new freedom. Her hands left him and went behind her head. Her lips were full, he had never seen them so full. She drew in her breath, sharply. "Come," she said, "come, my darling."

His mind was a caldron of impressions. Her body grew and grew. Its very expectancy made him shrink. He saw Tolachian — the torn side of Tolachian. He saw the field with the oddly outlined figures of the running deserters. He saw the hill and the shrubs, and Troy waving. He tried to direct his mind to her breasts and the dark curls of hair in her armpits. He forced himself to kiss her ears and her throat, her live, pulsating throat. The more he tried to channel his thoughts, the farther they went astray.

He broke into sweat from the hot fear which filled his bowels. It was fear of ridicule, fear of the disappointment he was to her, fear of impotence.

He threw himself on her, seeking help from her body. He felt her willingness, as she closed him into her arms. But it was like the dead man's embrace he had feared when he carried him.

"Karen," he said, "forgive me, Karen."

She patted his back, lightly. "It makes no difference, darling. None at all. Stay that way, be quiet."

He sobbed, one dry sob of unrequited excitement.

He felt her draw away from him slowly. She picked up her shirt and covered herself.

"Can I help you?" he asked miserably.

Her lips brushed his forehead. "No," she whispered, "it is all right." She was slipping into her clothes.

"I'm such a — such a ridiculous — "

"You are not," she said firmly. "We just weren't made for one another. These things must work themselves out. It was a bad day. You must not take it so hard. I'm not taking it hard, either — you see? It is much worse for me than for you — after all, I'm the woman in the case, and I wasn't able to make you love me. . . ." She laughed. "It isn't your fault."

"I love you, Karen," he pleaded.

She shook her head. While applying her lipstick, she said, "Listen, darling — the world is so much greater than the two of us. And now, let's cut out the big words. It was still very beautiful."

She went away. He looked after her as she walked toward the Château. And now his eyes could see her — he saw the movement of her hips, and her shoulders. It was as if her clothes were transparent. He wanted her, wanted her with all his heart and soul and body.

He dug his fingers into the ground. The sharp pain under his nails was wonderful.

Book Two

PARIS IS A DREAM

I

FARRISH was giving an interview to the correspondents.

He stood picturesquely before his own tank that bore the names of the battles of North Africa and Sicily in which he and his Division had participated. A new name was added now; the paint was not yet dry: *Avranches.*

Still posing, but I like him, thought Karen.

"Avranches," the General was saying, "is one of the turning points of the war. Imagine a great door, firmly closed in our face, and containing us in the two peninsulas of Cotentin and Brittany. As long as we were bottled up on those two land's ends of the European continent, the great danger existed that the Germans would mass sufficient troops and matériel to throw all of us back into the ocean. Well, Avranches was the hinge of this door. We have smashed the hinge and unhinged the door. We will now march forward."

Karen asked, "What about Le Havre? What about the other ports which the Germans have converted into strong points? When and where will they establish a line?"

Farrish flung out his arm in a motion that swept everything before him. "Whether and where the Germans will establish a new line, depends entirely on us — on our speed, our supplies, and the endurance of our troops. I picture a series of pincer movements such as we developed in the final stages of the North African campaign. Utilizing our superior mobility and the element of surprise, we will dance ring-around-the-rosy with the German divisions, corps, and armies, isolating and destroying them singly. You can quote me on that. You can not quote me on what I'm telling you now: The main push will be directed toward Paris."

"Yes — but that's the most interesting point!" another of the correspondents argued.

"I know!" Farrish beamed grandly. "Sorry, you can't quote it. But when you write your story on Paris, you may remember my words. Paris, ladies

107

and gentlemen, is Victory. It is the climax of all we have done up to now. For this, we have plodded and plotted, worked on the training grounds of our own country, fought on the deserts of North Africa and the mountains of Sicily. We will march in triumph the same road Napoleon took after his victories. In the clatter of my tanks, the sound of the German boots on the Champs-Élysées will be drowned out."

"He should never have to eat his words," someone whispered to Karen.

Farrish swung himself onto his tank. As it roared off, his gleaming helmet and waving arm remained visible above the clouds of dust.

"I bet he's enjoying this war," the same voice said, now completely unrestrained.

"He has a knack for happy phrases," Karen replied. "Saves you a lot of work."

The other, a wizened little man by the name of Tex Myers, shook his head. "It's so God-damned easy to coin phrases out of other people's blood. Oh, well . . ." And he disappeared, leaving Karen to her copious notes.

Long before the commanding general issues an order of the day or gives his interview to the press, the ordinary soldier, with his sharpened instinct for any turn of battle, has sensed what has happened, has stretched himself out on the ground, taken off his boots, pulled a cigarette from his sweat-soaked pack, and begun to catch up on his sleep.

This sleep never lasts long. Unless he is pulled out of the line, he is ordered forward. He climbs on trucks, finding a seat if he is lucky. He is jolted over impossible roads, his body shaken, his head bobbing as he tries to sleep some more. A new destination is reached, he is ordered off the trucks, and again hears the sound of battle.

In all this tiredness, there is a quiet exuberance. It springs from the experience that an enemy on the run is easier to fight than one who has his feet dug in. The campaign has not yet lasted long enough to compel the gray resignation that after every hill climbed, there are new and steeper hills, chains of hills, mountains, and Europe is much bigger than it shows on the map.

Troy's men are traveling that way. The platoon sergeant sits on the last seat, at the end of the half-track. He swallows the dust, and his eyes are the only spot of color on an otherwise sallow face.

Sheal says, "Maybe we're going right through to Paris. Oh boy." Sheal is young; he has a soft face and chubby hands.

Traub, who has tied a condom over the muzzle of his rifle to keep the dirt from settling in it, has his doubts. "We'll take Paris, and first thing, the place will be off limits."

Cerelli stretches his legs and tries to adjust his field pack so that the carrier straps stop cutting his shoulders. "When we have Paris, the war will be over. I read that somewhere. And it's logical, too. Look at the long front the Germans have in the East. And now, here, too. They've just got to give up. Look at the prisoners . . ."

They are passing a bedraggled line of German soldiers, walking back where the vehicles are rushing forward.

Cerelli continues, "When the war is over, I'm going to go into business. I know me a sweet racket in a certain line of secondhand cars . . ."

Nobody listens to him. They know the story of his secondhand cars and how they can be fixed up to run like new for forty-eight hours, or at least until the customer has driven them away.

Sergeant Lester wipes his face. He has been dreaming of a bed with clean, cool sheets, and a bath in which he can soak for hours, drawing fresh hot water as the old cools off. "Bullshit," he says, "I know where we're going."

"Where?"

"You never heard of the place. And I wish I'd never heard of it, either."

That's a damper, but not enough to keep them from feeling good. Lester is an old man with his thirty years; that's why.

Next to the driver, Captain Troy sits hunched in the corner of the seat. He wants to keep his eyes open, but he can't. His chin sinks on his breast. He is asleep.

Yates lay on top of a truck piled high with baggage. He was moving forward with the Detachment's advance party which was to enter Paris soon after its fall. Yates was fairly happy; after much dragging and pulling, he had succeeded in arranging the load in such a way that he could stretch out without having a tent pole or some other hard object poke his ribs each time the truck hit a hole.

The day was warm and sunny. The road was paneled with endless rows of poplars which flew by, forming two solid, wind-quickened walls of green. It was as if he were riding through a long, long cathedral whose roof was infinitely high and near God.

He thought of the age these roads must have for the trees to have grown that tall. He thought of bygone armies which moved over them before this one came along with its tanks and half-tracks and jeeps and bulldozers and trucks and self-propelled guns. In Normandy, these millions of wheels had counted much less. Men had hopped from hedge to hedge, and the taking of a village, paid for highly, was a major achievement. If he turned his head slightly, he could see the destroyed or broken-down German vehicles. They stood, as if obligingly, to the side of the road, the odd brown and buff and green design of their camouflage frequently singed by the flames that had burned out the steel shells. Sometimes, the muzzles of their elongated guns were split open like the petals of weird flowers; and the torn bogey wheels of their half-tracks created a picture of desperate disorder. Past these mute witnesses of hasty retreat rolled the Americans, past farmers plowing around abandoned antitank guns, past blasted road-blocks.

Yates never tired of these sights. Each mile forward, each smashed German vehicle, were witness and confirmation to what the wheels of the truck seemed to sing on the age-old cobblestones: *They can be beaten — they can be beaten — they can be beaten.* . . . Only now, and because he was going through virtually the same experience, did Yates begin to comprehend what the teacher of Isigny, Mademoiselle Godefroy, had said: *We had almost come to believe that they were the kind of men who could not be made to turn their backs. And then they ran.*

Normandy, despite the success of the initial landings, had also been a testimony to the staying power of the Germans. Yates, unlike the people of Isigny, had never felt the Nazis' physical presence; but the years of German advances, the ponderous reports of the American commentators, and the resigned and senseless sacrifice of position after position to the triumphantly loud, screaming Voice of Berlin had engendered in him, as in so many others, an almost subconscious belief in the qualities of the Germanic superman.

His people were not a warlike people; he was not a warlike man. The Americans were like workmen who had put their great shops and factories on wheels. They were digging a Panama Canal through the German Army, blasting, bulldozing, shoveling aside anything in their way.

The knocked-out German tanks and guns were like a beautiful token, perhaps not of the great victory, but at least of its possibility. And — this was the road to Paris. Yates recalled the instructions Colonel DeWitt had given upon arriving from England to take charge of the Detachment.

"The fall of Paris which we may anticipate," DeWitt had said, "will be a psychological shock to the Germans. Strategically, it is unimportant — it would be much better to win another channel port to bring in supplies. We know that the average German attaches great symbolic importance to the French capital. Therefore, its fall will be a blow. We must make them feel that blow — hard!"

You had to look fairly close at the Colonel's face to see his age. He had the robust build of an outdoor man, and a complexion that led you to assume he carried a hip flask. His straight, high, furrowed forehead forced you to take his words seriously.

"What's the matter with him?" Yates had asked Crerar. "Do his hands always tremble like that?"

"His nerves are shot," explained Crerar. "Some days it's particularly bad; and he's in pain."

"What's he doing over here, then?"

"Oh, I suppose he could have had a cushiony job in Washington," Crerar shrugged. "But he wanted it this way."

DeWitt had ended his instructions. "The task ahead is clear. But don't think, gentlemen, that it'll be an easy job!"

Somehow, Yates believed that with DeWitt around it would be easier. . . .

Paris was more than a target. Paris was a dream.

McGuire, driving the jeep for Loomis and Crabtrees, had his dream of Paris. Where the elements of this dream came from, he could not have said. Of course, there were magazines and the movies, photos and the stories that went the rounds among the men.

A wide-open town, with big houses, and beautiful women, and people who spoke much too fast. He had been in big towns; he had seen New York, on pass; and several times he had been from Rocky Creek, Kentucky, to Louisville. But if you looked at it honestly, Louisville wasn't much more than fifty or a hundred Rocky Creeks thrown together, and New York was a place for suckers; every damned thing cost a soldier twice what it should, and then you didn't get much. But Paris? In Paris the things of which you only thought at night were openly available and free, or almost free — he was willing to spend money within reason and to give the French a break. In Paris were liquor and shows and dancing and no questions asked, something like a perpetual fair, and it went on the whole night long.

Of course, he had not said a word about his feelings when Loomis had ordered him to get the jeep ready for the big trip to Paris. Now, glancing sidewise at the Captain without taking his eyes completely off the road, McGuire found Loomis all right. McGuire relaxed. He didn't mind driving for Loomis at all. At the end lay — Paris.

Loomis, traveling through the darkness, admired his own courage, but began to doubt his wisdom.

As long as they were back at headquarters, the advance had seemed simple enough. The Germans, he had been assured by everybody, were on the run, and it was unlikely that they would stop running so soon, much less turn on their pursuers. All you had to do was to hop into a jeep, and drive down the road to Paris at the approximate speed with which the Germans were retiring.

Paris was like a ripe fruit. If you wanted to have a bite out of it, you had to be there when it fell. And he wanted a big bite. He had sacrificed so much in this war: the lazy swing of his days; great opportunities for making a hunk of dough — Dorothy, his wife, wrote every week how people were piling up money back home — and the radio store he owned, in which he was his own boss. The war, the Army, owed him a lot. He deserved to be in Paris among the first.

Crabtrees smiled happily. "What'll they say in Philadelphia when they hear we've been the first ones to get into Paris?" The big bony sister who was continually trying to run his affairs; his mother who, bursting with pride and love, called him her little soldier-boy? This time, he was putting something over on them.

Loomis saw a clump of solid black in the transparent, silky blue of the summer night. "Easy now!" he ordered McGuire, "we may run into opposition any minute. . . ."

The opposition consisted of some trucks stalled on the road.

"Well," Loomis was relieved, "it seems there are still some troops ahead of us."

Thorpe, too, dreamed of Paris.

Paris was history — small streets with crooked houses, cobblestones over which the sewerage of the Middle Ages had flowed, and the blood of the musketeers of the King. He felt the humility of a man conscious of the fact that he comes from a nation which has hardly any history; he accepted the bad and the good things of old, and in his mind they gained great glory.

Also, he liked the largesse of Paris. It was so different from America, undertaking things on a grand scale — an avenue at home was built for traffic; in Paris, because it was beautiful to have an Étoile, a star, with boulevards radiating in all directions.

Mainly, however, Paris was a city with millions of people — civilians. You could lose yourself among them, you could almost believe that you were part of them, relieved from the dreariness of the Army, from associates forced on you, from a discipline which was geared to the lowest possible standard of mind.

In Paris, he dreamed, he would submerge himself in the colorful mass in order to become himself, an individual, again.

Crerar dreaded his entry into Paris. Yet he trembled in fear of any delay. He hoped that the Germans would not resist in the town — he knew that Paris had changed much since the time he had left it hurriedly; it couldn't help changing — the Germans leave their imprint on everything. How far had they succeeded in branding the live, quivering body of Paris?

No, the city must be left standing. He wanted to see again his old haunts on Montparnasse, the café where he and Eve had sat in the evenings, sipping crème de menthe, or the vile lemonades which belong to the hustle of the boulevards as surely as the clanging horns of the taxis. Oh yes, there would be no taxis. *Vélo-taxis,* they had now — bicycles with little cars attached. And what had become of the men he had known? Were they still alive, working on the stage or in their ateliers? How many of them had sold out to the Germans? How many of the girls — those mercurial creatures who always reminded him of quick burning embers and yet never seemed to burn themselves out — how many of them would have to be discarded because they had graced the bed of some stiff-necked, or elegant and worldly, German officer?

How unimportant, though, the people! He wanted the spirit, the fragrance, of Paris. This he must find again because this fragrance was part of Eve, and without it, she was not thinkable. Paris was the last station before he reached his farm, and through it recovered her who could not grow on the strange soil of New York, and who was shrinking away from him and withdrawing from him like his own youth.

Paris, at this time, seemed to lie asleep, but it was the sleep before the great stirring. Whether it contained the coveted Grail, nobody could say.

2

THE LEAD TANK stopped where the secondary road joined the main road to Paris.

On the map, the junction point was called Rambouillet, a small country town without particular character, similar to many in this part of France, with a *mairie,* a schoolhouse, a church, a brothel, a garage and a gas station; with most of its houses built in the uniform gray which made their age indeterminate. In the light of the evening sun, the gray had assumed a pinkish hue, and some of the windows were deep black, others golden.

The remnants of a German roadblock lay piled up on the sidewalk — heavy beams now splintered by demolition charges, slabs of concrete, and twisted barbed wire. Sergeant Lester was leaning against the wreckage, surveying the work of the detail he had been supervising. They'd done a pretty good job on that roadblock — they'd done a good job on the whole road, in fact, clearing it and preparing it for the advance of Farrish's Division.

As he loafed there, he saw the line of tanks approach and stop. Had he not recognized their typically American silhouette, Lester would have made himself scarce; but even so, the question of why a group of light tanks should come into Rambouillet over this side road bothered him. Moreover, the men in the tanks were careless; their main concern seemed to be to let the evening breeze cool them off.

Lester ambled over to the first tank. Then he recognized the French insignia painted on its side, the paint battered and partly washed off. Its commander lifted himself out of the hatch, jumped down, and began to pump Lester's hand enthusiastically. Lester found the handshake entirely too long and too warm. The tank man kept smiling and talking rapidly. He finally let go of Lester's hand and pointed along the main road leading to Paris.

Emphatically, Lester shook his head.

The Frenchman grew excited. He gestured eloquently, first toward his tanks and then, again, to the Paris road.

"No, no!" said Lester. "We —" his thumb touching his own chest — "Paris!"

The Frenchman threw up his arms. He broke into a torrent of angry words. He turned to go back to his tank, and his attitude indicated that he was determined to go ahead.

Excitable people, thought Lester. He pulled at the Frenchman's sleeve and pointed at his own submachine gun and said, "Bang! Bang! I'll have to shoot you, old man, if you try any monkey business."

The Frenchman pulled a small pistol out of his holster and also said, "Bang! Bang!"

Then they both broke into laughter, and Lester announced, "*Vous — avec — mon capitaine — là!*" He steered the Frenchman to the schoolhouse, which served Captain Troy as Command Post.

They had walked only a few steps when a second group of tanks drew up on the side road and parked behind the first batch. The latter clattered forward into the main road. At the point where the demolished roadblock narrowed the thoroughfare, the lead tank stopped to wait for further orders. At the same time, an American column of open half-tracks ground up the main stem, only to be halted by the effective barrier formed by the French tanks and the remnants of the roadblock.

Drivers began to shout at each other. Since the Americans could not understand what the French were saying, and the French were unable to understand the Americans, the Babel of languages and curses grew to a din. Nor could anyone withdraw, had there been willingness to capitulate on either side, because with every passing minute the two caterpillars of vehicles, their heads spliced and intermingled, grew longer.

Troy sat behind the teacher's desk, on the dais in the ground floor classroom of the schoolhouse. He was reading the algebra examples on the blackboard, checking on whether he still could do them, and carefully overlooking an inscription that ran across the top of the board: *Lieutenant Handler Is an Ass!* He hoped Handler would not come in. Handler would order someone to wipe off the blackboard, he would try to find the author, get nowhere with his investigation, and generally make himself ridiculous. Besides, Handler was an ass.

Troy wondered when the kids of Rambouillet had had their last algebra class. The Germans had been in town during the morning hours; they had erected the roadblock and then, for reasons of their own, had decided to pull out. Yesterday, the town had been shelled from the American side, some houses had been hit, and most of the people had run into the woods and fields. Few had returned, which made his job easier. You never could tell which side anybody was on; and he hated to take on Civil Affairs problems in addition to keeping the Paris road clear through Rambouillet.

When Lester brought in the French officer, Troy knew that something had gone wrong. The French were not supposed to be here at all.

He got up from the teacher's comfortable chair, saluted, and shook hands. "Go get Traub," he ordered Lester. Traub was the Company's specialist for negotiations with the French farmers for eggs, cider, and stronger stuff.

Traub reported.

While Traub parleyed with the Frenchman, Troy had time to study his ally. As unobtrusively as possible, he walked around the stranger. The man did not seem too well fed; his uniform and equipment were pieced together out of American, British, and old French supplies. Traub, apparently, got along well with him; they laughed together and shrugged and prattled on and on, as if the war left them endless time for amenities, as if the Germans were miles away, as if the most important thing in life was to spend it in agreeable company. Well, the French had no sense for the urgency of business; and that was probably why the Nazis had run all over them. The Germans were the only Europeans who had adopted American tempo.

Of the conversation between the Frenchman and Traub, Troy could make out only one word, *De Jeannenet.* But this was enough for him to feel even more uncomfortable — De Jeannenet was in command of the French Armored Division, and what the hell were elements of this Division doing at Rambouillet?

Troy's fears were confirmed by Traub. After exchanging the final pleasantries with the French officer, Traub turned to his captain. "Well, sir — I think I've got the story straight. This lieutenant's tanks belong to the forward elements of the French Armored Division. Their whole outfit is coming up behind them. They have orders to move ahead on the Rambouillet-Paris road and to enter Paris as soon as they can."

"Ahead of us?"

Traub translated the question to the Frenchman. The Lieutenant gave an expressive shrug and apologized volubly.

"Yes," said Traub.

"God damn these liaison people!" Troy took a piece of the teacher's chalk, aimed, and hit the spittoon in the corner. "Why doesn't anyone tell

us anything? Tell this man it doesn't matter to me who gets there first —
but I've got my orders. I can't let him go through until I get this thing
straightened out."

Traub began to interpret.

The Frenchman managed a smile.

"He says he'll wait a while in Rambouillet," translated Traub, "but not
very long. He must follow his own organization's orders."

"Now listen, Traub!" Small beads of sweat stood on Troy's upper lip.
"You've got to make it clear to this guy that he can't move ahead until I
tell him so. Make it very clear!"

"Yes, sir!"

Troy had visions of the road to Paris clogged up with broken-down
French vehicles, while Farrish's big tanks were trying to get through. He
turned to Lester. "Get me in touch with Regiment. Does the telephone
work now?"

"No, Captain — not yet."

"Try the radio, then! Get on the ball!"

In the waning light of day, a disheartening spectacle developed before
Troy. The street in front of the schoolhouse was jammed with French and
American vehicles of all kinds. On this road through Rambouillet, scarcely
wide enough for two horse carts to pass one another, tanks and self-propelled guns, trucks with trailers, half-tracks, bulldozers and prime movers
stood two abreast. The Americans had stopped the French — Lester had
made sure of that; he had stationed ten resolute-looking men near the demolished roadblock. The French retaliated by making it impossible for the
Americans to by-pass them.

The French drivers made noisy jokes. Some of them had taken up a raucous song. At the end of every verse they broke into peals of laughter. They
found the whole thing one hell of an adventure, while the Americans
leaned back in their seats, resigned to the hurry-and-wait procedure of the
Army. They had a good idea that a race was on — the race to Paris. They
were willing to do their damnedest to win that race. But as long as both
contestants were blocked on this lousy road, they took it easy.

My God, thought Troy, if the Germans knew! He was not gifted with
great imagination, but he had seen enough of the war to visualize the result of a German air attack on these vehicles, standing bumper to bumper,
and scratching the paint off their sides if they moved as much as a few
inches. And it need not come from the air! A company of infantry, with
hand grenades and machine guns, could create a panic in which nobody
would know where the real enemy was; in which everybody would fire at
everybody else, with bullets ricocheting from the houses; in which French
and American commands would make a unified defense impossible. The

wreckage! Steel and flesh smashed and mingled — the ammunition stored in tanks and caissons blowing up . . .

He was besieged by all sorts of officers and noncoms who wanted to know what was up and how long they would have to stay here.

Lester came out of the schoolhouse.

Over the heads of the clamoring gang around him, over the heads of the French and American soldiers who had begun trading cigarettes and liquor, Troy bawled out, "Are you getting through to Regiment?"

"Not yet!"

"Try again! Keep on trying!"

Sergeant Lester responded to the urgency in his captain's voice. He ran back into the schoolhouse and raised hell with the radio operator.

The operator defended himself. "Try it yourself if you think you can make it. Regiment's on the move, too — you know how it is. . . ."

The stream of vehicles and troops, coming from two sides, continued pressing into Rambouillet.

Night set in. With it came De Jeannenet.

The General, his tall emaciated body leaning on a cane, stood before the Café Montauban where, behind blacked-out windows, the French had set up a provisional command post.

A colonel, his tankist's helmet askew, was trying to make explanations. "*Les Américains* . . . They won't let us through. If we want to force our way, we've got to give them battle . . ."

"They won't let us through!" repeated De Jeannenet. "Who won't?"

"An American captain."

"A *captain?*"

The Colonel withered. "*Mon Général* — the American captain has orders from General Farrish! He is expecting General Farrish!"

"We shall wait!" said De Jeannenet. He waved to his adjutant to bring a field chair and set it next to a table on the sidewalk. "This will be my headquarters. Cider!" he said to the adjutant.

"Cider!" said the adjutant to the owner of the Café Montauban, who looked lost among the uniforms. The cider was placed on the General's table, and De Jeannenet began to drink, contentedly closing the small eyes in his beaglelike face. The Colonel attempted to argue respectfully that Rambouillet, being so far forward, was not the place for the General to be. "*Très dangereux! Très dangereux, mon Général!*"

De Jeannenet tapped his cane on the sidewalk and crossed his thin legs. "I've come here on my way to Paris. I will not retreat, not one step!"

Willoughby's jeep bounced into Rambouillet. Crerar, the kitten Plotz nestling under his field jacket, was holding on with both hands to the steel

117

frame of the rear seat. Crerar sighed with relief when the jeep had to slow down. "What's the hurry?" he managed to ask.

"Paris!" said Willoughby, and clicked his tongue. "Besides, I hate to keep the Old Man waiting for us."

The jeep stopped. Willoughby rose in his seat to survey the situation. "The usual mess, it seems," he remarked to Crerar and ordered the driver, "Let's go!" Between oaths flung impartially at French and Americans, he directed the driver past the blocked vehicles, over the sidewalks, behind lampposts, past stairways jutting out from the houses.

The jeep was being held up again.

"What're you stopping for?"

The driver pointed at the soldier Sheal who stood squarely in front of the car, his hands raised. Sheal was telling off the driver: Didn't he see that the road was blocked and that nobody was getting through? "Get the hell back where you come from!"

Willoughby swung himself out of the jeep and trod over to Sheal. Sheal saw the leaves on the grime-covered officer's shoulders. Willoughby did not raise his voice. "Now listen, young man," he said, "no need to shout at my driver. He's doing his best. Won't you kindly step aside so we can get through?"

After hours of being at the receiving end of all kinds of epithets, Sheal was short. "I've got my orders."

"Well," said Willoughby, "orders . . ."

Sheal became self-conscious.

"I could give you an order, too, couldn't I?" asked Willoughby.

Sheal didn't like the condescension.

Willoughby's tone became a shade sharper. "We happen to be in a hurry, young man!"

"So's everybody else, sir!" Sheal said, tired. "I get my orders from Captain Troy."

"Captain Troy," nodded Willoughby, "and who's that?"

"He's my C.O., sir. He's over at the schoolhouse."

"Fine!" smiled Willoughby. "I'll tell Captain Troy that he's got a good man out here. . . ."

"Thank you, sir."

The soldier Sheal made sure that the Major had turned his back. Then he spit.

The schoolhouse was the nearest large building. Past some of Troy's men dozing on the stairs, Willoughby and Crerar made their way into the classroom. Troy was asleep, his head pillowed in his arms on the teacher's desk.

Willoughby shook Troy's elbow.

Troy started up. His eyes blinking, he said, "What can I do for you, Major?"

"I'm Major Willoughby of Propaganda Intelligence. This is Mr. Crerar."

"Troy's the name, James F."

"We've got to get through to Paris, Captain Troy. You have a little man out there who stopped us."

"Uh-huh," Troy nodded. "I have several little men out there, and they're stopping everything."

"Do you mind telling me why?"

"Major Willoughby — do you have any recent dope that Paris has fallen?"

"It's about to fall, isn't it?"

"Well, it hasn't," Troy said slowly. "You see, sir, we are the people who're supposed to take it."

Willoughby took a closer look at the would-be conqueror of Paris. The skin of Troy's cheek was marked deeply where it had rested on his sleeve; it was a touch of sleeping child on the otherwise strong and broad features. The Captain's expression seemed to say, Here I am, and this is how it is — and what are you going to do about it?

Willoughby became careful. "You mean — there's nobody in front of you?"

The dimple appeared in Troy's cheek. "As far as I'm concerned, Major — if you're able to get through the blocked roads in this town — go ahead and good luck. You have my permission, sir. I'll give you one of my men along to tell the guard it's O.K."

Willoughby laughed. "Don't trouble yourself, Captain! Neither Mr. Crerar nor myself are that ambitious."

"Who is?" said Troy.

"You wouldn't know whether a Colonel DeWitt has come through here? We were supposed to meet him the other side of Rambouillet."

"Sorry, no," said Troy. "But nobody's gone forward of Rambouillet. I can guarantee that."

"Well — then you might tell us where we can be billeted overnight!"

Troy pointed at the classroom. "Help yourselves. But don't take up too much space. Some of my men are going to come in here later, and they've got to get some sleep."

"You haven't taken over any hotel?" Willoughby tried to see a way of squeezing his body into the seats of the children's benches. "No houses? Are there no officers' quarters?"

Troy looked at the unshaved, sagging jowls of the Major. "This is the front line, sir. It doesn't pay to make hotel arrangements if you can get thrown out of bed as fast as you get in."

"But everything's quiet!" said Willoughby, uncomfortably.

"That's because we don't know where the Germans are," said Troy.

"Oh!" said Willoughby. He pulled a bottle out of his Musette bag and offered it to Troy. "Might as well dig in!"

Troy held the bottle against the beam of his flashlight.

"It's good stuff!" said Crerar. "Tasted it on the way here. Try it!"

Troy had a big gulp, and then passed the bottle to Willoughby. From Willoughby, it went to Crerar and back to Troy.

Sergeant Lester came in, brimming with news.

Troy said, "First of all, Sergeant, have a drink." He glanced at Willoughby and said slyly, "It's all right, Major, isn't it?"

Crerar grinned. Willoughby kept from frowning. "Sure! Sure! Help yourself, Sergeant!"

Lester took a swig. Then he wiped his mouth, put down the bottle regretfully, and said, "Better hide this thing, Captain." He bent down to Troy and whispered something.

"Well!" said Troy, "finally! That'll break the deadlock."

He had just time to stick the bottle under the teacher's desk when the door was torn open and Farrish strode in, unmindful of the school benches in his way. Only Carruthers was with him.

"How long has this been going on, Captain?" he demanded. "This despicable mess out there?"

To Willoughby, the air seemed charged with new energy. There was a kind of esthetic pleasure in seeing the great man again, and in observing the way in which he came in and took over. It was the same magnetism that had attracted Willoughby in Vallères.

"How long have these French been blocking us?" Farrish tapped his foot. "Can't I get a straight answer from you, Captain?"

It was the first time Troy had met his General face to face. "Since late afternoon, sir, when their first vehicles came to the junction point. Your orders, sir, were to keep the Paris road free for our advance."

Troy's reaction to Farrish annoyed Willoughby. Too damned matter-of-course. Well, there were always the hacks — you could put them on top of the most beautiful woman, and they'd be too lazy to do anything about it.

"Do you call that keeping the road free?" the General demanded.

Any direct answer would have given Farrish the chance to launch a diatribe. Troy sidestepped it.

"General De Jeannenet is right in town, sir," he said, implying that the issue was now up to the two commanders.

"I know," said Farrish. "I'll see the man!" *And bust his ears and tear his guts out* remained unspoken. "Who talks that lingo?"

Both Crerar and Willoughby stepped forward. Over Willoughby's jowly face was shed the light of genuine loyalty.

"Aren't you the leaflet boys?" said Farrish. "Why the hell are you hanging around this God-forsaken spot? You want to go to Paris?"

"Yes, sir," said Willoughby, "if you'll take us along . . ."

"We were to meet Colonel DeWitt," Crerar informed him.

"DeWitt!" Farrish slapped his right fist into the open palm of his left hand. "It's a small world, isn't it?" He guffawed, and Willoughby smiled broadly. "Know him well, for years. How is he? Well, come along gentlemen! You did a good job on those little papers — prisoners, too — I remember, I remember! We'll show that Frenchman . . ." He knocked a bench aside. "Have this crap removed, Captain!"

Crerar lingered behind. "Captain Troy — if Colonel DeWitt shows up, would you tell him where we've gone?"

"Let's go, Mister!" shouted Farrish.

Then he was gone, cometlike, the tail formed by Willoughby, Carruthers, and Crerar.

Sergeant Lester dove under the teacher's desk and came up with the bottle. He handed it to Troy.

"Whew!" Troy wiped his forehead. Then he raised the bottle. "To more and better sleep!"

Lester looked sadly at the bottle's rapidly diminishing contents. "The General's a good man to keep away from," he said.

The encounter between Farrish and De Jeannenet began like an old-fashioned battle, with a meeting of the reconnaissance forces. Both men kept their main strength hidden.

De Jeannenet, who was on his third bottle of cider, offered a glass to the American. Farrish accepted graciously and reciprocated with a cigar. "Tell the General," he said to Willoughby, "that I've been looking forward to meeting him, that I've heard a lot about his exploits — you know the kind of bull."

"I do," said Willoughby. "I'm a lawyer." He went ahead.

The Frenchman bowed slightly from the waist. He paid back a similar compliment, but added that he wished the circumstances of the meeting were more propitious.

"Why?" said Farrish who wanted to find out how much De Jeannenet knew of the general plan of the advance. "You can follow us into Paris. It'll be an operation which will show the perfect unity and co-ordination of the Allies."

De Jeannenet's trouble was that the cider, of which he had consumed such quantities during his wait, was taking effect on his bladder. He was a man who valued etiquette; he didn't want to interrupt this important conference; now, he had to come out with the issue more directly than he liked.

"Co-ordination and unity!" he said. "Perfect, I agree. *Absolument!* However, the sequence, *mon Général,* the sequence! *You* will follow *us* into Paris; and I suggest that the necessary orders be given immediately. Time is short, and our situation in Rambouillet is untenable."

The arrogant bastard, thought Farrish. "Untenable!" he said. "You're damn tootin' it's untenable! Look at the way your vehicles are blocking the road! I wasn't here when it happened; but you've been sitting here for hours. Have you no eyes in your head? Don't you see that this place is the prize target of the war?"

Throughout the time he was talking himself into a fine frenzy — with interruptions, so that Willoughby and Crerar could get the essence of his words, slightly polished, into De Jeannenet's language — he was looking for an argument which would beat the trump out of the Frenchman's hand. Farrish knew only too well that De Jeannenet had the right of way, and that he himself had no business being in Rambouillet. Somewhere, the politicians had put their heads together and had decided that the first Allied troops to enter Paris should be French. So they had dug out De Jeannenet, with his banged-up secondhand equipment which wouldn't be able to stand up to a halfway decent antitank defense, and had handed him the triumph for which the Americans, for which Farrish, had fought.

"If anything happens," cried Farrish, "I'll hold you responsible!"

De Jeannenet held his finger to his long nose. He looked more like a dyspeptic bank clerk than a General. He had been the ranking officer in Rambouillet; Farrish was formally right in his reproach. On the other hand, De Jeannenet was fairly certain that Farrish's excited charges were mostly bluff to make him forget the main point: that Farrish was trying to horn in. De Jeannenet decided to hold his temper.

"*Mon Général,*" he said, "I am a reasonable man. I am an old soldier, like yourself. I operate under orders, and don't go ahead on my own."

Farrish crumpled his cigar and threw its remains into the cider glass. The word *orders,* Jeannenet noticed, obviously represented the weak spot in Farrish's line.

"My orders are to pursue and beat the enemy wherever I find him!" said Farrish. "And I'll pursue him into Paris."

"There's only one road open into Paris," replied De Jeannenet: "this road, here, through Rambouillet. You've taken an easy way of pursuit."

Farrish rose. "Damn it! This road is open because I've blasted it open! That's why!"

"Another cider," ordered De Jeannenet. He was moving restlessly on his chair, and his meager face was drawn tight with the effort of controlling his bladder. "Sit down, *mon Général!*"

But Farrish believed he had found the approach which would stymie De Jeannenet. Sure, he had circumvented the decision of the politicians by his own dash to Rambouillet — and with a little luck, with only a few hours in his favor, he would have rushed through it and right to the gates of Paris. De Jeannenet had blocked him — but De Jeannenet had nobody behind him, no real Government, no country, no industry. De Jeannenet had a mob of volunteers; he lived and ate and fought and was supplied by the goodness of Great Britain and the U.S.A. — mostly the good old U.S.A. — and Farrish would make no bones about it.

"So what do you want?" he asked, throwing himself back on the Café Montauban's shaky chair. "That I let you go ahead into Paris and let you act as if you had won the war? Who the hell do you think you are? We have fought this battle since the beaches of Normandy. My Division alone has lost over six thousand men — for what? To get you and your rattling conveyances into Paris?"

The tip of De Jeannenet's nose grew white. "General Farrish," he said — and turning to Willoughby, "and you, *mon Commandant,* will please translate this most precisely — General Farrish, my people have been in this war considerably longer than you. I have fled my country to continue the war. I have sacrificed my family. I have marched through half of Africa with men who were clad in rags and who had almost nothing to eat or drink. We have fought our way into Paris just as well as you have. And I wish you to keep that in mind."

Willoughby translated carefully. His voice, with its overlay of fat, sharpened, where possible, De Jeannenet's words. He wanted Farrish to clamp down on this man, for his own sake as well as for America's sake. Willoughby was discovering his national pride.

De Jeannenet's argument infuriated Farrish. Poor relatives should stay in the background. "And where would you be," he replied, his eyes stony, "where would you be, sir, if it weren't for us? Somewhere in the Tchad, roasting your damned hide? Every piece of equipment you have is from us, every shell you fire comes from us, every ration you gobble up is spared from our mouths — and now, you're going to take the victory out of our hands? Don't be ridiculous! We're Allies — all right. But even among Allies, a man's got to know his place!"

Jeannenet could not contain himself any longer. He got up and walked stiffly into the café.

Farrish was perplexed. Had De Jeannenet broken off? They couldn't remain as they were — with every passing hour, the danger that the Germans would discover the precarious situation in Rambouillet, became greater.

Farrish, too, got up, angrily signaled Willoughby and the others to stay behind, and went into the Café Montauban in search of Jeannenet. He looked around in the dim interior; finally, he discovered Jeannenet's head and shoulders, and his legs from the knees down — the rest of the Frenchman's body was hidden behind a kind of wooden half-door which still swung gently. Farrish joined De Jeannenet. Thoughtfully he stared at the black wall in front of them as their waters united and slowly ran into the drain. Farrish's own stream was strong and determined, the Frenchman's weaker and diffused.

He can't even piss straight, thought Farrish. The comparison made him more indignant — but less against De Jeannenet than against the politicians and the big operators at SHAEF, the real culprits who had tied his hands as he was about to reach for the prize. Never again, he swore, never again should they come to him with their sloppy talk of unity and co-operation and common strategy. From now on, it was every man for himself; and his eyes were sharp enough to look after his own interests.

De Jeannenet ordered his clothes. "I tell you," he said suddenly, "I don't care. We'll notify Army. Let them decide."

"You speak English?"

"Certainly."

"Oh."

Farrish pulled at his belt. "I may have been a little rough."

"Your interpreters were extremely kind."

In spite of the fact that De Jeannenet had fooled him, Farrish felt a kind of pity for the man. The Frenchman seemed so much older, worn out. Besides, Farrish could not afford to let the matter go to Army — had he not been blocked at Rambouillet, he could have defended his headlong rush by claiming the tactical situation necessitated it; but with Jeannenet and himself at the same jumping-off point, with Jeannenet refusing to take second place, all blame would fall on him.

"We might sit it out here," said De Jeannenet, holding the door for Farrish, "until we get word from Army. . . ."

"Hell, no!" said Farrish. "If *you* have no conception of the spot we're in — I have." He fell back upon his old grudge. "You may go ahead, under my protest. Get out of here — the faster, the better I'll like it."

De Jeannenet attempted to grasp his hand. "Teamwork, *mon Général!* Teamwork!"

The two Generals emerged from the café. De Jeannenet walked to the table and raised his glass which was still half full of cider.

Farrish, whose own glass had been cleaned and replenished, looked at it sourly. "The stuff is stale," he said.

He did not drink.

Farrish stood before the schoolhouse and watched De Jeannenet's units disentangle themselves from his own.

He had shooed away everybody; he wanted to be alone. From a tactful distance, Carruthers and a group of staff officers watched their General drink the cup of defeat.

Among them was Willoughby, full of sympathy. Despite the blow Farrish had suffered, Willoughby's belief in him had grown. After the argument between the Frenchman and Farrish, Willoughby was sure that Farrish had no leg to stand on; and he gave him credit for having tried anyhow. Farrish was his kind of man — and might be one of the best investments of his life. Farrish had the pluck to go all out after what he wanted. And if Farrish didn't punch through this time, he would the next. How often had Willoughby watched Old Man Coster of Coster, Bruille, Reagan and Willoughby, Attorneys at Law, accept undismayed a decision against him in the Lower Courts, sink his teeth all the deeper into the case, pull a few more strings, dig up a few more papers or witnesses, and come off victoriously in the higher courts! You've got to have the long view of things.

The General's eyes followed the French vehicles passing on to Paris; occasional sparks flew from the exhaust pipes, bogey wheels clattered, and the frequent backfire of the motors sounded like shots.

Finally, he seemed to have had enough. He turned abruptly and went into the schoolhouse.

In the room formerly occupied by Troy, an elderly officer, his field coat open, sat on top of one of the children's benches. The officer rose. With a few heavy steps, he reached the General. "Farrish!" he said warmly, "How're you doing?"

Farrish took his hand and held on to it while they walked to the teacher's desk. "Sit down, DeWitt!" said the General, pointing at the chair behind it.

"You sit down! You must be tired."

"Yes — I've been driving along, come to think of it. Hell. . . . I'm much too burned-up to sit and take it easy. You've learned of the dirt they've done to me?"

"I talked to Willoughby, briefly. He told me you might want to see me. He told me about the tiff with De Jeannenet."

"Tiff . . . !" said Farrish. He stepped to the desk and placed one finger near the inkwell, another near a piece of chalk a few inches away. "That's how close I am to Paris. A deal behind my back, and I'm as far away from it as ever."

DeWitt looked at the General with probing eyes. "What do you want me to say?"

The relationship between the two men was somewhat strained. Farrish, perhaps, was less conscious of this than DeWitt. Though younger, Farrish was senior in rank; his rapid rise from an obscure Tank Battalion commander to Commanding General of a battle-hardened Armored Division obliged Farrish to play the part, even toward the man who had known him when he was in his military swaddling clothes.

"What do I want you to say! . . ." he paraphrased. "What you think of it! Of all the double-crossing, no good, amateurish decisions —"

"If you want my opinion — but I don't think you're going to like it —"

"Say it! I can take it!"

DeWitt put his gloved hand on the ink well and pushed it aside, carefully. "It's only fair that the French be allowed to liberate their city." Before Farrish had a chance for a brusque comeback, DeWitt went on, "You're not on the football field — remember those passes you used to make?"

Farrish waved the memory aside.

DeWitt insisted, "But you were bad for the team. Now you've got to learn that you're on a team."

Farrish said heatedly, "I'm better than the others!"

DeWitt rose.

Farrish said, "No! Stay here for a while. I need someone to brace me up."

"What's the sense?" asked DeWitt. "You don't listen to me. You don't listen because I'm not telling you what you want to hear."

"I *am* listening!" Farrish said testily. He had taken the Frenchman's gaff, he might as well take DeWitt's.

DeWitt buttoned his coat. "You know, you're bound to be disappointed if you look at this war as a game for glory. Maybe I've been more fortunate than you; I had a stretch of civilian life before they pulled me in again. So I've dealt with people outside the Army racket. I want to tell you: This war is more than pushing soldiers over the map. There's also a battle that never shows on any of your maps. That's why it is good that they sent this French Division into Paris. That's why more things are bound to happen that'll upset you."

Farrish laughed, "They'd better not upset me too much . . . !" An undertone of threat had crept into his voice. "Where are you going?"

"We've got to push on," DeWitt said, trying to spare Farrish's sensitivity.

"To Paris, huh?"

DeWitt shrugged.

"To Paris!" Farrish badgered.

"Yes, among other places."

"You'll tell me how it was, won't you? You'll tell me because . . ."

"Because what?"

"Nothing."

"So long, Farrish. Good luck!"

"Hold it! Hold it!" said Farrish. "Let me ask you something before you take off for the Champs-Élysées. Tell me — where d'you get your high-falutin ideas?"

"I really don't know." DeWitt hadn't felt that his ideas were in any way unusual.

3

PARIS had begun to stir.

The bus in which Thérèse Laurent was riding home was filled to the bursting point. She was jammed in between a man whose torn shirt was coming apart at the shoulder seam, and another wearing a straw hat that showed a gray, greasy spot of indefinite boundaries where his fingers had touched its brim.

The man with the straw hat did not seem to mind the heat or the crowd. He sniffed the heavy smell of the wood gas and puckered his nose as if he wanted to say: What a perfume! He smiled at Thérèse and she liked the way he smiled — a good mouth, strong teeth — the thin, small mustache above it did not fit at all. Nevertheless, she looked right through him; he had no business smiling at her.

Suddenly the bus stopped.

"What's the matter?" asked the man with the torn shirt, craning his neck to get a look out of the window. "There's no bus stop here. Motor trouble, again."

The man with the straw hat tried to push to the rear of the bus.

"Stop pushing!" a woman with a market basket screamed angrily. "Can't you wait your turn? I waited all morning to get this food, waited in line — you can wait, too."

The man smiled at Thérèse. "The waiting is over," he said.

The bus moved again, jerkily. The driver was maneuvering it in a new direction.

"*Mesdames et M'sieurs!*" It was the man with the straw hat who spoke. He was very serious now, and his voice sounded clear and confident. "Please remain in your places. When the bus stops, leave quietly. You will be given sufficient time."

An uproar of questions, some outraged, some anxious. Someone cried, "Police! Where's the police!"

The bus came to a final halt; the motor was switched off. The silence of the motor silenced the passengers, too. In this silence, they turned to the man with the straw hat.

He took off the hat, wiped his face, coughed slightly. Thérèse saw that he had dense black hair and a scar on his forehead; his eyes twinkled humorously — perhaps he was a little embarrassed.

"*Eh bien,*" he said, "this is the end of the line. Someone else is taking over. . . ." He stepped on a seat and watched the people file out. They went quietly, almost as if under a kind of discipline. Even the conductor seemed to respect the new authority which had made its appearance with such suddenness — or had he known in advance the role which the man in the straw hat was to play?

Outside the bus, Thérèse lingered and heard the man being greeted by a group of armed persons. "Ah, Mantin!"

"Good you have come!"

"Boche patrols are all over!"

"Two armored cars!"

Mantin took the news in his stride. He seemed to know what was up. "Everybody out of the bus?" he shouted.

Ropes were brought and attached to the superstructure.

"Hoh ruck! Hoh ruck!" cried Mantin, pulling so hard that his face grew red.

The bus tipped over.

Men brought an uprooted fence. One appeared with a roll of barbed wire. Mantin gave orders to bring all the sandbags out of the houses where they were stored as protection against air raids.

"You!" he addressed the crowd of bus passengers, "either you help or go home! Don't stand around like fools! You see this is serious business."

But his eyes laughed.

"Mademoiselle," he said to Thérèse, "you can help. You'll be our nurse. When somebody gets wounded, you tie him up, yes?"

"Yes," said Thérèse, "of course."

Why she said Yes, why she accepted the request which was more like an order, she could not say. Her life, up to this point, had hardly been concerned with affairs other than her own. If you ignored the restrictions of the Occupation, if you kept away from the Boche, disregarded the inconveniences of the war, and concentrated on your job and what little amusement was left for someone who could not afford the black market, if you made yourself unimportant — who would interfere with that kind of existence?

Now she was thrown into the midst of this new thing where men tipped over busses one had been riding a moment ago; where it was expected that people would get wounded or even killed — and she liked it. She liked it and was puzzled by it. Though her brain took in and understood all her eyes saw and her ears heard, everything seemed to move on a plane other than her own. Her nerves tingled.

"Where will I get bandages?" she asked Mantin.

With his thumb, he pointed at a pharmacy across the street. The store was closed, the iron curtain had rattled down. Thérèse wanted to ask questions, but Mantin was busy emplacing his men behind the barricade. He had adjusted his hat at a rakish angle.

She went to the store, hammered at the corrugated iron. A small square in it came open. Through it, a man blinked at her from behind thick lenses. "What do you want?" he asked gruffly.

"Bandages, stuff for wounded. Everything you have, give." She was amazed at herself, at how strongly she could demand.

"For whom?" asked the druggist.

Thérèse nodded toward the barricade. "For them."

"You belong to them?"

She hesitated. Then she said, with conviction, "Yes!"

The small square in the iron curtain closed. She waited. Had she said something wrong? Did the druggist not believe her, didn't he believe how urgently she needed the supplies? Or was he also an enemy? Thérèse had never had enemies except the Boche — and him only in a very theoretical sense. Through Mantin, or through the way in which everything happened, she had suddenly gained many friends — but also enemies.

The iron curtain was rolled up slowly. In the door, the druggist appeared. He opened it and said, "Mademoiselle, this is precious material you want. I cannot get it again. You know how things are. And you want me to give it for people I don't know."

"We need it," she said. "For God's sake, hurry."

He went back into the store, and returned with an armful of packages. He gave them to her. A roll of bandages fell down, and he picked it up and placed it on top of the others she carried.

"*Merci, M'sieur!*"

"One moment," he said as she was about to turn. "Who will pay for all this?"

She had no money. The few francs in her pocketbook were not enough to pay for a fraction of what she was taking. The druggist certainly was not rich, and he could not afford to give so much and so freely. She tried to think what this man Mantin would have answered — probably he would say that everybody was sacrificing, in this hour; some, their blood — others, their goods. Suppose the store was burned or looted by the Germans, whom could the druggist ask to pay for that? But from her lips, the talk of sacrifice did not come readily.

"Mademoiselle!" the druggist pleaded. He did not want to demand back his wares, neither did he want to let go of them.

For a few seconds, she faced the druggist, at a loss. Then the answer occurred to her, an answer revolutionary to her and yet obvious.

"The new Government will pay!" she said.

"Ah, the new Government!" he nodded. "Yes. That is right."

Thérèse, carrying the bandages away from the store to the barricade, thought: *I, too, am part of the new Government.*

To a man like Erich Pettinger, *Obersturmbannführer* — or Lieutenant Colonel in the German *Waffen-SS* — the sudden activity of the people appeared highly anomalous. He saw it, heard it, sensed it, all the reports he received confirmed it — yet he refused to accept it. Wasn't it the very gullibility of the masses that had made him join the Nazi movement back in 1929? The people, all people, were essentially cowards who wanted to be left to the small pursuits of their daily life, their money, their beer, their worn-out women. They could be ruled by a combination of force and spiritual guidance. Since they desired nothing better than being ruled, the men who ruled could afford to be in a minority, provided this minority was well organized and centrally directed; as to the people's spiritual guidance, this was, under normal circumstances, no complicated affair.

Pettinger crossed the Place de l'Opéra on the way to his apartment in the Hotel Scribe. Everything seemed normal enough and, for a moment, he considered enjoying the sunshine. But as he looked at some of the men and women passing by, he forgot his pleasure in the weather. He had the distinct feeling that, once past him, they sneered at him, although on walking toward him, they appeared noncommittal, even deferential. And there were some who did not bother to wipe off a sly and knowing grin, even when he looked straight at them. That was something new.

Pettinger felt like taking one or the other by the throat, shaking him, and choking him. He did not do it. That was something new, too. Two months ago, he would have followed his impulse, and everybody on the street would have hurried on his way and made it a point not to notice the incident. But today? Today a crowd would gather, and he would have to say something. Say what?

He held people in contempt; and yet he knew that the time when he could stop a man on the street and slap that man's face had passed. Here was a contradiction. This contradiction was in his own consciousness; and this he must settle first, before anything else could be undertaken.

He paused at the newsstand before the Café de la Paix. The headlines were as they should be: *Allies Making Limited Progress; Strong German Units Holding Back Attempts At Penetration; Prepared Positions Taken Up by Hard-fighting Germans; Solid Front Reorganized.*

The headlines emanated from last night's news conference; he, himself, had read the *Wehrmacht* Communiqué to the French journalists, using his customary tone of studied ease. Then he had interrupted the dry words of the Communiqué. He had conjured up the picture of the front as he wanted them to see it: men with a will of steel pitted against the ever re-

peated, vain onslaughts of the Americans, who relied only on their machines — men retreating, yes, when it was absolutely necessary, but even
in retreat, imposing frightful, forbidding losses on the enemy.

In the course of their long association with him, the French newspaper-
men had learned to ask cautious questions which he could answer with
candor. They knew that anyone who made himself noticed by embarrassing inquiries would soon have to look for another job, or would find himself on a transport of men going to Germany to perform tasks vital to the
welfare of the New Europe. During these last days, however, they had become restless. "Will you have to give up Paris?" a voice had quavered.
Pettinger recognized that the man had not meant to be obnoxious — he
was afraid for his life. And so were many of the others who suspected that
they were on some list. Well, that was their hard luck. He, Pettinger, could
not protect them, if it came to that — they were living in an era in which
a man had to choose sides; and if the side he had chosen was defeated, temporarily or permanently, he had to bear the consequences.

Pettinger could not tolerate such fears coming into the open. Where
would that lead to? Nor could he answer the question about Paris. Very
possibly, Paris would have to be given up; everything depended on what
happened at the front. He had given them his interpretation of the military developments, and that was that.

He had done more. He had fought for, and received, permission for all
available German radio stations to jam Allied newscasts; all police organizations, French and German, were busy tracking down rumors and the
centers from which such rumors sprang. But where was one to begin?
With the front so torn up, all sorts of shady characters were moving from
one area into the other, and especially into Paris. They carried the news —
some of it true, some likely, some pure invention — of German armies surrounded and breaking up, of Allied spearheads piercing what lines the
Germans had managed to establish, of thousands of once-proud Germans
throwing away their arms and holding up their hands and marching off
into captivity.

Pettinger reached the Scribe. As he checked at the desk, the clerk told
him that a friend of his had inquired for him — a Major Dehn.

"Dehn?"

"*Oui, mon Colonel!*"

So Dehn was in town. What the devil was he doing here? "Did he leave
any message?"

"*Non, mon Colonel!*"

The voice of the desk clerk sounded as usual, efficient and with just
enough oiliness to create the image of a permanent and stable at-your-
service. As Pettinger slowly walked upstairs, he laughed to himself. In
and around Paris, a large number of people were thrashing about, bent

upon slitting each others' throats. They were making history, while inside the Hotel Scribe, ordinary routine was continuing. Such routine was nothing to sneeze at. It had no purpose except self-perpetuation. The clerk would be at his desk tomorrow, announcing visitors to the new tenant of the apartment, when Pettinger might be God knows where.

Apparently, two strata of life co-existed: one, to which this clerk belonged, and the grocer at the corner, and the peasant in the field — sowing, and handing out herring, and announcing visitors; and the other, of which Pettinger was a part, wherein armies clashed and newspapers were printed and great men released important speeches.

To Pettinger, who belonged to the strata of activists, the existence of this clerk was profoundly annoying. It proved that, despite his efforts to whip up a storm, the storm remained empty wind; and once it blew over, the permanence of the other strata reasserted itself. Even more unfavorable: In order to create the storm, one had to mobilize people, millions of them, who basically belonged in the category of the rooted ones, and whose deepest desire was to return to their roots, and to resume the announcing of guests, the selling of herring, and the sowing of barley or whatever it was.

A thorough change could be brought about only by uprooting that permanent strata of life — only then would the peasant, the grocer, the clerk follow blindly, because there would be no place for him to return. The mass migrations from west to east, from east to west, the destruction of home and town, the creation of a new type of man — the barracks man, who had no home and who existed only to be worked and mulcted — were the real guarantees of a new time. They were the guarantees of ultimate National-Socialist victory, regardless of the issue of battle. And the Allies, the fools, were helping this new world on its way, by their invasion that turned Europe into a battlefield, by their mass bombings that daily destroyed more roots and daily decreased the strata of permanence. Let them come, with their fagged-out, outmoded institutions, let them try to set up once more a world as they knew it! It was impossible.

Yes, the storm he had helped to whip up might be only a lot of wind; but even wind, if it moved fast enough, could tear out and carry away the strongest trees.

The door to Pettinger's apartment was unlocked. He had left it locked. He tore it open.

A man sprawled on the sofa.

"Dehn!" said Pettinger, "what are you doing up here? How did you get in?"

"The maid let me in. Maids are always good to me. I had to stretch out somewhere. Your place was the best, and I thought it wouldn't make much difference — you won't have it much longer anyhow." Without getting up, he pulled a chair toward the sofa and patted its seat. "Very soft! Sit down here, Pettinger." He pointed at the bottle standing on the floor next to him. "I've helped myself. You had only one bottle. What did you do with the others? No, no, no! Don't be afraid of me. I know how I look. My breeches are torn. The batman sewed them up, that was the last I saw of my batman. On this blouse hangs the dirt of a hundred holes I threw myself in, and on my boots, the mud of back roads and woods through which I ran. Even my razor's lost. And I didn't feel like going to a French barber. Somehow, I don't care to expose my throat."

"Don't be ridiculous!"

"I know what I know," Dehn said stubbornly. "I've seen them come out and attack us."

"Who?"

"People!" shouted Dehn. Then his voice broke. "They should all be shot. . . ." He sounded tired, and his postulate lacked force. He moved his legs, his boots muddying the fine sofa of the Scribe. "It's too late now. There aren't enough of us to kill them all."

"Where did you lose your razor? Where did you lose your unit?"

Pettinger remembered the impeccable Dehn in his bachelor days, before Dehn managed to crawl into the soft bed of Maximilian von Rintelen's daughter — what was her name? Pamela. Pamela's father controlled the German steel trust. Dehn, the impoverished Junker who formerly helped Pettinger beat up people on the streets of Kremmen and other Ruhr towns, had married a gold mine and become respectable.

"My unit . . . my razor . . ." Dehn frowned. "What difference does it make where I lost them?" He turned to Pettinger and scrutinized him. "Are you trying to check up on me? I don't know where. We were running all the time. You'll find out how that is. You'll have to run, too!"

"Not in your fashion!"

"*Ach!*" Dehn wanted to spit with contempt. He controlled himself and had another drag from the bottle.

"Leave some in there. I expect somebody."

Dehn put the bottle back on the floor. His hand shook. "You don't know what's going on. You sit here in Paris and send home yards of silk and cases of cognac while we get it in the neck. You just don't know. I was at Falaise. I thought I'd never get out of that trap. And I've been running ever since, clear across France. Now I'm sick of running. I'm tired."

"What do you want to do? Have you reported at the collecting point?" Dehn closed his eyes.

"You'd better report! They need officers!"

"For what?"

"For what? What *is* the matter with you! I'll make a certain allowance for your nerves. But there's a limit! You're an officer! I should turn you over to the Field *Gendarmerie!*"

Dehn half raised himself. "What is the matter with me . . . ?" He laughed. "Now there is an interesting question. I've been thinking about that, too. You've got a lot of time to think when you're running."

He reached into his pocket and pulled out a crumpled, worn sheet of printed paper. He smoothed it. "Listen to this. The Americans shot it over one fine morning: . . . *A nation of free men, equal before the law, and determined to govern themselves. . . . For these rights and liberties, we are fighting today. . . . Wherever the dignity of Man is affronted, we feel that it happens to us. Wherever people are oppressed and suffering, we are affected. Because we are that kind of nation, we have come to Europe to stop a tyrant from imposing his will on a nation, on Europe, and on the whole world. . . ."* Dehn read softly; the words came almost too glibly.

"Give me that thing!" said Pettinger. He glanced through it. He was angry — the disorganization of retreat! That leaflet should have been in his hands long ago, so he could have counteracted it; this was the first copy he had seen. "I'm keeping it."

"Help yourself!"

"And you want to tell me," asked Pettinger, "that you believe that hoary stuff?"

"No."

"Freedom! Dignity of Man! A fine freedom, knocking at doors that are slammed in your face; a fine dignity, holes as big as five-mark pieces in the soles of your shoes, and a worn summer suit in the December cold!"

"Funny!" said Dehn. "I never heard you talk that line. Are you afraid of becoming a bum again?"

Pettinger looked up sharply. He had not been conscious of giving himself away.

"No!" Dehn went on. "Of course I don't believe a word of it. But that's not the point. They're not going to convert us. But when you're running, when you feel yourself beaten, you begin to ask yourself: What makes those fellows that strong? They have material superiority. So we are being told we have superior morale: we fight better because we're fighting for a great idea. Now I don't believe that either; we're fighting for Maxie Rintelen's profits; and one day, I'm going to inherit part of them. But many of the men believe it. And they believe it when they're told that the Americans have nothing to fight for. But there comes this slip of paper, and it says that the Americans, too, have a cause. And we Germans are a crazy people, always inclined to look at the other side of things if it is presented to us. So, *they* have a cause, and Goebbels says *we* have a cause. But they're beating us, therefore their cause must be stronger. You see how it works? A man has lots of ideas when he's running away. . . ."

He picked up the bottle and drank. Pettinger let him.

"When your front breaks, maybe you can throw in new Divisions," Dehn continued, "or you retreat and shorten the front and link up again. But what do you throw in against words?"

He lay back.

"Let me sleep some. Ten minutes. This is nice and soft. Then I'll go."

"Against words you throw other words," said Pettinger. "I'll think up some!"

"Collecting point!" Dehn said drowsily. "What for?" Then he seemed to fall asleep.

Pettinger looked at the sleeper, and at the slip of crumpled paper in his own hand. He folded it carefully, and put it into his breast pocket. Words! . . .

He went to the phone. It took him some time to get through to the Transportation Officer of the Paris garrison; and when he did get through, the only person holding down the desk was a harassed lieutenant who promised to send around a truck, provided he had one available. "I have top priority!" Pettinger shouted into the phone. But the lieutenant answered that everybody claimed priority, now, and that he had no time for checking up. *Heil Hitler.*

Organization was breaking down, with or without enemy propaganda. Dehn was no exception. There he lay on the sofa, grunting, sweating, probably dreaming of being chased.

Pettinger had been in the retreat from Stalingrad. He had been with the troops who were supposed to relieve the encircled Sixth Army of Paulus — and they had to fall back. He had not been panicked then, and he would not be panicked now. He consoled himself with the wisdom of having conquered so much territory that one could afford to retreat, pull in one's horns, without having to withdraw into the essential inner ring, the Heart Land. There was still much fat between the present front and the Heart Land; and as long as one held Germany and the adjacent territories, the war could be carried on.

The men who yammered and were depressed by a few defeats went to pieces not so much because of nervous strain, but because their horizon had the approximate reach of a toilet seat. When Pettinger compared the present state, even considering all that had happened in the last year and a half, with his pre-Nazi days — next morning's breakfast an uncertainty, no job, no future in sight, tramping the streets of his own country, turned away from the doors of factories and offices by men who claimed to be his countrymen — he knew that then he had known fear; and he shuddered even now, when he thought back to it. That had been the real fear: the fear of starvation, of becoming chaff, of losing one's hold over oneself, of dirt and disease and decay in a gutter. Since then, his life had been dedicated to fighting off a repetition of that threat. He, Pettinger, would stay on top no matter what. He had not made the world that way; the world had made him.

He saw Dehn start up with a gasp. "Oh, it's you!" said Dehn.

"You'd better go now," said Pettinger, more mildly than before. "Stragglers are being organized at the Engineers Barracks. You'll report there."

"You're not telling me where to go, are you?" Dehn put on his peaked cap, but did not bother to button his blouse. "I hope your truck comes in time. And thanks for the hospitality, the nap did me good. And don't let them get you!" He turned on his heel and was gone.

Pettinger's face fell. So Dehn had heard him order a vehicle. He permitted himself a sigh; then he straightened. He now could hear sporadic firing a few blocks from the hotel. He shut out the sound. Regardless of how the battle for Paris ended, it was not the final, the decisive battle. He could hear the noise of trucks clattering down the streets in haste. This, too, he shut out. The retreat was tactical—he was concerned with bigger issues. And if a thin, nagging voice within him whispered that many such retreats created a flow of events which he could not stop, which nobody could stop, and that people like him were on their way out—he shut out that voice, as well.

The telephone rang. The desk announced the arrival of Prince Yasha Bereskin. Pettinger said the Prince was to come up.

Pettinger put the half-empty bottle back in the wall cabinet. Then he placed himself in the armchair behind the small mahogany desk, opened a book at random, and began to read.

Prince Yasha came in on soft soles. "An idyl!" he said. "A study in reading habits! Don't you know what is happening outside? Or do you have knowledge of events impending which can change the picture?"

Prince Yasha spoke a perfect, grammatically correct French. But after twenty years, it remained a foreign language to him, a language into which he translated his native Russian, stilted and somewhat pompous. Had he tried to correct it, he probably could have spoken as lightly as any other Parisian; but Prince Yasha believed that this style suited him, suited the brushlike, iron gray hair on his long, rectangular skull, the straight nose with the broad tip; the carefully horizontal brows.

This style had been most helpful to him. It had saved him from being submerged in the mass of refugees from a Russia long gone. It had preserved the clean appearance of his hands, however muddy the waters in which he fished. And without visible effort on his part, it had carried him into the best circles and, by a number of shrewd manipulations, onto the chair of President of the Board of Delacroix & Cie.

"Any news aside from what I can see?"

Pettinger shook his head. "I feel good, today. Can I help it?" He closed his book, picked himself up from his chair, went to the wall cabinet and took out the bottle.

"You have diminished your stock?" Yasha asked.

Pettinger took a drink and offered the bottle to Yasha. "I've told these hotel people dozens of times to keep liquor glasses in my room — they always take them out."

Prince Yasha helped himself. He wiped his lips. "There seems little sense in complaining, now."

"As long as I'm here, I have the right to demand service, haven't I?"

"No doubt." Yasha was in no mood to argue small matters. "How long do you think you will be staying?"

Pettinger was silent.

Yasha said, "Our long acquaintance should have shown you that I can keep secrets. On the other hand, I really don't want to know."

"I expect to be evacuated soon." Pettinger pointed to the cabinet. "That's why I've disposed of the stuff."

"Well, my dear friend," said the Prince, "since we are not sure of how much time you have left, you won't mind if I delve into the business for which I have come?"

"No, I won't."

Pettinger, in fact, was very much interested. He had worked with Yasha ever since coming to Paris. Dehn had brought them together; there were cross-connections between the Delacroix and the Rintelen interests in the steel and mining industries. The relationship had started with Pettinger suppressing certain news which Yasha considered unfavorable to Delacroix & Cie., and it had blossomed into a smooth and far-reaching arrangement. During the last few months, however, Pettinger had heard and seen less of the Prince, and had assumed that Yasha was quietly preparing to adjust himself and his business to a new master. Pettinger had therefore kept his hands off when Army Ordnance began removing to Germany certain important machinery from the Delacroix Works in France.

"Somewhere east of Paris, and west of the Rhine," Yasha slowly began, "your Armies will succeed in re-establishing a front. Any offensive is bound to lose momentum the farther it proceeds from its base, and come to a halt; any defensive is bound to become stronger the closer it comes to its own base. Right?"

"Right."

Pettinger was pleased that Prince Yasha, who was a cool observer and a military man — he had served in the Czar's and Kerenski's armies and under Kolchak — estimated the situation exactly as he, himself, did.

Yasha went on, "Concretely, this means to me that part of the Delacroix investments will come under a new authority, while the other part still remains under your people."

Pettinger saw where Yasha was aiming.

"At this time," the Prince continued, "it is more important for me to stay in Paris and get in touch with the Americans, who probably will have most to say about what is to happen to our industries. The Americans have an adage: *One must always be in on the ground floor.* You understand?"

"Perfectly."

"There will be men on your side, my dear Pettinger, men of limited outlook and jealous character, who will claim that I am a traitor because I am staying in Paris and dealing with the new power. Of course, I am no traitor."

"Why not?" Pettinger asked bluntly.

"Because I have no loyalty to one or the other side," the Prince explained. "In order to become a traitor, one must have had some loyalties, isn't that so?"

The logic was irrefutable. Pettinger did not answer.

"These envious and stupid men" — Yasha reverted to his main subject — "may try to lay their hands on what Delacroix owns in German-held territories, under the pretense that I have sided with what they call the enemy."

"These envious and stupid men could be very powerful?" asked Pettinger.

"Precisely," confirmed Yasha. "That is why I have come to you. I know you, your influence, and your connections. You can prevent any such interference, and I have come to ask that you do so."

Pettinger studied the label of the bottle. The next question was up to him. He could split hairs, talk about how little time he had, and that this work was not at all in his line — but this kind of game was tiring. Yasha's candor, he decided, deserved equal frankness.

"How much?"

"I will give you a note," said Yasha, "which will entitle you to draw up to — let us say — one million francs on any of our accounts."

"Two."

"Listen to the firing outside," said Yasha. "One."

"Two. If they weren't shooting outside, you would never have come to me."

"We both are men of sense and of tact. We will come to a reasonable arrangement."

"One moment," said Pettinger. "Something isn't quite clear to me."

"You may ask any question you like. . . ." Yasha's face was inscrutable.

"I will have your note. It will be good?"

"Signed by myself."

"Suppose I'm unable to do the job?"

"Then you would not be able to cash the note. If the Delacroix Works in German-held territory are taken over by someone else, my note would not be honored, of course."

"But if I cash it and then fall down on the job — "

"I have thought of that possibility," admitted Yasha. "I have the greatest confidence in you, but one must consider all aspects. Frankly, Pettinger, I do not think you will cash the note unless you are sure that Delacroix remains Delacroix and does not become, let us say, Goering."

"Why?" said Pettinger. "Why should I be so interested in your properties once I've cashed in?"

"Because, on any payment received by you, there will be records. And these records will fall into the hands of any — *any* German receivers. The Goering people would certainly ask you quite embarrassing questions, and either take away your money, or demand a cut. You would like to avoid that, wouldn't you?"

"It's still two million francs," said Pettinger.

Dehn burst in, the terror of the streets written on his face. His sullen insolence had gone.

"Why, Major Dehn!" said the Prince.

Dehn rushed past Yasha. "We must get out of here, Pettinger!" he said breathlessly. "We must get out of here right away. Everybody is pulling out. Do you want us to be stuck?"

"*Us . . . !*" Pettinger was furious over the man's lack of discipline and self-restraint.

"They're fighting in the streets!" Dehn screamed. "Armed French gangs everywhere — the police have mutinied — the garrison's retreating — "

"Shut up!" said Pettinger. "I am in conference. Get out. Wait outside."

Something in Pettinger's voice slapped Dehn out of his hysteria. "Sorry, sorry." He discovered the Prince. "Oh, how are you, Prince? Bad business, this. . . ." He turned to Pettinger. "You must take me along. I can't make it alone, I just can't. When are you leaving?"

It didn't pay to put the man in his place. "There will be a truck to pick us up."

Dehn laughed. The laugh sounded grotesque because his face remained as torn as ever. Yasha, who until now had remained studiously unconcerned, looked up.

"Have you gone completely crazy?" Pettinger's mouth became very ugly.

"Truck! What truck?" Dehn pulled a slip of paper out of his pocket. "The desk clerk gave me this. The call just came in. Message from the Transportation Officer. No truck."

"I gave you an order!" Pettinger said. "Get out of this room! Wait outside!"

Dehn turned and left, wordlessly.

"Kind of panicky, our friend?" Prince Yasha said. "It *is* very disturbing, this kind of breakdown."

Pettinger's anger turned from Dehn to Yasha. Even though he did business with him, Yasha was still a foreigner — a Russian, or an adopted Frenchman — in any case a member of an inferior race without right to pass judgment on a German officer.

"I'll straighten him out, all right," Pettinger said sharply.

"You won't have much time for that," Yasha replied. "In the near future, he may be taken out of your hands."

The Prince was right. By blurting out the news of the missing truck, Dehn had dealt a severe blow to Pettinger's position. On the other hand, Pettinger reasoned, if he did not get out of Paris, Prince Yasha would have nobody behind the German front to take care of the interests of Delacroix & Cie.

Pettinger smiled. "It seems that I will need some kind of vehicle."

Yasha nodded. "May I use your phone?"

Pettinger pushed the instrument across the desk. The Prince lifted the receiver, began to dial — stopped.

"One million francs?"

"You're a hard man."

"I am not," said the Prince. "I am a humanitarian." He completed the dialing, received an answer, and gave certain instructions. Then he asked Pettinger for a sheet of stationery. For a short interval everything was quiet while Yasha wrote out the note for his agent. Having finally finished and set his square and stiff signature under the letter, and waved the sheet to let the ink dry, he handed the paper to Pettinger.

Pettinger read.

"Satisfied?"

"Under the circumstances," said Pettinger, "yes."

There was nothing more to be said. The two men sat, facing one another. Time seemed to drip heavily. The windows rattled with a burst of fire from near by.

"Too big, those windows," said Pettinger.

"Really," said Yasha, "I don't think so. I've found that smaller panes break just as easily."

Someone knocked. Both men looked up. Dehn was at the door with a slight man in mechanic's overalls.

"This is Sourire," said Yasha.

Sourire nodded and smiled, showing bad teeth. His eyes closed when he smiled as if they were afraid of belying the rest of the face.

"You can trust Sourire," said Yasha, "I've known him for years."

"Bad times and good," said Sourire, "always friends."

"He is on the black market, our friend Sourire," Yasha continued his recommendations. "He should know the roads."

Pettinger took belt and holster out of his desk. He reached for his cap. "*Au revoir,* Prince!"

"No baggage?"

Pettinger waved. "My baggage was sent ahead more than a week ago. . . . Monsieur Sourire, we will have to pick up a few men before we can leave town."

Sourire shrugged as if to say: You're the boss, now. As they were leaving, Yasha heard Sourire — "I hope you don't mind the state of the truck, you and the other gentleman. You see, it was rather a hurry-call, and only this morning, we were carting a load of swine. . . ."

The Prince, alone, reached for the bottle. The stiffness had gone out of his face.

4

FREEDOM!

Bells ringing out, flowers, kisses, wine.

Every street is so much wider, every breath comes so much faster, the sun is real, and you are my brother.

How I have waited for this day. Long ago, in my mother's arms, I learned to speak; but only today, the sweetness of the words she taught me has returned. I cannot sing, to tell the truth, but I feel I must; so I shall join the others who are singing.

I have lived on this street, in this house, with these people, a long time. Today, they are not the same — they are finer, better, more beautiful. So it must be that my eyes have changed.

All the things I now can do! I don't know where to begin, I don't know whether I want to do them at all, or even which ones I want to do. Perhaps none. But I come alive in the thought that they are mine to do, and that mine is the choice.

I must start anew because this is a new world and I can move everything and form it to my liking. God has nothing on me.

For the first time in his life, McGuire saw a barricade. He had been driving along a wide street lined by ramshackle stores and cheap bistros and faded signs. But he had been forced to trail French tanks which proceeded slowly and garnered most of the honors and welcome.

As the jeep neared a comparatively empty street veering off to the right, Loomis, to whom the tanks had been a nuisance and a frustration, directed McGuire to make for it.

"Let's get through!" he urged. "We'll miss the big show!"

Where, and what, the big show was going to be, Loomis could not have said. On the last lap of the road from Rambouillet, nearing the outskirts of Paris, he had felt the flush of liberation fever. Its crisis now made him say, "Crabtrees! We're liberators! God-damned liberators! God damn it!" Something he had sensed back in his school days, in his history classes, stirred in him.

McGuire, following Loomis's order, found himself face to face with the barricade. He studied it: the overthrown bus, the mattresses and sandbags, the pieces of iron fence and the few strands of barbed wire — nothing that any man-sized tank could not have pushed aside — a few rifles sticking out from the whole makeshift and pointing at him. And though he never before had heard of a barricade or the kind of people who would use one, he felt a slight thrill and a sort of pride. That enemies could be hiding behind it never entered his mind.

Neither Loomis nor Crabtrees were as sure. Loomis was for speedy retreat and was about to give such a command to McGuire, when a man jumped on top of the barricade and, waving exuberantly, shouted, "*Américains!* Hurrah!"

McGuire had to laugh. The guy was a human jumping-jack on top of a junk pile, and, McGuire realized, he was a kind of signal, too. In a matter of seconds, the entire picture changed. The street, which had been empty and quiet, filled up with people. They came out of the houses and from behind the barricade, shouting and gesturing, climbing and jumping over the obstacle they themselves had built.

The first "*Américains!* Hurrah!" was taken up and acted out in a dozen ways. An old woman, her gray hair flying, threw kisses at McGuire. A number of kids, breaking through the grownups, boarded the jeep, crowded the hood, and screamed words that nobody, themselves included, could understand. A man in a black suit and a stiff hat, obviously assuming himself to be a dignitary, presented McGuire with three bottles of wine and began a speech which was soon drowned out by the pandemonium of roaring, singing, whooping, shrieking, hailing — the individual welcomes of the crowd.

The donation of wine was the beginning of a whole trend: a basket containing chicken, presented blushingly by a housewife to whose skirt two babies clung, their big eyes staring roundly at the strangers, their little fingers poking their noses; then, more wine from a man who seemed to be a butcher — at least he had blood on his apron; liqueur from a lady who apparently was explaining that the bottle was a last witness of the better days she had known.

And then flowers. McGuire never could figure out how so many flowers of so many varieties had come into this poor and drab part of Paris. Roses and carnations and flowers McGuire had not seen before — white ones and yellow ones, blue and red and purple and orange. At first, he tried to display the bouquets on his jeep; after a while, he gave up because the flowers came in such profusion and such quick succession that there was neither time nor space to arrange them.

Loomis and Crabtrees good-naturedly decorated themselves with the overflow until they looked like prize bulls at a county fair. But their attention was soon diverted from the flowers to the women.

"Look at them!" said Crabtrees, awed. "Just look at them!"

The girls who now had succeeded in pushing to the forefront of the mass weaving about the jeep were blatantly beautiful. How they had managed to outfit themselves in the short time since the barricade's surrender to McGuire's jeep, or whether they had been dressed long in advance, in expectation of the liberators, or whether they wore such clothes and hair-dos all the time, were questions unasked and unanswered. They were there! Their hair upswept to miraculous heights; their light, colorful, flowery dresses exposing the curve of their breasts; their knees and thighs showing below their short skirts as they excitedly bobbed and wiggled to get through to the three Americans, to shake their hands, to hug them and kiss them! Any semblance of restraint vanished as soon as the first girl laughingly threw herself into Crabtrees's arms.

Through its young women, the street, the *arrondissement,* the city, were giving themselves to the liberators.

Nothing like it had ever happened to Loomis. He bounced and grinned and kissed and hugged, and when he found breath, he slapped Crabtrees's shoulders and shouted, "Didn't I tell you? Isn't it worth it?"

And Crabtrees gurgled with joy and cried, "*Liberté! Fraternité! Egalité!*" and stuffed another nosegay behind his ear.

"I'm for that!" roared Loomis, and grabbed the girl who was climbing on the jeep.

It was Thérèse.

She had come through the barricade. Mantin had ordered it partially removed so that the jeep could pass through when the crowd on the street was done with its welcome.

She had remained in the background, at first, watching the carnival. She was swept forward by the milling mass, and with each fumbling step, she had become more and more gripped by the spirit of the moment. By the time she reached the jeep, she was as joyously eager as the others. A new time was beginning! People were laughing again and loving one another and living!

She felt herself lifted high. She felt the strong arms of the big, jaunty, laughing American embrace her — he said something she could not understand, then he bent his face over hers. A warm happiness made her close her eyes.

The air was torn by the crack of shots.

They echoed and re-echoed between the walls of the houses, and somewhere, a bullet ricocheted and sent a piece of stucco clattering down into the street.

Loomis froze. His lips, half-open and soft and ready to kiss Thérèse, became stiff and cold. He had the sudden and terrible feeling that he, alone, was exposed to the invisible, vicious, stabbing threat.

Involuntarily, he shoved the girl in front of him and slid down behind her to his seat. "Start the car!" he yelled to McGuire. "Get us out of here! Step on it!"

Again, shots rang out. McGuire thought he could locate the roof from where they came.

The first round had held the crowd motionless. The second threw them into frenzied action. They began to disperse in all directions, the women dragging their children; some children were caught between the running legs of the grownups, and thrown to the street, and trampled.

Mantin ran up to the jeep. "Help us!" he shouted in broken English. "The fascists!" He pointed at the roofs. "Snipers — French traitors — Germans leave them behind. . . ."

"Let's go!" screamed Loomis.

McGuire turned and saw that Loomis was using the girl as a shield. He muttered, and grabbed the Captain's hands, breaking their frantic grip on Thérèse. Loomis winced, but let go. McGuire forced the girl to the floor of the gift-filled jeep just as a third volley of shots burst out.

Then he made the car spring forward, his thumb pressed on the button of the claxon.

Mantin had to jump aside. He looked after the jeep racing through the opening which he, himself, had ordered torn into his barricade. He closed his eyes as if to squeeze out an ugly sight.

Some of his men were still behind the barricade, crouching in the protection of the bus and the sandbags. Mantin gathered them and led them into the building from which he had seen the fascists fire into the people.

The clerk at the Hotel Scribe registered Loomis and Crabtrees, and asked no questions about Thérèse. Both men were loaded down with field equipment and the bottles contributed by the grateful people of Paris. Thérèse carried the basket with the chicken.

She was hungry. The cheesecloth covering the chicken had come loose during the fast drive from the barricade to the Scribe; Loomis, in his bones the peril of stopping to accept the people's welcome, had permitted no further halts. Crammed into the jeep along with the Musette bags, sleeping bags, bottles and flowers, Thérèse had seen and smelled the chicken throughout the drive. She could not help swallowing painfully; a grayish roll at breakfast had been her last meal.

Looking at the complacent, restful, fat breast of the chicken, Thérèse, for the first time in the course of this day, took stock of the change in her world. So fast had the change occurred, so intensely had she participated in it, that she had not reasoned it out until she found herself swimming in this new, fast-moving stream. The motion was exhilarating.

Yet — she had the dim feeling: I don't belong here, with these total strangers, these soldiers — God knows where they're going and what their plans are. The barricade, in spite of its tension, had been a comparatively quiet pole, a rock in the stream to which one could cling. She had let go of it, at a moment when shots were still falling — no, these shots were the last ones ever, the fight was over, the liberators were here, and she was riding with them.

And the car was speeding too fast, and the smell of the chicken was too heady, and the whole thing was much too big an adventure to step out of now. Ever since the remarkable Mantin had ordered the bus to be overturned, ever since she had found herself involved in making the new world, she had felt the touch of fate and the futility of trying to oppose it.

All she had missed, in the years of staying away from things, now rushed to catch up with her. The fruits of freedom! Giving and receiving are one. We are suddenly so rich that the abundance forces our hearts to open, to shed what we have, and in turn to receive, enriched a thousandfold.

"Aren't you coming up with us?" asked Loomis.

She was still in the trance of her thoughts. Loomis put his arm about her waist, in a way at once possessive, protecting, and urging.

"Yes, I will come up," she said in her school English. Obediently, she followed the two American officers to the elevator. The new world, into which she had come, was still unreal to her — the soft rugs, the deep, warm tints of the furniture, the polished brass. But she had begun to like it.

"This is *something!*" said Loomis. He fell on the bed, the hooks of his leggings catching in the gold embroidery of the dark blue silk of the bedspread.

Something included everything — the luxury, the plumbing, the peacock design on the wallpaper, Europe, the gilt frame around the mirror, the girl, the liquor, the feeling of *We Have Arrived* and *Here We Shall Stay* — and the hell with *How Long?*

145

Crabtrees kissed the girl. He explained laughingly that he had to get his share of kissing — the snipers had cut into his quota.

Thérèse permitted his embrace. He was so young. He had not even a real beard — the stubbles on his chin, on his soft upper lip, were hardly more than down.

Loomis took off his coat and helmet. Thérèse saw that he had sparse, dark hair, and that his hair was disheveled from the helmet. For some reason not clear to her, she felt pity. She freed herself from Crabtrees. Out of her pocketbook, she took a comb; she went over to Loomis, ran it through his hair — softly, softly, her fingers playing over his forehead.

He stretched and purred and called to Crabtrees, "These women! These women!" Then he sat up, grabbed hold of her thighs, pulled her close to him, forced her between his legs, and pushed his head playfully against her stomach. His hands wandered upward along her sides.

Thérèse withdrew despite herself, despite her wonderful feeling of wanting to give.

"*Tu ne veux pas . . .*" Loomis said, "*coucher?*"

She laughed, throwing back her head. How blunt they were! Strange men in a strange country! They had crossed an ocean, they were lonely; and she was so rich in her new world, she could afford to let them feel her and touch her and kiss her . . . but *doucement!* Not that way. . . .

"I am hungry," she said.

That, Loomis could understand. He was hungry, too. He reached for the basket, and they pulled out the chicken and tore into it, the fat dripping down their chins and over their fingers. Loomis picked up one of the bottles and told Crabtrees to fetch glasses from the bathroom. He broke off the neck of the bottle against the edge of the table. The red wine spilled over onto the rug. Loomis laughed. He thought of home, of what Dorothy would have said, had he spilled wine on their rug. But this wasn't home, thank God!

They toasted and drank. Only now did Loomis realize how parched he was. He downed the wine, refilled his glass, and poured another for the girl.

"Your name's Thérèse? Very beautiful, *très beau, très joli!* You must drink. Drink it down, it's good stuff, didn't cost us a penny."

She sipped her wine.

"Drink it all down. Bottoms up! Like this, see? In America, you keep pace!"

He laughed some more and pulled her over on his lap. He held her glass to her lips and poured the wine into her.

She struggled, but then gave in. He meant well. He wanted her to have what he had, and she must not disappoint him. So he was crude — how

146

else could he be? He was a soldier. But he was a soldier who had come to bring a new world to her and to Mantin and to the people behind the overturned bus. That made him a much better kind of soldier. That's why he wanted to share the chicken, the wine, everything, with her. Naturally, he had some difficulties expressing his feelings *doucement*. He was a soldier.

Crabtrees, greatly admiring Loomis's bold bottle opening, had practised the trick and was eager to show it. Soon, there were bottles and bottles of wine open, and the three of them had to continue drinking long after the chicken was finished and its bones shoved beneath the rug under the bed.

Thérèse was leaning her head against Loomis's chest. Crabtrees had taken her feet on his lap and was stroking her ankles and her calves and her knees; and he was reaching slyly toward her thighs. She tried to fend him off, but she felt lazy and tired, and his touch was pleasant and lulling.

Loomis was telling a long story, most of which she could not understand: Something about America, where he was a very important man. He must be an important man, she thought; he had been driven into Paris in a car of his own, had gone to this big hotel, and had taken the most wonderful, luxurious room.

He gave her a cigarette. She had not had a cigarette for a long time, for weeks, perhaps months. She inhaled the smoke, and the wine and the smoke made her head swim. What was he saying? He was talking of women, women he had had. Whether he was bragging, whether it was true — what of it? He was a big, strong man, and many women must have liked him. She liked him, too, in a way. The other one was now stroking her thighs; his fingers tickled her. She slapped his hands. He laughed. Silly, how he laughed. Well, he was just a boy; and there, they had taken him away from his school and stuck him into uniform and shipped him here, far from home, so he could help to kick out the Boche, so that she could come to the wonderful hotel and rest her head on the chest of the important American, drink wine and smoke cigarettes and begin a life which was worth living.

Loomis had opened a bottle of cognac, and they were drinking the cognac from the water glasses.

Thérèse tried to explain that one could not do that — the liqueur one drank with reason, in small sips, from small glasses; one held it a while on one's tongue and then let it slowly roll down; one savored it and felt the warmth go into one's limbs. But not this way! It was too strong! It wasn't water! Neither was it wine!

But she had to keep pace with them. They were ugly about it. How could she teach them in so short a time? And whatever they did not want to understand, they answered, "No *compris*. . . ." The little one was kissing her knees and her thighs; his tongue was too wet, and his lips were clumsy. She still rested against the big one. He was saying something.

"My name is Victor Loomis, do you hear? Your name is Thérèse, *très beau, très joli,* and my name is Victor — call me Vic!"

"Victor Loomis," she said, "Vic!" and she had an uncontrollable desire to laugh. She put her hand on the little one's head; he had curly hair which felt fuzzy under her fingers. The little one was very foolish; he would get himself into trouble somewhere, some woman would take advantage of him. But she was glad that he was here, that she wasn't alone with Vic, now.

The big one had laid his hand on her breast. She felt her breasts change, the way they did when she stood before her own mirror and studied herself and touched her skin. It wasn't a good mirror; some parts of her always appeared distorted. Her breasts were a little too heavy for the rest of her body, she knew that. But Vic, the big one, seemed to like that. Her head, also, was too heavy for her body. It was a very heavy head, and she wished these two men would let her go to sleep. The bed in here was so great and soft and wide, much better than her own, even though the spread was soiled by the boots of the one she was to call Vic.

Vic said something to the little one. She could not follow the strange, slow drawl. But she could see the big one's arm pointing toward a door — the door to the bathroom. Later, she would have to go herself, she had so much wine and cognac in her; but if the little one had to go first, let him go, he was still such a child.

But why was Vic sending him there? Maybe the little one was already too drunk to know what was good for him.

Then she and the big one were alone.

Loomis reached for the cognac bottle. It was empty. The necks of all the other bottles were broken — nothing in there, either. Loomis creased his forehead with the effort of forcing his thoughts away from certain channels and into others. Finally, he saw his way clear. He swayed to the telephone and asked for McGuire.

"My driver, yes, naturally — he must be outside — before your damned hotel — in a jeep. . . . Don't know what a jeep is? A small car, low build, you'll find it — get him, tell him to bring me stuff to drink — Captain Loomis. . . . *Ell — double oh — emm — eye — ess!* . . . Naturally, he's got stuff — those people — they're giving it away — you just sit in a jeep and collect. . . . *Liberté Egalité* — let's go, let's get on the ball — d'you understand? . . ."

He turned to Thérése, "See? All I have to do is order, and there it comes!"

He took her into his arms. Her dress, fresh in the morning, now showed the wear of the barricade, the ride in the jeep, the handling in the room.

"Oh, your beautiful dress," he said with genuine regret, "*très joli* — all mushed. *Pauvre petite.* . . ."

He began to undress her. She resisted.

He put his hands on her naked shoulders, and his eyes met hers. The red rims had become deeper, there was a glint in his pupils.

"Look here," he said, "this is enough now. You came up here, you know why you came. Quit stalling. Where I come from, we don't play it that way. And this is Paris, God damn it."

She held her finger to his lips.

"Damn it!" he shouted.

"Do not shout. . . ."

The little one was still gone. Maybe the big one had really sent him away, and they had arranged it between them.

She was so tired, she could hardly stand on her feet.

"That's good, that's much better," Loomis said. "You're a darling."

"Don't — don't tear!"

"I'll be careful, Honey. Don't you worry. I'll get you a new one, a brand-new dress . . ."

His hands were all over her.

She pointed to the window. It was wide open.

He nodded, he understood. He grabbed two glasses from the table; a sediment of cognac was left in each of them. He handed one glass to her, and, arm in arm, they walked to the window to lower the curtain. Arm in arm. It was almost friendly, almost gay.

They stood at the window. Thérèse looked down at herself. She was nude to her waist. She wanted to run back into the room, but she couldn't. Loomis was holding on to her, his arm a vise; and her breast was cupped in his hand.

"The curtain!" she said.

Then she saw he was waving at someone.

Across the yard of the Hotel Scribe, at a window facing them, stood another couple, entirely nude. The man leaned out of his window and shouted, "Hello, Loomis!" and pointed to the naked woman beside him and raised his glass.

"Hello, Willoughby!" shouted Loomis. Enthusiastically, he toasted back.

"Fine day!" Willoughby called. "You fellows having a good time?"

"Not bad, sir, not bad at all! We're trying our best!"

At this moment, McGuire entered. He had knocked, but the knock had not been answered. He got the full view. He saw Loomis and the half-naked Thérèse, and through the window, the Major with his woman. He saw Thérèse wrench herself loose from Loomis, and run toward him. She seemed to recognize him, for she stopped dead and then fled to the bed, tore off the cover, and hid herself.

McGuire quietly placed a bottle on the floor and left.

He was sorry he had brought it. The man who had given it to him, while he was waiting before the hotel, had seemed like such a nice guy.

All the way down, in the elevator, McGuire had time to get mad and to make up his mind what to do about it. McGuire never had found Captain Loomis particularly likable; but Loomis was an educated man, and an officer, and he must know what it was all about. Apparently, then, McGuire had misunderstood this liberation business. The people who had welcomed them were part of a great amusement park without restrictions, and for their gifts and handshakes and kisses they expected something in return and would present their bill. If he waited around much longer, exchanging greetings and grinning like an idiot, he would just cheat himself out of his share of the fun.

If the Captain thought him that kind of sucker, Loomis was mistaken. Wait around in a jeep, stand before the hotel like a God-damned gentleman's chauffeur, collect liquor for Loomis while that jerk was having himself a time — no, sir!

McGuire tore into the crowd of people inspecting his jeep. He chased them off, all of them, except one. This one had yellow hair and protruding knees which showed fully below her short skirt, and she swung a black-lacquered handbag on her arm. Her, he gave the high sign, and she ambled over to the jeep.

"Well, Babe?" he said.

She slid into the jeep and sat close to him; her skirt moved up higher. He pulled out a pack of cigarettes, almost full.

"Want one?"

She grabbed the pack.

"Oh no — not like that!"

Her eyes questioned. "You — me — zig zig? Cigarettes?"

McGuire heard "zig zig" for the first time, but he knew what it meant. "Zig zig first — then cigarettes. . . ."

She nodded agreement.

He put his arms around her. She began to move, expertly, so expertly that it didn't disturb him at all that she was dressed. Neither did it disturb him that a new crowd had collected — different from the previous one: People interested in the performance, some snickering, some making remarks which he did not understand but which were probably funny. He did not care. They were part of the amusement park, and soon they would ask for cigarettes. He sniffed her smell; it was sharp and it excited him. She wasn't bad at all; she was at least as good as what Loomis and the other guy had upstairs. That was the whole difference — they did it on a nice bed, five flights up, and he did it down here. Paris was wonderful. In

150

America, you couldn't do it this way, you had to go out with the woman and spend money on her and go through a lot of waste motion. Zig zig! He had driven a long way for zig zig, but it was worth it.

Then she was quiet and stretched out her sweaty hand with the pointed, painted finger nails. "Cigarettes?"

He threw her the pack, magnanimously.

She lit one, sucked in the smoke. "You—again zig zig? Cigarettes?"

"Get out of here," he said. He now felt the eyes of the crowd. Their laughter and remarks had died down. The people just looked at him, and he didn't like it.

"Get away from here! All of you!" he shouted.

But they didn't understand, or they didn't want to understand, or they made a point of staying and staring at him, and he couldn't order them around any more—he knew that—because he had done something which made all his shouting and ordering so many words without meaning.

"Zig zig!" he yelled, starting the motor. "Zig zig you all!"

The girl stepped out hurriedly as the jeep began to move. She seemed afraid of him.

5

FINALLY, he let go of her, and she was free. Thérèse wanted to remember nothing and, thank God, most of what he had done to her was shrouded in her mind. But enough remained to make her feel soiled for the rest of her days—the scene at the window; how he had forced her on the bed; his breath, sour and hot; the fumbling caresses, uncouth and stupid; and the end, which came fast and painfully.

When she had said No and had cried, he had threatened her: What was all the fuss about? You don't want it? I'll make you want it.

And now he was finished and asleep. Through the door of the bathroom came the soft, soblike snores of the little one.

Thérèse put on her slip and her dress and her shoes. Quietly, quietly, for God's sake, don't disturb him. He might wake up again. . . .

That was her first need: To get away. Her mouth was parched, her arms and legs felt as if hammers had been hitting them, her head ached. Her mind was full of misshapen thoughts, nothing was in place or in proportion.

Yes, she had come up to this room with the Americans. What had she expected? They had accepted the wine and the food of the people, she had seen them take it; why shouldn't they take the bodies of the women? But that wine and that food had been given freely, hands had reached out; hearts had been full of relief and gratitude.

God, they had never let her have the chance to give. . . .

If only he hadn't had that wheezing breath, that stench. The sheep, last year when she had gone to Neufville and the farmer led her behind the house, the sheep had smelled that way. The farmer had pressed her against the fence with his flabby stomach — I'll give you eggs, two dozen, three dozen, and butter. *Étienne — Étie-e-ennnne!* His wife cackling like a hen. He had coughed and sputtered and his fat paunch had suddenly released her. She had laughed and run off, but the smell of the sheep remained.

We stood at the window and drank. The room was hot, or I was hot — what was the difference. . . . The wind had come and touched the naked skin. That was good. The wind had tender hands. Of course, I could have jumped out. How many floors was it down? Three, four, five. They would have come and carted me off. Snickered, too: Why was she bare to her waist? Drunk. . . . Of course, I was drunk. Bottoms up! *Doucement —* you roll the liqueur on your tongue, hold it, slowly. Appreciate the gift of God. God's gift . . . they never worked for it. They got it for nothing, for coming into Paris on their olive-drab cars and for bringing freedom, for chasing out the Boche and for laying her on the fresh sheets of the Scribe and for falling asleep, drunk. So they gulped down the liqueur — why not? *Mon Dieu!* Who is there to say No to them?

And the little one with his tickle-tickle fingers. They had fixed it between them; yes, they had; but the little one must have passed out in the bathroom and was unable to come back and get on top of her. They are all the same, but maybe he would not have stunk that much. Now, he will come in and find the big one sleeping and nobody there but him. *Pauvre petit.* Coming all the way across the ocean to find the bed empty. Coming all the way across like heroes.

They looked magnificent. Yes, they did look magnificent. The sun was behind them as she came forward from the barricade and saw them flooded in light, standing up in their car like conquerors. Who could resist them? What could you do but throw yourself at them — everybody was doing it, and what did you get out of life until they came with the sun behind them? You threw yourself at them — and then there were shots. She laughed to herself. Yes, that was it. The big one, the conqueror, had hidden behind her.

Freedom!

Bells ringing out, flowers, kisses, wine. Only today, the sweetness of the words my mother taught me has returned.

Honey, if you don't wanna, I'll make you. What do you think you came up here for? Now, be reasonable. Here's another drink. The bottle's still full.

She found the servants' staircase and walked down, embraced by the smell of dirty wash and stale food. She did not mind the smell. It suited her, it was fitting. And suddenly, she could not go on. She sat down on the stairs and wept.

After she had cried herself out, she felt easier. She could no longer bear to be alone with herself. She wanted to be among people — her kind of people. Where did she belong?

To the barricade. To the barricade that never had been attacked by the Germans. But she and the men behind the overturned bus had been ready to fight, and she had been accepted into their community because of this readiness of hers.

Mantin had explained it to her, during a quiet moment. "Thérèse Laurent," he had said, "expect nothing, not even glory. Glory is one of those things — you get as much as you hand yourself. This is a dirty and hard and dangerous business. Some of us have been at it for years; others, like you, have come only today. You should know what you are letting yourself in for. You still want it?"

At that time, everybody had been at highest alert. A German half-track, machine guns mounted, had been sighted and reported only two blocks away.

She had asked, "You aren't worried that I'll run away? You know, I have never been in anything like this."

"No," Mantin had said, "but you might want to leave now, when there's still a few minutes' time. They are very desperate, the Germans, and the fascist militia they're leaving behind. And I'd hate to see you caught."

"I am no better than you," she had answered.

And Mantin had said, "*Ça va!*" and had turned to bawl out a man who was letting sand get into the mechanism of his rifle.

How far off this seemed! The stress of the anticipated fight had given way to the all-inundating relief of victory, with reservations swept away, with everybody joining together, with jubilation shared, with doubts and hesitations obliterated. She could not really be blamed for running away afterwards!

She left the hotel and began to look for Mantin. Find a man like that among the millions spilling into the streets! But there was nothing else for her to do. She drifted, with a mass of people, toward the Madeleine, looking for the man with the straw hat. Whenever she saw his kind of straw hat, she tried to run, to push herself through the crowd. She would reach the man. It never was Mantin.

But something of Mantin was in all those faces, straw hat or no straw hat. A new hope, a new strength, a sense of common aim and common achievement. An illusion, perhaps. Something she had felt and lost and needed to regain, because once you felt it, you could not live without it.

Yates arrived in Paris in the early hours of the afternoon. By this time, the city was in a frenzy of joy; except in those streets where snipers or a few lost squads of Germans were giving futile battle, the masses of people were like solid, colorfully dotted walls along the sidewalks, pressing onto the pavements, weaving in and out between the Army vehicles, clamoring, shouting, singing, dancing.

The spirit infected Yates. He was trying to get his truck through, to find his headquarters if it had been set up; he knew that he should get to work immediately — every unutilized hour, with the city immersed in this kind of celebration, meant the disappearance of certain persons, the covering-up of tracks, the destruction of much-needed documents. Yet — he couldn't help himself. Never in his staid life had he felt the outgoing warmth of thousands, eyes that seemed to thank *him,* hands that seemed to reach for *him;* he stepped on the truck's running board — hanging on with his left arm, he waved his right in wild acknowledgment of the welcome, yelled nonsense from the heart, and thought, Jesus, I'm glad I could see this. *Le jour de gloire est arrivé!* The great Crusade. We've come to stop a tyrant, we've stopped him, he's driven out. The final chorus of the Ninth, *Seid umschlungen, Millionen,* I embrace you, peoples of the earth — hold that high note, you can hear it swing above everything. . . .

But he had to tear himself away. He parked the truck in a garage requisitioned by a French Antitank Company, left it under their protection, and hoped that most of its load would be there when he came back for it. He had to get in touch with DeWitt and Crerar. He tried the places where they had told him to report — no trace of them. He went into the Hotel Scribe and asked for Loomis and Willoughby; the clerk at the desk would only tell him that the house was full of American officers. Yates asked for a room for himself.

"So sorry," said the clerk who, during the last weeks, had boned up on his English. "You are too late, *mon Lieutenant.* You will have to try elsewhere."

Yates hated to have his affairs unsettled. What the hell was Loomis good for? Loomis had wangled himself a place in the advance — couldn't he have made some effort, at least, to have a definite assembly point and to look out for the physical needs of the Detachment?

Yates was tossed between the elation of the victor's welcome and the depression of a strange tourist in a convention town; kissed, one moment, and told, the next, that there was no room. Finally, he found a place for himself and his driver in the small Hotel Pierre. They carted their stuff over creaky stairs to the fourth floor rear; and Yates threw himself on the bed.

But he did not want to sleep. He wanted to throw himself again into the whirlpool of Paris, to get the feel of the city, to drink in the heady excitement of liberty.

He shaved and washed in cold water, and felt better. Then he went out. As soon as he stepped out of the quiet side street on which the Pierre was located, into the boulevard, he became part of the festive crowd, although a very special part. He was onlooker and showpiece both; with the jubilant eyes of the people, he saw the stream of Allied vehicles pour into the city — the stream of which he had been a drop. At the same time, his own hands were squeezed, his cheeks kissed, his shoulders slapped more often than he would have believed possible. He began to forget his search — Loomis, Willoughby, Crerar, DeWitt. What if the whole bunch were lost in the shuffle?

He was pushed and jostled, without direction, since the people themselves had none. He didn't mind, it was good. His impressions were not distinct — he saw colors rather than details, listened to the swelling and ebbing of sound rather than to words, caught the drift rather than individual movements. And he wondered at having been accepted and absorbed so quickly and so completely.

For some time now, he had been swaying next to a man with a straw hat. The man had a small mustache that did not quite belong to the strong face, the scar over his brow, the critical and yet friendly eyes.

Yates smiled at him.

The other smiled back over several people's shoulders. He said that they were certainly being pushed around, but that it was worth it.

Yates nodded and grinned.

"*Parlez-vous Français?*"

"*Certainement!*" said Yates.

The man made his way to Yates. "My name is Mantin, Monsieur. I'm a cabinetmaker. Allow me to welcome you. You don't know how we waited for this day."

Mantin had a wonderful capacity for creating elbowroom. His sturdy body plowed through without being inconsiderate; Yates trailed him.

They were leaving the thick of the crowd behind them, and could walk slowly.

"We waited and waited," said Mantin. "Only this morning, I was behind a barricade. The Germans were still in the city — organized, some of them . . ."

"Barricade!" said Yates. He rather admired these men who, with the technique of the Commune, had helped to fight a twentieth century war. "Seems you people never really warmed up to the Nazis — "

155

Mantin looked at him. "Do you know what they're like?"

"I've met quite a few, in the war — prisoners."

"Ah, when they're prisoners! That's different. But when they're holding *you* prisoner? . . ."

"It wasn't really that bad? I see your city, as beautiful as ever — "

"You will not understand. You are an American." There was just the slightest trace of contempt in Mantin's tone. "In America, you have not had anything like it."

He thought of the two American officers in their jeep whom he had welcomed, for whom he had torn down his barricade, and who had driven off through it when the snipers became disagreeable. He understood them. They valued their lives. It wasn't their mission to go out and kill snipers. If they hated better, they would kill better.

"I'll try to explain," said Mantin. "I knew a woman, Madame Grosset. She ran a small boardinghouse in Clichy, very nice, very clean; good, wholesome, home-cooked food. One day, two gentlemen appeared and took a room. They were well-dressed and well-behaved, and she was glad to have such nice boarders. Only, they didn't pay their bill. At the end of the second week, Madame Grosset said, Gentlemen, I am a poor widow, I cannot afford to keep you for nothing, please pay. They answered that it was true enough she was a widow, but that they knew she had a pretty good bank account and that she was making a fine profit on her boardinghouse and could well afford to keep them. They had pistols and they demonstrated how the pistols worked, and one of them showed her a document stating that he had won a prize as a sharpshooter only a year ago. All that was requested of her was a little food and one room, modest enough. In fact, they told Madame Grosset, she should be happy to have them; there had been some robberies in the neighborhood, and the streets were none too well-lighted at night, so that they were a kind of protection for Madame's establishment, weren't they?"

Mantin seemed to enjoy his own story so much that Yates decided to play along. "Why didn't Madame call the police?"

"*Mon Lieutenant!*" Mantin closed his eyes slyly. "They had thought of that, too! They told Madame Grosset, in case she had any idea of visiting the police station or of using her telephone, that one of them was going to stay in the house at all times and keep an eye on her. The week after that, they had another talk with Madame Grosset and pointed out to her that, since one of them was needed in the house, their earning power had diminished by 50 per cent, for which it was only fair to be reimbursed. They demanded whatever money she took in over and above what it cost to feed the boarders and themselves, and the running expenses of the house. They showed my friend, Madame Grosset, that each of them possessed a pair of brass knuckles and explained that brass knuckles could split a person's skull without making the slightest sound — not like a pistol which, if used, made a loud bang and aroused everybody. Madame Grosset handed over the money."

"What else could they take away from her?" asked Yates, beginning to appreciate Mantin's views on the Nazis.

"Wait!" said Mantin. "The next week, the two gentlemen raised a new point. They said it was criminal to spend good money to feed and house the other boarders in whom neither they nor Madame Grosset had any personal interest. They could live much more comfortably without them — each one of the gentlemen could have one floor of the house to himself, and Madame could occupy the top floor. Look at the saving in laundry alone!"

"Except that they cut their income," Yates remarked dryly. "Stick to your own logic, Monsieur Mantin."

"I will come to that," answered Mantin. "The two gentlemen brought up precisely this thought the following week. They were now running the house at a deficit. They suggested, therefore, that Madame should withdraw her funds from the bank. They would accompany her to the bank, because an elderly lady, with so many francs in her pocketbook, should not be left to walk alone. To convince her, they tied her to a chair and let her sit that way for thirty-six hours. Then, out of concern for her weakened state, they treated her to a taxi to the bank."

"And then?" Yates was amused, but at the same time he felt a slight horror at the neatness with which Mantin developed his story.

"Oh, next week, they made Madame Grosset sign power of attorney over to them so they could sell the house in Clichy."

"Did it bring much?"

"It wasn't sold," said Mantin. "Madame Grosset poisoned the two gentlemen with cyanide which she kept on her shelf from the previous year when she had had rats in her cellar. It was a celebrated case because the court had only Madame Grosset's testimony to go by."

"But if she had had no rat poison?" insisted Yates.

Mantin smiled. "These days, *mon Lieutenant,* you've got to keep something like that handy."

They were close to the Place de la Concorde when they heard firing.

Yates unslung his carbine. They hurried toward the Place and ran into groups of people watching a street battle from vantage points near buildings which afforded some protection.

The whole scene wasn't quite real to Yates — a battle with ringside seats, with a policeman as usher walking from one side of the street to the other, keeping the curious out of the Place. Yates wasn't curious, he wasn't eager to rush in — but he was the only man with a carbine in the crowd; the men who had guns were out there using them.

157

Mantin seemed cool enough. He said, "Same thing that's happening all over town. Snipers. We cleaned them out in our quarter."

Yates could see only a sector of the Place. Two armored cars drew up and commenced firing at some building on the left, outside his line of vision. A group of men in berets sprang forward from behind the armored cars. They carried a machine gun and spurted across the sector.

Some spectators near Yates began cheering.

Yates felt Mantin's eyes on him; it was as if they were deftly challenging him. And they were. Mantin was gauging Yates against the two liberators at the barricade.

"Well, let's get in there," Yates said, with resignation.

Mantin followed him. Mantin was suddenly brandishing a pistol. Yates frowned. You don't like your new friends to march at your side with weapons concealed. Then he smiled; he supposed Madame Grosset wasn't the type to use cyanide, either.

The policeman stopped both Yates and Mantin. He argued volubly, using his hands so that his blue cape fluttered like the wings of a pelican before its take-off. "Everything is under control!" he shouted because he thought Yates would understand French if it was spoken loudly enough. "The forces of law and order are prevailing. We are cleaning them out from the roofs of the Ministry of Marine and the Hotel Crillon — desperate, desperate! Monsieur, do not go in there, I beg of you. We do not wish to have more men on the Place than necessary. One might get hurt. . . ."

"All right!" Yates put his carbine back over his shoulder. "All right, don't upset yourself."

The cape stopped fluttering. Relieved, the policeman grabbed Yates's hand and shook it. "Welcome, Monsieur, welcome to Paris!"

The people cheered. Yates turned around, embarrassed. He had done nothing to deserve being cheered — on the contrary. Just because he wore a helmet and had a carbine, they presumed he was a hero, while in reality he was only a spear carrier in a mob scene.

He looked around for Mantin and saw him standing in a doorway, with a girl. Mantin waved to him.

Yates walked over. He noticed that the girl, on seeing him approach, gripped Mantin's arm as if seeking protection.

"Bon jour, Mademoiselle," Yates said, and gave her a smile.

She did not greet him. She turned to Mantin and broke into rapid, colloquial French.

Mantin quieted her down. He addressed Yates, "This is my friend, Thérèse Laurent. She was with me at the barricade."

The girl regarded Yates with dubious, almost inimical eyes in which he could detect traces of fear. He thought, Perhaps she's been on the Place de la Concorde and the bullets came too close for her comfort. But if she had been on the barricade with Mantin, she should not be scared that easily. On the other hand, he was certainly the last one to underrate the effects of sudden firing. And then, a girl — frail she was, too — quite lovely in a way new to him — she had no business being on the barricade or out in the battle on the Place.

He said he found her courage admirable. "But, thank God," he added, "the days when women have had to do that kind of thing are about over."

"What kind of thing will women have to do now?" she asked, bitterly.

Again this antagonism. . . . Yates saw that her hair had been hurriedly done after having been thoroughly disheveled, and her dress was crumpled. Her face, which had kept some of its sweetness, had the look of exhaustion he knew so well from the field. It was sullen, too, at least when it was turned to him. Under her arms, next to her bosoms which were somewhat too large for her slight figure, were the splotches of dried perspiration.

"Exciting day?" he remarked with intended casualness.

"Terribly," she said, "and terribly long." Then, facing Mantin, she asked, "Can you take me home, Monsieur? That is, if you have nothing more important to do. . . . I've got to talk to you."

The plea in her voice made Yates feel unaccountably sorry for her. She seemed to be so excluded from the jubilation of the day.

Mantin said, hesitantly, "Ça va. . . ."

Yates guessed that the relationship between the girl and Mantin was not a personal one. Yates was footloose, he had no plan, no program. And she attracted him. He could see her, with her hair done, bathed, and in a fresh dress. In fact, it ought to be fun to dress her up. Chartreuse would go well with her eyes.

He laughed at himself. He, too, could use a bath, and the dust of the road was still settled in his clothes.

"If you show me the way, Mademoiselle Thérèse," he suggested, "perhaps I could take you home."

"*Non!*"

She almost spit it out. Her smudged hand went to her face. Yates saw that the hand trembled.

"Thérèse!" Mantin said soothingly. He touched her elbow. "This American is my friend. . . ." And to Yates, "The day has been too much for her."

"Seems so," Yates agreed. Women cracked easily. On second thought he felt that this wasn't the answer, that there must be something more behind her hysteria.

"I'm thirsty," she announced abruptly.

"That's an idea!" said Yates. "Don't you know a place away from this

159

infernal firing, Monsieur Mantin — a quiet place where we can have a cool drink?"

Mantin nodded. He knew of one, only a few minutes' walk.

It was in a cellar. The long day had almost gone, and only a fraction of its waning light penetrated down here. The dark brown background fitted the fading of the day's pitch of nerves.

"Water for me," said Thérèse.

"*De l'eau,*" said the waiter indifferently.

She drank in long, thirsty gulps. Then she wiped her face. Yates wanted to ask her why she was afraid of him — afraid on a day when everybody who found an American embraced him.

Instead, he said, "What made you decide to join Monsieur Mantin at the barricade?"

"Eh?"

"I mean — have you been in this work for a long time? Fighting the Boche? In America, women don't generally decide on the spur of the moment to do a little shooting."

Thérèse studied Yates's face. Shadows had laid themselves over it, but beneath them, she could still see what kind of man he was and that he wasn't Loomis. When he came toward her, at the entrance to the Place de la Concorde, he had looked to her like Loomis, Vic, the big one. All Americans had looked like that.

Why did this American, now, ask her about the barricade? What did he want from her?

"That's just what she did." Mantin was answering for her. "She saw us building the barricade and decided to join us. Wasn't it so?"

"Yes," she said.

"We didn't have to fight, though." Mantin laughed a little. His scar was a darker gash on his dark forehead. "The Boche ran without attacking us. So we lost no blood. We did not gain much glory either. Thérèse was to be our nurse. She fetched the bandages and was in readiness to do her share."

"Why?" asked Yates. "What made you do it?"

"I don't know," said Thérèse. "I went to the druggist and told him to give us bandages."

She felt the relief that lay in talking of the good things she had done this day, of the community to which she had belonged. A luster came back into her eyes.

"The drugstore man wanted to be paid. I had no money. So I told him the new Government would pay him. Who is the new Government? I don't know. Have I done wrong, Monsieur Mantin?"

Mantin sensed that she needed to be assured not only about her promise to the druggist. His hand closed to a fist. "No. You did right."

"I really thought I could say it honestly, because I felt I was part of the new Government. That's stupid, of course. I have nothing to do with the Government. On other days, I work in an office."

"On this day," Mantin said gravely, "you were part of the new Government. Yes."

"But then I ran away," she said, audibly only to him.

Mantin, who understood how much to expect from people, patted her hand, "*Ça va. . . .* We were almost done with the job. We had no trouble."

She smiled.

It was the first time Yates had seen her smile. He saw her beauty. But he felt uncomfortable. A cabinetmaker and a stenographer pretending they were any kind of Government . . . It reminded him of Ruth, who also understood Government in a highly personal way, who took civic affairs most seriously, and who had no conception of how big these powers were and how little she was.

He said, "I still don't know, Mademoiselle Thérèse, what made you get involved in the business behind the barricade."

"Why do you want to know?" asked Mantin.

"I am interested in people."

"Interested . . ." shrugged Mantin. "You should feel with them."

"I can't explain it," said Thérèse. "I can't explain anything I did today. I suppose because everything was so sudden. There was a sound in the air, like music in church on Easter — "

"Yes," said Yates, "that I can understand." He really thought he could — see with her eyes, feel with her senses; but not because she was *people*. Because she was this particular woman, with this particular beauty of her own. Jeanne d'Arc, thought Yates.

Mantin said, "People seem to have an instinct for when the time is ripe."

Yates picked up his carbine.

Jeanne d'Arc — nonsense. She was just a little stenographer who had gone wild with the adventure of liberation. And Mantin was just a cabinetmaker who had had a day that made him seem important to himself. Yet, they had done a great job, even if they had only helped to trap a few Nazis. People . . . They hated the Boche, and they wanted to be the Government, and they had done something to free themselves. More than he had ever done.

"And now," said Mantin, "we will both take Thérèse Laurent home."

6

The kitchen of the Hotel St. Cloud lay quiet and almost deserted in the early afternoon.

Sergeant Dondolo sat behind the cleanly scrubbed meat table, his fingernails idly pursuing the scars which generations of meat cleavers had left in the soft wood. He was reading an old comic strip magazine that had found its way into the kitchen. Dondolo got stuck in the middle of the Dick Tracy installment; he leafed through the much-fingered book and found he could not go on — the crucial pages were missing.

Disgusted, he put it aside. It was like everything else in this lousy Hotel where the Detachment, after much moving and unrest, had finally settled. He looked up. Through the barred windows, he could see a collection of legs and feet. A dozen or more elderly men and women pressed around his garbage cans, searching for the remains of food which the soldiers had knocked out of their mess kits. The scavengers would scramble and pick until the MP guards came and chased them away.

Poor people, Dondolo thought complacently. The men of the Detachment, who were always kicking about the food, didn't know what they had. As long as they left stuff for the French to scoop up, they were obviously too well fed. If Loomis ever again said that the diet was insufficient for the men, he would simply show the Captain the scene at the garbage cans. Loomis was impressed by something like that. At the next formation, the Captain would bawl out the men for their constant complaining, and after that, Dondolo would have his peace.

Dondolo was not the man ever to have harbored illusions about the French. His limited share of the enthusiasm they displayed during the first days after his arrival had hardly touched him; and after it wore off, he easily made his adjustment to every day realities, keeping on the lookout for the opportunities which a starved city naturally would offer. For any man who still said "Paris!" with a dreamy look in his eyes, Dondolo had only a condescending smile.

He tossed the comic book into a can. It was about time that he collected the things for Sourire. Funny about Sourire — Dondolo never could fix the precise moment when Sourire had attached himself to him. It could have been at the corner bar of the Rue Giannini, it could have been much later when he was trying to find his way home. Anyhow, the first clear impression of Sourire, in Dondolo's mind, was the picture of both of them sitting at this same kitchen table, Dondolo with a splitting headache which seemed to concentrate behind his eyeballs, and Vaydanek preparing steaming black coffee for his sergeant and the Frenchman. Sourire claimed laughingly that he had carried Dondolo home; but that was hardly probable since Sourire was even shorter than Dondolo and didn't have the American's stockiness. So, other people might have been involved — friends of Sourire. Dondolo didn't care about Sourire's side of the business, as long as everything continued smoothly. That night — rather, that morning — as the black coffee returned his power of vision, Dondolo noticed Sourire's shifty eyes shrewdly appraising the supplies in the storeroom — Vaydanek had left the door open when he took out the coffee — the shelves laden with sides of bacon, powdered eggs, sugar, flour, canned meats and all the staples to which Dondolo had the keys.

"You don't know what you have there," Sourire had said admiringly and smiled, closing his eyes.

"Oh, don't I?" Dondolo had been sarcastic.

Whatever else Sourire had wanted to say, Dondolo had stopped by a motion of his head toward the eagerly listening Vaydanek; and Sourire had immediately understood. This little motion of Dondolo's head had established their relationship.

And now, Sourire was a regular visitor to the kitchen of the Hotel St. Cloud. Dondolo had his scruples about the deals — what he had done in Normandy was small stuff compared to the supplies going into Sourire's bags to be loaded on Sourire's worn-out truck. But Dondolo had a simple way of disposing of his scruples; he told himself that everybody at home was making money on the war, and that he had to compensate himself for the opportunities he missed. He owed it to Larry and to Saverio, his little one. With each hundred dollars that Dondolo sent to Marcelli to salt away in the bank, the Sergeant said to himself: Here goes another couple months of college. It takes a lot of dough to send two kids through school.

Dondolo unlocked the door to the storeroom and surveyed his shelves. How to plan his meals so that he could keep up the delivery he had promised Sourire? He was lost in thought, even worried about how often he could serve beans instead of meat and keep up the semblance of a balanced diet. . . . Balanced diet! Sourire once had told him what the French soldiers got to eat, and Dondolo began to envy his counterparts in the former French Army; but then it occurred to him that a French mess sergeant, or whatever they called themselves, would not have so much to choose from in the first place.

Somebody coughed politely behind Dondolo's back.

"Sourire?" said Dondolo. "Hullo."

Sourire smiled. "What are we having today?" he said cheerily. "Any news from home? How's the *bébé* Saverio?"

"Not a drop of mail!" complained Dondolo. "Ever since we moved into this damned town, not a letter, nothing."

"It will come! It will come!" Sourire consoled him. "When I was in the French Army, in 1940, we never got any mail, we were running so fast."

"Yeah," said Dondolo, "but we aren't running."

"That is true," admitted Sourire.

"It's because they have no consideration for guys like us. We're so much dirt."

"Well," said Sourire, "there's one thing you learn in the Army, and I say it's the same in any Army: You've got to look out for yourself."

The remark was too pointed for Dondolo's taste. This stinker Sourire thought only of his own business, and his interest in Dondolo's *bébé* was a lot of hooey.

"Let's start!" said Dondolo. "This is what I can give you today." He motioned Sourire into the storeroom and pointed out the items he thought he could spare. Sourire reached for a side of bacon.

"Uh-uh!" said Dondolo, "I want you to get out of here fast, but not that fast. How much?"

"The whole thing?"

"Yes."

Sourire calculated. Then he said, "Four thousand."

Four thousand francs, thought Dondolo. Not even a hundred bucks. "Do you think I'm crazy?" he asked. "I'd rather eat it myself."

"But it isn't worth any more!"

"Don't tell me," said Dondolo. "I've been around. I know the prices on the market."

"It is you who force the prices up!" Sourire was having a flurry of social consciousness. "I think of the people who've got to buy this!"

"Don't worry," Dondolo assured him, "they'll pay."

Sourire had to agree. He knew they would pay the price, any price. "All right, five," he offered.

"That's better," said Dondolo. "Give me the dough."

Sourire pulled a bundle of anemic-looking notes out of his pocket.

"Damned unhandy, this size," commented Dondolo, as he folded the thousand-franc notes and tried to jam them into his wallet. "Why don't you people print some decent-sized bills? Look here, like this!" He showed Sourire a dollar bill, the one he carried in his pocket as a souvenir of the States and as a reminder of his obligations. "That's solid, that's real stuff!"

The Frenchman fingered the dollar. "Give you hundred francs for it!"

"Nope!" said Dondolo. "That one is mine." He added, "Stop dawdling, let's get this stuff packed up. I've sent Vaydanek off, but he won't be gone forever."

For a while, Dondolo and Sourire worked hard, reaching up to the

164

shelves, dropping the bags and cans into the sack Sourire had brought with him. The sack seemed to expand endlessly.

"Do you think you'll be able to lift it?" Dondolo asked.

"Watch me," said Sourire. He dropped the coveted side of bacon into the sack. "The girls say I'm made of steel."

He laughed.

The laugh died in his throat. Somebody was outside in the kitchen.

"Anybody here?" the person in the kitchen called.

"Don't move," whispered Dondolo. "Maybe he won't find us." But the light of the storeroom shone plainly through the open door. Dondolo thought of switching it off, but that would have aroused the intruder's attention all the more.

The idea of coming out of the storeroom and simply locking Sourire in occurred to Dondolo too late. Thorpe stood at the open door.

Of all people, Thorpe, thought Dondolo. If it had been Vaydanek, or almost anybody else, they could have gotten together, made an arrangement, cut the man in, on a modest scale, or promised some other favor. But Thorpe! . . . Dondolo clearly remembered the staircase of Château Vallères, the moment before the German planes came over — the beating he had given Thorpe. . . .

"What do you want?" he said. "What do you want down here? You've got no business in the kitchen. Get the hell out!"

"I'm hungry," said Thorpe.

"I can't give you nothing," said Dondolo. "Chow's at six."

"All right, all right." Thorpe retreated, always facing Dondolo. "I just wanted a sandwich."

"Give it to him!" whispered Sourire.

But Thorpe was walking away, faster and faster.

I'm driving him away, thought Dondolo; my God, what am I doing? The moment he's out of here, he'll holler it all through the hotel. "Come back here!" he called.

Thorpe stopped.

"I'll give you your sandwich."

This offer, finally, connected in Thorpe's mind. He had come down to the kitchen, expecting to find Vaydanek. Dondolo usually took off after noon. Vaydanek would have fixed him a sandwich. But if Dondolo offered a sandwich, he had his own reasons, and his reasons concerned the civilian and the bulging sack. Now, the thing made sense: the meager meals, the rumors which had been making the rounds.

What could he do about it? He couldn't go to Loomis. Well, he could talk to some of the men and tell them what he had seen, or maybe Yates was the man to stop the racket.

"Come here," repeated Dondolo, "I want to talk to you."

Thorpe recognized that the Mess Sergeant had made up his mind. The skin over his swarthy face was taut. Thorpe became aware of his danger.

I can run, Thorpe thought. But they were two, the civilian and Dondolo, and they were inching up on him. And he didn't want to run; something inside told him not to. He had to face them. In Normandy, he had been defenseless — that was because the coffee Dondolo had poured over him had conjured up his old wound and old fear. He had come through that night remembering only that some horrible thing had happened afterwards, and that Dondolo had been connected with it. But the details were lost in a kind of yellowish fog that sometimes poured into his dreams, suffocated him and, without ever dissolving and showing the features of the threat, catapulted him into screaming awakening and, for days after, haunted him and riddled him with shudders.

Dondolo came up and said, "Maybe you think this isn't so kosher, huh?"

Thorpe stepped back to maintain a distance between himself and the Sergeant. He saw too late that Dondolo had cut him off from the exit.

"Well, I don't give a damn what you think," laughed Dondolo. "So what are you going to do about it?"

"Me?" asked Thorpe. "I don't mix in your affairs."

He was sorry the moment he said it. He saw Dondolo screw up his thin lips.

"But I'll tell you what I think of it," Thorpe went on. "That food belongs to us. All right, if you'd give it to the people out there who dig in the garbage cans — but they don't get it. Only the black-marketeers get it. The rich get it."

"So what are you going to do about it?" repeated Dondolo.

Thorpe said nothing. He watched Dondolo.

"Let's make a deal," suggested the Sergeant. He didn't take his own suggestion very seriously. He couldn't trust Thorpe outside the kitchen door. But perhaps the guy wasn't so honest — the man hasn't been born who'd resist an offer if it was big enough. Perhaps Thorpe could be kept quiet until Sourire had scrammed and Dondolo had covered the shortages in the week's ration. After that, nothing could be proved against him.

"What kind of deal?" asked Thorpe. It was probably just a ruse of Dondolo's to get close to him and to beat him up and to knock him out for good. "A deal for me to keep my mouth shut?"

"Yes," said Dondolo, offering a greasy hand. "There's enough in this for you and me, both."

"What do you think I am?" said Thorpe.

"All right," said Dondolo, "have it your way."

For a moment, Thorpe was glad that the fight had started, that the lines were drawn. Dondolo had been not only Dondolo, but everything haunting and pursuing him through his restless nights, and his days without

166

peace. And now, this Dondolo turned out to be a cheap crook. It made him more human, less menacing, as if a ghost had turned man.

Thorpe caught the glance Dondolo gave the civilian.

The civilian sidled up to Thorpe. Thorpe got the essence of their tactics — the civilian was to drive him into Dondolo's arms.

Thorpe faced the civilian.

Sourire measured Thorpe with his eyes and retreated hastily. He looked almost funny as he scampered back, a short, frightened man. Thorpe grinned.

At this moment, Dondolo was on him.

Dondolo's arm, its muscle bulging, pressed itself underneath Thorpe's chin; Dondolo, choking him, was trying to jerk his head back.

But Dondolo had forgotten that Thorpe, although not as compact as he, was the taller, more agile man. Thorpe managed to twist his body. The move deprived Dondolo of his footing; he felt himself lifted high. He crashed on the floor.

Groaning, he got up. The blood rushed to his head. Thorpe's image became blurred; there were two, three Thorpes, all glaring at him.

The brief respite gave Thorpe time to think. Dondolo could not possibly believe that he would keep quiet, even if he were beaten within an inch of his life. Then, what was Dondolo's plan? To kill him? There would be a search for him; Abramovici knew that he had gone to the kitchen. How could they dispose of his body? Then it hit Thorpe that the civilian must have a vehicle; he could not transport the stolen food on his back. So his body would be stowed away on some cart or truck, dumped in the Seine or some sewer — No. Dondolo was an American soldier. An American didn't do that kind of thing. . . . But Dondolo was desperate, a desperate fascist. He would not only kill him, but kill him slowly, if he could, and stand over him and watch him until the last drop of life had passed from his pulpy body.

Thorpe did not suspect that Dondolo might operate on the theory that, if a man was sufficiently beaten, he was also sufficiently cowed. In fact, there was no time for any further thought, because Dondolo threw himself against Thorpe with the force and the fury of a man fighting for his life.

Dondolo managed to hit Thorpe's old wound. The wound immediately sent waves of pain through his whole body. Dondolo held on to Thorpe, determined to permit no more tricks. And while he embraced Thorpe, the little civilian kept hammering some instrument against Thorpe's kidney. At first, the hammering was annoying; but as it continued, the pain grew and grew, it united with the waves emanating from Thorpe's wound, it unnerved him and weakened him, and Thorpe suddenly realized that all his energy would flow out of him if the little civilian were allowed to go on with his vicious hammering.

He felt that, in another moment, he would grow panicky and scream. He decided to scream now, while he was fully conscious. The scream forced Dondolo to use one of his hands to close Thorpe's mouth. Thorpe bit that hand. It was disgusting. It tasted of sweat and of all the entrails Dondolo had ever taken out of any carcass. Thorpe bit deep.

Dondolo tore his hand from Thorpe's teeth. He leaned back and smashed his fist with such force into Thorpe's mouth that Thorpe was thrown — thrown away from Dondolo and the little civilian.

Thorpe screamed again, this time from the excruciating pain in his mouth and in the hinges of his jawbones.

"Shut him up!" he heard Dondolo say, the voice sounding muffled. It was the Vot-eees-it voice.

Still, there was no fear in him, this Thorpe knew clearly; and he knew that as long as the fear did not come, as long as that feeling which froze his arms to his sides, and his feet to the ground, did not return, he was all right.

He saw Dondolo come at him again.

Thorpe laughed — Dondolo was so wide open. Thorpe raised his foot and with deliberate force kicked Dondolo in the groin.

Dondolo doubled over, but he did not fall.

This time it was Dondolo who screamed. In the scream was everything: pain and fear — fear for himself, and fear for Larry and Saverio, the little one.

Thorpe heard the scream — like music. Then he blacked out.

The instrument which Sourire had been using to hammer against his kidneys — a leather-covered lead ball attached to a rubber handle — had hit him squarely on the skull.

Thorpe came to when Dondolo poured a bucket of water in his face. An MP guard, the one who patrolled around the hotel, stood next to the Sergeant. A second MP was keeping himself close to the little civilian.

At first, what they were saying sounded to Thorpe like a low humming; it was an effort for him to pluck apart words, and then to connect the words into sentences.

"Stealing food from the storeroom," he made out, "black market — noticed shortage for long time — caught him in the act. . . ."

Dondolo was speaking.

Thorpe heard the MP say, "You sure gave him the works!"

Dondolo laughed, "He didn't like it — have a look at my hand."

Yes, that's what they're saying. Thorpe was sure of it. But it still made no sense. Thorpe struggled to get up from the floor. He tottered, held on to the wall.

"Watch him!" he heard Dondolo warn the MP. "He's dangerous."

He felt the MP grip his arm. "Come along, Bud! No trouble, y'understand?"

Come along? Where to? What for? Thorpe's head was incredibly big. It was so big that the thoughts he managed to have lost themselves in its expanse.

"Where you going to take me?" asked Thorpe. His words came slowly. His swollen mouth ached with each syllable. "I've done nothing."

"You heard the Sergeant!" said the MP, still friendly.

Dondolo said, "He plays dumb."

"I know! I know!" said the MP. "They all do. Think they can get away with it. But they learn fast. We teach 'em a thing or two."

Thorpe shook his head in an attempt to force his thoughts to hold.

"Say that again?" he asked.

"Say what again?" The MP thought, The guy really got a going-over.

"What Dondolo told you — about me."

"I'll tell him!" Dondolo shouted hastily. "I catch him with the goods — selling all these foodstuffs to this French fellow — there, the whole bag full! Flour, and bacon, eggs, sugar, canned stuff. I catch him and I say to him, Well, there, I finally got you! So he turns on me! Look at my hand — I'll have to go on sick call."

"All right," said the MP, "no more arguments. Let's get moving."

Thorpe tore his arm away from the MP.

"Listen," he said, "it's a lie! A God-damned lie! What he says about me — *he's* the one who did it! I caught *him* selling the food!"

The MP looked at Dondolo. "Well?" he asked.

"Say, what do I look like?" said Dondolo. "If I sold anything that belonged to the U.S. Army, do you think I would have this kind of guy catch me?"

Thorpe felt the fear creep up on him. The large, gleaming white walls of the kitchen began to move, to press in on him. "He's lying!" he managed to say.

"Why don't you ask the Frenchman?" said Dondolo. "He speaks English, all right."

The MP looked questioningly at Sourire.

Sourire and Dondolo had decided their line in the brief moment between Thorpe's sinking unconscious to the floor, and the arrival of the MP's, who came running at the noise of the fight.

"With whom did you deal?" the MP asked gruffly.

Sourire pointed at Thorpe. "This man!"

"He's lying," whispered Thorpe.

The MP did not even hear him. Once more, he gripped Thorpe's arm.

Now, the kitchen walls were not only moving in on Thorpe, they became transparent. He could see whole armies of Dondolos and Sourires, marching up and down, smiling, grinning, maneuvering. He was surrounded by their columns, caught, not a break through which he could escape. And even had there been such a break, he could not have run through it, because his legs would not move. Then he said to himself, All this is a dream. Curl up, sleep, make yourself small, and you will wake up on your mother's soft, warm lap. Nothing has been true since you left your mother's lap. Growing up was a dream, and going to war, and being wounded. But underneath, he knew that it was no dream. The armies of enemies were too much for him to take and stand up against.

He went along with the MP, his feet dragging.

Dondolo took himself to Loomis. Dondolo didn't like to go. Back home, in the Tenth Ward Association, it had been drilled into him by Marcelli, the Boss, that the fewer the people who knew of a deal, the better for everybody concerned, and the bigger the profits. But Dondolo was not fool enough to delude himself; the MP's entry into the fight and the arrest of Thorpe raised the whole matter out of his, a sergeant's, level.

And it was questionable how long Sourire would stick to his story, once he discovered that it wasn't so easy to get out of an MP can and into the comfort of a French retention jail.

Dondolo gave Loomis substantially the same report he had given the MP's.

Loomis didn't believe a word of it. He knew Thorpe, and he knew enough of Dondolo to make a pretty good guess at the truth.

"Where is Thorpe now?" he asked.

Dondolo shrugged, "At the MP station, I think."

For the moment, Loomis asked no other question. He was worried about something else: What did Dondolo want him to do?

Dondolo could not be treated like an ordinary man in the outfit. In his small way, ever since England, Dondolo had operated like a politician. He had built himself a tight little machine; he had made friends and furthered his friendships with favors from his office. A soldier's main concern was food, and food flowed from Dondolo. Loomis, himself, had participated in midnight snacks; delicious steak sandwiches for the officers, which Dondolo fixed with deft hands, putting slices of pickles on the meat before he slapped the second piece of bread on top. It all came out of the men's rations. God knows how far this had gone, how many threads Dondolo had spun to how many men and officers in the Detachment.

"Very bad thing," Loomis said finally, "very grave offense."

"Yes, sir."

"Selling Government property, attacking a noncommissioned officer in the course of his duties, Articles of War 94 and 65. . . . Let me see — five and a half years minimum if convicted."

Dondolo's eyes followed Loomis's hands as they turned the pages in the little book. He didn't feel too good. He thought of Larry and Saverio, growing up with their father in Leavenworth. Then he pulled himself together, determined to beat the rap, if it meant killing Thorpe or any number of people.

"I can't figure it," said Loomis. "All right, Thorpe is crazy — but not that crazy. And if you ask me, Dondolo, I would say that a guy who goes in for selling rations isn't crazy at all, but very calculating. Your story doesn't jibe."

"I guess it don't, sir," said Dondolo, filling his voice with dejection.

It improved Loomis's mood to see the usually self-sufficient Dondolo with eyes downcast, head hanging, hands clumsily stroking his knees.

"You've got to help me," said Dondolo.

"I'm always here for my men," said Loomis. "You know that. If you're in trouble, you'd better tell me."

Dondolo kept back a smile. "I'd rather come out with the truth," he said. "This Frenchman, he came to see me . . ."

"What Frenchman? Where did you meet him?"

"In a bar," said Dondolo. "He was very nice, and he paid for my drinks."

"I see," said Loomis. Obviously, the Frenchman was going to be the villain of the piece.

"Today he came around," Dondolo continued, "and he begged me for food. He said he had a large family, and under the Nazis, they'd been starved. Two of his children were sick, he said — rickets or something like that."

If Larry and Saverio were starving — Holy Mother protect them! — he would have gone out killing.

"His wife," Dondolo went on, "his wife, he said, was so starved that her breasts wouldn't give milk to the baby. Two months old, that baby," Dondolo added.

"Things are tough all around," said Loomis. "But we can't give to just anybody that comes along!"

"Captain, sir!" said Dondolo, and his appeal was genuine, "I invite you to come out behind the kitchen, any time after a meal, and look at those French going over our garbage cans. Garbage they eat! How long can a man stand seeing that?"

"So the Frenchman came to you . . ." prodded Loomis.

"We got plenty rations. I gave him some. Why not? What's the sense of liberating these people if we let them starve?"

"You took money?"

"A little," admitted Dondolo. "The Frenchman forced it on me. He said he wasn't a beggar, he was making money, it went against him to take things without paying for them. I didn't want an argument — and if it made him feel better to give me money? I'm just a sergeant, sir, I just make a few bucks, and I've got to think of my family, too!"

"Sure! Sure!" said Loomis. "But how did Thorpe get mixed up in it?"

"Thorpe came into the kitchen. He had no business there in the first place!" Dondolo's old outrage broke through again. "But in this outfit, they stick their noses into everything!"

Loomis grunted. He appreciated Dondolo's feelings. Tolachian had poked his nose into things that didn't concern him. . . . Tolachian was dead.

"So Thorpe comes in there," said Dondolo, "and he sees me give the stuff to the Frenchman, and he starts hollering: I steal from the Army! I sell our food! He calls me a crook and everything. Why, you know Thorpe, sir — he's crazy. I ask you, sir — was there ever anybody in this outfit, who didn't have enough to eat? Haven't I always looked out for everybody?"

"Sure," said Loomis.

"He gets himself into a real stew," Dondolo went on. "He gets red in the face and then white — and then he jumps on me. I tried to hold him off, for the longest time. But then he kicks me, down here, I can have a damage from that for the rest of my life, sir — and then I got mad. Finally, the MP's came."

"That is all?"

"Yes, sir!" Dondolo said, proud of his story.

Loomis thought, It listens well. But nobody in the Detachment would believe in Dondolo's charity. Besides, Dondolo had admitted the main fact.

"You can't get away from it," Loomis said, "you sold the stuff to the Frenchman, and you were caught at it."

Dondolo nodded.

"And I don't think Thorpe attacked you. He isn't that kind of man."

"What's the difference?" Dondolo was annoyed. Loomis didn't have to rub it in.

"I don't like your tone!" said Loomis. His mind turned in a new direction. At some time or other, these privileged characters in the outfit always ran up against him and made trouble. Dondolo's wheat had shot up pretty high. It was ripe to be cut down.

"I don't like your tone, Sergeant! And you're not in a position to tell me whether my statements make a difference or not. In fact, you are in no position at all! I've been getting plenty complaints about insufficient food — so, this wasn't your first contact with that Frenchman, or maybe there've been a number of Frenchmen who appealed to your heart and your wallet."

Loomis saw the quip had hit home. "Let's stop kidding ourselves!" he demanded.

"Yeah — let's stop kidding ourselves!" Dondolo came back. His beady, dark eyes became like pin points. His mouth shut tight, his whole face showed overbearing insolence. "Are you going to help me, Captain, or aren't you?"

"Help you!"

"Sure! I want no trouble!"

Loomis shook his head, slowly, as if in amazement. "You're beginning to interest me, Dondolo. Whatever gave you the idea that I would interfere with the course of justice? Articles of War, it's all printed. For your suggestion alone, I could have you court-martialed."

"I said let's stop kidding ourselves, sir!" Dondolo announced quietly. "Have me court-martialed! That's O.K. But when I'm on the stand, I'm going to blow this whole thing wide open!"

"What whole thing, Sergeant?"

"You don't think I'm the only businessman here! When I had the first real talk with that Frenchman — Sourire's his name, you may know him! — he gave you as a reference. He said he was dealing only with first-class people."

Dondolo chuckled. "I'm careful who I do business with. Then I checked with Lord, the Motor Sergeant. Lord said there were double gasoline requisitions, and that lots of gasoline disappears before it ever reaches this outfit. And you ask me what gave me the idea!"

Loomis felt a violent need for the latrine.

Dondolo studied the effect of his words. He had put all his eggs in one basket, and he wasn't sure whether the handle would hold. All he knew was what Lord had told him, and he knew that Loomis had something to do with the requisitioning of gas.

Dondolo said, "It's not me that wants trouble, sir. But I think some of us should stick together."

Loomis wished fervently that he had never come to Paris. Everybody lived high in Paris. In any restaurant, a halfway decent dinner cost a week's pay, liquor was beyond reach, and the beautiful things you could buy in the shops to send home *From Paris* were beyond what anyone could afford. You just had to have a private income. He didn't know how the others managed; Willoughby seemed to have no trouble. You couldn't always be somebody else's guest. What was the point of winning the war if you remained as poor as you had been? And the gas deal had been such a natural!

You could out-argue your own conscience, sure. But if you went back to the things you learned in school — and there's a lot to the stories they tell kids — you knew that your conscience has a way of catching up with you.

With an undertone of despair Loomis said, "I don't know what I can do!"

Dondolo stood up. Everything was hunky-dory. Larry and Saverio, God bless them, would keep their father.

"Between the two of us, Captain," he said sociably, "we'll be able to fix it. Don't worry."

Loomis resented the familiarity, but he needed the reassurance.

"If only those MP's hadn't come in!" he said.

"Remember how Thorpe busted your party, back in Vallères?" Dondolo leaned over the desk. "The guy is nuts! Everybody in the outfit knows he's Section Eight. I can't figure why he wasn't put in a strait jacket in Normandy — breaking in on you gentlemen like that and buttonholing Lieutenant Yates and pestering everybody. And he's been acting up ever since. He thinks everybody's putting the finger on him. He's dangerous to have around!"

"All right — so we put him in a hospital. There are still the MP's."

"Yeah — but they've got *my* story. And who's going to believe what Thorpe says when he's under observation for how many screws are loose in his head?"

"I don't like it," said Loomis. "I don't like it."

"What do you want!" Dondolo said, disgusted. "Make up your mind, sir. If you don't do it, I'll have Thorpe on my neck — you and me, the both of us are going to have him on our necks. If you know what I mean."

Loomis closed the little book containing the Articles of War. "I'll make a report," he said.

7

Bing brought the news to Yates.

"When did they take him to the hospital?" Yates asked.

"Last night. They kept him in the MP station all afternoon; and in the evening, they transferred him to the hospital. I've telephoned and I've been there and tried to get permission to see him — no dice."

Yates rubbed his right palm over the warts on his left hand. "Jesus, the poor guy. . . ." Thorpe's face, as he broke into the officers' party, claiming his help, was etched in Yates's mind. "Well, Bing, you've done what you could. Thank you."

Bing stared at him. "No thanks necessary."

"I'll see what I can do," Yates added hastily.

Bing said, "I kind of expected that, Lieutenant."

"You did?" Bing's attitude and the implication of his words irritated Yates. Why was it that everybody turned to him for help, and that everybody he tried to help ended on the junk pile?

"There's no guarantee I can do much," he said.

Bing misunderstood. He thought Yates was about to renege. "You don't mean that," he said. "Look, Lieutenant, somebody fixed up Thorpe so that he had to be taken to the hospital — "

"Thorpe was always, well, kind of irrational."

"I thought . . . Lieutenant, the men know a lot more about what's going on in the outfit than you think they do. We know, for instance, that you tried to replace Lieutenant Laborde on that Fourth of July mission."

"So I stuck my neck out," Yates said angrily. "What did I achieve? Whom did I help? That's just proof of how little a man can do."

Bing considered. "Maybe you tried when it was too late. Maybe you didn't try hard enough. Anyhow, you tried."

Yates thought that Bing was nearer the truth than he knew, with his naive attempt to goad him into action. In Tolachian's as well as Thorpe's case, he had gone part of the way, and then stopped and said to himself: Somehow, it'll work out. Well, it hadn't. It never did, because you couldn't let things ride you; you had to be in the saddle.

"I promise I'll try to see Thorpe," he said grudgingly.

"Thank you, Lieutenant," said Bing. Yates wished Bing would stop thanking him, but Bing went on, "I know Thorpe isn't your responsibility. Captain Loomis and Major Willoughby are responsible for what happens to the men in this Detachment — but you know how it is. That's why I've come to you. Things are going on that somebody should look into. The night after that bombing at Vallères, Thorpe finally came up to his bed in the tower — beaten up, badly. . . ."

That God-damned night of the party, thought Yates.

"Beaten up," he asked, "by whom?"

"I couldn't make him tell me. He'd get furious when I questioned him, and go into one of his silent acts."

"Well, we can't do anything about that. It's too late, now."

"It's too late for Tolachian," said Bing.

"And Thorpe's still alive. All right, all right! I told you I'd do what I can!"

"Thank you, sir." And he was gone.

Persistent sonofabitch, Yates grinned. Then his face became serious. *Too late!* Just another excuse for himself to do nothing. . . .

Yates called the hospital and insisted that one of the doctors come to the phone. At length a dry, not unkind voice stated that Captain Philipsohn was on the wire. Yes, he knew of the case; Yates shouldn't worry too much; they were trying their best to bring Thorpe back.

"Bring him back?" asked Yates.

"Well," said Captain Philipsohn, "he's in a kind of daze. He's suffered a severe shock. Physically, too, in bad shape. He got a beating, you know?

But don't worry, don't worry, Lieutenant — everything will be all right."

"Can I see him?" Yates asked, not very hopefully.

"I'm sorry, no," the voice was hesitant. "We don't want him disturbed."

Yates made the doctor promise to notify him as soon as Thorpe could have visitors.

"Thanks for your interest," said Captain Philipsohn, "Roger. Out."

For a few minutes after the call, Yates remained motionless in the sleezy Orderly Room chair, fingers flat against his temples. So it wasn't red tape on the hospital's part; Thorpe was actually too sick to see anybody. Yates would have felt better, had the gesture of a few kind words to Thorpe been permitted him — but that was out. And, more important, he wouldn't be able to get Thorpe's side of the story. That left him only the Frenchman who had been buying the food.

Yates left the Detachment's Orderly Room in the St. Cloud. The air outside felt sweet and clean after the sordid atmosphere of the hotel, where the smell of long-departed guests mingled with the more recent smells of soldiers and their equipment. Yates hoped that the Frenchman had not been released. He did not know the customs of the French civil authorities — if they stuck to any since the advent of the new regime.

Loomis drove up, in McGuire's jeep. He greeted Yates effusively; at the moment, the Captain was interested in mending his fences with everybody. Yates decided to use Loomis's expansiveness to borrow his jeep. The Captain was only too glad to oblige. "Take it, by all means!" he said — and ordered McGuire, "I want you to drive the Lieutenant wherever he wants to go!"

McGuire grunted.

"It's not far," Yates said, more to assuage the driver than to please Loomis, "just to the MP station."

Loomis, who was almost at the door of the hotel, stopped. "Where?" he asked. But he had understood perfectly, because he continued, "What do you want at the MP station?"

Yates wished he had kept his mouth shut; Loomis would immediately suspect interference in an affair which he had settled.

"Nothing exciting," Yates said, trying to appear as offhand as possible. "A routine check-up with the Military Police on somebody. . . ."

"Is that so!" said Loomis. He couldn't afford to question further. "Well, good luck!"

"Thanks," said Yates.

The streets, crowded with people, still reminded Yates of the first days in Paris, the honeymoon of liberation. True, the Army had settled down, and the front had moved farther east; yet the war cast a heroic shadow over Paris, the city was still close to the fighting. The sniping had ceased. For the most part, the fascist militiamen had been captured or had given up on realizing that the German chances for return were few. Most of the Parisians who had fought for the freedom of their city had turned in their arms and, more or less grumblingly, returned to the daily drudgery of finding work and something to eat.

He must ask Thérèse what had become of Mantin, Yates thought, and he was glad that he could think of the shy Thérèse, now, under the pressure of the Thorpe business.

He had seen her only once since the Place de la Concorde. Thérèse's first comment had been that she was not interested in love or love-making; that if he had this kind of thing in mind, and she suspected he had, they might as well say *adieu* right then. So he had told her that he was married, that he loved his wife, and that all he wanted was Thérèse's companionship. He had even believed it when he said it. He had felt that the girl had chosen a rather naïve way to avoid appearing cheap and to heighten his eagerness; he didn't take her very seriously, but he didn't mind — when it came to women, he enjoyed a challenge.

He called himself to order. Even though he and Thérèse had done nothing more than take a walk, and sit on the street before one of the cafés, sipping synthetic orange lemonade and somehow feeling good toward one another, it was almost indecent to let his mind play around her, to anticipate the pleasant prospect of being with her, while Thorpe was in the hospital, a mental case among many, and probably with little chance of recovering as long as he was kept there.

Yet — why not? His mind worked that way. Ruth had sometimes marveled at — and objected to — the ease with which he went off chasing a happy dream in the middle of a problem affecting both their lives. She had called it adolescent. He had defended himself by saying that it helped him to preserve his balance. Ruth had replied that these fantasies were a trick by which he continued to lounge in the comfort and peace he loved above all. Someday, she would say, Life will put you in a spot, and I won't be around to bring you your slippers. And he would laugh and tell her he would manage all right.

He had not managed so well. Tolachian was dead, and Thorpe in the psychiatric ward. He was after a girl who had told him that she didn't want him. And as for the war, he certainly had not distinguished himself.

McGuire was saying something.

"What was that?" Yates asked.

McGuire repeated, "Seems I'm running a shuttle service between the hotel and the MP station. . . ."

"Who's been shuttling?"

"Well," said McGuire, "I just came from there when I picked you up."

"Captain Loomis been at the station?"

"Yeah. Sure."

Yates said nothing. But McGuire was in the mood to talk. Since the day he had seen Loomis and the girl celebrating liberation, at the window in the room of the Hotel Scribe, he had restricted his conversations with the Captain to official business. After one or two rebuffs, Loomis had accepted his driver's taciturnity; but he didn't like it and began to complain about dirt in a corner of the jeep and other trifling matters — which indicated to McGuire that Loomis was looking for a ready excuse to get rid of him. McGuire hoped that maybe Yates, who had no vehicle, would try to get the privilege and take him and his jeep.

"I don't know what Captain Loomis was doing there," the driver obligingly explained. "But you can guess — it was about Thorpe."

"I don't think so," said Yates. "Thorpe was transferred to the hospital last night."

"You've got something there," McGuire said airily. And after a while, he added, "That boy was framed."

The very casualness with which the statement was uttered made it biting. McGuire, plain, primitive, faced it without hedging — but he was going too far. Yates said severely, "Listen — I didn't hear that remark. But I'd advise you to be careful of what you say about Captain Loomis or any other officer!"

"Me?" McGuire slowed down the car. "I didn't say a word about the Captain."

Yates started. McGuire was right. McGuire had accused no officer, and especially not Loomis. He, himself, had injected the name. It was one of those slips that told more about the workings of your mind than you liked to admit. "Well, be careful anyhow," Yates said.

McGuire announced, "Here we are, this is the MP station."

Yates stepped inside. The dreariness of the reception room reminded him of the police stations back home; only the tarnished brass spittoon, with mementos of those who had tried hard and failed, was missing.

He asked the Desk Sergeant, a youngish man whose face was peppered with large, black pores, whether he knew where to locate the Frenchman who had been brought in with an American soldier named Thorpe.

"Oh, him!" said the Sergeant, "there's been more trouble about him than the whole matter is worth. Yes, we're going to release him, but I can't let him go until our lieutenant has okayed it, and the lieutenant hasn't come around yet."

"You mean, the Frenchman is here?"

"Sure!"

"Why do you want to let him go?" asked Yates.

"*I* don't want to let him go. To me, it makes no difference one way or another." The Sergeant was impatient within the limits of what he could say to an officer. "But just a few minutes ago, a captain was here — I don't know his name, I can check it though, if you want me to . . ."

"Thanks, I know who he is," Yates assured him hurriedly. "So, what did the Captain want?"

"Well — he said the guy whom we sent to the hospital, this Thorpe, was *non compos mentis,* and so he was dropping all charges, and we didn't need to hold the Frenchman. You know, sir, our can is crowded as anything — we got 'em sleeping in shifts. We're glad to get rid of anyone!"

"I can see your point," laughed Yates. He had come just in time. Perhaps, since he had made up his mind to stop shilly-shallying, and to go ahead with what he considered his duty, things were beginning to break his way.

"Do you mind, Sergeant, if I have a word with this Frenchman before you let him go?"

"Not at all," said the Sergeant. "There's an empty room next door; I'll have him brought in there."

Yates went into the room; it was smaller than the reception room, but just as dreary. The windows had not been washed since the days of the Third Republic, and the paint was peeling off the walls. Yates shoved his fingers under some of the loose paint and began to break it off in slabs. He was furious that Loomis, without waiting for further investigation, had ordered Sourire's release — it was either abject negligence, or worse. He wheeled in surprise when the Frenchman's steps sounded behind him.

Sourire broke into a swell of words.

"Hold it! Hold it!" said Yates. "I understand French, but not that well. Take it slow."

"I can speak English, sir," said Sourire. "I am an educated man. I have been wronged, gravely wronged. Ah, you don't know my name — Sourire, sir, Amédée Sourire."

The stay in jail had not improved Sourire's appearance, but had made it easier for him to give the impression he wanted to achieve. Under the stubbles of his beard, his cheeks were thin. He hunched his narrow shoulders forward, a crestfallen man, a victim of forces beyond his control. Only those moments when Sourire forgot to keep his eyes veiled showed Yates how shrewd, how sly the man was.

"Have you come to let me out?" asked Sourire.

Sourire was accustomed to quick service when he got in trouble, but nobody had come to his aid this time. He'd been in jail for going on twenty-four hours; and Yates was his first visitor. He expected that the Lieutenant, somehow, was the envoy of his influential friends.

Yates acted on impulse. "What makes you think, Monsieur Sourire, that the American Army is going to let you go like that? . . ."

Sourire fell out of his assumed role. "Oh, they aren't?" he said. He straightened, and, with a quick motion of his head, threw back his long, thin hair. "I'm not going to be made the scapegoat — not me!"

Yates watched him silently. He knew those fits of temper. Whenever one of the German prisoners he had dealt with flew into a tantrum, it was a fairly sure thing that the man wanted to avoid answering a question he could foresee. The best policy, then, was to give the fellow a little more rope on which to thresh about.

"Scapegoat!" Yates paraphrased. "You're making yourself interesting."

"What else would you call it?" asked Sourire, accusingly. "But I'm telling you — " He interrupted himself. "Say, who are you anyhow?" he asked.

Yates parried the question. "I have a lot to do with whether you get out of here or not."

"I've done nothing wrong," Sourire said carefully. "I was offered some food to buy, I came to look at it — and then they arrested me. Exactly like the Nazis. And if you think that this jail is any better than a Nazi jail, you should try it yourself."

"Who made the offer?"

"One should think you Americans ought to know what's legal. If you offer to sell your food, that's your business. Why arrest me?"

"Who made the offer?"

"I don't know the name."

"You don't know or you don't want to say?"

"I honestly don't know."

It sounded like the truth; in these transactions, names were rarely given.

"Describe him," Yates demanded.

"He — he was quite tall, lanky, sort of pale, rings under his eyes, what we call *un visage de la nuit.* . . ."

"Hair?"

"Sort of blond." Sourire tried hard to remember Thorpe's features; if you beat up a man, you don't bother to study him at the same time.

Yates thought, It's Thorpe all right. He felt sick at heart. He wasn't inclined to judge a man too harshly for making some money on the side. The great American moral principle was: *If you can get away with it.* . . . Only, if you had liked Thorpe, it was a disappointment.

He turned to the door to call the Desk Sergeant.

"*Mon Lieutenant!*" he heard Sourire say. "Will I get out now?"

"No," lied Yates. "Why should you?" Loomis's order would be carried out soon enough — meanwhile, Yates would let the little crook do some fidgeting.

"Sergeant!" he called.

"*Mon Lieutenant!*" Sourire ran to Yates, shuffled at his side, imploringly, pleadingly. "I want to tell you something!"

The Sergeant stuck his head into the room.

Yates swallowed. Hoarsely, he said, "It's all right, Sergeant. I'm sorry, I'm not quite through."

"Anything I can do for you?" asked the Sergeant.

"No. Not now."

The Sergeant disappeared.

Yates said to Sourire, "I don't have much time. Lying doesn't go well with me. You'd better be sure of what you say."

"Will you let me go if I tell you everything?"

"Yes — if you tell me the whole truth," Yates said blandly.

Sourire let go with one of his oily smiles; his eyes closed.

"Don't you believe me, Sourire?" Yates prodded. "Have you had such bad experiences with the Americans?"

"The worst," said Sourire. "There's a sergeant I was doing business with — he promised he would have me out of jail in no time. And look at me — where am I? Stuck."

"Sergeant Dondolo?"

"Yes."

Yates stepped to the wall and broke off another slab of loose paint. He'd been plain lucky. But you've got to have luck.

"You know the Sergeant Dondolo?" asked Sourire.

"Of course. So it wasn't the man you described who sold you the goods — it was Dondolo?"

"Yes. . . . You're a friend of Dondolo's — "

"I know him well."

"And you're sure you'll see to it that I'm released?"

"Positive."

Sourire stared at him. He stopped being humble. "Because if you don't," he threatened, "I've got friends in high places."

"I don't doubt it. In your business, you get around."

"The Prince will get me out if you don't!" Sourire warned.

"Which prince?"

"Prince Yasha Bereskin." Sourire's hand shot out, his index and middle fingers straight and closely pressed together. "We're like that! A real prince! From Russia — they used to have thousands of princes."

Yasha, Prince Bereskin — somewhere, Yates had heard the name, but he couldn't quite place it.

"Well, if you have all those connections, Sourire — why are you still in jail?"

For a little while, Sourire said nothing, but the muscles of his face worked rapidly. Then he exploded, "Why! Why! How do I know? I've risked my neck for him dozens of times — "

"On the black market?" smiled Yates.

181

"For that man, I've been running people through the front lines!" Sourire caught himself. "I don't do it any more," he added hastily. "I've settled down. I'm strictly in the grocery business."

"What kind of people?" asked Yates. "When? Through what lines?"

"You will let me go now, won't you?" Sourire was worried.

"Answer!"

"German officers. A Colonel Pettinger. That was the day the Allies entered Paris."

"The Prince told you to get the Germans out of here?"

"Sure! I was paid. I hate the Boche. Do you think I would have done it on my own?" Sourire spit. "And I couldn't dump them either. This Pettinger had his pistol at my ribs during the whole trip. What can you do under those circumstances?"

"Very little," said Yates.

"Will you let me go?"

"I think I will," said Yates.

He called the Desk Sergeant and said, "As soon as your lieutenant comes, you can let this Frenchman go. There are no objections on my part," he concluded pompously. A vindictive idea reared up in his mind: If ever Sourire's release was questioned, it would be Loomis who was responsible.

Then he thought of Thorpe, and of Dondolo. What kind of war was this into which he had stumbled!

He lingered at the desk waiting for the Sergeant to return from locking up Sourire. He thumbed through the logbook that lay open on the desk. There it was: *Sourire, Amédée* — and the date — and the address. Sourire had given no home address; the entry read: *Care of Delacroix & Cie.*

It connected. Prince Yasha Bereskin — Delacroix . . . It was the name of the French steel and mining trust. Yates didn't even attempt, for the moment, to sift and order the amount of information he had received from Sourire. Delacroix — this had thrown an entirely new light on it.

Yates left before the Sergeant came back.

Delacroix & Cie. maintained a suite of offices near the Place de l'Opéra.

Major Willoughby fingered the letter in the inner pocket of his blouse, as he studied the dilapidated pillars and stone masonry of the building. It struck him as a rather poor home for a firm which, before the Nazis had settled in Paris, controlled much of the iron ore mining, processing, and steel production of France, and might still be controlling it. That, at least, was the information he had received in the letter from Coster, Bruille, Reagan and Willoughby, Attorneys at Law. In a hand-written postscript, Old Man Coster had said that it was of the greatest importance that Willoughby see Prince Yasha Bereskin of Delacroix personally — if the Prince was still alive—and that he should consider himself as having full power to conclude any preliminary agreement Prince Yasha might care to make with Amalgamated Steel. Coster needed to add no further information; Willoughby was only too conscious of the fact that Amalgamated Steel was the biggest client of CBR & W, and that the war would be won sometime, and that Major Willoughby would revert to being plain Clarence Willoughby, Esq., with the bills and obligations attendant upon his desired standing in life.

Looking at the present headquarters of Delacroix, Willoughby's hopes for an easy future were not particularly high. Not much could be left of the firm. On the other hand, the heaviest concentration of Delacroix mills and mines lay east, in Lorraine. Perhaps they maintained more sumptuous offices there and considered the Paris organization a branch. Or there was a possibility that this was exactly the manner in which Delacroix would conduct their business—they were more conservative in France; they didn't blossom out into steel, glass, and concrete structures resembling the lines on their profit graphs. After all, Willoughby told himself, French industry had been working at peak production for the Germans—and even with all the taxes and levies, they could not have failed to prosper. Why should French accountants have less practice in hiding assets than the accountants elsewhere in the world?

By the time he reached the second floor of the building he began to feel better. An elderly man in a cutaway, looking like a well-bred cross between executive and secretary, led him into the anteroom of Prince Yasha's office.

Yes, the man in the cutaway was glad to say, Prince Yasha was very much alive, and had weathered the inconveniences of the Nazi regime without great damage either to his health or his business.

"Of course," he added pensively, "the years aren't too kind to anyone, life takes its toll—did you know the Prince before the war?"

"No," said Willoughby.

The man in the cutaway regretted that. "He is such a loyal friend, the Prince is. He never forgets anybody."

Through a glass-paneled door, Willoughby could see the whole suite. He recalled the hustle and bustle of offices back home, the doors constantly opening, clerks rushing about with papers, the "silent" typewriters which sounded as if hundreds of open-mouthed people were chewing gum. None of that here.

"Not much business, now?" he asked.

"We are managing," the man in the cutaway smiled. "We are re-establishing our ties. Much of our property is still in German hands—not for long, I trust." This was said with a significant glance at Willoughby's uniform.

The suave manner, the smooth, even voice, soothed Willoughby. The effort to make up his mind on how to approach Prince Yasha had left him disturbed. He was still very much the junior partner; and his rank and position in his Army organization could not change his relation to Coster, or even to Bruille and Reagan. This was the first time they had let him handle a matter of such vital importance to CBR & W. He could almost hear Old Man Coster: *Well — we just have to let Willoughby do it. He's the only man on the spot.*

And what kind of person would this prospect turn out to be — Chairman of the Board of Directors, and a prince at that? Should he address him as Your Highness? It bothered Willoughby, but he couldn't make himself ask the man in the cutaway. Royal Highness. . . . Lah-de-dah! This was no operetta, it was business, Big Business. He should be wearing one of those natty, conservative suits on which Old Man Coster laid such stress — well, his uniform didn't look bad, either; except that it was also a reminder that by no stretch of imagination could his mission be called *in the line of duty*. All right — nobody knew of the visit.

Yasha himself appeared at the door to his private office to greet Willoughby. Very cordially he said, "Please enter, Major — I have been expecting you." His English was as mannered as his French.

The office was large; its walls were paneled with a light-colored, expensive wood which gave the room an atmosphere of warmth and comfort, while maintaining a businesslike air. Yasha, walking beside Willoughby with quick steps, ushered him to a chair near a smoking table, on which decanter and glasses were set.

"Sit down!" said Yasha. "Scotch? I always keep it around; I punctuate the hours with moderate drinking. A day is like a page in a book; one cannot read it without commas and periods."

"How true," smiled Willoughby. He sank back into a deep easy chair. Yasha had reserved for himself a straight-backed chair that gave him the advantage of being able to look down at Willoughby.

"I'll have a drink," said Willoughby. He tried to appraise Yasha's face. Willoughby had the theory, proved in the selection of many a jury, that there were only a limited number of types among humans — thirty-five to forty, at most — and within each type, the characteristics of every person belonging to it were generally the same. Once he had classified a man, Willoughby felt reasonably sure of himself and his tactics.

But Yasha didn't fit into any of the types Willoughby knew. He had elements of several. There seemed to be something too angular about Yasha, too ingrown for a businessman — still Willoughby thought he might be entirely wrong. After all, Yasha was something of an Asiatic.

"You said you expected me," said Willoughby; "did you, really? By the way, you must forgive me — I don't quite know how to address you. We have no family titles in the States, you know. . . ."

Yasha gave a tight-laced laugh. "It is of no consequence, Major. My title is a long-forgotten item. I am a simple citizen of a democracy reborn. My friends call me Prince." He seemed unconscious of the contradiction. "To return to your question — I naturally expected the visit of a representative of your splendid Army. I do not doubt that the various industries which I head can be of considerable help in bringing this war to a victorious conclusion."

Willoughby's mind registered the fact that Yasha had not yet been approached officially. So much to the good.

"I've got a letter for you," said Willoughby, and handed Yasha the thin sheet of air-mail stationery on which Coster had written his introduction. The Prince looked at the signature, and then at Willoughby, but said nothing.

Willoughby felt compelled to explain, "I am, first and foremost, a messenger."

"Quite," said Yasha. He pulled out a pince-nez and pinched it on his long, straight nose.

Willoughby sensed the Prince's similarity to the man in the cutaway who had received him. Well, it was natural that the servant aspire to the appearance of the master — but, in the behavior of the servant and the Prince, there was a kind of snobbery which bordered on arrogance and which began to annoy Willoughby. Coster, of course, would have dealt with it easily. However, Yasha very evidently wanted contact with the American Army, and Willoughby decided to play that for all its worth.

"And now," he said, although Yasha had not finished reading, "having delivered the note, I am no longer a messenger."

"What do you want to be?" asked Yasha without looking up.

"Suppose you tell me?" Willoughby said smoothly. Coster's letter had introduced him in no uncertain terms as a man well-suited to the transaction.

Yasha folded the note carefully and put it into his pocket. "I have had, always, the most cordial relationship with the representatives of Amalgamated. I am happy that we are to resume our friendship."

"Then I take it we can discuss concretely the proposals contained in the note?" Willoughby relaxed. "Personally, Prince, I like to conduct business at leisure. Do you play golf? You do? Good. To plunge into the quagmire of international cartelization in one afternoon — " His pudgy hands became eloquent. "But — these just aren't normal times."

"Not very," said the Prince.

"What we have in mind is simple," Willoughby said. "The destruction brought about by the war, especially in Europe, and the distortion, let me call it, of production, which has come about because our productive capacities are devoted almost exclusively to goods designed for destruction, will result in several years of postwar boom in our industry."

Yasha rested his bony fingers on his chin. "You certainly pursue a long-range policy," he commented.

"We do," said Willoughby, utilizing the Prince's admission to push farther ahead. "Modern industry in America does a bit of planning in its way."

Yasha nodded approval. "The last years have brought increasing difficulties in maintaining fruitful contacts," he observed. "I am pleased to learn that, in America, industry has not been lagging."

Willoughby laughed. "How do you think we ever got into Paris? The war has become a test of strength between the two most advanced, most powerful industrial combines — and we are winning it."

"Quite," said Yasha.

For a moment, Willoughby had forgotten that his vis-à-vis probably wanted to belong to neither of the combines and, having been forced to adhere to the one, having just been liberated from allegiance to it, was now being asked to join the other. He corrected himself. "That doesn't mean that we underestimate the importance, and the future role on the world market, of Delacroix & Cie."

"Ah, the world market!" Yasha said with a longing which somehow missed being fervent. "When last did I hear that phrase?"

"The world market is no phrase," Willoughby countered, "it's our only chance. After the war is won, after we've reconverted — what are we going to do with our productive capacity, our money?"

"Make new wars," said Yasha.

"I don't know," said Willoughby. "I think we'll want at least a period of normal business. We Americans believe in a liberal conception of economy, free enterprise, free trade, unfettered exchange of goods, the greatest benefit for the greatest number of people."

"If it succeeds — fine." The Prince's face remained unchanged. "You must forgive me, Major Willoughby, if I am no longer well-versed in these matters. For the last few years, I have been told what to produce and where to ship it; I had no choice. And, somehow, my thinking has become adjusted to this method of business. Very unpleasant it was, I wish to state, very unpleasant."

"Well," Willoughby said cheerfully, "that's over, now!"

"Thanks to you," said Yasha, with a slight bow. "Now I am occupied with picking up the threads, and tying them, and seeing what has remained and what can be done. I have become very modest."

Willoughby wished Yasha were as modest as all that. "About that future boom, now. . . ." He wanted to turn the conversation back to its original channel.

"Oh yes, the boom — what were we going to do about it?" Yasha asked harmlessly.

Willoughby went straight to the point. "You will understand, Prince, that in the delicate balance of the play of free economic forces, lack of harmony, undue competition, and so on can be damaging not only to your House and to my friends whom I represent, but to the general task of reconstruction which confronts all of us. This, we wish to avoid."

Yasha could not help being amazed at the American. What ability to blend a concern for the welfare of mankind with sound business practice! The Germans were orphans compared to it; they had covered their unashamed bullying and grabbing with love for the Fatherland — lately, they had dropped even that pretense. But the Americans really believed their own liberalism, at least this Major did. A healthy people. They had achieved the perfect amalgam of God, democracy, and the interest rate. Too bad that they were running up against the unashamed decadence of Europe.

However, he was no wet nurse for the budding American hopes. He said, "I am glad to inform you, Major, that our interests coincide."

"Wonderful!" The glow of satisfaction rose from Willoughby's jowls. "Then, I believe, we may come to a preliminary agreement on percentages of production, prices, exports — all the items which make for unhealthy conflicts."

"I should like that very much," said Yasha, "really, I should." He stopped. Regret oozed out of every feature capable of expression in his elongated face.

"What's stopping you?" Willoughby burst out.

The Prince shook his head. "You don't know what has been happening here! In Europe, my kind of man is not master in his own house."

"The Nazis are out!" said Willoughby.

"The Nazis are out," repeated Yasha; "and what kind of people are in? My dear Major Willoughby, yours is the first visit of a man whose good will I can see. Aside from you, who has come to this office? Investigation commissions, control commissions, state industrial commissions, God-knows-what-else commissions. They are persecuting me!"

"All French?"

"Naturally! You have nothing like that in your country, I hope! I dare say I have had more freedom in my affairs under the Germans! I am sorry, sir — I cannot make any commitments at present, and I don't know if ever."

187

"Well," said Willoughby, patiently, "these things will straighten themselves out. It's a new Government; a large part of the country is occupied by the enemy; they're nervous."

Yasha laughed shrilly. "Government!" Then he controlled himself. He pushed away his straight-backed chair and put his right hand on Willoughby's shoulder. "They accuse me of having dealt with the Germans. Well, in the name of God, with whom else could I have dealt? Do they think I liked being told how much I was to profit on every hundred francs expended?"

He withdrew his hand from his guest. "Suppose I had refused," he speculated. "Do you know what that would have meant?"

"Well, what?" said Willoughby.

"The Germans would have taken over all of Delacroix & Cie. What little I was able to save for France, would have been lost. Both Rintelen and the Goering Works tried — literally dozens of times! But that is what these gentlemen with radical manners and patriotic talk do not see — that the true patriot keeps on working, and suffers in silence."

Willoughby didn't believe the Prince had suffered too severely. However, he was much interested in the information that the new French Government was sticking its collective nose into the business of Delacroix. Should it keep its nose there, the firm of Coster, Bruille, Reagan and Willoughby, Attorneys at Law, would be out in the cold; because, in that event, any international arrangement became a matter between Washington and Paris. Had anyone come around to poll him at that moment, Willoughby would have expressed himself strongly in favor of the separation of Business and State.

"As an example," exclaimed Yasha, "it could very well happen that I am told to pack my few belongings and move out — the Government is taking over, and behind this desk, a Commissar will sit. Nationalization! Socialization! These things are always in the air when people still have the feel of rifle butts in their hands. You do not know these dangers in America, and may the merciful God preserve you from them — but I do know, believe me, I do. I have seen them happen in the country of our great ally in the east. I can sense them."

"I don't think anything of the sort need happen," Willoughby said, giving each of his words its proper weight. He hinted that he might be able to make the right man in the Army drop the right word, at the right time, to the right person in the right agency of the new French Government. This Government was dependent on the good graces of the American Army; certainly, the Army had not invaded Europe to bring socialism. One dictatorship was as bad as the other.

"Isn't it your alleged principle," complained Yasha, "not to interfere in the internal affairs of a so-called liberated country?"

"Delacroix & Cie. aren't an internal affair," Willoughby announced positively. "Our Army, I'm sure, will have occasion to call on the facilities of your mills and shops. There's still a war on, isn't there? Nationalization, socialization — I don't give a damn what you call it — in effect, it means a decrease of efficiency which we cannot tolerate in an emergency situation. The Army needs the know-how of Management."

Willoughby wasn't speaking for anybody, but he sounded authoritative. He noticed that the Prince was impressed.

He was about to utilize his advantage, when the telephone rang.

"Pardon me!" Yasha picked up the phone. His first words were, "I told you I didn't want to be interrupted. . . ." Then he listened quietly, glancing several times at Willoughby. Finally, he covered the mouthpiece. "Major — do you know a Lieutenant Yates?"

"Yes," said Willoughby, "sure I know him. What's it about?"

The mention of Yates threw him off his course. Here he had been sailing along smoothly, talking to Yasha with the weight of the Combined Chiefs of Staff, secure in the knowledge that nobody had any idea of his whereabouts, much less of what he was discussing — and there, on the telephone, was Yates! Was he being traced? What was going on?

Willoughby asked, "Is it Yates himself? What does he want?"

"Just one moment," Yasha spoke into the phone, and covered it again. "He wants to come up and see me."

"Ask him what he wants!" Willoughby whispered, although no one but Yasha could possibly hear him.

"About what do you wish to see me?" Then, once more covering the mouthpiece, "He says he cannot explain it over the phone. But he says it is important."

"Well, he just can't see you!" Willoughby tried to hide his exasperation. God knows what Yates wanted from Yasha! It didn't matter — in no case must something as delicate as Willoughby's visit to Delacroix & Cie. become the gossip of the Detachment, the object of questions from DeWitt or Crerar. "You tell him, Prince, that he can't see you!"

"But he is an American officer!" The Prince was doubtful.

"Let him be an Admiral of the Swiss Navy! I'll take care of him. Tell him you're busy."

"All right," shrugged the Prince, "your responsibility!" And into the phone, "I am sorry, sir, I am extremely busy. No, not tomorrow, either. I am in touch with representatives of the United States Army. There is nothing I could possibly discuss with you. Thank you. Good-by."

He hung up. "Tell me, Major — what does your insistent Lieutenant Yates want from me? And why do you prefer that I do not see him?"

Willoughby saw that Yasha was out to use the incident to stall and to put himself into a better bargaining position. He smiled. "My dear Prince,

189

I did not discuss my suggestions with your doorman. I came to you. Similarly, you don't want to deal with my lieutenant, but with me, directly. Isn't that so?"

"Certainly."

"Let us continue, then," Willoughby proposed tersely. "As I said, you don't have to worry about interference from your Government. We'll take care of that."

He has lost some of his flourish, thought Yasha.

Willoughby floundered. "It should be easy to reach an agreement between you and my friends whom I represent. We know very well — we have to take into consideration the present unsettled conditions. . . ."

He sensed that the Prince, also, felt the intrusion of a disturbing element — if Yates was just a doorman, why expend so much effort to keep him away?

As a matter of fact, Yasha was not too much concerned with the incident. He was calculating that trading a few concessions to Willoughby, meaningless until perhaps a year from now, for some immediate American protection, was a good bargain. If Willoughby was not the man to deliver, somebody else would come along. The larger the liberated part of the Delacroix empire, the more bidders there would be; and once the Lorraine mines were returned to him, he'd control the situation. He could afford to wait. The threat of nationalization was not as black as he had painted it. He had used it with purpose — Americans were congenitally averse to radical measures. He could well afford to wait. Of course — if his real deals with the Germans were ever discovered . . . ! *Eh bien!* There is always a loophole.

"Major Willoughby," he said, "I will study your proposal and communicate with you. I am favorably impressed by it."

They parted — the Prince a trifle condescending, Willoughby maintaining a perfectly good front even though it was difficult.

Outside Yasha's office, guarded by the man in the cutaway, sat Yates.

Willoughby had the presence of mind to show pleasant surprise.

The man in the cutaway seized upon the emergence of Willoughby to say, "As you see, *mon Lieutenant,* Prince Yasha *is* in touch with representatives of your Army; there is no further need for him to see you. Why do you not direct your inquiries through the Major?"

Yates disengaged himself from the sofa to which he had been pinned, and gave Willoughby a dry "Hullo, sir!"

Willoughby cleared his throat. "Hiya, Yates! What do you want? Can I help you?"

Back in the days of the landing in Normandy, Yates would have spoken out, expecting a fellow officer to help him. But that was before the surrender at St.-Sulpice, before the Fourth of July leaflet, the death of Tolachian, and Paris. Until he knew where Willoughby stood, until he knew what Willoughby's ties to Yasha were, he was saying nothing.

He suspected that Willoughby had been closeted with Yasha when he phoned. And Yasha would hardly have had the gall to refuse the interview, had he not been backed, coached, or possibly ordered to do so, by Willoughby.

Why?

"Can you help me? Of course, Major. I want to see the Prince. This museum piece in the cutaway has been handing me a line."

"What do you want to see the Prince for?" Were they checking on him? And who? Just Yates — or DeWitt, through Yates?

Yates took the first answer that occurred to him. "I'm conducting a sort of survey — public opinion on the liberation and its prospects. Taking men in all walks of life — workers, tradespeople, even a few Big Shots. The results ought to give us some hints on how to direct the conduct of the troops."

"Never heard of such a survey."

"Didn't it come through channels?" Yates asked innocently.

It *was* possible, Willoughby thought, with misgivings. He was no longer the sole person through whom instructions came down, now that DeWitt had taken over command, now that the Detachment had been enlarged and split up into several groups. . . . But Yates's prompt arrival, in the middle of the steel negotiations, smelled.

"Personally," Yates continued, "I'd like to ask this Prince a few extra questions. . . ."

Willoughby felt increased discomfort. Yates was too good an interrogator to be unleashed on Yasha.

"Where does he get off refusing to see me?" said Yates. "I have the courtesy to come up here, myself, instead of sending a noncom. I figure he's Big Business, so I give him the privilege of looking at a couple of bars. And then he gets on his high horse — he's got no time, he's busy. . . . In my eye!" Yates was getting quite proficient at lying. He had no conscience about it; it was for Thorpe.

"Now, look here." Willoughby put his arm about Yates's shoulder. "We've got to be tactful in this business. I've just been with the man. He's an important guy in this funny country. If I only had known, I would have taken you in with me; we could have killed two birds with one stone. Why doesn't anybody tell me anything?"

Yates said he was sorry.

"Now it looks bad if one after the other of us troops in to pester him.

You've got to consider their feelings, too — right? Pick some other Big Number — how about René Sadault, the automobile man? Or let me submit your questions to the Prince the next time I see him."

Damn it, Yates thought — smothered in kindness. I can't even lie effectively. "Unfortunately, Major," he said, "there is no formal questionnaire. We make up the questions as we go along."

Willoughby took his arm off Yates. "Perhaps there is no survey at all?"

"And if there weren't," Yates said sharply, "why shouldn't I see the Prince?"

"Because it so happens, Lieutenant, that Prince Yasha Bereskin is *my* man. And I wish you to keep that in mind."

"Yes, sir!" said Yates, and followed Willoughby down the stairs.

Outside the Delacroix building, Yates took leave of Willoughby. He crossed the Place de l'Opéra to the Café de la Paix and sat down at one of the tables on the sidewalk.

So Willoughby was mixed up in it, too. It was a whole conspiracy. Thorpe wasn't the centerpiece, but the accidental victim who had got in the way and had to be eliminated. The conspiracy had several levels: Sourire and Dondolo on the lowest; Yasha and Willoughby on the highest; Loomis, somewhere in between. And who was Pettinger and where did he belong?

The waiter brought Yates a cup of *Ersatz* coffee and a small *Ersatz* croissant. Soldiers in every possible uniform, women, civilians, passed by on the street, Army trucks conked their horns, vélo-taxis jingled their bells. Things seemed to blur in front of his eyes. He closed them.

Three little monkeys, he thought, the one holding his hands to his ears, the second to his eyes, the third to his lips. See no evil, hear no evil, speak no evil, Ruth said when she brought the cheap little statuette and placed it on my desk. . . . Not on my desk, it's cluttered up as is, and besides, you're not being subtle! . . . That was when I refused to come out for Spain because I knew damn well Archer Lytell wouldn't like it, and the Board of Trustees at Coulter wouldn't like it, and who was I to buck a man like Lytell, the Head of the Department? So along comes the war. And believe me, Ruth, guys like Willoughby, or even Loomis, are a lot more powerful than an old fogy like Archer Lytell. And Tolachian is dead, and Thorpe's gone insane. . . . Give me your three wise monkeys, my dear — they are right, dead right, one hundred per cent right.

Give them to me. I'll smash them.

8

SHE LED him gently along the quay.

Some of the bookstalls were open again and did a slack business; the dealers, mostly elderly men with an instinct for the transitoriness of anything not printed and bound, leaned against their stalls or against the stone railing of the Seine embankment. Several openly turned their backs on prospective customers and displayed a desultory interest in the anglers who, without visible results, stood close to the level of the water or sat in flat-bottom boats, patiently casting their lines.

A lazy day, far removed from the war. The sun-soaked air seemed to dissolve into tiny specks, and Yates began to understand those French painters who achieved their effect by putting thousands of infinitesimal dabs of color on their canvases.

A great, blessed tiredness came over him, a complete negation of drive. At this hour, he was quite satisfied with things as they were; he was having a holiday from himself. He should have been trying to break through the isolation the hospital had set up around Thorpe, he should have been doing many things other than walking along the Seine quay. But this was better; and a man had the right to be just a small dab of color on the great canvas that was the War, or Paris, or whatever.

He felt that he belonged. And Thérèse belonged. A little hefty around the bosom, her hazel eyes deep-set, a few strands of her soft hair straying and casting trembling shadows over the tender skin of her neck, she fit the mood and the day. He felt tempted to kiss the back of this neck, the slight valley which lived there. But he didn't kiss her because he didn't want to see her withdraw. He wanted no arguments, as when she had indignantly refused the chocolate and the cigarettes he had brought her — *I will take nothing from you; I don't want it; I give you nothing; you give because you want me to give* — he wanted no arguments. He was happy enough just being with her and being led along by her, on this summer day.

Thérèse felt the peace and contentment of the man with her. As long as he made no demands, being with him was healing. Both of them avoided the subjects which would be upsetting to the tender balance of the relationship they had achieved.

Sometimes, Thérèse asked herself why she agreed at all to meet and be with another American, and she found no definite answer. Of this she was certain: In her breast was a lightness all its own, something which wanted to flood her, and which grew stronger and lighter with each approach of the days they were to meet; until it pressed her heart against her ribs and gave her a slight, but not at all disagreeable, pain.

And then, when she did see Yates — once, they had met before the Café de la Paix, and today, at the Pont Neuf — she had to hold her breath, and busy her hands with her pocketbook, so as to rein in her impulse to let him take her into his arms, and keep her there. And she would fight against him and hurt him, and he wouldn't know why — until she quieted down, because her fight was like the foam that beat on the sand.

"I don't like Paris," she said.

"Not even today?" he smiled.

"You don't meet the right kind of people."

"What people do you want to meet?"

"When the country is free again — and when you are gone," she added — "and one can travel again on the railroads, I am going to leave Paris and settle in some small town in the provinces."

"Why?"

"That is where you meet the right kind of people. Honest, hard-working. Young men who work to start businesses of their own, or who have one. I don't want an exciting life. I have had my fill of excitement. I want to grow old quietly, and in the evenings I am going to sit before the door of my own house and watch the sun go down without regret because I know it is going to rise again, tomorrow."

"And children and cooking and the same faces every day?"

"Children, cooking, the same faces — yes!" she said obstinately.

"And how do I fit into the picture?" he asked.

"I won't even think of you. Do you think I have you on my mind when you are not with me? Oh, I control myself. And you are easily controlled. No, don't touch me, please, I don't like it."

"How do you control your feelings?"

She did not answer. Just rip off the dressing and let the wound feel its rawness. Just close your eyes to recall the picture of Call-Me-Vic bending over you, reeking of sweat and liquor, his hands at you, and then the feel of his body, tearing you.

Of course, she was not fair to Yates. But who had asked him to attach himself to her? She, perhaps? Who had ever been fair to her? She was punishing Yates for what the other man had done. No, it was not fair to Yates — but it was fair in terms of a general straightening of accounts. He was a man, and an American, and it had to be. Even if it hurt her, it had to be. And the kinder he was, the more it hurt her, the better it healed her — his kindness healed her, and his need for her healed her, both.

"Thérèse," he said, "I won't be here forever."

"I didn't expect you would," she said pertly, though she felt the quick sinking of her heart. "Soldiers are here one day, gone tomorrow. A woman who hangs her heart on a soldier is a fool."

"Before I go back to war, before you go to the provinces to sit before your house in the evenings, we could be very happy," he said.

"Fine kind of happiness," she answered. "And afterwards you are left with the feel of the man in your hands, on your lips, and you know that you will never feel him again."

She had betrayed herself, *pauvre petite,* and he used his advantage. "How would *you* know! . . ." he said.

She spoke softly, "I thought how it would feel if we loved one another and you left me."

It had never occurred to him. He wanted this girl, with every gland he wanted her. And he was kind to her, he did not insist, he was a scholar, an officer, and a gentleman; but he had never thought how it would feel if we loved one another — and then parted — and all that remained would be the feel of a hand once touched. Had he left behind even that much with Ruth? He knew why she had kissed him when she did, why she had laughed, and why she had wept. He had permitted neither her kiss nor her laughter nor her tears to penetrate too deeply — why? He had gone through life feeling only his own feelings; analyzing, perhaps, the other person's feelings, but never letting the other's feelings intrude on his own. Was he afraid that a genuine emotion would tear him out of his expensively bought security? But what about afterwards, when there was no more security, when he knew he would have to go overseas, into the invasion? Why then?

There must be an alliance between women all over the world, he thought. And he resented it. They acted and spoke for each other, and defended each other, against men. Thérèse, so different from Ruth, blended into her.

"You see, my little Thérèse, I don't know how it feels when a man leaves his woman. I'm a very poor man, that way. I left my wife to go to war. And what you said about your hands being empty . . . It gave me the first inkling of what she might have felt and might be feeling now."

Unnatural people, these Americans — the one, completely without restraint, the other, caught up by memory and bad conscience.

"If I wanted you, I would take you," she said, startling him.

The other woman was so far away that she took nothing which would have deprived the other of possession; his wife did not possess the man who walked with her, Thérèse, now, in summer, here, in Paris.

"If I had been your wife," she went on, "I would not have let you go to war. . . ."

"How could you have stopped me?" He smiled at her bravado.

"I don't know. Perhaps I would have put something into your food to give you ulcers. Women are too weak. They do not hold on to their men, not strongly enough — if it were otherwise, there would be no wars, be-cause not enough men would be able to go. If I loved a man, I would hold him; or if I couldn't, I would follow him to the end of the world."

It was a nice romantic idea. Yates was half-attracted, half-repelled by it — women wanting to possess their men so desperately.

"You want to keep your man away from war," he said, "and you, your-self, went to the barricade?"

"That is different," she answered, "you know nothing about women. You didn't know how your wife felt when you went away from her. Her feelings left you unmoved."

It wasn't that, he thought. He had loved Ruth, and he loved her now. He was not an egotist; other people did matter to him if only there was space for them in his mind that was mostly crowded with himself.

"No, Thérèse," he said, "you are wrong. It was just that I was so con-cerned with myself."

"You were afraid of the war?" she asked, compassionately. It must be terrible for a man to have to go and not know if he would be killed, or wounded — and yet, always they went.

"I was afraid," he admitted.

She took his hand. They stopped walking and she held on to his hand as if it were all of him, as if holding it would protect him.

"Don't worry," he said. "I'm over it. I was lucky. There are other things which are much worse."

He thought of Thorpe. The fear that had been his was also Thorpe's fear — a fear as unpredictable as a bullet. Whom would it hit: the man next to you, or you?

"Yes, there are worse things," she confirmed, and her hand left Yates's. "You want to forget them, but you can't. Always, they come back, even at the most beautiful moments."

She had been taking him literally; she was referring to something defi-nite. "What things?" he asked. "What disturbs you?"

"Something ugly. I don't want to talk about it."

"Worse than fear," he said, "is the inability to handle it. It's very com-plicated." He didn't know how far her understanding went.

"I like you ever so much," she said, her voice growing husky. "You must have confidence in me."

"I have."

"You are not happy. Is it because you must leave here to fight again? Is it that you don't like what you are doing? Are the men with you not good to you?"

"There are certain things I must take care of, and I'm afraid of starting them. There are certain people who are bad, and I'm afraid of tackling them."

"Like the Boches?"

"Well — similar."

"You will punish them," she said with certainty. She half wished she could tell Yates of what had been done to her, so that he could go out and punish Loomis. But the shame of it was so great that it would never be spoken. "You will punish them," she repeated with relish. She could see them brought to justice by Yates.

"It isn't so simple," he said.

"Why not?" she asked. "When you make up your mind, it is simple. I found that out. When the people here made up their minds to get rid of the Boches, they got together and did it. I, too, didn't know it was that simple — but one day, I found myself behind the barricade, with Mantin. All you need do is to forget about yourself."

What could he say? That it took three armies to land in Normandy, to fight great battles, to drive all the way to the outskirts of Paris, before she could ever get behind her barricade with any chance of success? Even if he said it, she would not really believe it, because she saw only herself and her barricade, and that was a great, unforgettable moment in her life.

"I will try," he said. He could not get away from this thing. It was burned into his flesh. He had accepted the doctor's refusal to let him see Thorpe because he was afraid of seeing Thorpe. He had accepted Willoughby's refusal to let him see Yasha because he was afraid of an open conflict he could not avoid anyhow.

Again, he had the sensation of Ruth and Thérèse blending into one. Ruth, like Thérèse, had wanted to tie him to what she thought were his responsibilities, while he had clung to the comfort of his study. They were all the same, these women — or was it that he was still the same, and that any woman, any person concerned about him, could react toward him only this one way?

"Your thoughts have gone away from me," she said.

Poor Thérèse! She did not know that she was sending him off into a kind of war.

"I must go now," he said, "to do one of the things I have to do. Will you kiss me *au revoir?*"

"No," she smiled, "no rewards."

He did not insist.

The General Hospital was in a drab building near the outskirts of Paris. It looked more like a prison than a retreat where people were to be nursed back to health. Yates, walking through its corridors, could see that the Army had taken over the installation from the Germans; the walls were still decorated with the labored *Strength through Joy* cheerfulness which operated on the theory that a flowerpot could make you forget your stomach, and a picture postal card, your wife. The most encouraging statements of the leaders, lettered in an ornate but precise Old German script and framed by garlands of poison-green oak leaves, adorned the whitewashed expanse of hall. Between the verbiage were simple, colorful murals showing the more humorous side of the German soldier's life, his efforts at learning the goose step, his troubles with his straw mattress, and others which reminded Yates of Gasoline Alley adjusted to the war effort.

He found Captain Philipsohn in a little room whose door carried a penciled sign PSYCHIATRY.

Philipsohn was a small man with troubled, sympathetic dark eyes and wavy hair which he stroked back, every few seconds, with a nervous, patting motion of his hand. Yes, he remembered Lieutenant Yates — hadn't Yates called him in reference to a patient named Thorpe? Very tough case, that; yes, indeed. . . .

Yates asked if the state of the patient had sufficiently improved so that he could be visited.

"I'm afraid not," said Captain Philipsohn, casting an almost professional look at Yates. Yates moved uneasily on the small, collapsible chair the doctor had offered him.

"Look at it this way," said Philipsohn. "You have an open wound. Naturally, you put a dressing on it to keep out dirt, and foreign bodies, bugs, and what have you. A boy like Thorpe is one great open wound. We hope it will heal in time," he added, seeing Yates start.

"I've got to see him," Yates said stubbornly.

From a pile of papers on his crammed field desk, the doctor took a small file. "I know very little about the case — suppose you tell me what you know, Lieutenant."

"Hasn't Thorpe told you?"

"Thorpe doesn't talk," Philipsohn said matter-of-factly, "at least, he doesn't talk sense."

"Is it that bad?" Yates felt his heart constrict.

Captain Philipsohn disregarded the question. "I've tried to get some information from the officer on whose orders the boy was brought here — "

"Captain Loomis?"

"Yes, Loomis. But he didn't seem to know much, or, perhaps he didn't want to say much."

A quick glance from Yates: What do you suspect?

Philipsohn, however, changed the subject immediately. He said: "It was unfortunate that the patient was brought in during the evening. I wasn't here. The doctor who looked at him at the time, and who patched up the cuts and the bruises on Thorpe's head and face, reported that the patient seemed somewhat disturbed, but otherwise all right. They kept him in the ward. In the middle of the night, he started raving and throwing anything he could grab and shouting about fascism, about a conspiracy. The doctor on duty, again another man, had him transferred to a separate room."

"Kind of solitary?" asked Yates.

"Kind of," sighed Philipsohn. "These things are all sad, Lieutenant. We're dealing with the shadowy side of life, don't forget that."

"When did *you* get to him?"

"They didn't call me," said Philipsohn. And then, in defense of his colleagues, "Why should they? I couldn't have done any more than they did — quiet him down with a hypo. In the morning, he was in his present condition, and he hasn't come out of it."

"Such cases frequent?"

"Fairly."

"Someone should have talked to him as soon as he was brought in here!" Yates was embittered.

Philipsohn came back sharply, "Someone should have done something for him before he was ever taken to the MP station! Someone should have been at the MP station, who had some understanding of the boy's problems! Someone should have prevented the beating he got, I don't know where! Someone should! Someone should! Stop throwing around your recriminations, Lieutenant — they'll never get us anywhere." He stopped ranting and said with sudden control, "You must leave yourself out of the picture entirely."

Yates took the slap.

Philipsohn looked at him. "Let's understand each other, Lieutenant. We both want to help the patient. But I am handicapped because I don't know enough of his background. I know his service record — North Africa, a wound. No treatment for combat fatigue there — but combat fatigue was very possible, it is often not diagnosed. Then, the arrest and the beating — perhaps, the order of events was reversed. Then the outbreak at night, here, in the ward. What does it add up to? Nothing new. Nothing we haven't seen again and again, nothing that might not happen to anyone in this war. But why the cry against fascism? It is still a foreign word in our national make-up — it is, let us say, something strictly on the rational level. The soldier Thorpe, who could only have a superficial knowledge of fascism — he is American-born, isn't he? — has transferred some original trauma from the depth of his subconscious into the surface idea of fascism. It is a process of identification. But then other elements enter. Anything he doesn't like, anything he can't master, is shoved under the same heading until the thing rises so big that it haunts him and drives him into this —

this stupor, which, you must understand, Lieutenant, is nothing but his defense against what troubled him originally. A defense, a refuge. Do you follow me?"

"Yes," said Yates, "something like sleep?"

"Approximately."

Philipsohn wanted to go further, but Yates interrupted him. "If the body, or the mind, adopts this tactic of defense, maybe it's better to let him sleep out this strange sleep?"

"They don't wake up from it," smiled Philipsohn. "In the second place, there are certain defenses we cannot permit. A man steals a hundred dollars. It's his defense against poverty, it is probably easier than finding a job and working until he's made a hundred bucks. We still clap him into jail."

"I don't see the parallel."

"An acute neurosis, or a psychosis, Lieutenant, is not considered a legitimate way out. The illness eliminates the man as a useful member of society — in this case, as a soldier who can be shot at. I am under the same discipline as my colleague who sews up the shrapnel hole in a man's body. After our patient, Thorpe, was wounded in North Africa, he was patched up again so that he could be exposed again to the same thing."

"Kind of vicious circle?" Yates's conception of medicine had been different. To aid, to heal a sick or wounded man, was as much a human obligation as what he had set out to do. It was all tied up in one: Thorpe's reaching out for him, in Normandy, when the madness was encroaching on the boy; his own need to see him healed; his own fears; the fear of the "Fascism" that had wrought the destruction in Thorpe's mind; and war itself.

"Sure it's a vicious circle," said Philipsohn. "It's war."

"Well, to me it makes no difference, Captain, why *you* want to get him well. Professional ethics, military necessity . . . Just do it!"

"Have you any particular reason?" Philipsohn asked.

Yates thought awhile. Then he said, "An injustice has been done. And to correct it we need a fully responsible, mentally sound Thorpe. As a witness."

The doctor's eyes questioned.

"It may sound trifling to you," Yates said. "Thorpe is being blamed for a certain black market transaction. I got hold of a Frenchman who admitted it wasn't Thorpe at all, but the very American sergeant who is accusing Thorpe. The Frenchman was let go; I've been unable to find him again. So, you see, I need Thorpe."

"Stickler for justice?" said Philipsohn.

"Never thought I would be!" Yates frowned. "But you've got to start sometime."

Captain Philipsohn nervously patted his hair. "You'll get nowhere."

"I promised," Yates insisted, "mostly to myself."

Philipsohn began to like Yates. "What is your relationship to the patient?" he asked, professionally.

"Rather an odd one," Yates said slowly. "I'm one of the officers in the Detachment to which Thorpe belongs. One night back in Normandy, we had a sort of party — officers mostly, and a woman, an American newspaper reporter. In the middle of it, Thorpe appeared — he broke in, you might say, in a state of great excitement. He didn't speak too coherently, and I don't remember exactly what he said — but the gist of it was that the fascists were all over, in our own ranks, too; kind of conspiracy, I suppose; and that we were losing the war even if we were winning it . . ."

"Was that the first time you heard him speak that way?" said Philipsohn.

"Yes. He sounded crazy. Everything about him was like — like a man who tells you that he's seeing white mice, and watch out, there's one right in your pocket."

"And you, Lieutenant, where do you come in?"

"He came to *me* for help. Picked on me. He said that people like himself and me, we'd be the — victims."

"What did you do?"

"Nothing."

"I see," said Philipsohn. He looked at Yates's hands, at the warts.

Yates tried to hide them. "They're psychosomatic," he said, apologetically.

"I see," Philipsohn said again. "So — what happened?"

"The Sergeant of the Guard was called, and Thorpe was led off. Then the Nazis came over and bombed us. The man who slept next to him reported to me, much later, that Thorpe went to bed that night beaten-up."

"Do you know who did it?"

"Thorpe never spoke about it. By the way — " the scene had come sharply alive to Yates — "the Sergeant of the Guard, that night, was the same man who is now accusing Thorpe of the black market deal."

"And you didn't talk to Thorpe after he was led away from the party? You just left him to himself?"

"I tried. I tried too late." Yates saw that Philipsohn again was looking at his warts. "Go ahead! Say it! Tell me what you think I am!"

"Don't be childish. The patient's probably been out in left field since North Africa. I'll tell you, Lieutenant — the more I see of the war and what it does to people, the less I know about the border line between the sane and the insane. That goes for the men who do the fighting and for the others. Have you ever dreamed of killing somebody? You don't need to dream it any more — you can do it! Ever dreamed of stealing, whoring? What do you want to dream it for? Do it! Now take Thorpe. He's had this fear — and he's been having it in this fantastic war atmosphere, in which the most insane dream becomes reality!"

Yates didn't want to follow Philipsohn. He had the distinct feeling that the doctor, himself, had inherited a touch of his patients.

"However," said Philipsohn, "that's neither here nor there. I have decided that I'll let you see your man Thorpe."

"Thank you."

"You want to know why, don't you? I have a thin hope, Lieutenant — mind you, nothing but a thin hope — that through you, the patient can find the bridge back to our side of life. For reasons of his own, Thorpe saw in you a kindred soul at one time in his trouble. If we can re-create that feeling, or a part of it . . ."

"Now?"

Now that he was to face Thorpe, or rather, what he had permitted Thorpe to become, Yates would almost have welcomed a refusal from the doctor. He sensed that seeing Thorpe would be a milestone in his life, crucial and decisive, and he shied away from it.

"Now!" said Captain Philipsohn. It was like a command.

Yates fought it. "I'm not your patient!" he said.

Philipsohn rose and waited for Yates to get out of his chair and follow him.

Behind him, Yates heard the door fall into its lock. After a few seconds, his eyes grew accustomed to the semidarkness; the only window of the room was heavily curtained, but in such a way that no one on the inside could get at the hangings.

The room was full of an offensive smell, a mixture of feces and urine, sweat and vomit. The smell persisted, although the bare room, apparently, was kept clean. The only thing resembling furniture was a rack, which probably served as a bed, but which now was pulled up and screwed to the wall.

Yates hoped that, after a while, the smell would lose its pungency. It didn't. He had to overcome a squeamishness in his stomach.

Because the room was so bare, it looked larger than it was, but not large enough to eliminate the sense of being shut in, a finality, something inescapable. Yates had expected friendly, cheerful surroundings; a well mind would grow sick in here, he thought, and he was determined to bring that point up with Philipsohn.

Somebody coughed.

It was quite an ordinary cough, like that of a man who wanted to bring attention to himself and open a conversation.

Yates shrank together just because this cough sounded so normal, so without pretense. He had seen Thorpe. He had forced his eyes away from Thorpe, to the inspection of wall, window, rack, and floor; he had forced them because of the morbid attraction of the heap of man sitting, or cowering, in the dead center of the room. You can't stare at him, he thought; hunchbacks mind being stared at, and men with bulbous noses. He didn't want to realize that Thorpe, probably, was beyond the stage where he was able to object to anything.

"Hello, Thorpe!" he said.

This had come out nicely; he had managed to give his voice a casual tone.

"Hello, Thorpe — how are you? They feeding you all right?"

He now could distinguish head and trunk; Thorpe's face began to stand out, whitish. The skull had been shorn. It was swollen in one place, and the pale mouth seemed swollen, too.

A slight change came over the face. The eyes were now open, but not alive; they had a dull gleam, like amber.

The head was raised slowly and came to rest in an oblique position. It was trying to hear, to understand. From somewhere a sound had come, touching a familiar chord; but was there a sounding board left, or had it all been smashed?

Yates gabbed on. "Everything is all right. Soon we'll come to get you out of here. You're getting better, much better. The boys want me to bring you their regards — everybody, Bing and Clements, Abramovici, everybody. . . ."

It moved its hands. They were like a blind man's hands — long, sensitive; they were trying to feel the world, but all they touched was the thick, foul air of the room.

The gesture cut into Yates's heart.

"Thorpe!" he cried, "do you hear me, Thorpe?"

The swollen lips moved. The face became more alive. The amber went out of the eyes and the pupils became distinct.

"Say something, Thorpe!" Yates's voice lost all timbre in its urging. "Do you recognize me? It's me — Yates — "

All of his will went into these words. It was like sending and receiving. He must strengthen the transmitter to reach the weak, poor, battered receiver.

"Yates!" Thorpe said.

He had got through! From now on, everything would be easier. The important thing was not to lose the contact.

"Of course — it's me! You knew I would come to see you, didn't you?"

It didn't matter what he was saying, as long as he kept talking, as long as he tied down Thorpe's attention and guided him along the thread he had thrown to him.

"You are Yates . . . ?"

"Certainly I'm Yates!" Poor guy, he isn't sure yet. But I'll get him around. "I've come to visit you. You're not so well, you've gone through a lot, but you're getting better. **You're** getting better all the time."

"You can't be Yates."

"Now don't be . . ." Foolish, he had wanted to say. "Now look at me, closely! Open your eyes. Take your hands, feel me! I'm Yates! I'm your friend."

"Uh-huh."

"You see! You recognize me. Now, I've brought you something." He hadn't brought anything. He had come directly from Thérèse to the hospital, on the spur of the moment. Frantically, he tried to think of something he could give Thorpe.

"A handkerchief. I've brought you a handkerchief. Thought you might want one," he added, helplessly.

Yates placed the handkerchief before Thorpe and waited for him to pick it up.

"Yates is dead."

For a moment, Yates was dumbfounded. The vagueness with which Thorpe had been speaking had given way to something else. That he, Yates, was dead, came out firmly, positively.

Yates tried to laugh. "Nonsense! Who told you that? I'm not dead, I'm right here with you. Can't you see me? Feel me!"

He took Thorpe's hand and brought it to his sleeve. He remembered that a long time ago, Thorpe had grasped those sleeves, held on to them.

The hand fell back. The hand did not believe.

"Yates is dead. Killed. Beaten to death. You aren't Yates."

"What have they done to you?" What a question! Had he not helped? He had stood by. He was as guilty as the others.

"The uniform!" said Thorpe. He began to laugh, slyly. "You can't trick me. I know. I won't say a word. Yates is dead."

Could be, thought Yates. Yates is dead, the Yates who lived in that boy's mind.

That was the funny thing about it: the Yates of Thorpe's imagination had never lived! But he must have been something, that Yates — a man to whom Thorpe could cling in his despair, a man of integrity, courage, loyalty, and understanding — such a great person, that Yates, that his failing Thorpe could only be explained by his death.

"You're wrong," said Yates. "Yates isn't dead. He's alive!"

He felt the words come back from the walls, hollow.

"Listen to me, Thorpe!" he said desperately, "Yates is alive!"

He saw that the listening was again in Thorpe, but the boy was clearly receding into himself, sinking back into the great indifference whence he had come.

Thorpe began to slobber. A thread of spittle developed and hung down from the left corner of his mouth.

9

THE BAR was not as crowded after dinner as it would be later. Colonel De-Witt, who was a heavy eater and, in general, no scorner of worldly joys, liked this time for the one or two drinks that helped along his digestion. He lounged at a small table in the corner, Crerar's back all but screening him from casual strollers into the bar.

At first glance, DeWitt appeared a most plain man. His uniform was simple regulation; he didn't go in for brass and ribbons. His square features showed a certain integration of desires, effort, and fulfillment. His lips were surprisingly full for a man of his age; he had quick, observant eyes. Crerar, who had worked with him in England, had an idea that the outward serenity of the man was the camouflage of a searching mind that had wrestled for each of its opinions. In War Department circles, some called DeWitt an "odd egg," but hastened to explain that he really wasn't — he was a fairly good mixer, a conscientious officer, but with a conspicuous lack of the give that would have made him one of the fellows.

Once, on Grosvenor Square in London, in the hustle of the many uniformed Americans who had taken over the adjacent buildings in preparation for the invasion, DeWitt had turned to Crerar and said, "I've seen all this before, in the previous war. I was young then. I found it quite exciting, but stupid, and a waste. And here I am again. . . ."

"What does that prove?" Crerar had asked.

With an undertone of disappointment, DeWitt had replied, "I'd hoped people were more intelligent."

Of course they weren't, in Crerar's opinion. And, if he had felt that way in London, Crerar had no reason to change his opinion now, after his return from his despoiled farm north of Paris. The conversation during dinner had been revolving about his trip — Crerar saying, "I should never have gone there, should have kept it in the back of my mind as it was, or as I had seen it — " and DeWitt consoling him, "The land is there and the buildings. Start over again! You've got the money! I'm from the New England coast, where storm and flood ruin whole villages. They're always built up again."

"I'm not going to do a damned thing," sulked Crerar. "They cut down the trees, you know, for their artillery. After they cut them all down, they didn't even fire a single shot; they just moved out."

"Plant other trees," DeWitt said patiently.

"Have you any idea how long it takes for trees to grow? If I planted them today, I'd be a dead man before they gave a decent shade."

DeWitt understood. With the farm, a part of Crerar's life had gone, irretrievably; and Crerar was painfully conscious of it.

Crerar went on, "The leaves of those trees used to cast very fine shadows. It's got something to do with the atmosphere, you know? My wife would sit under a tree and read, or play with her kitten."

"What became of Plotz?" DeWitt asked suddenly.

"I left him on the farm," smiled Crerar. "Left him all alone, except for the mice and the rats. Anyhow, he'd grown too big to cart around."

DeWitt drank, to avoid looking at him. He and Crerar must be about the same age. He knew these crises — they happened each time a period came to its close and the gate banged shut behind you. A son married — you got drunk and sensed that life was on the wane. The wife came home with her hair dyed Titian red — you realized that it had turned gray. You made your adjustments, you made a point of being useful, you insisted on going overseas with the younger men.

"It isn't me!" said Crerar. "Hell, what do I care! But Eve — I won't be able to take her back to the farm."

That was the difference, thought DeWitt: Crerar had a young wife. "If she loves you," he said, "she'll love you anywhere. You don't have to have the trees."

"I suppose you would have had them chopped down, too!" Crerar snapped.

"If I needed them for a gun position — sure!" DeWitt was intentionally hard. If Crerar brought home to his Eve the whole beauty of France and shed it over her, it would not necessarily make her happy. Just because the man was worried about her, he conjured up his own destruction.

DeWitt changed the subject. "Farrish was in Paris, last night. I saw him, but I didn't want to talk to him." He shook his head. "Raging mad."

"Isn't he always?" Crerar thought of the General's visit to his tent in Normandy, and of Rambouillet — Farrish moving in, spreading himself, taking over.

"I know what the retreat must have meant to him."

"Retreat?" asked Crerar.

"It was a retreat. After almost taking Paris, after sweeping across France, to have to stop at Metz and pull back though you know there is hardly any organized resistance in front of you — because the last drop of gas in your tanks is burned out."

"But the gasoline is coming in! What about the pipeline we're building?"

DeWitt said, with a trace of bitterness, "It's coming in. And it's being sold, right here in Paris."

"A few cans, yes. I've seen it myself, right on the Champs-Élysées. An

Army truck, loaded up with cans of gas. Then it stopped and the driver handed a couple of them to some civilian."

"Why didn't you step in? You're a simulated lieutenant colonel!" De-Witt scrutinized his glass, with disgust. "Everybody talks about the black market, nobody does anything about it."

Crerar resented the reproof. If these Army people couldn't hold their own men in line, they should shut up.

DeWitt's laugh was unpleasant. "It's an attitude," he said after a while. "A few cans here, a few cans there. By the time the supplies reach the front, they're half gone. I tell you what it is: We can't take success. The same men I've seen working like sonsofbitches when the stuff was flying around — look at them now, watch 'em swagger, throwing their weight around! *Nobody can touch us, we're tough!* Sometimes I'm afraid of what will happen if and when we win the war."

"We're a young nation," smiled Crerar.

"But it's a grown-up world. I never allowed my son the excuse of being young and not knowing better. I told him: You have all your senses and a mouth to ask questions. I'm beating your pants off because you were too lazy to make use of the faculties God gave you."

Loomis and Crabtrees came into the bar. Loomis headed for the Colonel's table, but DeWitt didn't look up; Loomis hesitated and finally swerved to the right and found place for himself and Crabtrees at the opposite end of the room.

The four poker players who had begun their game on the LST coming across the Channel entered and marched through the room in single file, headed by the radio officer. Loomis waved to them, but they marched on, sat down at another table, ordered Scotch and cards, and proceeded to shift piles of invasion francs from one side of the table to the other.

Loomis had begun to crave company. He had Crabtrees; but Crabtrees didn't count. He felt ostracized, though nothing had occurred to make him seek the comfort of being accepted. No repercussions had come from Dondolo, Sourire, the MP's, or the hospital. He wished he could do something for Thorpe.

"What *is* the matter with you?" asked Crabtrees. "Something wrong with your stomach?"

"Leave me alone," said Loomis. "Go get me a cognac — a large one. The service here stinks."

There were people who blamed him for Tolachian's death; now, he supposed, there'd be others who'd try to hang Thorpe's going nuts on him, too. Why on him? Why not, for instance, on Willoughby? Willoughby had luck. With everything; even with the Fourth of July leaflet, Willoughby had come out on top. DeWitt himself had said that it was a neat job, conveniently forgetting that SHAEF had been left out of the picture. Willoughby never ran into trouble.

Crabtrees returned with the cognac.

Loomis gulped it down. "I'm sick and tired of the war," he said moodily. "Nothing good can come of it."

Crabtrees stared at him. "What's wrong with the war? You've been having a wonderful time in Paris! Now take that girl — "

"What girl?"

"The one you never gave me a chance at. All right, I was drunk. Didn't you have fun?"

The question hurt Loomis. The incident with Thérèse rushed back at him, the memory joining and aligning itself with his other self-reproaches.

"Some fun!" His voice was despondent. He could see the girl's face, it was flat and distorted, her eyes protruding in her effort to shake him loose. But he had held on to her.

Crabtrees wanted details.

Loomis fended him off with generalities. He became more and more restless; he had the uncanny feeling that the Colonel and Crerar were discussing him. He wished he could get up the courage to go to their table and force himself on them, or at least hear what they were saying.

He saw Yates come into the bar.

He waved at him as he had waved at the poker players. Yates went directly to the Colonel's table.

"Shut up!" Loomis exclaimed as Crabtrees asked still another question about his success with Thérèse. But Crabtrees's offended silence was no help against the steady bidding of the poker players, the convivial laughing and shouting of the drinkers, and the methodical clink of the glasses as the bartender washed them, wiped them dry, and replaced them on the shelves.

DeWitt looked up at Yates not as if he were an intruder, but with curiosity. The Lieutenant never had sought his company — probably didn't want it said he was currying favor.

"Sit down, Yates," he said. "How's everything?"

"I've just been at the General Hospital visiting one of our men," Yates began.

He was surprised at the ease of this beginning. He had been priming himself for it ever since leaving Thorpe's cell. What could he prove? He had few facts and many suspicions; and DeWitt would accept no speculations. There had been a moment when the difficulties seemed so overwhelming that he considered dropping the whole thing. Thorpe was beyond the realm of hope. But he had shoved the idea aside; it was so typical of him to think of it at all.

The Colonel was waiting.

"The man will be Section Eight — if he ever gets well enough for that," Yates resumed.

"Thorpe?" asked Crerar. "I heard of it. That was the boy who suddenly appeared at that party Willoughby gave at Château Vallères?"

Yates nodded. "It was my first visit to an institution like that. It threw me. And I'd rather not talk about it. It's the history of the case which interested me, sir. I've looked into it in my spare time, and I've established certain angles." He looked straight at DeWitt. "I thought I'd better let you know them, too, Colonel."

DeWitt listened to the story of Thorpe and Sourire. Gradually, his face became drawn. "Why don't you let the situation be handled by the men whose job it is?" he grumbled. "What's your special interest in Thorpe, Lieutenant?"

Yates wanted to state that justice is the job of everybody. But DeWitt was old-fashioned Army. Carefully, Yates said, "At that party Mr. Crerar mentioned, Thorpe directed himself to me — I don't know why. Perhaps he thought I could help him out of his trouble. That kind of appeal gives you an obligation, doesn't it?"

DeWitt seemed satisfied. "Is this Sourire still in the MP jail?"

"I'm afraid not, sir. I got hold of him just in time. Captain Loomis had agreed to Sourire's release, and the MP's said their jail was crowded and they were glad to get rid of him."

"Then we ought to grill Dondolo," said Crerar.

"And if he denies it?" the Colonel asked. "Were there any other witnesses?"

"No."

"So we can get only one story — Dondolo's."

"There's another aspect," countered Yates. He felt more certain of his tactics, since DeWitt seemed to be thinking in terms of an investigation. "I found out that Sourire wasn't working entirely on his own. He had a boss, for whom he had done several jobs — one of them was getting some German officers out of Paris, by truck, at the time we were entering the city."

Crerar whistled softly.

Yates continued. "The senior of those Germans was a Lieutenant Colonel Pettinger. I've checked with the Order of Battle people at G-2. They know the name. He's an SS man; but that's about all I could get from that source."

"This is getting interesting!" said Crerar. "If Thorpe had to go insane to protect Pettinger. . . ."

"Don't jump to conclusions!" DeWitt said angrily. "The black market operation might be something Sourire ran on the side. Who's the boss?"

"A Prince Yasha Bereskin."

"Prince Yasha!" exclaimed Crerar.

"You know him?" Yates asked.

"Know his name."

"All right, all right!" DeWitt tried to keep the conversation in hand. "Tell me some more about this Prince. What's his racket?"

"He has no racket," said Crerar. "He's Chairman of the Board of Directors of Delacroix; and Delacroix, in France, means steel."

"Sounds incredible," said DeWitt. He had a healthy respect for Big Business — not that he lacked the courage to treat it on his own terms, if that was necessary for the war. But he believed that the size of its transactions lifted it automatically to a higher level of ethics.

"We could question Prince Yasha," suggested Crerar. "We could ask him if he knows Sourire, and where we can get hold of him."

Yates hesitated to take his next step. He had involved Loomis as far as he could without stressing his own suspicions. Willoughby was something else again. He was DeWitt's second in command; he was the Colonel's closest collaborator and probably enjoyed the Old Man's unlimited confidence.

"You haven't by any chance been in touch with this Yasha Bereskin?" DeWitt asked Yates.

"Perhaps Major Willoughby can help us," Yates evaded a direct answer. "He knows the Prince."

Yates expected DeWitt to ask: How come you know that? But the Colonel got up from the table and, in a tone heralding nothing pleasant, announced, "Shall we adjourn to my room?" And, as Crerar seemed to be reluctant, he turned to him, "I want you along, Crerar."

Loomis saw the Colonel leave, followed by Crerar and Yates. Something in their manner indicated that they were not bent on private celebration.

"Look at Yates!" he said to Crabtrees. "Brown-nosing!"

Crabtrees watched the procession. "Wouldn't you think the guy would have at least enough decency not to do it in public!"

Major Willoughby was busy with his letter to Mr. Coster, giving the results of his interview with Prince Yasha. Willoughby injected optimism into the letter. He wrote that he would pursue the matter as energetically as his other duties permitted; for the time being, he was stymied, since Yasha had left Paris to go to Rollingen in Lorraine, which had just been liberated. Rollingen, he explained to Coster, was the Pittsburgh of the Delacroix empire.

The phone rang. With a grunt of impatience, Willoughby picked up the receiver.

"Yes! What is it?" he began; but he made a quick change to civility upon recognizing DeWitt's rasping voice on the other end of the wire. "Yes, sir. I'll come immediately," he said.

He went back to his desk. He read through his letter, then signed it deliberately, sealed the envelope, and shoved it between the blotter and the desk pad.

The Colonel had sounded laconic, as always. In all probability, DeWitt just wanted him for conversation. The Old Man was lonely; he should have stayed at home by his fireside and played backgammon, or whatever they played at that age, with his wife.

He was relieved to find the Colonel in company; but his relief was instantly jolted when he began to ask himself the reason for Yates's presence.

DeWitt went straight to the subject.

"I hear you know Prince Yasha Bereskin."

"Yes, sir," Willoughby managed to keep his face expressionless. "What about him?"

DeWitt saw no point in concealing anything from his major. "I want you to get some information from the man," he said.

"In reference to what?"

The Colonel said, "I understand there's been some black-marketeering in the organization. I won't stand for it! I'd like to know why I have you and a pack of officers around, if you can't stop it!"

"We're checking! We're checking!" Willoughby placated.

"Anyhow," DeWitt continued, "I'm informed that a fellow this Prince Yasha knows very well — Sourire is his name — has been dealing with some of our men; and I want to get hold of Sourire, and I want to have him questioned so we can find out who's at the bottom of it. Damn it!" he broke out. "I hate to waste time on this stuff! We're supposed to fight the war!"

Yates saw that the Colonel was being sidetracked by his anger. . . . Ask Willoughby how he knows Yasha! he wanted to plead. Don't throw your cards on the table! Let me put him on the griddle; I can do it, and we'll get much further! . . . And then he thought: My God, now he'll come out with the Pettinger deal. . . .

DeWitt did. He said to Willoughby in a friendly, man-to-man fashion, "I want to warn you about this Prince Yasha. There's a report that Sourire, on orders from Yasha, supplied a truck for a number of German officers fleeing Paris after the Allies entered town. Among them was a Lieutenant Colonel Pettinger of the SS, in whom we're interested. So you'd better be as careful with the Prince as possible."

Willoughby perked up his ears. No doubt, the dope came from Yates. The little snooper was shrewder than he had suspected; it might pay to get together with him.

"I'm always careful, sir," he said. "I'm a lawyer."

The chair under Yates was the hardest he had ever sat on. The matter had slipped completely from the Colonel's hands; Willoughby would pick it up the next moment.

He threw in, "With your permission, sir, I would like to ask Major Willoughby something."

DeWitt and Willoughby were startled, DeWitt because of the junior's interference, Willoughby because he felt that this was it; the little snooper had saved his coup for last.

"Shoot!" said DeWitt.

"It's really a request, Major. Next time you go to see Prince Yasha — will you take me along?"

No, thought Willoughby, this was still not it. But almost. He said, "Delighted! But I'm afraid we'll have to wait, Yates. My latest information is that Yasha went to Rollingen in Lorraine, where the most important Delacroix mills are located."

The news unsettled Yates. God knows when they would get hold of Yasha, and how long it would take to extract from him the information on Sourire; and then he would have to go back to Paris to hunt up the black-marketeer, while the front had moved somewhere else and work was crying to be done — impossible. Delay was defeat. Words tumbled from his lips. "Then why the hell did you stop me? Why couldn't I go in to see Yasha?"

"Wait a minute," said the Colonel. "Say that again!" His voice became threatening. "What have you two been holding back from me?"

His face was brick red, his hands shook.

Crerar whispered, "Easy, now. Lieutenant Yates will explain."

"Lieutenant Yates had better explain!" DeWitt said. "Well?"

"As I told you, sir," said Yates, feeling his way, "I knew from Sourire that Yasha was possibly involved in the black market, and most certainly in the escape of Pettinger. So I checked on who Yasha was and where I could find him."

"In the meantime, you let Sourire get away?" interrupted the Colonel. "Why didn't you report then and there?"

Now he was being blamed for Sourire's premature release, too. It was almost funny. "Sir," Yates defended himself, "I knew you wouldn't want me to pass the matter on unless I had all my facts. Besides, Captain Loomis is responsible for the release of Sourire. He gave his permission to the MP's."

So Loomis is involved, too, Willoughby thought. You've got to watch these guys like a hawk.

"We'll take that up later," DeWitt was saying. "You went to this Prince?"

"I phoned the office of Delacroix and asked to speak to Prince Bereskin. I got him on the wire, but he said he was too busy to see me. I made it urgent, he still refused. So I went up to the office — " Yates paused. He couldn't afford any reflection on Willoughby. The Colonel would misconstrue it.

"Go on," said Willoughby encouragingly. "What happened then?"

Yates swallowed. "Major Willoughby came out of the Prince's private office. . . ."

Willoughby picked up the fat under his chin and rolled it forward with his thumb. "And I told you it wasn't necessary for you to see Yasha."

"Yes, sir."

Yessir, yessir, yessir — the old Army game. You couldn't stand up against them — they were always on top of you. A pyramid; the higher a stone, the heavier it was on your neck, the less you could move.

"And what were *you* doing in that office, Willoughby?" asked the Colonel.

Too late, thought Yates.

"What was I doing there?" Willoughby shook his head indulgently. "Asking the Prince about Pettinger, among other things," he lied. "It was really quite simple — in fact, the Prince told me of the incident as an example of Nazi methods. It seems that Pettinger forced the Prince at pistol point to supply him with a truck. So the Prince called a truckman." Willoughby turned to Yates. "Apparently this was your Sourire, Lieutenant."

Yates felt his gorge rise. It was a glib story, all right — but why had Pettinger come to Yasha of all people? And what else had Willoughby discussed with the Prince? . . . He couldn't ask. He was the junior, and in the doghouse, at that.

"Well, that's that," said the Colonel.

"Not quite," said Willoughby. "I wish to clear up something, for the record, sir, if I may. Lieutenant Yates — what was the reason you gave me for wanting to see Prince Yasha?"

"I said I wanted to see him for the purpose of a survey." Smile, thought Yates. Keep smiling.

"You think this is funny, Lieutenant?" asked DeWitt.

"No, sir."

"Then wipe that grin off your face."

Willoughby looked as if he pitied Yates. "And what answer did I give you?"

"You said the Prince was an important person, and you didn't want to have him bothered."

"Right," said Willoughby. "Thank you, Yates. . . . You see, Colonel," he turned to DeWitt, "had I known what Yates was after . . ."

Crerar stood up. "Wonderful!" he said. "Can I go now?"

"What's wonderful?" said the Colonel, peeved.

"Everything!" Crerar answered. "The Army, life, what do you want? Excuse me, gentlemen. Good night!"

"Let's have Loomis," the Colonel said.

Loomis, entering the Colonel's room, felt as though he were coming before a court of law. The two men ranking him were judge, jury, and prosecution combined; Yates was obviously the cardinal witness for the prosecution. And while the defendant in any civilized court at least can rely on reassuring glances from his attorney, Loomis had nothing by way of support. He cast about for an expression of sympathy—Yates's mouth was set sharply; the Colonel was studying his hands, using his left to suppress the trembling of his right; and Willoughby was thoughtfully massaging the folds of his chin.

Perhaps, thought Loomis, it was best to make a full confession and throw himself on the mercy of the Colonel and Willoughby. Not that Loomis expected much mercy from DeWitt; but Willoughby had an understanding for people.

The Colonel folded his hands. "Captain Loomis—do you know a man named Sourire?"

There it was. Yates had found out everything. Yates had reported everything. And he, himself, had supplied Yates with the jeep to go to the MP station . . . !

"Sourire!" demanded the Colonel. "Do you know him or don't you?"

It was ridiculous. Loomis frowned: At this moment, when his whole future depended on his finding the correct answer, all his thoughts clustered about that one little mistake—giving the jeep to Yates.

"Yes—I know Sourire . . ." he said vaguely.

Willoughby's fingers had stopped moving. If Loomis blabbed about Sourire, DeWitt might stumble on a lead that could take him from Sourire to Yasha to the projected Amalgamated Steel deal. His eyes, from above their dark rings, were like pinpoints. They caught and held Loomis's glance. Loomis sensed something in them—a warning, perhaps; he wasn't sure.

"Do you know this Sourire personally?" asked the Colonel.

Loomis wavered. "Sir, I had no intentions—"

"Intentions!" Willoughby broke in. "We're not interested in intentions. Stick to the facts, Loomis, will you?"

Willoughby's cutting tone pricked the bubble of Loomis's illusions and hopes about mercy and understanding; it stripped him of everything but a cold, sober fear of what might happen to him if he admitted to anything.

"No, I don't know him personally. Of course not. Where should I have met him?"

DeWitt unclasped his hands; they had stopped trembling. Loomis *was* a gentleman. DeWitt hated the disagreeable job of questioning. He nodded to Willoughby.

Willoughby took the nod for what it was, the go-ahead signal. But it was more than that: It was the proof that he had won his case, won it to such an extent that he was entrusted with its further prosecution. Unfortunately, he knew neither Loomis's nor Yates's side. Warily, he proceeded, "Now, Captain Loomis — of course you know that there was some black-marketeering in the organization?"

Yates fidgeted. Willoughby was coaching the man!

Loomis wiped the sweat off his upper lip. Perhaps, the gesture served to hide his relief. "I stopped the black-marketeering," he said with resurrected dignity. "I stepped in and stopped it the moment I got wind of it."

"Why haven't you reported on it?" Willoughby asked sternly.

"There is a complete report on my desk, sir," Loomis said, turning to the Colonel. "It was delayed because I had to have it typed. I wanted to hand it in to you tomorrow."

DeWitt noticed that he wasn't getting to his point. He waved Willoughby off.

"Captain, do you know where we can get hold of Sourire?"

"No, sir — sorry." Loomis congratulated himself on his wisdom in having seen to Sourire's release.

DeWitt's face darkened. "That's quite regrettable!" A faint suspicion took hold of his mind. Much as Yates had been discredited, the impression of his sincerity when he had placed his evidence before DeWitt in the bar had remained with the Colonel. And Yates had stated that Sourire had been let go on Loomis's say-so. "It was you who gave permission to have the MP's release Sourire, wasn't it, Loomis? Before you'd turned in your report. Before the investigation was closed. Before, in fact, it had ever been started!"

For a moment, Yates felt hope.

But then Willoughby took over again. "You were God-damned hasty, don't you think so, Captain Loomis?"

With a flash of intuition, Loomis answered the Colonel, "Sir, I accept your reprimand. Perhaps I was too hasty." He saw the suspicion fade from DeWitt's face. He glanced at Willoughby and added, "Hasn't Thorpe been punished enough? Should we hound him beyond the line? I mean, he's cracked — he won't sell any more Government supplies. . . ."

Yates jumped up. "Thorpe never sold any Government supplies, Captain Loomis!"

Loomis lost all color.

"Lieutenant Yates!" DeWitt's hand came down on the arm of his chair.

"You've made a fool of yourself once, tonight! Will you kindly keep out of this?"

"There seems to be some doubt that Thorpe was on the black market as you assume, Captain," Willoughby offered. His voice was quiet, smooth. If only he could get out of Loomis some acceptable explanation for the accusation against Thorpe! It was another loose end — if DeWitt grabbed it and pulled, he might still unravel the whole untidy mess.

"We have Sergeant Dondolo's word, sir!" Loomis was defending himself. "And the statement which this Frenchman, Sourire, made to the MP's, corroborates Dondolo's story. I've got it attached to my report — "

DeWitt interrupted, "Hold it! Yates, you told me the Frenchman confessed that he bought the food from Dondolo!"

"That's the truth, sir!" said Yates.

Loomis smiled vapidly. They had him. His every word was counting against him. "I had no intentions . . ." he began. But he'd said that. He stopped.

"The truth?" Willoughby shrugged. "These French! They'll tell you anything you want to hear." He turned to Loomis. "You questioned Dondolo?"

"Severely, sir," Loomis said contritely.

"Do you have any reason to doubt his word?"

"No, sir."

"But you didn't get Thorpe's side, did you?" Willoughby prosecuted.

"I couldn't, sir! Thorpe was in no condition to be questioned. And what good is the statement of a man who ends up in a nuthouse, twenty-four hours later?"

"Don't say nuthouse!" said DeWitt.

"I mean hospital, sir. What I mean is — we couldn't court-martial an insane man — so what was the sense of holding Sourire?"

Willoughby looked at the Colonel. DeWitt was again studying his hands, his eyes angry. It seemed he had nothing more to ask.

"I suggest," said Willoughby, "we take Sergeant Dondolo out of the kitchen. Transfer him. Make him a driver. We always need drivers."

DeWitt agreed. "Regardless of who stole the food and sold it — it was Dondolo's job to watch it," he said sharply.

Willoughby ordered, "You take care of that detail, Loomis!"

Loomis said, "Yes, sir!" enthusiastically.

The Colonel was looking at Yates. Yates's chin was sagging; his fine, sensitive lips were turned down. DeWitt felt some sympathy for him — after all, Yates had been trying to do the right thing. "Well, Lieutenant," he said, "seems to me you've been going off on the wrong tangent. No harm done. We've cleared up a lot of business."

It was a well-meant sop; but it sharpened the defeat. "Yes, sir," said Yates, mechanically.

"Now, as to the Prince and the SS Colonel," DeWitt continued, "I want you to make a report to G-2 on that, Lieutenant Yates. And I want you, Willoughby, and you, Yates, to look some more into the matter. We're going to move up, closer to the front, and a trip to Lorraine can be easily arranged. And will you gentlemen keep in mind that I don't forget things, and that I don't like any of you to operate behind my back. All right, I've got a stiff neck — comes with age, you know — but occasionally, I do turn around!"

Yates thought of Thorpe, rotting away in his cell. He thought of Tolachian, his white hair smeared with blood. He thought of Thérèse, who had helped to push him into this; and of Ruth, who had always wanted him to get into the fight for causes he considered lost.

That's what he had become, now — a champion of lost causes; and he wasn't cutting too good a figure at it.

But wasn't the whole war being fought for lost causes?

10

So it was all over. The brave fight Yates had undertaken against what he now liked to call "the combine" had ended disastrously. Only DeWitt's kindness had made any face-saving possible.

He called on Captain Philipsohn and learned that Thorpe had grown worse. Philipsohn put it bluntly — he doubted very much that Thorpe would ever be sufficiently well for release; in any case, such treatment as psychiatry had devised, would better be given in the States; as soon as Thorpe was in shape for it, Philipsohn would arrange for his removal to America. Yes, he recommended that the parents be told the truth.

"I want to write a letter to his parents," Yates said.

Philipsohn suggested, "Why not let the authorities handle it?"

"No," said Yates, "I'll do it."

It was all he now could do for Thorpe; it was his duty, not Loomis's, not Willoughby's; it was like the lowering of the flag at surrender. It was something that had to be done.

Yates took the defeat and searched his mind and his heart for the fault within him. As with the letter to Thorpe's parents, he didn't choose the easy way out; he didn't blame the combine for his defeat — they were entitled to protect themselves.

However, he could see no fault but his initial one: failure to act in time as reason and conscience had directed; complacency, laziness, love for mental comfort; pretending this is none of my business. From there, disagreeable as it was, he took the next step. He asked: Why? Why was I that way?

Was it the Army influence? The spirit of doing nothing unless you were ordered, which was systematically nurtured by the strictly departmentalized pyramid? How long had he been in it? Two years — two and a half, going on three; you even forget to count time. Was that enough to bring about a basic change in character? It might strengthen certain tendencies, but it wasn't enough to cause a qualitative change. Other men had remained themselves. Bing, for instance, had done the Fourth of July leaflet practically against orders. And regardless of the strength of Farrish's pressure, without Bing's initiative, without Bing's acting on the impulse of his own conscience, the leaflet would never have been written and fired. So it *was* possible for a man to keep his integrity even in the Army; he needn't compromise. He had to risk something — Thorpe had risked, too, in a rash, emotional way, and had ended badly. The base from which Thorpe started had been cracked — and yet, he had acted and he had risked.

To get at the root of it, Yates decided, he must go back further — to a period of his life before the Army swallowed him up and tried to mold him. There was Coulter College. Red and white brick buildings between lawns and elm and maple and chestnut trees. The paved walks under the trees from Winston to Thorndyke halls and back to the library. Peace and security and years of life in which nothing more exciting should or could happen than graduation exercises, football games, and the occasional, sedate funeral of a super-annuated professor who had died unspectacularly.

The first time he had put the city behind him and reached the campus, a satisfaction with this kind of life had filled him. He had felt this almost painfully each time he returned to the college from his increasingly rare trips to the city. No price was too high to achieve it and, once achieved, to cling to it. His marriage to Ruth, in a way, was part of the yearning for the quiet life; it was better for a young, good-looking instructor to be married; and he had picked the prettiest and most mature, though certainly not the richest, among his students.

But the peace of the college was veneer, as Yates discovered after he had wriggled his way into Archer Lytell's Department. Over the five o'clock teacups in the social room, the atmosphere was charged; those who had been in the Department for any length of time considered their years a vested interest to be defended against the newcomers. Discussions of who was to teach Advanced German A, or Advanced German B, would lead to explosions of long-stored hate. When the academic year approached its close, men who always had been civil became poisonous as jellyfish. You had to watch your step, guard your tongue, be everybody's friend. And lording it over the whole thing: Archer Lytell, dropping little hints, pouring bits of oil on the fire — mighty, unapproachable, and holding the whip of tenure.

Thinking back to it, Yates could see the parallel to the Army. DeWitt was no Lytell, but he had the same power. And if Willoughby or Loomis were let loose in Lytell's Department, the atmosphere would not have changed, for better or worse. Yates smiled — of course, there *was* a difference. In the Army, your superior ruled over life and death; Archer Lytell controlled a man's measly three thousand bucks per year. But weren't the three thousand bucks life and death, security under the elm and maple and chestnut trees?

Yates — and for this he took credit — was able to see things as they were. He could adjust himself, if he wanted something badly enough. It took him less than a week on the Campus to get the feel of conditions and to decide that, if he wanted to stay in this College, he'd have to become a good mediocrity, mind his own business, take it easy, and bide his time. One day, perhaps, he would step into Archer Lytell's shoes after a short, dignified eulogy on the achievements of the deceased Head of the Department.

It was this which annoyed Ruth and led her on to attempts at changing him. He knew just as well as she did how much was wrong in the world; she didn't need to be a gadfly.

"I'm not going to come out publicly for Spain or any of your causes," he would say. "One College professor more or less doesn't make any difference."

"You're afraid," she had answered; "you're just afraid Lytell won't like it."

"I know he won't, and the President won't, and I'm not going to risk my job."

"Three thousand dollars!" she had said, sarcastically.

"Yes, three thousand dollars! This little house, and food in the icebox, and at least some of the things we want for ourselves."

"I don't want them at that price!"

"Don't be ridiculous, Ruth!"

"You'll probably lose it all, anyhow," she had prophesied. And she had bought him the three little monkeys.

It looked as if Ruth had been right, at least partially. The war had come — how far back lay the college, in another world, the elm and maple and chestnut trees, the small problems, so utterly unimportant. But Ruth had been wrong, too. America at peace was different from the war, from Europe, the invasion. Here you had to act on what you felt was right — you had to, because human lives were at stake. But life at college would go on interminably. It was a gradual ascent, all very well organized and set up, traditions and future, and you had to fit yourself into it and to make your compromises.

It was insane to presume that Tolachian had died because Archer Lytell had the power of decision over Yates's tenure. And Thorpe certainly had not lost his mind because Yates, years ago, had striven to teach Advanced German B.

They sat on the street before the Café Gordon on Boulevard Montparnasse. Yates's straw chair creaked when he moved, but he was too lazy to get up and take another.

Thérèse's arm rested on her lap; very lightly, he stroked the thin down on her skin.

"Nothing you could do to help him," she said; "*pauvre petit. . . .*"

Whether the *pauvre petit* was meant for Thorpe, of whom he was telling her, or for himself, Yates didn't know. Probably for Thorpe; but he accepted it as an indication of her mood, a mood of compassion. Women compassionate were women willing to help; women helped most easily by giving themselves.

She allowed him to caress her. She liked it. The tenderness of this man had become like a gift, offered humbly. A nonsensical gift, nothing useful — a bouquet of flowers which would wilt soon, and of which nothing but a slight fragrance would remain. It would not lead anywhere; but while it lasted, it was beautiful.

Before them floated the life of the Boulevard. Soldiers of many nations, caps in many colors, striding and laughing, girls with artificially high hairdos, on high heels, tripping by and laughing. Life floating by, and yet — seeming to stand still. There are minutes which don't end because we don't want them to end.

"*Je t'aime,*" he said.

He could not have said, I love you. But the French expressed exactly what he felt.

She took his hand and played with it. He wanted to withdraw it, fearing his warts would offend her; but he didn't. Her fingers were well-formed; they made his body shiver. Ruth never touched his hands that way — or was it that he had forgotten?

He looked at her face. In the dusk settling over the Boulevard, it had no sharp outlines; it was a sweet face, not pretty, but sweet in a manner that touched him. I wouldn't hurt her, he thought, not for anything.

"*Je t'aime,*" he repeated.

She shook her head, but said nothing.

"I am going away," he said.

"Yes?" Her hand stopped moving. "When?"

The orders had come that morning — a part of the Detachment, with

220

himself, was to move up to Verdun. At Verdun, they would be closer to the front. Yates was glad of it, especially after the defeat administered him by Willoughby. He felt that the front, despite its blood and strain and filth, was somehow cleaner than the rear. Men would be more decent, not because they became different men, but because they were out of the corrupting influence of Paris, of Victory Unchallenged.

"When am I going away? Perhaps tomorrow, perhaps a day later."

"Where to?"

More out of habit than out of fear that she would spread the information, he lied, "I don't know. They don't tell us."

"I won't see you again?" she asked, her voice small.

"No, Thérèse."

She seemed to be waiting. He didn't know what to say next. Of course he knew what he wanted to say — Let's make love, this is the last chance, let's grab it, life is this way, and we're fools to miss out on it.

"It was like a dream," she said.

She would say that. She was very young, younger than her years and her body. If she hadn't spoken of the damned dream, he probably would have come out with it and asked her to go to bed with him.

"Or like a poem," she said, "meeting you, seeing you, being with you. . . ."

A poem. In Paris, on a summer night on Boulevard Montparnasse. What a line to pull. And he fell for it. No, he didn't fall for it, but he couldn't make himself talk brass tacks to this girl.

"Unfinished poem, don't you think?" He smiled.

She nodded seriously. "But beautiful. You've been good to me."

He sipped his thin, too sweet lemonade. It tasted like this whole story. He could never tell it to anybody. People would laugh at him.

She thought of his going back to war. They would shoot at him. She had been behind the barricade, and she had been on the Place de la Concorde, and she knew how bullets sounded, and she had been afraid. But her fear had been erased by the movement of that day, by what they had been fighting for, and by the shock of what had happened to her, in the Hotel Scribe. Battle, probably, is like that: you forget your fears over what you have to do and what is done to you.

But the fear she felt for the man next to her, this man, would stand by itself; nothing would come to break its weight. If she could become small, very small — so small that she could hide in his pocket and go with him — then she would have no fear. If she could creep into him, become one with him, be like a talisman resting on the skin of his chest, she would banish the fear, and not be left with it.

And then there was pity. He would go to war and be very alone, because he was that kind of man. She did not care what memories he carried from the far past; they were no longer strong enough to break through his lone-liness. If he had the last line of the poem, the final rhyme and rhythm which gave sense to it and rounded it out and made your heart light . . .

What was there to it? What little effort!

They had hurt her, hurt her terribly, and the scar was by no means healed. But the man next to her was tender, his hands would not go tear-ing the new, still raw tissue over the wound. And she must test the scar, test life, sometime — why not now? And being this kind of man, he would help her to heal. It could not be that it was ugly always, that it left you al-ways with the taste of vomit in your mouth, and the feeling that your whole body had been dirtied.

She said, "My room is not beautiful. I have so little money. But if you want to come. . . ."

The honesty of her offer made him feel its dignity. He had to think to find the right answer. Not: Sure, kid, let's go! Not: *Je t'aime*. He had to reach the level to which Thérèse had raised everything.

He said, "You're very dear."

They walked up the Boulevard, quite naturally falling into step. Yates felt so close to her that he thought, I've never been so close to anyone. He felt her confidence, and her joy, and they began to permeate him.

Her room was even less than she had promised — in a third-rate hotel, really a rooming house — furnished with the cast-offs of a second-rate place. The bidet stood brazenly under the washstand. Thérèse hastily pulled a screen forward to hide the corner, but the middle part of the screen was torn.

Yet, there were a few touches in the room which seemed to want to atone for its seedy past, and which showed that its present tenant consid-ered it her home. On the shaky chest of drawers, the paint of which showed the imprint of a hundred hands, stood a bunch of flowers in a wa-ter glass — yellow and white and red roses, their buds half opened. Be-tween two religious prints behind glass — the dust on their nicked gilt frames somewhat lessening their glaring cheapness — hung a good repro-duction of a Renoir; Thérèse's property, as she was quick to point out. However, these touches were not enough to overcome the impression of poverty which blew its evil smell from the faded, torn wallpaper and the ragged quilt at the foot of the bed.

Yates made up his mind he would leave her some money; she needed it badly, and he would find a way of giving it to her without her having to feel offended.

He took off his blouse and hung it over a chair and helped her out of her jacket. She seemed apologetic and embarrassed.

"Do you mind it?" she said.

"This is better than lots of places I've been in," he answered with a smile meant to dispel her reticence.

"I have books, too," she said, "not many. I had to sell most of my things. Everything has become so expensive. . . ."

Yates was not in the mood to let the conversation shift to the economic difficulties of France. He must take the initiative, subtly and considerately. He sensed how slim was the margin on which he had to operate. With Ruth, things had been much different. He could not remember ever having to think about what to do next; she had always led him, with a light but firm hand. However, there was a definite sensation in having to plan. It pleased his maleness that he was called upon to decide when and where to do what.

He placed his hands on Thérèse's shoulders and felt the suppleness of her flesh through the thin silk of her blouse. His eyes sought hers and held them. Imperceptibly, almost against or without her will, she came closer to him. Then he kissed her.

Her lips were soft, warm, giving. Her body seemed to lose all energy of its own, it entrusted itself to him, he was holding it, to do with as he pleased. He tasted her mouth, her tongue, the kind of sweet taste which made him thirsty with a peculiar, never experienced thirst.

Had Ruth kissed this way, had she allowed herself to be kissed like Thérèse, who gave, and gave? He opened his eyes, he wanted to see Thérèse to blot out the thought. It was easy. The girl in his arms, he felt every part of her body, her breasts; her breath caressed his chin; he saw the skin of her face, live, warm, a tiny drop of sweat between her brows.

Then she slipped from his arms, gently winning her freedom. She knew, at that moment, that she wanted him, more than she had wanted anything, ever. She asked him to turn away.

When she called him again, she lay on the bed and was naked. She saw him swallow. She followed his eyes as they took in her body; her shoulders, hips, thighs.

He sat down on the bed. The mattress gave a little under his weight. She heard his shoes fall to the floor, first one, then the other. Then he stood up again, opened his belt. She saw every one of his moves.

His hands were too hasty; he wished, as she did, that the technicalities, the preparations, were over and done with.

And then, with a suddenness which left her shaken, it all returned. Ugly. Body was body, ready to throw itself on her, to pin her down, weight her down. Ugly. If he only would speak, say a word, make his voice break her obsession, as a stone smashes a mirage in the water. But he didn't say anything; he was intent on getting out of his trousers. It was as if something in her dried up, a beautiful big green leaf, suddenly withered.

She said, her voice hardly above a whisper, "I can't do it."

He had been about to lay himself down, next to her.

"Darling," he said, "what's the matter?" And as she didn't answer, he replied for her, "You're frightened. There is nothing to be afraid of, it'll be very beautiful, feel my hands — I'm caressing you. . . ."

She shrank from him.

He stopped. He looked at her, trying to understand her. But he didn't understand. . . . They were two grown-up people.

He tried to kiss her.

Thérèse's head moved, as if she wanted to wrench it free.

He had a puzzled, still patient smile; but she didn't recognize that. She saw Loomis. Man was Loomis. While one part of her mind made her withdraw further and further, another part kept thinking: This is terribly wrong, I love him, *je t'aime,* and he'll never forgive me.

She knew that if she were able to talk it out of her, ask Yates for understanding, Loomis would be banished, perhaps forever. But how could she talk of her shame? Wasn't she as guilty as the man who had done that to her?

Yates sat very quiet. He lit a cigarette, and gave her one. "We'll wait a little while," he said kindly, "it's one of those moods, it'll pass."

She shook her head, gave a little sigh. "I don't think so. . . ."

He pleaded. He had reached the stage where he saw only the opportunity, which threatened to glide from his hands. All these weeks in Paris, and before in Normandy, he had lived like a damned monk. He didn't want the cheap thing. He wanted it nice, at least the illusion of friendship and sympathy and of some love. All the time he had wasted on this girl! And there she lay, ready, and he was ready. He looked at his feet, moved his toes. He hadn't consciously examined his toes for ages. Sometimes, after having made love to Ruth, he would lie on his back, cross his legs, move his toes and study them. Studying toes was the symbol of satisfaction, peace, relaxation. He turned to Thérèse, determined.

"Listen, Thérèse," he said, "let's stop acting like children. We like one another, don't we? You and me — that would be the most wonderful thing. We want it; you want it, I want it. I don't know what's in the back of your mind, but whatever it is, we don't want it to interfere with you and me. If we had time, if this were normal life, peace, for instance, I'd say: It doesn't matter, let's get dressed, have dinner, go to the movies. But don't you see — this is war. Tomorrow, I won't be here; at the latest, the day after tomorrow. Only this evening, this night belongs to us, you've got to get hold of yourself."

"*Pauvre petit,*" she said.

"*Pauvre petit!*" he mocked.

She looked away from him, at the blackout curtain which was pulled tight and on which age and rain had drawn fantastic designs.

She thought, he is right. It is only this evening, only this night. This is all he has. And what does it take away from me? I can lie still, I can grit my teeth, I can control my breath — it is all one and the same, and if he goes away tomorrow, let him go light, whistling a melody, at peace with himself.

"All right," she said, "come to me."

Her resignation was so complete that it excited him by its very passivity. He was the master, he ruled, she was his. Or was she? Wasn't this, rather, the final, the absolute withdrawal? Everything in him ached to take her, to take advantage of her. They had made a bargain, and she was living up to her end of it.

He stamped out his cigarette. The ash tray, he noticed, once had broken into four pieces, and had been carefully mended. Then he pulled up the sheet and the blanket and covered her and tucked her in tenderly. He felt noble doing it, sacrificing; it was the only satisfaction he got out of it.

A wave of warmth slowly flooded Thérèse. It began at her feet and spread through her entire body. She felt like weeping.

He dressed. She watched him, wondering whether he despised her or what he felt about her.

He wasn't clear about his feelings, nor about his reasons for acting as he had. He called himself a damned fool and, simultaneously, believed he had done the right thing, believed that had he acted differently, he would have taken away only uneasiness.

"Come here, please," she said after he had finished dressing. He pulled up the rickety chair and sat by her bed and held her hand like a doctor.

"Good-by, Thérèse," he said.

Her hand tightened over his. "I will never forget you," she said. "Won't you kiss me good-by?"

He kissed her, and stroked her forehead, and then got up to leave. "I want to thank you," he said. "I would have been sort of lonely without you. But now I must go."

He put her hand back on the cover.

He left her, closing the door softly. For a minute, she lay still and thought that the thing which had withered up in her, had disappeared. In its place was an even, smooth feeling — the feeling she once had had in a small boat, on a quiet pond, in summer, letting her hand trail in the water. She knew that Loomis had gone, never to return, never to haunt her again. She knew that she was healed, and that this man Yates had healed her. She imagined herself jumping out of the bed, running to the door, calling after him, calling him back — and how wonderful it would be.

But she remained stretched flat, feeling her breasts swell and her warm body touch the cool sheets in many places. She was quite happy.

Then she fell asleep, a deep, dreamless sleep.

Book Three

IMPROVISATIONS
ON A WELL-KNOWN THEME

I

SOMETIMES, the past injects itself into the present with a peculiar force. It is as if strong hands were clamped on your skull. The mute witnesses, long dead, gain voice and raise their voice so loud that puns and laughter, songs and small talk, cease.

Most of Troy's men on their advance beyond the city of Verdun felt this; nor was it limited to the sensitive and thoughtful among them. It wasn't so much the Monument which they could see from the hills — the tall soldier of stone, his hands resting on the knob of the sword before him; and neither was it the neat perspective of rows upon rows of crosses which were like quills on the backs of the hills.

What affected the men were the trenches which, grass-overgrown, still scarred the land. True enough, they had been flattened, and their sharp edges were gone; but almost thirty years had not been able to wipe them from the face of the earth, to remove the scar of hundreds of thousands of men bled to death, in a carnage which proved nothing.

Troy's men knew very little of Verdun. Most of them had been children, or unborn, when that battle was fought. They had heard about it in school, or from fathers and uncles who, in their time, had read the headlines dealing with yard-by-yard advances and the strange names of forts and villages. Now, the strange names were once more on the map. They actually existed, including the ruins which had been left standing and which somehow looked liliputian compared to the ruins the men had seen and helped to make in this war. In Normandy and northern France, the battle had moved over virgin soil, soil where nobody had fought within human memory. Now, they were coming through this land. . . .

And fall was in the air. Last night had been biting cold. They were still advancing, oh yes, but the end seemed farther off than ever. Christmas at home! A bitter laugh. Some of the men remembered the ride toward Paris, after Avranches, when the summer had been young. Gone was the cocksureness, gone were the hopes — and what remained? Plodding, plodding on.

They were coming through this fallow land. The last plowman's shares had been the guns of yesteryear's war. And a thin rain began to come down which laid itself, sticky, on their faces and hands. The rifles, muzzles turned down, became heavier, and drops fell from the helmets.

They had by-passed the town; other units had invested it. Somewhere east of Verdun, they stopped for the night. Troy went from platoon to platoon. He had noticed the silence, and he didn't like it; he knew from his own feelings what bothered the men.

He said, "I know what you're thinking, because I've been thinking it, too. The God-damned lousy war, there's no end to it, and what for? Look at those trenches from 1916 — for what did those guys die? And twenty or thirty years from now, will other armies march over this ground again? That's what you been thinking."

They looked at him, Simon and Wattlinger, Cerelli, Traub, Sheal, and Sergeant Lester. Their faces were relaxed and expectant; also a little skeptical. Troy thought how similar these faces had become, the sameness of experience had put its stamp on each of them.

"I've got no pat answers," said Troy. "And I don't think there is anything like a readymade solution. Now, look at this Company. We've settled down for the night — so what did we do? We placed guards, and some of us will give up some of our sleep. When we've won this war, I imagine we'll have to do the same thing. It takes people a long time to learn, and we don't all learn with the same speed. You got to see to it that you're learning something, now, while it's time. War is educational."

"Ain't it?" said Sheal.

"Shut up," said Lester, "the Captain's still talking."

"No, I was through." Troy shoved back his helmet; he appeared younger now than his men.

In the late afternoon of the next day, Troy's Company came to a group of buildings which, to judge from faded signs, once had been French Army storehouses. More recent markers indicated that the Germans had been using them.

Some of these buildings were still gutted with fire, others had tumbled down in part, and others, again, were virtually intact. There was an eagerness and excitement in the faces of the men. The destruction they saw did not deceive them; they knew this kind of set-up, they smelled souvenirs, loot, the chance of a search.

Lieutenant Fulbright, a short man with the forehead and shoulders of a football player, led the First Platoon through the area, ready for a trap. Fulbright, who had joined the Company after Normandy, didn't like to take chances; but surveying the buildings, and without saying as much, he agreed with the judgment of the men: The Germans had pulled out, trying to take along as much as they could, trying to destroy the remains. Only there hadn't been time to complete the demolition job — the Americans were still advancing too fast.

Fulbright's men found nobody but a few French, who emerged from the buildings, wearing giant fur caps, fur-lined vests, fur-lined pants, and fur coats. The Frenchmen grinned sheepishly, tried to scrounge cigarettes, and slunk away when Fulbright shouted, "Get the hell out of here!"

"Nice winter stuff," said Lester.

"Government property," said Fulbright slowly and regretfully, "I guess we have to post sentries all over."

"I guess we have to," agreed Lester. He wasn't worried as long as the guards were from C Company. They would keep out everybody else and leave first choice to the boys.

Similar thoughts must have gone through Fulbright's head, because he added, "Better be careful. And watch for booby-traps."

Sheal, a light in his eyes, said, "Nah — they been pulling out too fast. I can smell booby-traps."

"The Lieutenant says there are booby-traps," said Lester, "so you look out for them. You can get your ass right over there — see that building with the windows out on the first floor! You'll be guarding it."

"Tough, huh?" Sheal spit out a piece of gum.

"Double time, march!" said Lester.

Fulbright listened to the altercation in silence, a kind of smile playing around his lips. It had taken him some time to learn from Troy what these men were about, and that discipline was nothing you could glean from the manuals; once he had learned it, he had grown into the Company and become an integral part of it.

"Get the other guards posted," he ordered.

Lester picked the men, and shouted "Fall out!" at the others. They disappeared almost instantaneously to make the most of what daylight remained.

Traub and Cerelli and Sheal came out of one of the buildings, sporting black ties and German sailor caps.

"What's it mean?" asked Sheal, spelling out the gold lettering on the black band around the cap. "What a language!"

"*Kriegsmarine*," laughed Traub, "their Navy."

"Anchors Aweigh!" sang Cerelli, swaggering over some slabs of concrete and twisted steel rails. Then he began to operate an imaginary steering mechanism. "Full steam ahead!" he shouted. "Man the torpedoes! Zzzzzt! Beautiful shot! Hit the bastard! Sank him with all hands aboard!" He turned to Traub. "I'm in the wrong place. I belong in the Navy." He stopped dreamily. "Gimme a ship and the seas!"

229

"Shut up, Admiral," said Sheal. He listened. On the road farther down, a number of tanks rattled through the evening. "Going to send this cap home, got a little sister, she can wear it."

"What size head she got?" said Traub. "It's going to be much too big for her."

"Jesus," said Sheal, "I don't remember. No, the kid must have grown, their heads grow too, don't they?"

"But not so fast as the rest of 'em."

"She's going to be proud of it," insisted Sheal, "if I write her I took it from a Nazi."

"You shouldn't lie to a kid," said Cerelli. "It's all right to lie to grown-ups, but kids get bad habits soon enough, without your helping them."

"But she wouldn't know I was lying!" said Sheal. Then he threw the cap away. "Hell, where am I going to get stuff to wrap it? Never got time for yourself, never — "

"Better go over there," advised Cerelli, "and liberate some of them furs."

Four men stepped out of the vanishing day and blocked their path. They wore rifles slung over their shoulders, and an odd assortment of clothing, half-uniform, half-civilian, and none of it in good shape.

Sheal, who saw them first, was startled. He leveled his carbine and ordered, "Halt!"

The four men stopped obediently. The one in front stretched out his open hands — either in a gesture of welcome or to show that they were empty.

"Hello, Americans!" said the man, and his face was one broad grin.

"Don't you move!" Sheal shouted, and motioned Traub and Cerelli to advance on the strangers and to cover them while the man in front, who seemed to be their leader, gingerly stepped forward.

Pointing at himself, the man said "Russky!" Then, pointing at two of his fellows, he repeated, "Russky!" and, at the last one, "Polack!" Then he grinned again and slapped Sheal's shoulder with such hardiness that Sheal felt his knees give; and then, brushing the carbine aside, he embraced Sheal. Sheal was kissed on both cheeks, the man's rough stubbles rubbing against his own, softer ones; Sheal, embarrassed, shook himself free.

He looked at the Russian; the man wasn't so much taller than he. But what a chest! What hands, and arms, and legs!

The Russian pointed at himself and announced, "Kavalov! Andrej Borisovitch Kavalov!" And stared questioningly at Sheal.

"Sheal's the name," Sheal answered.

The conversation stopped there. The next move was obviously up to Sheal, and Sheal didn't know what to do.

Finally, it occurred to him that he should notify Lester or the Lieutenant. But when he asked Cerelli to fetch them, Cerelli grunted, "Where the hell am I to find them?" and Sheal could see that the objection made sense — they could be in any of a dozen buildings, searching for fur coats and things. The thought brought Sheal back to his original purpose. He didn't want to miss out on the booty; he had seen enough foreigners in the course of the war.

"Hey, you clucks!" he shouted to Cerelli and Traub, "take their rifles and let's get going!" He reached for Kavalov's weapon. Kavalov's big hand went to the stock of his rifle.

"Come on!" said Sheal, and pulled.

The Russian shook his head. He held on to the rifle, not in a hostile way, but stubbornly.

Sheal was fazed. The Russian and his companions weren't the kind of men you liked to tangle with, unless you had to. Reluctantly, he withdrew his hand; the Russian grinned apologetically.

Sheal nudged him to go ahead. Kavalov obeyed; his head high, he fell into the easy step of a man who had marched much.

Sheal found his Company Command Post in a small house, a few hundred yards along the road which led into the warehouse area. Some men were sitting on a bench in the corner, playing cards. Troy was shoving wood into the kitchen stove, while an old woman in a blue apron and wood-soled shoes was clattering over the stone floor, fetching kettles and pots and pans.

Troy looked up, a stick of wood in his hand.

"I've brought you these men, sir," reported Sheal. "Russians, I guess."

"Fine!" said Troy, and rose. "Tell them to hand their weapons to the First Sergeant."

"Well, sir, you'd better kind of talk to them yourself about that; I've tried." And then, since he wanted to get out of this and back to his furs, Sheal mentioned that he was really supposed to guard one of the warehouses.

"O.K.," nodded Troy. Sheal and Cerelli took off; but Traub, smelling warmth and coffee, preferred to stay.

Troy studied the four men. Their faces were haggard and showed traces of what they had been through. Gradually, Troy's mistrust wore off. A German, or anyone who had been on the Germans' side, would look less lean and wouldn't show the quiet, hopeful confidence that was in the eyes of these men.

Troy picked the most military-looking among them and motioned him to come to the table.

The Russian saluted. He said, "Sergeant Kavalov, Andrej Borisovitch." Then he grasped Troy's hand and shook it, seriously.

Troy pointed to a chair next to the table. "Do you speak English?"

Kavalov smiled. "*Neponemaje.*"

"Nep—what?"

"*Neponemaje. Nix verstehn!*"

"Uh-huh!" Troy was puzzled.

"*Dajtsch! Ich sprech dajtsch!*" Kavalov tried to be helpful.

Traub called from the card players' corner, "He means he speaks German!"

"Well, come over here!" Troy said impatiently.

Traub ambled over.

"You understand the lingo, so you translate," said Troy.

"I don't know German," said Traub. "My folks came to America from the old country, and they speak Yiddish."

"Is that so?" said Troy. "Why the hell are you classified as German-speaking?"

"Yiddish is kind of a German," said Traub, to conciliate the Captain.

"Try anyhow!"

Traub and the Russian began an animated conversation. Troy broke in, "I want to know how these guys got here!"

Traub said, "He speaks Yiddish. He thinks he learned German in a concentration camp in Lithuania, and when I ask him who taught him, he says some old Jews were his teachers. The old Jews died in a quarry, he says, he couldn't save them."

"He couldn't?" said Troy, and he wondered about a guy who, in a concentration camp, thought of saving others. "What kind of sergeant is he anyhow? And tell him to hand over their weapons."

Traub gave Kavalov a cigarette and resumed his questions. Between answers, Kavalov pulled a big knife out of his pocket, judiciously divided the cigarette into three butts, and held them out to his men.

Troy looked at the Russian, and the Russian looked back at him, and smiled. "All right," said Troy, as if Kavalov could understand, "I've been a lousy host." He pulled a pack of cigarettes out of his Musette bag and handed it to Kavalov.

"*Spassibo!*"

"All right—*Tovaritch!* . . . Isn't that coffee ready?"

Traub pieced Kavalov's story together for Troy.

Kavalov had been a Sergeant in the Russian Marines, had helped to defend the island of Oesel in the gulf of Riga and, wounded, had been captured by the Germans. He had escaped and made his way back to the Russians.

"Well," said Troy, "how did he get here?"

"Guerilla," explained Traub. "The Russians sent him back through the lines to work as a guerilla. In Riga, the Germans caught him and tortured him."

"Tall story!" said Troy.

232

He was accustomed to a different kind of war, more orderly, more civilized. You didn't torture prisoners. Guerilla war was a romantic invention, a propaganda item in Soviet news-reels which he had seen back in the States.

Traub said something to Kavalov. Kavalov took off his thin jacket with the patches on the elbows. Underneath, he wore an old, sweaterlike shirt, cleanly laundered, with thin, light blue, horizontal stripes. He stripped off the shirt. Then he turned his back to Troy. The skin was striped, almost like the shirt, but in red.

Traub looked at this skin. The card players came out of their corner and stared at it, too.

Troy swallowed. "Tell him to put on his things. Tell him I believe him."

Traub said, "He wants you to know, Captain, that he killed many Germans. He and his men were working in a mine in Lorraine. They broke away from there and killed Germans with their hands. They took the Germans' weapons and used them to kill more Germans."

Traub's translation carried some of the earthiness of Kavalov's feelings and of his way of expressing himself. Kavalov said a few words to his men; they began to take things out of their pockets and to pile them on the table in front of Troy — watches, fountain pens, wallets, papers. . . . "German!" Kavalov said, and his hand swept disdainfully over the loot. The loot was his proof, as much as his rifle which he still held tightly.

Troy glanced at the pile — debris of men garroted, knifed, shot in the dark, men who would no longer fire at *his* men. "I believe you," he said, "I believe you." Then he pointed at the brass buckle of Kavalov's belt.

"Russian!" said Kavalov. "Russian Marine!" He showed Troy the hammer and sickle design.

Traub explained, "It's the last piece of his uniform, this buckle and the shirt. Even the Germans couldn't take it away from him."

Thoughtfully Troy put a cup of coffee into Kavalov's hand. "Traub! Tell him to take back all this stuff. They took it from the Germans — they should keep it. And tell Sergeant Kavalov we're going to outfit him, from head to foot! We've got a whole German Navy depot — very fine material, pants and blouse and jacket and all."

Kavalov, pocketing the loot, his eyes intent, said something to Troy.

"He wants to fight," translated Traub. "He wants to join our outfit."

Troy held back a smile. He told Traub to explain that this was the American Army. Kavalov and his men would be taken back to Verdun, and other Americans would decide what he was to do.

"Fight?" said Kavalov.

"Yes, sure!"

Suddenly Troy thought of a Company of such men. It might be as good as his own. And that was damn good!

"Now, Traub, tell him I've got to have those rifles. We can't have this kind of thing behind our lines."

Traub tried to make the matter clear to the Russian.

"Fight?" Kavalov asked again; and this time he spread his hands in complete lack of comprehension.

Troy could see Kavalov's logic. But he had to have those rifles. The war here was different from Kavalov's war — more orderly, more civilized.

2

YATES AND BING crossed the yard of the Displaced Persons camp in Verdun. Yates buttoned the collar of his field coat. Then he looked at the sky over which a busy wind was driving rags of dirty gray clouds. "Doesn't look as if it's going to stop today, either."

"Nope, doesn't," said Bing, and switched the subject. "Did you get any milk out of the administration?"

"No."

"Why not?"

Yates sighed with annoyance. This had been the third attempt, and the third failure. "Officially, the French are in charge of this place, and they say they haven't got it. So I spoke to Major Heffernan, and Heffernan said he tried to get powdered milk from the Army and couldn't; it's a French camp."

Bing said nothing. He tried to balance between two deep puddles of water, slipped, and swore.

The yard had never been paved. At one time, when French troops were quartered in the profusion of one-story barracks which fenced the yard, the soil had been hardened by thousands of feet marching up and down, columns wheeling to the right and to the left, platoons and squads drilling for hours on end. But that had been long ago. The army which had tramped this ground had been defeated and broken up. Weather of all kinds had beaten against its barracks, had split the roofs and cracked the walls and broken the windows. And now it was raining, had been raining for days, the miserable fall rains of Eastern France which fill men and sky with monotonous melancholy.

Over the administration building, the only solid stone structure of the camp, the French, American, and British flags drooped, wet and limp, stirring only when the wind slapped them against their poles. The ground was soggy. Between large puddles of water, never quiescent because fresh drops of rain constantly created new eddies, groups of men and women, some children among them, huddled or circulated slowly, heads pulled in

234

between their shoulders, the collars of their thin jackets turned up, their hands in the pockets of dilapidated coats or pants.

"Damn it, Lieutenant," said Bing, "if this is liberty, it isn't going to mean a thing."

"You can't let them run around loose, can you?" Yates said gruffly. "They've got to be grouped, processed, organized. . . ."

"But the way they live!"

"My God, how do you think they have been living?"

"That's just why!" insisted Bing.

"Shut up, for Chris'sake, will you!" Yates said savagely. "I'm trying to do what I can!"

"Yes, sir — I guess you are," Bing admitted. Bing had seen Yates trying to do the best he could — Yates had his pockets full of K-ration candy which he passed out to the thinnest of the children.

After two days of interviewing the inmates of the camp — with new ones being brought in constantly — Yates had learned that he was running his head against a very soft, a very elastic wall. Major Heffernan, the American Liaison Officer in the Camp Administration, made promises, the French made promises, everybody was friendly and eager to help, and everybody explained his limitations. Each noon, before going to lunch, Yates would talk to one or the other of the administration people, and would leave them with his mind sufficiently eased to enable him to swallow his food. And when he returned to the camp, and saw and heard and smelled the DP's, the food would rise from his stomach and gag him.

Officially, the job of Yates and Bing was to interview as many DP's as they could, to establish a cross section of their opinions, morale, and state of mind. These in Verdun were the first Hitler's Europe had disgorged; millions of others were slaves behind the German lines and all over Germany. One had to find out whether a substantial part of these millions could be counted on as Allies in the Nazis' rear.

Yates tried to be callous, he had a job to do, there was a war on. But there were the children with old faces and swollen bellies, children who didn't run and shout and jump, but who searched the mud for God knows what; who hung around the kitchen shed and sniffed the smell of boiling cabbage, a thin stream of saliva running down their chins. There were the old people with childish faces who touched his field coat, rims of dirt on the crinkly skin of their necks and foreheads, the dank smell of musty clothes and unwashed bodies and decay about them. There were the women, some emaciated, some with the flabbiness of potato diet, staring at him, smiling, swinging shapeless hips, barefoot most of them, the mud oozing between their toes and spreading over their grimy, cracked, misshapen toenails. There were the men, their faces a curious mixture of hope and mistrust, some trying to maintain a kind of dignity, others groveling — filthy, hungry, and afraid.

Where are you from? was Yates's opening question. The answer, almost always, was an industrial town in Lorraine. Not Warsaw, not Belgrade, not Bratislava — but the place where they had been slaves and lived in barracks.

"Once, they must have had homes," said Bing. He was about to reopen his harangue that something must be done.

"When was that?" said Yates, sarcastically. "Something new has been added. I tell you, a whole new species of men has come into existence — barracks men. The Germans took them and put them in barracks and made them work, reduced them to the essentials — some sleep, a pot of soup, and loads of work. At least we don't make them work. Blame the Germans, if you want to blame somebody, but give us a chance to get things straightened."

Yates was puzzled; his position in relation to Bing was the same as Heffernan's in relation to him.

"Give us a chance . . . !" mocked Bing.

"What do you expect? Who was prepared for so many?"

"All right," said Bing, "we do the best we can. We improvise. This is only the beginning. What are we going to do when we have millions of these DP's on our hands, instead of thousands? And what about the Germans? . . . Didn't we know what Europe was going to look like?"

Yates seized on the word *improvise*. "We're a great people at improvising!" he said. "American ingenuity. You're not American-born, so you may not have the feeling for it. But we opened up a whole continent improvising. Nobody planned it. It worked out all right, didn't it?" Unconsciously, Yates compared the ragged people in the camp with what America was — they were Europe, they had made their Europe, or had allowed their Europe to be made into what it was. And there they were, wreckage, freezing, stinking, starving, and waiting for American charity.

Bing did not answer. He could have said that this was no American push into the wilderness of virgin prairies and virgin forests. That the Germans, in uprooting these people, had had a plan and that, therefore, a plan was needed to undo what the Germans had done and, maybe, create something better. He did not answer because Yates, in his anger, had declassed him and disputed his right to speak as an American; presumably, Bing was unable to attune himself to that mythical pioneering spirit that made it possible for Americans to find patent solutions for the ills of everybody.

A man came forward, shapeless military cap in hand. In tolerable English, he addressed Yates. He was a Yugoslav, and his name was Zovatitch, he said. He wanted to ask the American gentleman to help him and his comrades.

Yates replied that he was not connected with the administration of the camp.

"But you—American!" insisted Zovatitch. He had dark, hungry eyes, and his Adam's apple moved rapidly up and down in his stringy throat.

Yates smiled at Bing; Americans, apparently, could settle everything.

Zovatitch explained—excusing himself and hedging a great deal—that all the Yugoslavs had been placed into one barracks.

"Well," said Yates, pleased that at least this much organizing work had been done, "what's your complaint? What's wrong with it?"

Zovatitch's mouth was tight. "Wrong? Everything wrong! We escape German fascists to live with *our* fascists? We find stool pigeon for Nazis, we accuse him, he has friends, many of them—*Tchu!*" he spit. "We fight, crack his skull with leg of stool—so!" He showed how the stool had been swung; his angular face glowed with hate—"Crack! Stool breaks, man down, then fighting, then come police. . . ."

A second man detached himself from an anxious group near by, and limped over. He began a heated argument in Serbian with Zovatitch. The two forgot Yates and Bing were there. Yates realized there was murder in the limping man as well as in Zovatitch. It was in their faces, the poise of their bodies, the tautness of what was left to them of muscle.

"I don't understand!" shouted Yates. And turning to Zovatitch, "You translate!"

"He lie to you!" said the limping man, in broken English. Apparently, he had been selected by his group because he could speak it, but had forgotten his mission upon coming close to Zovatitch.

"He lie to you!" he repeated. "He is a Tito man, they lie, steal, kill. They try kill poor Karel this morning—"

"A Nazi," said Zovatitch, and shrugged. He glowered at his compatriot. "Go ahead—*you* tell. The American, he not believe. He knows! America for the people!"

"What are you?" Yates asked the limping one.

"Mikhailovitch!" he said proudly.

"Traitor!" said Zovatitch.

"Communist!"

"Hold it!" cried Yates.

There they stood, equally threadbare, equally starving; they had been through the same German mill.

"Why don't you get together?" said Yates, but he didn't believe very much in his own advice.

"No!" said Zovatitch.

"No, Mr. American!" said the limping Mikhailovitch man.

Hatred. Yates felt again as he had felt in the dim past of Normandy, in the house of the watchmaker Glodin. But Mademoiselle Godefroy, the schoolteacher of Isigny, had hated the Boche, the enemy — that was all right. It helped the war, and the Germans deserved it. But these two guys — both Yugoslavs, both former slaves of the Nazis, liberated maybe a week, maybe ten days . . . It was the same as if he, Yates, were to hate enough to kill another American. . . .

And then — he did not know how or why — the faces of Loomis and Willoughby appeared before his mind, as they had sat in DeWitt's room in Paris, and between them not only had driven Thorpe to insanity, but also had settled the guilt of theft on the helpless boy in the isolation cell.

But that was vastly exaggerated, he said to himself. A couple of bandit leaders, down in some Balkan mountains, competed with one another; and their jealousies and animosities were reflected in these two poor saps. Anyhow, it was a political matter. What was political about him and Loomis and Willoughby?

Zovatitch and the limping Mikhailovitch man were still waiting.

"What are we going to do?" said Bing.

"We?" Yates said angrily. "You are going to go off and finally start working on the Hungarians as I told you. Remember?"

"Yes, sir. But what are we going to do about these people?"

Yates's lips thinned in irritation. If the Yugoslavs in their barracks killed one another, so many less DP's would have to be cared for. That was improvisation, all right.

"I will speak to the Camp Administration," he said.

"That's going to solve everything," remarked Bing, saluted, and went off toward the right, to the barracks where the Hungarians were lodged.

Yates crossed the yard. Four times he was approached for something to eat, once by a girl of about fourteen, with pointed breasts, who offered him any kind of love-making he desired.

The Spaniard Manuel spoke English in measured tones. He coughed frequently, with a hollow rasp, and spit into a dark blue handkerchief which he held in his right hand. This hand, in spite of its dark tan, seemed almost transparent.

"We are a small group," he said, "not many of us are left. We are soldiers. We fought at the Jarama River, in Catalonia, in the Pyrenees. What are you planning to do with us?"

Yates looked at his shrunken body and sunken eyes. "I don't know. I don't know that we have any plans for you. You're in free France now, this is a French camp, maybe the French have made some arrangements. I will ask them."

"No, they haven't," said Manuel, quietly. "Besides, we can't trust them.

They betrayed us, handed us over to the Germans — do you know that we held off the Germans for weeks, at the Jarama?"

"The past isn't going to help you," argued Yates. "You must consider the present, and present conditions."

"But we do!" said Manuel, and coughed. "Forgive me, I was very strong once, I was Captain of a Spanish merchantman. I'm not talking for myself, I will die soon enough; I am speaking for the others. They cannot go anywhere. You will win the war, and everybody is going to go home. We cannot go home."

He was a depleted man, he made no demands. But as the Spaniard sat before Yates, on an overturned box, his onetime shoes held together with rope, his jacket encrusted and in tatters, he presented a claim.

"What do you want?" Yates asked.

"We want to join your army. We're soldiers. We haven't been at it for a long, long time, but we can pick up what we missed, fast enough. Let us fight."

"Your country is neutral."

"Our country is allied with your enemies, Lieutenant."

"I am sorry."

"Lieutenant, you are an American. We were fighting your war. You didn't help us. We lost it."

Funny, thought Yates. Ruth used to say that.

"We came across the Pyrenees to find a place to rest our heads," Manuel continued. "Then came Pétain. You know what happened. You cannot let us rot here, we don't deserve that."

"I assure you, you have my sympathy."

"We need beds, we need bread, we need clothes."

"How long have you been here? Give us some time. You're a soldier, you know what it takes to fight a war. Our Army needs its supplies. There are relief agencies. . . ."

The Spaniard shivered. He spoke with effort. "Charity — we thought we had some rights. We were slaves, granted; we lived like them, worked like them, and the Germans never forgot what happened at the Jarama. That's why so few of us are left."

"You're free, now." Yates said it sincerely, he wanted to help the man.

The Spaniard began to laugh, but his laugh was caught in his coughing, tears rolled down his cheekbones, and his whole body writhed. The other Spaniards, who had been waiting at a respectful distance in the corridor of the barracks, came closer. One of them stepped over and shook Manuel. Manuel's convulsions stopped. He sat for a while, his eyes closed.

Then he said, "I am sorry. I was beaten, so I get fits, can't control myself. Don't hold it against these men, Lieutenant."

"Why did you laugh?"

"Did I laugh? I didn't. What if I laughed? I laugh because I'm happy. Happy to be free. Do you know what it is to be free? These men and I, we had a taste of it, long ago, at the Jarama River."

He bent his head.

Yates saw that he had a purple scar on the top of his skull, deep and jagged. "I will see what I can do for you," he said. "I will speak to the Camp Administration."

"We will be grateful," said Manuel.

Yates could have escaped his assignment. DeWitt would not hold him to the work if he claimed he was not up to it, and gave the reasons. But he stuck to it, doggedly; because he still thought he could do some good; and because these people filled his mind and obliterated the picture of Thorpe drooling in his cell, of Willoughby coming out of Yasha's office and killing his efforts to uncover the truth, and of Thérèse lying before him — that, too.

During the trip from Paris to Verdun, Yates had attempted to analyze his resignation to her mood. The farther away Paris moved, keeping within its orbit the opportunity to satisfy his urges in somewhat civilized surroundings, the less clear became the motives for his renunciation of what had been in his grasp. For an empty gesture of magnanimity, he had thrown away bliss, joy, whatever you wanted to call it. Of course, in retrospect, missed opportunities always appeared much sweeter than those one had taken — but what consolation was that?

He looked at the women in camp. He could have almost any of them for the picking. You'd have to feed her for a week or so, bathe her, dress her, comb her, get her some lipstick and powder — rehabilitation on an individual scale. The Polish blonde, for instance, had all that was needed. She belonged to the MP Sergeant, and the Sergeant had put her in a separate room — very convenient arrangement.

What held him back, Yates reasoned, was that any such relationship would have to take place before the eyes of eight thousand people who looked upon him, and Americans in general, as beings from a higher, better plane. The Nazis had taken these women in such fashion, some of the girls had told him so — master and slave, he didn't want to perpetuate this kind of world.

He wanted to forget Thérèse, he wanted to forget Ruth, he wanted to forget what had been. He stuck to his work. But the work pushed his nose back into the problems.

Yates thought, If ever there was going to be peace, these people — the Spaniards, the Yugoslavs, everybody — would have to disregard what had been and start anew. But how could they?

We would have to teach them and lead them. But where were we to begin? And who was to teach and who was to lead?

Major Willoughby, perhaps?

He entered Barracks Eight — Russians. He opened the door to the first room. The solid whiff of human stench nearly drove him away. It was a mixture of rotting wood and wet plaster, of fouling straw and unwashed bodies, of food and excretion and sweat and something indefinable which had been in the hedgerows of Normandy — although there were no dead here, none that he could see.

The broken windows had been patched with paper; a strong draft intensified the cold, and Yates wondered why the cold and draft didn't kill the smell.

The room was crowded with men and women. They looked up as he entered. They had their share of curiosity, but they managed to seem self-contained. In the other barracks, he had been surounded immediately by pleading people elbowing each other in a rush to claim his attention. Here, they kept to themselves.

Probably a question of temperament, he thought.

They let him inspect the room — the corner which could not be used at all because the roof leaked and water dripped into banged-up cans; the thin layers of dirty straw which served as beds; a few double-decker bunks — mere wooden frames, wired across, straw bags instead of mattresses. These seemed to be reserved for married couples; the inmates of the room had tried to screen off the family homes with sheets of paper and burlap.

Yates walked around, saying nothing. He attempted a smile, and he saw that some of the people lying about in odd heaps were smiling back at him. He was conscious of the eyes following him.

Then the total picture broke up into its details. He saw a plump girl resting in a young man's arms. They clung to each other in a kind of desperation as if, together, on their bed of filth, they were a world apart from the cold and the dirt. A woman nursed a scrawny child which, with its remaining strength, tried to force every last drop out of her hanging, baggy breasts. A very dirty man of indefinable age, sucking on an empty pipe, looked at her and nodded, and kept on nodding as if this would encourage her milk glands to exert themselves.

Out of a corner, suddenly, sounded a guitar. A male voice began to sing a boisterous tune. Other voices joined. A group of *babushkas,* sitting like blackbirds on a telegraph wire, their heads bound tightly by dark kerchiefs, began to sway and softly clap their hands. A youth, with pasty white skin and red hair and protruding eyes, started to dance, whirling and sinking on his knees and jumping up again, until he collapsed and was picked up, and leaned against the post of one of the double-decker beds to pant in exhaustion.

Yates suspected that the performance had been given in his honor. He applauded and handed a cigarette to the dancer, who lit it, drew in the smoke hungrily, and coughed.

A barefoot girl with serious face, her hair close-cropped, approached him. As he shook his head to her Russian words, she changed into German. "I don't like to speak it," she said.

"I wouldn't transfer my dislike for a people to their language," said Yates, in a professorial tone. "It's the language of Goethe — but I don't suppose you have heard of him. . . ." He stopped.

"I have heard of him," said the girl. "I was a student once, at the University of Kiev."

"I was a schoolteacher," said Yates, "before I got into the Army. You should agree with me, then — at least on Goethe."

"Look at us for a while," she invited, "and see how his countrymen have dealt with us."

"I know."

"You look at my hair?" she asked. "It was shaved off."

"It will grow again," he said, after a pause.

"It will," she confirmed.

"Why did they cut it off?"

"Some say because the Germans used it, some say it was so we couldn't run away."

"But you did run away?"

"The Nazis ran. They wanted to take us along, but we refused to go. They could not force us; they were in too great a hurry."

"Were there many of you?" Yates asked.

The girl pointed at a group of women sitting in the center of the room, on a kind of dais. "Some of us are here now. We walked for three days."

"No men with you?" Yates inquired.

"Very few. Most men had gone off two days before, when the Germans began to get nervous. The men killed some of the Nazi guards and took their guns and went off."

"Where was that?"

"In Rollingen. We worked in a mine."

"You worked in a mine? These women, too?"

"Yes."

"Underground?"

"Yes."

She was sturdy enough; or, at least, she must have been before they put her to this work. Then he thought, only Russian women could be used for that and survive, they're more primitive.

"How many hours a day?" he asked.

"Ten, sometimes twelve. But we didn't work very hard." She laughed, short, bitter.

"Didn't you have to deliver a certain amount of ore?"

"Andrej took care of that."

"Who is Andrej?"

"He was the checker," she explained. "He's not here with us. He went with the men. I don't know where he is. Andrej organized it."

"He must be quite a man," said Yates, patronizingly.

"He taught us," she said. "The mine belonged to a Frenchman, but the ore went to the Germans."

"Delacroix?" asked Yates.

"That may have been the name. I don't know. They're all the same."

"Yes, I guess they are," said Yates. Conviction and a measure of hate had come into his voice. She looked up at him, and her eyes showed that the argument over Goethe was forgotten.

She led him to the other women. They brought him a box to sit on, and he opened his field coat and indicated that he was making himself at home. The smell seemed less unbearable; perhaps he was growing accustomed to it.

She introduced him to the women. "This American officer has come to see how we live."

They edged toward Yates, and he saw an unwashed profusion of feet and heads. He took the last chocolate from his pocket and passed it around.

"Good!" they said, and "Thank you!" and divided it into very small pieces, one to each.

The girl turned to him, "It is the first time someone has come to see after us. . . ."

Yates couldn't tell them that he had come to draw them out, not to improve their lot. Then he saw that they were no longer looking at him; even the girl from Kiev was staring at something else.

Yates followed their eyes, to the door.

There stood a barrel-chested man, his face one wide grin, his long arms outstretched as if he were embracing everybody in the room.

"Andrej!" said the girl, and flew to him, "Oh, Andrej. . . ."

He put his arms around her, not like a lover — rather like a protector. She was very small beside him. Her short-cropped head hardly reached the level of his chest where his blue sailor blouse parted and the horizontal blue stripes of his shirt became visible.

She broke into excited Russian, and he patted her to quiet her. The other women crowded around him, until he waved them off to gain space and come into the room.

Yates was sitting on his box. So this was Andrej the teacher, Andrej the organizer, who had gone off with the men. He was obviously a soldier and carried himself as one, erect, and yet easy of limb. He had dense, white-blond hair which grew thick and straight like a little roof over his square, hard forehead. He had a well-formed, small mouth. His chin, like his forehead, was square and strong and prominent. He blinked his eyes to adjust them to the half-light of the room; then he approached Yates, stopped, and waited for Yates to address him.

The personality of the man was so overwhelming that Yates could not disregard him. Besides, he was unquestionably of interest. He must have undergone the same experience as the thousands of other DP's in this camp. How had he maintained such strength, such exuberance, such spirit? And were there more like him?

"I'm an officer of the American Army," Yates said, in German, feeling more than ever the oddity of a situation in which two Allies could make themselves understood best in the language of their common enemy.

He expected the girl student to translate, but Andrej answered for himself. "I'm a Sergeant of the Red Marines, sir, name Kavalov, Andrej Borisovitch."

"You're wearing a fine uniform!" commented Yates. "Saved it throughout your time over here?"

"No," laughed Kavalov. "An American captain gave it to me. He is my friend. When we came to the American outposts; my comrades and I" — he included the several men behind him in a gesture, and Yates only then noticed that Kavalov had not come in alone — "we wore rags and rifles. Now I wear this."

He felt the cloth of his pants. "Not bad! German sailor's. . . . These are Russian." He slapped his belt buckle with one hand, and with the other the striped shirt over his chest. "Nobody could take them away from me."

"How did you find your way here?" asked the girl. "What have you been doing since you left the mine?"

Kavalov answered slowly, directing his remarks to Yates. "We killed Germans. We lived in the woods and moved at night. Partisan — you call it partisan, in America, too? I was trained for it; many of us are. It comes in well. After two days, we had taken more weapons from the Germans than we could carry. We could have gone on for a long time. But I say to my men: It is time to get back to the Red Army. We go to the Americans, tell them who we are, and they will send us back."

The man isn't as naïve as that, thought Yates. How does he imagine the war is run?

He said, "I'm afraid, Kavalov, it isn't so simple. Once you enter this camp, you're a Displaced Person like everybody here. . . ."

Kavalov waved the objection aside. He was in a high good mood, and

244

nothing could dampen it. He had escaped the Germans; he had solved more difficult problems. "Well, anyhow, here we are."

"Were there many guerillas — I mean partisans — or just your group?" asked Yates.

"We met some French ones. They were in the woods four months, and they had some old rifles. We were fighting four days, we had two machine guns, many rifles, loads of ammunition. I gave them the machine guns."

The women listened approvingly. They were satisfied. They knew that their men would be better than anyone else.

The girl said, "Tell the American officer how we had the strike."

"Where did you have a strike? When?" Yates grew excited. If there had been a strike, there must be more men like Kavalov behind the German lines. This was the kind of thing he had come to the camp to learn.

Kavalov said to the girl, "You tell. I am tired." That was final. He closed his eyes.

"He does not like to talk about himself," said the girl. "It was the First of May — you know, it is a holiday. It was in Rollingen. So Andrej said, We will celebrate. We are far away from the Soviet Union, he said, we are prisoners and slaves, but we will show the Germans that this won't last forever. We were housed in barracks outside the town — every shift, a train would come and take us to the mine. The morning shift came on at five. We gathered all the red cloth we could find, the girls gave their underclothes, and kerchiefs, and we cut up some stolen German flags, cut out the swastika, and left the Red. The First of May train rolled to the mine, flags out of every window, red flags, our flags, the workers' flags, you know?"

Yates rubbed his fingers, feeling his warts. He did not approve of demonstrations; theirs had done them no good, either, in any practical sense.

"At the mine," the girl continued, "the police took the flags by force and tore them up. They would have shot us, but they needed us to work in the mine. We went down. We didn't work. We had a meeting underground and Andrej told us of the First of May, and what it meant, and that we were soldiers, too, fighting side by side with the Red Army." She smiled. "And with the Allies," she added.

Yates could see these people meeting down in the earth, in a tunnel of the mine — the ill-lit darkness, the faces of women and men directed to Kavalov, the power that they were, even as slaves, together. He envied them a little. They knew what they were fighting for.

He thought of the Fourth of July leaflet: I went to Farrish and I gave him a line of hokum to keep him and everybody from telling the enemy that we, too, in our way, know what we're fighting for.

The girl was going ahead with her story. "Then they took some of us women and put us in solitary, and grilled us and starved us — I was among

245

them; Dunja here, too. They wanted to know who organized it. But they never found out."

Kavalov came awake. "You didn't starve," he said.

"No," said the girl. "We never ate so much in all our time with the Germans. Andrej saw to that."

"It wasn't anything to speak of," said Kavalov.

What is it about this guy? thought Yates. He's like a catalyst.

"I don't like it here," Kavalov was saying. "I won't stay here."

Yates took him seriously, now. And he understood. In this camp, the rot to which the Germans had condemned these people simply continued.

"Don't let me know about it," he smiled. "But I want you to give me your word of honor that you will stay another twenty-four hours. Tomorrow, I'll come back and take you out of here. I want you to tell some of our people what you have seen and done. Then, I'm going to return you to the camp. After that, you can do what you please."

He felt Kavalov's eyes rest on him, and he knew that he was being appraised.

"It's an invitation for dinner," Yates said, and wondered what Willoughby and DeWitt and the others would say when he trooped into mess with this Russian Marine.

"I accept," said Kavalov. "In the name of my comrades here, I accept, because I see it is impossible for you to invite us all."

3

BING saw Yates come out of one of the DP Camp's barracks, and hailed him. Yates seemed tired and discouraged.

"I'm glad I found you, Lieutenant," said Bing. "Couple of things I want to tell you."

"What's wrong?"

"Nothing's wrong! First of all, I got a dame waiting for you."

"You got a what?"

"Not bad-looking, Lieutenant."

"Now listen, Bing — I'm a very tolerant officer, I think you know that. I treat you and everybody else like grownups and human beings. But you've got a hell of a nerve to go out and fix up my sex life. I'll do that myself."

"O.K. Let her wait! . . . I certainly didn't mean to intrude." Bing dug into his pocket and finally came up with a crushed pack of cigarettes. Lighting one, he said, "The other matter is a rumor I heard, or maybe more than a rumor. I got it from the MP Sergeant who has that Polish blonde. They picked her, too, but he had her struck off the list."

"What Polish blonde? What list?"

"They're planning to send a lot of those DP's back where they came from — to the mines."

Bing waited. Yates was rubbing his fingers.

Suddenly, Yates's eyes focused and he asked sharply, "You said a dame was waiting for me? Where? Here in camp?"

"No, outside, of course!" It had never entered Bing's mind that Yates might suspect him of procuring one of the DP women. He laughed, "I'm not in that business, Lieutenant!"

"Dame — dame! What kind of woman? Do you know her name?"

"Sure I do. She gave it to me — Thérèse Laurent; and if she wasn't so starry-eyed about you, I'd say she was my kind of dish."

"Thérèse!" Yates's heart began to pound; he thought he could hear the sudden singing of his blood, everybody could hear it. The dismal, drab camp sank back beneath his feet; it was as if he stood alone on a wide field — and Bing, who was directly in front of him, faded out like a wisp of smoke.

"Where is she? How did she get here? Where did you meet her?"

He began to walk away from Bing. Bing ran to catch up with him.

"Now take it easy, Lieutenant. She's waiting at the gate. You're going the wrong way!"

"The gate — oh, yes. That's over there. . . ." Yates smiled. "She's come here and she's at the gate — "

"Lieutenant! Don't you think we should do something about the DP's?"

Dutifully, Yates stopped and listened.

"They just got through being slaves — and now . . ."

Bing's words made no sense whatever. Again Yates walked off, this time straight across the yard, bumping into people who did not get out of his way fast enough.

Bing plodded along next to him. "Maybe you should take it up with the Colonel! At least you could ask him. . . . Wait a minute, Lieutenant! The girl's not going to run away. She's come all the way from Paris, she'll wait a while longer."

"How did you meet her?"

"Before the billets. I came out of the house on my way here, and she stopped me and asked me if I knew a Lieutenant Yates. David Yates."

"David Yates," Yates nodded.

"I said, Sure, Mademoiselle, come along. That's how it was. Simple, no? Do you want *me* to talk to Colonel DeWitt? Even if they need workers in the mines . . ."

"How did she get to the house? All the way from Paris — "

"Hell, I don't know! You'd better ask her yourself. I must know what you want me to do about the DP's!"

"The DP's?"

247

Jesus Christ, thought Bing, the guy's hard up for it. "I tell you what I'll do," he said. "I'll say to the Colonel that you sent me to report the matter to him."

"What matter? What are you talking about!"

"This stinking plan they have — to send the DP's back to work — "

Yates's face finally showed a measure of understanding. "I'll take care of it, later."

"Let me handle it, sir."

They had come close to the gate. Only a corner of the Administration Building hid the gate, the police, and Thérèse from Yates's sight.

He stopped.

"What's it now?" Bing asked.

Yates was reluctant. He had to take someone into his confidence. He hated to; he had a natural distaste against men sharing a secret over a woman, though it was quite customary in the Army.

Yet — Bing was the logical choice, not only because Thérèse happened to have run into him, but because he was one of the few men Yates had come to like and trust.

"I've got to have a room, and it's got to be a decent room, and I don't want to be disturbed."

So he wants me to fix up his sex life after all, thought Bing; but he didn't make the obvious comment. He simply asked, "For when?"

"Tonight, about 9:30. I'm having the Russian marine I told you about for dinner at the mess — I can't get out of it, and I don't want to get out of it. Afterwards, I'll have Abramovici escort him back to camp — and then I'm free."

"How about hotels?" said Bing. "Do you want me to check?"

"You know they're either cathouses or requisitioned!"

"Well, that leaves us only one choice. . . ."

"Where?"

"I'll arrange everything, sir."

"I said, Where?"

"In the house, naturally."

"No, that's out." Yates was quite determined. "I don't want the whole Detachment in on it. It's bad enough that you're mixed up in it."

"I wouldn't bother with it for anybody else but you," said Bing. "What's wrong with the house? With any luck, I think I can keep the others away. You like the girl, don't you? Anyhow, what do you expect in this war? All the polish should stay on nicely?"

Yates felt that perhaps he should have stuck to his own caste. But he couldn't see himself going to DeWitt; and Willoughby would have delighted in holding any favor over his head for the rest of the war.

"She's a very nice girl. . . ." Yates said.

"I know; I could see it."

Bing reflected. The man was disturbed, didn't know where to turn; kind of Displaced Persons, too — Yates and this girl.

"I'll take care of it," he said officiously. "Tonight, I'll have the room ready for you, and I'll see to it that no one butts in."

"I can't do much else, can I?" Yates took the Sergeant's hand. "Thanks. It's because of this — this barracks atmosphere . . ." Yates was afraid of Thérèse's sensitivity. He couldn't have stood a repeat flop.

"You know what I mean?" he asked.

"I do," said Bing, and went away.

He saw her before she saw him. She had given up peering into the gate and had moved away from the inquisitive French policemen who guarded it. He saw her through the iron bars of the gate — her neckline, the touching, childlike curve, the slight hollow. He saw her soft hair under the small, black Basque cap. He brushed by the guards and called, "Thérèse!"

She turned around.

It was all so different from what he had imagined. They did not rush to one another, they took each step that brought them closer slowly, almost hesitatingly, as if they were treading a thin, loosely suspended bridge.

Only when she was in his arms and he felt her body, and felt the relief in her, did he trust the present.

"I am so happy," he said.

He did not understand her answer. She spoke many French words, very fast, like little caresses.

Then he kissed her. The French sentries at the gate had turned discreetly away.

"What great good fortune!" Thérèse exclaimed. They were leaving the camp behind them.

"Yes," said Yates, unquestioningly. He was content to drift along. Although he wondered how she had come to be in Verdun, how she had found the house in which the Detachment was billeted, the very fact of her presence, and the secure knowledge that whatever had kept them apart in Paris had disappeared, filled him so completely that his curiosity could wait. A great calm had replaced the singing of his blood.

But Thérèse brimmed over with the sensation of their having found one another; also, she was proud of having braved the war and conquered it through her own initiative.

"When you left me — " she began.

He pressed her arm to his side.

"I know, you don't want to be reminded," she said, "and I'll never again talk of it — just this once. When the door closed and I remained all alone,

249

I suddenly knew that I loved you, and that this wall between us was gone. It was gone because you went. If you had stayed, then, and taken me, I would never have come to you — never, I know that."

She placed her hand on his, and quieted his objection.

"Something made me that way, something I have forgotten; it has gone out of both our lives, and we need never worry about it."

He did not worry at all. It was the first time that he was so victoriously sure of his mastery over his own life.

"You had not told me where you were going."

"I couldn't, dear," he said. "We're not allowed to."

She nodded. "I went to the Hotel Scribe and asked for you. I thought I might find somebody who knew you and could tell me where you had been sent."

She did not mention that she had asked to see Loomis, and that she had been willing to face the man once more — so deeply had she wanted to find Yates. But Loomis had not been at the Scribe.

"Everything is good now that you're here," he said.

"An American woman helped me," she continued. "She writes for your newspapers. Karen Wallace was her name. She was very kind to me, very understanding. She said she knew how it is when you love a man and cannot have him. I liked her. She told me I might find you in Verdun."

"I know Miss Wallace," he confirmed, and smiled to himself over that fine-spun alliance between women; they're so superior to men once they make up their minds about what they want. And he wondered, How much had Karen told Thérèse about him? Had she told her that, long ago, she had slapped his face, and why?

But if Thérèse knew, she made nothing of it.

"Then I went to Monsieur Mantin and told him I must go to Verdun to see you. He asked me if I was sure that this was what I wanted."

"What did you answer him, dear?"

"I said I was sure. I said I was left with the feel of your hands, and that wasn't enough to go on with."

"It isn't enough," he said, "you are right." And he felt humble before her.

"Mantin gave me a pass, and he put me on a truck going to Verdun, and he gave me the address of a family where I am staying — I sleep on a cot in a room with their two daughters."

"Everybody helped you. . . ." Through her, Yates felt part of a loose and yet delicately woven community.

"It's because of the war," she said. "Everybody has someone whom he's looking for. You understand?"

"Yes."

"Even some of your people tried to help," she went on. "When I came here, I found there were thousands of American soldiers; so many, I lost hope. I began to ask, and nobody knew you. I've asked for days. I began to think the woman in Paris had told me wrong."

"*Je t'aime,*" he said.

"It was hard. Some of your soldiers were angry. Some said to forget about you. One said, Lady, we've got more lieutenants than we need. You won't find him."

"But you did. I am very happy."

"Then someone sent me to the Town Major. They said they had no time for me. But I waited. At the end of the day, they wanted to go, and they saw me still waiting. Then they looked through many lists, and finally told me the house where you were staying."

She loved him that much. He added up her courage, her devotion, her willingness to throw herself into the melee of an Army on the move, with nothing but a thin hint to go on — and the total was so great that he had to examine himself: Where have you been? If this is possible, how little you know of the human heart. And how little you can give her. . . .

"And then you came out of the camp," she said jubilantly — and, almost inaudibly, added, "I knew it was you before I turned around. I knew, I could sense you. But I didn't dare to turn unless you called me. I was afraid."

"You are no longer afraid? Are you happy, now?"

"Yes," she said, "very."

4

ABRAMOVICI, his clarion voice filling the *salon* which served as the Advance Detachment's orderly room and as office for Willoughby and De-Witt, said to Bing: "No — Colonel DeWitt isn't here. He's gone off to the headquarters of Matador, to see General Farrish. He will not be back until tonight — "

Bing edged away from him. "All right, all right — it isn't that important."

At a table in the corner, Willoughby's frowning face rose above the papers on which he was working.

"Sergeant Bing!"

"Yes, sir!"

"What do you want from the Colonel?"

"Nothing, sir. It can wait."

"Come here, Sergeant."

Bing slowly walked across the *salon*. He didn't feel too good. Since the surrender of the fort at St.-Sulpice, there was no love lost between him and Willoughby. Bing knew the Major's opinion of him; few things of this kind remain secret when men are constantly with each other, observe each other, rub shoulders, clash, and compromise. Bing knew that Willoughby had called him *precocious, impertinent, arrogant,* and upon Loomis's complaint had promised, "Give me a man with the same qualifications, and I'll bust your Sergeant Bing and send him to the Infantry in no time flat."

At one time, Yates had warned Bing. Yates had said, "You're a funny fellow. Your open-mindedness and your shrewd judgment are fine — but aren't you a little ahead of yourself and, what's worse, ahead of everybody else? Why do you give opinions on matters that the others have just begun to mull over? Don't you ever see any If's, any But's? Let me tell you: With your damned sharp tongue, you're making more enemies than is good for you."

No doubt, Willoughby was one of them — because the elements of which he and those of which Bing were composed didn't mix; because of Karen; because of the Fourth of July leaflet; and because Bing was irreplaceable at this stage of the war — which must irk a man like Willoughby who could see only one irreplaceable person on earth: Himself.

"Sergeant Bing," said Willoughby, "in the Army, you don't just bust in on your commanding officer. Ever heard of channels?"

"Yes, sir."

Bing hoped that would be all. But Willoughby didn't dismiss him. He seemed to wait.

"All right, what did you want, Sergeant?"

"It's not urgent."

"You rushed in here, all hot and bothered, to see Colonel DeWitt. And suddenly you backtrack. What is it?"

"Lieutenant Yates — "

"Lieutenant Yates sent you?"

"Yes," Bing said uncertainly.

"Did he specify that I should be left out of the picture?"

"No, sir. Of course not!" Bing felt roped in. He cursed Abramovici's loud mouth.

"Where is Lieutenant Yates? Why doesn't he come himself?"

Willoughby's heavy-jowled face went sour when Bing replied truthfully, "I left him at the DP Camp."

"So he sent you — about what?"

Bing knew that if Willoughby demanded it, he had to give the report. During the Colonel's absence, the Major was in charge.

"Something's brewing in the camp. They seem to have a project there — to return the strongest of the DP's to work in the Lorraine mines."

"And Lieutenant Yates doesn't like it?"

For a moment, Bing said nothing. He was sure that Yates had not even comprehended what was afoot.

"Lieutenant Yates felt that the Colonel should know about it."

"And what do you think?" asked Willoughby.

"I think it stinks."

Willoughby nodded.

"The camps are bad enough," Bing continued, surprised at the Major's apparent sympathy, "but that would top it all. Just because we don't know what to do with these people, we have no right to — "

"I'm glad you informed me," interrupted Willoughby. "We can't afford to let something like that go through. Of course, you and Lieutenant Yates would approach it sentimentally. What we must constantly carry in mind, is the great aim of winning the war. If we force the DP's back into the mines, the Germans are sure to learn of it — and, Boy, will they use it! Who's our liaison officer in the Camp Administration? — Major Heffernan? Good."

Willoughby reached across his table for the leather case that contained his field telephone. He pulled out the lever to ring the operator, and turned it.

Fast action, thought Bing. He had hardly hoped for such success, and certainly not with Willoughby. And Willoughby was right — the Germans would make their own way of dealing with DP's seem like charity in comparison to the Allies'. He got a kick out of observing Willoughby's mind at work and having the Major, for once, on his side.

The operator seemed to be taking his time. Willoughby rang again and, still waiting, turned to Bing. "Have you any idea where the DP's are to be sent?"

"From what I've learned — most of them are supposed to go to the vicinity of Rollingen, to the Delacroix mines. . . ."

Bing could hear the thin quavering of the operator's voice in the receiver of the phone. Willoughby did not reply. Softly, he replaced the receiver in the case and rang off the call.

"There's something else we should consider. . . ." he said, and settled comfortably in his chair, the short fingers of his pudgy hand grasping each other over his stomach, his shrewd dark eyes staring mildly from above their bags at Bing.

"But, sir . . . !"

"We forgot that the mines produce ore, and that ore is made into steel, and that we need the steel for the war. Winning the war is what counts — I said that, didn't I? Besides, I know Major Heffernan. These people won't be coerced — only volunteers will be taken, and they will be paid proper wages. We aren't like the Nazis!"

"No."

Willoughby spoke to Bing with a measure of benevolence. "You're a good man, Sergeant. Quick, and on the ball — I kind of like seeing eye to eye with you on something. Why are you so — contrary, sometimes? It doesn't help you, you know?"

Bing was still puzzled over the Major's sudden switch, and didn't trust it.

"You're a good man yourself, sir, if you permit me to say so."

Willoughby smiled.

"You can see a problem — and its implications. . . ." Bing paused. "But as to my being contrary or — " he emphasized the word, "impertinent: It's a matter of, as you call it, seeing eye to eye on an issue — "

Willoughby stopped smiling.

"Who the hell do you think you are? Get out!" he said coldly.

Bing left without a word. Willoughby was a good man depending on what and whom he worked for; and you were a good man if you worked for him.

DeWitt was inclined to humor Farrish. You must take people as they are, he felt; you can mold only as far as the material on hand will permit. Not that the Colonel saw his mission in molding people; he felt neither authoritative nor superior enough for that. But when DeWitt saw that a man was wrong and that the error, in turn, would subvert the events influenced by that man, he attempted a more or less subtle correction.

It was a bad time to try the experiment on Farrish. DeWitt last had talked to the General at Rambouillet, but had kept in touch with him during his sweep across France. Farrish, in the forefront of the advance, had been the first to feel the slackening of the push. Now he was stymied before Metz. He had planned to by-pass the town quickly, to surround it as rushing water will surround an island, leaving it to be inundated by the wake. But his troops had been bogged down, supply had not kept up with the Division, and the tanks, bare of gasoline, had to be pulled back.

The Germans, at first quite willing to evacuate the fortress town, had sensed the lack of impetus; they had brought up reinforcements and strengthened the forts around and within the city.

When the supplies for which Farrish had begged and wheedled and threatened and cajoled finally arrived, the period of by-passing was over. Each of the fortified works in and around Metz had to be assaulted and taken singly, at great loss; Metz, instead of an island engulfed, had become a pivotal point in the German defense.

Farrish felt himself free of blame.

"You just might have outrun your supplies," DeWitt reflected aloud. "It's a problem of logistics. A certain number of miles requires a certain amount of men and material. You can't argue with figures."

Farrish came out of the hot shower in his trailer, his lobster-red skin still steaming, and wrapped his blue bathrobe around his ample frame. "You want to take one?" he asked DeWitt, "help yourself as long as the water's hot."

"Thanks, I will," said DeWitt. "I've got a fairly decent house in Verdun, but the plumbing is antediluvian."

"Towels are over there!" Farrish pointed to the chest behind his bed. "Who says I want to argue against figures? I know all the figures, old man, and my figures are right. But it makes me sick — actually sick!" — his flat hand came down on his naked thigh — "to have to send my men against those God-damned Heinie forts, when I know I could have starved them out, at will, if my gas hadn't been sold on the streets of Paris. Yes! Don't tell me it isn't so! Carruthers was in Paris and he saw it, with his own eyes. Other men of my outfit saw it, too."

"What?" shouted DeWitt. The steam of water rushing down his back was louder than Farrish's voice.

"Sold!" cried Farrish. "God-damned Judases! All the blood I have to spill should come on their heads!"

DeWitt turned off the water and began to rub his chest.

"You're getting fat!" said Farrish. "You lead a sedentary life, old man. I keep moving around — backward, mostly, it seems now."

DeWitt dried his feet. He groaned a little at having to bend. "Wait till you reach my age," he said, "you'll stop bragging."

"Twice, in one week, I've had to pull back this CP," said Farrish. "Something's got to be done about it, and I'm the man to do it."

"What can you do about it?" asked DeWitt, "short of turning the great American character inside out?"

"Get dressed," said Farrish, slipping into his trousers, "I want to show you something."

Farrish was a self-willed host. DeWitt did not bother to ask what he was to see. He put on his uniform, and followed the General out of the trailer.

Inside the car, Farrish touched his arm, solicitously. "I'm going to take you to the hospital. I go there frequently. Cheers the men, I think. And to me it's like a — like a shot in the arm. I come away from there fighting mad. I want you to get some of that spirit."

"Think I need it?" asked DeWitt.

"Oh yes, you do!" asserted Farrish. "Listen, if we don't scream our heads off — you and I and the few other honest guys who aren't afraid — nothing will ever get done!"

DeWitt glanced at Farrish. The General sat straight as a ramrod, his nose and chin jutting out, his eyes directed ahead. There was no grace about him, no forgiveness, he was almost inhuman.

Farrish said, "I don't intend to take it lying down. I've been persecuted

255

since Rambouillet — since they ordered me to avoid Paris and stole my show and handed it to that windy Frenchman."

DeWitt listened to the screaming sirens of the four motorcycles that preceded Farrish's car as it rushed down the bumpy road. The General mechanically answered the salutes of men and officers who froze to attention as the car sped past them.

"I'm a soldier," said Farrish, "I'm willing to accept orders — "

"Well, that's that!" DeWitt wanted him to stop there.

"But," continued Farrish, "soldiers' orders, not politicians' — whether the politicians wear uniforms or not."

"This is a citizens' army, and we're servants, servants of the people." DeWitt disliked clichés, but, in this case, they were so eminently applicable.

Farrish did not answer; it was obvious that DeWitt's words had rebounded from him like pebbles from an armored car.

They stopped in front of a large building, one wing of which had collapsed under a bomb. The roof of what remained was painted with giant red crosses on white fields.

Farrish entered, curtly brushing aside the medical officers who ran to greet him. He seemed to know his way and strode down the hall, turning into the first ward on the left.

"Oh God, there he is again!" DeWitt heard a nurse whisper.

On field cots, covered with rough blankets, lay the wounded. A perceptible move went over the beds, somewhat like the wind rippling over a burned wheatfield. The wounded who could move were trying to straighten themselves.

Farrish picked a man at random. The soldier looked at him, his eyes a hopeless jumble of fear and expectancy.

"Chest wound," said a respectful major, "recovering nicely, sir."

Farrish paid no attention to the Major.

He asked the soldier, "Where did you get it, son?"

"Metz, sir," the man said with visible effort. "Fort Elizabeth."

Farrish took the soldier's hand. He held it between his own, as if he were holding a young bird. DeWitt thought, he shows tenderness; he wondered whether it was all show, or whether some part of it, at least, was genuine.

"What outfit?" asked Farrish.

"F Company of the 37th," said the soldier.

"Captain Lombardo?" asked Farrish. "I know what you've been through."

"Captain Lombardo is dead, sir," said the soldier.

"Oh, yes, he's dead, quite." Farrish dropped the hand. "Who commands F Company now?"

The man was sweating. The nurse, who had groaned at the General's entrance, stepped forward and wiped the wounded man's forehead. "He shouldn't talk that much, sir."

The soldier didn't hear her, or he thought the General was more important than the nurse. He said, "When they took me away, the First Sergeant was heading the bunch."

"Not many left?"

"Few. I sure hated to leave them, sir."

"You'll get well, soon." The General dropped a pack of cigarettes on the blanket.

"He can't smoke, sir," said the nurse.

"Who asked you?" said Farrish, but he didn't say it viciously, more out of habit. He seemed deep in thought. "Well," he added, "give them to someone else here. I can't spare any more. I only draw my ration."

He went on. He passed down the line, stopping at various beds, asking questions, making rough remarks he thought encouraging.

"Why, Jimmy!" he cried suddenly, turning to a bed near the end of the ward, "what on earth have they done to you?" And to DeWitt, who had followed him, he explained, "Best God-damned Bazooka man I have!"

The man called Jimmy, his forehead and skull wrapped in bandages so that his head seemed supernaturally large on his emaciated shoulders, gave no answer. A smell of pus emanated from him. His hands, which were above his blanket, moved in slow semicircles, as if he were trying to find something long lost.

"Can't you hear me, Jimmy?" asked Farrish, heartily.

Jimmy's eyes came open, staring blindly from under heavy lids.

"What's the matter with you, Jimmy?" Farrish's voice was without confidence. The General, who could move thousands of men, could not wake this one; the man was beyond his power, and it puzzled Farrish.

"He's doped up," said the Major, softly. "He feels nothing, not even pain."

Farrish looked at the slowly moving hands. "Does he do that all the time? Where I come from, they say it means he's going to die."

"That's a superstition, sir," the Major hurried to assure him. "It's not a medical symptom."

Farrish didn't listen. He bent down, a great man over a small bed, and kissed Jimmy on both his sunken, stubbled cheeks.

The doctors and nurses and wounded were absolutely quiet. DeWitt could hear the soft, scraping sound of Jimmy's hands on the blanket.

"Well?" said Farrish. "What are you staring at? You said he feels nothing!" He tucked one end of Jimmy's blanket, which had come loose, under the mattress.

"I want this man to live!" he announced, in his old voice.

"Yes, sir!" said the Major.

Farrish stood before the cot as if he were defending it from an invisible enemy. "Lives are precious, you understand! More precious than —" He could not find a fitting comparison and hesitated. "Than anything!" he concluded.

Then he strode out.

Back in the car, he said to DeWitt, "They're all children. They're all my children. That's why they fight my way. That's why I demand that much. That's why I hate to be double-crossed."

"Tell me something," asked DeWitt. "Why do you put on that show? Where does it get you? You don't have to pretend before me, I've known you too long."

Farrish laughed. "You think it's a show? Huh-uh. I mean every word I say. That's why the politicians don't like me. They can go take a ride on a bucket. I win their battles, don't I? I know my business. Morale, great factor. Those poor guys in there, most of them will be patched up and go out again, and when they come back to their outfits, they're going to tell about how Farrish came to see them. It's a long war. You've got to think ahead."

"What do you really want? Where are you really going?"

DeWitt was acting on a hunch; Farrish, he felt, was becoming a lone wolf.

Farrish raised his brows. "Haven't thought about it — not much."

DeWitt felt hot under his heavy coat. "Don't evade the issue — General!" Never before had he addressed Farrish as General. Its significance was not lost on Farrish.

"All right!" Farrish sighed. "I'll tell you. I've seen a lot and thought about it and learned a lot. We must have a purge. We must weed out the undesirables — the crooks, the politicians, the guys who talk back and always have dozens of considerations. There is too much democracy in the Army, and that doesn't work. It costs the lives of men. Men like my Jimmy."

"What do you mean by democracy?"

"What I said. Talk, inefficiency, politics, double-crossing, stealing my gas. A war has got to be run on the basis of dictatorship —"

He noticed DeWitt's disapproval.

"You can't get around it, old man! Afterwards, when there's peace, they can have it all back — the politicians their politics, and the crooks their graft. We've got to take our lesson from the enemy — much as we might hate doing it. God, if one tenth of the gas sold in Paris had been stolen on *their* side, hundreds of them would be lined up against the wall, and justly so! My record is spotless, and yours is spotless, and there are many others like us. Let's get together and clean out that stable!"

"Fascinating idea," said DeWitt. "You know, of course, what it is!"

"I don't care what you call it. As long as it works."

"But it doesn't," DeWitt said sharply. "You just don't know the facts. I happen to get the documents on my desk — captured documents and orders, and what the prisoners tell us. You complain about corruption — why, it's rampant with the Germans. Peanut politicians, inside and outside the Army — they've got more over there than we could dream up. Inefficiency — how the hell do you explain their defeats? Because we're brave, and good boys, and have more artillery and air force? Fascism is the most corrupt system ever — that's why they have it."

"I didn't say I wanted fascism," said Farrish, choosing his words with care. "If we want to win this war, it's got to be a soldiers' war, it's got to be handled of, by, and for soldiers. Citizens' army . . . Sure, we've got to have citizens in it — whom else? But soldiers have got to run it, according to the laws of a soldier, and with a soldier's iron — iron — "

"Iron fist?"

"Yes! That's it! Iron fist!"

"We once did a leaflet for you. Remember what was in it?"

"Sure! I approved of it! Fourth of July! That's what we're fighting for — America, a strong America, a clean America, a country fit to be proud of!"

"Equality before the law?"

"Sure — but we've got to be the law. We must have a soldiers' caste — "

"Democracy?"

"I'm for it. But it's got to be the kind of democracy that is like a shield, shining, strong, a democracy a man can look up to and be proud to fight for."

"It takes more than soldiers to make a country. You couldn't advance a mile without the labor of thousands of people you've never seen, never heard of, on whose co-operation you must depend. We have an — an industrial society. What you want is, well — medieval, maybe. . . ."

"I don't know about history. I'm just a Division commander. I have fifteen thousand men or so, many of whom I've never seen, never heard of. I make them co-operate, don't I? I even make them go out and die, which is more than those people you mentioned are asked to do!"

"I'm afraid your scheme is just not going to work." DeWitt spoke slowly, emphasizing every word. "We're Americans. We're not that kind of people."

"People!" scoffed Farrish. "People are selling my gas. What I'm afraid of, old man, is that you're just too old for these times!"

DeWitt went back to Verdun. He was glad he at least had had the hot shower.

5

THE INVITATION to Kavalov, made on the spur of the moment, took on an entirely different character on reconsideration — Yates could almost hear Willoughby's *sotto voce,* "What's Yates up to now? Why's he bringing that tramp around?" And if the question were put to him openly, Yates would have had no clear answer. What was he trying to prove, and to whom was he trying to prove it? And was it so important? As important, for instance, as Thérèse who was waiting for him?

But Kavalov behaved with such ease and dignity that, after a few minutes, Yates's misgivings vanished and he began to enjoy the party — the introduction which was a little like the arrival of a new puppy in the kennel, with mutual sniffing and growling; the flare-up of human interest; and finally the effort at making the stranger feel at home.

Yates knew that the venture was possible only through DeWitt's tolerance and because DeWitt had organized the life of his men in Verdun with the work, and not the ceremony, in mind. For the small group — the main body of the Detachment was still in Paris awaiting further orders — he had requisitioned this fairly large house which was living and working quarters at once. Over Willoughby's objections, he had ordered that enlisted men and officers eat in the same room, though at different tables. And it was DeWitt's acceptance of Kavalov that smoothed the way for Yates — "I was brought up in the tradition of hospitality," DeWitt said to him; "we're living together; your guests are my guests." And he was the first to offer his hand to the Russian.

Willoughby studied Kavalov's build and muscles, and said dryly, "Impressive. . . . But why didn't you bring us an average specimen, Yates?"

"I wasn't looking for specimens," Yates shot back. "I brought the man because he'd done something to help us, and the least we can do is to give him a decent meal."

"My God, if you start that, we'll have to feed half of Europe!"

"Damned cheap way to pay back for blood," said Yates.

"We can only do so much," said Willoughby; then, regarding the grayish mass on his dish with critical eyes, "We should go and draw some decent rations, we really should, sir. . . ."

With his fork, the Colonel picked idly at the pork patty that had been heated in the ration can and tasted like it. He looked at Kavalov and observed that the Russian methodically cut his own patty and ate the slices neatly.

"Hungry, Sergeant?" He smiled.

Yates translated the question into German, for Kavalov.

"Not too, thank you," the Russian smiled back at DeWitt. Among cultured people one didn't wolf one's food, even if one felt like it; he was very conscious of the fact that his Government and his people were being judged by his behavior.

"Have mine!" said DeWitt. "I'm not hungry, and why should it go to waste?"

Yates gave the guest an encouraging nod.

Kavalov glanced at the others' plates. Nobody had more than one pork patty. His own was almost gone. "Thank you, no," he said, and set his mouth firmly in refusal.

DeWitt shrugged. It was annoying that he was unable to talk directly to the Russian; he liked the man from what he could see of him. Magnificent physique — that counted for much in a soldier. And he saw that the man's eyes, as they studied his new surroundings and the people about him, noted everything, and that he adjusted himself quickly to what he felt was the custom. A gentleman, no doubt — whether he was brought up to be one or not. Soldiers should be gentlemen.

Kavalov turned to the Colonel.

"What does he want?" asked DeWitt.

Yates leaned forward to make himself heard over the general hubbub. "He wants to know what we feed the Germans we have taken prisoner."

"Why?" asked Willoughby.

"They're not getting very much over at the DP Camp."

"They'll be out of there, soon," said Willoughby, "and earning money. Some of the DP's will be employed locally — in the Lorraine mines, I understand."

Yates frowned. Darkly, he remembered Bing having mentioned the plan. There was something wrong with it, but he couldn't put his finger on it. His mind see-sawed between Kavalov and Thérèse, between the strain of making a success of Kavalov's visit, and the expectation of something too joyous for him to believe fully.

DeWitt ceased picking at his patty. "Yates, you'd better tell Sergeant Kavalov that our prisoners get exactly the same food as he's been eating here."

Kavalov's face went through a scale of emotions: from amazement to disappointment and disgust.

"Tell him about the Geneva Convention!" said DeWitt.

Yates tried. But he felt that all his fine words about fair treatment of a beaten, unarmed enemy fell flat in the presence of Kavalov.

Kavalov slipped back the sleeves of his blouse, showing the scars around his wrists, scars like sharp lines drawn in purple ink with heavy pen. "Shackled with wire," he said. Then he folded his hands behind the back of his chair and explained how he had been hung up by his wrists.

"That was in Riga," he said. "I headed a group inside the city. We were to blow up the powder plant the Germans had taken over."

". . . The powder plant the Germans had taken over," repeated Yates, in English.

"Sabotage behind the lines," said Willoughby. "We'd get nasty, too."

"We do not torture prisoners," said DeWitt.

"Of course not," asserted Willoughby. "But the war in the East seems to be different."

Kavalov waited. When DeWitt's quick eyes again rested on him, he went on, always giving Yates time to interpret. "At that time, a new man joined our group. . . . He had been expected. . . . He had the right identifications. . . . He was to replace me. . . . I had orders to leave Riga before the explosion. . . . I went to his room to hand over my job. . . . I shall never forget that room. . . . A plain wooden table . . . a naked woman crudely carved on its top. . . . He was sitting behind the table and stood up. . . . We shook hands, his was cold. . . . Our hands were linked, the room filled with Germans. . . . He never let go of my hand. . . . When they tortured me they said I could admit everything. . . . They said they knew everything. . . . They said they caught our man who was to replace me . . . and substituted their agent. . . . They said other people couldn't take torture as well as I. . . . They laughed, they thought it was a joke. . . . Perhaps it was."

"Perhaps it was," Yates ended. Except for the occasional clatter of tableware, the mess was quiet.

Willoughby broke the silence. "Ask him, Yates, how come he survived?"

Kavalov cut a thin slice of American cheese, placed it on a cracker, bit off a piece, chewed thoroughly, and swallowed. "I did not confess." And after a pause, "I survived."

Willoughby contemplatively pushed the loose skin of his cheek upward. "I wouldn't like to have you as my enemy, Kavalov!" He laughed.

Yates turned to Kavalov. "The Major says he wouldn't like you as his enemy."

Kavalov laid his knife aside, softly. "We are fighting together, against the same enemy. Together, we will win."

The heavy air suddenly seemed dispelled. DeWitt raised his cup of coffee. "That's an excellent toast! Sorry I ran out of liquor."

The toast was drunk seriously, formally.

Then the Colonel said, "I'd like to do something for the fellow. Ask him, Yates!"

Yates asked. Kavalov's large hand, which had been lying flat on his lap, came up. The fingers bent and formed a grip, as if he were taking someone by the scruff of the neck.

"Yes," replied Kavalov, "there is something I would like. . . . Put me

262

in charge of a camp . . . a camp of German prisoners. . . . I would follow your Geneva Convention to the letter. . . . I would do exactly what you want me to. . . . Give me one day of it."

" . . . One day of it," echoed Yates.

DeWitt had inclined his head so as to catch Kavalov's every intonation. He sensed the urgency, the deep, absorbing hate which came through Kavalov's courteous tone.

"He'll ask for a commission in the Army next," chuckled Willoughby. "Tell him, Yates, his job is all cut out for him. Man with that bone structure, and those arms — he'll be very useful as a miner. . . ."

Yates brushed away the dishes in front of him. The coffee in his cup spilled. He saw that Bing and the men at the other table were looking at him.

"Major!" he said, "I think you're out of luck. You don't know Kavalov. He worked in a mine, under German management. And he didn't produce for them, either."

At the enlisted men's table, someone laughed.

The Colonel raised his hand. "A soldier is a soldier. We have no authority to make him a prison guard, and he shouldn't become one. But if he wants to stay with our Detachment, we'd like to have him. Ask him, Yates."

"Sir . . . !" Willoughby's brows were knitted.

"Well — why not?" DeWitt said, suddenly uncomfortable. "We'll be contacting more and more DP's. He can translate, can't he, together with Yates? Besides, he's a damned good soldier!" His assurance returned. "How are you behind a machine gun, Willoughby?"

"Bad, sir. It's not my job, either." Then, his eyes opening wide, Willoughby asked, "You want to have Bolshevik cells in this organization, sir?"

"Have — what? Major Willoughby, I think our democracy is strong enough to hold its own." Farrish's outburst flashed through the Colonel's mind. His eyes narrowed. "Or aren't you convinced that our way of life and thinking is the best?"

"I am, yes, sir."

"Then why not give the same confidence to the men!"

Kavalov had sensed the clash and suspected that he was its cause. He waited for its end. Then, quietly, he spoke to Yates.

Yates translated. "Kavalov wants me to thank you for your offer, Colonel. He says he'd be proud to serve under you. But he wants to go back to his own Army."

"How'll he get back?" asked Willoughby.

Yates smiled. "He'll manage."

DeWitt lit a cigarette and drew on it. He was kind of let down. DeWitt

263

wanted witnesses to his belief that Farrish's plan could never materialize; he wanted them close; and he didn't care where they came from — what country, what class, what color — as long as they bore out his conviction that man was basically a decent animal.

"I should have liked to keep him around," Yates said.

"Would you?" Willoughby asked, hoarsely.

"Well, Major, if you should send me to a difficult spot — with this man along, I'd feel secure."

Willoughby rose and clicked down the handle of his canteen cup. "I only rely on myself."

By the time Yates and Thérèse reached the house, darkness was complete. The blackout regulations were in force. Yates recognized the house by the small spire on the corner of its roof, but he could hardly find the handle to the garden gate. He had to feel his way through the garden to the stairs leading to the entrance.

"Take my hand, Thérèse," he whispered, and, feeling her hand small and trusting in his, he recaptured the thrill of his boyhood, of the first girl he led to the porch of her parents' home, on a summer evening. They had sat on the porch and listened to the rustling of the leaves, and to the sound of the cars on the road. Then, they had trembled because they were afraid that their being together was something forbidden.

Nothing was forbidden in his relationship to Thérèse. Had he cared to announce it to any of his superiors, he would have had their noisy approval. A man has to exert his natural instincts; war reduces such necessities to an animal level. But this was just what he wanted to avoid — for the sake of his own self-respect and for Thérèse's sake. And then there was Ruth to think of. Walking through the garden with Thérèse, the pebbles on the path crunching under their feet, the memory of Ruth was painfully clear. He wanted to drive it away, it had no business here — Ruth was part of a different life; and she would not object because she would want him to stay normal in the life he now was leading. And his feelings for Thérèse were entirely different from those he held for Ruth. One thing had nothing to do with the other. He was true to Ruth, he said to himself, because he would not allow Thérèse to touch the part of his heart and his mind and his memory which was reserved for Ruth; and in a few days, the stream of the war would reach him and carry him off again — and that would be that.

All these thoughts were out of place, he chided himself. Why couldn't he be like everyone else, taking what came his way, accepting it gladly, enjoying it, without racking his brain over its possible implications? Ruth was none the poorer for his giving Thérèse what Ruth could not have anyhow.

And Thérèse knew very well how shortlived their happiness was bound to be, and she didn't complain about it and was willing to grasp what life gave her!

"Your hand is cold," she said, her voice small and tender.

He blamed it on the weather.

The door was opened for them. In the dimly lit foyer stood Bing. Bing smiled and said, "Good evening, Mademoiselle — please, follow me."

Through the glass door at the left, Yates heard the voices of the men from the messroom beyond. He recognized Abramovici's blaring tenor, but could not understand what was being said. Someone was snapping the cards of a deck, in preparation for shuffling it.

Bing said, "The Colonel and Major Willoughby have gone out — there's a staff meeting somewhere. Everybody else is in the mess. I told them to cut their racket, but you won't hear it anyway. You're on the third floor."

"Thanks," said Yates. He observed the light, graceful steps of Thérèse. Under his boots, the stairs were creaking, she seemed hardly to touch the boards. He wanted very much to hold her close to him. He told himself to wait; in a few minutes they would be alone, a door would close out the world and the war.

They reached the top floor.

"There's only one room up here," explained Bing. "It isn't much of a room, as you will see. . . ."

He opened the door, and Thérèse, stepping in, smiled with pleasure. "How nice!" she said. "*Charmant!* You're very good to us, *Monsieur le Sergent.*"

In the light of the bulb which he himself had provided that afternoon, Bing studied the girl. He liked her, and he was satisfied with his arrangements and glad that she admired them. She stepped on the rug; it was really the worn pelt of a polar bear and it had become bald in spots.

"That's from under the piano!" Bing whispered to Yates. "I've sort of stripped the house for what we needed. There are sheets on the bed — don't ask me where I got them. And we have a tablecloth, not so clean, of course, but it covers the hole in the table."

Thérèse went around, touching the chest of drawers, the carvings at the foot of the bed. She straightened the lace doily on the easy chair. She was like a bride entering the house her man built for her; she found joy in everything.

"You wanted to make me feel at home," she said. "This is like home, really!"

"Don't sit down on that chair!" said Yates. "It's got only three legs." He saw, only too well, the shoddiness of the room, the ramshackle condition

265

of every piece in it. He knew that Bing had done wonders, but wonders were not good enough. He had only one wish — to turn off the light which had no shade and shed its straight glare over all the deficiencies.

"And here," Bing pulled back a curtain, "is your washstand. Water in the pitcher, towels on the rack." He reached into the top drawer of the chest. He smiled. "This is the best — a bottle of '34 Sauterne. A good year, they tell me. And glasses."

He had three glasses; apparently he expected to share the toast of welcome.

But Yates turned to him and said, "For God's sake, scram! You've been awfully decent to do all this, and I want to thank you — but quit acting like a God-damned Madame!"

The moment he said it, he could have bitten off his tongue. He saw the pained expression around Bing's mouth. Bing smoothed his hair. Then he left quickly.

Bing went down to the next floor and sat on the stairs and took up his vigil. He would sit there until everybody had gone to bed.

He kept his guard in spite of his disappointment. He had seen the whole thing in a romantic light; it was his own fault that reality had shown its edges. He had wanted to create a little magic castle, even if it was not for himself, and out of its magic, a ray was to fall on him. He had wanted to fool the war and give it a little beauty, as he had fooled it with his leaflet in Normandy, and given it a meaning it probably didn't have.

Abramovici came by on his way to the faucet, towel over his arm, toothbrush in his hand.

"I'm going to conk you over the head if you gargle tonight!" announced Bing, and as Abramovici was pulling in breath for a defense of his gargling, Bing said, "Not a squeak out of you, you understand!"

He heard Willoughby and DeWitt return. DeWitt came up the stairs, heavily.

"What you doing here, Sergeant? Why don't you turn in?"

"I can't sleep, sir, I'm not tired."

"Well, go downstairs. Sit on a decent chair!"

"Thank you, sir, perhaps later."

DeWitt shrugged and went to his room.

Bing sat and thought of Karen. He imagined Karen and himself in the attic room, undisturbed, finding one another. She was so much more mature than he, and he had behaved like a stupid, stubborn, self-centered, arrogant boy. That was all over, and he had only regrets to keep him company. But he could dream, dream of her head bending back, of her throat, and of her hands touching the nape of his neck.

The moon came out. The night was fairly warm, and Yates had opened

266

the skylight window. A shaft of pale light fell on the half-empty bottle and the glasses on the table.

He listened to Thérèse's regular breathing. Her head rested on his shoulder. His hand lay on her breast, feeling its roundness, its warmth, its life.

He was very quiet. The blood, which had beaten against his temples until he believed they would burst, until he had felt her body surge to his, had come to rest and was flowing through him evenly, relaxing him down to his toes and to the tips of his fingers.

"*Chéri,*" she had said, "how will I ever be without you?"

"You won't," he had answered.

Her hair was soft. The smoothness of her skin was like that of fresh grass in spring. He had buried his mouth in the flesh of her thighs and the inside of her elbows.

Thérèse stirred. She turned and her face came against the side of his chest. Her lips moved. She was kissing him in her sleep.

Yates felt strong and at peace with himself. She had given him strength and peace. He loved her for it.

6

Yates leaned back in the car. The wind, saturated with the dampness of the ground, was beating against his face. The hilly fields changed into woods. The purr of the motor droned on. He slumped in his seat, giving his body to the rocking of the car, the unevenness of the road.

In him was the dull pain of his good-by to Thérèse; she had said "*Au revoir*" with a pitiful courage in her voice; but they both had known that they would not see one another again.

"So soon. . . ." she had said when he told her he was ordered to move on.

"Yes, so soon. . . ."

In him had been rebellion against the brutality of being torn from her, against the signature on a piece of mimeographed paper that cut and killed something so tender and beautiful, something just begun. Rebellion and the dull realization that their own lives were neither in his nor in her hands.

Then he had attempted to talk sensibly. He had told her that what they had been to one another would live on and enrich their lives, like a melody that sank into your heart and remained there and made itself heard again, always. She had nodded bravely, and said, "Yes, dearest," and clung to his hand.

She had given him so much and he had given her nothing of what a man should give a woman: the house he had offered her was an attic furnished by Bing; the security he had brought her was a few nights in his arms. If he had not taken her, would it have been better?

He remembered something he had not understood. She had said, "You don't know how much I owe you. You've made me well."

She had refused to explain. How can I make anyone well, he thought, the kind of person I am. . . . And he thought how little he knew her, how little he knew anybody, including his own wife, Ruth.

Funny that he should think of Ruth. She had been pushing herself more and more into the foreground of his mind. He thought back to his attitude toward her — when he landed in Normandy, and even before that time, when, on a foggy morning, the ship glided down the murky river to sea, to Europe, into the great adventure. He had been afraid then, almost crazy with fear. He had said to himself that it was unlikely he would ever again see that sky line, or Ruth, or anything that had been. He had looked at the other men and officers aboard; they were taking it in their stride, or acting as if they did, and even appeared happy in an exaggerated kind of way. He had then decided that he would have to banish the past, and Ruth with it — the less you thought of what you left behind, the less you felt the loss of it. The best, the only way to take what was coming, was to take it as an adventure and to live untroubled while it lasted.

Of course, the plan worked only in part. You could shed the things which had been outside yourself; you could not get rid of what you were and what had made you. If you tried to bury it, it broke through the vault and resurrected itself. And there it was — you had to live with yourself, all of you.

Here, perhaps, lay the essence of what Thérèse had been to him — she had made him bridge the gap between Yates, the man, and Yates, the soldier afraid of death, who had therefore geared himself to it. She had transplanted into him a tiny part of herself, and this would stay with him. If, similarly, a part of his being had gone over to her, then, maybe, the futility of their love would lose its knife edge, and a reflection of beauty would remain to them both. She had helped him to outgrow the self-centered adventurer and to return to life.

Outgrow? She had made him grow a little. For the first time, he had sensed toward a woman that he was the stronger, that she relied on him. He had been happy in her trust, and he worried about what would become of her, and that he could do nothing for her, though he wanted to, very much. For the first time, he was concerned more about the woman than about himself.

With a sense of catastrophe, he felt that Ruth might well have looked to him for the very thing he had given Thérèse, and which he had never given to her. Had he forced Ruth into the role of mentor which he resented? Was she, perhaps, patiently waiting for him to become all that was her right to expect in her man?

He had not known how much Ruth loved him — because he, himself, until now had not fully understood the meaning of love. For this, he had to come to the lonely road from Verdun to Rollingen.

"I want you to go to Rollingen," DeWitt had said to Yates. "Take a couple of men and a loudspeaker truck. Twice or three times a day, make some news announcements on the market square — they must have a market square. Get in touch with Civil Affairs, get their co-operation and offer your help. Your main mission is to make a survey of the population — their opinions, their loyalties, on whose side they are, how far they can be counted upon to help us."

"When do I start?"

"Tomorrow morning, I suggest." And he had handed Yates the mimeographed orders.

Yates had managed to fold them and put them neatly into his pocket. This had given him the chance to overcome the first quick, sharp hurt of *That's the end for Thérèse and me.* But fussing with the papers, the pocket, the button to his pocket, also helped him to hide the other thought: Rollingen is the center of the Delacroix empire. Prince Yasha will be there; and I will have him for myself.

He had glanced at DeWitt, trying to find out whether the same thought was in the Colonel's mind. But DeWitt's face had been set in its usual lines; no sign that the man implied more than he actually said.

"One thing more," DeWitt had continued. "You'll be on your own, so be careful. No extraneous activities, please."

That could mean anything, Yates had figured. It didn't exclude a visit to Yasha, whose opinions were as important as those of the baker and the butcher. Could it be that DeWitt had chosen the pattern of a survey in Rollingen because, back in Paris, Yates had given Willoughby a similar survey as his reason for wanting to interview Yasha? DeWitt had a sense of humor.

"No extraneous activities!" Yates had affirmed.

"The people, I understand, can be classed as border population. Lorraine is bilingual. In Rollingen, they speak German, mostly. Now here's your problem, Yates: How German are their feelings?"

"Check," Yates had said. "I'll take Bing and Abramovici, if you don't mind. McGuire as driver?"

"Settle that with Willoughby," DeWitt had said coolly.

When Yates had spoken to Willoughby, he noticed how ill-at-ease the Major was. Willoughby had paced through his room, "So you're going to

Rollingen? Very good! Very interesting assignment — wish you all the luck in the world. Sure — take any man you like. And let me know what you find out."

Then he had stopped. His dark, sharp eyes had been somewhat blood-shot.

"I bet you think you're putting one over on me!"

He had sat down, draped his feet on his desk and said complacently, "My dear Yates, your animosity against me is very stupid. I know, I know — you got a rotten deal in Paris; nobody enjoys looking like a fool. But don't you see I had to do it? Either you were going to look foolish or I was — so I had no choice. Wouldn't you have done the same in my place?"

"Sir, looking foolish wasn't the issue involved."

"Whatever . . . ! We should be friends, Yates. I can help you a lot. After all, we both want to win this war and get it over with. . . ."

He had sounded sincere enough.

But Yates had not committed himself. And as he left Willoughby's room, he had heard the Major resume his pacing.

A row of blast furnaces rose out of the valley. They lay quiet in the autumn sun. A few men, insignificantly small, were busily scraping away at their sides. To Yates, it seemed that their labor could not possibly have any effect.

He ordered his jeep and the loudspeaker truck stopped at the first inter-section in town. Few people were about. Rollingen was subdued and peaceful, an ominous peacefulness which laid itself around the small group of Americans like a pall of invisible fog.

Bing got out of the loudspeaker truck and walked over to Yates's jeep.

"How long since the Germans left?" Yates asked a man who, a much-washed blue apron over his big stomach, looked like a shoemaker but could have been the grocer or even the owner of the *Schwarze Rabe* beer cellar at the corner.

"Five days!" said the man. "That was the last time they came back. They've been in and out for three weeks."

"How many, the last time?"

"Not many. Just a patrol, maybe. . . ."

He tried to retreat.

"*Kommen Sie her!*" shouted Bing.

The man advanced timidly.

"What's going on here? What's the matter with these people?"

The man looked around to see if he was being observed. Then he leaned into the car and whispered to Yates, "The Americans are retreating!"

Yates, who had no such information, said, "Nonsense! Where did you hear that rumor?"

"I've seen it with my own eyes! As truly as I stand here before you, I've seen it! They came in here on Thursday, with armored cars and tanks and guns, and stayed till Saturday; and then at night, they left."

"Sure!" said Bing. "Did you think the troops would stay here forever? Most soldiers go to the front, to fight, you know?"

"Maybe!" The man spread his hands. Everything is possible, he seemed to say. "But they went that way!" His thumb pointed over his shoulder, in the direction of the road across the mountain which Yates and his team had traveled. "No protection for us!" The man suddenly yammered. "And we have wife and child. What is going to happen?"

Then his expression changed. A wan smile of hope went over his large, dreary face. "You're going to stay here?"

"Probably!" Yates said to encourage the man.

It was a ridiculous situation. He and his three men couldn't defend Rollingen even if they wanted to. But to this man, and perhaps to quite a number like him, the jeep and the loudspeaker car — total armament: one pistol, one carbine, two rifles — were a token that the Americans were here to stay. At Verdun, Yates had been told that he would find an Armored Infantry Battalion in Rollingen — apparently, it was this Battalion that had pulled out. The direction, which spelled retreat to the local population, of course meant nothing — but how could he explain to this man the intricacies of an army in battle? God knows where the Battalion had been needed.

Meanwhile, a dozen or so citizens with equally anxious faces had assembled.

"How are things at Metz?" someone wanted to know. It was a thin, resentful voice, ready to pounce.

"The Americans are in Metz!" Bing said firmly. Since they were to broadcast news anyhow, he saw no reason for keeping the information to himself.

The thin voice stopped being resentful and became sneering. "Oh no, they aren't. We know!"

A woman came to the other side of the jeep, tapped Abramovici's arm, and whispered, "He's the owner of the *Goldene Lamm*. All the Nazi bigshots stayed at his place. Don't you trust him."

Abramovici said nothing. He decided he would trust nobody and would keep his rifle handy at all times.

The thin voice continued, conscious of its own importance. It was not quite clear whether the owner of the *Goldene Lamm* was lecturing his townspeople, or the Americans. "Is there any water in the upper part of our city? The upper part gets its water from Metz, everybody knows that this is so!"

He paused.

271

"But it isn't getting any water. The Germans have shut down the pipe. Therefore, the Germans are in Metz."

Bing left the side of the car and made his way through the small crowd, to the speaker. The man stepped back. Then, feeling himself isolated and without the protection of the others, he began to talk fast, "It's the truth! Look at the water uptown! I'm not saying that the Americans are *not* in Metz — but the Germans are in there, too. A few Germans only, very few, and they're going to get out fast. They always get out fast, they always run, the cowards! We've seen them run from Rollingen, haven't we?"

He laughed, hysterically. His laughter stopped when he saw Bing wave him closer.

"What's your name?"

"Reuther, *Herr Feldwebel.*"

"How many rooms in the *Goldene Lamm?*"

The man stuttered.

"We need four rooms, and we need fresh sheets," said Bing flatly.

"But, *lieber Herr,* I have just had American soldiers in the house. Why don't you go to the *Schwarze Rabe?* That's a first-class hotel, and it's also recognized by the Association of National German Hotel Owners!"

"Come here, my man, come closer!" Bing said in his kindliest tone. He and the owner of the *Goldene Lamm* were now the center of the crowd, which had grown considerably.

"We're bringing you a great many presents," expounded Bing. "Freedom and security and the long-desired opportunity to rejoin France. You ought to be happy to take upon yourself a few little inconveniences."

Hearing the word *inconveniences,* the crowd thinned out; but those who remained were grinning.

"All right, Herr Reuther — hop into the car and show us the way to your first-rate establishment also recognized by the Association of National German Hotel Owners. I hope their recommendation is trustworthy."

Bing turned the man around, almost playfully, and gave him just enough of a shove to propel him at a good speed to the car.

"I've solved the housing problem," he announced to Yates.

Yates and his men walked down the street to the *mairie.* It was the only building showing a French flag.

They were welcomed by the Mayor, who was a local *avocat.* He wore a red beard which did not fit in with his well-cut pin-striped suit. He said he had been in the woods until the town was evacuated by the Germans, and since he did not know how long his new grandeur in office would last, he would rather hang on to the beard.

The Police Chief, much elated by the addition to the local forces of liberation, shook Yates's hand long and fervently, and assured him that the situation was excellent, and that police reinforcements, promised from Nancy three days before, could be expected momentarily.

"A whole squad of Gendarmerie!" he said, awed. "And well-armed and uniformed."

He himself wore coveralls and a Basque cap, and a German pistol was strapped to his belt.

"I'm not really a policeman," he confided to Yates, "I'm a foundry worker. We were about sixty FFI men from here, but most have gone to their homes. Very understandable, *n'est-ce pas?*"

"As soon as the gendarmes from Nancy arrive," said the Mayor, "we're going to organize a liberation parade. Of course, you'll be in it, Lieutenant — the gentlemen of the Civil Affairs Detachment are going to march, too. We'll have the police in front, then the Americans, then the Fire Department, then the Rollingen *Société des Jeunes Femmes* in their national costumes — really very pretty, very, I assure you; and then any part of the remaining population that cares to join. The *Curé* is going to have the church bells rung, and we're trying to find enough instruments for the band — the Germans stole the best."

He looked so pleadingly that Yates said he would be very glad to parade.

"I wanted to have the flags out, too," said the Mayor, "but the Police Chief advised against it. Up in Villeblanche, the people hung out the flags, and the Germans came back, and the heads of those families who had shown the French flag were forced to go with the Germans, and one has not heard from them since."

"Is that so?" said Yates. "Well, that won't happen here."

The Mayor said nothing.

Yates asked, "The situation here is different, isn't it? The front line. . . ."

"*Mon Lieutenant,*" said the Police Chief, shoving back his cap, "*we* are the front line — we, and you, and your Civil Affairs Detachment that is quartered across the railroad tracks."

"And the Germans?"

"We don't know. They could be fifteen miles from here, or five miles. It is a quiet sector, we hope."

"Suppose they infiltrate?"

"You mean, march in here, *mon Lieutenant?* They could, easily. Nothing to hold them — except maybe thirty or forty FFI men in a farmhouse east of town."

"You see how it is," said the Mayor.

Yates could see how it was. These people were trying so hard to make a go of it, on pretty slippery soil. And they were whistling in the dark. Well, if they could, so could he.

"I'll be in the parade," he said, "and my men, too. Sorry, I've got only three. . . ."

Just as Yates stepped out of the *mairie,* an ancient truck, its rear crammed with Gendarmes, came rambling down the road. Yates never had had much love for the police; but he was glad to see the truckload of Gendarmes, and stopped to talk to their sergeant.

Yes, they would be in the parade, said the Sergeant; they had already had two parades in towns along the road. But then, they would have to push on. Of course, sufficient forces would be left in Rollingen.

"How many?" inquired Yates.

"Four men," said the Sergeant, and excused himself because he had to confer with the Police Chief.

Yates began to see a grim humor in the Rollingen situation, and he thought he might as well get into the spirit of it. He ought to be able to rally at least as much fatalism as the French Mayor. If things were as precarious as they seemed, he had all the more reason for getting in touch with Yasha immediately. But the parade would take up the rest of the afternoon. . . .

He would send Bing to Yasha's villa.

He called his men. Only Abramovici and McGuire, both munching apples, reported. Abramovici said righteously that Bing had become tired of waiting and had gone off to take a look around town.

Yates blew up.

The whole tenseness stored in him broke out. Then, in the middle of his tirade, he stopped. No sense in crushing Abramovici who, thanks to Bing's irresponsibility, would now have to go to Yasha.

Bing, if given the right instructions, would have come through on this mission with flying colors and, if necessary, would have brought in Yasha by his ear.

But Abramovici — with his natural obedience to anything smacking of authority?

Perhaps even McGuire would be better. No, McGuire knew no French, and the visit to Yasha's house on the hill might require considerable parleying with guards, butlers, or maids — and maids, definitely, would be McGuire's finish.

"There'll be a parade," Yates said, and added that the four of them were to represent the armed might of the United States.

Abramovici blossomed; his chest expanded. Yates could see that the little man was preparing himself mentally for the part.

"Not now, Abramovici," Yates said; "we have about an hour's time until the thing starts. . . . McGuire, you can take off. Try to find Bing, and report here in front of the *mairie* in exactly an hour. . . . For you, Abramovici, I have a special job."

Balefully, he studied Abramovici. Then the thought struck him that the martial enthusiasm and the deadpan seriousness of the man might be the very thing to impress Yasha who, as a European, must be imbued with respect for the military. If Abramovici remembered to keep his pants pulled up, he could look quite formidable.

"Do you see the big house up on the hill? Yes, the one that looks like a stage set from Wagner."

When the furnaces are going, thought Yates, the house must be enveloped in smoke — perhaps Yasha enjoyed the grime that promised profits.

"Take the jeep; drive up there and ask for Prince Yasha Bereskin." Hastily, Yates added, "We're Americans. We don't give a damn about titles. Is that clear?"

"Yes, sir!" The tone assured Yates that Abramovici was full of the spirit of '76.

"If the Prince is there, you make certain that he stays there. You tell him that I'm in Rollingen and that I want to see him tomorrow at 2 P.M. sharp. Mention that he'd better be waiting for me. Don't take any excuses; if anyone tries to get funny and wants to keep you away from the Prince, just sort of show them that you carry a weapon."

Abramovici slapped the stock of his rifle.

"That's right!" Yates kept his face very straight. "Precisely as we represent our Army, our people, our Government, in the parade, so you represent the same things, and me in addition, in your mission to the Prince."

Abramovici was grave. "The Prince is a dangerous man?"

"Not physically." Yates couldn't afford to let fear creep into his messenger. "Prince Yasha is dangerous in a political sense."

"A Nazi agent?"

"The Prince is a very rich man," Yates explained carefully. "He owns three quarters of this joint, and his politics are questionable. I rely entirely on you, Abramovici, on your diplomacy and forceful personality."

"Yes, sir!" blared Abramovici.

He was finally coming into his own — an independent mission, and a parade to follow it!

He ran to the *Goldene Lamm* to fetch the jeep.

Driving up to the house on the hill, Abramovici squirmed in his seat, restlessly. His feelings about very rich people were mixed; he had a deep envy and resentment toward them because they were Haves and he was a Have-Not; on the other hand, he admired them because they had achieved what he aspired to. Back home, he had piously delivered the few dollars he saved from his meager wages to the Long Island Savings and Trust Bank; with quiet satisfaction, he had watched the growth of his account. Over here, however, he had devised for himself a different scale of values, based on the fact that he was a soldier in the liberating and conquering Army. In this scale he, as a member of this Army, held a position higher than even the richest Prince, and the size of his own bankbook had nothing to do with it.

But in the hall of Yasha's villa, dark with heavy furniture and deep rugs which gave underneath his boots, his self-confidence was sorely tried. The servant, who had gone to announce him to the Prince, had looked at him very much askance, and another servant lurked near by apparently suspicious that the soldier under the big helmet might be interested in some of the *objets d'art* as souvenirs.

Abramovici stared at the servant belligerently. He tried to make the butt of his rifle resound on the floor, but the rugs interfered. This Prince — was he a real Prince? — living in such surroundings, would not take kindly to the orders of a Technician Fifth Grade. Abramovici was kept waiting. The longer he waited, the less sure he became. Perhaps he was being trapped. Yates had said the Prince was politically questionable. What if some Germans were hidden in this large, dark house? There were practically no Allied troops in Rollingen; Yates should never have sent him up here, all alone. If he disappeared — what could Yates do? Abramovici gripped his rifle more firmly and advanced toward the man watching him. Hoarsely, he said, "I don't have time to wait. I want to see the Prince, now, and get out of here!"

It must have been the way he held the rifle — the man flew and came back with the first servant and brought the Prince's apologies, and the Prince would see him now.

"Aha!" said Abramovici, "that is better!" and allowed himself to be ushered into the Prince's presence.

Yasha sat deep in an easy chair, a silk robe around his bony frame. At his feet lay a sheep dog, the size of Abramovici; the dog rose, growling, and pushed his wet nose against Abramovici's cartridge belt.

"Grishka!" purred the Prince, "come here, Grishka." The dog retreated, slowly lay down, and was petted by Yasha. "Grishka doesn't like strangers," and it came out as if it were spoken for the dog's owner as well.

Abramovici cleared his throat. He took up a position which would enable him to face the dog as well as the Prince. Finally, he remembered something. He pulled back the bolt of his rifle and let a cartridge glide into the chamber.

Yasha started up, he didn't like the clicking sound. "Why do you do that?"

Abramovici explained, "A bullet fired at such close range, would tear a hole the size of my fist into your dog." His knees were trembling and he was glad that his baggy pants kept the Prince from realizing it.

"Sit down," said Yasha, "consider yourself my guest. Drink?"

"I never drink," Abramovici said truthfully, and he would have told the Prince of the damage alcohol did to a man, had not every word meant such an effort to his constricted throat.

The laconic visitor, the bullet in the chamber of his rifle, made Yasha feel extremely uncomfortable. It was the first time that anyone not an officer had dared to approach him; even the Nazis, on their frequent black-mailing attempts, had observed the niceties due his station in life.

"What do you want?" he burst out.

"Nothing much," gulped Abramovici.

Nothing much, thought Yasha. What was this — a hold-up? He had come here to take inventory and to get his mines and mills going. He had done nothing that could displease the Allied authorities: he had received the red-bearded fool of a Mayor and the American captain who was head of Civil Affairs, he was in the clear with the powers-that-be; and this visit was highly irregular, if not actually ominous.

"My commanding officer," said Abramovici, who had finally managed to collect enough breath for a longer sentence, "wishes you to hold yourself in readiness for tomorrow afternoon at 2 P.M. sharp."

"But why should he want to see me? I am a citizen of the French Republic, I am a highly respected businessman. It is most certainly my right to attend to the properties entrusted to me. . . ."

"I don't know," said Abramovici, shifting on the chair and accidentally pointing the gun in the general vicinity of the Prince.

"Take that rifle away, will you!" the Prince demanded nervously. "I am not accustomed to this kind of visit!"

"The rifle," said Abramovici, who felt safest with statements of basic value, "is an essential part of the soldier's equipment. In wartime, a man should not part with his rifle; even when he sleeps, he must keep it within easy reach."

Yasha took the words for irony. The little man with the big helmet and the big feet, whom he first had thought ridiculous, was a serious threat. And the worst of it was that he didn't know the source of the threat, and that he was unable to find out.

"Do you mean to say that I am under a kind of house arrest? Hold myself in readiness — for what? I don't understand! This is not Germany where a man can be arrested at all times and under all pretexts!"

The more anxious Yasha became, the more relaxed Abramovici felt. Abramovici remembered the importance of the mission entrusted to him. He remembered his scale of values.

"You're very rich," he said, "aren't you? I've always wanted to meet real rich people. How does one become rich? How did you get rich?"

A gangster, thought Yasha. America is full of them. Naturally, they'd be in uniform, too. He wanted to ring the bell, call the police, call Civil Affairs. *A bullet, fired at such close range, would make a hole as big as my fist . . .*

"What do you want? How much? I have no money with me. I have been here a few days only. . . ."

Abramovici didn't understand the offer at all. His question had been theoretical. Finally, Yasha's purpose penetrated the thick pelt of his absolute honesty.

"You dare bribing me? Sir, I could arrest you on the spot. In wartime, in the Zone of Operations, any American soldier has the right of arrest!"

"If you don't drink, you don't mind if I do?"

"No," said Abramovici, "spoil your health if you wish." Then he rose, followed by the dog. I must not be afraid, he thought. Dogs smell fear. When they smell fear, they jump you. He retreated toward the door, slowly, strategically.

"Tomorrow at two!" he warned. "Don't forget. And you'd better be here!"

As soon as the door closed, the Prince rushed to the window. He tried to see the men who must be surrounding the house. Seeing no sign of them, he suspected that they were well-camouflaged.

A strange feeling had overtaken Bing as, waiting before the *mairie,* he saw the little boy with the apples. He traded a roll of Charms for three apples. He gave an apple each to Abramovici and to McGuire, and then took off.

The various sensations of the morning began to fall into place, and created one total sensation, deeply disturbing to Bing: he was meeting his lost childhood. He knew why — Rollingen, though in the French province of Lorraine, was the first town he had reached which bore the visible imprint of the Germans: not of the Germans as conquerors, not of the Nazi boot, but of the Germans who had lived here and dominated the province for generations. He could see it and hear it and feel it and almost smell it; the systematic cleanliness; the iron fences, well-painted; the titles before the names on store and house signs; the beer mugs in the *Goldene Lamm,* name-plated for the man who always drank from them; the cobblestones laid out like mosaic on the streets; thoroughness and solidity, pettiness and limitations, clearly defined; and the curve with which a man doffed his hat calculated exactly to fit the station in life of the man being greeted.

Now, Bing didn't like any of that because he had grown into a more

278

generous nation and had become a part of it. Yet, in such surroundings he had had a more or less happy childhood until the Nazis came to power; he wondered how much of it had been ingrained in him. The peculiar flower of Nazism had grown here, perhaps could grow only on this soil where out of the meanness and grudges of their daily existence, people yearned for a romantic and cruel power; where subordination and evasion of responsibility were singularly paired with the desire to be more and better than the next guy. He understood these people all too well; he had to have only one look at men like Reuther, the owner of the *Goldene Lamm,* to know how to deal with them. Did he have this instinctive understanding because there was, in *him,* the residue of *them?* And if so, what was to become of him since he hated them for what they were, for what they had caused, and for what they had allowed to happen? Did he have to hate himself?

He could find no answer. But he knew that the question must be answered sometime, that it would follow him and become more urgent as the armies crossed the border into Germany proper, and as they pushed deeper into it. He decided then that, if ever the armies got that far, he must make it possible to go to the small city of Neustadt. There he had been born, there had been his childhood, and there he would discover whether he had outgrown the German in him, whether the roots which once tied him to the poisonous soil had been destroyed.

He had been wandering without destination, and now had come into the side streets. His train of thought was disrupted by a woman in a shabby calico dress. He could see she had been running, from the way her rough woolen stockings hung around her ankles. She collared him and panted, "He'll kill her! He'll kill her! You must come, *Herr Soldat,* and save her!"

Now he heard the screams coming down the street, and though he should have asked questions and been careful of what he let himself in for, he went with the woman.

She led him through a door into a dark back yard surrounded by workers' tenements. Laundry flapped on lines hung from one side to the other. Before the entrance to the rear tenement stood a hushed crowd, fringed by children. They were listening to the screams shrilling through the open first-floor windows. The strokes of a flat instrument against something soft sounded clearly. "Mercy! Mercy!" the cry came from inside. Then a door falling, glass crashing, hurried steps, a man's voice, "Come out of there, you bitch!"

A man in the yard, arms crossed, smacked his lips and said, "What a beating! What a beating!"

The woman who had fetched Bing implored, "My sister! He's killing her!"

279

A slovenly, gray-haired woman, part of her hair pinned up, the other part in straggling curls, said, "What if he is killing her! So much the better! She deserves it, the whore!"

"A regular *maison publique!*" said a big-bosomed girl in a silk blouse, sidling up to Bing. "German soldiers coming in at all hours. Drunk! Disturbing people's sleep!"

"And her man up in the woods, fighting the Boche!"

"There he goes again!"

Inside, a door crashed and a cry rose and became a wail. A dull blow. The wailing ceased.

Bing went to the entrance of the tenement. The people gave way willingly. He hesitated. Liberation, he thought; this, too, is liberation — the backwash of it. A man coming home, finding his wife has become a Nazi whore, perhaps because she couldn't do without it, perhaps for money, or favors. Now he beats her to death. Why should I interfere? I've got my own problems.

The people were watching him — what would he do?

A child came up to him, shyly, *"Schokolade?"*

"Later!" he said, and went in.

The rooms of the flat were built around a winding stairway, so that the woman could have given her returned husband a merry chase. Bing went from one room to the other; whatever movable furniture there was, had been thrown over. He picked his way to the kitchen. There, on the floor, more dead than alive, her head against the gas stove, lay the woman; the man was standing over her. Her face was swollen and discolored. Blood ran down her cheek and her chin. Even discounting the evidence of the beating, she was by no means a handsome woman, not with those thin lips, that snout-like nose, the Punchinello chin, and that flat chest. Funny taste these Germans have, Bing thought.

"Come on! Quit that!" Bing said. "You've given her the works, that's enough."

The man shook his head. He seemed unable to place Bing's right to interfere.

The woman moved sideways, slowly, slowly — and then, seeing that her husband was concentrating on the American, she jumped up and ran. The man lumbered after her. Bing guessed that they would come his way again; and they did: the woman first, her mop of hair flying, crying "Help!" — the man at her heels.

She stopped, because Bing barred the way with his rifle. The man bumped against her, and immediately gave her a vicious clout over the head, which sent her reeling.

"Stop!" shouted Bing, "I told you to stop!"

The man growled that he had his rights.

"I'm French!" he cried. "Damn you! I fight for you! I get my home destroyed! I'll kill her, the lousy whore!"

"No, you won't!" said Bing, significantly tapping the stock of his rifle. "I'm the authority here, you see?" The man dripped sweat, his hands were stained with his wife's blood. Bing had no desire to tangle with him. Now, a few people from outside had come into the flat, the woman's sister among them; they were staring at him and at the man.

The woman, recovering from the last blow, had risen to her knees and was embracing Bing's legs. He couldn't move, and if the man were to attack him, he would have to fire, probably hitting the spectators.

He pushed the woman away, but she held on. He let the butt of the rifle drop, and it fell on her knee. She yowled and crept back. Then he jammed the muzzle in the man's stomach and said, "Go!"

The returned husband obeyed.

"You come along, too!" Bing ordered the woman. She groaned and rose and limped after them.

It was quite a parade which came out of the side street onto the main road of Rollingen. First the man with the bloody hands, Bing's rifle still pointed at him; next to him his wife, dragging her beaten body. After them, Bing, representing law and order — and behind him, that portion of the neighbors able to leave the tenements. The procession, marching in the general direction of the Mairie, was joined by numerous passers-by. Most of them seemed genuinely happy over the misfortune of the couple; and Bing, who understood their every remark, felt conspicuous and thought: That's how they behaved when the Nazis marched their prisoners through town.

He looked back — at least two hundred people were following him. "Get away from here, all of you!" he shouted, "get back!" The mass swayed slightly, but kept its footing.

And then he heard music and saw flags coming up the road. The Marseillaise, at first a few disjointed sounds, took form and swelled and became powerful. Involuntarily, the prisoner, his unfaithful wife, Bing, and his followers fell into step.

The French gendarmes, flags, drums, and dignitaries, leading the Liberation Parade, were now only a few yards from Bing. The two columns swerved, Bing maneuvering his to the right, and the gendarmes leading theirs to their right. The colorfully dressed young ladies of the Rollingen *Société des Jeunes Femmes,* their laces and ribbons softly ruffling in the wind, eyed Bing and his two protégés with shocked surprise and not a little curiosity.

And there marched Yates, and McGuire, and Abramovici!

Bing shouldered his rifle and snapped to attention.

But Yates looked straight past him and failed to return the salute.

The effect of the liberation parade, short as the line had been, was noticeable. A few French flags began to blossom out of the sun-filled windows. The crowd that gathered around the loudspeaker truck on the market square was larger than Yates had expected.

McGuire had parked the truck close to the church. The sound of the six o'clock bells trembled in the air. Inside the truck sat Bing, anticipating the hell Yates had promised to raise with him as soon as the broadcast was over.

Yates stood outside and, with studied aloofness, observed the people. He caught fragments of their conversation. Fear still colored their curiosity; they expected either a speech of the Allied *Führer* or orders. The hushed quiet of some, the harassed expression or overconfidence of others, showed that many of them felt their slate was not as clean as it should have been. There was an almost audible relief when they finally realized that the clear, assured voice was announcing nothing more than news items.

Yates's mind was like a caldron in which boiled the general tension in town, the expectation of getting to Yasha, the anger at Bing, the gradually tempering pain at the loss of Thérèse. He fidgeted over the length of the broadcast. When it was over, he looked into the truck in which Bing was busy locking up the apparatus and putting away his manuscripts, and called out the Sergeant.

All right, here goes, Bing was thinking.

"What was the idea of taking off on your own?" Yates began. And he asked if he needed to point out to Bing the situation in Rollingen — with a good part of the local Nazis still in town expecting a German comeback, with no one quite sure what the next hour would bring. This was the front line! Under these conditions, he demanded discipline, especially from Bing, who ought to be able to see these things for himself — "And what about that bunch of hoodlums you marched down the road?"

"Hoodlums? People. A man came home from the woods, found his wife had become a Nazi whore — I don't know how I got into it. I just did. And why I took off? I don't know that either. I don't like this town. It gives me a funny feeling in my stomach. I had to go and see for myself."

"See for yourself? See what?"

"I don't know. . . ."

"Oh, for Chris'sakes! None of us like it here! I needed you for a job. You were not available. I don't stand for that — "

Yates broke off. What was he talking about? What did he know about a man's reasons for going off or staying, for doing or not doing what was commonly called duty? Why had a Bing stood guard at the foot of the stairs to an attic room in which he slept with a girl, and why had the boy been compelled to go through this town, alone?

"All right!" said Yates, "I want no more of it. Is that clear?"

"Yes, sir." Bing had his own way of getting over disagreeable incidents which did not interest him. He could stand in front of a man, his eyes open, and yet be deep in a kind of sleep, his thoughts wandering elsewhere. He had learned that in school, in Germany, under the tutelage of vindictive, puffed up, self-glorifying professors.

Bing had sounded neither sincere nor convincing, and Yates was trying to think of what he could add to his sermon, when the street and the square began to shake with the approaching rumble of a column. Bing double-timed it to the corner, followed by Yates.

And there they came around the bend — an armored scout car in the lead, then half-tracks, then trucks, filled with men — men hunched and silent, the last light of the day throwing shadows over their tightened faces; men going into the line. They were taking the road to Metz. Yates glanced at the markings on the vehicles: Farrish was throwing in his reserves.

In one of the cars, a tall, blond officer, his face powdered with dust, stood up and waved at Bing; Bing shouted something and waved back.

"That was Captain Troy," he said to Yates, a kind of light coming into his eyes.

"You know him?" Yates said, uncomfortably.

"Yes," Bing answered simply, "I practically puked in his lap, last July Fourth. . . ."

"I see."

"I don't think we'll have any trouble from the Germans, tonight."

About a half-dozen of the vehicles at the tail end of the column sheared out and drew up on the square; their men dismounted, apparently waiting for something. The main body disappeared up the road, occasional sparks flying from the exhausts.

"I'm beginning to feel better," Bing smiled. "D'you mind if I talk to those guys?"

"Go ahead!"

But Bing stopped short. Out of the same direction from which the Armored Infantry had come lumbered four old-fashioned, creaking civilian trucks, their rears packed with men and women, body to body, head to head.

They, too, stopped on the market square. The soldiers came forward, unlatched the ramps, and watched the new arrivals pile out.

Neither Bing nor Yates said anything. They went close to the scene, and stared.

Yates began to curse. "Let's go!" he said, finally. "Let's get away from here!"

283

"Why?" asked Bing. "You knew they were coming! I told you that."

"Did you see that girl?" asked Yates. "The one with her hair cropped? The Nazis did that; maybe they used hair for something, maybe so she couldn't escape. She was a student, at the University of Kiev. She knows about Goethe, too."

Bing began to laugh.

"What's so funny?" Yates's voice broke in anger.

"I was just thinking how handy that's going to come in when she starts digging again for Delacroix & Cie."

The soldiers pushed the foreign workers into groups and led them off. The hills around Rollingen, usually illuminated by the fires in the blast furnaces, were crowned with the lightning of far-off guns.

7

IN THE LATE hours of the next morning, Willoughby arrived in Rollingen. He came into the *Goldene Lamm,* radiating amiability. He pulled up a chair, eased himself into it, stretched his legs wide, and smiled, "Had a good night?"

The sonofabitch, thought Yates. "Thanks, sir. We slept all right after our troops came in. You must have gotten up early."

"Uh-huh!"

"You should have been here last night when they brought back the DP's to the mines," said Yates, looking straight at Willoughby.

The Major's face remained unruffled. "Is that so?" he said. "Well, that's none of our business — so let's not argue about it."

Yates did not argue. Willoughby's sudden appearance rendered the DP matter quite secondary. In the back of his mind, Yates had expected Willoughby all along. The Major's farewell wishes in Verdun had been too loaded to be genuine. He could have guessed that Willoughby wouldn't leave Yasha to his tender mercies. The damned parade! He should have told the red-bearded Mayor to be satisfied with Civil Affairs and the Fire Department and the *Société des Jeunes Femmes.*

Now, Willoughby would try to repeat his old Paris trick; run interference, put himself between Yasha and anyone who attempted to make it hot for the Prince.

But this time, Yates promised himself, he would fight it out.

Willoughby, as if reading his thoughts, said, "Now, let's talk about this thing like two reasonable, grown-up men who know where they each stand, and who appreciate one another. Yes, I've come here to see Yasha.

I consider the Prince as sort of a — well, as my special pet. . . . And I won't let you handle him alone. Do you understand?"

"I understand, Major. Are you making this an order? I've got to know, for the record."

"Record! Record! Don't be childish. If you're going to be stubborn, Yates, if you don't want to listen, we'll never get anywhere."

Willoughby paused.

"You haven't seen him yet, have you?"

Yates could gain nothing by lying. "No," he said, "I haven't."

"Good! You see, Yates, you labor under a misapprehension. I've done some checking in Paris. I spoke to Loomis, on the QT; I even spoke to Dondolo."

Yates stared at him. "Well, and did you come to the conclusion that Thorpe was framed?"

Willoughby glanced up, smiling jovially. "Is that all you're interested in — Thorpe?"

"Thorpe stands for a lot — or his case does!" Yates rubbed his warts and walked around the table, close to Willoughby. "Major, something pretty big is involved here, aside from the life or death of a human being — Integrity, honesty, decency. . . ."

Integrity, honesty, decency! My God, thought Willoughby, I'll help him to feel good about that kind of tripe! Or — *did* Yates know about the Amalgamated Steel deal and was he keeping it to himself as a last trump?

Willoughby said, "You're right, Yates. I feel the way you do, most of the time. But I don't make so much noise about it. When I spoke to Loomis and Dondolo and whoever was around, I came to certain conclusions. I began to find out what you really were after. . . ."

Thoughtfully, Willoughby tweaked his jowls. "You can't accuse people on a hunch, either in or outside the Army. You've got to have your witnesses and your documentation — preferably both. You have no documents — otherwise you'd have handed them to the Colonel. And Loomis and Dondolo —"

He shrugged.

"What about Sourire?" said Yates. "He's Yasha's man!"

"Try and find Sourire!"

"I will try!"

"I'll help you, Yates, if you'll let me. You know why? In thinking over the whole matter — our, well, dispute in the Colonel's room in Paris; all the hints you dropped; and what Loomis and Dondolo told me — something else occurred to me."

"Yes?"

"You suspect me of belonging to that ring, if — and I say *if!* — there is such a ring. Now, isn't that pretty far-fetched? You know me fairly well.

Do you really think I'd go in for such piddling stuff? Black market! As if I couldn't dream up more remunerative and less dangerous operations. . . ."

Yates crossed over to the bar. He had to drink a glass of water. To have suspected Willoughby of a connection with the frame-up of Thorpe was so juvenile, to have gone off the deep end on the strength of this suspicion was such a howling boner! He, himself, had fallen for the mistake for which he once had blamed Bing: The mistake of seeing people in black and white.

"Looks like you've misjudged me on two counts!" Willoughby raised his voice so that his every word would clearly reach over to Yates. "Once, by underestimating my abilities, and the other time, by assuming that I could be involved in a shady deal of that kind."

He shook his head.

"Don't you admit, Yates, that I have every right to clamp down on you? — Then why don't I do it? Well, that's the funny part of it: I happen to like you. When you went to DeWitt — and you were neither tactful nor very successful — you went because you're a decent guy who wants to do the right thing. I appreciate that. We need such people. They're what pushes us forward. You don't trust that coming from me? Come on! Speak up!"

"Well, to tell you the truth, Major: I trust you — sometimes."

Willoughby laughed.

"Galahad!" he said. "The pure knight, running after the Grail, upsetting every apple cart in the process! But likable."

"How do you fit in that picture?"

"I don't look for Grails. I'm too busy. Back home, people who knew used to say: Watch Willoughby! The war interrupted that. I want to get it over with. . . . Well, I'm going to prove how I feel toward you. You and I will go to Yasha together — and I'll let you do the questioning. How's that?"

Yates noticed that Willoughby had invited himself and was making it sound as if he were graciously inviting *him*. But there was some sincerity behind what he had said.

"My appointment with Prince Bereskin is for 2 P.M."

"All right!" said Willoughby. "I'm looking forward to seeing you work."

"Why, it's you!" said Yasha and grasped Willoughby's hand. "I didn't know whom to expect after the visitor I had yesterday."

"This is Lieutenant Yates," said Willoughby. "Prince Yasha Bereskin — Lieutenant Yates."

"Honored!" said the Prince.

The blaze in the fireplace cast an occasional orange glow over Yasha's features, softening their sharpness. In his velvet jacket and slippers, the

286

man gave the impression of a thoroughly solid citizen, with perhaps a touch of the eccentric about him. Yates found him rather civilized, suave, a good host probably, a man with whom one could discuss business, politics, art.

"Whom *did* you expect, Prince?" asked Willoughby.

"A gangster, an extortionist — "

"Didn't the Corporal tell you it was I who wanted to see you?" Yates asked.

"So it was your man, Lieutenant Yates! I wish I had known! Your Corporal used Gestapo tactics. I was unable to sleep all last night. He threatened me with his gun!"

"Who did that, Lieutenant Yates?" Willoughby frowned.

Yates shrugged. "I sent Abramovici."

Willoughby glanced quickly at the Prince. Abramovici wasn't able to scare a church mouse. If it was true that Yasha hadn't slept all last night, it was not because of Abramovici, but because of something Abramovici had announced. He said to Yasha, "My friend Yates, who was unable to see you in Paris, wishes to direct a few questions at you. That is all."

Yasha looked up quickly. Then he smiled. He knew Yates's type: eager young officials from the Tax Bureau, coming around to investigate your books, imagining they'd found something. Ultimately, they all ended up on the pay roll. And Willoughby was present — obviously to protect his own future business.

"What do you wish to know, Lieutenant?"

Willoughby had stepped to the window, apparently disinterested in what Yates and Yasha might have to say to one another. He looked out at the industrial landscape at the foot of Yasha's hill — the furnaces, the mills, the network of cables dotted with cable cars now suspended, motionless. He asked himself whether it really had been necessary to accompany Yates. So much effort — for what? So much tongue wagging to pacify Yates's suspicions! As if Yasha couldn't be trusted to be smooth and discreet — a man didn't get to where Yasha was without being able to take guys like Yates and tie 'em up in knots.

"Do you know a man named Sourire?" Yates began.

"Sourire . . . Sourire . . . !"

Sourire led to Pettinger. Yasha saw the angle. This was not going to be so agreeable. And Willoughby was still standing at the window, disinterested.

"Yes — I do recollect him, Lieutenant. A driver, isn't he?"

Had they caught Pettinger? Had they caught Sourire? Which of the two had talked — or both?

"A driver, quite right," said Yates, "among other things."

Yasha came to a decision. There was no sense in trying to conceal this

287

matter. Either Pettinger was free and safe with the Germans — or he was an American prisoner. In neither case could Yasha protect him. As regards Sourire — the man was a small-time racketeer who deserved to be dropped if he was asinine enough to get himself into trouble.

The Prince sprang his countermove. He asked, "Do you know an SS Colonel Pettinger?"

He caught Yates unaware. Yates had wanted to lead up to Pettinger slowly.

"What do you know about the man?" Yates asked back.

"Oh — a very smart and ruthless and rude fellow. Approximately as rude as the Corporal you sent me yesterday!"

Willoughby coughed.

"Is that so?" said Yates. "Tell me more about Pettinger, please!"

The Prince pressed the fingers of his hands against each other. The hands were too big for the Prince's size, too thin, too clawlike.

"There isn't much to be told. I think he had something to do with the French newspapers — censorship, I suppose, or propaganda. I met him because I complained. You see, I was being blackmailed to give advertising to certain newspapers which the Germans supported. To be a rich man, Lieutenant, is not always roses and beauty — so many envious people; one is so exposed!"

Willoughby grinned. He had heard this kind of talk back in America, and he had dutifully sympathized with the respective millionaire; CBR & W clients had the right to expect sympathy from their attorneys.

Yates didn't take to the *poor rich man* stuff. "Go on, Prince," he prodded.

"Pettinger paid me the honor of a visit. He made clear to me that I would better — how do you call it in English? — come across, yes, come across. . . . You see, Lieutenant, how the Germans were. I was very glad to be rid of them."

"That was your only contact?"

"Oh no!" said Yasha.

He was like a ship. He had eased out of dock and had gained the channel and was going at good speed.

"And now we come to Sourire. It was during the last days of the Germans in Paris. The last day, in fact. I remember it as if it were today — the shooting, the excitement, the expectation of being liberated, finally!"

He breathed deeply and exhaled; Yates saw a small feather, which must have blown off some pillow and attached itself to Yasha's coat, fly away and sail through an orange field of light.

"This Pettinger — he was only a Lieutenant Colonel, by the way — came unannounced. He had a pistol, and he threatened to shoot me unless I got him a truck. Lieutenant, I am a noncombatant! My life, certainly, was worth a truck. I called our garage and had them send a truck over for Pettinger. The truckdriver's name was Sourire."

Willoughby had been listening intently. For a moment there, things had been hanging precariously. But Yasha told a story well. And what Yasha had said tallied exactly with what he, himself, had invented and dished out to DeWitt and the others in Paris! Suppose it hadn't? But then, anybody thinking of the Nazis would automatically assume that they threatened people with violence and got their bidding done by force. His mind and the Prince's had followed the same beaten path. And perhaps — who knows? — it was the actual truth!

Yates continued to press. "Did you see Sourire afterwards, Prince — I mean, after Pettinger used him?"

"No, sir, I did not."

"Do you know where we can get hold of Sourire?"

"No — not unless our Paris garage keeps a record of the men's home addresses. You must remember, Lieutenant, I am what, in your country, they call an executive. I really do not know how that garage operates. I presume the men report for work in the morning. Don't you think so?"

Yates felt frustrated. "Do I think so? . . . Prince Yasha, I want to know from you! What about Sourire's activities outside his job as driver in your garage?"

"Lieutenant!" Yasha looked bored. "Do you believe your Mr. Du Pont personally follows the private life of a driver in one of his celanese plants?"

The Prince's manner indicated clearly that he was saying just as much as he wanted to and not one word more.

Yates came out sharply, "May I point out to you, Prince, that, on the face of it, you are guilty of having connived with a German officer to help his escape" — and, waving off Yasha's objection before it could be made, he said bitingly, "You claim Pettinger had a pistol? Thousands of your countrymen faced German rifles and didn't collaborate. And *collaborate* is the word that fits here — let neither of us forget that!"

Yasha looked to Willoughby for help. Willoughby was leaving his vantage post at the window and approaching Yates. But before he could speak, Yates stated, "Sourire is a black-marketeer. How come that of all people, Sourire appeared conveniently to furnish the truck for Pettinger's escape? How come that of all people, you were the one Pettinger asked for a truck? You're more deeply involved than you admit!"

"Major Willoughby!" cried the Prince. "I refuse to accept another word of this! I am a man of position and reputation, and if you wish to do business with me — "

Willoughby raised his hands. "Now wait a minute, wait a minute! Gentlemen!"

It had happened. Yasha had slipped.

"Let me handle this, Yates — will you? You're losing your temper; you can't get results that way. You're throwing about recriminations — no good! The Prince has been perfectly willing to tell us what he knows, anybody can see that — in fact, he's told us more than we knew. Take the advice of an old lawyer — there's no sense in bullying a man, particularly not this one."

He turned to Yasha.

"Now, Prince, let's hear a little more about this Pettinger — "

Yates cut him short. "I'm sorry, Major, we had an agreement — I was to do the questioning here. All right, Prince Bereskin, what exactly did you mean by *If you wish to do business with me* . . . What kind of business?"

Yasha had calmed down. He glanced at Willoughby, whose lips were pressed tightly together.

"Why," said the Prince, "it was just a manner of speaking. Business, Lieutenant, is my favorite pastime. The word, quite naturally, slips into my speech. . . ."

"Business with whom, Prince?"

"With you, Lieutenant — with anyone else. . . . To my kind of man, all human relationships ultimately resolve themselves into business." He nodded sadly.

Yates had enough; Willoughby had dulled the shock of his attack too thoroughly for Yasha to be caught off guard, again.

"Your witness, Major!" he said caustically.

Willoughby considered whether he should go through the act. Yasha seemed willing enough; his elongated face was overlaid with a quiet, self-satisfied smile. In the end, Willoughby discarded the thought. It was much more important to settle with Yates.

They were back at the *Goldene Lamm*. They went into Yates's room and sat down, Yates on the bed, Willoughby on the grandfather chair in the corner next to the wash stand. Through the open window, the excited chirping of a family of sparrows sounded into the room.

Yates was evaluating the results of their visit to Yasha. The Thorpe incident would have to be left buried because he couldn't pursue Sourire any further. He felt depressed about it — but not as deeply as he had expected. Was *he* getting dulled? Or was it that he began to see it in a greater frame of reference: as part of a picture which showed itself with equal bluntness in the chicanery over the Fourth of July leaflet and in the muddle of the Verdun DP Camp?

Willoughby was not at ease in his soft, wide chair. He suspected that Yates was analyzing the interview with Yasha, particularly Yasha's unfortunate reference to business, and was coming to unfavorable conclusions.

"Go ahead!" he taunted, "why don't you ask it?"

"Ask what?"

"Why I protected Yasha. . . ."

"I have no right to ask."

"Don't be finicky. I give you the right."

"Well," asked Yates, "why did you?"

"For two reasons — the one personal, the other universal. Let's take the personal one first. The law firm of which I was a member takes care of the Delacroix interests in the States."

Willoughby knew he was presenting his hopes as a reality; but the difference between future and present business was too fine to bother with, now.

"You don't want to antagonize your clients," he continued, "even though, at this time, you're in the employ of the Government. Right? Besides, this peculiar position of mine enables me to state definitely that Yasha is not a collaborationist. From a certain level on up, business becomes international. You don't collaborate, you belong to a cartel. So, this was my personal reason. Do you follow me?"

"Yes, it's easy enough."

"More important, however, is my second reason — the consideration of whom do we want to work with over here: we, the Americans. Have you ever thought about that?"

"Not very much," admitted Yates.

"As I see it, this war upsets the very foundations of European society. The Nazis, being confirmed thieves and driven by the lust to grab what they could while they could, did the spadework. The actual fighting, the uprooting of millions of people — of which you've had a taste — the expropriation of these and other millions, are undoing whatever the Germans left standing."

Grudgingly, Yates had to admit that there was a lot to Willoughby's analysis.

"So, we're faced with the issue," Willoughby went on. "What do we want to resurrect — things as they were, or something different? Granted, many of us, up to the highest echelons, don't see the issue at all. This doesn't mean that we won't have to face it. Now, I believe that a nation constituted as we are, will have to deal and will deal with the constructive forces of Europe to bring about an order as closely resembling our own as possible."

"And you include this Prince Bereskin among the constructive forces?"

"Sure."

"Despite what we know about him and Pettinger?"

"What do we know? Nothing. Much more important that *he* knows something about steel, and can help to get French industry going."

Yates was silent.

"You don't like it?"

"No."

"What, then, is your alternative? Let some bums from the underground, or from the FFI, run the show?"

Yates remembered Mantin and Thérèse, the dark bistro in Paris, close to the Place de la Concorde; their claiming that they were the new Government. *Je t'aime.* He had slept with the new Government.

"They helped us. They helped us more than your Prince Yasha did. He supported Pettinger."

"You're putting it so crudely, Yates. I admit they're helpful in war. But they aren't, in peace. No, I'm not cynical. But we've got to make up our minds on what we want. Do you want chaos, anarchy, Bolshevism? Do you mean to tell me, in earnest, that the American people sent its Army over here to establish Communism in Europe?"

"No," conceded Yates. He didn't want it, either.

"Well, I ask you again: What *would* be your alternative?"

"Democracy. . . ."

Willoughby was annoyed at so much stupidity. Yates was the first man in the Detachment to whom he had spoken so openly. And Yates refused to think logically.

"Democracy, Yates, is purely a matter of form. What we're concerned about, is: Will Yasha Bereskin, who knows about production and management, control the Delacroix mills? Or will it be a committee of the great unwashed, men from that DP camp, perhaps, who know only one thing — to work with their hands?"

"That is not the alternative!"

"Well," said Willoughby, "what is?"

Yates wanted to say that there was a third force which somehow would emerge to be the carrier of the future — men like himself, men of good will and sincerity, with no axes of their own to grind. These men he was going to support.

But he couldn't make himself say it. He knew it was no argument in a contest with Willoughby.

And as long as he had nothing concrete with which to oppose him, he couldn't fight Willoughby. You can't fight established institutions with a hope. He had to recognize Willoughby's justification in propping up Yasha, though everything in him cried out against it and against any measures like it.

"No answer?" Willoughby chuckled. "Then I suggest you stick to your duties, Yates, until you come up with something better."

"I know my duties," Yates said darkly.

"Now you're angry at me. . . ." Willoughby raised his hand and let it fall. "Man, I've given you the score so that you know what you're at. You ought to be grateful. I mean well, I really do! After all, we're on the same side! . . ."

He rose and looked out of the window. Over the roofs of the town, he saw the tops of the blast furnaces.

"There's still a great future here!"

"You mean there's lots of dough in that!" scorned Yates.

"What's wrong with it?"

He turned to face Yates. But he suppressed what he wanted to say about money. Yates's expression showed that he couldn't take any more lecturing of this kind.

"Anyhow," shrugged Willoughby, "let's win this God-damned war, first — "

"It'll be over soon enough. . . ."

"Anybody who hopes for a walk into Berlin had better revise his schedule! No, Yates — the war isn't over by a long shot, and it's going to be tough."

Willoughby's eyes blinked sharply, and his jowls seemed less sagging.

Yates went to the window, broke up a cracker into small bits and threw the crumbs to the sparrows. The birds chirped excitedly and fluttered over the food. Yates saw Willoughby's point. He saw that, for the present phase, they had to be allies.

He looked up at the sky and said, "It's going to rain."

"It's going to rain all winter," said Willoughby. "It's that kind of country."

8

FARRISH finally moved in for the kill.

Monitor's Company C under Captain Troy was ordered to take a series of three pillboxes whose continued existence in the Southern outskirts of Metz was one of the General's several tactical headaches. They dominated a hill bearing the number 378, and from the hill a small but necessary road leading to the Moselle river.

Troy traced the gracefully winding lines that terraced the slope of Hill 378 on the map, and compared it to the aerial photographs of their target. He spoke of interlocking fields of fire, and said, "Let's not kid ourselves — this isn't going to be an easy job."

Sergeant Lester said, "If they can make such beautiful photographs — why can't they bomb 'em?"

Troy shrugged. "If they could do it by air, they would have. We will have close artillery support — half an hour before we attack, they're going to lay it on and keep the Germans pinned down inside their pillboxes.

293

Now, here's how the thing will shape up: The second and third platoons will take pillboxes B and C, respectively, located on the flanks. The center and strongest pillbox, which I'm calling A, will be handled by the first platoon. I consider our forces more than ample, if we co-ordinate the attack properly. Lieutenant Fulbright, you wanted to say something?"

Fulbright, his low, strong forehead creased, grumbled, "It's getting kind of monotonous, isn't it? C Company gets the toughest nut and I get first crack at it. . . ." Fulbright liked to grumble because he thought it was a man's good right to kick. On the other hand, he knew that Troy had picked him and his first platoon because he was the least likely to get rattled, and because his bunch of men were the best.

"You want to have a change?" asked Troy, unconcerned. "Would you want me to make different dispositions?"

Fulbright grinned at the Captain. He liked Troy, an easy man to get along with.

"Don't trouble yourself," he said, "I'll manage. We'll need some engineering equipment, mainly pole charges."

"It's all taken care of," said Troy. He knew he could count on Fulbright to calm down as soon as the man had his responsibilities. The Lieutenant was like a foreman who knew his machines and the men working the machines, and so could estimate the result of the labor. Troy had watched Fulbright develop. In the beginning, when he came to the Company from a Replacement Depot, a Ninety-day Wonder from OCS, the man had felt lost and handicapped. But he had had the sense to let Sergeant Lester run the platoon, once he recognized that the Sergeant's experience in Normandy made him superior to himself. He had learned from the Sergeant. And now, the gangling Lester and the sturdy Fulbright were a team, the men with them were a team. Their comfort — what little there was of it — their protection, their lives, depended on one another; that they had learned. Naturally, their personal grievances against one another, their dislikes, peculiarities, and frictions, had sharpened and deepened. When you constantly live with a man, eat with him, sleep with him, but can't get away from him, your hate against him grows more violent than hate against an outsider. Troy had seen Lester and Fulbright, Sheal and Cerelli, Traub and Wattlinger, lash into one another on the most trivial pretext. None of them could be called *nice;* what breeding they had brought with them from their homes and Sunday Schools was ground off fast enough by the dirt, and by the absurd tiredness which was with them always, by the shells and the bullets which landed close and never lost their shocking power.

What remained was the rationalization that, alone, a man was lost. What grew was a new sense, a new bond, entered into unwillingly; a man help-

ing another and, at the same time, calling him from the depth of his heart
a sonofabitch; Lester, mercilessly lambasting Simon and then sharing his
last cigarette with him.

Why did this go through Troy's mind? Was he worried that some of
these men might not come back from the attack against the pillboxes on
Hill 378? Was he trying to justify his decisions? He had made so many of
them, he had seen so many men disappear — half his Company consisted
of faces which had not been with it in the beginning. It made a difference
inside a man who had an eye for such things. Troy hardly gave direct orders any more; he made suggestions. His men believed in him. Whenever
he was conscious of this belief — he doubted himself, often — he wanted
to give up in despair. He said Fulbright's platoon was to tackle the strongest pillbox. If Fulbright fell, or Lester, or Sheal, or any of them, it was he
who had sent them to their death. And if he switched platoons, the same
applied.

Troy felt the strain of it; he didn't show it much, and he would be able
to go on for a long while, until the war ended, or until he was hit — but inside him, his heart corroded.

Lester could hear Fulbright cursing; he couldn't see him because the
hill curved to the right, and because Lester was keeping his head down.
Last night's rain was still in the soil, the earth was wet and slippery; and
after a few minutes, his clothing was soaked where he tried to hug the
ground. In summer, the earth had been a friend; now it rejected him. It
made him feel helpless and angry, but he wasn't afraid.

His fear had gone as soon as he had begun the climb up Hill 378. Corporal Simon, Wattlinger, Cerelli, Traub, and Sheal were following him up
the hill. These were the men who, together with himself, were to make
the critical dash over some fifty yards where there wasn't a grass-blade of
cover, directly to the wall of the pillbox. Once they reached the wall and
crouched close to it, the defenders could not touch them because the German weapons could only be operated through the apertures. Fulbright
had said, "You've got twenty-five men and the mortars covering you when
you go across that field . . . ," and Lester had said, "Yes, sir!" — but he
knew that they could not cover him because the Germans behind the concrete would be safe from their fire.

Lester crawled, taking care that he didn't expose himself more than necessary. He had all the time in the world to wonder why he wasn't afraid,
and he guessed it was because he had reached the point where it was impossible to feel anything. Through the long hours of the night, he had
tossed around unable to sleep; his mind had pictured the dash over the fifty
yards to the pillbox; he had imagined the feeling of being hit — like a fist

meeting you with full force; he had seen himself throw up his hand, and topple over, and lie there, and the blood oozing out of him, and himself getting lighter and lighter until he could almost fly away. He was fully awake when they roused him for the attack. He had gone through everything a man could go through in his final agony, and he was just empty, except for a headache which was splitting his skull.

He went through the same procedure before every action he knew about in advance. But the longer he was in the war, the more thorough, the more detailed was his anticipation. Before the first hedgerow fight, his fear had expressed itself in general terms; by now, he had seen so much he could equip it to perfection.

He had walked the last half-mile to the jump-off point conscious only of the necessity of moving his legs and of keeping a poker face in front of the five men whom he, personally, had picked to go with him. He did not talk to them; they had already been told exactly what each of them was to do, and who was to do what in case the first-choice man kicked the bucket or was otherwise out.

And now he was spent and free of fear.

The slope which the pillbox topped was gentle but pock-marked with the shellholes of the artillery barrage. The shellholes were a temptation. Lester avoided them; he felt, once in there, he would never want to get out again. He was terribly tired — moved knee after knee, elbow after elbow, and he had to push himself into every move. Small sharp stones hurt him; why he should bother about such little pains, he didn't know — but there it was.

He looked at his watch. Only four minutes had passed since they had started. Half the height of the slope had been climbed, and nothing had happened. He was suddenly impatient. He wanted to get through with this. He weighed his chances.

If they got up and ran, they would offer a bigger target to the Germans. If they kept crawling as they were, the target was smaller, but remained an incomparably longer time on the sights of the Germans in the pillbox. One was as bad as the other.

He half-lifted himself. The German machine gun fired.

"You crazy?" he heard Simon shout. "Get down!"

Afraid, he thought — the hairiest man in the outfit, big chest, **big** mouth.

Lester rose, waved the others to follow him, ran forward a few steps. Now he was gaining ground! With every step he was gaining ground, although the slippery earth robbed each step of his gain by inches. He struggled against the mud. His heart was high up in his throat, it pounded against the insides of his ears.

Yet, he heard the thin scream, as if a child had cried in terror. He wanted to keep on going forward, but he couldn't. He thought if I turn around, all this beautiful progress will stop. He turned around. He saw the big body of Simon roll down the hill. Its limbs seemed loose and relaxed; rolling, the body gathered mud. Finally, Simon came to rest in a shellhole and sprawled there, grotesquely, already part of the earth.

The machine gun cackled. Lester saw the mud splash up in front of him. "Down!" he shouted. "Down!"

Again he was on elbows and knees and belly, mechanically moving upwards. With Simon out, they were only five, including himself. For the living Simon, he would have gone through a hell as bad as the one he was passing through now; the dead Corporal counted only as a number — from now on, the Germans would have to concentrate on only five men, especially during the final dash. His individual chance had lessened.

He heard someone panting behind him. Between each breath, Sheal was saying, "I've got to get Simon — wounded — he's wounded . . ."

"Hell! He's dead!" said Lester.

"He was hit — in the knee — I saw it — went out — like a light!"

"God damn it!" shouted Lester. "You stay here! With me!"

Sheal stayed beside him. He looked miserable. "You bastard!" said Sheal.

Lester crawled on.

"I wish *you*'d gotten it!" said Sheal.

Lester felt whipped. He crawled on.

"Got to run upright!" said Sheal. "Got to bleed to death!"

"The medics will fetch him," Lester said hoarsely. "Stop bunching up."

Sheal fell back.

Lester looked at his watch. Two more minutes had passed. They had almost reached the end of the slope.

Those who survived that last dash — Cerelli, Traub, Sheal, and Lester — would never forget it. Till the end of their days, there would be times when they would start up out of their sleep, and see the shell-torn stretch of plateau, ending at the gray concrete block, its edges tapering like the front view of a coffin.

Wattlinger didn't make it. Both Cerelli and Traub saw him die. He disintegrated before their eyes, and went to his Maker in flame and smoke, to the deafening sound of a detonation. They believed they had seen parts of him sail through the air, but the experienced men to whom they told this, shook their heads and said: Impossible. He stepped on a mine, didn't he? Well, if there were parts of him left big enough to see, they would be flying too fast for you to see them.

The event itself rooted them where they stood. Cerelli heard pieces of metal whizz by and thought This is the end, and wondered that he kept on thinking and deduced from it that it wasn't the end; and felt a sob in his throat which had to come out but didn't. Not that he had been close to Wattlinger; what fascinated him and held him was that there was nothing where a man had been — nothing except a gash in the ground.

Traub was hit with full force by a clump of wet dirt; it hit him in his kidneys and took away his breath. He found that out later. For the moment, he was too numb to analyze. He fought for breath. He had the crazy idea that Wattlinger and his explosion had sucked off all the air, and that he was in a vacuum, and nobody can live in a vacuum. Oh God oh God oh God! he wanted to say, only he had no voice. He could see the other three men: Cerelli, who was standing; and Lester and Sheal, who kept on running. But he saw them as through inverted field glasses — very small, very far away, and unreal. And he saw the pillbox, wisps of smoke coming from its slits; over there, they were firing away, firing at him.

It was now that Lester turned around. Lester had only another ten yards to go to reach the safety of the corner formed by the wall of the pillbox and the ground. The Germans could not shoot straight downward from their apertures; lying close to them, separated from them by the layers of steel and cement, and planning their extermination, he could not be touched. Ten yards.

Then the sound of the detonation registered in his mind and, still running, he turned around. Sheal, also running, was diagonally behind him. Farther back, two men were standing, like cattle before a closed gate; and where the hell was the third man? The third man and the detonation belonged together. One had had an effect on the other, and so the third man was gone. Cerelli and Traub were carrying the charges; so Wattlinger was gone. But why did they stand like dummies? Men come and go, men are killed, this is serious business, you can't stand there and wait till you're hit.

He shouted at them; but either they didn't hear, or they heard and what they heard didn't impress them.

Lester saw the security of the pillbox, of the small niche which waited for him. He longed for this security with all the strength left in him, and with the despair of a hunted animal. Yet, he turned and ran back to Traub, ten, fifteen, twenty yards, skirting the hole where Wattlinger once had been. He pushed Traub, he beat him over the back, he shouted, "Go ahead, you sonofabitch! Get going!" He made Traub stumble forward. "Faster!" he yelled and he saw Traub pick up speed, jogging oddly between the bullets, bent to the load of explosives, which would blow him to hell if they were hit.

Then he rushed over to Cerelli. Cerelli seemed afraid of him, and it gave Lester a thin moment of grim satisfaction. Cerelli dodged and spurted forward. Much later, he told Lester that he had never seen the Sergeant, murder in his eyes, come at him; he had noticed Traub go forward, and he hadn't wanted to remain back there, by himself.

Now Sheal was alone out in front, alone against the pillbox. Sheal was angry with a deep anger which flooded him. He knew this kind of anger. In his childhood, when it came over him, he would lie on the floor, on his back, and kick his feet savagely, and defy anyone to approach him. He was angry over Lester, who had left Simon behind — Sheal had forgotten the incident, but the anger had remained, and had increased over the unfairness of the whole deal: Here he was, one man alone, unable to fight back, running toward the pillbox from which they were trying to pick him off. He envied the Germans nicely encased behind their walls. He hated them, now, though he didn't know their faces, whether they were old or young, or how many they were. He called them the most vicious names he could summon to mind, and hoped they could hear him and understand him; he wanted to kill, to murder, not fast and clean, but taking his time and doing it dirty. He wished he had white phosphorus. He hated them because he was delivered into their hands, and because they wanted to kill him, and he was defenseless.

Lester was the last to reach the pillbox. He looked at his watch. Eight minutes and thirty seconds had passed.

The quiet, then, was astounding.

Fulbright had ordered the men covering Lester's advance to cease fire; and the Germans inside their box could see nothing and were waiting and watching.

Cerelli pressed his ear against the concrete.

"You can't hear them!" said Lester, but he said it in a half-tone as if the Germans could hear him. Then he said, "Let's go — before they come out of the hatch and bump you over the head! Give me the thing."

Hand over hand, carefully, the pole charge passed from Cerelli to Sheal to Lester. The Sergeant grabbed it with both hands, seemed to weigh it. There was a moment when he would have his head and shoulders before the aperture, staring into the muzzle of a German gun. He imagined how he would look to the German behind that gun — a black shadow, very black. Perhaps the German would not know what it was, and would do nothing.

"If it doesn't work," said Lester — but he meant, If I am killed — "Sheal is next." *If I am killed*. . . . But he didn't believe he would be killed. His mind shied away from the possibility and from the acceptance of the possibility, although he had to make arrangements as if he could be killed.

"O.K.," said Sheal, "I know."

Then Lester lit the fuse. He jumped up. He pushed the pole and the TNT wound around it into the aperture of the pillbox, as the baker shoves his shovel into the stove, with the dough on it which will rise and grow hot and still the hunger of man. Lester made no such comparison; but he felt that, after all the crawling and running and cajoling and waiting, he at last was doing something good.

Nothing happened. Perhaps, inside, the man behind the aperture and the men with him were too surprised over the sudden messenger from the outside world. After all, it was a silly thing — they were in there, behind their safe wall, with the most modern weapons in the world — a field piece, some machine guns, carbines — and there was this pole being stuck in, reaching for them. . . .

Lester shoved it all the way through.

Then he dropped to the ground, exhausted. He kept his eyes closed.

The earth shook. It jarred them back to the realization that they had finished the job, that it was over, that they had won this battle. Cerelli jumped up and cheered hoarsely.

Traub, looking at him, laughed. Lester huddled on his haunches, motionless, but relaxed.

Sheal said, "I wouldn't like to look around, inside there." His hatred was gone. He felt as he had when he was a child, after his attack of screaming and kicking was over.

Book Four

AN OBIT FOR THE LIVING

I

IN THE MIDST of the German retreat, Field Marshal von Klemm-Borowski had been appointed to command the German Army Group which took in the entire Central Sector of the Western Front.

Pettinger, who had arrived at Group Headquarters a few days after the Marshal took command, sometimes wondered what made Berlin pick on Klemm-Borowski to inherit the wreckage and the stupendous task of reorganization. The Field Marshal was not a fighting man; he had never led so much as a company into battle. He was a mathematician and a specialist in logistics, with a love for medals whose help he sought to give his meager chest more weight. Pettinger, who had an eye for such things, despised the Junker's attempt at elegance, his way of pulling tight his belt and achieving only the bulging of his stomach above and below.

Yet, there was more to Klemm-Borowski than Pettinger's first impression conceded. The fact that the Marshal had thrown out his predecessor's entire staff could be interpreted as superstition, as fear that ill luck, once it attached itself to men, clung to them and made them carriers of defeat — but it could also be an indication of supreme self-confidence and the perception that a staff, once so badly defeated, needed more time to change its pattern than the military situation allowed.

Hearing the Marshal's pompous announcement, "My dear Pettinger, the day I take over anywhere is operationally speaking the beginning of a new era," one was tempted to brush him aside and rue the day when the Witzleben revolt broke and caused Berlin to mistrust all but a very few of the top generals. But Klemm-Borowski's measures to strengthen the front, to slow the retreat, showed that the Marshal meant what he said and that he had good reason for being the first high-ranking officer to cable his congratulations to Hitler on the Führer's escape from the assassin's bomb. Pettinger himself analyzed the Witzleben revolt as the open expression of a cleavage on top, between those who believed the war lost and who wanted to get out of it as inexpensively as possible, and those who thought a German victory still within reach. And while telegrams were cheap, Klemm-Borowski had done more: he had accepted this difficult and probably thankless command.

To Pettinger, defeat was inconceivable. This was a fixation for which he constantly sought foundation in fact. Despite their contrary natures, the search compelled him to ingratiate himself with the Marshal, to get close to him. He submitted a number of proposals he thought would be attractive to a man of Klemm-Borowski's caliber — if accepted, they had the additional advantage of affording Pettinger ample opportunity to travel, to take care of the Delacroix interests, and to cash the remainder of Yasha's draft.

Eventually, the Marshal sent for him. He questioned him carefully. Pettinger offered only the least sensational details of his flight from Paris: the safe delivery of himself and his men at the Command Post of a German Artillery Battalion, which he subsequently left to proceed to Army Group. He omitted all of the facts which might pinch the Marshal's sensitivity toward men on the run: his escape; the disheartening detours with the Artillery Battalion; his forcing his friend, Major Dehn, at pistol point into the arms of the commander of a straggler-collecting post. As for his stopovers at several Delacroix plants for conferences with the local managers — these were none of Klemm-Borowski's business.

Klemm-Borowski listened. He seemed to be the kind of man who liked to listen. Suddenly, he shot, "I've had you checked, you know?"

Pettinger looked at the Marshal's indistinct pupils which disappeared behind thick, horn-rimmed glasses. He didn't question the check-up. He was an SS man; and after the Witzleben revolt the Marshal would suspect him of having been attached to Group Headquarters as a special policeman.

"The Party says you are in excellent standing," Klemm-Borowski said, after a pause.

Pettinger nodded. If the little owlish man was afraid of him, so much the better.

"I'm a mathematician," said the Marshal. "I can tell you how much space we can trade for how much time, provided the factors are constant and no accidents intervene. I can prove to you that one good soldier equals three bad ones; and that a bad soldier equals a good one under certain favorable conditions — for instance behind the wall of a concrete bunker. But I know nothing about people."

"People?" said Pettinger.

"Yes, people. All of your proposals concern people. I think your proposals are revolutionary. I think they can get both our necks into nooses. And I'd like to be sure that I'm not the only one to stick out his neck."

Pettinger understood. The logistics expert did know about people, if not as a mass, then as individuals.

"But your proposals fit in with my plan," Klemm-Borowski continued.

"What is your plan, sir?"

The Marshal chuckled and reclined comfortably in his chair. "Suppose you tell me, *Herr Obersturmbannführer?*"

Pettinger hesitated. A lot was at stake — not only his own job and personal plans, but the long-range view.

"Well?" asked the Marshal. "You're an old soldier. . . ."

"The plan is simple," said Pettinger. "You put it into operation the moment you took over. The shock of the Allied offensive is being absorbed by a cushion of second-rate, expendable troops. I've seen them ground to pieces — old men and youngsters, Croats, Slovaks, Alsatians, Hungarians — the backwash of the Europe we conquered."

"And then?"

"You are trying to pull together two elite armies — "

The Marshal rose. "And I'm getting them, Pettinger! First, a limited objective for my counteroffensive, but big enough to gain us another six months. After that, the final blow with completely new weapons!"

"V-bombs?" asked Pettinger, doubtfully.

"Something much bigger! Absolutely earth-shaking — it will wipe the Allies off the map. It will win the war!"

He saw the animation in Pettinger's eyes. "We understand one another, I see . . ." he said, and his manner was almost personal. Then he became factual again. "I'm planning my push for some time in December. The Americans are warm weather soldiers."

Pettinger smiled. The moment had come to put in his own oar.

"And until then, your Excellency," he said carefully, "you'll be selling space for time."

"Exactly."

"But we want to sell it dearly, isn't that so, sir?"

"Well — naturally!" A slight impatience was in the Marshal's tone.

Pettinger sensed that Klemm-Borowski felt he was being guided. But he pushed on. "There are people living in that space!" And, pointing at the wall map, "The territory through which we are now pulling back is inhabited by Germans or, at least, German-speaking people. This, sir, is where my proposals come in."

"I know! I know!" said Klemm-Borowski. "I told you I was considering them."

"But now is the time! We must destroy what we can destroy!" Pettinger tried to hold the Marshal's attention. "We must leave the enemy nothing but scorched earth. If the Russians could do it, we certainly can!"

303

"What will you do with the people?" Klemm-Borowski asked.

"Evacuate them! What difference does it make? As long as we don't leave to the enemy well-ordered communities! Germany must live whether people sell herring and grow barley or not! . . ." Pettinger's old hate against the rooted ones broke through; he wanted to uproot them, to disperse them, and to create the disorder that would insure his kind of final victory regardless of the success or failure of Klemm-Borowski's plans.

The Marshal put his glasses back into their case and snapped it closed. Without them, he looked less like an owl. "And have you thought of the administrative confusion, *Herr Obersturmbannführer?* Things must be done in an orderly manner. Throwing millions of people out on the road —" He stopped, his myopic eyes staring vacantly.

Throwing millions of people out on the road could very well be interpreted as another part of the Witzleben plot, Pettinger finished the Marshal's sentence in his mind. And Berlin was sensitive. . . . Klemm-Borowski *was* scared of the noose.

Pettinger shrugged. "If your Excellency doesn't trust me, I understand."

"That's not it," the Marshal said half-heartedly.

"But don't forget — you have the chance to become the savior of Germany, the real victor of the war. You've got to rely on some men!"

The Marshal stroked his chin. Pettinger had sketched his position exactly: If he succeeded, Germany was saved. The question was whether he should let Pettinger handle the program.

"We can't be squeamish!" argued Pettinger. "Time is running out! If we leave the people where they are, they'll find out that it is possible for Germans to live under Allied occupation. People accept any police!"

His thin lips were curling.

"And trust the Americans to make the most of it — we let them have the radio station in Luxemburg; they'll din the beauties of their rule into our ears. The population, instead of backing your armies, will sap their strength. Sir, I say: Not a soul to the enemy!"

Klemm-Borowski glanced up. His eyes had become sharp. Pettinger saw that he had kindled something in the dry soul of the logistics expert.

He saw more. He saw his new slogan, *Not A Soul to the Enemy!* splashed on the walls of empty villages and blasted towns. Willing or not, finally all of the people would be involved in the war. The fact that the installations of Delacroix & Cie. in the border areas and in the Saar basin would be left carefully untouched would escape attention when the trickle of refugees flowing east broadened into a stream.

It took him a moment to get the full meaning of the Marshal's oblique question, "Well, do you think you can handle this matter on the side?"

"On the side?"

"Of course — these civilian affairs will have to be managed mostly by civilian authorities. . . ."

"I don't quite follow you, sir."

"My dear Pettinger — " the Marshal toyed with the ribbon of his *Ritterkreuz* — "I've had you in mind for an even bigger job!"

Pettinger bowed, warily. Apparently, it was both jobs or none.

"It's a little operation of mine. I'm going to call it *Buzzard*." He cocked his head, questioningly.

"Nice name. . . ." Pettinger was not going to tie himself to anything unless he knew what it was.

"Do you know Skorzeny?" the Marshal asked. "I admire the man! This kidnaping of Mussolini was a wonderful stroke — that's what gave me the idea! What planning! What precision in action!"

"I thought it was a good show. . . ."

The Marshal whinnied. "We'll do the same thing, only on a larger scale. Simultaneously with my offensive, we're going to launch the greatest diversionary attack in military history. Buzzard's going to do the diverting — and you are going to lead it, *Herr Obersturmbannführer!*"

"How?"

"Simultaneously with my offensive, we will send through the lines specially selected men in Allied uniforms." The Marshal smiled. "You have experience in getting through the lines, haven't you?"

Pettinger frowned. He's afraid I'm his special policeman, and that's how he wants to get rid of me. "Through the lines?" he said. "I did it only once."

"That's enough. Some will go through the lines, others will be dropped by air. They will speak perfect English, like you. I've checked on you, you see. They will disrupt enemy communications, blow up bridges and dumps, transmit wrong orders, eliminate isolated command posts, and kidnap or kill the most important Allied commanders — *die Herren* Eisenhower, Bradley, Patton, Farrish, for instance. Inside of twenty-four hours, Pettinger, Operation Buzzard will have created such havoc, and my *Panzer*-Armies will have broken the Allied front so extensively, that the American defeat will have become a rout. A rout, Pettinger!" he shouted, and glared at the SS man as if he wanted to hypnotize him by the force of his own personality.

"I think Skorzeny ought to do it," Pettinger said calmly.

"Skorzeny's in the East, I can't get him."

"There's the Hague Convention," said Pettinger. "It forbids this kind of warfare."

"Bah!" said the Marshal. "The Hague Convention forbids the bombing of civilians, too."

305

"It can be enforced against us. The Americans are stronger. They've taken more prisoners than we have." It was no argument, Pettinger thought. He was just worried that he, himself, might be caught. On the other hand, it was a kind of thrill: Strike silently in the night, strike from the back — the old technique he had helped to perfect in dozens of street battles, before 1933; and it had paid off.

The Marshal sounded estranged. "Suppose the enemy *is* stronger! You are willing to drive millions of Germans from their homes, many of them into their death — perhaps it'll help us. And I'm willing to let you do it. I'm going to break some outdated rules — perhaps it'll help us. I'm telling you, Pettinger: Either this offensive and Operation Buzzard and your evacuation program reverse the trend — or we'll be done for. I've calculated and weighed all chances. As Caesar said, *iacta alea est!*"

Caesar! Pettinger shuddered. He was worth more than a pair of dice. And there was nothing he could do to stop Klemm-Borowski! With sudden perspicacity, Pettinger saw that his empty talk of the Marshal as Germany's savior had buttressed the old mathematician's compulsions. And he saw the terrible danger which lay in the fact that Germany's fate and his own fate, at this critical phase of the war, were in the hands of adventurers — adventurers of which he, himself, was one. He was tied up with them on two counts: As planner and as prospective victim. And though he saw the abyss which opened itself before them, he found himself rushing toward it, propelled by them.

Götterdämmerung was at hand! He had to pile adventure on adventure, in the hope that one of them would turn the tide. He had to accept the Marshal's proposition to save his evacuation program and to save his own skin.

Pettinger stared at the Marshal's silly hair, his vapid eyes, and the stomach which bulged above and below the broad, silver-embroidered belt. "I think it's the greatest plan ever conceived!" he said with determination.

"I knew you'd think of it that way," said Klemm-Borowski. "Because you'll be the hero of it, son."

At this moment, it became clear to Pettinger of whom the Marshal reminded him: A teacher he once had had in the *Real-Gymnasium*. The man was beloved by the boys because he recounted ancient Germanic lore with an enthusiasm that fired each of them with the desire to go out, single-handedly, and overpower Attila's hordes and avenge the Nibelungs. One day, the professor failed to come to school. The boys heard he had been taken to an institution, screaming that Siegfried was being betrayed and that he must go to warn him.

2

THE ABANDONED mine dated back to the time when coal was plentiful and you didn't have to dig deep into the bowels of the earth. It ran like a tunnel underneath the chain of stony hills that divided the town of Ensdorf from the village of Schwalbach. It could be entered both at the Ensdorf and Schwalbach sides; but to cross from one end to the other was difficult because of the water that had collected where the tunnel was deepest. There, for a distance of some eighty yards, you would have to walk up to your hips in cold, black water, guarding your light carefully — the heavy air laid itself with equal weight on the struggling flame and around your chest.

Now the tunnel had become the haven of about five thousand people. Miners and children of miners, most of them had played in its dark caverns when they were young; then it had been forgotten.

Elisabeth Petrik, the shoemaker's wife, was the first to remember it. For days the evacués from the border villages, fleeing the front, had been coming through Ensdorf, plodding the road, without aim and organization, panicked, their pitiful possessions thrown on carts and wheel barrows and perambulators. For days, Elisabeth Petrik and her lame son Paul, standing before their house, had watched the unending procession. "People without houses," Frau Petrik had said, pulling her old shawl tighter around her gaunt shoulders. And Paul, conscious and afraid of his crippled leg, had asked, "Where will *we* go?"

And then, suddenly, the front reached Ensdorf. Government, in the person of Mayor Konz, took off in the official limousine. The pimple-faced Franz Seidel, janitor, file clerk, and general factotum at the *Rathaus,* blossomed out as Deputy Mayor, running up and down Ensdorf's streets, shouting, "Evacuation today! Evacuation today!" A shell had landed in the middle of hundreds of men and women waiting before the *Rathaus* to be issued refugee identification cards.

It was then that Elisabeth Petrik remembered the mine. She packed her bundle and took her crippled son and her complacent husband and led the way to it; she was followed by the girl Leonie and by most of the Ensdorfers. The people sensed that here was someone who gave them direction. It had not been planned. It was simply that one authority had broken down and another was taking its place; or perhaps, as with Frau Petrik, the old mine came to mind with men accustomed to spending part of their lives underground.

Once inside the mine, the question of authority became vital. A committee crystallized out of those who, at the sudden influx of thousands of excitedly milling, crying, frightened people, had stepped forward and said,

"This is your place; and your family will camp here; and the goats will be kept there." Without wanting it, the venerable Father Gregor, Elisabeth Petrik, the miner Karg, the teacher Wendt, the baker Krulle, drifted into the job of organizing community life in the mine, in the almost total darkness of the narrow, low tunnel.

The Committee was lucky insofar as it had to deal with an orderly people accustomed to discipline and obedience to authority. Abandoned by Franz Seidel and the Nazis, the Ensdorfers accepted the new regime almost without questioning. Twelve years of fascism bore unexpected fruit.

Also, as Paul Petrik observed sarcastically to Leonie, they accepted their miserable existence the same way. "They've heard of and seen so many people disowned and driven from their homes that they can't really complain now their turn has come."

Leonie felt her child move inside her. She couldn't think of people, only of herself. She had been in the Labor Service in Saarlautern and had fallen in with Hellestiel, the Hitler Youth Leader, and his whole gang. It had been fun; but now it was over. Nothing had been left her but to go back to Ensdorf and wait for the child; Frau Petrik had taken her in.

Leonie said, "What did you want the people to do? It just happened. We couldn't help ourselves — and we can't, now."

She and Paul huddled in a small, dark niche, close to the Ensdorf entrance. A miner, long, long dead, must have hacked it out of the rock so he would have room when the coal carts, drawn by blind horses, came crawling by. The daylight at the entrance seemed far away, no bigger than a pin point, but radiant like a diamond.

"Can't help ourselves," Paul mocked. "I can't help myself, with my leg — but all you others, healthy and well! Whom do you now blame — your leaders? But your leaders have gone! If I weren't in this myself but could watch it from somewhere, I would laugh my head off!"

"Paul," she said, "I am carrying a child."

She could feel him move away, as far as the small niche permitted.

"From whom?"

"Hellestiel, probably — I don't know."

She waited for a reply. None came. A group of men stumbled by. She heard Frau Petrik's quiet, flat voice. "As soon as it gets dark, you go to the village. Karg will lead you. You milk the cows and give them food and hurry back with the milk. I'll take some women. We'll be cooking at Konz's house and at the baker's house. People must get something warm to eat."

"Your mother's a wonderful woman," said Leonie.

Still no answer from Paul.

"Why don't you speak?"

"What should I say? Didn't you tell me you couldn't help yourself?"

"It was because of the Race," she whispered.

"They're all bad," he said. "This Race must perish."

"Your mother is getting milk for them!"

"It will turn to gall at their lips!" he said prophetically.

"You shouldn't talk like that," she said, seeking his hand. "They're your own people."

"That's what's making me crazy!" he cried.

The bright star of day had vanished. Except for the occasional flare of a torch or candle, the cripple and the pregnant girl were steeped in velvet blackness.

The community in the mine had sprung from a common purpose: To save the lives of its members, and to keep from being scattered on the roads. But minute by minute, hour by hour, the darkness, the foul air, the hunger, the cramped living were taking their toll. When the immediate danger of shells and bombs was removed, the people began to feel the misery of their existence.

The Committee soon sensed the wane of its authority. It was the little disturbances: A man refusing to go on an errand, a woman grumbling when she had to take care of a child whose mother had been killed. The authority was so new, so untried; and, perhaps, the Committee members were not the people to exert authority and to enforce it.

The miner Karg, the teacher Wendt, the baker Krulle, and Frau Petrik sat near the Ensdorf entrance of the mine, looking out at the puffs of smoke, the trees of dirt and stone rising and falling where shells landed and blew up.

"Still fighting everywhere?" asked Krulle, his full face topped by a brush of whitish blond hair.

Karg, who had just returned from the Schwalbach side of the mine, stared at the cuffs of his pants from which water dripped into his cracked and broken shoes.

"Take off your pants," said Elisabeth Petrik, "you'll catch cold."

"Same thing on the other side," Karg said in reply to the baker.

"Well," said Krulle, rubbing his doughy hands, "if somebody wants to leave through there, let him! I won't be responsible for what happens to the fools!"

Elisabeth Petrik spoke up. "Why don't you get clear about what's going to come? If there's a stampede out of the Schwalbach side, we can't stop it. Many will be killed. But quite a few will get through. And we will be left, we and whoever sticks to us."

"The more room we'll have!" said Krulle.

"Yes. And the easier it will be for the Nazis to pick us up. They'll come back — they have to! What we have done is a — revolt. Whatever way you look at it, we haven't followed their orders. Seidel's orders."

"We've saved the lives of thousands of Germans!" said Wendt, the teacher, who was a patriotic man, a veteran of the First World War, and whose preferred subject was the Bismarckian era.

"They don't care about lives," said Karg. "Remember the explosion in the Friedrich Wilhelm pit? There was a good chance that the men buried underground were still alive, but they ordered the level where it happened walled up, and told us to go down again, deeper, and dig coal."

"We haven't followed their orders," Frau Petrik insisted, "and they can't let us get away with it. But what can they do to five thousand people who stick together? They'd have to send a regiment of police down into this mine, and they don't have the men and they don't have the courage. Sometime, the fighting must stop. The front must move on one way or the other. Until then, we must hold the people together. There is no other way."

Krulle tried to comprehend the frightening possibilities which Elisabeth Petrik had presented. His main concern was his bakery with the new oven that had cost so much money. This he didn't want to give up; this was why he had stayed and would do anything to remain. "I've done nothing wrong!" he said, his lips firm.

"Historically, you haven't," said the teacher. "Legally, you have."

"I don't understand these fine differences," said Frau Petrik. "All I know is that we'd better get some men to stand guard at both entrances, so we can be warned when somebody comes. For the rest, let us hope and pray. . . ."

"Maybe Father Gregor can hold services tomorrow," suggested Krulle.

Karg said, "It's not Sunday, tomorrow."

The teacher Wendt, erect, the hair on the back of his head cropped Prussian-style, said, "God is on duty at all days and all hours. Let's hope the Americans finally make some headway."

"*You* say that?" Krulle's mind was not yet accustomed to the thought that their lot depended on the success of what had been the enemy.

"I'm judging this as an old soldier," said Wendt. "The military specialist observes, but takes no sides."

Karg shrugged. He could not follow the drift of the conversation.

That same evening, after dark, Franz Seidel came into the mine. With him was a high-ranking SS officer who kept equal distance from Seidel and the people camping along the walls; his rubber boots that reached up to his hips shone from the water through which he had waded. Behind the two men, carefully feeling their way, groped some twenty armed Field Gendarmes.

The Ensdorfers' guard at the Schwalbach entrance had alerted the Committee, so that shortly after the visitors forded the water, they were met by the Committee, backed solidly by a mass of miners whose rows filled the narrow span of the tunnel.

"Seidel!" someone hooted, "where you come from suddenly? It's not warm here! It's not plushy!"

The light of a torch glided over Seidel's narrow, pimpled face; he was unnaturally pale. "Where's the priest?" he demanded. "Where's Father Gregor? We want to talk to him." A few inches above Seidel's head was the ceiling of the mine, roughly hewn and wet. Blende and drops of water reflected the beam of his flashlight; he lowered the beam only to have it reflected from the eyes of the people who crowded the depth of the tunnel. Behind the first rows, they were standing on their toes, or jumping up and supporting themselves on their neighbors' shoulders, to get a glimpse of what went on in front. The eyes seemed phosphorescent to Seidel, not at all the eyes of the people he had known when he had swept the stairs of the *Rathaus*.

Then the human wall parted and Father Gregor stepped forward, in priestly white. His voice, alternately held and thrown back by the crags and crevices, had an unearthly quality. "Whatever you have to say, Franz Seidel, you can say before these people. I have no secrets."

Seidel, looking too small for the officer's raincoat he was wearing, grasped the priest's hand and kissed it. Then he stepped back, stretched himself as tall as he could, and began, "I've come back to you in spite of the danger to which I expose myself. I've come back because I'm sure that you will do as I say. I order the immediate evacuation of this mine. Nobody will stay in here. At the Schwalbach entrance, you will be picked up by trucks. Provisional shelter has been supplied by the Party in the Province of Rheinfranken. The Gendarmes are here to assure the orderliness of the evacuation. We will begin immediately."

Seidel saw the eyes direct themselves at the priest. Father Gregor was silent. He did not move. If the people were to evacuate, they would have to step around or over him.

"What are you waiting for?" Seidel asked nervously. "*Obersturmbann-führer* Pettinger has come down here with me to assure all of you that evacuation is the best, the only course for the preservation of your lives."

Frau Petrik said, "You talk of trucks. Three days ago you promised trucks would pick us up in Ensdorf. Are these the same trucks?"

Seidel recognized her voice. Angrily, he shot back, "What difference does it make what trucks they are?"

"We just want to know! There've been too many promises that were never kept."

The teacher Wendt said, "Herr Seidel — if you assume you can put twenty persons and their belongings on a truck, you'd have to have 250 trucks to evacuate the five thousand people in the mine. Do you have that many trucks waiting outside?"

Seidel, who actually had two cars at the Schwalbach entrance, was not prepared for Wendt's mathematical precision. He stammered something.

"I don't believe you have them," said Karg. "But even if you had, it's madness to try loading five thousand men, women, and children under fire."

Krulle, the baker, his fat voice deep with indignation, asked, "What do you take us for? Haven't we talked with enough people who've left their villages? Don't we know — and don't you know — that no transportation, no shelter, no food were ever supplied them?"

"Why don't you go back where you came from?"

"Why don't you leave us in peace?"

"We can take care of ourselves!"

"Nobody shoots at us here!"

"We're safe here!"

A woman, cackling shrilly, broke through the crowd. "I want to go!" she shrieked.

Father Gregor turned to her. It was Frau Biermann, the postmistress. He smiled, and blessed her. "You may go," he said, "no one is holding you. And whoever else wishes to follow her, may go, too."

Pettinger watched the crowd. But only two men followed the hysterical Biermann woman. The human wall behind the priest closed again.

Frau Petrik breathed deeply. She had tried to hold back Frau Biermann; she had thought, One break means all will break. . . . How come, then, that the wall held? Were the people stronger, or were they more afraid of the war outside than she had assumed?

Her husband Johannes, standing next to her, supplied the answer. "If Frau Biermann gets through, and the two with her, we'll go, too. Everybody will go. But we've got to be sure, first."

Seidel was saying, "Herr Pastor! We've always gotten along so well — why don't you co-operate?"

Pettinger shoved Seidel aside. Still aloof, not threatening at all, rather friendly, he said, "*Herr Pastor!* And you, people — I respect your love for your soil, your love for your homes. These are feelings every German is proud to have. We have discussed your case — your Mayor Konz, the *Kreisleiter,* and other high officials in Saarbrücken. In their name, and as an officer of the SS, I give you my word that you'll be returned to your homes as soon as the enemy is beaten back, and as soon as it's safe for you to come home. Meanwhile, you must evacuate the mine."

"Under fire?" asked Karg.

In the darkness, Pettinger couldn't see the man who had spoken. He turned toward the sound of the voice and said, "It's your damned insistence on staying in the mine that has made evacuation dangerous. If you had gone when you were ordered to, by now you'd be in emergency shelters prepared for you in Rheinfranken. You'd be living in clean barracks, you would have light, air, water, hot food, your children would be in kindergartens — "

He paused. What was he doing? Begging these people — begging them instead of ordering them! He thought of the twenty Gendarmes. He thought of how many they might be able to kill in this tunnel — and he thought that he would never get out alive, either.

"Look at yourselves!" he shouted. "Living worse than animals in this dark trap, water seeping from the walls, the air foul and poisoned, coal gas that makes you sick to your stomach, that may explode into open flames — where are the miners among you who'll confirm what I've said?"

"We don't like it down here," came Elisabeth Petrik's calm voice. "But it's the only safety we have. We're just little people. We don't have the fine fast cars of Mayor Konz and the other big men. We're willing to go. But we want to live. In all respect, we ask you, *Herr Obersturmbannführer:* You go to the Americans and get us a three-hour truce so we can leave the mine without being killed!"

"You're out of your mind, woman!" He turned to the priest. "You have the welfare of your people at heart, Father — tell them to follow orders!"

The people receded. Father Gregor stood alone. "Seidel and the *Herr Obersturmbannführer* want you to leave," he began slowly. "Yet, before God and my own conscience, I don't know how to advise you. You will not know from where the next meal is to come. You will walk the roads from place to place, your children hungry and cold — "

Violently, Seidel tugged at the priest. "Stop!"

Father Gregor shook him off. "Is there anything smaller, anything more insignificant than man under the wheels of war? And can you run away? The tanks are faster than you, the wagons of destruction. . . ."

Pettinger was rattled. For the first time his own people, Germans, were not pliable; they attacked him, attacked him from the flank! They were not worth saving! All right, he didn't care whether they were saved or not — he had to have them out of the mine, away from where the Americans could reach them, out on the road — anywhere but here. . . . He must remove the priest. The priest was the heart and soul of the revolt. Without his leadership, it would crumble. People could not move without leaders.

"*Herr Pastor*," he said, his voice controlled, "will you come with us? The *Kreisleiter* and the other officials in Saarbrücken wish to confer with you, wish to show you their good will so you may convince the people that they have nothing to fear."

He saw Father Gregor hesitate.

313

"I assure you, I, myself, will return you here to the mine, to your people!"

Elisabeth Petrik felt the wavering of the priest; the old man was too straight-thinking to see the pitfall. She said, "*Herr Obersturmbannführer,* our Father Gregor is a very old man, and the *Kreisleiter* is much stronger, much better able to get around. It is right, isn't it, that the young man should come to see the old one?"

They certainly aren't worth saving, thought Pettinger, and shouted, "One should put that woman against the wall!"

"You want to see blood, *Herr Obersturmbannführer?*" came her quiet answer. "Why don't you go up front where enough of it is spilling?"

"You're coming along, *Herr Pastor!*" ordered Pettinger.

"You'll have to employ force," said Father Gregor.

"I am forcing you!" Pettinger grabbed the priest's arm.

The priest was obstinate and, in spite of his age, stronger than Pettinger had estimated. He wrenched himself loose. "Not that way!" he said. He stretched out his hands. "Handcuff me!"

"What?" Pettinger beat down Father Gregor's proffered wrists. "I haven't brought any handcuffs."

Then he heard the catcalls. He saw the people press forward, their mass swallowing up the priest.

"Coward!" he screamed.

He heard the woman's riling voice, "If the old man were a coward, he'd be back where you are, where all of you are!"

It was a defeat. Pettinger turned away. Pursued by derision and scorn, he retreated and escaped the angry voices only after he had waded through the water. Its chill sobered him. Nothing had happened that couldn't be corrected by a squad of engineers and some dynamite. As soon as he was back in Saarbrücken, he would give the necessary orders to blot out the mischief.

Johannes Petrik followed Seidel and Pettinger and the Field Gendarmes at sufficient distance to enable him to keep sight of them and the thin, wavering beams of their flashlights, and yet to remain unseen.

He was not clear about why he was following them, except for the indistinct notion that his wife's measures and advice could not be quite the thing. Certainly, she was a good woman and a good housewife, sound of mind and body, thank God — but a woman, and his wife at that, whose every weakness he knew, and with only four years of schooling! The responsibilities she took over — which men like himself, who had spent their lives at a skilled trade requiring sound judgment and thrift, would not dare to accept! In the end, though she was now acting big enough, the responsibility would fall on him. . . .

He stumbled through the water; in trying to straighten himself, he swallowed some of the cold, thick fluid still muddied by the boots of the Gendarmes; he coughed and sputtered and spit attempting to rid his mouth of the flat taste of coal. He almost lost sight of Frau Biermann and her two followers, who were trailing the official party. He arrived at the Schwalbach side breathless and in such shape that the people at that end of the tunnel took him for a messenger of bad news and came on after him and followed him to the exit.

So it was that Johannes Petrik and some of the people in the Schwalbach side of the mine became witnesses of Frau Biermann's end. They saw the Gendarmes disperse and, singly or in small groups, hop downhill toward Schwalbach. They saw Pettinger get into his car and drive off. They saw Franz Seidel invite the postmistress into his car, while the two men who had decided to leave with her stood by, with nobody to tell them where to go or what to do.

Seidel's car started and made good progress in the direction of Schwalbach. Johannes Petrik envied the woman a little — how comfortably she was being driven into exile!

And then a shell hit the car squarely and neatly. What was left burst into flames. Its twisted skeleton stood out black against the fire. Nobody had come out of the car — neither the driver nor Franz Seidel nor Frau Biermann, the postmistress.

And nobody from the mine ran over to see whether help was possible. Nor did anyone comment. The people stood in silence and watched the car and the bodies burn.

One of the men who had deserted the mine with Frau Biermann ran across the field and disappeared in the dusk; the other returned to the Schwalbach entrance, his steps slow and faltering. Later, after he and Johannes Petrik came back to the Ensdorf side, he said to the miner Karg, "Where was I to go? What was I to do? It was like a wilderness. . . ."

Crossing the hill to the Ensdorf entrance of the mine had taken the four German engineers and their corporal an hour. They were tired from lugging their heavy load. They sat down behind a mound that concealed them from the Americans, took bread and wurst out of their knapsacks, and began to eat. The Corporal lit a pipe, carefully, because the enemy was close. They deserved a good rest, he said; they had all night to rig up the explosives, and he wasn't going to hurry a thing, he wanted the job well done.

Inside the mine, Karg, acting for the Committee, was checking with the two miners posted at the Ensdorf entrance. They reported that soldiers carrying cases had suddenly appeared. Karg asked himself whether this was the sequel to Pettinger's abortive appeal; but he discarded the thought when, on ambling out, he saw the Corporal and his men — relaxed, listening to the occasional shells, and expressing by their attitude that they had the world's best conscience.

"You ought to be ashamed of yourself," the Corporal said, without changing his position.

"Why?" Karg sat down with the soldiers, snipped a blade of grass and started to chew on it.

"You're a deserter, aren't you?" said the Corporal, but his voice showed no condemnation. "Know what we're going to do?"

Karg spit. "No."

The Corporal touched one of the cases with his well-worn, stubby boot. "That's dynamite." He winked shrewdly at Karg. But he was disappointed; Karg's face showed that he didn't understand the warning.

"You're not only a shirker," the Corporal continued, "you're also a *Dummkopf*."

"Why do you call me a deserter?" asked Karg.

"Why!" The Corporal shrugged. "Let me tell you: You'd better get out of there. I don't like you. But I think there are nicer ways of dying than being shut in there. That's what the dynamite is here for, do you see it now, *Dummkopf*?"

Karg saw it. But he was not quite able to grasp the whole weight of the Corporal's casual information. "Deserter?" he said helplessly.

The man next to the Corporal wiped the liverwurst off his knife and snapped it closed. "I wouldn't like being in the *Volkssturm* either." He laughed.

The grass blade fell from Karg's lips. "My children are in that mine!" he said. "There are five thousand people! Women! People who live here! *What* are you going to do?"

"Jesus!" said the soldier with the knife, forgetting to pocket it.

The Corporal raised himself slightly. "Everybody in this district has been evacuated."

"We haven't gone," Karg said in a low voice. Then he spoke louder, "You! You have a home somewhere, wives, maybe children. You wouldn't want them to be driven away from there?"

The Corporal, who had served in Poland and had seen it with his own eyes, said No, he wouldn't.

"Come and look at them!" said Karg. "It's only a few steps. Come and look at them!"

It was growing dark. The Corporal didn't want to move, he didn't want to look. He heard the shells landing between Ensdorf and the mine. He saw the flashes of the American guns. A house was burning in Ensdorf, its flames shooting up steeply in the windless air.

"I don't believe you," he said. "I've got my orders."

Karg got up and ran toward the black hole of the mine entrance.

The Corporal shouted after him, "Get out of there! Get out of there! I've got my orders!"

Karg stumbled into the mine. He was running so fast that his feet, accustomed to the slippery, uneven ground, lost their sureness; yet he kept going.

He was stopped by Elisabeth Petrik.

"Come!" he urged, "come with me. Right away, now, hurry. For God's sake, hurry!"

He took her hand and, together, they ran to the entrance, past the squares allotted to the families, past anxious men and women rising from the dark; he, elbowing his way, she, still unaware of his purpose, trying to keep up with him, calling "Quiet! Quiet!" to the questioning people.

Outside the mine, Karg confronted the Corporal with Frau Petrik. "Here! She's a woman! Now do you believe me?"

The Corporal rose. He looked at the woman, he even touched her. "Many like her?" he asked, willing to believe, unable to decide.

"You can't blow up the entrance to the mine!" said Karg. "You can't! We've gone in there to be safe! We can't go out! You can't make us die — like that!"

Elisabeth Petrik understood what the soldiers were about to do. She grew deadly calm.

"We're five thousand people," she said, "human beings, like you — and you — and you. . . ."

"I know, I know," said the Corporal, "but what about my orders?"

Yes, what about his orders? Elisabeth Petrik knew what orders meant, she was a German; she might have disobeyed orders, but only in a personal way, and only when there was absolutely no alternative — and to expect the same from other Germans, especially soldiers, was far from her mind. She fully appreciated the danger that lay in the fact that the Corporal had orders.

"I'm not responsible," said the Corporal.

He had his orders, so his orders must be changed. "Where's your officer?" she asked. "You must have an officer!"

"The *Herr Leutnant* is on the other side — Schwalbach, I think," the Corporal said eagerly. He realized that she was showing him an out. "It's an hour's trip; we've just come over the hill — "

"It's shorter through the mine," said Elisabeth Petrik. "You wait here, Corporal!" She was not pleading, she was commanding, and he was accepting it. "You wait here and don't move until I come back!"

"Hurry!" said the Corporal. "I can't wait long. I've got my orders."

The Engineer Lieutenant was a reservist named Schlaghammer, a swarthy man past the prime of life, with a pockmarked face and indecisive eyes, a man of few convictions, a good father and good husband. He had no reason to disbelieve what Pettinger had told him — that the *Ober-sturmbannführer* had inspected the mine and had found it might very well be used by the Americans to infiltrate from the Ensdorf to the Schwalbach side. He wondered, though, why an officer of such high rank should have made it his personal business to reconnoiter the dark and dirty hole and to get his pants wet in the process; but he wasn't the man to question a Lieutenant Colonel's reasons.

Pettinger had added to his instructions, "There might be a few people in the mine — *Volkssturm* deserters, hiding down there to escape duty."

Schlaghammer had said, "Yes, sir." He had had a momentary vision of men walled up inside the mine, trying to scratch at the rock that blocked them off from light and air, with pocket knives and finger nails, until they dropped back, too exhausted to go on. Then he had shut out the vision. He had three sons at the front, whose lives might be jeopardized because these very deserters were shirking.

He had promptly taken off from Saarbrücken to Schwalbach. Having studied the terrain, he had sent half his squad, with two cases of dynamite, to the Ensdorf side of the mine, telling them to make their way over the hills. He didn't want his dynamite carted through the stretch of underground water. He had kept with him two other cases, tightly packed with enough explosives to bring down a good part of the hill over the Schwalbach entrance.

Lieutenant Schlaghammer stood there listening to Frau Petrik. *Die sind ja auch Menschen,* he thought; they're human, too. A few deserters, Pettinger had said — my God, they were women and children and old people who had fled the war. The Americans might infiltrate. . . . How? By clubbing and bayoneting these people and stepping over them? But he had orders. . . .

"You see," he said, "it's not that we want to hurt you people. But the Americans are on the other side of the hill. They've taken part of Ensdorf. If they go through the mine, they will attack the rear of our own troops. It's a military necessity."

Military necessity carried a terrible weight. Germany was more important than five thousand people. Elisabeth Petrik felt weakness settle in every blood vessel. Against military necessity there was no argument.

"Well," said Lieutenant Schlaghammer, "if we blew up only one side — that would give you a chance."

"It's not just a tunnel," she said; "it's an old mine. Unless you have some draft, there'll be coal gas, firedamps. I know. I've lived in a mining town all my life. We've got to keep both sides open."

Schlaghammer frowned. It was not up to him to judge Pettinger, Pettinger's reasons, Pettinger's lies. But it *was* in his province to interpret orders. He was to blast the entrances of the mine, not to kill five thousand people — Pettinger had said nothing about that — but to keep the Americans from infiltrating, small as that chance might be.

"It's only a question of time," she pleaded. "The front is moving. Then we can come out, live again. . . ."

Schlaghammer opened his collar.

If the mine became a kind of neutral territory used by neither side, that was as good as blocking it by demolition. Who was going to check on how he had achieved the purpose of his order? His own command was far back in Saarbrücken. And Pettinger would hardly return here.

"I must have a guarantee," Schlaghammer said sharply, "that the Americans will not use the mine. Can you bring me such a guarantee?"

"We can try!"

"Who is *We?* I mean you — Frau . . . What's your name?"

"Petrik."

"You, Frau Petrik!"

"I'm only a woman," she said, rather mechanically, anticipating objections on the part of the Committee, her husband, the men in the mine.

Schlaghammer was impatient. "That's just why! If they listen to anyone, the Americans, they'll listen to a woman. A man is always suspect — why doesn't he carry a gun?"

She looked straight at his face. "I'll try."

"Maybe they will listen to you," he said hopefully, and thought, *Die sind ja auch Menschen,* and repeated, aloud, "They're human, too. Go and try, Frau Petrik."

"Thank you," she said, "thank you. . . ."

He held her back. "I'll give you forty-eight hours. That's all I can do."

"Forty-eight hours. Yes, *Herr Leutnant.*" Then she braced herself, and went.

He watched her go toward the mine, an old woman, walking firmly. And if she never got through? If, on the other side of the line, they didn't understand what she wanted? Laughed at her? What he had done was — unorthodox, to say the least.

Well, forty-eight hours from tonight the dynamite would be as effective as it was now.

"I know what I have to do," Elisabeth Petrik said to Father Gregor and to the Committee.

They listened to her arguments. To her surprise, they raised few objections, and these half-heartedly. In the end, they agreed that it was she who must go.

The priest went to the small valise he had brought with him into the mine. He knelt down stiffly, and took out a garment. He brought it to her, carefully folded on his outstretched hands.

"You will need a white flag," he said.

She saw his gift. "Your chasuble! You need it yourself!"

The priest's veined hand stroked the heavy silk of the offering. "Perhaps it will protect you," he said quietly.

Then she came to her own family's plot. Neglect was everywhere. Her husband sat on his haunches amid the disorder that marked the small square assigned to them. Her quilts, once Frau Petrik's pride, were strewn about; the dishes, unwashed, were stacked loosely; a candle slopped its drippings as it burned. Paul and Leonie, hand in hand, sat apart from Johannes.

Frau Petrik felt she had failed in her housewifely duties; even down here, she should have seen to it that the family was kept together and cared for. Now she would have to leave them.

Johannes Petrik greeted her with complaints.

"I can't tear myself to pieces," she defended herself and sensed at the same time the estrangement that had set in between them. "I am going now," she said, half hoping he would offer to come with her. "I am leaving the mine and going to the Americans; they will help us."

Johannes Petrik jumped up. "You're crazy! I've had enough of this. You're not an official! You're not a man! I forbid you!"

Paul came over, the girl hesitantly following him. She didn't know whether she was sufficiently close to the family to partake in the argument.

"I forbid you!" the shoemaker railed. "Look at us! Look at the misery we're in! We need you. . . ." He paused helplessly. "I've been a good man to you, always. . . ."

"Yes, you have."

He pleaded. "You can't leave us now. You'll be killed out there! And what's the good of it? How are you going to deal with the Americans, you, a shoemaker's wife with four years of school! They're out of their mind, that fine Committee of yours, to send you — they're men, and they're afraid to go."

"A woman has a better chance," she answered.

He stepped in front of her, his arms spread, as if he could thus block her way to the exit.

"Be quiet," she said, "the neighbors will talk."

"I'll come with you," said Paul.

She looked at her son and smiled. It was the smile she had given him after the accident that lamed him; Paul remembered it clearly. He felt his heart ache because the smile was so full of love and because he was betraying her at this moment — he didn't want to go with her, he was afraid of

320

the shells and the noise and the lightning of the night; never had life been so precious to him, his own life and the life he wanted to lead with Leonie. He would take the child and accept it as his own; it would be a healthy child and it need never know that he wasn't its father.

"I'll come along," Paul repeated. It was a question of honor and manliness and of the front he must show to Leonie. But he couldn't move. His leg buckled under him. He clung to his mother.

She felt his full weight. "You're very good, Paul. But you see — " She didn't know how to go on, she didn't want to hurt him. "Your leg, you see — you couldn't run fast enough, and it's a long way to Ensdorf, and the fields full of shellholes — I'll be back soon. . . ."

"Mother!" he cried and hid his face at her shoulder, ashamed, and glad that she could not see his relief.

Elisabeth Petrik kissed him, and she kissed her husband, and she kissed Leonie. Then she left, the chasuble pressed under her arm. She wore a pair of men's shoes that Karg had given her because her own had not withstood the water and the rough floor of the mine. Her faded, shapeless, gray pullover was covered by a thin coat. The people whom she passed and who knew of her mission, saw how drawn and bony her face had become.

She breathed deeply of the fresh air outside the mine. The Engineer Corporal and his men, guarding the dynamite, saw her go by; she was unfolding the chasuble and tying it to a stick of wood.

She swung the flag of truce and surrender; but to her, it was a symbol of personal victory. Then she heard somebody calling her, stumbling after her. She slowed her steps, disregarding the shells that began to fall closer.

It was Leonie.

"I couldn't let you go by yourself," the girl said.

Elisabeth Petrik looked toward Ensdorf.

"You've come this far," she said, "you might as well come along."

They walked on together.

3

COMPANY C HAD penetrated the western part of Ensdorf. There had been some house-to-house fighting the previous evening, but by nightfall Troy had decided to hold operations. He wanted to avoid sending his men into the eastern part, as long as there was reasonable hope that the Artillery, doing a methodical job ahead of him, would drive out the relatively weak holding force of the Germans.

Cerelli saw the chasuble first. He was lying on Herr Krulle's bed which he had moved next to the blasted second-floor window of the bakery. He was keeping his head down so that only his helmet and eyes showed above the sill. He was motionless, observing the road, thinking of the second-hand cars he was going to fix as good as new the moment the war was over and he was back home; he was trying, with this pleasant vista, to fight off the sleep which kept encroaching upon him, forcing his head to nod every so often. He saw the chasuble, white and filled with an aura of its own, like a ghost weaving down the road. It was unexpected and unnatural; he didn't know what to make of it; and his first thought was, I haven't done anything bad, have I? . . . and his second, Take a shot at it and see what happens.

Then he perceived that the two figures underneath the floating white-ness were women, dragging themselves rather than walking.

Cerelli was damned if he was going to show his face. It could be a trap. "Hey, you!" he shouted.

The two stopped dead. The chasuble ceased moving and hung down limply. Cerelli figured it was a kind of flag, a white flag, sign of negotia-tions or surrender.

Cerelli's shout brought up Corporal Clay who had replaced the wounded Simon since the attack on the pillbox. Clay threw himself on the bed next to Cerelli. The springs creaked; Clay was a heavy man.

"What d'you make of it?" asked Cerelli.

Clay creased his freckled forehead and squinted. His thick lips moved as always when he was thinking.

"Civilians," he said, "Kraut civilians. Probably caught in some cellar and sick of the noise. So now it's night and they come out. I go fetch 'em; you cover me."

Cerelli felt the mattress of Herr Krulle's bed come up as Clay moved off. Then he saw Clay dash across the street, gain the cover of the nearest house wall, and work his way to the strange pair. Clay motioned them on. They came gingerly to the wall against which Clay was pressing his bulk; using his rifle, the Corporal herded them down the street toward Cerelli's window, and then past the bakery so that Cerelli lost sight of them. The street was empty again and all was quiet but for the consistent drumming of the artillery.

After a while, Clay rejoined Cerelli. "Crummy dames," he reported. "One was pretty old. She kept yammering for *Offizier*. I put 'em up with Sheal, he's got two Kraut PW's to guard anyhow. What do they want me to do? Take 'em to the Captain in the middle of the night? Let Troy say tomorrow what he wants done with them. . . ." He cursed suddenly. "Why don't they keep out of the way?"

Cerelli laughed. His open, boyish face turned to the Corporal. "Maybe they know where there's some liquor around here? You didn't ask 'em, did you?"

"No," said Clay, "damn it, I forgot."

"You're new in this racket," Cerelli consoled. "You oughta pick up the local customs. . . ."

In the morning, Troy received orders to lay low for the day. They wanted to bring up the flanks before pushing on further in his sector. He felt relieved at the chance to dig in and consolidate, but his relief was marred by apprehension. The push went more slowly with every passing day, and he had a notion that the Germans on the other side were up to something. He had nothing to back up his idea; there had been a conspicuous lack of patrol activity on the part of the Germans, and they ought to be out patrolling if they planned a show. He thought of his grandmother who could foretell a change in the weather by the pain in her knee; his knees were all right, and yet the feeling persisted.

He heard a jeep drive up before the house he had picked as his Command Post. He heard boots on the stairs, heard the glass splinters grind under the boots — someone should sweep out that hallway! A sergeant entered.

"I owe you a pair of pants and a shirt," said Bing, "remember — from Normandy?"

Bing dropped a package on a chair.

"Why, the hog-caller!" exclaimed Troy and got up to shake Bing's hand. His own suddenly stiffened. "My God, you haven't brought those damned loudspeakers again?"

"Hell, no! This is just a friendly visit to return old favors. I'm glad to see you alive, sir!"

"I'm surprised to see *you* alive! You aren't with that lieutenant any more?"

"I managed to shake him off. I've got another one now, fairly decent guy named Yates. I was supposed to meet him at your Division cage, but he didn't come in on time — so I decided to drive down here. There were no prisoners in the cage, anyhow."

"Shouldn't have come. They're shooting around here. And I've got enough pants."

"Well, Captain, I got those pants from your own Division supply, so they're no sacrifice to me. And I've had it in my mind to drop in on you since that day you passed me in Rollingen — "

Troy looked at Bing. He understood. "You've grown older. Cup of coffee?"

Bing sat down. The hot canteen cup felt good to his fingers. He blew into it.

"How do you like the war?" asked Troy.

"Kind of slow, isn't it?"

"What are the Germans up to?"

323

Bing took a careful sip. "Do you know anything?"

"No," Troy said heavily.

"I talk to the PW's. They drop hints, sometimes, particularly the tough ones."

"What kind of hints?"

"You can't put your finger on it. But if you ask me, Captain, they're going to start pushing."

"Have you reported on it?"

"Sure. And I hear the same thing from interrogators all along the front. But it may not mean a damned thing. Sometimes the Germans will start rumors among their own men to keep up their morale. They talk of new weapons, offensives, everything — you can't take them too seriously."

"H'm," said Troy. "Far cry from the tour across France?"

"It's winter!" Bing smiled into his cup. "In winter, war should be fought inside the hall. . . ."

"I've got two Kraut prisoners," said Troy. "My own man Traub, who usually deals with them — you know, he speaks Yiddish, but the Germans understand him, isn't that funny, them being against the Jews? Anyhow, Traub got nicked in the arm and he's back at the aid station. Do you care to have a look at them after the coffee?"

"That's the first good break I've had this trip!" Bing drank now in hasty gulps. "Thanks a lot, I will!"

Sergeant Lester came in. Troy introduced the two soldiers. Bing liked this touch which was so entirely civilian.

Lester said, "Captain, two German women came in during the night, with a white flag. Sheal reports they've been asking all night to see an *Offizier*. You want me to have them brought up?"

Troy glanced at Bing. "If it isn't asking too much. . . ."

"White flag?" Bing was interested.

"Not really," said Lester. "I saw it. It's gold-embroidered and real pretty and Sheal says he wants it as a souvenir. Kind of thing priests wear in church, you know?"

"Don't bring the women in here," said Troy. "Bing will go with you and talk to them."

"Took you a hell of a long time!" said Dondolo, as Bing and Lester stepped out of Troy's Command Post. "It's cold out here."

Bing cursed the luck that assigned Dondolo as his driver for this trip. At the first sign of Dondolo's bucking he had made it clear to the former sergeant that he was the boss; but it took Dondolo a while to adjust himself. Now, Bing countered the complaint, "Yeah, isn't it tough — you out of the warm kitchen and driving up here where it's so dangerous and all. . . .

Park the car and come along. We'll be inside and you can warm your delicate ass."

Dondolo said nothing; he could bide his time and he figured it would come soon.

Bing installed himself in the empty house next to Troy's Command Post. There were three rooms on the ground floor — the best one he picked for his interrogation; another was the waiting room in which Dondolo made himself useful as a guard; the third remained empty.

Bing was soon finished with the two German soldiers. They had been recently thrown into a second-rate *Volksgrenadier* unit and had gotten lost during the retreat — they knew little aside from their company number, their division and the name of their lieutenant, who had run away first. They seemed even more dejected than the average man from such an outfit, and said that the war was lost, as far as they were concerned; and the sooner it was over, the better.

Sheal came to take the two soldiers off Dondolo's hands. Then Bing called in the older of the women.

"You're not an *Offizier!*" were her first words.

Bing pulled up a chair for her. She sat down, exhausted, pale; the night's waiting, the worry, and hunger — she had eaten nothing since noon the day before — lined her face like an overly etched plate. But her eyes were alive; sleepless, rimmed eyes, their lashes almost invisible.

She tried to tidy her coat and skirt, without success; the floor of the cellar in which she had spent the night had dealt her clothing the final blow.

"Why do you want to see an officer?" said Bing.

"Because of the mine — because of five thousand people — it'll be blown up — they'll perish and die — and the *Herr Leutnant* said I should go and see the American commander — word of honor — "

It gushed out of her.

In the long hours of the night, her flesh aching from the stone and the icy dampness, her mind tortured by the futility of time running out, she had planned her speech so sensibly. But now, all her rhetoric was gone. The fears of the night were on her tongue, and she even resented such sensible small questions as the American managed to interject: What her name was . . . and whether she was from Ensdorf . . . and how come she had been chosen for the difficult mission. . . .

Bing had not listened to more than a small part of her disjointed story, when he got its significance and grew excited. Here were five thousand *Germans* in revolt, or if not in revolt, at least consciously opposing orders the Nazis had given; here the Nazis were proposing to exterminate them, *their own people;* here was the chance to support these miners and their families, stiffen them, stiffen the resistance; here was an example in fact to be given to the entire German nation, a cleavage between rulers and ruled, between the Nazis and the people; you could widen it if only you drove in the wedge with quick, determined strokes. And what a devilishly appropriate time it was, now that the Armies had entered Germany itself and the people all over the country were faced with the choice of sticking with the Nazis, or rising against them — or, at least, dissociating themselves from their war lords!

"I have only thirty-eight more hours," Elisabeth Petrik said. "Then I must bring word to Lieutenant Schlaghammer that you won't go through the mine. Will you help me? Will you get me to your Colonel, your General? Lieutenant Schlaghammer said, a soldier's word is a soldier's honor. It's our only hope. . . ."

Go through the mine! thought Bing. He was not familiar with the local map or military situation. Troy would be able to say. But he was inclined to take the whole infiltration idea as a hoax to get the Ensdorf people out of the mine, or to give this Schlaghammer a well-sounding reason for exterminating them. Any American commander would think twice before sending his men into a long dark tunnel that could be blocked by three men and a machine gun.

In the other room, Dondolo appraised Leonie.

He could see beyond her shabby exterior; the small triangle of skin under her throat was sample and promise of white expanse, curves, shades; she had the light skin and yellow hair that could drive him, the dark and swarthy man, crazy. Her pregnancy had brought out thin veins on her temples, and he expected that kind of skin at her breasts and at her thighs close to where these joined her pelvis. That she was dirty and unkempt meant nothing; where he came from, women often slopped around all day.

To Leonie, it was clear what this American wanted; Hellestiel had sometimes glowered at her that way, as if she were given entirely into his power. She moved away from the soldier and laid all her pleading into her eyes, and her fear came out, too — and that was what goaded Dondolo into action.

He drove her into a corner, slowly and methodically, and suddenly grabbed her shoulders and pressed his body against her and whispered, "We'll have some fun, *Fräulein,* huh? Quiet, quiet! Now you co-operate — stop kicking, you! — or I'll make trouble for you — plenty, plenty trouble . . ." Her topcoat came open and through her thin dress and sweater he felt her full breasts and her arched belly. The German bitch! Let her kick! Let her pant! Let her eyes pop — soon they would pop even more.

He reached down to raise her skirt, and for the fraction of a second he felt her soft warm flesh.

She screamed.

"Shut up!" he shouted.

It was too late. Bing was in the room.

Dondolo saw the old woman behind Bing, heard her call something unintelligible. Women should be killed off after a certain age; they were good for nothing.

Dondolo turned to fence Bing off. In this moment, the girl escaped him. She was fast as a rabbit. Dondolo saw her flash by, he heard the outside door bang shut, heard the running steps on the stairs, on the street — then quiet.

Beads of perspiration stood on his face. He laughed hoarsely and ordered his pants.

"You aren't going to get away with this," Bing said. His lips were white.

"So what are you going to do to me?" said Dondolo. "There's nothing worse than being where I am now. The MP can is a safer spot, ain't it?"

In a way, Dondolo was right. What greater punishment was there than being a soldier and going where you might be killed?

"*Kommen Sie!*" Bing said to Frau Petrik and shepherded her back into the other room and closed the door between himself and Dondolo. He didn't know how to begin.

"I am sorry," he said finally, "terribly sorry. I have no excuse to offer for the man. He will be punished."

The woman seemed to be listening, but not to him. Frau Petrik hoped Leonie would have the sense to come back. She listened for the odd shot indicating that some soldier, American or German, was attempting to stop the girl's escape. But this single, isolated shot did not sound.

"Your daughter?" Bing asked.

"No."

Elisabeth Petrik placed her fingers on the rim of the table; he saw her square-cut nails, the dirt collected around the cuticles.

"Leonie is a girl from this town," she said tonelessly.

"Very brave of her to come here with you. Were there no men?"

"We felt women might be better. . . . What time is it?"

There was something inhuman, something very German in her singleness of mind, her determination, her clinging to the idea of the *Offizier* and the infiltration of the mine. Bing asked, "Your family in the mine?"

"Yes."

That explained something, but not all.

"I can't go search for the girl. . . ." he said.

She knew that. She glanced at him. The loss of Leonie, the girl whom Paul loved, made her drive to save her son and the thousands in the mine all the stronger. And this American was her only hope, her only contact with that American commander who could give her and Schlaghammer the assurance that the mine would not be used.

327

"What time is it?" she asked again.

"Ten-thirty," said Bing.

"Take me to the *Offizier,* please!"

Bing gave Troy the complete story. Together, they plotted the mine on the map — it had been abandoned so long ago that their up-to-date maps did not carry it.

"What do you think," asked Bing, "is there a possibility of your going through the tunnel to the Schwalbach side?"

"Possible," said Troy, "but not probable."

"Why?"

"Hell, I'd take any approach sooner than the one through that mine. You yourself said that this tunnel — or any tunnel — can be blocked by a machine gun and three men. I know what it cost us to take the forts of Metz, to work our way through the underground passages there."

He paused.

"You can tell the dame she should stop worrying and go back and tell her people that we're not the ones to bring the mountain down over their ears!"

"I'd like to hold her until Lieutenant Yates comes. I finally reached him at Division cage and he said he'd be down immediately."

Troy shrugged. "Suit yourself!"

The telephone rang, then Lieutenant Fulbright came in, and other matters took Troy's attention. Bing waited quietly, trying to think of ways of putting his hunch into practice. If the woman and the people in the mine were an indication that something was cracking up on the other side, it was high time to hook in and to develop the crack. But as usual, as it had been with the Fourth of July leaflet or with the DP's in Verdun, nobody had anticipated this development. Yates, probably, would talk some more of improvising.

Yates came in; he and the Captain shook hands. Troy's hulking frame made Yates seem slender, almost elegant.

Yates said, "I'm very grateful, Captain, that you called us in so quickly."

Troy, who carried an indistinct memory of Laborde and the encounter over the placing of the loudspeaker truck, had expected a man of similar caliber, despite Bing's remark that Yates was different. There was also Troy's natural antagonism against men who lived the more sedentary and less risky life in the rear.

"If the case is what the Sergeant said it was, over the phone," Yates went on, "well, maybe it will help you and ultimately save the lives of some of your men."

Troy didn't attribute that much importance to the woman of Ensdorf — but he was pleased that Yates should think at all of the men in C Company.

"It's all the Sergeant's work," Troy said. "He spoke to her. What are you going to do with her that's likely to benefit me?"

"Frankly, I don't know yet. I have an idea. But first, Bing and I should have another talk with the woman."

That Yates didn't know, and admitted it, was an added point in his favor. Troy had learned that in this war most of what you did was guesswork, and that you were lucky and should thank your God if it turned out well.

"Whatever it is you're planning," said Troy, "just make it good and strong."

"Bing always has ideas!" Yates grinned.

Bing remained serious. "Captain, if you found the sector in front of your company undefended, no enemy troops — just a vacuum — wouldn't you move in?"

"Provided there's no trouble on the flanks. . . ." Troy laughed. "I've been looking for something like that since D-day."

"Well, that's exactly the situation we have!" Bing knew he was oversimplifying the matter; but he wanted both officers to follow him all the way. "The leaders of those people have run away and taken along all the illusions. If we don't move in, if we leave those people leaderless, if we don't give them new ideas, our ideas, to rally around, they'll fight on because there's nothing else for them to do. What does the woman of Ensdorf tell us? Very plainly, that now is our chance."

Troy smiled a little, amused. "I'm in favor of anything that saves us a day of fighting. It might be just the day the slug is fired that hits me."

Yates said, "Cut out your theories, Bing! We have an immediate problem. There are five thousand people about to be suffocated. I want to speak to this woman. Captain Troy, is there a room I can have? Perhaps upstairs?"

"Sure!" Troy went so far as to put his broad hand on Yates's shoulder. "Only do me the favor and get rid of her for me."

"It won't take long," promised Yates.

Bing went along with Yates. He wasn't happy. Neither Yates nor Troy had understood him or had grasped the change that was taking place on the other side.

By the time Elisabeth Petrik told her story to Yates, it had jelled into definite form in her mind; much of the emotion with which she had recounted it to Bing gave way to a soberness that struck Yates as callous.

Only later did he realize how right Bing had been in seeing the issue in its full implication; only later did he wish that the woman of Ensdorf had come to him at a time in his life when he was ready for her. His reactions at the moment were personal and emotional. He wanted to ask her why her people in the mine hadn't thrown themselves on Pettinger and torn him to pieces — Pettinger, Yasha's man, who kept reappearing almost like a personal enemy.

When she told him that Pettinger was willing to annihilate his own German people with the same ruthlessness the Nazis used against the French of Isigny and the DP's of all Europe, and not even the excuse that these were enemy nationals or Jews — when Bing added that the threadbare pretext of an American infiltration through the mine was so much eyewash — Yates felt his hate grow and encompass not only Pettinger but the whole Nazi setup.

He said to Frau Petrik, "I can assure you, there won't be any attempt on our part to go from Ensdorf to Schwalbach through the mine in which your people have taken refuge." And he gave her the military reasons and added, to make it doubly clear, "Can you imagine our tanks, our guns, our vehicles creeping through that hole in the mountain? We'd be stuck at the first turn, at the first narrowing of the tunnel."

"*Jawohl, Herr Leutnant.*" She understood.

"Furthermore, Herr Schlaghammer, your Engineer Lieutenant ready to blow up the entrances and to seal you inside the mountain, knows it — must know it as a military man. Pettinger couldn't be an *Obersturmbannführer* in the *Waffen* SS without knowing it. All they want to do is get rid of you, one way or another, because you have risen against your Government."

Bing found that Yates was putting it neatly. If Yates saw this far, why not farther?

Bing said in English: "Lieutenant! You say it yourself — this *is* a revolt! And it's over something as simple as houses and staying where you've lived all your life. If this can be spread, if we can push part of the German people into liberating themselves — I'm not only thinking of how much it's bound to help us, I'm thinking of much later, of what are we going to do with Germany? *Now* we must give them a program, *now* we must tell them what kind of democracy we want them to have, and where they'll fit in, provided they *do* something for themselves. . . ."

Yates was having trouble enough keeping his thoughts and words reined for the job on hand. "We have a concrete case here, Bing — this woman, the people in the mine; and we're going to settle this thing first. If you don't see how Pettinger has been playing into our hands, and how we can play it up — that's just too bad. Your politics can come later."

"Damn it, Lieutenant — it's always the same story. We come into Verdun and get into the DP mess, because nobody bothered to think ahead of what we'd find, and because we still believe that armies fight apart from people. But if we make the same blunder this time, with all of Germany at stake — we'll just miss the boat, and there'll never be another."

"This isn't Germany, it's just one woman I have to deal with. And I'm only a Lieutenant, and you're only a Sergeant, and for Chris'sake, stop solving the whole world's troubles." He turned back to Frau Petrik. "What were you saying?" he asked.

The woman had been trying to adjust herself to the new light Yates had shed on Schlaghammer. "What are we to do?" she said dejectedly. "What are we to do?"

She had clung so firmly to the thin hope the German Engineer had extended her. She had only this one hope, and it had made her leave her family and the people she knew, her crippled son; it had made her discard her responsibility toward Leonie who had come with her on her hard road through bullets and shells; it had made her throw herself at the mercy of what was, after all, the enemy — and now, this American officer told her that Schlaghammer, in giving her that hope, had betrayed her.

"Coming back to your friend Schlaghammer," said Yates. "Suppose he means what he says! What if he's replaced tomorrow, or has been replaced already? What if any of his superiors come to check up on him? Do you honestly think a man like Pettinger will leave something he's started, unfinished? Can you answer me, Frau Petrik?"

She couldn't.

Perhaps it was cruel of him to put her on this rack, but Yates knew he must, if he wanted to make her see beyond her singleness of purpose.

She began to weep quietly. She had no handkerchief. She looked around and finally, embarrassed, wiped her nose on the sleeve of her old, gray pullover.

Yates grew impatient. He raised his finger, involuntarily falling back into the style of lecturing.

"How can we stop the Nazis, how can we stop Pettinger? Why, *you* can stop him! We're interested in saving the people of Ensdorf, not for their sake — but because that's the kind of war we're waging. And we can save them within the time limit you have set yourself, Frau Petrik. You and we, together — we can do it. And incidentally, save thousands of others, too. Isn't it logical to assume that, in other towns, people are also trying to stick to their homes, to hide when the Nazis come around and want to drive them away? Don't you think there are other Pettingers willing and prepared to kill them rather than see them live under another Government?"

"Yes — yes. . . . But I'm only one woman, a *Hausfrau*. I've only four years of schooling. . . ."

Bing smiled at Yates. She was only a *Hausfrau,* and Yates was only a Lieutenant, and he was only a Sergeant.

Yates didn't seem to notice. He said sincerely, "You stopped being a

Hausfrau when you led the people of Ensdorf to the mine. You have taken a responsibility upon yourself, and you must carry it out."

"What do you want me to do?"

"We took the radio station in Luxemburg, one of the most powerful in Europe. You will speak over the air. You will tell your story to the whole German people. You will expose Pettinger and what the Nazis are planning to do to your people. If you tell your story, and tell it right, if all of Germany knows it, the Nazis must let your people live because they cannot admit, now, when they need the support of the people more than ever, that they are killing Germans for their own ends."

She sat stunned. Her head began to wag like a very old woman's. She had never before thought in these terms, and she had to arrange all these new ideas in her mind. It was difficult.

"Did you understand the Lieutenant?" said Bing.

"*Ach, mein Herr,*" she asked, "how can I do that? Radio! My husband is a shoemaker!"

"Forget that," said Yates. "You must think not only of the people you know in the mine, the five thousand people of Ensdorf and Schwalbach. Think of all the others! The American Army is going to march forward. Nobody can hold us. What you are facing today, every German will have to face tomorrow and in the weeks and months to come. Even the Engineer Lieutenant Schlaghammer said, *Die sind ja auch Menschen!* Think of them — they're human, too. . . ."

"Clever stunt," Bing said to Yates. And he thought: Accidentally, it might even start things going the right way. Still, it was surface scratching. It was expediency. And Yates was trying so hard and so honestly!

"What time is it?" Elisabeth Petrik asked.

"Quarter of one," said Yates. "We can be in Luxemburg tonight."

Leonie, escaping from Dondolo, had done the most sensible thing. She had run into the street but had ducked out of it and into the nearest empty house. Panting, half-blind with fright, she crouched in the hall, among the odd pieces of furniture, pictures, lamps that people had wanted to take along and had finally abandoned in their hasty exodus to the mine.

She waited for the pursuers. To run up the street, toward the German lines, toward the mine, would have been fatal in broad daylight. That she didn't do it was not because she reasoned it out, weighed her chances, and chose the wiser course. She was too upset to think much. But there was in her something of the hunted animal's instinct — she had had it ever since Hellestiel mated her and then dropped her as soon as she told him she was pregnant.

As she cowered in the dark hallway which shook and shook with the

332

impact of the shells tearing into the earth outside, and as nobody appeared to search for her and the realization came that, perhaps, she had not been seen, the temptation grew to lie down and die. Then she thought of Paul who had wanted to help her with his poor means; but Paul was only a cripple, and Leonie had the subconscious contempt for the weak and maimed that Nazism bred and that Hellestiel had expounded when preening his perfect body in preparation for her. She pitied Paul a little, but pitied herself more. And then, frightened, she started up at the thought of his mother, still in the hands of the Americans, and now left alone with them.

Only, at this moment, the child in her moved. Poor worm, she felt its kicking all through her.

And then she knew that she could not go after Elisabeth Petrik, back to the swarthy, sweating thing that had assaulted her. She wasn't alone, she couldn't afford it. It was her child, though she had it from Hellestiel; it was in her and lived and kicked and asserted itself, and she had to protect it.

She was hungry. She dragged herself to the kitchen, to the cupboard — empty. She climbed upstairs and opened the first door and almost cried out — she could have stepped into space. A shell had sheared off the upper corner of the house. The door in her hand was there, and the wall to which it belonged with a sink jutting out senselessly and a hook next to it from which a coat dangled. She wanted the coat, it would warm her, but she could not reach it and did not dare to try.

But if she kept the door open just a slit, she could see the house where Elisabeth Petrik was.

Leonie stayed at her observation post. After a time, she saw soldiers hurriedly crossing the street. Then Frau Petrik, accompanied by the swarthy one and the other soldier who had stopped the swarthy one, came out and went up the street, and entered another house.

Leonie waited and waited, her eyes strained. Her legs hurt and her back felt like a string drawn too taut. Finally, a car drove up before that house, and then another. She saw Elisabeth Petrik get into one car; she saw the cars drive off and grow smaller and disappear — out of Ensdorf.

Leonie did not attempt too much reasoning about what was going to happen to Frau Petrik. They had been two women under the cloud of war; and what would the Nazis have done to them — Hellestiel, or Pettinger?

Only the return to the mine was left to her. There, at least, were people she knew; although no one could say how long they were going to stay in it or when they would perish amidst falling debris from the slow change of air into thick, choking matter.

She had to bring the terrible news to the mine. They had not seen an

Offizier. Frau Petrik had been taken prisoner. The white chasuble had counted for nothing.

After nightfall, Leonie crept more than walked to the mine. She arrived there, bleeding from hands and knees, and fainted in Karg's arms.

4

DESPITE the late hour, Yates found Colonel DeWitt at his desk. His office, located in the studio building of the Luxemburg radio station, was overheated; DeWitt had opened his collar and was working in his shirt sleeves; he looked more like a country doctor than an officer. He continued shuffling through his papers while Yates began to report on his find and the possibilities he saw in Frau Petrik and the people of Ensdorf. Gradually, however, the papers came to rest under the Colonel's muscular arms; his hands were folded, and only an occasional twitching of his fingers belied the statuesque repose of the man.

Then DeWitt called Crerar from the adjoining room. Crerar, his creased face, his shrewd eyes attentive, his leggings awry as always, took the chair next to the Colonel's desk.

Yates swept to his conclusions. He was elated and didn't see how his listeners could fail to agree with his proposals: "We'll expose the tactics of the enemy to his own population and keep him from exterminating the people of Ensdorf and God knows how many others in similar circumstances. We defeat his intentions to scorch and depopulate the areas we occupy. . . ."

DeWitt swung his chair around. "What's your opinion, Crerar?"

"God, it's a wonderful story!" said Crerar. "Imagine those people in the mine, waiting for the trap to close. Having to choose between being killed outside, caught in the battle — or being choked in the darkness underground, with the oxygen and the food giving out. What a clever, simple threat this Pettinger pulled! By the way, isn't he the guy who got away from us in Paris?"

Yates, though he expected little more of Crerar, was furious at the man's detachment. As if the Ensdorf people weren't human, but shadows on the screen! "Yes, it's the same Pettinger!" he snapped.

"And this Lieutenant Schlaghammer," Crerar went on, "torn between his orders and his conscience. Classical character, classical situation. . . . By all means, let's dramatize this thing on the air, this shoemaker's wife who dared to defy her Government!"

DeWitt grimaced, "You should have gone into show business."

"Always wanted to, Colonel. But there's more money in advertising. And it's a steadier income."

They would never change, Yates thought nervously. They went off on tangents; they really took nothing very seriously. And once he'd been like that. . . .

DeWitt saw Yates squirm. He said matter-of-factly, "I am in favor of letting the woman of Ensdorf speak, if one of us prepares the script. Maybe Bing can do it. But I want to point out — particularly to you, Yates — that you're all wet if you assume that this is going to save the people in that mine!"

Yates was startled. "Of course, there is no guarantee," he admitted uncomfortably.

"That's putting it mildly!" smiled DeWitt. "I should say Frau Petrik's speech is the death sentence for the Ensdorfers!"

"Obviously!" exclaimed Crerar. "Quite a curtain!"

Fear rose from Yates's stomach to his head and burned his cheeks and forehead. "Could you enlarge on that?" he asked tightly.

"Certainly."

DeWitt shoved all his papers aside with the exception of one blank sheet on which he wrote, in large block letters: (I) *Military Necessity*.

"I believe the Nazis are motivated by the principle of military necessity. Not that the mine itself is a military objective, but the people in it are. If, as we know, the Germans plan to leave us nothing but bare fields and uninhabitable ruins, they must do away with anybody opposing that."

Crerar said, "It's a ridiculous plan! It's atavistic! It's the old Nibelungen concept of taking along to your doom as much, and as many people, as possible!"

DeWitt ignored the interruption. He wrote: (II) *Covering Up*.

"Furthermore, Yates, if their plan in its application to the people in the mine is exposed by your Frau Petrik, they will have to eliminate these people to get rid of the witnesses of a revolt. I don't see any other alternative for them."

Yates, on whom the whole recognition of these self-evident facts and of the pointlessness of his own illusions fell with a sudden, staggering weight, stammered, "Then we — we can't do it."

DeWitt crumpled the sheet.

"We can — and we must do it. It's our job to use any means to split the German people from their Government. Frau Petrik will show them it is possible to resist the Nazi machine. That's what we're interested in."

"Even at the cost of five thousand helpless people?" said Yates.

"We know military necessity, too. If their deaths save us the lives of five American soldiers, even of a single one — that's perfect!"

DeWitt said it with a cruel superficiality. He knew that the harder he appeared to Yates, the easier it would be for the younger man to blame him for the consequences.

335

"Once we talked about the trees on your farm, Crerar," the Colonel continued. "You complained the Nazis had cut them down to create a field of fire for their guns. And I told you I'd have done the same, didn't I?"

"Very beautiful trees, too," said Crerar.

Trees! thought Yates. "But Colonel, sir — I sold the woman the idea of the broadcast. I promised her it was the only way to save her people."

"Perhaps it won't work out so tragically," Crerar said soothingly. "So much depends on the course of battle, on the local situation."

"*You* don't have to see her again, Yates!" shrugged DeWitt. "Let Bing handle it!"

"I can't," said Yates. "I'll have to carry it through myself."

"I'm afraid that's a matter for you to settle with your conscience. We'll have the woman on the air tomorrow morning."

Bing was open about his intentions. He had a hasty, late supper with Dondolo and announced across the table that he was going to see Loomis that very evening and make his report.

"I don't want to do it behind your back. If you want to come along, that's fine with me."

Dondolo picked up a lukewarm frankfurter, whose skin had shriveled, and waved it thoughtfully in front of his eyes. Then he stuck it into his mouth, bit off a piece, chewed, and spit out the skin.

"Vot ees it? Maybe you'd like to come visit me in the hoosegow?"

"No," said Bing quietly, "I'd like to see you strung up by your balls."

Dondolo leaned back and contemplated the general vicinity of the part of his body by which Bing wanted him strung up.

"You don't say . . ." he answered, equally quietly; "and you pretending to be an educated man. I don't know when it's going to come — but when it does, and you and your kind are put where you belong, it'll be a pleasure to me to do the same to you and to skin you and break every bone in your body. . . ."

Bing knew he meant it.

"Like you did to Thorpe?"

But Dondolo didn't bite.

"I didn't do nothing to Thorpe. Nothing. Put that under your hat."

"Shall we go?" asked Bing.

"Might as well," Dondolo said amiably. He even held the door for Bing as they left the mess.

They found Loomis alone in his room, playing solitaire. He gathered up the deck. "Nice of you boys to have come!"

"This isn't social, sir," said Bing. "I want to make a report."

"Salute, will you?" said Loomis. "I didn't think it was social."

He snapped the deck and let his eyes rove from Bing to Dondolo and back, as he listened to the story of Dondolo's attempt on Leonie. He found it picayune. So the old woman was upset! . . . Old women were bound to be upset in wartime.

"You got anything to add?" he asked Dondolo.

Dondolo squinted at him, an amused smile playing about his thin lips. "Hell no, sir!" he said. "Of course I tried to make her. It wasn't fraternizing either. If you have to, you have to."

"It was attempted rape," said Bing.

Dondolo looked at Bing with cold hate. "I didn't know the dame was that important to Sergeant Bing. Why didn't he tell me? I could have waited until he was through with her."

Loomis started to deal himself another hand. "Well, Bing — you realize, of course, that denouncing a man for a matter like that is a rather unusual procedure. You don't want me to forget about it, now you've got it off your chest?"

"I insist that charges be preferred!" said Bing. "If it were anybody else, I'd skip it. But not with this man. Not after what was done to Thorpe. It was Dondolo who turned Thorpe in — according to the official version."

Loomis wanted to ask: What do you mean, Official version? But he bit his lip and turned his head away from the light. He thought the matter over. He remembered the girl in Paris. He understood Dondolo's need to find a piece of nooky once in a while; but anything the guy touched was the root of some trouble.

"You know," Loomis said to Bing, "you'd have to produce the girl in question — because it's your word against Dondolo's."

Dondolo spoke up. With a cynicism unsettling Loomis, he said, "You forget, sir, I admitted it!"

"Oh yes, yes — you did." And then, facing both men, he cried, "By Christ, what do you want me to do?"

"Prefer charges!" Bing insisted.

"I don't care," said Dondolo, staring straight at Loomis. Jesus, he thought, it takes this jerk a long time to catch on.

Loomis did catch on. It was the solution to all his problems. He worried, for a moment — Dondolo had made his wish so God-damned obvious. Well, maybe Bing was interested in getting Dondolo out of the way, too. . . .

"All right!" he said. "Technician Fifth Grade Dondolo, you're hereby severely reprimanded. I'll have you transferred out of this outfit, and you'll be sent to the Replacement Depot. I'll make it official tomorrow morning."

Loomis looked at Bing. If Bing wanted to make it tougher than that, there were ways of making it tough on Bing. But Bing seemed satisfied. Replacement Depot, to him, meant the speedy conversion of Dondolo into an infantryman.

Bing forgot what Dondolo knew: That his classification was that of mess sergeant; that, if worse came to worst, they would put him into the kitchen of some other outfit. Dondolo was reasonably sure, however, that his long experience in the Army would make it easy for him to wangle a safe job, far in the rear — possibly even a return to the States. There were so many corpses buried all over the Army — you just had to sniff around a little. The Army, after all, wasn't so much different from the Tenth Ward Association back home, and nothing would happen to a fellow who knew his way around.

But Bing, Dondolo gloated, would continue to go on his dangerous expeditions, with some other sucker driving him — not Dondolo, thank God. And somewhere, the bullet with Bing's name on it was being cast. Dondolo hoped it would have a good-sized caliber.

Yates got DeWitt's permission to take Frau Petrik back to Ensdorf.

"We owe it to her, sir," he said, "at least I think *I* do. I can't send her back there alone."

"You're a glutton for punishment," said DeWitt. "Go ahead!"

Yates saluted and turned to the door.

"Hold it!" DeWitt called. "Is she waiting out there for you?"

"Yes."

"How did she do this morning?"

"Wonderfully. Very composed. She was frightened of the mike, and the men around, and the machinery. But that let up after a while."

"Bring her in, please," said DeWitt. "I would like to see her."

Yates returned with the woman of Ensdorf. The Colonel rose.

"This is *Herr Oberst* DeWitt," Yates said to her. "He's the man who made it possible for you to speak over the radio." Then he turned to DeWitt and translated what he had said to the woman.

The Colonel's face was compassionate, and his hand shook slightly. "That's all right, Yates. I'm prepared to take the responsibility. . . ."

He motioned the woman to a chair, and studied her face and her dress and her figure. She sat stiffly at first. Then she began to feel easier; the American *Herr Oberst* seemed like a good man. He reminded her of Father Gregor, except that Father Gregor was much older and had the gentleness that came with the thousands of times he had forgiven people's sins.

DeWitt, too, felt a kind of affinity for the woman. She wasn't quite like the New England farmers' wives he knew, although in her face was something of their earthy quality, lines like the furrows on the hills, sorrow for what had grown and was constantly threatened.

"Yates!"

"Yes, sir!"

338

"Tell her I'm sorry for the war. Tell her that we are fighting it so that there'll never be another, so that people like her and myself can live out the rest of our days in peace. Tell her that I respect her and what she did, and that I thank her for it in the name of those whose lives she may have saved by her decision."

He paused and waited for Yates to put his words into German. He saw Elisabeth Petrik's eyes come to life and her lips move.

"And tell her that, from the depth of my heart, I hope she finds her people alive and well. . . ."

He saw Yates hesitate. He said sharply, "I can hope for it, can't I?"

Then DeWitt took the woman's hand and accompanied her to the door.

To Yates, the trip back to Ensdorf seemed endless. Elisabeth Petrik had stopped asking him about the time; she knew that they were just within the forty-eight-hour limit set by the German Engineer Lieutenant, Schlaghammer. She spoke of her happiness in having succeeded in her task, of her joy in seeing her son again. . . .

"What a shame I lost the chasuble. And we won't be able to get another one."

The road wound between hills. Patches of dirty snow flew by. The sky became darker and heavier, and here and there, they drove through rags of fog.

"It's going to snow," said Yates.

"*Ach ja*," sighed Frau Petrik, "maybe we can return to our houses soon. The roofs will be damaged, and the windows will be out. It will be a cold winter. But we will manage."

Yates wished she would stop talking, but he didn't have the heart to order her. He tried not to listen.

"It's high time that I come back," she continued her prattle. "My son, he has a lame leg, he needs me badly. And my husband, too, though bless the Lord he's perfectly healthy. Men are so helpless — I don't mean soldiers, soldiers have learned to take care of themselves — but ordinary men, if they're away from home and don't know where to find their things. They mustn't have had a warm meal all this time. My God, *Herr Leutnant,* can you imagine the life in that old mine — no light — filth — water dropping around you all the time; it's a wonder everybody doesn't come down with pneumonia. And poor Leonie . . . It's the people that suffer most in war. You're very lucky, you Americans, that the war is over here. . . ."

Then she told stories about the mine — the family that moved in with their three goats, and how the goats broke loose and began to eat their neighbors' shoes; and the child that was born in the mine, and how they christened it. . . .

She was not disheartened; she said that life in the tunnel was better than wandering lost and homeless and aimless over the roads of Germany, especially in weather like this. She was actually homesick for the mine — no, not really for the mine, but for Ensdorf and the people with whom she had spent her life. Never again would she want to leave, and exciting as it had been to speak over the radio, she was a shoemaker's wife and never would she do it again, not for all the money in the world.

Yates would intersperse her chattering with a monosyllabic "Yes." She was building herself up for a terrible fall. He knew it, and he couldn't prevent it. Even DeWitt hadn't had the courage to say to her face that she would come back to Ensdorf to find her people exterminated — exterminated because she had made their annihilation inevitable. And DeWitt could have told her the truth much more easily — he was not bound to her by the promises Yates had given.

What would be his role? To stand by and hold her while she broke down? To hang on to her and try to keep her alive — her whose life had lost all sense? He could see this life as it really was — wrapped up in the crippled son who would be dead, in the shoemaker helpless without her, little personal things — how the house was, and the furniture, and all that — all these things that were destroyed first, in a war. To some people, he thought — to Mademoiselle Godefroy, the teacher back in Isigny — this destruction was part of a picture that, as a whole, had meaning; it was the price they paid for the freedom they had lost and regained. But to the Germans, it could make no sense; to them, destruction was nothing but destruction, they paid the price and got nothing in return, because that was the war as they had started it and fought it; and even if one of them like Frau Petrik rose above herself, it still was of no use.

When they arrived in Ensdorf, it was snowing in big, wet, sticky flakes. In the house that had been Troy's Command Post, Yates found a major who told him that Company C had pushed a few miles forward against little resistance; they were at the outskirts of Schwalbach, he said.

"Do you know anything of those people in the mine? Do you know what happened to them?"

"What mine? What people?" The Major reconsidered. "Oh, I know what you mean, Lieutenant. Troy said something about it — people who had taken refuge there? I think he said they were gone when his men got there. . . ."

Elisabeth Petrik still waited in the car. Her hands gripped the steel frame of the jeep's front seat; she half lifted herself when she saw Yates come out of the house.

"It's too dark to drive across the fields to the mine," he said to her. "We'll have to walk there. You'll show me the way."

Stiffly, she got out of the car. For a moment, she seemed at the point of falling down, whether from the cramped ride or from sudden weakness, he couldn't say. He supported her, and after a few steps, she recovered. She asked something, but her voice was so low he didn't understand.

"What?"

"Can you — can you go to the mine? Isn't it dangerous for you?"

"Not at all," he said. "We've pushed farther ahead. We're almost in Schwalbach."

She stopped. Her hands searched for something to hold on to. They found a post, wet and rusty, part of a crumbled fence. Then her hands moved to her face and covered it, and when they sank down, it was streaked. It had a comic effect in all the mute despair.

Yates pulled out his handkerchief. He knew what must have gone through her mind: If the Americans were beyond the mine, and if her people had been saved — Why hadn't they come back to Ensdorf? Why was there nobody in the town — nobody but a few American soldiers who went through the houses, seemingly without aim and order?

She didn't see the handkerchief. He wiped the smudges off her face and thought, Now it's beginning, she won't survive it. I ought to arrange for an ambulance. And if she survives it, where's she going to go? What am I going to do with her? Bring her to a DP camp? She's a German, she doesn't belong there. Leave her in Ensdorf, all by herself?

"You'd better prepare yourself, Frau Petrik," he said, and put his arm around her sagging shoulders. "Perhaps things haven't worked out quite as we planned. . . ."

But he felt her shoulders straighten. She laughed. "Of course! They wouldn't come out unless somebody told them! I have to tell them. I have to tell them they can come home now. The front has passed over them. . . ."

She began to run through the slush and the mud. She stumbled where the pavement was torn by shells, got up and forced herself forward. Yates panted, but he kept up with her. He heard her breathe in short gasps. Her shawl trailed behind her. Her men's shoes, too large for her, made the puddles splash; her coat, now come open and soaking wet, beat against and around her bony legs; and the snow came down more densely, its flakes mingling with the hair straggling over her forehead.

The last houses of Ensdorf sank back behind them. They went uphill over a field whose furrows were partially covered with snow. The stubbles of last fall's harvest gave under Yates's boots; he slipped and cursed, and almost lost her.

"Hold it! Take it easy!"

And there were the shellholes he had to look out for, treacherous land in this early semidarkness of December. But she went ahead as if driven and pursued, she looked neither backward nor to the ground, but kept her face tensely forward.

In front of them yawned the entrance to the tunnel. Out of the side of his eye, Yates noticed a couple of American soldiers standing there, but he did not look at them. He didn't want to let the woman get out of his sight.

"Hey, Lieutenant!" somebody shouted.

Then Elisabeth Petrik stopped. Nobody was in the entrance, not a soul, nobody to welcome her, no voices, only the black opening, as if the mountain had a mouth, a pain-torn toothless gaping mouth.

She stood stock-still.

Yates noticed a case standing to the side of the entrance. He couldn't read the inscription, there wasn't enough light for it. But he was fairly sure that this was the dynamite which the German Engineers were to have used.

"Well, they didn't blow it up," he said to the woman. "At least we prevented that!"

She did not answer. She stared into the black mouth as if, any second now, people must come tumbling out of it, jubilant people, free of the terror of war.

Somebody did come out. At first, they saw a light, like a thin white point, it became bigger and bigger, and as it approached the outside world, it was switched off.

"Oh, hello, Yates!" said Troy. "Good to see you. I went in there a few hundred yards. Nothing. It's empty. Nobody remained — God-damned fools. They went out on the other side, you know, toward Schwalbach. They were caught badly. They came out, I think, about the time when we prepared to cross the hill. It was quite a barrage. And it was aimed just at the area between the village of Schwalbach and the mine entrance on the other side."

He shook his head.

"What a mess. Children, too. Lots of them."

Somebody said, "They should have stayed in there!"

"They were perfectly safe!"

Yates, listening to Troy, had taken his eyes off the woman. Troy was saying, "My men had to dig in right among the bodies, the shot-up baby buggies, all the trash they tried to carry with them. . . ."

Yates turned to the woman. She was gone. The space where she had been standing was empty.

Her screams came out of the mine, "Paul! Paul! . . . Paul . . . !"

Yates ran after her into the blackness.

"Paul!" Much thinner, much farther off, re-echoing, "Paul . . . !"

"Frau Petrik!" he called. "Wait! Frau Petrik, come back here!"

No answer. Even the cries for Paul had ceased.

Yates stood and waited, in absolute pitch-blackness, he didn't know for how long. He thought, Old horses that have done their duty are shot. There was something of the old work horse about her. Why hadn't he done her that last service?

Finally, there was a light around him. Troy was letting his flashlight glide over the walls and the rubbish-littered ground.

"Why don't you let her go?" he said. "You can't help her any."

He stooped and picked up a torn, colored postcard. It was a picture of Hitler, sitting on a white charger, a golden shield with a big swastika protecting his left side, the sun rising behind him.

Troy let it flutter down and stepped on it.

"What the hell," he said.

5

THEY WERE the strangest unit in the German Army. They had no flag, no Home Military District, no name — only a code designation: Buzzard. They were kept isolated from all other soldiers; their barracks were strictly shut off and securely guarded. They had orders to speak only English, even in their most personal and most trivial conversations; they received pre-aged photographs of newly assigned wives and sweethearts: Ethel from Baltimore, Honey Lou May from Oklahoma City, and Dotty from Oshkosh; and letters from the dames, which they were to carry with them at all times. They went through a concentrated and rigorous training in anything requiring stealth and trickery; they learned to move in silence and to kill in silence. They studied the details of American weapons and American vehicles. They were subdivided into small groups according to the localities in the United States from which they were supposed to have come — some were actually born there; they were instructed in the lore, the customs, the names of the Big Shots of their community; they knew more about their Congressman and their Senator than the average American did; they could tell exactly what streetcar line to take from the West Side to downtown, and where to transfer if you wanted to go to Sears Roebuck.

They were picked men, picked from all over the German Armed Forces and brought together in secrecy; Ensign Heberle had been taken off his minesweeper in Kiel; Sergeant Mulsinger came from the *Luftwaffe* — he had been helping to repair a Messerschmitt when he had been told to pack up his things and report at a certain town in the West of Germany. They had been screened and double-screened, tested and examined. Pettinger was a thorough man and he was making this thing as airtight as humanly possible.

Field Marshal von Klemm-Borowski's big Mercedes drove up before the barracks and turned through the gate into the yard. Drawn up in there, in ironic contrast to the Germanic slogans over the doors and to the bas-reliefs of Prussian Hussars from the 1870 war adorning the space between the second and third-floor windows, were the men in American uniforms, the jeeps, trucks, and armored cars of the parading nameless unit.

"*Achtung!*" shouted a man wearing corporal's stripes, giving the command in German to honor the Field Marshal.

The men stiffened more rigidly than any American battalion that ever came to attention.

Field Marshal von Klemm-Borowski slowly walked along the ranks, stopping here and there, shaking his head at a man's open shirt, the easy fit of the coat, the boots that couldn't be shined.

Pettinger enjoyed the disciplinarian's disapproval. He apologized, "We must make them look genuine, sir. That's the kind of Army the Americans have!"

"I understand," said the Marshal.

He planted himself in front of a thin, blondish youth with narrow-set eyes.

"Name?"

"Ensign Heberle, sir."

Pettinger shook his head from behind the Marshal.

"That's my — my German name, sir . . ." stuttered Heberle. And then blurted, "Sergeant Howard Bethune, sir!"

"From where?"

"Chicago, sir!"

"Chicago, Illinois!" corrected the Marshal, proudly.

"Chicago, Illinois, sir!" echoed Heberle. His pinched mouth was even more pinched than usual, his narrow, steep forehead poured sweat.

"What's he supposed to do?" Klemm-Borowski whispered to Pettinger.

Pettinger took a long list out of his pocket. He showed it to the Marshal, his finger pointing at a certain line. Next to the names of Heberle and Mulsinger was marked another name: *Farrish.*

"Do you know your mission?" Klemm-Borowski tried to pull up Heberle's ill-fitting American Army overcoat. Heberle stood motionless. The coat was as awry as before.

"Yes, sir."

"Suppose you're not able to get back?" asked the Marshal, inclining his head benevolently so that part of his jowl fell loosely over his stiff, gold-red embroidered collar.

344

This was precisely the problem Heberle had been pondering ever since learning that he and the horse-faced Mulsinger were to dispose of the American *Panzer-General* Farrish. For himself, Heberle had found no answer. For the Marshal, he said with the strength of his parade-bloated chest: "We will die, sir!"

The Marshal grunted something, satisfied, and moved on to the next man, Mulsinger.

Mulsinger's long, horselike face shriveled under the Marshal's glare. With tremulous voice, he identified himself as Corporal McInnerney from Newark, New Jersey, and at Klemm-Borowski's request reported that, in civilian life, he had taken the Hudson Tubes every morning to get to his job in a New York brokerage house.

"Intelligent fellow!" said the Marshal. "What happens in case you're captured — by the Americans, I mean?"

Mulsinger hesitated. He knew he would be in trouble if the Americans got him; the men of Buzzard had received a lecture on the Rules of Land Warfare; but they had been told that, in the first place, the Americans were too stupid to catch up with them, and in the second, too soft and democratic to do much about it.

"Well?" said Pettinger, examining Mulsinger with the same studied interest he used when he had had to deal with a recalcitrant French editor.

"They will not get us!" said Mulsinger. "We will get them, sir!"

"Excellent!" said the Marshal. "Wonderful men!"

"Reliable!" said Pettinger.

Of course Pettinger knew that these rigid, well-drilled men were not the best. He had combed everything to find them; but how thin the ranks had become! The years of war, the winters in Russia — and the summers, too — Normandy, and North Africa, had eaten into the substance. The best weren't the best any more; and this show for Klemm-Borowski's benefit, successful though it was, could not make up for that.

The Marshal was really pleased when he came to the vehicles. They were captured material, now cleaned and scrubbed, their engines in splendid order, their white stars in the white rings shining with provocative freshness.

"They'll get dirty soon enough," said Pettinger with suppressed anger. The Marshal was a meticulous ass.

Klemm-Borowski said, "Let's get through with this, now."

They returned to the men of Operation Buzzard, who were standing as stiffly as before. It began to drizzle, depressingly.

Pettinger pulled himself together. This was his last chance to instill these men with the absolute certainty of success.

He addressed them.

"I suppose you know that the privilege of being inspected by His Excellency, Field Marshal von Klemm-Borowski, means that you are to be started on your way, that Operation Buzzard is about to begin. You men have been selected for your reliability, initiative, knowledge of English. You have been trained in the tasks of demolition, disruption, and sabotage. You have been equipped with correct documents, with the genuine uniforms of the enemy, and with what the Americans call 'dog tags.' You will be indistinguishable from any American once you have crossed the line. Don't forget that if you look like an American to the Americans, you will also look like an American to our own troops. If you are attacked by our troops, take off your helmets and wave them. The line commanders are being informed that this is the sign of recognition."

He paused. This show would more than make up for the humiliation he had received in the Ensdorf mine. He glanced along the ranks, at Ensign Heberle, at Sergeant Mulsinger. If they, if all these men came through . . . They must come through.

"You have been informed of your mission. Your group leaders have received detailed orders. Some of you have been chosen to kidnap or kill certain high Allied commanders. The hour of attack has been set. Above all, keep in mind, that you are not isolated. Simultaneously with Operation Buzzard, whole armies, fresh armies, elite armies, will strike. They are equipped with an abundance of the latest weapons. You will have the advantage of the disruption and confusion on the enemy side. Never has any military undertaking been started under more propitious circumstances."

Klemm-Borowski growled applaudingly. Pettinger sensed the Marshal was priming his brain for a speech.

"One more word!" said Pettinger. "If any of you feel unequal to the task, step out now. You won't be punished. I will have you returned to your original units."

He waited. The lines of men, presenting their weapons American-fashion as they had been taught, remained without a ripple.

"Good!" Pettinger's face was as immobile as the ranks of these German soldiers in American mask. "I expected nothing else! His Excellency, Field Marshal von Klemm-Borowski, wishes to speak to you!"

The Marshal, small and awkward next to Pettinger, coughed. He wanted to say something big, something inspiring. But he wasn't good at it, and Pettinger had stolen all his thunder. He clasped his hands behind his back, and coughed again.

"Men!"

They waited.

"German soldiers!"

They waited.

"You will go forward! You will strike! Very significant — "

He looked at Pettinger. Pettinger said nothing.

"*Heil Hitler!*" cried the Field Marshal.

The echo came back, clipped and precise.

"Hurrah for the *Herr Feldmarschall!*" commanded Pettinger.

"Hurrah!"

" — rah! . . ."

The rain had become stronger. Klemm-Borowski turned up his collar.

The Marshal was happy about the show, even if Pettinger wasn't. Buzzard was the tip of the dagger he was going to wield. Klemm-Borowski rocked himself in the cradle of his most logical, finely spun plans. But he wasn't so deeply immersed in his gratification that he failed to notice the expression on Pettinger's face.

"Unburden yourself!" the Marshal said with an attempt at chumminess. "You've done splendidly! Splendidly!"

Pettinger wiped the raindrops off his forehead and nose. "I wish I could be half as sure as I've made these men. People are easy to sway — "

He stopped. Not even that was true any more.

Then, seeing the Marshal fish for his glasses, Pettinger said, "How's it going to go, sir?"

Klemm-Borowski looked at him over his heavily rimmed spectacles. "When I was a boy, we used to play a guessing game, with marbles. I always won. In the end I had so many marbles I sold them back to the kids."

"Is that so?" said Pettinger. He didn't know why the Marshal brought up the marbles; and at that early age, young Pettinger had been more interested in pulling girls' pigtails. But on the chance that Klemm-Borowski was serious, he said, "How did you always win?"

"Well — here was this little boy, let's call him Gustav. Gustav would hold a number of marbles in his closed fist, either two or three. If I guessed the number correctly, they would belong to me; if not, I would forfeit an equal number. But I always guessed right."

The anecdote about the little smart aleck irritated Pettinger.

"Don't you want to know how I did it?" Klemm-Borowski chuckled. "I took a guess at my friend Gustav's level of intelligence. Suppose, the first round, he had two marbles in his hand — if I decided Gustav was on the lowest level of intelligence, I knew next time he would have three marbles. If Gustav was on the next higher level, I knew he again would hold two marbles!"

"Why?" asked Pettinger. He was getting interested.

"Because he would have enough brains to try to be one step ahead of me. He would think that after two marbles in the first round, I would guess at three in the second. Therefore, he'd keep two in his hand. But I knew that. So I won the two."

Pettinger laughed.

Klemm-Borowski delved further into his psychology. "Now, let us assume little Gustav was a really clever kid — top level. Then, he would hold three marbles in the second round. He would think I could figure out that he was going to fool me by sticking to the original two marbles. So, to throw me off, he would change to three. But I would know that, too — and win!"

Pettinger began to see where the moral of the story lay.

Klemm-Borowski's eyes seemed to sparkle behind his thick glasses. "I am willing to give my American colleagues a lot of credit. I pre-suppose that they are as smart as little Gustav on his top level. Remember two marbles and three, Pettinger. In 1940, we used two marbles — we pushed from the Eifel through the Ardennes. They just won't believe that we'll do the same in 1944. They'll bet on three. I outguess them again. I use precisely the old road!"

"Very good!" said Pettinger. "Guess and counterguess! Fascinating!"

"Isn't it? A science! Absolutely!"

And Pettinger wanted to be convinced. The people of Ensdorf had dealt him a greater shock than he admitted. Perhaps that was because he had spent the last years in France, had not observed the fissures in his own country, had gone ahead, blithely and against his own reason and skepticism, on the presumption that the Germans were the same as when he had left them, and that the war could have no other effect on them than to make them close their ranks all the tighter around their leadership. No, that wasn't it; that was a false excuse to himself. He *had* seen it. Dehn stumbling into his room at the Scribe, panicked, doing him out of one cold million of Yasha's francs . . . Panicked, without faith, without backbone! And Dehn had been one of his own crowd!

With an undertone of worry, Pettinger said, "You know, *Herr Feldmarschall,* we must win this one."

The Marshal took off his glasses. He snapped the case closed. "I do not have to be reminded!"

"I beg your pardon, sir."

The Marshal spoke fast. "I have done the greatest pre-operation maneuvering in the history of modern war. You know perfectly well, until I took over this Army Group, Eifel and Ardennes were considered by us as well as by the enemy as a sort of rest area. Bad roads, woods, early snow, hard for armor to operate; a sector for tired troops, second-rate troops, holding forces. I've known we are under constant enemy air observation. I take that into account. I pull troops into these woods and I pull troops out of these woods — the same numbers. On the other side, the enemy adds up the figures. He thinks everything is in the best order. What he doesn't know is that they are not the same troops. Into the woods come the Fifth and

Sixth *Panzer* Armies, out of the woods come the worn-out old men and the youngsters whom, at best, I shall use at the flanks."

Klemm-Borowski unhitched his belt.

"What do you say about that?"

"I said we must win. Time is running out."

6

IN DONDOLO's pockets were his records and his orders, signed by Loomis and approved by Willoughby.

Much to the Captain's relief, his decision was not questioned. DeWitt, who might have looked into the matter, and insisted on real disciplinary action, was not in Luxemburg. He had gone to Paris the previous evening for a conference. And as for Willoughby, the Major had taken no particular interest in the case, or at least had found nothing objectionable in Loomis's disposal of it. Willoughby merely raised his heavy brows and with a sly glance said, "The old guard sure is vanishing, isn't it?"

Some of that old guard surrounded Dondolo as he stood in front of the courier's truck that was to drop him at the Replacement Depot — among them Lord, the Motor Sergeant, and Vaydanek, the assistant cook who had been made Mess Sergeant. The truck was loaded and ready to go, but Dondolo was delaying its departure. He told the courier, "I got to say So Long to somebody. Keep your shirt on. I want to get away from here, too!"

When Bing arrived at the studio building to report for his day's work, Dondolo came forward, broke into a shrill "Vot eees it?" and, followed by his entourage, blocked Bing's way.

"Vot ees it?" mimicked Bing. "I'll tell you what it is — you're out! You've played your last dirty trick, and this time you didn't get away with it. That's what it is!"

"Heard the latest?" asked Dondolo.

Bing, who hadn't heard it and wasn't interested in getting his news from Dondolo, didn't answer.

Dondolo said, "The Germans are attacking, all along the front. East of here, they've broken through! Fifteen minutes ago, it came over the radio!"

"What is it . . . ?" The question was like a mechanical reflex, involuntary.

"Vot eees it?" Dondolo, Lord, Vaydanek, the whole group, even the courier who was a stranger, broke into raucous laughter.

Bing's mind reeled under the news so that he seemed to feel it physically. And here he'd been hatching schemes to make the Germans rise against their regime! He had the uncanny notion that he had expected it; he remembered saying as much to Troy, that day in Ensdorf. But now it had come; Dondolo blared out the words as if the German offensive were his personal revenge.

Dondolo came to mock attention before Bing.

"Brother, my ass bleeds for you! When the Krauts come in here and it's getting hot, just think of me. I'll be in the kitchen of the Repple Depple. I'll sweat it out there. Or maybe I can get myself shipped home. And when I get home, I'll tell 'em what great guys you are, and how you're fighting your war. It ain't mine no more, thanks to you, Sergeant Bing!"

Bing controlled himself. He wasn't letting any Dondolo panic him.

Dondolo was perspiring freely, in spite of the cold morning. It was an oily sweat that made his face glisten. He wanted to go on, he wanted to describe how Bing would be taken prisoner by the Germans, and what he hoped they would do to him; but the courier, anxious to get out of the enemy's reach, stepped to his truck. Dondolo jumped in, waved, and as the truck pulled out, he crowed over the din of its motor one last "Vot eees it?" and was gone.

The first reports reaching General Farrish in his headquarters at the border of the Saar Basin were disjointed and as foggy as the weather. The only thing clear seemed to be the fact that the front farther north, between Monschau at the left wing and Luxemburg in the center of the American armies, had come into violent motion. In his own Division sector, everything was quiet and uneventful, and if Carruthers's reports were to be trusted, promised to remain so.

And the whole affair, doubtlessly a large scale offensive, had come as a complete surprise! To the politicians in uniform — not to him!

He called in Carruthers.

Together, they went over the last two weeks' reports — there it was, black on white: Estimates of the situation; interrogators' reports; Enemy Capabilities — *The enemy is capable of launching a major counteroffensive.* Carruthers, whom Farrish had promoted to major and who had taken over all functions of G–2, pointed out that, at this headquarters, they certainly had seen the threat and had warned the higher echelons.

"You're sure you've forwarded all this to Army and Group?" Farrish asked.

Carruthers confirmed it.

Farrish stormed through his trailer in triumphant rage. "The swivel-chair strategists, the politicians that stole my gas — there, they have it! Echelons so high they have their heads in the clouds, if they have any heads! I told them so, didn't I? But they don't listen. They think I'm nuts. I'm just a soldier's general, just a tank fanatic — what the hell! What's the sense! They're going to lose us the war yet because they don't want to step on anybody's toes!"

Carruthers nodded careful approval. Perhaps he had too little imagination to gain personal gratification out of the jam in which others found themselves; perhaps, unlike his chief, he didn't see the war as a ganging-up process against General Farrish. Carruthers said, "Except that the trouble up there is likely to get us into a stew, too!"

"And don't I know it! Want me to tell you what we'll have to do? We'll have to pack up here and go north and beat them out of the mess they got themselves into."

He slumped into his chair and picked up the phone to call his Chief of Staff. "Listen, old boy," he said, intensely conscious of the dramatic moment in his announcement, "this is preparatory to something big. I want you to get every available man out of the line. All advanced units are to be pulled back. Shorten the line, make it as straight as you like, I don't care. Just hold it thinly. Orders are: Be ready to move on a moment's notice. Check? — Check."

The reports came in more frequently. They were longer and the picture began to shape up clearly.

Farrish studied his maps. The danger was obvious. He saw the beautiful simplicity of the German plan, and he reveled in it because, as a maneuver in his kind of mobile warfare, it was well-nigh perfect. In his enjoyment of the problem he did not overlook the threat it presented to his side; but emotionally, he somehow didn't feel it.

"Cutting us in two — just like that! Grandiose!" he muttered and, turning to Carruthers, said, "I want a conference. Immediately. Everybody down to battalion commanders. There's this barn down the road, ought to be big enough to hold 'em. Have the maps brought over there and lights set up."

Farrish could have chosen a decent house for the meeting, but the picturesque, rough barn struck him as proper for the emergency. It was bitter cold; the wind blew through the cracks between the beams, and most of the straw had been stolen long ago. A kind of catwalk running around three sides of the barn formed a gallery. Since the light was directed against the maps which took up the biggest part of the front wall, only the dangling legs of the officers on the gallery were visible. Many had to sit on the floor, the thickness of the layers of straw under their posteriors denoting their rank.

Farrish stood in front of his maps like an impresario. Above the audience hung the vapor of breaths and the humming of subdued voices. They talked; mostly of the cold, much less of why they had been summoned.

Finally, Farrish was satisfied that almost everybody was at hand. He coughed, and the audience grew quiet.

"Gentlemen!" he said, "it gives me great pleasure to inform you that the war is on again."

The corners of his mouth came up in sarcasm.

"Unfortunately, the initiative did not come from our side."

He began to pace. Whenever he turned, he paused a moment to whip up and down, from the heels to the balls of his feet and back.

"Some people have been caught with their pants down." Whipping. "I'll have you know that this implies no criticism." More whipping.

Laughter in the audience.

"And it is no laughing matter, Goddammit!" Again whipping.

Dead silence.

"It costs lives, you know. The poor sonsofbitches caught up there" — his crop beat against the map, at the Ardennes mountains — "are at this moment being cut to ribbons."

The crop whistled through the cold, thick air.

"This is how I figure it. The Germans are pushing approximately here" — his right hand, fingers extended, slapping the Ardennes — "on a front extending from somewhere here — to there. . . ." Both hands being used, the crop being held between his teeth.

"The main effort is here!" Fist on northern Luxemburg and Bastogne. "The plan, obviously, to cut northwest, get out of the mountains, take back Antwerp, Brussels — fork off; maybe, take Paris."

The crop, again in his hand, following the pincers indicated.

"That's how I would do it; and I'm sure, on the basis of my admittedly scanty information, this is their plan. Tactically, they're trying to cut off the British and the Ninth Army from the First and Third Armies; if possible, they'll try to destroy the First. They have broken through successfully, gentlemen."

Facing the audience, crop in both hands, again whipping up and down.

"There are islands of resistance. They may hold out, I don't know how long. I don't know the exact German strength either; it is considerable, and it is mobile. What we have left to oppose them are rear-echelon troops —quartermaster, depot troops, MP's, God knows what."

Now he stood motionless, to let the significance of the catastrophe sink in. The men in front of him — he had picked almost every one of them himself — seemed to sag under the weight. The legs on the gallery ceased to dangle and hung limply.

"Jesus Christ!" somebody said.

Farrish pressed out his breath. It sounded like something between a hard cough and a forced laugh.

"Now, gentlemen, I show you how we can lick them. It's a problem that will be taught as I am teaching it now, in the military academies of the future, regardless of whether we'll do it or not. I'm giving you the solution."

He turned to the map. "It seems that here — and here" — the crop pointing to Monschau and Luxemburg — "at the flanks of their push, at the shoulders, so to speak, the Germans are being contained. They are not strong enough to roll up the entire front; they're only strong enough to push forward."

His hand was raised, his finger extended. "Gentlemen! I say, let them push! There'll be a sack" — his arms embracing the sack on the map — "and gentlemen, it will be up to us to pull the string tight and form the most gigantic trap of military history."

His voice cracked orders. "Push down from Monschau! Push up from Luxemburg! Meet at Bastogne! Cut them off! Close in! Hack them to pieces!"

The men in the barn were tempted to applaud. It had been a wonderful performance. The histrionics of the General captured the imagination. And withal, he had proposed the only sensible countermove, the only tactics that could turn the apparent German victory into a defeat, or at least into a draw. And he had given them a kind of vision, a hope to hold onto, in a situation that otherwise appeared completely black.

With a short, quick motion of his hand Farrish cut off the whispers that had started up.

"Gentlemen, I didn't like the war these last months. It was like the hedge business in Normandy, little progress at great cost. Now the Germans have stuck their head out, right into a noose. When General Patton calls on us to pull tight that noose, I want my Division to be the first one ready for the job.

"Thank you, gentlemen."

The convoys moved north. Day and night, without break, they kept moving. There was no speed limit. The roads shook under the weight of the tanks, the holes torn in the roadbed became deeper and deeper; the melting snow splashed high; the fenders were caked with mud, the trucks were spluttered with mud, the men were covered with it.

Its wetness penetrated your clothes. And the wind, this lousy ice-cold wind, spurred to a fury by the sixty-mile speed, cut through everything and made you feel as if the mud were frozen on your skin. Half the time you couldn't see a thing, because the fog was so dense you hardly recognized the shape of the vehicle before you. There was no warm food. There was no warmth anywhere, unless you crept close to your neighbor and tried to borrow what little his body gave out. Your teeth chattered, and your hands became numb, and you couldn't touch the metal parts of your weapons for fear your fingers would freeze to them. Your feet rested on the steel floors of the trucks, and the cold seeped through to your soles as if your shoes and your socks were so much paper. What good were the shelter halves and the coats and the sweaters? After a while, you gave up seeking protection and tried to sleep because the cold made you so God-damned tired, even more tired than you were, and you thought that, perhaps, in sleep you could escape it. But it got into your dreams. And it wasn't real sleep at all, just a dozing-off that neither refreshed nor gave you the illusion of warmth. And the nights without stars; and your only comrade the roar of the engines before and behind you . . .

Yates was in this mass race north. He had been with Troy in Schwalbach when C Company got its orders. He had taken Troy into his jeep since the Captain had turned over his command car with its upholstered seats to some of his men who had refused to go to the hospital and who had insisted on coming along with the Company.

Yates was glad he was with Troy. Crowded in between the Captain and the baggage and the driver, he realized that it would have been hard for him to take the ride north alone.

Despite the cruelties, the stupid and senseless and horrible things he had been exposed to in the war, there had been, at least since Paris, the certainty of military victory. Though he had taken it so much for granted that he had been hardly conscious of it, that certainty had been an essential. He was sure he would have cracked under a constantly hammering threat of being on the losing side. He thought of the countless times he had suggested and approved leaflet, broadcast, and loudspeaker appeals to the Germans: *Give up, put an end to it, you're losing the war anyhow!* And now, the coin had been reversed, or it was being reversed. It was a question either of adjustment or of going to pieces. He, and everybody, had to become winter soldiers, now — figuratively and literally. Not that it had been so easy to be a summer soldier in this war; but this was much, much worse.

"I wish we knew some more about how it's going," he fretted.

Troy, bundled up in his field coat, said, "How what is going?"

"Forget it!"

The Captain's muffled voice became louder, "If I knew, what good would it do us? Wouldn't change a thing. Wait and see. I've become an expert at Wait and See."

But rumors traveled faster than the column; the radio men listened in between communications to the news from both sides. By the time the column approached Luxemburg, the men knew the approximate score. And since the rumors emphasized the dark side of the picture — as if there were any but a dark side! — there was a slight note of panic in what was whispered or grunted or griped.

Cerelli mentioned the Tiger Tank and said there was nothing we had to oppose it. Then his mind swerved back and he reminisced, "Remember the way we rode through France?" In retrospect, it seemed like a joy ride.

The fuzz on chin and upper lip of Sheal was coated with the frozen vapor of his breath. He held his gloved hands before his face, trying to keep it warm, and his voice sounded hollow. "I don't like trips. I've moved around plenty. When this war is over, I'm going to settle down and stay put in one place, Goddammit — in one place!"

From Traub's eyes came an annoying, steady trickle of tears. He wrapped his shawl tighter around his head, pulled down his wool cap and let his helmet sit on top of the whole of it. "We sure look swell!"

"Where we headin'?" asked Sheal.

"Why don't you relax?" said Lester.

Cerelli began to fight because Sheal, in turning, had hit him with his entrenching tool. Lester swayed over and separated them; Clay took Cerelli's part, and Traub shrieked it hadn't been Sheal's fault, and soon the argument became general, only to peter out because you couldn't keep your fists up in a bucking, kicking, shaking half-track crammed with men and baggage. So they sat, clammy and exhausted, glaring at each other, hating the day they'd been thrown together, hating this particular day and all the days to come.

The city of Luxemburg had been under fire that morning. It hadn't been much; some shells from long-range guns — but it hadn't happened before and it had come upon the town with shocking suddenness. It broke out of black, low-hanging clouds, reviving the talk of secret German super-weapons, and breeding rumors that German paratroopers had been dropped on the city.

Yates saw the change in the people — the same people who only two months ago had derided the German troops fleeing on stolen bicycles and in carts pulled by borrowed horses; who had welcomed the Americans with all the enthusiasm their stolid, staid natures permitted. Now they stood glumly along the curbstones and the street corners; the German defeat that had seemed so final wasn't final at all; and the first American troops coming up from the south to be thrown into the breach, tired and dirty and freezing, didn't look like the victors of two months ago, but like a desperate last levy.

For a man as sensitive to the mood of others as Yates, it took conscious effort to show an indifferent face in that air charged with depression. He wanted to see DeWitt. He needed to get a clear and sober and truthful picture of what actually had happened and what was likely to come. He needed to be assigned a place, a sensible activity, in the ranks that now must be tightened under the force of the catastrophe and in preparation for some countermove.

355

The sentries at the studio building had been doubled, and his papers were checked, which encouraged him. But on finding the Colonel's office empty, and on learning that DeWitt had gone to Paris the day before the breakthrough and had not been heard from, he felt disappointed, even resentful. DeWitt's absence left him without the assurance he wanted; and it left Willoughby in charge of the whole works. Willoughby was a first-rate conniver, and he had his wits about him when it came to figuring out tricks and slants and policies. But how strong would he be under the real and terrific weight of the enemy? And in this crisis not only the fate of the Detachment's operation depended on Willoughby, but also Yates's own life. . . .

Yates found the Major chatting animatedly with Crerar; he looked cheerful and composed; only the bulges under his eyes seemed deeper, and the shadows under his jowls grayer.

"Welcome back!" he said. "I trust you've heard the news. . . ."

"I have," said Yates. "I've come up with a unit that's to go into the line somewhere close to here, but I don't know the exact state of affairs."

"It stinks," said Crerar.

"You nearly missed us," said Willoughby, and then laughed. "The Germans were already astride the main road into the town of Luxemburg, and they could have made it in an hour and a half. . . . But the Fourth Division stopped them. They were supposed to be resting up, they came out of the Huertgen Forest. . . . Very few of them left, but they stopped them, cooks and clerks stopped them, MP's stopped them, and what not."

"What're we going to do?"

Willoughby said challengingly, "Nothing. Sit tight!"

"O.K.," said Yates, "that's O.K. with me." He began to appreciate this man; it was the Willoughby who in Rollingen had predicted, *The war isn't over by a long shot, and it's going to be tough.* . . . Perhaps it wasn't so bad to have Willoughby next to you. It was another element making for optimism, after Troy's absolute stoicism on the icy race up to Luxemburg.

Willoughby continued, "We're on the extreme left wing of the German push. I don't think they're going to make a real effort to take the city of Luxemburg; there's nothing here but the radio studios and the prestige of reconquering the first of the many capitals they've lost. But they'll grab it if it falls to them as a result of advances further north."

"And what's happening up there?"

"A bulge," said Crerar, "a bulge. . . ."

Willoughby elaborated, "There's no more line. The 101st Airborne is still at Bastogne."

"They're holding?"

Willoughby shrugged. Then he said, "I want to tell you that you did a swell job on that Ensdorf woman. . . ."

"Kind of *passé*, isn't it?" joked Crerar. "Who's worried whether German civilians stick to their homes or not? We were up in the clouds. From now on, I'm for every one of us spending part of his time up front — you know, keeping in touch with the war. . . ."

Yates objected, "I never sat around in offices!"

"I didn't mean you," Crerar placated him.

"Mr. Crerar," Willoughby chuckled, "Mr. Crerar's joined the reform boys. What are we kiddin' ourselves about? . . ."

It was empty chatter; Yates felt its emptiness oppressively. They were in touch with the war all right, the war had reached out to them.

"All right, Yates," Willoughby said in a suddenly changed voice, "pack up your things and be ready to move. I've given orders to everybody. I don't know how long we're going to stay. I understand Farrish is coming up from the south; he'll take over this sector of the front, and we'll be nominally under his command. So he'll decide. But naturally, it's up to us to look after ourselves."

"And when's Colonel DeWitt coming back?"

For a reason not clear to Yates, the question upset Willoughby. The Major pushed back his chair, and Yates saw he was carrying his pistol strapped to his belt.

"I don't know! Hell, I don't know whether he'll be able to get back — at the moment, there are only two roads open, and they're choked with troops — and how long they'll remain open, nobody can say. I'm not going to have this Detachment cut off. We're irreplaceable!"

He came around his desk and tapped Crerar's thin chest. "Irreplaceable, right?" And added, "At least some of us, right?"

There was something unhealthy in Willoughby's insistence.

"What do you want me to do, Major?" Yates asked.

"I told you, get packed!"

"And then?"

"Wait."

"I don't want to wait. I want to do something!"

Willoughby's dark, veiled eyes were expressionless. "Fine! I had something in mind for you . . . ," he said slowly. "Go forward, down to Company; further, if you like. I want to know what the Krauts are thinking, now. We've got to re-evaluate and re-adjust all we've been saying. Take a good man along who can get your reports down and serve as liaison. Want to do that?"

It was obvious, the man was improvising. But the suggestion was what Yates needed. One taste of this headquarters under the cloud of defeat was enough. If you had to run, it was better to run with people who occasionally turned back to fire; and if you had to die, you might as well make the last trip in company you liked.

Interesting that the thought of death occurred to him only now, in the heated office, where he could peel off his coat and field jacket, and stretch his legs, and warm his feet. In the jeep with Troy, he somehow hadn't thought of it.

He would go and find Troy.

He couldn't take Bing along; Willoughby said Bing couldn't be spared. He'd take Abramovici. There was an almost perverse satisfaction in taunting fate with Abramovici — the little man was the perfect mascot.

Abramovici didn't like it. He explained to Yates that he wasn't the outdoor type.

Yates, remembering his feeling about winter soldiers, quoted Paine; to which Abramovici replied with something that also sounded like a quote, but that was, in reality, an opinion of his father, that veteran of the Rumanian Army, on the undesirability of warfare in general, and during winter in particular.

After Abramovici had suggested a list of likelier candidates for the jaunt, and after each of them had been turned down patiently, he resigned himself.

He reported, equipped with an assortment of gear that showed he had carefully saved up everything ever issued to him by the Army, and with a number of items he had acquired privately. A pair of green-and-white-striped ski socks, made of merino wool, stuck out pertly from the top of his boots. His face, except for the nose and the eyes, was covered by a kind of knitted mask that kept slipping down over his lids. The whole man was enveloped in what seemed to be a giant pillow slip which he lifted daintily to climb into the jeep. When he finally had rolled into his seat, he explained to Yates that it wasn't a pillow slip at all, but two linen sheets he had stitched together.

"A snow suit," he said, "is supposed to be worn in winter warfare. It is natural that white from white, especially at a distance, cannot be distinguished easily. I can pass for a rock or any small ground elevation covered with snow."

"What happens if the Germans overlook you?" asked Yates. "They attack, they pass you, and you're left behind, a small ground elevation covered with snow?"

"Well, you'll be around, won't you?" Abramovici was worried.

Yates left the question open.

The columns rushing north from the town of Luxemburg were thinning out. It was possible to by-pass them singly and make greater speed. Yates wanted to catch up with Troy and his men; altogether, he had spent about three hours in the town, talking to Willoughby, mobilizing Abramovici, eating a hasty meal that had the one advantage of being warm, and

358

changing his clothes. Now, his exhaustion made itself felt, but he couldn't afford to give in to it. He had to remain on the alert.

Somewhere to the east lay the Sauer River. The night before, a *Volksgrenadier* Division, on the extreme left flank of the German push, had crossed it and had been contained on the west shore. But nobody knew definitely how the engagement had ended. Meanwhile, armored infantry of Farrish's Division continued to feel its way in a northerly direction, trying to test out the strength of the German left flank.

The further north Yates and Abramovici drove, the more frequently they encountered the signs of what had taken place. It was the reverse of what had been France — American vehicles, instead of German, broken down and shot to pieces, lined the road; American guns, their muzzles smashed, or their barrels torn, or their wheels crushed, stood abandoned in their last position. Freshly fallen snow, and the softness of fog, took away much of the jaggedness of destruction; but they added a melancholy touch.

And then Abramovici saw the first dead — in a ditch, as if stretched out to rest. Abramovici's first thought was, How unhealthy! He'll catch himself death! — and it took a few seconds before he realized that the man was dead, that snow had settled on him, too, and that the black on his coat was not a shadow, but the terrible reality of the shrapnel that had torn into him.

The road up ahead was blasted and the vehicles were working their way around the hole — the troops going up and the ambulances coming down.

Abramovici leaned forward. "Lieutenant!" he said, in a voice swinging between huskiness and tenderness.

Yates turned around.

"I don't want you to look to the right just now."

"Why not? What's the matter?"

"Just don't do it, please."

"All right!" Yates was irritated. But he did glance to the right and, out of the corner of his eye, he saw what was there in the ditch. And he saw that Abramovici had wanted to spare him this, and he turned around once more to the lumpy figure in white and patted its knee.

There had been something in Abramovici's action that made him think of Ruth. She knew he was in Luxemburg. He had made it easy for her to guess from his letters his part of the front. Now she would read in the home papers of the break-through; and their headline technique, their panic-mongering would bring her natural worries to a pitch. He thought of her — no longer as a woman so grown-up, so independent, that she would be able to take it all right — but: There she was, and her man was in this; with all his shortcomings, his vacillations, his unwillingness to commit himself, her man. And his heart went out to her, suddenly, and more strongly than it had ever gone out to anyone, even to Thérèse. And when it came to this, this wretched, terrible point where you didn't know if you'd be alive tomorrow, in an hour; or what would happen to you; and if it got you, where would you go; and what remained once you became like the dead boy in the ditch. . . . Now you knew it was Ruth you wanted, because you would find strength in her and she in you; and two's a team; and there's no friendship, no comradeship, no relationship that could ever take the place of that Belonging Together.

It was almost a year since he had seen Ruth, and yet, she was stronger in him now than when he had left her. It must be that he had called to her out of this great need of his, and it was crazy but true that she had responded to him — through Abramovici of all people, through the most unsentimental, the most self-centered of all the unsentimental, self-centered men around him. It was a kind of miracle. It was nothing he could mention to anyone, except perhaps to her when he came home, if he came home. . . .

Now, the trucks ahead of him were stopped completely, the men were getting off and disappearing into the woods to the right and left of the road. The woods looked as if they had been gone over by a giant comb led by the hand of a giant, brutal barber. Splintered trunks, treetops broken at tortured angles, brush plowed up and under, naked roots rising like gnarled, threatening fingers — and all of this interwoven by hurrying wisps of fog, screening here, exposing there, lending the torn woods a new, uncanny, shifting life. Only the voices were real: Men shouting orders, cursing, questioning. They were assembling here. Guns were being brought up and placed in position. Somewhere an overanxious machine gun cackled tentatively.

Yates drove on, passing the trucks. He saw that he was approaching the end of the woods; for a mile or so, the road wound through naked, snow-speckled hills whose tops were shrouded in yellowish fog.

The deadly quiet belonging to this landscape was ripped by the crash of shells, a noise dry and hard and more frightening than on an ordinary day, because the country had this spectral quality.

Now the trees to the right and left of the road were like the posts of a portal; and Yates, doubtful whether he should pass through, had the jeep stop. A soldier came from the right.

"Where you goin', Lieutenant?"

Yates pointed vaguely ahead.

"Huh-uh!" said the man. "No good."

"Why?"

"Jerries."

"Oh."

The soldier turned. He seemed little interested in whether or not Yates followed his advice.

"Where's C Company?" Yates called after him.

"Right here!" the soldier yelled back.

"Where's your CP?"

"Through there — cut through the brush and keep on going!"

Abramovici muttered that he was very tired. "A soldier, before going into battle," he said, "has got a right to rest."

7

Night set in early, a gray-black, wet-cold night.

Sergeant Lester moved ahead, crouching over his submachine gun, barely visible to Sheal who was behind him. In back of them, to the right and left, the staggered lines of the squads, silent; only the slushing of feet through fresh snow and muddy loam; the occasional crackle of thin ice under the groping boots of the men. They could hear each other, but they could see nothing more than the dim outline of the figure next to them.

They had come out of the woods into the bare hilly land ahead. They didn't know what lay in front of them; but Troy had said they must go forward, and that the night and the fog protected them as much as it protected the Germans, and that they might come upon the enemy suddenly and have the advantage of surprise.

Fulbright was somewhere in the center of the advancing wedge. He tried to keep in contact with his flanks and with Lester at the tip of the wedge; at times a man would come out of the formation, and break across, and try to find him to say that as yet, nothing had been encountered.

Somewhere behind them was the remainder of the Company, coming out of the woods, following the tracks of Lieutenant Fulbright's wedge. The arrangement was to keep in touch by runners and by walkie-talkie, if other contact was lost, as was likely in the darkness. If Fulbright met with strong resistance, he was to fall back on the main body of the Company. Otherwise, decisions were pretty much up to him.

The men were slowly advancing over the hillocks, weaving up and down like the little flags of a fisherman's net in the tide.

Lester was all alone. He listened to his steps, as if they weren't his at all but somebody else's. How long can a guy stand this without going nuts? Wattlinger had been a good boy but it got him and he was blown to smithereens; they say they'd seen his arm sailing through the air, higher and higher, an arm alone, rising to meet God. He wondered whether, up there, they'd accept an arm in place of the whole man. His soul couldn't possibly have been in the arm; it was in your heart or in your guts or in your brain, but not in your arm. Or, perhaps, your immortal soul was all over you, and it didn't make much difference if only the nail of your little finger remained, a particle of soul was attached to it, must be, because the soul couldn't be like a bird nesting somewhere inside of you.

"Sheal!" he whispered.

Sheal edged forward.

"Where d'you think your soul is?"

"What?"

"You heard me!"

"You're nuts," said Sheal, and fell back.

Sheal called to Traub behind him.

"Hey, Traub!"

"Huh?"

"Lester wants to know where his soul is."

Your soul . . . You could find it in a back alley of Rivington Street, a little girl, smudged face, playing among the trash — big eyes that go all the way through you. But Lester never in his life had been on Rivington Street, it wasn't his kind of soul.

"Cerelli!"

"What do you want?"

"Go up to Lester, he wants to ask you something."

Cerelli stumbled forward.

"Hey, what's the matter, Lester?"

"Nothing. Something wrong back there?"

"No, everything's O.K. They said you wanted something."

"Me? Hell, no! Wait a minute! Do you see a light — over there?"

"No."

"Hear anything?"

"No."

"What's the difference between dreaming and waking?"

"Hell! I don't know!"

"How long we been going this way?"

Cerelli looked at his watch, but the dial was blurred.

Lester said, "D'you ever try to follow your own thoughts?"

"Where d'you get the liquor? Lemme have some! I wanna be happy, too!"

"Get back there!" ordered Lester. "Get back, you, or I kick you back!"

"All right! All right!"

You can't determine how these things get started. Whether it was Lester's sudden mysticism that set them off, whether it was the wading through the milky, misty night — even Sheal, even Cerelli, even the most realistic, the most hard-boiled felt their shells soften; each in his way became thoughtful.

The ground under Lester's feet became suddenly hard. He immediately came fully awake. Beneath the snow, there must be a kind of roadbed; and if he looked to the right and to the left, something like a straight strip of white stretched into the darkness, and the shadowy streaks at its edges might be trees or telegraph poles. It was a road, and it ran from east to west; and, somewhere to the left of him, it must cut into the main south-north road from Luxemburg which they traveled up last night. Now he was oriented. He gave word through to Fulbright that he had hit this road, and that it seemed nobody was on it.

When word reached the Lieutenant, he told the walkie-talkie man to get in touch with Troy and let the Captain know that they had reached the road and that he was going to cross it and push ahead farther.

Meanwhile, Lester had gone across the road, the men behind him pressing after him. He struggled up a slight dam and was again caught in the undulating, frozen waste. He cut down his speed and didn't resume his stride until he was reasonably sure the whole platoon had made it across the road.

If you're in the field long enough, you develop a sense for the sudden changes that may come upon you. It's like the instinct of a boxer who ducks before he actually sees his adversary's blow.

When the roar became audible, when the tanks were on them in a matter of minutes or possibly seconds, nobody told them — and there was nobody to tell them — that a German column was coming down this east-west road they just had crossed with such care; that the German tanks were racing not only along the road proper, but spread out over the field like a dragnet; that the tanks would be between them and the other platoons of their company; that they were cut off, thirty or forty men with infantry weapons, against perhaps as many armored, heavily armed tanks. But they knew it.

It was one of those mobile columns with which the Germans had punctured and gashed the front and with which they were pushing the great bulge westward. Fulbright's platoon was no more than a pebble in their way; he had dared ahead too fast, led on by the quiet of the night. And five minutes sooner or five minutes later, his path and that of the tanks would never have crossed.

The mind of Lieutenant Fulbright, safely lodged behind his low, sturdy forehead, chewed on this and on other things. He hoped, for a short moment, that he and his little band of men might escape the attention of the German *Panzers,* that these might by-pass them in the night and the fog.

But the Germans had seen them. They maneuvered around him, and cut him off from three sides, and began to take him under fire — the deadly whip-blows of the machine guns, spraying the ground indiscriminately. They even let loose with their 88's. Ridiculous. Like throwing bricks at a fly on the window sill.

Fulbright didn't have to give any orders. He noticed gratefully that his light machine gun and his BAR-men took up the futile fight. He wasn't frightened. He was carrying a ball and trying to break through a whole Eleven of gray-chested guys, each one twice as big as himself. They were unfair. They struck him where his body was soft and vulnerable, they fought against the rules, and where was the referee? . . . There he was. Only he looked like Professor Cavanaugh, who once said, I'd never give you a passing grade, Fulbright, except for the fact that you're such a wonderful tackle. But Professor Cavanaugh wore a long white beard and he wasn't really Professor Cavanaugh at all; he looked like Charlie, the colored man who tended the furnace in the Fraternity House, and he sang *Go Down Moses,* and then the cheering section went into action: Rah! Rah! Rah!

Lieutenant Fulbright turned over in the snow, his helmet safe in the crook of his arm like a football, and was dead.

Sergeant Lester saw fields of color like the marble top of the counter in Pete Dreiser's drugstore when the fluorescent light was turned on. He leaned against the counter and felt its hard rim against his shoulder. It was a real pain. It grew and became terribly sharp; and then there were no more counter and no more light, only the pain and Lester writhing with it.

Cerelli and Sheal and Traub kept on firing. They fired against the moving skyscrapers that were German tanks, because they had been taught to fire, and because they knew that it would be all over once they ceased firing.

Traub fixed his bayonet. Traub wanted to die on his feet. It was a stupid notion and Cerelli and Sheal tried to hold him back when they saw that Traub was getting up. But Traub tore himself loose and marched forward. It looked as if the bayonet was pulling him. He picked a tank and marched toward it. Somehow, the tank's spewing machine gun failed to hit him. He kept on marching until they were face to face, little Traub from Rivington Street, and the black cross set off against its white field, on the German tank. Then bayonet and rifle splintered. The tank moved on.

Corporal Clay saw German infantry coming from all sides at him and Cerelli and Sheal and the few men left of the platoon. The infantry must have been riding the half-tracks that trailed the German tanks. The Germans fired and closed in, fired and closed in. Corporal Clay wanted to live. There was in him, at this moment, an all-conquering voice that said, No! No! No! This isn't the end, this can't be the end, not here, not this way, not now. He looked around for someone higher than himself for orders. Had there been someone to order: Fire! Fight! he would have fired and fought because he wasn't a bad soldier, only a man accustomed to being led. But no one was there to give orders, no one but the voice in him crying out that any sort of life was better than hitting this ground, these furrows and stones and bodies and patches of snow dyed in mud and blood, and never getting up. And there's a point where the force of the enemy becomes so overpowering that your relationship to him is turned inside out — it's like drowning; finally you cease struggling and give yourself to the strength of the waves.

Corporal Clay dropped his weapon and raised his hands. And the men of Fulbright's platoon, those that were left, dropped their weapons and raised their hands, and a German major came forward and slapped Clay's face with his leather gloves, right and left, and Clay, really, found nothing objectionable in it. It was as if his father were punishing him for something bad he had done, though Clay couldn't figure out, much as he tried, of what his sin had consisted.

The rage Major Dehn vent on Clay passed as quickly as it had come. Perhaps, in punishing this complete stranger, this American corporal, who stood before him, his face gray as the night, trembling, Dehn wanted to punish himself. During these last months, on the flight through France, and in Paris where he met Pettinger and became conscious that his insides were broken to pieces, there had been times when he wanted only to raise his hands and surrender and end it all and find peace, rest, and security in some dreary Prisoner of War Camp.

But he had gone on. Pettinger had made him return to one of the many collecting points, and some Prussian compulsion had kept him in line; he had suffered being assigned anew, and whenever there had been a chance for a safe post somewhere in the rear, a higher power had prevented it. It was as if the great impersonal machine that was his Army became personal when it dealt with Major Dehn; and he suspected, with or without grounds, that it was his friend Pettinger who viciously directed his fate. His suspicions were confirmed when Pettinger, remarking, "I've a rendezvous with a Buzzard group at the Meuse," attached himself to Dehn's column at the very hour it was to move into the offensive.

Which made Dehn hate the Americans all the more. They always had it so easy. When they were winning they never had to win the hard way — always the horrible superiority of air force and artillery which made you powerless to do anything but watch your nerves peter out. And when they were losing, all they had to do was raise their hands in order to be sure of a royal welcome and of achieving the restful life without responsibilities that Dehn ached for and could not make himself go after.

Now that the immediate fighting around him had ceased, he could hear the sound of firing from the South where the squadron covering his left flank must be engaged by the Americans. Dehn didn't like the situation. His mission was to push ahead as fast as possible and leave the cleaning-up to the infantry units following him. The prisoners he had taken impeded his progress; he had no space on his tanks and half-tracks for them; neither could he let them go.

Pettinger stamped up to him, shaking the snow off his boots.

"How many?" he pointed at the Americans bunching together miserably, as if their closeness could give them protection.

"About fifteen," said Dehn.

"Well — what are you waiting for?"

Dehn kicked his knee against the inside of his stiff, black, shiny leather coat; it was so stiff and new that, from the belt down, it stood off his thin legs like crinoline.

"I don't know . . ." Dehn said, drawing out his words.

Pettinger glared at him. Dehn, aristocrat, muscle-man, parasite. Falling back into his congenital decadence. Well, nothing surprising about that! He ratted in Paris, too, and lost me a million francs.

"You don't know!" Pettinger aped. "You're in command here, remember?"

"I've got no sympathy for them," Dehn said, "by God, I haven't! But I can't do that. . . ."

"Why can't you?"

"Because they're prisoners. Because they're unarmed, damn them all."

"If you hadn't acted like such a bloody *Dummkopf,* if you'd kept firing from the tanks instead of having the *Panzergrenadiers* dismount, you'd have no problem."

Dehn didn't reply.

"So where is the fine moral difference?" jeered Pettinger.

"I *had* the infantry dismount. These men are prisoners." Dehn, once he had gotten himself into an impasse, was stubborn.

"How long are you going to wait here? You can't take them along, can you?"

"*Verflucht noch einmal!*" Dehn cursed. "Give me time to think!"

Pettinger squinted with distaste.

"So your advice is . . ." Dehn didn't finish.

"Yes. Definitely!"

"Then *you* give the order!"

Pettinger laughed. The Americans heard him laugh.

"You're a coward," said Pettinger. "I always knew it, and I tell you, you're going to end like a coward one of these days."

He lit a cigarette. "*Unteroffizier!*" he shouted.

The Sergeant dashed up.

The glowing end of the cigarette described a little arc. "Have 'em shot."

The Sergeant saluted.

Cerelli saw the two officers turn and disappear in the dark. He heard the motors of the German tanks roar up.

Then he saw a number of figures come out of the dark and take position. He pushed Clay, and Clay saw it, too.

"No!" shouted Clay. "Don't! No!" And then, pulling together what little German he knew, *"Nix schiessen! Nix schiessen!"*

But they didn't hear. They didn't want to hear. Like robots, they followed their orders; or perhaps it seemed logical to them, a kind of justice; or perhaps it was even something good, like harvesting, the mowing-down of the wheat in the fields, and seeing it bend over and fall and lie quiet.

Sheal lay warm. The smell of blood was all around him, and slime was over his face; with each breath it was sucked into his nostrils, and his mouth was full of it. He tried to raise his arm to wipe it off, but he couldn't. Something heavy, immovable had fallen over his arms and over his legs, and it kept him down. He coughed and sputtered and finally a convulsion rose from his stomach. Everything that was in his stomach spilled out of him and flushed off the soft slippery stuff that had been on his mouth. He could open his eyes. The darkness was even darker than the night, but he could see two opalescent points. He raised his head and the opalescent points became larger and were like the insides of clamshells, only convex — the same consistency, the same sheen. He touched the thing giving off the gleam, touched it with the tip of his nose still covered with the slippery, slimy matter that was growing cold rapidly, touched it with his lips that were bitter from the sourness of his stomach.

And then his brain began to work; it figured out the distance between the gleaming clamshells; it took into consideration the feel of the thing he was touching, a feel like cold rubber or gelatine.

Sheal's nose and lips were touching the dead eyes of Corporal Clay.

The last Troy had heard from Fulbright was that he was crossing the east-west road ahead. That had been his last message.

After that there had been the sound of tanks, the sound of firing, and a lonely green flare that rose into the fog and hung there a while in a vain attempt to materialize before it was smothered in the dense, whitish soup.

Troy pushed his men forward. They stumbled uphill and down, down-hill and up, a race without course.

He shouted, with a wild voice that came deep from his chest. "Hurry up! God damn you! Forward!" It was mad. He whipped himself and he whipped his men. He must get through. He must get through in time. It was his fault. He should have ordered Fulbright to wait. He should have gone faster himself, kept in touch with the forward platoon that now was cut off.

He strained his ears. They were still firing, still fighting, he still had a chance. When he came upon the armored squadron on the Germans' left, he was not so much worried about himself and the two platoons with him as he was agonized that here was a wall, a block preventing him from breaking through to Fulbright.

He had sense enough to radio back for armored reinforcements, but he didn't wait for their arrival. He began to attack, regardless of cost, regardless of the natural consequence that the Germans would counterattack and had the power to plow him under.

Abramovici found the forced march over the naked, cold, foggy hills disagreeable and unnecessary. He still wasn't clear about why he was with Troy's men, except that he had picked up and gone after Yates when he saw his Lieutenant join the Company. The wind billowed his homemade snow suit, the sheets stuck between his legs, his rifle became heavier and heavier, and his feet more and more difficult to move. He stuck close to Yates, and Yates heard him mumbling from time to time, "An Army as highly motorized as the American should adjust its tactics to its technical facilities. . . ." or, "Night blindness can be reduced to a deficiency of vitamins." Abramovici seemed completely oblivious of the reasons which led Troy and his men and Yates into the headlong race; to him, it was one of the vagaries of the military mind, much the same as the dash to make a formation and then the wait in line for an hour to listen to the speech of some high-ranking officer.

It took Abramovici a while to realize that the enemy's fire was directed at him. Then he hit the ground with an instinct for self-preservation that shook every bone in his body. He very quickly overcame his natural reaction of They Can't Do That To Me; they were doing it to him all right, and he had to do something about it. His adjustment took the form of a dogged determination to give blow for blow, and luckily, at that moment, he could hear and understand and make sense of and follow the hoarse orders of the sergeants. He could discern the moving shadows of the German vehicles along what seemed to be the horizon. The sky was lighting up by several shades, it was getting toward morning, and he could see the dim outlines of little men moving close to those vehicles — the enemy that was shooting at him.

Abramovici aimed and fired, aimed and fired.

He was very cool about it, not heroically cool — later on, he could never properly express why he had behaved that way — rather, it was mechanical with him: In this and this situation, a soldier has got to act thus and thus.

What went on around him went on as through a veil. He observed it out of the side of his eyes, as it were — a man holding his belly and crying and then the crying getting weaker, like a kitten's, and ceasing altogether; a German armored car being hit and starting to burn fiercely, a small figure trying to crawl out of it and catching fire and waving its burning arms and legs and falling down, like a burnt-out ember; a mortar being dragged into position on his left; a man dropping the shells into the tube, systematically, regularly; *whuiit, whuiit;* and then suddenly no mortar and no man, just a heap of flesh and a twisted tube and the hot breath of an explosion.

Abramovici was reloading his rifle when he noticed that a sudden quiet had set in. He looked for the shadowy enemy and saw that the shadows had disappeared; far over to his left a machine gun was barking and that, too, stopped abruptly. It was new and inconceivable. The fog settled deeper and enveloped him; close to his right lay Yates, not quite clearly visible, and Yates was getting up on his knees, heavily, using his hands to support himself, like an old man.

And out of the quiet it came to Abramovici that the battle was over, it had left him alive; it had been a battle — a battle! You know, where people go out and push little buttons and pull little triggers and figure out targets and aim with the intention to kill, to tear your guts, to blow out your brains, to put great, ragged holes in the body you've been taking care of and feeding and washing all your life, holes out of which your blood comes pouring, more blood than you ever could wash off, hold back, stop with all the bandages in the world!

Abramovici looked at his snow suit. The earth on which he had been lying had colored it brown and gray. He pulled it off. He tore at the seams he had stitched, he heard the thread rip with an ugly sound, he saw the sheets fall down around his feet. He lifted his feet and stepped out of the ring of dirty linen. It was as if he were stepping out of a magic circle. He lifted his left foot — step! His right foot — step! One step after the other — he began to run, his knees sagging, but he kept on running, like a drunkard.

He ran away from the battle. He was an ordinary human being that didn't want to kill or be killed, so he ran away from the battle. He had actually forgotten that he had fought in it.

Yates saw him and ran after him, caught him and brought him back. Abramovici didn't resist. He was docile as a lamb.

Every moment of the battle, Yates had been fully conscious not only of what was going on around him, but also of his own reactions. His kind of brain would either cease functioning completely or would function with all its diverse faculties, imposing on his heart the terrible job of holding out, unrelieved by Troy's burning drive to make up for a fault, or by Abramovici's field-manual precision.

He saw what was happening around him, each picture impressing itself indelibly on the photo-cells of his brain, making him wince and shudder, and forcing him to overcome his deep desire to run or to hide. And since he was completely awake and rational, conscious and responsible, his staying power had to be based entirely on intellect and morale, on his sense of duty, on convincing himself that he must hang on. Had he been a more primitive person, a man held by instincts or by the habit of drill or even by the community bond, the *esprit de corps,* or at least by the necessity of setting an example as an officer, it would have been easier for him. But his had to be a bravery of conviction, an enlightened bravery that eats up the substance of your nerves and leaves you limp and fagged, but somehow a little proud of yourself.

Troy and a sergeant named Bulmer went on patrol. Yates offered to come along. He thought that waiting for Troy's return would be more difficult than going forward with him to see what had happened to Fulbright and his men.

Troy had changed for the worse. The cumulative effect of what he had gone through since Normandy seemed to break out all over him. His face was puffed and yet sharply lined, his eyes sat deep in their hollows, and he kept grinding his jaws nervously.

"Take a smoke," said Yates.

Troy didn't answer. After they had crossed the road — it lay still and harmless and only its ruts showed that it had carried catastrophe — he said, "D'you think it's worth all that?"

Sergeant Bulmer said, "Over there!"

They saw a dark lump against a small, snow-covered roll of ground; the snow was trampled and beaten. The dark lump was Lester. And Lester had managed to stay alive; he was wounded in both legs and in his shoulder; he was unconscious.

Yates took off his coat. They bedded Lester on it. Troy said, "You and Bulmer carry him back. Return here as fast as you can, and bring along about ten men. I'll go on by myself."

Yates stared after him until he disappeared behind a hill.

When Yates returned with the rescue party, Troy was not alone. He was dragging Sheal, Sheal's arm over his captain's shoulder, Sheal's face a mess of blood and dirt, Sheal's free hand shaking wildly.

"Go over there!" said Troy, pointing behind him. "You'll find them." He pulled up the weight of the sagging Sheal. "You stay with me, Yates!"

"Yes, Captain."

And as Bulmer moved off with the other men, Troy called after them, "Hey, you!"

They stopped.

"I want you to remember what you're going to see! Don't any of you ever forget it!"

They didn't reply. They walked slowly up the next elevation. Yates saw them break into an odd canter as soon as they reached the top of the hill.

"They lay all in one pile," said Troy.

Yates waited.

"They lay all in one pile," Troy repeated in a tone so monotonous that Yates was reminded of Thorpe in his cell.

"Fifteen of them," said Troy.

He laughed to himself.

"Fifteen. All that was left. Knew every one. Why did they do that?"

He didn't wait for an answer.

"They didn't have any weapons. They'd given up. They were prisoners. They were all in one pile."

He put one arm around Sheal as if he were hugging him.

"I go down on my knees," he continued, "I dig in the pile. I go through pockets where I can find pockets, I tear off dog tags, I'm their captain, I'm the captain of a pile of dead men. . . ."

He stopped and, in a voice suddenly normal, said, "They never had a chance, God damn it, they never had a chance. . . ."

And falling back into the recital, "Then somebody throws himself on me, starts wrestling with me, starts choking me. Sheal here!"

He chuckled.

"Thought I was a Nazi, didn't you, boy? . . . He was right out of the pile. He couldn't really grab me. His hands were so slippery, and numb."

He pulled off Sheal's glove and showed Yates the hand, stiff, discolored, almost black.

"So I holler: I'm Troy! I'm your captain! But he keeps on fighting. I had to knock him out. . . . You didn't recognize me, did you? I understand. I don't hold it against you, Sheal."

Yates couldn't say anything. The grief of the man had something frightening in it. It held you back from making general remarks about treachery, or, We'll pay them back with interest.

"I want you to do something for me," said Troy.

"Anything."

"You speak their lingo, don't you?"

"Yes."

"There must be witnesses," said Troy. "There was a whole column of armor, hundreds of men who know. We will catch one or the other. Keep on the lookout for them, Yates. I'm not going to kill them, not all of them. I don't say an eye for an eye and a tooth for a tooth. I'm a Christian, and I'm going to stay one. It's hard, but I'm going to stay one."

Sheal seemed to be coming to. His feet stopped dragging and tried to make real steps. Troy's burden became lighter.

Troy straightened himself. For a moment, he stood upright, towering over Yates and over the soldier he was supporting.

371

"But I want the man who gave the order!" he called out. "I want that man and you're going to find him for me!"

"Yes," said Yates, "I will." It was an oath.

8

FARRISH was at the front.

The men hated him. They knew he would drive them forward. Day and night, where he was, they would have to keep going; no rest, no sitting down, no stretching out. The woods began to burn, the hills to change their contour, the men at the guns were kept firing till they dropped, nerves taut as the strings of some whining, misshapen instrument.

Farrish was like an evil big bird; where he swooped down, there would be death. They began to wish that a bullet would get him, but he was untouchable. He had no fear. In one attack, he was said to have walked along, swinging his crop like an elegant walking stick, occasionally firing away with his pistol. He came out of it unscratched, though the Germans kept them nailed down halfway from the objective.

Slowly, slowly Farrish was trying to push north. You couldn't say that the tide of battle had turned. The Germans were still going ahead toward the west, pouring in fresh troops to exploit their wedge and to deepen it. The sky was still overcast, and the air force was tied to the ground, and the whole Army was like a blind man groping his way, stumbling, rising again, only to fall once more.

But the Germans, too, were far from their goal. They hadn't taken Antwerp. Some armored spearheads had reached the Meuse River, but no gain had really been solidified, and the Americans blew up their own gas dumps and with them some of Marshal von Klemm-Borowski's fondest hopes.

Farrish came to Company C. It was down to half its strength. Someone said, "The hell with him. I ain't going to get up for nobody, and for him neither."

Farrish didn't ask anybody to get up.

He leaned against a tree and, with the tip of his boot, traced a design in the snow.

"I know how it is," he said. "I'm tired, too, God damn it. This is the worst thing that ever happened to us. If we don't push on, we haven't got a chance. If we go back, we haven't got a chance. I'm telling you, this war is being decided right here and now. We've got to go forward. That's how it is."

Afterwards, Troy said to him, "Sir, you ask for more than the men can give!"

"I didn't ask for your opinion, Captain Troy."

But Troy was in a rebellious mood. "Sir, I'm giving it to you. They're my men, sir. They aren't just figures."

Farrish looked at him and grinned. He had wonderful teeth, brilliant, white; Troy was tempted to smash them.

"They're *my* men," said Farrish, "every single one of them. And don't you forget it."

That evening, they attacked again, and again were held short of their objective.

The front was so close to the city of Luxemburg that, at four in the afternoon, you could have a piece of *Ersatz* apple cake and a cup of *Ersatz* coffee in one of the cafés, thumb a ride and be back on duty in the line at six. The Germans shelled the railroad depot and the road junction at Arlon, and it looked as if they were trying to get into Arlon in order to encircle Luxemburg.

So close was the front that the prisoner cage was installed in the field of the local sports stadium. Bing and Yates interrogated in the soccer players' dressing room under the grandstand. The dusty washbasins were excellent shelves for papers and other odds and ends; and at noon you had only a fifteen minutes' walk to the mess. Things were as comfortable as they could be in a beleaguered fortress, even though the latest dope picked up at dinner was by no means reassuring: One of the towers of the cathedral had been hit squarely. The Germans had offered their highest decoration, the *Ritterkreuz,* plus two months' leave, to the commander capturing the radio station; the transmitter of the station now lay within easy range of medium artillery.

The man being shoved into the dressing room for interrogation wore an American uniform. Two Negro soldiers, from a Quartermaster Laundry Company that had been thrown into the line, had brought him and his wounded companion to the cage. The Negroes also delivered a note from their lieutenant explaining that these men had been stopped at a roadblock — there was something fishy about them. And then they had attempted a getaway; that's when one had been wounded.

Bing studied the note and from time to time glanced at the prisoner standing before him — his button mouth, his large cheeks, flabby despite his youth, his narrow, steep forehead with the shimmering black and yellow bump at its side. The man was trembling, but it could have been from cold. He'd been kept waiting outside on the field where the wind, striking unimpeded across the bare expanse, whipped into you. His uniform was American, all right, and in a sorry state. Evidently the men of the Laundry Company had given him a good going-over.

"*Setzen Sie sich!*" said Bing without looking up, pointing at the stool in front of him.

The man didn't move.

"*Setzen Sie sich!*"

"I don't know German."

"Sit down. How did you know I was talking German?"

There was a moment's hesitation. "It sounded like it. I've been near Aachen and the people there sounded like what you said. Listen, Sarge, this is a lot of nonsense. These niggers went crazy because I called them niggers; that's no crime, is it? So they shoot my comrade and say that I'm a spy. How can I be a spy? My papers are in order, my dog tags — you have them all there in the washbasin, I've seen them — "

Had Bing not received the letter from the Laundry Company Lieutenant, had he encountered the soldier sitting before him accidentally, he would never have suspected him. But, his ears sharpened, he noticed slight discrepancies — the occasional hissing *s* in the man's speech, his using slang like *Sarge* and *Nigger* on the one hand, and calling his wounded driver *Comrade* on the other — only a German would translate *Kamerad* into *Comrade*.

"Tell me a little bit about yourself. Tell me what you've done in the Army."

The man rattled off his complete Army history, camp by camp, unit by unit. He did it by rote, even as he had done after his capture, surrounded by the mass of dark faces, his mind seething with the stories, dished out so amply among the Germans, about the barbarism and the cruelty of colored troops. Even under those circumstances, even in the face of the Negro Lieutenant — they made officers out of those apes, too! — he had steadfastly maintained that he was Sergeant Howard Bethune from Chicago. Maybe he should have added *Illinois,* as Marshal von Klemm-Borowski had added at the final parade of the Buzzard men. . . . Heberle found it no job to keep up the story, now, when he had to repeat it for a man who was at least white, like himself. If only Mulsinger, wounded, didn't give them away in some delirious fever! . . .

Bing heard him through. Everything was correct, everything checked; but it was too detailed and it came out too smoothly. Once more Bing looked at the Negro Lieutenant's note. Popeye, he thought. The guy couldn't tell the Lieutenant who Popeye was. And he didn't know who had won the World Series. Well, there are people who just skip the comic strips. There are even people who aren't interested in baseball.

"What's *T.S.?*" Bing asked.

A guard in the background laughed.

Heberle moved nervously on his little stool. *T.S.* were initials for something — but what? He wasn't cold at all, now; he felt hot and unzipped his field jacket. He could see the letters as if they were chalked up on black in front of his eyes. Only they were elusive. They teetered and danced and became blurred.

An officer came in, a Lieutenant. The officer placed himself next to Bing and looked at Heberle, quite sympathetically and obviously puzzled that a man in American uniform was being gone over.

"*T.S.!*" said Bing, excitedly. "Tell me what *T.S.* means and I'll let you go!"

"Sir!" Heberle jumped up and saluted more smartly than Yates had been saluted since the States. "I'm an American Sergeant, and I'm being treated like a prisoner! Worse than a prisoner, sir!"

"Aw, don't get fancy!" said Bing. He motioned Yates to one side and in hasty whispers told him how the man had been brought in and what his questioning had led up to. "I'm sure the guy's a German; he and the one with him were completely outfitted GI-style, and they were in an American jeep — that's an organized job — and on a big scale. . . ."

Yates's tired face grew hard. Only the previous night, he had come back from the remnants of Troy's company. He had hardly slept, and what little sleep he had managed, had been disturbed by images of what he had seen, of the pile of murdered men Troy had described. And what had hit those men, day before yesterday, might hit him tomorrow.

He looked at the prisoner. Heberle's face showed a remarkable mixture of truculence and groveling. It was this expression that made up Yates's mind that Bing and the unknown Negro Lieutenant could be right — too often he had seen that truculence and that groveling, and the swift change from one to the other, on the faces of German prisoners.

Yates came toward Heberle.

"So, what is *T.S.*, Sergeant?" he asked. The question sounded ridiculous within these bleak walls.

"I know! I know, sir!" Heberle said desperately. "I just can't remember at this moment."

The guard in the background couldn't contain himself any longer. The two words burst out of him.

Heberle's eyes focused. "Yes," he said. "Of course." Then, feeling that such language was not appropriate in the presence of an officer, he coughed and raised his hands apologetically.

"A bit late, isn't it?" said Yates.

He stepped close to Heberle and twisted the last button the men of the Quartermaster Laundry Company had left on the man's coat.

"Now, suppose you are a German," he said.

Heberle wanted to protest, but Yates cut him off.

"I don't say you are — but just suppose. In that case you'd be liable to being shot, because you were caught in an American uniform. Is that clear?"

"You make a terrible mistake, sir! I'm an American!"

"We'll find that out. Every American soldier is fingerprinted. If you're Howard Bethune from Chicago, it can be checked, and you have nothing to fear. If you're not, I suggest you tell us the truth about how and why you got into this uniform and who ordered you to do it, and what you were supposed to accomplish. You will be tried, but your case would be considered differently in the light of your confession. . . ."

Heberle felt weak. Then his wits returned. Even if they had fingerprints of Howard Bethune, whoever he was, it would take them time to check. The German Army was going forward, the Americans would be beaten. . . . Let them try to prove something! The more time they were forced to spend on him, the better became his chance of being liberated.

"I can't confess. I have nothing to confess. If you'll have a look at my dog tags, sir, at my papers — they are in order!"

"Perhaps you think it will take us a long time to check your finger-prints," said Yates, "and much can happen during that time?"

Heberle's tongue went dry.

Yates continued, "We could simply call the Company to which you say you belong. Inside twenty-four hours somebody will be here to identify you."

Yates knew it would take more than twenty-four hours to produce someone to identify this Sergeant Bethune; he wasn't even sure, at the rate things were going at the front, that anyone in that company was left.

Twenty-four hours . . . "Yes!" said Heberle eagerly. "That would be the best thing. And I want to thank you for your fairness, sir. Am I through, now?"

"No," said Yates.

He was coming to the end of his rope. He had made the last possible threat for breaking the man. He took Bing aside. "I'm going to do something I'll never be able to answer for, if that man is an American. You think he's German?"

"I'm sure," said Bing. "But if you have any doubts —"

Yates had his doubts. Yet, if the man was a German, if the Germans had sent men in American uniforms through the lines, it was essential to know — this very minute, this hour — how many had been sent, what their mission was, and a dozen other items. On them depended the lives of thousands, perhaps the outcome of this battle.

"Go out and get me a detail of four MP's," Yates said. "The biggest and toughest you can get."

"Wonderful!" said Bing.

"What's so wonderful about it!" said Yates.

It was a long shot and a great risk. But if the man was a German it was likely to work. Any German knew — even if he didn't admit it — of the Gestapo, of concentration camps, of the beatings, and of their effect. An American probably didn't. Lacking the experience, he would be curious about the preparations. He would wait and see. But a German would know what it meant. And unless this one had more guts than they usually had, he would buckle under before the procedure actually started. At least that was what Yates hoped.

Bing came back with four praiseworthy characters. If he had scoured the ranks of Deputy Sheriffs of a mining county during a strike, he couldn't have done better. Yates felt an almost comic relief that it was he who could give them orders.

"Brought your sticks along?" he asked.

"No, sir," said the Corporal, a man whose bulging neck was more prominent than his head. "Haven't got much use for them around here."

"That's all right," said Yates, "you can use your bayonets. Flat side at first. If that doesn't work, I don't care how you handle them."

It was very quiet in the dressing room. Heberle looked around, hysterically. The concrete walls were thick, absolutely bare, as rough as when they had been poured. It was like the cellars he had heard of, whose walls would stifle any human cry.

"See him?" he heard the Lieutenant say. "He's a German, but he refuses to admit it. The kind of guy who comes around to hit you boys when you're not looking, and when you can't fight back. Take his clothes off. Tie him to this chair. Good and tight. And one of you get a bucket of cold water, just in case he tries to faint."

Heberle felt his heart beat against the back of his head and behind his eyes. He tried to tell himself that he was a German, and that such things weren't being done to Germans. But he saw the four butchers come at him. They were terribly real; one of them carried the bucket with the ice-cold water that would revive him, should he escape into unconsciousness. He saw the bayonets; they weren't gleaming like German bayonets, but dull, hard — harder than any bone in his body; they would fall on his back, on his belly, on his skull; and all the stuff . . . that you were a hero because you were a German, and the glory that was in it, and Fatherland and *Führer* . . . was like jelly, sweet rosy jelly that would squirt out of him at the first blow.

The sweat was pouring down Yates's forehead. Oh God, he thought, oh God, oh God, if I should be wrong. And it wasn't that he feared what might happen to him — the inquiries into why he had ordered the beating of an American soldier, the judgment, the disgrace. It was that the man who would have to take this beating would be destroyed forever, a wreck, spiritual more than physical, stirring out of the sleep of his later years, screaming — an American destroyed by another American, as thousands of people here had been destroyed by the Nazis, as Thorpe had been destroyed by Dondolo. . . . Yates leaned against one of the washbasins, his hands gripping its dust-covered, cold rim.

Heberle felt his clothes being pulled off, the clothes that had been so nice and new and carefully cleaned when they were issued to him in the meticulously scrubbed supply room of the German barracks. He tried to say something, *I'm an American! Don't!* — any words that might come and form themselves; but he had no voice. He felt the nails of one of the men scratch the skin of his back, his naked, twitching skin.

He screamed.

With an effort so great, so sudden that the four slow giants tumbled, he tore himself away from them, ran to Yates, fell down at Yates's feet, hands raised imploringly, and stammered: "*Ich bin ein Deutscher. Ich hatte Befehl, General Farrish zu töten.*"

Yates pushed him back.

"Take notes, Bing," he said hoarsely. "*I am a German. I had orders to kill General Farrish.*"

Yates rushed back to the studio building. He went straight into Willoughby's office. There was no time for amenities. He said, "I've run into Pettinger again. Yes, your friend Yasha's friend."

"So what!" said Willoughby, aggressively.

He was nervous. The transmitter and its costly, irreplaceable equipment were in acute danger, and still no word had come from DeWitt.

"Still chasing old stories!" Willoughby went on. "If the Nazis break into this town tomorrow, we're all sunk — and all you have in mind is Yasha. I'm not interested in him. Submit your report in writing."

He fell back into the brooding which Yates had interrupted. Willoughby needed DeWitt. Events were reducing him to the mental attitude of a junior partner; he still hadn't outgrown Coster of Coster, Bruille, Reagan and Willoughby, Attorneys at Law; and he was conscious of it. And here Yates came storming in, reminding him rudely of better times when victory had been bulging in a man's pockets and you could speak up securely and make plans for the future.

Yates threw himself into the big executive leather chair that the Major had appropriated from some other office, and looked at Willoughby with detachment.

"I'd go see General Farrish myself," he remarked, "if I didn't know that, afterwards, you'd try to get me for having jumped channels."

"Farrish? What's he got to do with it? Can't you make a clear, straight report, man?"

378

Yates continued in his vein. "And I'm not ambitious either. When you came to see me in Rollingen and explained to me what you thought the war was all about — "

"Ancient history! Ancient history!"

"I'm paying you a compliment! I was just about to say that I think you were right at the time — it has turned out to be a long and tough war."

"That's some news!"

"Anyhow, at that time I decided to play along with you."

"Very kind of you," Willoughby said flatly. His mind registered that Yates had changed. Galahad was getting too positive for his taste. Was it the pressure of the Bulge? Did it affect different people differently? Did it serve to make Yates stronger while it attacked and weakened his own stamina?

"Get to the point, now!" Willoughby ordered, summoning his authority. "What did you want to see Farrish about?"

"To tell him that we discovered a German plot against his life. And Farrish isn't the only one — there's a whole list of much bigger guys that are to be bumped off."

Willoughby was speechless.

"I don't have all the names. The man we caught and squeezed didn't know them all. But we know a gang of Germans is loose behind our lines, in American uniforms. About four hundred or so, if every one of them got through. They call it Operation Buzzard."

Willoughby still said nothing.

"There's a joker in it, Major. The man at the head of it is your friend Yasha's friend Pettinger. The same Pettinger who got away from us in Paris, and who suddenly popped up in Ensdorf, down in the mine —"

Willoughby caught his breath. He shouted, "Stick to the main facts, please! God-damned professors that can't hold to a point without bringing in everybody and his uncle!"

"Pettinger isn't everybody, sir, and Yasha isn't his uncle. I still say we should have shot Yasha even though you might have lost some business."

"Leave my business out of it! Here we've got the biggest break of the war — Aw, you'll never understand. . . . Here, get to this typewriter!"

Willoughby pushed a portable across the desk and pulled sheets out of a drawer so hurriedly that the top ones tore.

"Write it out, will you? Everything you know."

"Give me some carbons."

"Yes yes yes! Only hurry it!"

Yates fitted sheets and carbons into the machine, and began to peck away.

"Mark it TOP SECRET!" said Willoughby. He looked over Yate's shoulder. "Jesus!" he said, "do you suppose they're after us, too?"

Yates said, "I think they'll wait till they capture us the regular way." He typed on. "But if you're worried, Major, why don't you double the guards?"

"Guards!" Willoughby gestured his disdain. "We need more than guards!"

He rushed to the phone and gave the code names that would connect him with Farrish's headquarters. "Yes, most urgent!" he said.

Yates only half listened to Willoughby's call. Then the harsh voice was close to his ear, "Aren't you through yet, Yates? I don't think you realize what is at stake!"

Yates stopped typing.

"Go on! Go on!" urged Willoughby.

"Now look here, Major. It strikes me that, during this whole campaign, I've been the one who realized what was at stake. In Normandy, with the Fourth of July leaflet, I had the funny feeling that something was wrong in your attitude. And in Rollingen I found out. At every turn, when I tried to do something — who stopped me? So let's face it!"

"Will you finish that report! When I've come back from the General, I'll be available for your gripes."

"I'll keep that date, thank you."

Yates turned back to the typewriter.

Willoughby felt better in the presence of the General. If you looked at Farrish, just returned from the front, still grimy and mud-stained, you sensed that with this man around, you didn't have to bother finding your way. That was his job, and he was on the job. Of course, the fact that you didn't come to him with empty hands, but with a report that would obligate him and that was proof of your loyalty, improved matters even more. And then, there was curiosity: How would Farrish take it? Willoughby had seen the General accept defeat from the Frenchman, De Jeannenet, and to him Farrish had come out the stronger. This, now, was a graver test. How Farrish was going to take it, was a personal thing to Willoughby.

The General kept putting down the pages of Yates's report to blow into his still numb hands. When he finished reading, he leaned back in his chair and laughed uproariously. "So they're after me!" he exulted. "The little men are after me! That's great! In fact it's flattering! At least we're appreciated by somebody! — Carruthers! Why didn't you tell me of that sooner?"

Carruthers, who had ushered Willoughby into the General's sanctum, grinned back happily at his chief's mirth.

"And by the way, Carruthers," snapped Farrish, "why didn't you inform me of it? That's your job, isn't it?"

The sudden switch in the General's mood took its immediate toll of Carruthers. As he twirled his mustache, his small head seemed to sink between his large shoulders.

"Why does a report as important as this have to come from somebody else, huh? . . . Major Carruthers, I'm asking *you!*"

Carruthers stammered, "They had — a lucky break. . . ."

Bitingly, Farrish said, "There are no lucky breaks! In war, everything's hard work — blood, sweat, and tears!"

"Yes, sir!"

"Suppose Willoughby here hadn't had the brains to rush to me with this report! Suppose those two spies had gotten through to me! Yes — what then?"

"But they didn't get through!" Carruthers said meekly. "They were caught!"

"And who tells you they're the only ones prowling after me? Do you seriously think that to get rid of me they'd send only these two jerks that got themselves in trouble with a couple of Boogies? Maybe they were just decoys, huh? Where's your Intelligence, Carruthers? Where are your interrogators? Asleep? Well, if they're asleep, it's your God-damned fault!"

Willoughby had listened stony-faced to the altercation. Much of Old Man Coster's authority rested on his keeping everybody else strictly in line; but it paid to keep out of his way at such moments.

"Say, Willoughby — What's your first name, by the way? . . . Clarence? Fine. Say, Clarence, how d'you like to have a job with me? I can use good people. I've got the best people in the Army, all hand-picked. Would you like to join?"

"I'd like to think about it, sir," Willoughby stalled.

"I'm a soldier," the General said, a little disgruntled. "Soldiers have to be able to make quick decisions."

But he wanted Willoughby. Not that Farrish was afraid for his life. He believed, if you faced it, a bullet wouldn't hurt you. An assassin's bullet, striking suddenly, out of the dark, or in close quarters — that was something else. A clever, watchful guy like Willoughby was the right man to have around.

"Well?" he asked.

Willoughby weighed the offer. The future, military and otherwise, was not with DeWitt. The future was with strong men. On the crest of the wave Farrish would beat up, a man could ride far. Funny that in the midst of the German offensive, not knowing where he'd be tomorrow, he was contemplating his future. . . . No, it wasn't funny at all; he had to consider everything. Willoughby knew that regard for the security of his immediate staff never kept the General out of all sorts of places where no man in his right mind would go. And around Farrish, the mighty fell exceedingly fast. And there could very well be other German teams lying in wait for Farrish. . . . This was not the season to hitch your wagon to the General's star.

"Sir," said Willoughby, "I'm more than flattered by your offer. I'm deeply moved."

On the other hand, this was a golden opportunity to demonstrate to Farrish that he was the man to stick to his job, and at the same time to build what, in military parlance, was called a reserve position.

"At present, however, my duties are such that I cannot desert my post, sir. I'm holding down two jobs — my own and that of my commanding officer, Colonel DeWitt."

"I'll talk to DeWitt!" The harder to get Willoughby made himself, the more Farrish wanted him.

"Colonel DeWitt isn't here at the moment, sir. And if I may ask a favor — please don't talk to him about me. The Colonel might think I started this myself, and behind his back. . . . Sir, would you permit me to work it out in my own way?"

Farrish, though disappointed, appreciated Willoughby's honor-and-duty-soaked line. "I don't want Yes-men!" he agreed. "Any other thing I can do for you, Major?"

"Our studios are very much exposed, sir. We could use a couple of platoons. . . ."

"Could you?" said Farrish. His face broke into a sly grin. "I could use a couple of regiments. Don't you be worried about yourself, Clarence Willoughby. A man who can look out for the welfare of his general certainly ought to be able to look out for his own! Right?"

"Right, sir!"

But Willoughby was full of misgivings as he left, and not at all sure whether he had played his cards well. One thing, though, was certain: In a pinch, Farrish had hinted, he was to use his own resources.

9

CRABTREES returned from the transmitter. He had been under fire; shells had landed a few hundred yards from where he stood; and his pretty face showed traces of how badly shaken up he was. He said to Loomis, "It was almost like the snipers when we came into Paris, except there was more of it, much more. . . ." He sat down and tightened the belt around his small waist; but the buckle kept slipping, and he gave it up finally. "Why don't you say something?"

"What do you want me to say?" asked Loomis.

"How long is this going to go on?"

The Captain shrugged gloomily.

"Remember the girl in Paris?" said Crabtrees. "I wish we had a girl now."

Loomis said, "And then, what?"

"On second thought, I couldn't, these days. . . ."

"Aw, shut up!"

"I've got to talk to someone!"

"What for?"

"I don't know. . . . So many things turning around and around. I feel like in a trap. I didn't come across for this!"

"None of us did."

"Out there, at the transmitter, they went about their work, even the civilians. . . . I didn't let on. I locked myself up in the latrine—but then I had to come out because I got afraid the place would be hit with me inside it. . . ."

"And no chance to flush!" said Loomis.

Crabtrees looked at him unbelievingly. "You're a sonofabitch . . ." he said, and wandered out.

He trudged through the empty corridors and ended up in the maproom. Yates was studying the map. The line looked as if the front had developed the gout, a protuberance ugly and disproportionate, and it didn't take much imagination to see the blood and the pain that went into it.

Crabtrees sidled up to Yates.

"What do you think of it?"

Yates took one glance at Crabtrees and knew what the man was up against. But he felt no sympathy. An Abramovici he might have tried to help, but not this hanger-on of Loomis who, even when things went well, wasn't worth the paper his records were typed on.

"I guess it's going to work out all right," Yates said indifferently. "The 101st Division's still holding at Bastogne. They're cut off."

"We might be cut off soon, too. . . ."

"How's it look at the transmitter?"

"Desperate," said Crabtrees.

"What do you mean? Are the Germans attacking it?"

"They're shelling all around it."

"Oh."

Crabtrees became hostile. "Why don't you go there, sometime? You wouldn't act so smart if you had to face it!"

"Pipe down."

"I don't like you!" Crabtrees said with sudden spite.

"You know what you can do with yourself."

"Yeah, I know!" Crabtrees spoke heatedly. "I can go and get myself shot up for you."

"For me?"

"For you! Sure! You like this war, don't you?"

"Go and lie down."

"Yes, I'll go, I'll go!" It sounded like a threat.

Crabtrees went into the cubbyhole in the basement that served as his office. Out of the pocket of his shirt, he pulled a pigskin picture album, opened it, and placed it in front of him on his small desk. On the photograph was written: "To my little soldier boy — *Maman*." He stared at the picture of his mother, a dowager with severe features, who stared right back at him out of her sharp, small, appraising eyes.

He wasn't a soldier, and Maman knew it — Maman always had exaggerated ideas of everything, including herself. And now she sat back in Philadelphia and prattled that she, too, was doing her share, that her little boy was now a little soldier boy. She got something out of the war, everybody got something out of the war, everybody except himself who was stuck with it in the Bulge.

He hated Yates and he hated Loomis. He wished he could punish them both; he thought up schemes, but they were all no good. And the Germans were coming anyhow.

Cut off. That was the beginning of the end. He could see how it would be: The whole town overrun by the Nazis; they would close in on the studio buildings. . . . *Sorry, little soldier boy, caught with this outfit, hung with it!*

No, if it came to that, he would defend himself. He pulled out his pistol and reached into the drawer of his desk for the cleaning utensils. He weighed the weapon in his hand; a big thing, trustworthy. His mother probably would cry out if she saw him with it.

You had to be careful. Men wounding themselves while cleaning their pistols was a common accident. But it was ugly. They said a man had to have real courage to maim himself. If you were wounded in combat, you didn't know what hit you when; but here, you knew; you fixed the time. . . . Very practical, the Colt, really a little marvel of modern technique. You had to pull like that to let the cartridge slide into the chamber — click! — and the thing was cocked at the same time. And you can see how good a weapon it is, and what care has been taken against accidents! You have to grip the handle in a certain way so that the safety catch — just a piece of metal band, very easily depressed — comes down, before you can fire.

He laid the pistol on the desk. Little soldier boy, cut off and shelled and having nobody . . . If you looked at it in the bright light of the sun, of course it wasn't so bad — but there was no sun. Down here, in this cubbyhole, you had to have the electric light burning, regardless of the

384

hour; and outside, the sky was dreary and overcast; and if you listened sharply, you could hear the rumble of the front.

He sighed and turned back to his pistol. He tried to shake the cartridge out of the chamber, but it was stuck. He shook the pistol again. He knocked it against the corner of the desk. He opened it and glanced critically at the little round, shiny, stubborn thing in the chamber. He held it far away from himself, with both hands — pointing downward as it was prescribed. And then something slipped and the shot rang out, loud against the low walls of the cubbyhole. A pain so unbearable surged through the little soldier boy that his brain seemed to swell against his skull. Acrid smoke floated around him. He heard the weapon tumble from his weak hands and fall to the floor. Then he fell, too, and blacked out.

Loomis didn't believe for a moment that it had been an accident. Crabtrees had shot himself neatly in the foot, and the doctor said he might have to amputate. They were sending him back to the General Hospital in Verdun; the road through Arlon was still open.

Loomis wondered where Crabtrees had raised the courage for it. It was really extraordinary, and he wished he had known Crabtrees was able to do it — he wouldn't have kicked him out of his office. He would have listened to the poor slob. What a happy-go-lucky kid Crabtrees had been! Never complaining, always ready for a joke — and now he was gone.

Crabtrees had managed to go, and *he* was left here — just when things got thick, and you felt you couldn't look up without getting a waft of catastrophe, like a wet rag, thrown around your head! Maybe he overestimated Crabtrees's sensitivity. . . . Anybody could add up the entries on the map, and the faces of the men returning from or going into the line; and Willoughby had ordered: *Be packed!* Loomis was packed, ready to move out at a moment's notice. What was the good of that? You could sit here on your duffel bags, and sit just one hour too long, and you'd be caught, bag, baggage, and all. Loomis had to hand it to Crabtrees: The kid had made a decision and gone through with it, like a man.

But Willoughby shouted that it was a scandal and that he would make it tough for Crabtrees to prove that it was an accident. Cleaning his pistol! In my eye!

"He just pulled out," Loomis said hopelessly. "That's easy to understand. . . ."

Willoughby became vehement. "Either all of us pull out, or none!"

"He was just back from the transmitter. He saw how it was. He talked to me. A man can only go so far, then he sees it's useless."

"I've been trying to get in touch with DeWitt," Willoughby said, seemingly changing the subject.

"No success?"

"Not a word."

"So we're alone in this. . . ." The corners of Loomis's mouth were pointing downward.

"We're under Farrish." Willoughby sounded as if he were following this course of thought for the first time.

"What does *he* know about broadcasting?" said Loomis.

"He's been very kind to me," Willoughby said, tentatively.

"After all, this outfit saved his life!"

"In a way. . . ." Willoughby stroked his jowls. Sure, Farrish would ultimately be responsible if the station was closed down; but in the pattern of human relations within a unit, it wasn't necessarily the man signing the order who counted most. There was a moral responsibility.

Loomis left, his shoulders sagging.

Willoughby reached for his phone. "Try again!" he demanded. "Try to get through to Paris, to Colonel DeWitt. Or find out if he's left and when!"

"Yes, sir," said the operator.

It would be of no use, Willoughby knew it. The grab for the phone had become an automatic reflex.

He leafed through the messages from the transmitter. Their similarity was depressing. *Received fire at 0500; at 0540; hit on RR crossing Junglinster* — Junglinster was the village closest to the masts; *Sighted enemy armor mile and a half NW; 0622 sporadic fire from enemy heavy artillery.* . . . These were only the top sheets of the batch; Willoughby put the whole sheaf aside.

There were millions at stake, millions of dollars — equipment, men, all irreplaceable. What would DeWitt have done?

Willoughby scratched his jowls. Maybe he should take a ride out to the transmitter and see for himself. But how could he judge whether a situation was untenable or not? Maybe they weren't firing at the transmitter but at the local spur of the railroad. Maybe the enemy tanks had gone in a different direction, or they weren't enemy tanks at all. Everything was guessing, guessing. . . . How the hell can a man decide with no facts to go on? No, there were facts — plenty facts, and all bad. Whole divisions smashed; the Germans still pushing after so many days; the Air Force still tied to the ground, which meant that the Germans were always stronger wherever they chose to attack; and nobody could predict when Farrish would be able to consolidate and re-establish something remotely resembling a coherent line.

No, he wouldn't go out to the transmitter. What was the sense? The only thing that could happen out there was that he himself might be hit — and then who would take over? Loomis?

Or he might call a conference. Talk it all out, get some fresh views, see what the general feeling is. At least, if some conclusions were reached, the whole burden wouldn't sit on his own shoulders!

War is almost like peace — he'd said it so often. This was one time when it wasn't. Conferences were no good in the Army, there was no majority rule in the Army, what the Commanding Officer said went, and he was the Commanding Officer.

All right — in any case, some other opinions! But he knew who'd be there: Crerar, Yates, Loomis. . . . He could discount the rest — they'd have nothing to offer, anyhow. Crabtrees would be missing, Crabtrees already had had his say with a bullet.

Major Willoughby, commanding, would open the conference. He'd give both alternatives — what would happen if they went on broadcasting and the Germans exerted the little effort needed to take the transmitter and to take the town of Luxemburg and the studios. And what it would mean if the station were closed down, unexpendable equipment and men removed to the safer rear — to Verdun, for instance. He'd be fair about it — he was in doubt, he needed advice.

But he knew what they'd say. Crerar would play up his civilian status: *I disqualify myself. I know nothing about the military situation.* After that introduction, his position would depend on whether and what he'd dreamed last night about his child wife, so-called.

Yates would bore him with his dramatizing. He'd say that we'd managed in Normandy and fell apart in Paris. Victory does that to us. But in defeat we're wonderful. And then he'd talk about obligations — This station is the voice of the American people and of the liberated peoples, you can't silence it, silence is the open concession of defeat, everybody in France, Belgium, Luxemburg, and the few acres of Germany we still hold, will be panicked — look at the consequences! Stick it out! Don't give up the ship!

It would be the truth, too. But not all of it. In war, as in peace, you retreated and you advanced; sometimes you retreated in order to advance. And even if the station were shut for a while — look what it would mean when it opened up again!

Maybe that's what Loomis would say. Of course, Loomis couldn't admit that he wanted to run — so he'd be the voice of reason, slightly nasal, and debunk Yates's heroics.

And in the end, Major Willoughby, commanding, would sum up and say *Thank you, gentlemen,* and *I think we ought to take it up with General Farrish!* Crerar and Yates would remain doubtful — Crerar wouldn't show it, but Yates might come forward with a crack like *Don't you think, Major, that everything depends on how it is presented to the General?* He might go further. Willoughby could hear him: *I'm for waiting for Colonel DeWitt!* Well, who wouldn't like to wait for him!

The telephone rang. Willoughby felt his heart pound.

"Sir — sorry. Been trying all this time to get through to Paris. No luck."

"Thank you, operator. . . . No, wait a moment. Ring up all the officers and Mr. Crerar, and ask them to come to my office for a conference."

Willoughby sat back and folded his hands. In the final analysis, it would be up to Farrish. Let him decide!

Abruptly, at five in the afternoon, the station was silenced. Even the carrier wave, that breath in the ether, was dead.

The men charged with the dismantling of the transmitter's vital equipment — American soldier technicians and Luxemburg civilian engineers — worked with blind haste. They were the same men who had been ready to stick it out until the Nazis were at the master switch; but now, their courage was deprived of its meaning and turned into the fallow feeling of *What's the sense?* The civilians resented the soldiers and those in their own ranks fortunate enough to be on the list of evacués; the soldiers resented the civilians because they were civilians. Even Laborde, selected by Loomis to command this rear guard activity, fluttered about like a disturbed sparrow, cluttering up the technicians' progress with his constant goading to hurry, hurry!

Then the trucks with the transmitter's metal, plastic, and glass guts came lumbering into the yard of the studio building. Willoughby had arranged for the personnel to leave in two convoys — Loomis would take the first one carrying the radio equipment and some of the men, including Crerar. The second, following twelve or twenty-four hours later, was to be led by himself. This was Willoughby's concession to the voice inside of him that said: If you run, at least do it decently.

As Loomis cleared his desk, he caught himself soliloquizing — talking to Crabtrees, as it were, laughing at him out of the corner of his mouth: So what good did it do you to smash your foot? Softly, he whistled, "Where Is the Kiss of Yesterday?" He liked the song. It had a sentimental charm. He placed his papers neatly into a carton and tied the package securely. He did not hurry. There was more than enough time. He could say a cheerful good-by to the men who were staying on; to Yates, for instance, who was hanging on though Willoughby had offered him a place in the first convoy.

Yates was not alone, Loomis found. Bing was with him. Their silence at his entrance was acute, and he sensed that his head in the door was the cause of it.

He wasn't wrong. Yates had been saying, "I wish I knew what mistakes I made. I certainly tried hard to keep them from closing down. . . . No dice."

388

Bing had argued that Yates was crazy to sit around and blame himself — "You always blame yourself, you always look into yourself, as if your belly button was the center of the universe. There are times when you feel you have to do that kind of thing; but not all the time. Certainly not this time — the General gave his orders — period."

"Be consistent!" Yates had answered. "When everybody was against the Fourth of July leaflet, I remember that you went ahead on your own, spoiling all of Willoughby's tidy plans, including what I was supposed to do. I was kind of mad at you then — I've forgiven you since. Don't sit there and grin, I don't like it."

"But don't you see? I had that wonderful chance! It just worked out that way. . . ."

"Why do your chances work out that way — and not mine? Why do I screw mine up?"

Bing shrugged.

"All right," said Yates. "There is no answer. I know."

"You couldn't do a damned thing, Lieutenant — you tried! So take it gracefully. Be happy you're getting out in time. I am."

Bing saw the door open. "A visitor . . . ," he observed, and the two fell silent.

Loomis was ready for travel — weapon, musette bag, everything. He said with a gayety that was genuine enough, "Well, it's good-by for a short time. Tomorrow, when you arrive in Verdun — I think it'll be tomorrow for you — I'll have everything set up."

"That's awfully kind of you, sir," Bing offered. "I can speak for the enlisted men — we aren't accustomed to it."

Loomis took it straight. "Glad to be appreciated!"

Yates stopped rubbing the wart on his left index finger and asked, "Is that what you've come in here for?"

"Yes. To say So long!"

"Well — So long!"

Loomis felt affronted. His intentions had been good. He hesitated and then repeated, "So long. . . ."

"Get out!" Yates said tersely.

A fatuous smile spread over Loomis's face. "You should thank me on your bended knees for saving your life, Yates."

"Thanks. I'll do my own saving when I feel like it."

"I'm only trying to help you!"

"The way you helped Thorpe?"

Loomis stormed out. But he had forgotten his gloves. He came back, picked them up from Yates's desk, and repeated his exit, mad that the repetition made it a flop, but not mad enough to freeze his hands off on the ride to Verdun.

Outside, the engines of the heavy trucks roared up. The convoy began to move.

"Let's celebrate!" said Yates.

"Celebrate what? Loomis's departure?"

"Yes, why not? I've got a box of candy — good stuff from home, not GI. And I've got sardines and crackers and a bottle of rye. I don't want to drag it along, and I don't want to leave it here for the Germans, if and when they come. Did you ever notice how happy and well-fed the guys are who surrender after siege? I know the answer to it — they've been having a whale of a time, eating and drinking up everything they'd saved. So now it's our turn. Call in the boys — anyone you like. Anyone who's remained here."

Bing came back with Abramovici; Sergeant Clements, the loudspeaker man; and McGuire, the driver. Others pressed in after them, the mechanics, the announcers, and the few officers left, Willoughby among them.

"I've been getting lonely," Willoughby announced, almost in apology. He put one of his own bottles on the table. "Real Scotch!"

Nobody said anything.

"How about some music?" said Willoughby.

"BBC all right?" asked Bing, fingering the dials of Yates's receiver.

"Sure! Anything!"

The music came over, sweet and rhythmic. Someone began to hum. There was a clink of glasses and the clatter of an empty sardine can being thrown into the wooden wastebasket.

And then the music faded out. A voice announced, "This is the Allied Forces Network. BBC London. And now the news!"

"At ease! Shut up! Let's hear the news!"

The woman announcer had the kind of voice that belonged with knitting needles by a fireside, mellow and full of sympathy. She gave the communiqués from the front, and somehow, she made them sound as if the German advance were only half as bad; and perhaps, her listeners thought, she was right.

Then she said: "We have just learned that German forces have taken Radio Luxemburg and are using the station. Radio Luxemburg was one of the most powerful broadcasting stations of the Allied forces. Nothing is known of the fate of the valiant men who have been operating Radio Luxemburg. It is presumed that they are safe. Attention! Any announcements coming from Radio Luxemburg originate with the enemy. . . ."

"Oh my aching back!" said Bing.

"Shut it off!" said Yates. "I'm not interested in our own obituary."

A cracker with two anchovies symmetrically placed fell from Abramovici's hands. "Something is wrong here!" he said, reaching for his rifle. "The Germans are in the building!"

"Nonsense!"

"Why did you shut it off?" protested Bing, first to regain his wits. "Maybe they had some more nice things to say about us!"

Willoughby pressed through the crowd to the radio set. He switched it on and dialed the wavelength of Luxemburg, his own wavelength. "Here it is!" he cried. A voice came through, quite faint, but clear, speaking in German. "Here it is. . . ."

Everybody listened, sick at heart.

Willoughby said, "The bastards! They've put a transmitter on our frequency."

"Smart," said Bing.

Yates turned to Willoughby. "That's only the beginning. Don't say we haven't been warned, Major."

Willoughby said sharply, "Are you criticizing an order of General Farrish?"

Yates waved him off with a motion expressing how tired he was, physically and mentally. He didn't want to dispute, he didn't want to fight. He pleaded for a little quiet to be alone with his thoughts. His thoughts were with Ruth — who at this minute, back at their house in the small university town, would be listening to the announcement that her man was in German hands, or dead.

He stood up and said, "All right! All right! Let's break it up! The party is over!"

The German voice still spattered the air, guttural and insistent. Yates turned the dial until it snapped. He was alone, and he felt as if he had just come through a crying jag.

IO

ABRAMOVICI ran into Yates's office. He was flushed with a happy excitement that made him clumsier than ever. As he straightened to report, the butt of his rifle knocked against Yates's desk with a sudden thump.

"The Colonel's back!" he said. "The noise which can be heard outside is caused by the worms rustling to their holes due to the arrival of the chicken."

"Abramovici!"

"I just thought I'd let you know so you can stop packing."

This was exactly what Yates felt; but he couldn't admit to Abramovici what he thought of Willoughby's orders, and that he anticipated they would be canceled now that DeWitt had returned.

"Are *you* all packed?" he asked Abramovici.

"Yes, sir, of course. I've been packed since the day the Germans started their attack. I live out of my musette bag — but then . . ." Abramovici's round face looked so ingratiating that Yates felt its appeal. ". . . I am, perhaps, a more careful man than you are."

Yates smiled. "Anyhow — thanks for letting me know!"

"Lieutenant Yates — " Abramovici's voice went down almost to a whisper. "There's a small matter I'd like to take up with you, just a little favor . . ."

"Yes?"

"Remember, when we went into that crazy expedition of yours — I don't mean it was crazy of you to go, but it was crazy of me — and the Germans came suddenly out of the night, and we had to take them on . . ."

"I remember, Abramovici."

"You see, I ran away."

"Did you?"

"Didn't I?"

"I've forgotten."

"No, I didn't run away, sir. I stood there and fought as long as I could, honestly . . ."

"I believe you."

"Now, I don't think you'd tell the Colonel, not intentionally, you wouldn't. But it may slip out in conversation. You might tell it like a story. . . . I know, Lieutenant, some people think I'm funny. Maybe I am — but I'm just careful because there is so much to live for. . . . So, you'll keep it to yourself?"

"We all are careful, in our own way," said Yates, feeling something inside him well up. "Do you think I'd have taken you along to a spot as bad as the one we found ourselves in, if I thought you just a funny person? The only man with me? The man on whom I had to rely? No, I had confidence in you, and — I was not disappointed."

"Sir, I don't want to die for anyone." Abramovici's light eyes began to shimmer vaguely. "But if I had to, I'd rather die for you than for anyone else!"

Yates couldn't laugh. He said, "Well, Abramovici, I think you're offering me your friendship. I want to be your friend, too. Shake!"

DeWitt and Willoughby closeted themselves. Both men felt that what they had to say to one another had better be kept between them.

A growing change in Willoughby had set in from the moment he saw

DeWitt drive into the yard, listened to the Colonel's steps, heard the deep, strong voice sound through the corridor. All the reasons he had given himself and Farrish about the need to close down the station failed to hold the instant he realized that DeWitt was back, that DeWitt would question him, and that no answers, no matter how concise and packed with military data, would be sufficient. And because he was conscious of that, he was frantic, trying to think up better reasons, better answers, even before De-Witt called him in. He was on the defensive without having been attacked.

DeWitt didn't open as Willoughby had expected. The Colonel didn't say: Why have you done this? Neither did he explain why he had been delayed. Instead, he said, "Well, Willoughby, what are we going to do now?"

Willoughby was not prepared to answer this question. Had things panned out, he would have been gone in twelve hours; but somehow, he couldn't make himself say to DeWitt: What do you mean — What are we going to do now? We're going to get into a car and drive back to Verdun, or wherever, and wait till the worst has blown over.

"You must have had something in mind?" said DeWitt. "You didn't think you'd close shop and call it a day?"

"Of course not! Of course not!" Willoughby hurried to reply. "But I didn't want to make any plans without you. I saved such of the equipment as could not be replaced, and I saved the personnel — after that, it's up to you. . . ." And as DeWitt silently stared at the middle of his desk, Willoughby added, uncertainly, "At least I thought so. . . ."

"Well, you've made a very grave decision without me," DeWitt said. His eyes, in which there usually was some residue of humor, were cold and serious. "I just wanted to know if there were any other decisions, not yet carried out, but already made."

"No," assured Willoughby, "none whatever. You seem to suspect that I've overstepped my authority. I haven't, sir. Here we were, in this predicament, and no word from you — God, I've moved heaven and earth to get in touch with you! And something had to be done — so we put it up to General Farrish. . . ."

DeWitt's expectant silence made Willoughby's words spill out. "It was the General who ordered us to remove the tubes and the other parts of the machinery. They're irreplaceable. You know that, sir. And the transmitter *was* under fire; every man, every officer who was out there, will confirm it. And only the road through Arlon was open, and that was in danger of being cut off any time. I'm so happy you got through all right, sir! Take all these factors, put yourself into the situation here, and I'm sure you'd have given the same orders yourself. There was nothing else to be done. I discussed it with everybody, with Crerar, with Loomis — everybody; I didn't rely on my own judgment alone; though in the end, of course, neither I nor any of the others did the deciding. General Farrish made the decision.

393

If he had said *Stay on!* we would have stayed on. But he said *The equipment and the men are more important than a few days of Blah Blah on the air* — so — here are the orders, sir. . . ."

He shoved a sheaf of papers across the desk at DeWitt. DeWitt picked them up with two fingers. He didn't read them. He just let them swing, right — left — right — left, looking at Willoughby, whose eyes followed their movement.

Then Willoughby tore his eyes away. He had done nothing out of line. Did DeWitt think he could punish him by silence? Emphatically, he concluded, "So, one group of men left last night, sir; and the other is leaving tonight. . . ." He paused. "That is, if you agree."

DeWitt dropped the orders; then, as if reconsidering, he handed them back to Willoughby.

"Of course, you explained to the General what it would mean if we closed the station?"

"Naturally. I put the question to him in all its aspects. I stressed that some people would feel it was like admitting defeat — but he didn't see it that way. He laughed it off. He said there was no defeat as long as his men were in the field, and the war would be able to get along very well for a few days without our Blah Blah. . . . I'm repeating myself, I'm sorry, but that's what he said."

For the first time since his return, DeWitt smiled at Willoughby. "I'll admit that you've acted correctly. No blame can be attached to you. There is nobody in this Army who would, or could, find you guilty."

Willoughby smiled back at DeWitt; but at the Colonel's next words, the smile froze on his face.

"The fault, I would say, lies with me." DeWitt again stared at the center of his bare desk. "Not in my going away to Paris — nobody could foresee the beginning of the German offensive. Not in my inability to come back in time — I tried hard enough, but most roads were blocked, and spare me the details of my trip. My fault lay in the selection of the man I trusted. Because I am responsible for you and your actions — not Farrish. At least that's the code I believe in."

Code! Willoughby thought. He wants to live by a code. He admits that I can't be blamed and in the same breath he blames me and absolves me by taking the blame upon himself. He thinks he's Jesus. I wish I knew what happened on his trip; he's not all there.

"Those men," said DeWitt — "those men who were where the Nazis attacked — do you think they didn't stand and fight? Or at least try to?"

"Some stayed and fought, and some ran. That's only human. What do you expect from people?"

"Perhaps it goes deeper. Perhaps it depends on what you believe in."

394

"I can handle a situation only as I see it," said Willoughby, "and with the men I've got. One of them shoots himself in the foot and gets himself taken off to the rear. That's Crabtrees. And Loomis comes to me and says . . ."

"What did he say?"

"I don't know any more. But it was clear that he wouldn't be able to stand the pressure. That's incidental. The main thing is: A radio station isn't an artillery battery. Tubes aren't howitzers. Howitzers can be replaced, these tubes can't. I had to think of another day — of the day when we'd come back and speak up once more! What a day that'll be! Let the Nazis laugh now, we'll see who laughs last!"

He waited for DeWitt's reaction. There was none.

Suddenly he cried out, "I don't give a damn how you feel about me personally! I'm satisfied that I've done what I thought right, and if you don't approve — well, you shouldn't have gone away. What do you think the men thought when they learned you were gone just when things were getting disagreeable?"

"I said it was my fault."

"Yes, you say that — but the way you say it! You try to shovel the guilt on me! All right, I can take it. I've got Farrish's orders, and he's the General, and what he says, goes."

"Certainly!"

"Then what's the complaint?"

"I suggest you calm down. I suggest you apply for a transfer after you've calmed down. I will endorse your request, favorably."

"So that's it. You can't afford a real accounting either, so you want me out. Well, perhaps I should say now that General Farrish has asked me — "

Willoughby stopped. It occurred to him to ask himself why DeWitt sat there, taking all this vituperation, all this insolent, insubordinate ranting. Jesus, again. Willoughby was furious. He bit his lips.

"I'm sorry, sir, I lost my temper. Nobody likes to be called a coward."

"I never used the word."

"You implied it."

"Not even that," disputed DeWitt. "A man must act according to what he is and what he believes in. Shall we drop the subject?"

"As you wish. . . ."

"I wish to drop it. And as long as you're under my command, will you please give orders to the men still here that they are to stay, and will you recall the group that has already taken off?"

"Yes, sir. But General Farrish — "

"My responsibility, Major."

"And if we're cut off . . . ?"

"You have a weapon, haven't you? You've learned to fire it, haven't you? Save the last bullet for yourself!"

"I have every intention to live," said Willoughby, matter-of-factly.

"Yes," agreed DeWitt. "But how?"

Yates was waiting in the corridor outside DeWitt's office. He had no official reason for wanting to see the Old Man. He just felt the need to talk to him.

Much as Yates had opposed Willoughby's arguments for closing down the station and retreating into safety, he had been affected by them. Willoughby could have been right, couldn't he? Willoughby was shrewd, good at evaluating a situation.

Willoughby came out of the Colonel's office and walked past Yates without so much as a glance or nod. Yates knocked at the Colonel's door. There was no answer. He knocked once more, listened; when still no sound came from the room, he turned the knob.

DeWitt lay slumped over the desk, his head in his arms. It seemed like a gesture of utter fatigue. Yates felt like an intruder. He was about to retreat and close the door, when DeWitt looked up.

"Oh, Yates!" he said, "come in."

He blew his nose with a strong, trumpetlike sound, stroked his stubborn hair, cleared his throat, and was ready.

Yates sat down. He found a horsehair sticking out of the collar of his jacket and began to pull at it, and avoided looking at DeWitt's face. Give him the chance to set the stage, he thought. He still was not over the feeling of having caught the older man unaware.

DeWitt picked himself up. "Well — what can I do for you?"

"Nothing, sir." Yates was embarrassed. "I just happened to come by. So I knocked at your door. I wanted to say, Hello, and — we're glad you're back. . . ."

He half-rose.

"No, stay!" said the Colonel. "I want to talk."

Yates was afraid that DeWitt, discouraged and tired, might say something that he would regret at some later time. "We won't remain closed down?" he asked hastily.

"Hell, no!"

"Then — what's the matter, sir?"

"I've made a bad mistake."

Yates remembered Willoughby in Rollingen, smart, clear-minded, analytical — and in Paris, fighting for his position — and in Vallères, building himself up. "A man is mostly what you want to see in him," he suggested.

396

DeWitt said wearily, "I've got a war to fight. I have no mind to carry on additional little wars in our own ranks. . . ."

"You may have to. It's a complicated war."

"I've had a bad trip," DeWitt said. "I've seen men die, again. I've seen too many die, in my lifetime. I was in the first war, and now I'm in this one. You're born into a community, it gives you your chance — to develop yourself, to build a home, to raise a family — so you owe it something. If there's war, well, then it's your war. But in these wars, I've seen some of the nicest people I've known — wiped out. I don't object to it, you understand! If it makes sense! Tell me, do you think it makes sense?"

Does it? Yates asked himself. With Tolachian unnecessarily killed, with Thorpe in a ward for the insane, with Yasha in the saddle, with the liberated transferred into DP camps, the Spaniards without country, the Yugoslavs ready to cut each other's throats, with the people of Ensdorf murdered, with Troy throwing in his precious men, with Willoughby and Loomis choking off the station, the one voice that spoke and gave hope — does it make sense?

"I really don't expect you to give me an answer," said DeWitt. "How does your wife feel about it?"

"About what?" Yates didn't understand the question.

"Ever thought about what she's going through?"

"Yes. Particularly now."

"Mine didn't want me to go overseas," DeWitt said. "At my age, I could have stayed home. I went. I hurt her very much. If you've been with a woman for going on thirty years, ups and downs, children and crises, you rub off each other's rough edges, and finally you are like two smooth boards of wood so planed to each other that, if you hold them close, there's a natural adhesion. . . ."

Ruth, thought Yates. He saw her, now, in the perspective of life, of those two smooth boards fitting together. And Thérèse fell into her proper place, as a substitute, poor dear.

"I'm going to write Ruth that it makes sense," Yates said quietly, "and I hope the letter gets through. The thing can make sense if we put some sense into it — now, and after the war, too."

"Let's tackle the *Now* end of it first," said DeWitt.

Yates smiled. "I may have a little project for when we reopen the station. It involves two Germans we caught in American uniform. One of them, I myself put on the griddle. They belong to this Operation Buzzard. Their names are Heberle and Mulsinger. . . ."

That night the weather broke. The fog lifted. The stars and the plush-black, fresh sky appeared like new skin after a disease. The air became crisp and clear and dry, the slush turned into ice, and the snow became powdery.

And in the morning the sun rose with a brilliance rare in winter; there wasn't a feather of a cloud. Over the ground torn by battle rose an unblemished, light blue orb, magnificent in its height and transparence.

To the men it was more than a sign. It was real. For up there, coming from all directions, flying on different levels, were the bombers; even higher, surpassing them, the tiny silvery specks of the fighters; and close to the ground hovered the Cubs, seeing the earth as a neat arrangement of squares and lines and circles and dots.

A new and different roar added itself to the old sounds of the battle, something more frightening in its intensity than anything heard until now: the seed of bombs falling from the sky in pre-arranged patterns, sticks following each other like darts, arriving in close sequence, screaming, tearing up the ground, whining victory and blasting the Germans' tender lifelines.

The great protective cover under which the Germans had operated was torn from them. Every move they made was seen the moment it was started; every tank, every truck, yes, every man that stirred, was like a pin on a map, and the tracks on the snow were like arrows pointing to the target.

The Army, which had been fighting blind, had regained its eyes, and seeing, it could reduce the enemy to his proper proportions. It saw that he depended on a few roads which could be blocked at strategic junctions. It saw that he had not been able to consolidate his positions, that he had spread out like a thin-fingered hand, each finger vulnerable.

In the crisp, sober light of the day, the specter that had risen in the fog lost its terror; it was, after all, the same German Army that had been beaten since Normandy, with the same weaknesses as always — lack of motorized equipment, lack of air force, lack of gasoline and oil. As always, their tanks had to be dug in when the fuel gave out. Converted into artillery pieces, they were like sitting ducks to the American fighter-bombers. The hunt was on — at first against columns and squadrons, then against single vehicles, and in the end against single men running and scurrying for their lives. The armored spearheads which the Germans had driven up to the Meuse found themselves cut off; the trek back began. And while they were harrowed from the air, and harrowed from the flanks by the quick stabs of American light armor, the base of the German bulge was whittled down by Farrish and Patton hammering up from the south, by Hodges forming the anvil in the north. When the 101st Airborne at Bastogne was relieved, the battle was won.

Field Marshal von Klemm–Borowski blamed it on the weather; and true enough, with the lifting of his great ally, the fog, the tide had turned against him. But the Field Marshal was mistaken — he would have won regardless of fog, had he been able to roll up the American front to a greater extent, had be been able to broaden the base of the Bulge.

He was defeated by men. They were average men, without rank and name. But they had that remarkable American quality: They were able to put down their foot and say, *Wait a minute, Bud. Don't push us around. Let's see what this is all about.* Perhaps they didn't say it in these words. But they felt it, and they acted on it, and they stood fast, and many of them gave their lives. And this collective attitude came about in spite of the difference in personal background — in spite of the fact that some didn't know what it was all about, and what the Bulge Battle meant; that some of them did; that most were afraid, and few weren't; that all of them were miserable and cold and tired and worn with nerves frazzled. In the hour of crisis, they proved themselves citizens of the Republic.

I I

THE MILITARY COURT sentenced Heberle and Mulsinger to death, to be shot at dawn, as was customary.

It was not until the two men were informed that their appeals for mercy had been turned down that they began to believe they were lost. Heberle cursed Pettinger; he cursed himself — hadn't he had the chance to step out of ranks, to refuse the whole thing? Eventually, he settled into a deep despondency from which he emerged only once, to write an erratic letter to his mother. Mulsinger coughed and wept that his wound was painful, which was probably true, but which irritated Heberle.

"It's going to stop hurting you soon enough. If I were you, you idiot, I'd bless every minute that it hurts — as long as you feel pain, you're alive. Me . . . I feel nothing. . . ."

And he returned to his moody silence.

He listened for every step outside the heavy door of their cell. There must be someone above the Commanding General. The Americans had a President. Perhaps, at the last moment, there would be a reprieve. . . . Every passer-by evoked a shock of hope; and each spurt of optimism flickered out with the ebbing sound of the footsteps.

He jumped as the door was opened to permit two Americans to enter. In the light of the single bulb, encased in wire mesh, he recognized the Lieutenant who had interviewed him in Luxemburg, shortly after his capture, and who had ordered him beaten if he didn't confess.

Well, he had confessed! He had done everything demanded of him, and the end was the same as if he had said nothing and taken the beating. He was only a little man; he had let himself in for it, and now they were tramping all over him. Especially this Lieutenant. There was nothing merciful in his face. . . . Heberle started. This Lieutenant was the one who had hinted at mercy in the first place! Perhaps he returned now to bring mercy and life!

Yates pointed to the approximate center of the room. "Let's set up the mike here, Clements!"

Heberle saw that the door of the cell had been left open to allow an exit for the cable which ran from the foot of the microphone. For a moment, he considered making a dash for freedom; then, through the open slit of door, he saw the guard outside.

"I'll let you know through the mike when we're ready, Clements," said Yates. "I'll give you time enough to get the recording machine going."

Sergeant Clements nodded and left.

Heberle eyed the microphone dubiously.

"Well, remember me?" asked Yates.

"Yes, *Herr Leutnant*," Heberle said warily. "Are they going to let us live?"

"This is the other fellow?" Yates went on. "Wounded? How does he feel?"

Heberle forced a laugh. "How can you feel, sir, if you know it's going to be over in the morning? . . . Is there no hope?"

Mulsinger, reclining on his cot, raised his head.

It was an interesting problem, thought Yates. How did men feel who were to die in the morning? He probably would find out.

They wanted an answer, though. Yates wasn't going to play cat and mouse with them. He had no time for it, and he didn't enjoy that kind of game.

"Now, you know what you've done," he said. "You know the penalty."

Mulsinger's head sank back on the cot. Heberle grew paler and said, "Yes, sir. But you promised me . . . !"

Yates knew exactly what he had promised this man.

"Let's get this straight, Heberle, so that you don't go into the other world with an unnecessary grudge. I said we might deal differently with you if you confessed. But I had to beat your confession out of you — to be exact, you couldn't take even the threat of a beating and broke down beforehand. So that's for the record."

"I don't want to die," Heberle said miserably.

"D'you think the man you went out to kill wanted to die?"

"But we didn't kill him!"

"Not because you didn't try! . . . And do you think that all the defenseless people that your Army, your SS, your Secret Police have killed in the course of this war, and still are killing, wanted to die?"

"But I have nothing to do with that! Don't you see, sir — I only followed orders! I'm not responsible!"

Yates found that no understanding whatever was left in him for this man's problems, viewpoint, and feelings. And this was not because he had the man in his power, squirming, but because there was only one side that was right in this fight, and that was his own side.

He said sharply, "Let's get another thing straight, Heberle — and you, Mulsinger! The time has come when men have to stand up to the things they do. This hiding behind your superiors is no good any more — because, no doubt, they in turn will hide behind their superiors, and so on up the line, until nobody is guilty but one man; until all the suffering of the war is atoned for by one bullet in that one man's brain. It's not going to work that way. If you have a heap of dung, the lowest layer stinks just as much, even though you take a shovelful off the top. You're going to be judged by what you, yourselves, have done — every single one of you."

Heberle understood that he could expect nothing from Yates, and his anguish submerged every military taboo drilled into him. "Leave us alone!" he cried. "Take that thing with you! Go! Get out!" He pushed Yates and dragged the microphone toward the door.

The guard stuck in his head. "Anything the matter, sir? Need any help?"

"No, thanks," said Yates.

He took the microphone from Heberle's hands. Heberle seemed to have exhausted himself, and fell on the cot, next to the apathetic Mulsinger.

Yates considered the situation. He had gotten himself into a blind alley. He had eased his chest considerably; he had demonstrated to two guys, who had to listen, how tough he could be; but this was of no intrinsic interest to them, and it wasn't exactly part of his job.

He had to find an approach that would enlist their co-operation. It wouldn't be easy — this was their last night; he had made that very plain to them. He sat down on the other cot; between himself and them stood the waiting microphone.

After a long period of complete silence Heberle burst out nervously, "Why did you bring that thing in here?"

His tone was hostile, as if he didn't expect a reply. Yates, who had been waiting for this, said indifferently, "The microphone? That's to give you your last chance."

Heberle was on his feet. "What do you mean, *chance* — sir? What do we have to do?"

"The microphone is connected with a recording machine mounted in a truck that's down in the prison yard. . . . No, don't be worried, it isn't switched on. Not a word of what we've said up to now has been recorded."

"I get it," said Heberle. "You want us to say something. What do you want us to say? What are you going to do with it?"

Yates rubbed the warts on his hands. He didn't like Heberle's sudden willingness.

"I'm not going to tell you what to say — " he began, and was again interrupted by Heberle.

"If we say the right thing, will we — will you let us live? I know what you're going to use us for — propaganda. I don't care. Use us for anything. But if we help you, you must help us." He hesitated and then said, "You gave me a promise once, and you didn't keep it — how do I know you won't fool us again?"

"Because I'm not making you any offer. But I'm giving you the chance to talk to your people, to the soldiers of your Army, on this, your last night — to tell them what you went out to do, and who ordered you, and how you were tried, and why you have to die. I'll give you the chance to warn them — so that others won't have to go the way you will go. Do you understand?"

Neither Heberle nor Mulsinger answered. They seemed to be thinking.

"We'll broadcast the recording you make over the most powerful radio station we have. Everybody will hear you. Your voice will live after your death; maybe that's how you can do something decent at last."

Heberle chewed on the knuckles of his hand. Then he raised his face, ugly in its distortion, and in a cracked voice asked, "If I say the right thing, will you give me a week more to live — three days — twenty-four hours . . . ?"

A strange glow had come over Mulsinger. He lifted himself on his elbows; his horselike face pushed forward, figurehead of a sinking galleon.

"You said our voice will live after our death — is that what you said?" He coughed.

"That's what I said."

"Good! Good!" Mulsinger was keeping himself erect with effort. "I will speak. And he will speak, too. Don't argue, Heberle, you will. This is some joke! Our voices will live. Bring the microphone here. I can't get up without help, I'm wounded, you see, sir. I will speak — how we were betrayed, by this swine Pettinger who sent us into this — how they told us the battle was already won and the Americans would be rolled up and smashed — and how they broke their promise — and how we're paying for it — "

He had a fit of coughing. When his breath returned to him, he asked submissively, "Can I say a few words to my mother in Breslau?"

"Yes, you may, surely!" said Yates.

He wasn't clear about what had brought on Mulsinger's unexpected confessional mood; but he saw that it was carrying the other man, too. Was it that they recognized their guilt and were willing to accept it? Or was it that they appreciated the drama of such a broadcast, and so forgot the volleys that would make it a posthumous appeal? Or, did they still have the hope that, even without his promise, they would be spared if only they were very, very good in their performance?

But Yates had no time to puzzle this one out.

He placed his mouth close to the microphone and spoke into it: "Testing — One Two Three Four — Testing — Ready for Take? — Ready? — Take!"

Yates stayed half the night with Heberle and Mulsinger. The recording progressed not too badly — several re-takes had to be made; and, in the end, Yates had to restrain the two prisoners from wanting to do it over.

"This is not a rehearsed show!" Yates tried to explain, half-amused, half-annoyed. "Don't forget this is real life; it's you, talking under the strain of what you're living through! It's perfectly all right to fumble, to look for words — in fact, that makes it more effective!"

But Heberle didn't agree, and neither did Mulsinger.

"That's the difference between you Americans and us Germans," Heberle pointed out sincerely. "Whatever we do, we want to do thoroughly, as near to perfection as possible. It's one of the national German traits. We have to be better than anyone else, because we're jammed into the middle of Europe — we don't have the space and the natural resources you have in America, and we don't have the British colonies to fall back on. We have only our quality."

It was ludicrous. A few hours prior to their complete annihilation, these characters were rattling off the Pan-German line. Everything about them was a lie — it was just because they had not been thorough, just because their human qualities were anything but superior, that they had been caught and would be killed. But they didn't see it. They sailed through without any doubts in themselves; and the moment any outside influence took them out of their immediate fears, they reverted back to what they always had been. It presaged nothing good for a basic change in the national make-up of a defeated Germany.

Yates permitted them to polish their last statements to the very dots on the *i*'s. Why not let them have their fun if it made them co-operative? He would cut the recordings anyhow, and select the parts he considered best.

And when they were all through, Mulsinger pleaded that he had one last wish — if it could be granted?

"Is there a possibility of playing the record back to us?"

They would have to go down to the truck, Yates thought; but he saw no objection to that. Apparently, these men now believed themselves important cogs in the American propaganda machine — or was it just that Heberle and Mulsinger instinctively considered this turn-about a part of their lives, and one they wanted to live to the fullest as long as they were breathing?

Yates got the necessary permission from the Prison Commandant; complete, with guards, and with men to support the wobbling Mulsinger, they trooped down to the truck. Clements, patient and noncommittal, put the recording on the player — and the two who were doomed listened with fascination.

Yates saw them nod their heads in approval at each point they considered particularly well taken, at each phrase especially apt — "This will show them!" Heberle's face seemed to express, and Mulsinger had tears in his eyes as he listened to his farewell to his old mother. Even in going over to their enemies and in playing the enemies' game, they were still — German.

They returned to their cell, satisfied.

When Yates finally took his leave to find some hours of sleep before the execution, Heberle and Mulsinger were at the point of shaking his hand, and would have done so, had he not clasped his hands behind his back.

Yates was awakened by Clements after what seemed to him only a few minutes of sleep. "It's time," said Clements. "I've prepared everything. The mike's in the yard. We're ready."

"Did you get some sleep?"

"Not much," Clements smiled limply. "I'm sort of excited. It's my first execution."

"Mine, too — come to think of it," said Yates. "Feels funny, doesn't it?"

"Yes, sir."

"Would you think I'm cruel or brutal by nature?"

"No, not at all, Lieutenant. . . ."

"I used to say it was unnecessary, cruel, stupid to take men's lives systematically." He pulled up his tie and let his finger tips explore the stubbles on his cheeks. "I don't think so any more. To me, these guys are like bugs. You don't have any compunctions using DDT, do you?"

"Even after last night?" Clements asked.

"Particularly after last night. But maybe I'm just talking. Maybe I can't imagine what it means until I've seen it."

He combed his hair, and was through with his morning toilet. He gave his last instructions to Clements, "Keep the record turning all the way through — even if I make pauses. We'll do the cutting when we're back at the station."

Yates went down to the yard. Last night, the prison had seemed like a whole block of buildings, but in the faint, gray, first light of the January morning, it had shrunk.

404

It was chilly. The few persons assembled didn't say much beyond a laconic "Hello!" and "Damned early to get up!" as Yates shook hands with them: the Signal Corps photographer, the doctor, the chaplain, and the Major from the Judge Advocate General's office, representing the Court.

From far away, through the gateway to the yard, Yates heard the marching steps of the execution squad. He went to his microphone and began to speak:

"And this is the end of Ensign Heberle and Sergeant Mulsinger. We're in the yard of the Verdun prison where they've spent their last days since being sentenced to death — you're now hearing the firing squad march into the yard — a Lieutenant and ten men. . . ."

"Column — halt! Left — face! At ease!"

"Near the wall of the yard two poles have been erected — now Heberle and Mulsinger are being led in — Mulsinger, who was lightly wounded during his capture, supports himself on the shoulders of two prison guards — Heberle has made himself dead weight and is being half carried — they both know what is going to happen and why — they have spoken to their fellow soldiers in the German Army and to their people — a warning that the American Army doesn't tolerate any infringement on the laws of warfare — espionage, sabotage by German soldiers — now they have arrived at the poles and are being strapped to them — an American Major steps forward and reads the sentence of the Military Court — he reads it in English first, then in German — though both prisoners understand English very well — they were selected for their criminal mission because of their ability to speak it — now the Major has finished and goes back — the Chaplain takes his place — he talks to them. . . ."

"Vater unser, der Du bist im Himmel — Our Father, which art in heaven . . ."

"Their lips move, they are praying with him. . . ."

Yates fell silent. He caught himself, his lips were moving, too. It wasn't so easy. Now that the two men were strapped to the poles, had become part of them, had ceased to be the personalities they once were, they became quivering flesh that was about to be torn. Yates swallowed. He forced into his mind the image of Troy's dead men, murdered in cold blood; of the uprooted, homeless, and starved in the DP Camp; of the scars on the body of Andrej Kavalov, the Russian Marine; of the stern, condemning

405

face of Mademoiselle Godefroy, the teacher of Isigny. And the images came and blotted out this one, and he could go on:

"The Chaplain has finished — he goes back — a Sergeant comes and pulls black hoods over the prisoners' heads — now it's a matter of seconds only — the Lieutenant comes to attention — he is about to give the orders to his men — some of them carry blanks in their rifles — so no one will know who fired the fatal shot — the Lieutenant commands —

"Ready! . . . Aim! Fire!"

The volley rang out. Yates saw the bodies slump a little, just a little, their heads dangling.

With hardly any voice left to him, he whispered into the mike:

"The Chaplain and the Doctor go forward — the remains of Heberle and Mulsinger are released from the poles — laid to the ground — the Doctor kneels down — he nods — they're dead — dead. . . ."

"Coming along for a drink?" It was the Major from the Judge Advocate General's office.

"No, thanks," said Yates. "I prefer coffee."

"That can be arranged, too. They're serving coffee upstairs for the whole party. You know," the Major continued, "the trouble with these affairs is that they always come on an empty stomach."

The relief of Victory worked and fought for gives war its moments of compensation. However hard-boiled you may be, you cannot escape the emotionalism of such moments. You feel a fraternal tenderness for the men at your side. You are careful not to show it even though you are fairly certain that the others feel as you do. This isn't the kind of Army that goes in for speeches, handclasps, embraces, and kisses on ruddy cheeks. Wisecracks and drinking are the accepted mode of expression. Mostly, it ends up in a brawl.

For Yates, this moment came with the reopening of the radio station. It came faster than he had anticipated — the engineers worked prodigiously to install the giant tubes and the other equipment that had been ripped out and transported to the rear by Loomis. The engineers were still at work when the men at the studios gathered, waiting for the phone call that would tell them the transmitter was ready, tell them the station could go on the air once more.

Yates sat in the very chair he had used while listening to his obituary from BBC London, during the darkest, most hopeless hour of the Bulge Battle. He smiled nervously at Bing.

Bing laughed, "I guess those London monitors, who reported us finished and done for, are going to look like damned fools! I hope they choke when they have to eat their own words!"

He switched on the receiving set. The German station masquerading as Radio Luxemburg, and wobbling about on its usurped frequency, was still active — true, a trifle squeaky, but persistent in its falsetto.

Yates grumbled to Bing, "To hell with the British monitors! Keep the Germans in mind."

Clements nodded toward the receiver and reveled, "Are *we* going to drown *him* out!"

Only Abramovici was not fully happy. He remembered the delicatessen of defeat, and inquired whether everything really had been eaten up during that terrible time. "A typical case of panic resulting in the waste of food!" he commented.

Clements asked suddenly, "Say — do you hear what I hear?"

They turned their ears to the receiver. Above the feeble German voice another sound was coming through — a faint but steady sound, hardly audible, as if somebody with a terribly long breath was blowing into the air waves.

"The carrier wave! She works!"

And then the call came through from the transmitter — everything was clear! They were ready to go on the air.

Bing ran out and upstairs to the broadcasting studio. He was to pinch-hit as announcer — some of the regular personnel had not yet returned from Verdun.

DeWitt strolled into Yates's room. "As you were!" he said genially and perched himself on the corner of the desk. His broad hands came to rest on his thigh; he leaned forward, intently, and smiled, "Quite an occasion!"

Yates looked at his watch. It was two minutes to nine in the evening. He followed the second hand around the dial, twice. When it touched the *60* on top of the dial a second time, the room, at a stroke, was filled with sound.

They played the anthems of the United Nations — first "God Save the King," then "The Marseillaise," then "The Internationale" — and then the strains of "The Star-Spangled Banner."

Yates had heard it so often; and often, it had meant little. It spelled Legion conventions, and openings of Fairs, hullabaloo, and cheap, flat-footed patriotism.

But this time, he had a lump in his throat. It *was* still waving, and they'd done a little bit to keep it up there, and the flag was more than just a piece of gaudy cloth — it was how you lived under it, and who had died for it, and the meaning that those who carried it gave to it.

Army rule was to remain seated when the music of the hymn was canned. And certainly it was canned as it came over the receiver, as it obliterated the usurping German voice. But somehow, it tore them from their chairs. And as the last swinging fanfare, *the Home of the Brave,* faded out, they remained standing, each man alone, and yet each aware that his very absorption was shared by every other man in the room.

Yates was very close to his country, then; perhaps for the first time. It was a wonderful, sweeping feeling. And he thought he wanted to hang on to it; and dimly, he perceived that he might be able to do it. It depended on what kind of country it was and what kind of country you made of it, on whom it belonged to and who formed its destiny. He felt that you could reduce the great slogans, so seductive and yet so empty, to something real and human and warm and genuine, to something profoundly stirring — a call to action.

Book Five

MUFFLED VICTORY

I

"I just remained behind. It was as easy as that."

The German Major looked obliquely at Yates, his slender fingers latching and unlatching.

"How did you know our troops would come your way, Major — Dehn's the name?"

"Erich Wolfgang von Dehn."

Dehn had been advertised as a prize catch. On surrendering he had explained, in precise if somewhat halting English, that he had inside knowledge of the German Army's morale work, and wished to be taken to the appropriate American authority. The regimental interrogator had agreed and sent him to Propaganda Intelligence in Luxemburg.

"Well?"

Dehn smiled. "During these last weeks, I was attached to the staff of Field Marshal von Klemm-Borowski's Army Group."

"I see."

"Do you know the Rolands-Eck, Lieutenant?"

"I've heard of it."

"Beautiful place. Leave it to the rear echelon to pick the best. The Rolands-Eck lies right on the shore of the Rhine, near Bingen — a splendid hotel. It was almost like a sanitarium; that's where I really belong, in a sanitarium. . . ."

Yates looked at him. "I'm afraid our accommodations — "

"Oh, that's perfectly all right. Very nice house you're keeping me in, and your little man who's guarding me is most kind."

Yates thought he'd tell Abramovici to be a little less kind.

"I took long walks," Dehn continued, "and thought it all out. I love the German landscape. The Rhine, rolling between those wonderful old mountains. Spring had just come, and the hills were a magic light green, dozens of different shades, and the sun gleaming on the water as it has

409

gleamed for centuries — golden, the gold that's hidden in the Rhine, the gold of the Nibelungs. . . . I don't suppose you've heard of it?"

Yates didn't answer.

"It's an old German saga. We Germans go in for that — mysticism, National Fate — do you follow me?"

"Yes." Pleasant voice, thought Yates, cultured. "Get to the point."

"These are intangibles, of course!" said Dehn. "But you Americans will have to develop a feeling for them if you want to succeed. Germans listen to that kind of appeal. We're a nation of dreamers. That's where I can be of help to you. You are engaged in propaganda. But you are Americans. I've read your material. It is very good — but it has this tone foreign to us, too materialistic. It never quite breaks down the barrier to the German soul. So, in my lonely walks along the Rhine, I thought about that. And when the time came, and we were ordered to leave the beautiful Rolands-Eck, I just took another walk."

He nodded. He was a romanticist at heart. Pamela, his wife, always said so when his ineptness at managing the Rintelen Steel Mills brought down the wrath of his father-in-law, Maximilian von Rintelen.

"It was a long and satisfying walk, Lieutenant. And when I returned, everybody was gone. I sat in the lobby of the hotel and read and drank some wine and waited for your troops. I knew they were crossing the Rhine at many places."

"And you're offering us your services?"

"Yes," Dehn said blandly.

"Why?"

"It might help to save some lives. . . ."

"Let's stick to the facts!" said Yates.

"All right, we've lost the war!" admitted Dehn.

"So you wish to join the winners in good time?"

Dehn waved aside the question and its implications. "We've lost this war — but it's like losing a game in a match that will go on endlessly."

"Wasn't this one enough for you?"

"It was the wrong kind of war," Dehn explained. "Instead of fighting the East while being backed by the West, our leaders made us take on both East and West. But what can you expect from *parvenus?*"

"What do you think is going to happen?"

"We're out, now. And yet we aren't. This war, *Herr Leutnant,* merely postponed the great decision that has to come — the decision between your way of life, yours and mine, and that of our real enemy, the oriental despotism masquerading behind utopian slogans. By fighting us, alongside your Eastern allies, you've knocked down your own barrier against the advancing East, and you yourselves will have to erect a new one, and post your own men as sentries. And when the time comes, you'll have to call on us for help. You're too far away in your America. And you don't have any illusions about the strength of the British, I hope. . . ."

There he sat, his legs crossed comfortably, his long hand nervously stroking his knee well-rounded in his tailored breeches. Yates wanted to slap that decadent face in which every feature was just one degree too fine.

"Suppose we don't want to make another war?" he asked.

"I don't like war either, Lieutenant. This one has knocked the bottom out of me, and I won't be much good for anything to come. But the nations are lined up according to laws they can't change; and war seems to be the beginning and the end of everything."

He searched Yates's eyes for an expression that would show him whether he was safe. Then he went on.

"I've tried to help build peace. Many Germans have. We tried to unite Europe as a bulwark against the East. I've been in the administration of Occupied France. We wanted them to collaborate; and I, certainly, have used only the most humane measures. And what was the reward for our planning, for a policy with the perspective of history in mind? The nations were incited against us, and finally you landed and spoiled the European peace. And so it'll go on — and on — and on. . . ."

Yates made a mental note of Dehn's occupation service in France.

"I cannot decide whether we'll use you in any future war, Major," he said. "Get back to this one. When did you become convinced that Germany had lost?"

Dehn settled back. He felt on safe ground again. "That I've known for a long while. I saw it the first time in Paris. I was running away from you then — and frankly, I've been on the run ever since. Paris . . ."

His eyes narrowed, he seemed to stare back into the past.

"Unshaved, dirty, my uniform in rags, I sat in a room in the Hotel Scribe. I was with *Obersturmbannführer* Pettinger."

Outside, the spring sun cast its rays against the window, but inside this house, the damp cold persisted and now merged with the shiver Yates suddenly felt.

"Erich Pettinger?"

"Yes! The *Herr Obersturmbannführer* last was head of my staff section at Army Group Klemm-Borowski."

Thorpe in his cell, insane, yet clinging to his belief in the man he thought Yates was; Frau Petrik, running into the interminable darkness of the Ensdorf mine; Heberle and Mulsinger tied to their posts, their heads dangling — Yates felt his face freezing, but he made his lips smile.

"What kind of person is Colonel Pettinger, really?"

"What do you know about him?" Dehn asked back.

"Militarily speaking? Quite a bit." Yates's tone was one of idle curiosity. "I mean, personally, what's he like?"

"*Ein Schwein,*" Dehn said unequivocally.

Yates raised his brows.

"You think this is the first time I'm a prisoner?" Dehn's voice rose. "Well, it's not. He's been holding me all this time. He knew I was cracked to bits. He got a kick out of pushing me into duties I was unable to perform. I was his personal guinea pig, you understand?"

"How long do you know him?"

"Years. Know him since the '20's. Know his whole career. Long before 1933, he went around beating up Communists — that's good training because you really risk very little; you always have the police on your side. And he's been beating up people ever since, one way or another."

Yates said nothing.

"I'm a sick man. I've been running since Paris, always running. A man wants to stop sometime! I could have gotten out of the war — I married into the Rintelen family — big people, steel, you know? But something always interfered — Pettinger! He persecuted me — "

"You've already said that."

Dehn was frantically kneading his hands. "To take a sick man and push him into a field command, in the offensive — and he came along, too, just to watch me break down!"

It was a sad-sack story. But Yates listened, in the hope that Dehn would finally come forward with some concrete data on Pettinger. "Field command?" he asked. "What kind of field command?"

"An armored battalion. We got to the Meuse, too, and there we were ground to pieces — except that Pettinger fled in time. He dragged me with him. He didn't want to lose his private whipping boy."

"I see," said Yates. "And that's where you got your dose of battle fatigue?"

"No. By the time we got to the Meuse, I was already no more than a bundle of twitching nerves. The thing happened before. I know the exact moment. . . ." Dehn made his weak chin come to rest on his thumbs. "A lonely road north of Luxemburg — we were pushing west, running — running forward for a change. . . ." He chuckled. "You know the fog, and the hills there — we ran into some resistance, not much — a couple of squads or so — we caught them — "

Dehn stopped. How was he going to finish this story? He sensed the change in his interrogator.

He shrugged. "Well — these night battles are always enervating. . . ."

Yates was looking at him, hard. It was a hundred-to-one shot — or maybe, with Pettinger involved, it wasn't. Yates decided to play his hunch.

"You were on this east-west road, Major — about a mile before it hits the north road to Bastogne? Remember the telegraph poles? They were damaged, some of them leaning dangerously, held up only by the wires? And there was a hill to the right, with some brush — "

Dehn's head shot up. Then his eyes focused on Yates, questioning, terrified.

Quietly, Yates said: "Who was it who had those men killed?"

"You don't think it was me!" Dehn jumped up, leaned over the table toward Yates, swaying a little.

"Answer me, will you?"

"Pettinger," Dehn whispered. "That's what finished me . . . !" And, his voice growing stronger, "I refused to do it. I refused the responsibility. He gave the orders. Do you think I'm mad enough to desert to you with that thing on my conscience?"

"But you were in command, Major!"

"He was the ranking officer!"

"You took his orders? You permitted your American prisoners to be assassinated?"

"Lieutenant!" Dehn raised his long hands and let them drop in a gesture of futility.

Both men were silent. Yates felt the regular pumping of his heart. *And none shall escape* . . . A line he'd read somewhere.

Then Dehn said hoarsely, "I tried to plead with him."

"What did he say?"

"He laughed. . . ."

"He laughed," repeated Yates.

"Yes, he laughed!" Dehn insisted, as if Pettinger's laugh were his own exoneration. He slumped down in his chair.

Yates looked at his warts and compared his hands with Dehn's slim and elegant ones. "As for our appeals to the Germans, Major — I think we'll have to get along without your help."

"What'll you do with me?" asked Dehn, his voice strained.

"You served on occupation duty in France — " Yates thought of Mademoiselle Godefroy, the teacher of Isigny; of Mantin, the Paris carpenter; yes, and of Thérèse. He smiled. "We'll turn you over to the French."

Dehn's face seemed to shrink. "But why?" he said desperately. "Why?"

Nervous stomach, thought Abramovici. They're getting fancier and fancier. It used to be that a prisoner was glad to get a decently balanced American Army meal, with peaches for dessert. But this Major said, *Thank you, I've got a nervous stomach.*

Abramovici, peaches in one hand, rifle in the other, left the Major's room, slammed the door and locked it. It was a big, heavy oak door, and the lock was equally solid.

He went downstairs and out into the yard, leaving the dish with the sliced peaches in the shade of the house door. He sat down on an old box, rifle across his knees, the big helmet deep on his forehead. It was hot and he was sleepy. In an hour or so, he thought, he would take the peaches up again. *You are very kind,* the Major would say in his polite way. Abramovici creased his forehead. He wasn't kind. He hated being a guard, especially when most of the guard business consisted of being a waiter. And Yates had told him to stop being so God-damned kind, when all he had done was no more and no less than his duty.

Upstairs, a figure appeared at the window, shadowy, blurred by the reflection of the sun on the pane. The Major seemed to be looking out at the sky and the trees and the concrete slabs that covered the yard. Abramovici glanced up, but gave no sign of recognition. Then the window was empty.

Abramovici felt drowsy. His thoughts wandered off farther than he could trace them, they involved carbohydrates and vitamins and things that a body needed, prisoner or not.

He came to and wondered that all was so quiet. He looked at his watch. He must have dozed off. The peaches still stood in the door of the house, but the sun had shifted, the juice was almost dried up, and the slices had begun to shrivel.

Abramovici got up. He yawned, stretched his short legs, picked up the dish with the peaches, and trudged upstairs.

"*Why?* he asks me, *Why!*"

Yates grabbed the cigarette DeWitt offered him.

"They're no good to the world, they're no good to themselves. With the exception of the Ensdorf woman, I haven't yet met a German who didn't enjoy crawling on his stomach. And she became human only under pressure."

DeWitt laid his strong hands on the desk before him. "The man surrendered to us. He's our prisoner. We'll have to deal with him in our way. Be objective about it, Yates!"

"Back in Normandy, sir, I was an extremely objective gent. I believed we were about as vicious and as foolish as the Germans, and the war was unnecessary, and I, certainly, didn't belong in it. Now, I'd love to apply for the job of Extermination Commissioner."

"I'll keep you out of that job," said DeWitt, with a twinkle. "You might find a few people on our side you'd like to handle, too. It doesn't work that way. We don't execute without trial. We don't convict without proof."

"A pile of butchered men is not enough proof?"

"How're you going to prove that Dehn is responsible for the murder of the prisoners?" asked DeWitt.

414

"Pettinger gave the orders; Dehn permitted it!"

DeWitt smiled. "Let's hold the man. After the war, we'll find witnesses and we'll try him."

"After the war . . . !" Yates said angrily. After the war, they'd be even more detached. "Look, Colonel, I don't want you to trouble yourself about something that far in the future — all I want is your permission to hand Major Dehn over to the French. They'll take care of him."

"It's because of the future," said DeWitt, his hands trembling, "that I stand for deliberate justice and fairness."

"The future, sir? I thought I'd reported Major Dehn's theories on that. Unless we clean out his kind of people, he's going to be right, and we're going to tumble from this war into another. . . ."

"Don't you admit the possibility?"

"Sir, *this* war is not yet over! I refuse — "

The door to DeWitt's office was torn open. Abramovici stumbled in, his rifle trailing.

"Sir — I brought him the peaches — peaches for dessert — "

Yates shook him.

"The mirror was broken. . . . I thought there shouldn't be a mirror in his room — but there was nothing — nothing in the rules — "

"Corporal Abramovici!" The Colonel rose. "When you report to a superior officer, your shirt is to be correctly tucked into your pants!"

"Yes, sir!" A flash of understanding went from Abramovici's eyes to DeWitt's. He tucked in his shirt, pulled up his pants, came to attention, and said, "Sir, the prisoner has killed himself."

2

THE MAP SERGEANT at Corps Headquarters was very busy. The rapidly disintegrating symbols of German units in dissolution, and the unpredictable jumps of the Americans who, once over the Rhine, continued to be reported at unexpected places, kept him on his toes.

Farrish's Division, code name Matador, gave him the most trouble; that's why he liked it best. It appeared one day near Koblenz, the next it had crossed the Rhine and popped up in the hills East of the river. Its units seemed to dance around the dazed Germans. When officers came to inquire about the situation, the Sergeant would explain, "The last we heard places General Farrish here — but God knows where he is now. No, I can't tell you any more, sir — operational blackout, you know!" But operational blackout in most cases merely meant that neither the Sergeant nor the Corps Commander knew where Farrish was attacking.

Farrish no longer had to prod his men. Though the Germans resisted and continued to inflict losses, though they threw into the battle whatever they had — from the remnants of elite units to *Volkssturm* men who went into action in civilian clothes and with two *Panzerfaust*-Bazookas per man — the central direction, the drive, the sustained will, seemed to be gone.

Farrish established his headquarters in a small resort town overlooking a lake. He stayed in the *Kurhaus* and tasted the local mineral water. He spewed it right on the colonnade in front of the German *Herr Professor* who was the medical authority of the resort and who had recommended it in the unspoken hope that the occupiers would return at some time in the future as paying guests.

Willoughby laughed and explained to the Professor that the digestive tract of the *Herr General* was in absolutely perfect order. "In fact, Doc," he said, "you'll be amazed at how healthy we are. We're winning the war, Doc — that does your digestion no end of good!"

The Professor bowed and retreated.

Farrish reached for Willoughby's elbow and pulled him close. "Clarence, you certainly have a way with these Krauts. You almost treat 'em like people, but not quite. As soon as this chase is over, I'll put you in charge of Military Government in my Division area. That's what I'm going to do with you. Very useful citizen, Colonel Willoughby, very useful."

Willoughby took the praise in his stride. He had learned very soon upon joining Farrish's staff that any overdose of emotion annoyed the General and made him suspicious. When Farrish promoted him to lieutenant colonel, Willoughby had accepted almost too stiffly, coming to attention, and thanking Farrish huskily. That had moved the General. The trick, as Willoughby found out, was to teeter at the brink of emotion but to hold on to yourself in a show of soldierly restraint, and thus to give the General the chance to become emotional himself. If you followed this simple rule and dropped him ideas which he could pick up as his own, you were bound to rise in his favor. Carruthers, poor shnook, was too dumb to see it; he went around, pulling at his mustache, and discovering too late that Willoughby always outbid him.

All this was merely the basic condition for getting along with Farrish; to push him forward, and yourself in his trail, was another matter requiring constant thought, vigilance, and work. And Willoughby was smart enough to restrict his suggestions to intra-echelon politics and publicity, thus developing his own limited realm of endeavor exactly as he had in the firm of Coster, Bruille, Reagan and Willoughby, Attorneys at Law. Besides, he was genuinely fond of the General.

They were walking up the broad flight of stairs in the *Kurhaus,* on their way to Farrish's suite. The General was taking two steps at a jump, his entourage trailing him.

"When are we going to take the town of Neustadt?" Willoughby threw in at the first landing. "Carruthers says the Germans have very little to keep us away from the place. . . ."

The General turned his head to Willoughby, who, respectfully, kept half a pace behind. "I'm not going to take it at all," he said, "it's not in my sector."

They reached the top of the stairs and hurried to Farrish's rooms. In the door, the General stopped. "Why?" he asked. "Why just Neustadt? Do they make cameras there?"

"Not that I know of," laughed Willoughby. "Besides, I liberated a Leica long ago. . . ."

Farrish looked at him. "Come in!" he invited. And, closing the door behind himself and Willoughby, he said, "Neustadt, to you, isn't just any old place. What about it?"

Willoughby stepped to the map on the wall.

"Here's Neustadt!" His stubby finger covered the river, one of the tributaries of the Rhine, and the hill in whose shadow the town nestled. "And here" — his finger moved due East for a distance which Farrish's trained eyes translated into an approximate fifteen miles — "here's a place not entered on any maps, neither ours nor theirs. It's called Paula. God knows who that girl was; she can't have been very nice. Paula is a concentration camp."

"Uh-huh," grunted Farrish; "so it's a concentration camp."

"Paula would be the first concentration camp to be liberated by American troops."

The General strode to the map. He towered over Willoughby. He squinted at the distances. His eyes followed the curved line of dashes and X's that gave the boundary between his own and the adjoining Division.

"I suppose the poor bastards in that camp could stand some liberating," he said after a pause. "But the Krauts are going to evacuate them before we ever get there."

"I don't think so," Willoughby argued. "Not if we drive there fast enough."

"So the Nazis will kill them off!"

"According to the report we have, there are between seven and ten thousand prisoners in Paula Camp. Sure, the Nazis will kill them off without a second thought — but not if they know we'll catch them at it."

The General was listening.

"Some of the Division reserves should be enough," Willoughby observed. "Battalion strength, no more — we can spare that. How many guards will the Nazis have at the Camp, with their shortage of man power?"

"Division boundaries . . ." Farrish turned to the map. "A lot of nonsense. All theory." And, as if in explanation, he said to Willoughby, "If you push ahead like we do, you've got to protect your flanks." But he seemed undecided.

Willoughby avoided the problem of the boundaries. He said meditatively, "There'd be a kind of poetic justice in this."

"Poetic, huh?" Farrish grimaced.

"Well — the hand of God, quite visibly! After all, they were out to get you — and from behind. . . ."

It was a psychological bull's-eye. This *was* his chance to get even for that Buzzard thing. Not tank against tank, not Division against Division; but personal blow against personal blow — Farrish against the epitome of Nazism.

Willoughby said, "Shall I let the press know, sir? We could take some of them along, for the ride."

"That's your department!" Farrish growled. He preferred imagining himself in the midst of the liberated to thinking of the need to pose for the picture. Great moments in history must come spontaneously.

"I'll take care of all the details, sir," Willoughby assured him.

Out of the troops held in reserve by the Division, Farrish had his Chief of Staff submit a list of units and officers. He had to choose wisely for this mission — he couldn't detach too many men because he must not neglect his regular assignments; and this was strictly a bootleg affair that had to be conducted by someone who could be trusted, who was able to think and act independently, and who wasn't likely to get himself into a spot with the Germans, or with American units outside Farrish's command.

The name of Troy struck Farrish — that captain in the Bulge Battle? An officer like that was either very good or headed for a bust.

Troy was ordered to report to the General — urgent. He went as the messenger found him — none too well shaved, his field jacket badly in need of replacement. He hadn't seen Farrish since their encounter in the Bulge. Maybe the General was catching up with his old accounts; but Troy wasn't too worried.

He calmly stood Farrish's appraising look. In the background, he noticed Willoughby, whom he remembered from that night in Rambouillet; Willoughby was nodding encouragement.

Then he heard the General say, "Well, Captain Troy, I'm going to send a Task Force to liberate Paula Concentration Camp, about fifteen miles East of Neustadt. D'you think you're the man to head it, huh?"

"I'll do anything you order me to do, sir!"

"You didn't always feel that way, did you?" Farrish's lips took on a sarcastic line.

418

Troy decided to stick to his guns. "Sir, today you're asking me what *I* can do — not what my men can do."

Farrish laughed, not a very comfortable laugh. "To come back to this Task Force. You'll be on your own, Captain, and I won't be around to correct your mistakes. You'll be far ahead of us, and you won't be able to count on support, and I prefer you to use your radio only in an emergency — the Germans can pick up your signal as easily as we can. We'll catch up with you, don't worry; but it may take a few days. You understand all that?"

"Yes, sir."

"D'you still want it?"

"Yes, sir."

The General studied his man, and he approved of his selection. Troy was built too solidly to be hasty; he had intelligent, searching eyes, and a chin that promised firmness. Furthermore, an officer who had led his company from the beaches of Normandy all the way across the Rhine had proved that he could look out for himself and his men.

"All right — step over here!" The General led the way to the map. "Here is your objective, and this is how I want you to proceed."

Troy saw the General's finger cross his Division boundary line. So that was the deal. . . . But he didn't comment. Farrish must know what he was doing.

"Now, Captain, what do you take along aside from your own company?"

Troy glanced once again at the map, estimating the position of Farrish's advance units in relation to Paula Camp and to the forward elements of the adjoining Division.

"I've got to be mobile," he said, "I want to be faster than the fastest the Germans can put up against me — so I can run, if necessary. I want to be independent — that means I must have some medium artillery, mounted, and tank destroyers. Then I'll need engineers, and supplies — gas, lots of gas, and food. And what about if I get there? How many prisoners in Paula Camp? Seven thousand? How am I going to feed seven thousand starved people?"

"You should find some food at the Camp!" said Willoughby.

Troy looked at him doubtfully.

Willoughby added, "And we'll be there with all the supplies soon after you've taken the place. . . . But you'd better take along some extra medics; those people may need them. . . . And there's something else you'll have to drag along. . . ."

"What's that?"

"Correspondents," said Willoughby.

Troy hesitated. "Sir," he said finally, "this mission is ticklish enough without having civilians along."

"There are only a couple of them," Willoughby consoled. "The main batch will come with the General."

Troy fixed his eyes fully on Farrish. "These are your orders, sir?"

Farrish retreated to the map. "Yes, of course. . . ." He cleared his throat.

Willoughby cut the awkward silence. "I took the liberty of asking the two correspondents who will go with Captain Troy to come here. I thought it might be best, sir, if your instructions were given in the presence of everybody."

"All right — let's get them and let's get this over with!" said Farrish.

Willoughby picked up the phone. Shortly afterwards, a man and a woman, both in uniform, entered.

"You remember Miss Karen Wallace?" Willoughby said genially, as the General rose and shook Karen's hand.

"Why sure!" beamed Farrish. "Where have you been keeping yourself? I've missed you all during the winter. Been hibernating?" Reluctantly, he let go of her hand.

"And this is Mr. Tex Myers," said Willoughby, giving the wizened little man a slight shove that brought him close to the General.

"How're you, Tex?" Farrish said offhandedly, keeping his eyes on Karen.

"I've been thinking of you, General," Karen said pleasantly. "I was in Paris, for a while, and then I was sent to the Seventh Army, too far away from you for comfort."

"Paris is bad for women," Farrish stated unequivocally. "Bad for everybody. That's where they stole my gas. That's where they held up the war."

"I know," said Karen. "I didn't stay there. I like my soldiers to be sol-diers — "

Farrish took her arm and led her to Troy. "Well, meet Captain Troy, with whom, I hear, you'll be going to liberate Paula Camp."

"How d'y'do," said Troy, touching her hand and withdrawing his quickly. He felt her look at him, or perhaps through him. Everything about him was suddenly too big — his hands, his feet, his chest, his neck, everything.

She was again talking to the General. Willoughby saw that her eyes were going back to Troy. He nudged the Captain and whispered, "For Chris'-sakes, Troy, be your age! Haven't you seen a woman before?"

Troy shook him off.

She turned from the General. "Well, Captain, will we leave soon?"

"Do you really want to go?" he asked. "It's not going to be fun. And even if we get there, what we'll find will be kind of rough."

Her gray eyes grew warm. "I know that, Captain. I think I can take it."
She saw him smile, a good smile; he was thawing up finally.

He said, "My Company Command Post is just out of town, in a farm-house along Road 22. Why don't you and Mr. Myers drop by there to-morrow, around noontime. I want to start out at dark. We'll clear up all the details."

"We'll do that," said Karen.

The General claimed her attention again. "You'll be all right with Troy. How do I pick 'em, huh?"

She gave Farrish her sunniest glance. "I want to thank you and Colonel Willoughby for the break you're giving Tex and me. I know I always can rely on you two."

Farrish patted his hair. The wings of his nostrils trembled slightly as he pulled in breath. "I owe you a good story, Miss Wallace," he began, "to make up for the one somebody screwed up in Normandy — Forty-Eight Rounds from Forty-Eight Guns! Made up the title myself!"

"Yes, somebody screwed that up," she said ruefully. Her sympathetic smile expanded to envelop the General and to hold directly upon Willoughby. "But I guess it won't happen this time," she added pointedly.

"No, sir!" said Farrish. "This time nobody's going to interfere! This time we'll go right through, and I don't care how much china is broken in the process. Do you know the Nazis tried to assassinate me? I'm going to put the fear of God in them. We're going to take Paula Camp, this blot on the name of Christianity and civilization, and we're going to liberate what's in it, and we're going to take the Nazis and we're going to bring them to justice. How's that for a title, Miss Wallace? General Goes on Crusade — for Liberty and Justice!"

Karen nodded. She saw Troy's face grow stiff as a mask; she saw Willoughby's jowls puff up in self-satisfaction. She heard Tex Myers mumble something under his breath; it sounded like "Crap," but she wasn't sure.

3

TROY was the kind of man who kept his balance despite the friction that was bound to develop when units of different nature with their different problems were thrown together and had to be welded, for one common purpose, into an organic whole. He was not a diplomat, he made no con-cessions; he exerted his authority quietly, with a few words spoken to the point and precluding contradiction. And because of his ability to delegate jobs, reserving to himself the task of checking on performance, he was un-hurried and had time to answer special questions and wisecracks, and to get acquainted with the officers and key men whose confidence he had to gain if the jaunt to Paula Camp was not to end in disaster.

Inside, he wasn't without qualms. He had to fight down the fear that an event like the loss of Fulbright's platoon might repeat itself, possibly on a larger scale. Considered soberly, there was a good chance of that. His small troop of men was going to isolate itself voluntarily, practically issuing invitations to be surrounded and ground to pieces before help could reach it; only speed, co-ordination, and absolute level-headedness could make up for the odds against him. All this, he could reason out, and he could take measures to make the men see what they were up against; still, he was unable to wipe out completely his uncertainty.

He was sitting in the living room of the abandoned farmhouse on Road 22 leading to Neustadt. Around him was a welter of military gear, of old-fashioned furniture displaced in a half dozen hasty conferences. The floor was littered with maps and papers.

He was alone. The last details had been settled. The only people he still had to see were the two correspondents — Karen Wallace, with the reddish brown, short-cropped hair, and the little guy, Tex.

He sighed. He could call in a couple of men to straighten up the room, but he decided against it. The men were busy packing up their own stuff, and checking the guns and the motors, and loading the vehicles. He began to pick up papers from the floor. He shoved the table to the place where he believed it belonged — in front of the bench before the big, colorfully tiled stove. He set up the chairs. He kicked duffel bags and musette bags and bedding rolls into a corner; he discovered the flashlight he had lost last night; he found a can of cheese and felt suddenly how hungry he was — he hadn't eaten since morning, had had no time for it. He sat down and opened the can and was just beginning to cut a chunk of the cheese when he heard steps. Must be them, he thought, and quickly pushed the can under a batch of papers and snapped his pocketknife closed.

"Oh, it's you!" he said, audibly let down, as Yates entered with Bing close behind.

"Didn't expect us?" laughed Yates. "We thought we'd never find you. Looked all over the place — finally I got hold of Willoughby, old friend of mine, and he told us where you were and we should hurry because you were going to take off tonight."

Troy pulled out his knife and the cheese and began to dig in the can. "Want some?"

"Thanks, no," said Yates. "I've had all the K-ration cheese I want in my life."

"What kind of guy is he, this Willoughby?" asked Troy, munching. "How come you know him?"

"Used to be with our outfit," Yates answered. "We got rid of him. Seems we kicked him upstairs; Farrish snapped him up, and Willoughby says he's doing fine."

"Oh." Troy swallowed the cheese.

"What's the matter?" Yates frowned. "Have you had trouble with him?"

"Not exactly."

"He gets along all right with people," Yates informed him, "that is, with people he can use."

Troy nodded. "That kind of man. . . ."

"Yes, that kind of man."

Troy let the matter drop. He said to Yates, "You must have made quite a trip to get here. . . ."

"Took us two days to catch up with you."

There was a pause while Troy dug out the last morsel of cheese and then threw the can on top of the stove, where it came to rest with a clatter.

Bing had picked up a map from the floor and was studying it. "I know that neighborhood," he said casually. "I used to go hiking there, with my father. He was a great hiker and he dragged me along as soon as I was able to walk straight — I've hated hiking ever since."

"What neighborhood?" Troy asked, his interest sharpening.

"Neustadt, Captain. I'm from Neustadt. Born there, raised there, and kicked out of there. They didn't like my nose — "

"Neustadt . . ." said Troy. "Do you know of a concentration camp near there, Paula Camp?"

"They were still building it when we left. They told my father they'd have him in there for the housewarming."

Troy, picking his teeth, was attentive.

Yates said, "I wish you weren't so snotty about it, Bing."

"That's the way I choose to talk about it, if at all!" Bing answered, and continued busying himself with the map. "If I remember right, Captain, Paula Camp was built here. . . ." He had marked off a small square on a plateau surrounded by hilly, wooded terrain.

"That's it!" said Troy, comparing Bing's entry with the information on his own map. "It works out exactly."

"Are you going there, Captain?" Bing asked quickly.

"I'm taking a Task Force to Paula."

Bing turned soberly to Yates. "Lieutenant, would you give me permission to go along with the Task Force? I want to see Neustadt, I want to see the house I was born in — you understand that, don't you?"

Yates said, "That's not what we came here for."

"Well, what *did* you come here for?" asked Troy.

"I've come to deliver."

Troy looked up, his eyes narrowed.

"... On the promise I gave you one winter night, Captain!"

"Have you got him?" Troy asked tensely.

"No. But we know who he is."

Yates saw Troy's hand grip the thick wood of the peasant table; he saw the muscles of Troy's neck bulge.

"His name's Erich Pettinger, Lieutenant Colonel of the SS. He's the man who ordered your men killed."

"Where is he?"

Yates raised his hands. "God knows!"

"I want him alive!"

"Take it easy!" Yates said. "He's probably alive, and Germany is getting smaller every day. Let me tell you the whole story!"

When Yates had finished, Troy repeated, "I want him alive. It isn't just getting even. If I wanted that, I could have it cheaply — I'm going to Neustadt to bust open Paula Camp. That's good, and it gives me a kick, and I'm grateful I got the job — at least I know what I'm doing. But it isn't enough. I want this Pettinger."

"Is that all?" asked Yates. "Suppose we catch him. Suppose he tells you what his sidekick Dehn told me — they were advancing, and they were in a hurry, and they simply had no room for prisoners."

"That's a fat excuse!"

"You're going to Neustadt, Captain. You have a small, mobile unit. You can't take prisoners either — or can you?"

"I won't shoot any unarmed men!" Troy said flatly.

"I didn't think you would," said Yates.

Troy was stubborn. "I want him alive!"

He's really hepped on the subject, thought Yates. Big, strong, healthy man. War got them all.

Bing burst out, "I wish you'd let me go to Neustadt, Lieutenant. The Captain will need a man who talks the language and understands those people. . . ."

Yates wanted to say, Ask Troy! but he thought it over. He had been so intent on his news of Pettinger, and on Troy's reaction, that the full significance of the mission to Paula had not sunk in. Bing's request made him aware of it.

"The Sergeant has a good point there, Captain," he said. "In fact, I'd like to come along with you, too, and see the Camp."

Before Troy could answer, Bing broke in, "What do you want to see the Camp for? You've got imagination. We'll get all the reports and pictures we want. . . ."

Yates turned to Troy. "I think I could get some material there that my Detachment could use — I'm sure Colonel DeWitt would give his permission — I have my own jeep — and Bing and I *could* help you."

"I wasn't talking through my hat!" protested Bing. "I mean it, Lieutenant. Unless you know what's been going on in Germany, you have no idea what the interior of such a Camp looks like — you can't have. If I were you, for my own peace of mind, I wouldn't go in there unless I had to. I can live without having seen it."

"What are you so steamed up about?" Yates asked angrily.

Why didn't he listen to Bing? Why did he want to go to Paula Camp? Gathering material for propaganda purposes was something to tell DeWitt. What was it, then? Perhaps — that he was after the truth of the war, and Paula Camp was part of that truth, very likely its most terrible part.

Troy had made up his mind. "Come along at your own risk," he invited. "Maybe we'll be able to pick up Pettinger's trail. He ought to be the kind of man that hangs around where people are tortured. . . ."

"You and your one track mind!" Yates smiled. "But we'll come."

Karen and Tex Myers entered the house.

"Are we on time, Captain?" she said, and then turned to trace the suppressed sound, the sudden stir of the man in the back of the low-ceilinged peasant room. She recognized the familiar face though it remained in the shadow, and something near her heart gave a quick, painful jump.

"Karen!" Bing said. He came toward her, his hands outstretched, unmindful of Troy who looked askance at the scene, and of Yates who hid his embarrassment behind a grin. "Karen — I've been waiting for this . . . !"

The pain in Karen had gone as fast as it had come. She felt she had to make a decision, here and now, and before the boy could rush more deeply into whatever he was throwing himself.

"Hello, Sergeant Bing!" she called out cheerfully. "I'm glad you've come through all right since Normandy. And you, Lieutenant Yates — I've seen your friend Willoughby, so I knew you were alive — but it's good to see you."

Yates nodded. She had not changed much; the gray, aloof eyes that once frustrated him were still aloof, and the features that sometimes seemed about to break into a warm smile were still plain. Neither had the grip of her strong, almost male hands changed — the hands he had once felt on his face, ridiculous situation of which he didn't want to be reminded.

"It's a small war," he said with a man's friendly interest in someone who had shared a bombing with him. "Are you headed for Paula Camp, too?"

"Yes, if Captain Troy will assign places to Tex and me."

Troy had been feeling left out among these old friends. Now he spoke up, "I've prepared everything. You will travel in the main body. . . ." He was about to launch into a detailed description of what he wanted them to do, the things he wanted them to take along, the precautions he wanted them to observe. He had thought all that up carefully, and he was disappointed when Karen cut him short.

"Why don't you give all the dope to Tex? He's much better at practical things than I am. I'd like to have a word with the Sergeant, if you don't mind." She turned on her heel and walked out of the farmhouse.

Bing looked around, guiltily at first, then with the expression of the driver who's won the speed race — battered and strained, but smiling. He followed her, closing the door softly.

Tex Myers pulled up a chair and said to Troy, "Don't mind her. She's always that way, full of surprises. You should see her make Willoughby jump!"

Troy said tartly, "Well, he's *your* Sergeant, Yates. I don't want any trouble on this operation. It's too damned serious. And I don't want my men affected. Is that clear?"

"She'll take care of herself!" said Yates.

In the farmyard was an empty trough where the horses, long gone, had been watered. Somehow, their smell seemed to linger, not strongly enough to be offensive, just sufficiently to make you feel you were in the country, and to make you forget you were in the war, and that in a couple of days you might be breathing the stench of people rotting alive.

Karen was perched on the trough as Bing came out. He saw her, and hesitated. He looked at the picture of the slender woman, the graceful pose, the fine outline of her head. It refuted the memory he had of her.

He approached her slowly. "Karen," he said haltingly, "I want nothing from you. I have no claim, no rights. But give me a chance."

She had not expected this. She remembered him irrepressible and, even at bad moments, possessed by a kind of youthful confidence.

Impulsively, she took his hand. "I can't," she said. "Don't you see I can't?"

"Why not? Is there someone else?"

She shook her head. He saw her serious face, and he thought it was appealingly lovely.

"It isn't that at all," she tried to explain. "I've never forgotten you. . . ."

She came off the trough and faced him. "I've thought of you and reproached myself."

"What for? It was beautiful!"

"You must let me finish," she said gently. "We can't afford to misunderstand one another. I've reproached myself because you were you, and I didn't take you for what you were — it was as if I had a heavy gold bracelet and wore it with an assortment of cheap costume jewelry."

He wanted to object.

"It really was," she said hurriedly, although she wasn't quite certain that

426

her line would lead her to a decent, painless solution. "Think back, dear. Didn't you, yourself, have the feeling: What does it matter? Who knows if we'll be alive tomorrow?"

His mouth hardened. Of course, he had known it all along—but it hurt.

"I'll tell you something," he said. "A story that I think is sort of tender. We had a man, and he found a girl, and they fell in love, the way you fall in love in the middle of war. We had to leave, and she followed him, and they met again and they knew they had to be together, at least this one time. So I got them the room, and I fixed it up, nicely; I even got them a bottle of wine, and their bed had sheets. And then I sat on the stairs leading to that room, and I kept guard so that no one would disturb them. And all the time I really did it for you and me."

A number of soldiers came through the yard; they probably were reporting to Troy. Karen was glad of the interruption; she couldn't have said a word to Bing at that moment.

"I know," he said after a while, "I failed you once. But you mustn't forget what happened that day. A man was killed next to me, and I knew the man, and his body was horribly torn. . . ."

Was that it? she asked herself. Her heart was full of pity, a feeling so strong that, if you didn't keep your head, you might mistake it for love.

Bing said, "For Chris'sakes, don't misunderstand me. I don't need to prove myself. I've been to Paris, other places, too. I'm all right. In fact, sometimes I believe it wasn't Tolachian's death at all that caused the— the disappointment; it was something else. . . ."

"What was it?" she asked softly.

"That I loved you so much. I wanted you so much that when I could have you, it was so—surprising, so unexpected that—this thing happened, and I couldn't take you. I've grown up in America; Americans have an attitude toward love—it influences you, you can't help it—it inhibits you."

He was too young, not her vintage. "It was my fault," she said. "I knew the kind of person you were and yet I thought we could have this and then part and be the same as before. Well, you can't, not people like you—and I'm not so clear about myself any more."

His face lit up.

"Karen," he said, "the war will be over soon! We have a lifetime ahead of us—give us a chance—"

He was so eager, a wonderful kid. How could he fail to move her? He did move her, but like a puppy licking your hand; not like a man, her equal, offering to share his life.

And she could see a life thus shared. He was mature for his twenty-two years, surprisingly mature and independent in many ways—but not in the

427

one that counted. Grow as fast as he might, he would not be able to catch up with her. The puppy would become a beautiful male; and by then, she would be an old bitch.

"Would you want just another affair, warmed up from last summer?" she asked.

If that was the best he could get — why not? But he said, "Of course I wouldn't."

And it suddenly dawned on him that what he wanted was only to warm up last summer's affair. He really didn't want a permanent arrangement — but he couldn't say that either.

"Of course not!" he repeated.

"I was sure of it," she said.

Then she put her hands on his shoulders and came close to him. The scent of her hair excited him and once more made him feel how desirable she was, and how much he wanted her, and what he had missed — though he knew it was over.

For a minute she thought of risking his offer of a lifetime shared, so as to put the burden of the final No on him. But for this, she liked him too much. And she feared that, cornered, he would go through with it and postpone the great disillusionment for a time when it would cut deepest. You can't build on that.

"It wouldn't be a lifetime, and we can't just play at it. I'm thirty-three, and I've been around. All right, you can overcome that if there's a great love."

"I do love you," he protested.

"Don't make it hard for me," she pleaded. "I'm terribly fond of you — oh, why do I have to say these things!"

She broke away from him.

"There isn't enough here — " her hand went to her heart. "There just isn't." She pulled out her mirror and lipstick and mechanically did her mouth. The face that looked at her seemed old and ugly and she hated it. Why did *she* have to do this surgery? It took a lot out of her; and only he benefited by it.

"Then let's be friends," he said.

"Yes, of course."

He turned and went, as slowly as he had come. She felt sorry, not for him, but for herself; perhaps she had made a mistake. Chemistry was still chemistry — and who told her to be so God-damned moral and to cramp her own style when it hurt so to do it?

Or had her style become different?

The sun beat down on her. She went across the yard to the barn and sat in its shade, on an overturned wheelbarrow.

The soldiers who had come to see Troy while she had been talking to Bing now emerged from the main building, whistled at her, and took off. Then Bing and Yates came out.

Yates called over, "See you tonight!" and Bing waved casually. He showed no trace of emotional strain; but then, she was not close enough to observe the small signs that might very well be there.

She waited for Tex Myers. The little man with his crinkled face, his native wit and horse sense, his sober observations, would be good to have around now. But he didn't come. Instead, the tall Captain who was to lead the advance stepped into the door and looked around, blinking his eyes against the sharp light. He discovered her and came over, his shoulders slightly hunched, as if he were constantly ducking bullets. His shirt, obviously unpressed, was open at the neck and revealed the blond hair of his chest.

He stopped in front of her, and looked down at her and attempted a smile.

"Hot!" he said, and seemed to be stuck.

"Yes, hot, isn't it?" she said.

"The Sergeant gone?" he asked.

"Yes. Didn't you see him go?"

"Must have gone with Yates. I know them both. . . ." He talked more easily now. "Know Bing from Normandy. He came to me with some of his loudspeakers, brought in prisoners, too; but a man was killed. Some people don't get accustomed to that. Must have been the first time the kid saw a man killed that close. Took it hard. But he's a good kid."

"I know the story," she said. "I wasn't too far away myself."

"Yes? We could have met then. . . ." He paused. "What do you think would have happened?"

"Nothing much!"

"Yeah," he nodded. "I was very busy that day, and I've been keeping busy ever since. I'm still busy."

Karen laughed. "I'm not holding you from your work?"

"Hell, no! I'm taking a break. Your friend Tex, he's in my room pecking away on my typewriter. He's doing a story, he says. You write stories, too?"

"Why, yes!"

"Sometimes I wish I could write," he said musingly. "All the things I've seen in this war; somebody should write a book about it, or at least some short stories."

"Try it, Captain!" She thought she knew the type. They came to her often, with little stories or big ones, feeling that it had happened to them alone, forgetting that the war was the same, more or less, all over the front. Usually, they were bores.

429

"I'd call mine *The Valor of Ignorance*."

That was surprising.

"Why that?" she asked; and he noticed that, for the first time, her eyes had come alive to him, eyes he liked because they seemed the deepest he had ever seen.

"Only the dumb are really brave," he stated. "The moment you find out what you let yourself in for, you want to run like hell. I learned that back in Normandy, and I haven't changed my mind about it. The dumb are winning the war; but personally, I have a lot of respect for all the cowards that somehow hang on to themselves. You don't think I'm off my beam?"

She wanted to hear more from him, but he laughed off his own theory with, "Sometimes I think I'm a crackpot. I'm an engineer by trade, I was foreman in an assembly plant for agricultural machinery, and then they stuck me in the Armored Infantry. So how would I know? But I'm taking up your time. . . ."

"What *did* you want, Captain Troy?" He wanted something, and it wasn't what he was talking about.

He fell back into his shyness.

"That's all settled, now," he said finally.

"What was it?"

Carefully, he sat down next to her, on one of the handles of the wheelbarrow.

"I'm no expert at handling people," he said, "though I keep my own men in line; they like me. I don't want any trouble on this trip, I told it to Yates and I told him to watch his Sergeant. You know how it is — I have over four hundred men with me, and one woman — that's you, Miss Wallace. So I thought I'd have a talk with you and make sure."

She felt she ought to put him in his place. But he had been nice about it, in his awkward way.

"It's really not my business," he apologized some more, "except that it is — because the General put me in charge of this job and he palmed you off on me."

"Are you still worried?"

"No!" he exclaimed; the load was almost visibly off his chest.

"And are you sure," she said, "you didn't just pretend to be worried and didn't just come out to have a pleasant chat?"

"Now, if you put it that way," he answered, "I don't rightly know. I'm glad I came out, though. I must have been mistaken when I saw you drop into the house, and heard the boy hello you as if — "

"As if?"

"Nothing. I said I was mistaken."

She said tersely, "You were right, Captain, when you said I was none of your business. For your information, Sergeant Bing and I are close and dear friends!"

He continued blandly, "From what I know of the boy, he's worth being your friend. You don't meet genuine people very often, so if you do, you hold on to them."

It sounded as if he now were speaking for himself. But Karen wasn't sure. He was either so guileless that you couldn't hold anything against him, or he had much, much deeper insight than he pretended, and knew what he was after.

Tex Myers came out of the house and yoo-hooed.

Troy rose. "I'll be seeing you, Miss Wallace!"

She studied his gait. He must be very strong; and she was glad he was strong and the kind of man he was.

4

PAULA CAMP was a piece of arid desert in the midst of the live, green hills of this part of Germany. It could have been the dust rising from the tired tramping of thousands of feet in the enclosure; or the choking stench emanating from Paula; or the fact that the trees around it had been cut down to build the huts and to give the guards in their towers a free field of observation and of fire — whatever, Paula was like a cancerous growth that spread over the plateau and into the hills, ugly and forbidding, and no signs were necessary to tell those entering: So many have died here, you'll be sucked dry, too, and end on the bone heap.

The Camp included about forty huts, in varying stages of decay. They were built to hold a hundred men each, and the floor plan had been figured out with German thoroughness so that every inch of space was used for the rough triple bunks. Now, however, three hundred men were assigned to each hut. Even though the windows were kept open, the air was so thick and foul you could scarcely breathe it.

The Camp administration, the barracks trusties, lost count of their people. Corpses would lie in the bunks for days, next to the sick, until their own peculiar stench, finally overpowering the customary smells, revealed them. Then they were thrown out of the huts. The corpses were never heavy, yet it took at least three, and more often four or five of the living to carry one.

Not that the overflow particularly worried Schreckenreuther, the Camp Commandant. He received the same amount of provisions, whether he had four thousand or twelve thousand people in the Camp; and of these provisions, a good part was taken by the SS guards and directed to the black market. It wasn't the first time that his Camp had been overcrowded;

Schreckenreuther had implicit confidence in the ways of Nature which saw to it that, after a while, the number of inmates was reduced by a comfortable margin; and there were many ways of helping Nature along.

Schreckenreuther was a thin man with kinky blond hair and a nearly albino complexion. He was not particularly cruel — that is, he wasn't cruel for cruelty's sake; he got no fun out of it. He used it only for educational purposes, and when he was in a good mood, he would explain to his staff that the prisoners must be considered as children. They were either of an inferior race or, as enemies of National Socialism, of an inferior mind; in both cases, like children, not fully responsible. And a good father must punish his children. There were many methods of punishment — a whole scale, which, at one time, he had laboriously typed out on sheets of choice white paper, together with the crimes for which they were to be applied. He had his opus bound in fine parchment that one of his guards made from the tattooed skin of some prisoners. They had to be skinned after they were dead; Schreckenreuther insisted on that.

The booklet lay on his desk and was not used; Schreckenreuther didn't need to teach the finer points of his theories to his staff — they had their own and often improved systems. There was Biederkopf, Schreckenreuther's assistant, a dark man with a low forehead and bushy brows. Biederkopf used the concrete mixer. He would pick a fat Jew, a recent entry, and put him and some good-sized rocks into the drum of the machine. Then he would start the whole thing rolling. The punishment was not applied against the fat Jew, naturally; of him, soon enough, only scraps of flesh and splinters of bone were left. The punishment was given to those men who had to scrape out the drum; and Biederkopf saw to it that the job was done thoroughly. He was a stickler for cleanliness.

When the orders came to evacuate Paula Camp, Schreckenreuther was upset. He had not figured on it. Of course he knew that the Americans were coming close; he listened to the radio regularly, and he had learned to read facts out of the German newspapers. But he had assumed that, in the first place, a concentration camp was not a military objective, and he had expected that, if it came to this, he would be permitted to turn the Camp over to the Americans in good shape. What could the Americans do with the prisoners in the Camp but leave them there? They were no good for anything else. And perhaps, the Americans would even leave him in his job, with one of their men as Commissar, or whatever they would call it.

But the orders were explicit, and he was a German officer of a kind, and had to follow orders. The orders said that all traces of what had been going on in Camp were to be erased.

That would mean a lot of work, and he had little time for it. Even if he locked up every prisoner in the huts and set fire to them, there'd be the charred bodies. And the orders said that those able to march were to be marched off and to be used as munitions workers at the place of destination, in Thuringia.

Schreckenreuther shook his head. What did they mean by erasing all traces? And he didn't approve of having his children used in a munitions plant — they were too stupid or too full of resentment to turn out a good job. Things must be in a sad shape if the Government had to use the inmates of Paula Camp.

He called in Valentin, the Camp doctor. "You'll have to get busy," he said.

Rudolf Kellermann was digging graves. The place Schreckenreuther had chosen for the graves, on the basis of Dr. Valentin's estimate, lay about five hundred yards beyond the barbed wire, and another five hundred yards from the nearest hill in whose gentle slope were rooted the bent, dust-covered, slowly dying birch trees.

"You'll be able to take along about five thousand men," Valentin had said to Schreckenreuther; so, graves were laid out for the remaining seven thousand. The graves were laid out neatly; one of the SS guards who knew something about excavations had gone down on his belly, measured the ground, driven in pegs of wood, and drawn white string between the pegs. If you figured that you could easily pile three emaciated corpses on top of one another, and another three alongside, the digging work wouldn't be too difficult or too prolonged, even though the diggers weren't the fastest in the world because they, too, were emaciated.

The SS men didn't say what the digging was for; but the prisoners knew. It was easy to guess. It was equally easy, for a man of Kellermann's intelligence, to guess that the diggers, themselves, would end up in the ditches they were digging.

And Kellermann didn't want to die. He had managed to live through the fighting and the slave work of the 999th Light Brigade in North Africa — the punishment unit the Nazis had organized at the time. In North Africa, Kellermann had become convinced that the Nazis would lose the war, which meant to him that he would win it; and he wanted to see this victory. He had not died in the Gestapo jail of the industrial city of Kremmen. When, the torture in jail still fresh on his body, jammed into a truck, able to stand only because the pressure of the others held him up, he was brought to Paula, Kellermann was firmly determined to live through that, too.

He had learned, and he had learned fast. He had found that a concentration camp is not necessarily the end; that it, too, develops its form of society; and that you were completely lost only if you were alone. There were groups in Camp, groups of men — and probably it was the same on

433

the women's side — who were drawn together by the same bitter determination, by common experiences in the past, and by common ideas for the future. When they were sent out to do slave work in the local factories, or to construction sites, or to the farms at harvest time, they would steal for one another. They would cover up for a weak or sick one, against the trusties and against the SS, even though some of the trusties, prisoners themselves, were secretly on their side. They would spirit away a beaten and bloody one to the dark rear of some hut, and nurse him. And at night, they would whisper together — at first on how to escape, though they knew it would never pan out; then on means of sabotaging the work they were forced to do; and finally on the future, always on the future, and freedom. There was little talk of vengeance — it was taken for granted that the SS would be snuffed out, quickly, and without much ado. But there was a whole country, Germany, diseased to its core, that would have to be cleansed and rebuilt from the bottom up. And who were the men to do that if not they who had gained the moral right by years behind the barbed wire, surviving under and despite the whips and the truncheons of the SS?

A dying man in such a group, his body weakening by means called natural in Camp, or by torture, was not too sad; he knew the others would live through his having helped them to live. They were winning the fight to preserve sense and meaning for life — the sense and the meaning for whose destruction the Nazis had devised these camps.

For Kellermann, self-preservation was an obligation. Having lived through these past years, he would not now let himself be killed among the gravediggers.

He looked around the dug-up ground for a rock, and he saw one; but it wasn't close to him, and there was little chance that he could work his way to it. The man working near the rock, his baggy, pajamalike striped uniform soaked in sweat, seemed afraid to tackle it. Kellermann waited.

The man, his skull-like, slavic face clammy and red, fear written all over his subdued features and his doglike, beaten eyes, finally began to tinker with the rock. The metal of his spade scraped at it. The guard heard the sound and strolled over. The man worked faster, some dirt flew up, the rock remained unmoved. The guard beat the lead-filled rod of his whip playfully against the black, stiff leather of his boots. The man stopped working. He looked up out of the ditch, at the guard high above him. The guard easily weighed twice as much, a full chest, strong legs, and a face rosy with good, fresh air.

"Well?" said the guard.

The man continued to look up, as a bird might look at a snake, with terrified fascination, because he knew what was coming and was helpless against it.

434

Then Kellermann left his place and came over to the unnerved man. He seemed to ignore the guard, and this was what made the guard wait and watch. Had Kellermann tried an apology, or even glanced at the guard, seeking permission with his eyes, the guard would have refused and made his refusal tell with his whip.

Kellermann jammed the blade of his spade into the ground, close to the rock, to give himself leverage. He grabbed the handle with both hands, and pulled it toward himself with all the weight left him. He thought his sharp bones would break through his withered muscles; there'd be no fat to keep them from puncturing his skin. The ditch and the men digging began to swim at crazy angles. He saw things through a pink film. Sweat bit his forehead. A pain started in the back of his neck and spread over the surface of his brain, a pain so sharp and wild that he wanted to scream. But his tongue, mercifully swollen, gagged him.

Then the handle broke. He fell back against the wall of the ditch, still holding on to the stump in his hand. For a moment, he closed his eyes.

He heard the guard's furious scream, "*Dummkopf!*" And again, "Come out of there, come here, nitwit!"

Kellermann struggled out of the ditch. The guard gripped the collar of his faded, striped denims; Kellermann heard the seams rip.

He stood in front of the guard, arms raised before his face. "*Achtung!*" yelled the guard. "*Still-stann!*" Kellermann had to come to attention. He had to obey the command, refusal meant a shot in the back.

The SS guard's fury was abating. You either killed these people or sent them back to work. He didn't want to kill Kellermann because the mass graves had to be dug and, except for breaking the spade, the man was a better digger than the other wrecks who could hardly lift a full shovel.

So the guard raised his whip and slashed it across Kellermann's face — well-aimed, systematic blows, one — two — three — four, two on the left cheek, two on the right. The welts sprang up, and the blood trickled out of them.

"You know what this is for?"

"Yes," said Kellermann.

"The spade belongs to the *Reich*."

"Yes," said Kellermann. His eyes were full of stinging tears; he hadn't known he had that much fluid left in his body.

"Go, get another one!" said the guard. "Run!"

"Yes," said Kellermann. And ran. Each step was like a stab, deep, down to the center of his nerves. When he felt he was out of the guard's sight, he slowed down. He must walk. Other guards, seeing him run, might think he was trying to escape. He walked through the gate, reporting to the sentry that he had been ordered to fetch a spade for the digging detail out in the field. He was allowed to pass.

He wanted to crawl into one of the huts and sit there, quietly, until the pain ebbed. But he trudged between the huts, mumbling to himself, telling his damned body that it must not yield, that it had gone through worse, and that this was no time to let go and sink into painless black.

Then, between two of the huts, he saw the line-up — an endless line, thousands upon thousands of men in striped suits, dirty gray and dirty blue, blending into a single hue of nondescript dirt. It was a double line, with enough space between the front and the back rows for a group of inspectors to pass through comfortably. Instinctively, Kellermann knew what it was for: the double line was the complement to the graves he had been digging. And he had to be in this line, in spite of his pain, in spite of his overwhelming desire to faint. He had to be in this line and to stand there, if necessary for hours, and press out his chest and make himself appear strong — at least strong enough to be taken along on the march. Because those not chosen for the march were to fill the graves.

He continued behind the huts, pasting himself like a shadow to the rough, tar-papered walls. Each space between huts, where his outline could be seen, was a new risk he had to force himself to take, and he had to utilize the spaces to observe the backs of the men in the line, to find those of his own hut, his own group.

He reached the fourth or fifth such space and recognized the white, moth-eaten hair of the Professor. It wasn't really moth-eaten; some Nazi, offended by the dignity of that hair, had had the trusty barber shave a weird design on the old man's skull, and the hair had not fully grown back.

In a last spurt of energy, Kellermann dashed out and into the line. The Professor moved, as did the man next to him. It was no more than the merest ripple on a pond; then everything was as before, a stiff, rigid line of striped, dirty suits, in the sun of a spring day.

Dr. Valentin was no fool. As a medical man, he knew it was impossible to make a valid selection of those who were to march out and live, and those who were to die. But he didn't mention this to Schreckenreuther because he assumed the Commandant was aware of the Camp farce called medical care, and because he wasn't much interested in the procedure. Anybody chosen who did not stand the march would fall and be eliminated by the guards covering the column.

He didn't even get a kick out of being Fate. It was nothing new that a flick of his hand, a nod of his head, decided over life and death. Long ago, pleading, begging, silent eyes had given him the thrill of power; but it was always the same thing, and it wore off. To try to save lives, which was, after all, his profession, was nonsense in a place devoted to the liquidation of lives; all you were called upon to do was to sign death certificates stat-

436

ing the person had died of heart failure or pneumonia; or, in the rare cases of an investigation in Camp, to keep the bodies of those being investigated patched up and breathing for the processes of justice.

In his boredom, he fell back on the ambitions of his youth — the study of medieval Latin, and cancer research. Medieval Latin was his personal hobby, and it was a matter of his own particular luck that the Professor, an authority on it, was a prisoner in Paula Camp. The Professor was useful, helping him to explore the language and read the texts.

One night, after the studies had progressed nicely, Professor Seckendorff told Dr. Valentin why he had been sent to Paula. His children, Hans and Clara, had been involved in the students' revolt at the University of Munich — an amateurish if sincere enterprise, a protest of the young people against the slaughter of war, against being sacrificed at Stalingrad. They had been caught, of course, and Hans and Clara had been executed, and the father, the Professor of Latin at the University, against whom nothing could be proved, was brought to Paula.

"Life means nothing to me," Professor Seckendorff had said. "I would as soon die. . . ."

Dr. Valentin, closing the lesson as usual, by jabbing insulin into the old man's ridiculously thin thigh, had laughed and said, "I keep you alive, *Herr Professor,* first, because you must be punished for having had that kind of children, and secondly, because we intellectuals must stick together and preserve *Kultur* and science under the trying circumstances of war."

The Professor winced and said nothing. The longer the lessons went on, the more time he had to change his mind. Eventually, he got to know Kellermann and learned again to value life, and he began to believe in Kellermann's postulate that he was spared to carry on what his children had died for.

Dr. Valentin's cancer research was a more serious matter. He believed that the first step in learning how to eradicate the disease was to learn how to create it; and he never got over the first step. He took the prisoners, preferably women because of the frequency of cancer of the breast, cut them and tried to infect them, kept the wounds open and festering, grafted cancerous tissue from men and mice, working with ever-increasing skill and ever-increasing frenzy. Since his human guinea pigs were inferior anyhow, and in most cases died before he could achieve tangible results, he did not waste anesthetics on them. In the medical papers which he continually wrote but never completed, were extensive footnotes on the desirability of pain for the process of healing.

The evacuation order hit him particularly hard. It meant the end of three years of research. Before starting the inspection of the line-up, he had visited the hospital hut, standing at the cots of his most hopeful cases, observing those who writhed and groaned, contemplating the ones who had gone insane with pain. He said a silent good-by, looking, for the last time, at the wounds which his own hands had carefully inflicted, sniffing the pus, and nodding when he believed he discovered the trace of a growth.

Then, with a heavy heart, he began the review. He walked past the long, quiet line, trailed by Schreckenreuther and a group of guards — a tired, discouraged man. He rarely looked at a prisoner fully; most of them he took in out of the side of his eye. His left hand, index finger erect, pointed mechanically at odd chests. Then he and Schreckenreuther and the guards moved on — the chosen man stepped forward, to live and march if he could.

Dr. Valentin stopped when he reached Professor Seckendorff. The old man wasn't good for the march, that much was clear. Dr. Valentin had come to like him in a way, and for a moment considered giving him his chance. But then he thought that, as a scientist and officer, he was duty-bound to be objective. And besides, there would be no more lessons in medieval Latin, no more pleasant readings of the ribald songs of runaway students from the monasteries. Too bad. Professor Seckendorff's usefulness was over.

Dr. Valentin passed him by.

He chose the next man in line, who seemed strong for an inmate of Paula Camp.

Dr. Valentin and Schreckenreuther and the guards moved on. Kellermann stepped forward. He stepped forward and dragged with him the Professor, who resisted feebly.

"Please!" whispered Kellermann. "I know what I'm doing."

The column of evacués from Paula Camp marched out soon after Dr. Valentin had finished his selection. Armed SS men spurted about, yelling orders, pushing and kicking the prisoners, shoving them into the slowly forming rows, three abreast, and beating back the weaker ones, those Dr. Valentin had passed by. Rifle butts were jammed into bones, whips cracked on loose skin. The weaker ones now knew the meaning of Dr. Valentin's formation — they struggled against death, mercilessly beaten down by the SS — a pitiful struggle, like flies in autumn moving toward the last speck of sunlight on the window.

The big gate was thrown open. At the head of the column Schreckenreuther reclined leisurely in his car, taking the salute of Biederkopf and those SS men and women who were to remain behind to finish the job and fulfill that part of the order concerned with the obliteration of traces. Then came the Camp band, Schreckenreuther's pet and pride, kettledrum on a pushcart, trumpets and horns. They played, *"Muss I denn, muss I denn . . . ,"* a gay marching song about a troop of soldiers leaving a little town, leaving the girls behind.

438

Then came the prisoners, trying to keep step with the music, SS men marching on both sides of the column, their Tommy guns loaded and ready to fire.

Kellermann didn't look back. He couldn't look back because the SS guard on his right would have noticed the untoward move. And he didn't want to look back; the Camp lay behind him and, SS guards or no, the march would lead, must lead, into freedom. How many of the striped, beaten, starved men and women would make it, he didn't know, and he shut out that thought. But he would make it.

Then he heard the machine guns behind him. Their chatter came from the Camp, and the band in front could not drown out the sound. Back there, they were beginning to kill the seven thousand left behind; row upon row, they would be laid on the dusty, stained ground, the little blood left in them seeping into the earth.

"Sing, you bastards!" shouted the SS. "Sing!"

Kellermann heard the Professor's quavering voice. *"Muss I denn . . ."*

> Now I must, now I must march out from here,
> But you, my dear, remain. . . .

5

IN THE Middle Ages, Neustadt had been a walled city, depending for its defense partially on the small river in whose bend it nestled. Once, the great trade route wending from the Dutch ports, through Cologne, Augsburg, and Venice to the Near East, had led through Neustadt. In those days, the merchants traveling the tortuous roads, their slow carts bringing the rich cargoes of pepper and spices and rare fabrics, stopped over in Neustadt. The town was prosperous and had a fierce, independent pride. Later, when the Americas and ocean trade became important, when Augsburg and the Hansa League declined, Neustadt fell into a sleepy existence that outlasted the walls of the city, which crumbled by themselves. So it stood, that spring of 1945, its old churches bright in the sunlight, its towers mounted by little guard towers, its small-chested houses with their gables toward the narrow streets; ingrown and clannish, hiding its poverty behind its history; its people intermarrying and relying on their own handicrafts and trades — the rope factory, the brewery, the occasional tourist who might discover the timeworn beauties of the town.

"Very nice for photographing, but otherwise something to stay away from," said Bing.

439

Troy was lounging against his command car. He had stopped his Task Force some two miles outside of Neustadt, and was listening with Karen and Yates to Bing's discourse on the quiet town which, bedded between green hills, lay at their feet.

Before Bing could continue, the first of the reconnaissance patrols which Troy had sent ahead returned. Its commander, Lieutenant Dillon, reported with a bewildered civilian who, despite the warm weather, wore a heavy black Sunday suit and held on to a walking stick to which a white, embroidered handkerchief was tied.

Dillon made the man face Troy. "We caught this bird outside of Neustadt."

"Surrender!" said the civilian.

"All right, all right," Dillon waved him aside. "We drove up all the way to the river. Could have spit across into the town. No opposition. Didn't draw any fire. Unless it's a trap, it seems to me we can go right through. The bridge was intact, as far as I could make out. It should be able to carry our equipment."

"Thank you," said Troy. "Good job. Get some rest, Dillon, and get your men something to eat." He turned to Yates. "Want to do your stunt?"

"Glad to!"

Yates addressed the civilian. "*Kommen Sie her!*"

The civilian, his baggy face worried, obeyed instantly and bowed.

"Karl Theodor Zippmann is the name." He bowed again. "I'm the apothecary of Neustadt."

Bing broke in, "Are you still making elderberry schnapps on the side, and without license?"

Zippmann paled. How could a soldier of an Army from across the Atlantic know about his elderberry schnapps? "No! No!" he cried. "I follow the law!"

"Stop it, Bing!" said Yates, in English. "You befuddle the guy!"

A sly grin lit Zippmann's face. "But maybe I've got a couple of bottles left — if you gentlemen would like some when you come into Neustadt. . . ."

"He doesn't recognize me," Bing said to Karen, half disappointed, half glad of it.

Yates remained serious. "We have no time, Herr Zippmann, to try your schnapps. Are there any German troops in Neustadt?"

"No, *Herr Offizier,* that's just what I've come to tell you. This morning, four gentlemen in all, we went out of Neustadt to meet the *Herren Amerikaner.* I'm very happy and honored on this great day in the history of our town, that it was I who was chosen to encounter you first. Herr

440

Bundesen, the wine merchant — he's head of the Chamber of Commerce — he'll never forgive me because I'm only the apothecary, but Father Schlemm said I was to go, too — "

"Wait a minute!" Yates stopped him. "You're sure there aren't any German troops in Neustadt?"

Bing couldn't contain himself. Hands behind his back, he came at Zippmann from the side, so that the man didn't know which way to turn. Impatiently, he said, "Herr Zippmann, if we come in and find a single German soldier, I'll see to it personally that you're shot!"

"*Ja, Herr* — " Zippmann was squirming. "We had a garrison — that is, until last night we had one."

"How many men?" asked Yates.

"About forty. But they left in an awful hurry. And *Kreisleiter* Morgenstern went with them, and three men from his office. But his wife is still in town, though he took his secretary along — the bounder! And about half the *Volkssturm* left, too — those that were Nazis; the others just didn't report and stayed home."

Zippmann's detailed account sounded truthful to Yates. Why was Bing taking it out on him?

"And the bridge was mined!" Zippmann went on busily. "But Father Schlemm said to old Uli the fisherman that maybe he could cut the wires, and that's what Uli did, and so the bridge is still there."

"Who is this Father Schlemm?"

"He's the priest of St. Margarethen's. He said we must tell the Americans that the Nazis have gone and the soldiers have gone, and that we surrender the town, because otherwise they'll come with their guns and shoot everything to bits in Neustadt."

"Perhaps that's what you deserve!" said Bing.

"Cut it out!" ordered Yates. Switching back to German, he asked Zippmann, "This priest, this Father Schlemm, is a good man?" He thought of Father Gregor in Ensdorf, and he was hopeful.

"Yes, of course." Zippmann hesitated the fraction of a second. "You see, *Herr Offizier,* I'm a Protestant. But I get along!"

"I never heard of a Father Schlemm," Bing said in English. "Probably got into the parish after my time. But Zippmann is a fairly decent character. Under the Nazis, my father had to come to him after hours if we needed medicine. He always helped us."

"Why have you been riding him?"

"I know this town, Lieutenant. . . ."

Yates shrugged. Then he turned and gave Troy the essentials of the apothecary's information, adding, "I'd be careful anyhow, Captain."

Troy strolled over to the civilian and studied him. "All right!" he said at last. "What are we waiting for?"

He gave the signal to advance.

The Engineers checked the bridge and found that Zippmann had spoken the truth.

Then the guns and the armored cars and the trucks rolled into the old town, clattering over the cobblestones, their noise re-echoing from the quaint houses in the narrow streets. Otherwise, it was a silent welcome. It had a depressing note that didn't let you feel quite comfortable in spite of the old-fashioned, sunny, *gemütlich* atmosphere.

Yates could see the faces pressed to the closed windows, peering between shutters. From the gables, from the alcoves, from the beams of the wood-work, from wherever the inventive Nazis had discovered that flagpoles could be mounted, hung improvised white flags — bed sheets, towels, pillow cases. The people, apparently, wanted to make sure that their intentions could not be misunderstood. Still, the overzealousness in surrender was too obvious. It didn't inspire confidence.

But after all, Yates thought, neither he nor Troy nor the men with him had come here expecting confidence from these people. Surrender or no, postcard prettiness or no, Neustadt was part of the enemy, and the next-door neighbor of Paula Camp.

The road broadened to a fairly large, oblong square, at one end of which stood the Gothic city hall. Behind it loomed the two towers of St. Margarethen's, symbolically ruling the town; and just as the lead vehicles of the column pulled up before the city hall, the bells of St. Margarethen's began to ring, somber and sonorous, as they had tolled for Easter or for Hitler's birthday or the Emperors' birthdays before.

Some vehicles drew up on the market square; others went on to the end of town to guard the approaches to Neustadt. Troy got out of his command car and, pistol drawn, hurried up the steps to the main door of the city hall. He pushed against the massive door; it came open readily enough. Inside, the stone vaults were cool and dark, and they smelled of mold. The floor was littered with papers, some torn, some hastily burned around the edges, signs of disorderly retreat. His foot kicked them aside. Then he turned.

Outside the door, on the top of the stairs, he called over the din of the bells and the racket of the motors, "Lieutenant Dillon! Lieutenant Dillon! The flag! Let's haul down that God-damned bed sheet on the pole and hoist something with meaning in it!"

Bing did not participate in the conquest of Neustadt. He said to Yates,

"Please, let me go now. This is very important to me. I'm home. I'm back where I started from."

Yates let him go, saying, "Take it easy."

Bing walked through the streets that seemed so much smaller than he had carried them in his mind, and he thought, I bet I could close my eyes and still find my way. He passed by Zippmann's pharmacy. It was locked. He looked into the show window, which was much barer than he remembered it; but he thought he could smell the herbs Zippmann once mixed so dexterously.

And there was the house where he was born and had lived; the window on the first floor still had the iron bar across; his father had had it placed there to prevent the child, who loved to play at the window, from falling out. In that doorway his mother used to stand, waiting for him to return from school; he would rush to her, back to the security of the house, back from the adventure among so many strangers. A great longing surged through him, to go into this house, to sit in the room that had been his, and then to go into the dining room, to wait there until he could hear his father's homecoming steps, and his mother's soft-voiced greeting. He never knew what they said to one another; when he was small, he could not understand them, and when he grew to boyhood, he hadn't wanted to.

He rang the outside bell to the apartment. No one answered.

He rang all the bells, just ran his finger down the line of buttons next to the neat white row of names. People stuck their heads out of the windows, others came out of their apartments and asked what he wanted.

"What's the matter?" he said. "Nobody home on the first floor?"

They didn't know him; he had left a child, and returned a man, in a strange uniform.

"No, *Herr Soldat*," said a woman, "nobody's at home there."

"Where are they?"

No answer. The woman retreated a little.

He looked at the nameplate for the apartment. "Who's this Friemel living there?"

"He's an attorney, *Herr Soldat*," said the woman. "It says so right there."

"Nazi?"

Silence.

"Fled?"

Silence.

"I want to get in there."

"Nobody has a key, *Herr Soldat*," the woman assured him, with seeming helpfulness.

Then Bing recalled that once or twice, his father had mentioned the name Friemel. Friemel was the man who had forced his father out of

443

practice, and then taken over. It had been one of those deals: Either you agree, or I make you agree.

He cut through the people and went into the house. The door of the apartment was locked. He raised his foot and kicked, hard. The door gave.

He was inside, alone.

He had hoped that something of the old spirit of the rooms would be there. But they were different, shabby. The wallpaper had been changed, and there was new, cheap furniture. The only thing remaining was the metal cover camouflaging the radiator in the foyer. For a moment, he considered tearing off a part of it — but it would have been a sad souvenir. He walked through the rooms without pausing in any of them. He didn't belong here. The house that had been anchored in his life was gone, though, outwardly, it stood. The real home of his childhood was a picture in his mind.

He felt the shreds of what he had feared was in him, fall away. He had no relation to these people — not because a Herr Friemel lived where his youth had been rooted, not because he and his father and his mother had been driven away from here, but because he had changed and grown roots elsewhere.

He walked out without looking back. He left the door wide open and hoped that the neighbors, or soldiers passing by, would help themselves to Herr Friemel's possessions.

A woman ran toward him and stopped in front of him. She stared at him questioningly, and as he looked at her full face, she cried breathlessly, "Oh, it *is* you! they told me someone had come to the Friemel's and gone in there, and I knew right away it was you. Yes, I knew it. How big you have become, how strong! And how good you look in uniform! Little Walter Bing, how he's grown!"

A crowd gathered again, and Bing turned around and shouted, "Get away — all of you!" He reached for his carbine. They ran.

The woman laughed. "That's right, Herr Bing! Show 'em who's boss, now!"

"You're Frieda, aren't you?" he said.

"How's *Herr Doktor* Bing and your mother? I can't tell you how often I have wished that the good old days would come back. They were such nice people, and so kind to a maid — I've always said to Robert, that's my husband — yes, I'm married. . . ." She laughed, familiarly. "I've said to him, Robert, you can say what you want about the Jews, but they're the best people to work for. Well, your father wasn't Jewish, but your mother was, and if she wasn't the kindest, most good-hearted person. . . ."

"You haven't changed much, Frieda."

She looked down at her body. "I have two children, I didn't want

444

them, only Robert said we must have children, every German has children. I carry myself well, though, don't I?"

She pushed her breasts out.

Bing remembered her breasts. He must have been about nine, then. He had been told to call Frieda. He ran into her room and found her before the mirror, naked to the waist, combing her hair. He stood in the door, transfixed. She had kept on combing her hair. She had laughed, a deep laugh. "They're nice, no?" she had said. "If you're good, maybe . . ." But apparently, he had never been a good enough boy, and then 1933 had come, and she left the house, and his mother had to do all the work.

"Where's your husband?" he asked.

"Robert?" She laughed again. "Oh, he was so stupid. He let himself be drafted into the *Volkssturm*. He's gone. God knows where he is now. Will you visit us? We have a little place, very cozy, you know I keep house well, up on Breite Strasse, Number 9. You must come. Can you come now?"

"No," he said slowly, "I don't think I can. I don't think I'm going to stay here long."

"You can sleep in the house," she said. "A nice soft bed, with white sheets, like in the good old times, and two pillows for you. And if you want to, I'll tuck you in, like it used to be when you were a little boy. Such a good boy you were, never any trouble. . . ."

"I must go now," he said. "My Lieutenant's waiting for me."

"*Ach,* this war! . . ."

He went, and she called after him, "You won't forget the address?"

He didn't answer. He didn't feel as sure of himself as he had when he'd stormed out of his parents' home. He wished Frieda hadn't run into him, bringing back to him the boyhood he wanted forgotten. And how easy it had been for her to approach him! . . . Some conqueror!

Bing met Karen in front of the city hall. He was glad to see her, almost relieved; it was as if he'd stepped out of a sultry afternoon into the cool shade.

"How was the homecoming?" she said. "Did you meet anyone?"

"Just the maid that used to work for our family," he answered. "Gabby as ever. She gave me her whole history since I left Neustadt."

"And how do you feel?"

"About what?" he asked back, harshly.

"About being home?" And, as he said nothing, she continued, "I mean, if I came home to where I was born, after so many years . . ."

"It isn't home," he said; "that's just it. America is. And believe me I'm happy about it, Karen."

She felt the restlessness in him.

445

"And boy, was I worried!" he went on. "When I came into Germany, I thought I might find myself back in the old rut, liking their way of life — I don't mean the Nazi way. I mean what's good in the Germans — their pettiness, their thoroughness, their regulated days, their well-defined social scale — all that has its good side, too — and then the old town, the atmosphere. But it says nothing to me any more. I saw the house where I was a child, and it isn't the house where I was a child."

He was trying so hard to convince himself. . . . She said, "I'm sorry you went off alone. I thought I might come along with you. Maybe it would have been helpful."

"What's up, Karen?" he asked. "Are you reconsidering?"

"No, dear."

"Well — what then?"

"I want to see you back on your feet."

He didn't want that kind of relationship. He had been at Friemel's apartment; he was free of the past — all of it.

"I tell you what we'll do," he said. "I'll show you the town. We'll go to my school and you'll take a picture of me: *The Most Successful Graduate of Neustadt Gymnasium.* Nice caption? I am — you know? I survived! The boys who used to make it tough on me are dead, or prisoners, or still busy losing their war. Let's rip the town wide open!"

"Let's!"

The white flags had blossomed out into crude signs, *Welcome to our Liberators!* and Karen read the words with skeptical eyes.

"Liberation . . . !" said Bing, with the tongue in cheek intonation the men had learned in Germany. You couldn't very well stay on the level about the great word when these signs barged into view; when full-bosomed, freckled, well-dressed *Fräuleins* told you, first thing, how much nicer you were than the Nazis, how glad they were that you had arrived and not the Russians — and did you have any cigarettes; when well-nourished, roundheaded kids, so different from the spindly children of France and Belgium, greeted you cheerily, their stubby hands outstretched in the Hitler salute, and asked you for candy and chocolate in exchange for cheap souvenirs, or the promise to lead you to their big sister.

"You know," said Karen, "I'm not sure how these Germans made out as conquerors, but they're awfully good at being the conquered."

"Do a column on it, sometime — why don't you? We don't liberate these people — we liberate cameras, pistols, SS daggers. And why the hell not? The Germans are sort of willing to accept that kind of liberation. They know what their own men have done; and I think they're glad to get away that easily."

A group of soldiers came prancing down the street, sporting top hats, lifting them with wide, sweeping motions, and hollering, *"Guten Tag! Kommen Sie her, Fräulein!"*

"That's going to hurt the Krauts," said Bing. "In Neustadt, a top hat is what makes you a respectable citizen. Those pieces come down from father to son."

Karen laughed. "What about Troy? Can't he stop them?"

"Why should he? What fun do the men have? The trouble is, they take the top hat first, and then they start trading. Ultimately, the German ends up with both his top hat and our cigarettes."

"And then?"

"And then Troy moves on. And then the rear echelon takes over. That's when the liberation becomes organized." Bing shrugged. "D'you remember Mr. Crerar?"

"Faintly."

"I liked him. He got into Willoughby's hair. Now he's back in the States, left right after the Bulge. Anyhow, once, when I showed him the copy for the Fourth of July leaflet, he said: You've got to have an Army of crusaders if you want to make a crusade. Exaggerated, like all those hard-and-fast rules. To my mind, the stolen top hats are just as much part of it as the stand these men made in the Bulge Battle. It's all America."

Karen had no ready reply. And before she could think of one, Bing began to hurry toward two men in striped, pajamalike suits. One of them sat, exhausted, on the curbstone, leaning against the base of a street lamp; the other pleaded in vain with passers-by for help. The few civilians on the street went around them in a wide circle.

"Who are you? Where are you from?" demanded Bing. Then he saw the face of the old man sitting on the ground, the closed, sunken eyes, the sagging chin, the white hair growing in patches; the sharp, black whip-cuts on the other man's cheeks; the miserable weariness of both of them. He toned down his voice, and softly, he said, "Can I help you?"

"We're from Paula Camp," said Kellermann. "We escaped. . . ."

Inside the city hall, Troy had taken over *Kreisleiter* Morgenstern's office and had installed Lieutenant Dillon as provisional Military Governor of Neustadt.

"I can't leave you more than a platoon of men," he said to Dillon. "That ought to be enough to hold order in this town and to watch the road, so that we can maintain some sort of communication with Division. You've got to have curfew at 1900, and you've got to keep the streets patrolled. If you should have trouble with real German troops that outnumber you, pull out and retire and try to let me know."

"All right, sir." Dillon was a youngish man with thin shoulders and a long, anemic-looking face. "I'm much more concerned, though, about the

Krauts right here in town. I don't know anything about government — I only voted once in my life, straight Republican. And we've got to have a civilian government, so we can at least announce curfew."

"Get yourself a town crier, or something!" recommended Yates.

"What about that priest?" asked Troy.

"Waiting outside," said Yates. "I had Zippmann fetch him."

"Well, call him in!" Troy demanded.

The man who entered, and remained modestly standing at the door, wore his black frock and the silver chain and cross very consciously. His face was so carefully and closely shaved that his upholstered jaws and chin showed a rosy hue. The pink fitted well with his lively, light eyes and his short, drab hair that was parted at the side and held in place with pomade.

"Father Schlemm?" Yates asked.

"Yes. I'm the parish priest of St. Margarethen's, the biggest parish in town." He spoke perfect English, American English, and the factual tone with which he had introduced himself took away from the self-praise of the statement. "I speak your language, gentlemen, because I fear you have difficulties with the German. I studied for a number of years at a Jesuit College in New Jersey."

Dillon breathed easier. At least he had found someone with whom he could work.

"I understand you have been instrumental in surrendering this town?" said Yates.

Father Schlemm considered. "Surrender, sir, is not the word. The Church is like a mother, it prefers preserving to destroying."

"Well, what's the difference?" said Troy, averse to fine points at this time.

Father Schlemm raised his thin brows slightly. "The Church does not meddle in politics, sir. It is not of this world."

Dillon saw himself losing his interpreter before he had nailed him. He said hastily, "This is an emergency!"

The priest creased his forehead with some difficulty. "Certainly! But it's not of our making!"

"Does that mean that you refuse to co-operate with us?" Troy lifted himself out of *Kreisleiter* Morgenstern's big office chair, walked around the desk and up to the priest. Father Schlemm held his ground.

"On the contrary," he said. "Of course it depends on what you want us to do. Right now, we are the only organized and functioning body in a vacuum, aside from your troops who will pass on sooner or later."

"That's better," said Troy.

Yates noticed that Father Schlemm, in the few minutes since his en-

448

trance, had moved himself into a bargaining position. "We want order," he said impatiently. "Not the kind of order you had here — a democratic one. And by God, we'll have it. You have the choice, Father Schlemm — we'll establish it with or without you."

The priest bowed slightly and said nothing.

"Let's get the thing organized!" demanded Troy. "We've got to get going. What about a Mayor?"

"The *Bürgermeister!*" Yates specified.

"The Mayor we had, has left with *Kreisleiter* Morgenstern. So have the other top officials." Father Schlemm spoke factually, without implied criticism of the fugitives.

"Do you know of anybody who could fill the job?" asked Yates.

"Of course," said Father Schlemm. "On my way over here to see you, I took the liberty of compiling a short list of men who, I feel, would fill the key posts in the administration of Neustadt satisfactorily, both to you and the people."

"Why didn't you say so right away?" Dillon exclaimed, relieved.

The priest smiled benevolently. "I wasn't sure you wanted me to submit it. And in giving it, I wish to stress that the Church dissociates itself from all responsibility of what these men might do in office."

"Quit hedging!" said Troy. "Who are the guys?"

"Herr Bundesen, the wine merchant and president of the Chamber of Commerce, is the logical choice for Mayor," Father Schlemm explained. "He's widely respected and has great executive ability, as his position in the business world proves. The City Engineer, Herr Sonderstein, has chosen to remain at his post instead of fleeing with *Kreisleiter* Morgenstern. He is available as Assistant Mayor in Charge of Public Utilities."

"Very good!" said Dillon, happy that he wouldn't have to worry about garbage.

"Herr Kleinbauch, who is head of the Neustadt Central Savings Bank, a small but very solvent institution, is the man for City Treasurer."

"What about the Chief of Police?" urged Dillon.

"I was coming to him," Father Schlemm assured him. "The man I have in mind is a retired police inspector, *Polizei-Oberinspektor,* to be precise, by the name of Wohlfahrt. He has the gout, sometimes, but he's all right at present."

"You wouldn't have a younger, more active man?" Dillon asked, a little disappointed.

"No, I'm sorry," said Father Schlemm, again with the slight, benevolent smile. "Younger and active men are rare in Germany, these days."

There was something too pat about Father Schlemm's cabinet, Yates thought. Willoughby might approve of it — but that was all the more rea-

449

son why he should treat it warily, while he had the chance and could influence Troy.

He said, "Are you sure, Father, that these men would accept if we suggested their provisional appointment to office?"

"If I advise them to, yes," the priest said quietly. "They are good members of the Church."

"Tell me, Father," Yates asked, "were these men Nazis?"

It took the priest a second to relax the sudden tightening of his rotund face. Then he said, "Yes, they were. Everybody who was anything in Germany belonged to the National-Socialist Party. It was the same as — let us say — in the State of Mississippi, where anybody who wishes to maintain his position in society naturally is a Democrat."

Troy snickered.

Yates turned to the Captain, "Your men didn't get murdered in the Bulge so that we can re-establish what murdered them."

"You're right," Troy admitted, "only the good Father put it so neatly."

"But who's going to keep the electricity running?" asked Dillon. "I don't know how they work it here. . . ."

"Let's talk this over again," Yates said to the priest. "Sit down, Father, here's a chair."

Father Schlemm looked up at Yates. He found the American officer's fine face similar to that of the Apostle Simon whose statue was to the left of the main gate of St. Margarethen's. Sensitive, but severe. He promised himself to show the Apostle to the officer, if he stayed on in town. The American seemed the type that would be interested in that sort of thing.

Yates noticed the priest's stomach resting on his thighs, he noticed the hands folded over the stomach. "Have you heard of Paula Camp?" he inquired.

The priest lowered his lids. He seemed to be regarding his knees. "I know of it," he said, his mouth pained. "Some of my parishioners were taken there. I've tried to save them. . . ."

"And yet you dare to propose to us the names of men who belonged to the same Party that instituted Paula Camp?"

"You just don't know Germany, sir!" Father Schlemm remonstrated. "Neither Herr Bundesen nor any of the other gentlemen had anything to do with Paula Camp."

"Let's put our cards on the table, Father Schlemm!"

"Yes, gladly!" The benevolence was gone from the priest's rosy face. He nervously patted the small island of short hair on his head. "What kind of Government do you want? Who *is* there to take over the power? You should be happy that we have some men of decency and reputation left who are willing to help you."

"Well! Who, really, is this Government that you suggest to us?" All Yates's outrage was in his voice.

The priest gripped the seat of his chair.

"I am, Lieutenant!"

The door was torn open. Bing pushed two men in striped baggy suits into the room. "Go ahead, Professor! Don't be afraid!"

Then, turning toward Yates, Troy, and Dillon, Bing said, "I'm sorry to interrupt. But these two men escaped from Paula Camp. I thought their information so urgent that I went right through to you."

Troy wheeled around. The priest, Neustadt, Government, garbage disposal became so much unnecessary tinsel.

Yates looked from the two escaped men to the priest and back.

The priest noticed his glance. He rose. "Holy Mother!" he said, "these people must be fed and taken care of. I'll see to that."

"Sit down, Father Schlemm!" Yates commanded. "First let us hear what they have to say!" He addressed the younger of the two escaped prisoners. "You may speak German. What is your name?"

"Rudolf Kellermann." And, with a tired motion, "This is Professor Seckendorff of the University of Munich."

"You came from Paula Camp? How did you get away?"

"We didn't escape from the Camp. . . ."

"Well, where did you escape from?"

"From a railhead."

"Railhead? I thought you were from Paula Camp!"

"We are. We were being evacuated. Five thousand of us, the strongest. Seven thousand remained in Camp. . . ."

"And they're still there?"

Kellermann smiled. It was a smile that cut into you. "I don't know. . . ."

Troy was waiting impatiently. Yates gave him a preliminary report.

"Lieutenant Dillon!" called Troy. "Will you see to it that all unit commanders are notified: We're leaving in exactly half an hour?"

Troy gave his own chair to the Professor; he tersely motioned Father Schlemm out of his chair and shoved it behind Kellermann. "Half an hour, Dillon!" he repeated. "I'd like to save some of the seven thousand in Paula Camp — if any are left."

"Yes, sir!" Dillon hurried out.

Yates was again questioning Kellermann. "How did you escape?"

"It was dark," said Kellermann. "There was such a muddle at the railhead . . ."

"Can't you speak louder? Have a drink!" Yates passed his canteen to Kellermann and to the Professor.

Kellermann drank slowly. "They had marched us all day. At night we reached the railhead. As the train pulled in we made our break. They had no time for a long search, they were in a hurry. Then we walked west. West, we thought, that's where the Americans will be. When we came close to this place, we saw the white flags, and we saw an armored car with a white star on it standing near the big factory at the end of town. So I said to the Professor: We've made it. These are the Americans."

"And they came into this town," Bing continued. "Miss Wallace and myself, we saw them sitting on the street, and every damned German was passing them by, in a nice wide circle."

"Neustadt!" said Troy, in a tone indicating how academic anything but his continued advance had become to him. "We've got only a few more minutes to set up their Government, Yates. Let's get going!"

Yates turned to Kellermann. "How long have you been in Paula Camp?"

"Ten months."

"And before that?"

"Munitions factory. I was arrested for sabotage."

"Did you do any?"

"No, didn't have a chance. But I saw the Russians and Poles do it; they were slave workers there. I didn't stop them."

"A fanatic," said Father Schlemm.

Kellermann heard the priest's tone. He looked from Father Schlemm to Yates, and seemed to close himself up.

Yates said to Kellermann, "My name is Yates. I'm an American officer. And I tell you that, to us, your opinions are as valid as Father Schlemm's. . . . Where were you before you worked in the munitions plant?"

"Army hospital," said Kellermann. "I was wounded in North Africa."

"What unit?"

"999th Light Brigade."

"Wasn't that a punitive outfit?"

"Yes, sir, for political criminals."

Yates lapsed into silence. Neither he nor Troy had any directives about who was to become the new Government. He looked at Kellermann — the red-rimmed eyes, the hollow cheeks with the stripes of dried blood. Then he made his choice.

"Captain, I think I've got the right Mayor for this place!" And in German, "Herr Kellermann, will you help us to run Neustadt?"

Kellermann, who had just sat down on the chair the priest had vacated, got up. It was the first time in years that he had been addressed civilly. He had a choking feeling in his throat. The new time was beginning, the time for which he had hung on to life. "Perhaps you'd better take the Professor," he said. "He's an educated man."

452

"You're a little stronger," smiled Yates.

"I do not know how good I'll be as *Bürgermeister*," said Kellermann solemnly. "But I promise you, there won't be any trouble with Nazis."

Father Schlemm bowed and turned to go. Troy called after him, "What's the hurry, Father? If we decide to give the job to Mr. Kellermann, he will need your co-operation."

"I told you already," said the priest, "the Church cannot participate in politics."

Yates said cuttingly, "You mean: If you, yourself, are not the Government, you're going to sabotage it. Do I understand you right?"

"You're insinuating, sir!" Father Schlemm replied. "You may impose the rule of a man escaped from concentration camp on the city of Neustadt. But you cannot expect me to persuade the citizens of this community to accept and like that rule!"

Troy took Yates aside. "We can't afford trouble in this place as long as Division hasn't caught up with us."

"It's a matter of principle," said Yates.

"Dillon and his few men can't face a mutinous town."

"I'll leave Bing here," said Yates, cornered. "That'll give Dillon someone who at least speaks the language and can serve as liaison."

"Let's not be stubborn!" Troy's mind was on the road to Paula Camp.

"What security do you have with four Nazis in office?" asked Yates.

There was no answer to that. Troy walked to the window. He saw his column forming on the market square, he saw his car and driver waiting before the city hall. He saw Lieutenant Dillon rushing up the stairs, to tell him that all was ready to push off. He felt the eyes of everybody in the room directed at the back of his neck.

He turned around.

"Father Schlemm, was this druggist you sent us, this Zippmann — was he in the Nazi Party?"

"No," said the priest, "not that I know of."

"Then the druggist is your Mayor!"

Father Schlemm wagged his head. "It will be difficult, sir. Herr Zippmann, unfortunately, is a Protestant. And this is a Catholic community."

Troy's fist came down on the window sill. "God damn it, Father! Christ died for the Protestants, too!"

The priest bowed his head.

Bing's lips were curled, slightly. He caught Yates's eye, and Yates understood: We're improvising again — American pioneers, trying to make the best of it. We have no policy. But what the hell *can* we do? We've got to go ahead!

Dillon came in and reported.

Troy put on his helmet. "Sergeant Bing! Lieutenant Yates wants you

453

to stay here to assist Lieutenant Dillon for the time being. Dillon! You have your instructions. And have these two men taken care of."

Troy glanced once more at Seckendorff and Kellermann, and a worried look came into his eyes. He would have thousands of such people on his hands.

"Let's go, Yates!"

Bing and the priest followed them downstairs. Bing saw the column move out, the armored machines so out of place in the old streets. He listened until the last faint echoes died down.

Then he heard the calm voice of the priest, "You people will have much to learn."

"Yes?" said Bing. "From whom?"

6

THE CITIZENS of Neustadt followed the curfew regulations to the dot. After seven o'clock, every breathing thing, except stray cats and dogs and the occasional American patrols, was inside the houses. The windows were dark. Mayor Zippmann had been told to let the citizens know that the thinnest ray would cause the Americans to fire into the lighted windows. Dillon was very conscious of the size of his job; he had begun to feel his isolation as soon as Troy and the Task Force had pushed on.

But he had not been able to keep his few men keyed up. Or, perhaps, they were too keyed up. They sprawled on the chairs of the dining room of the Hotel *Zum Adler* that had been taken over as billets, and proceeded to get drunk. There was nothing else to do, and the liquor made you feel big and good, and it couldn't be taken along when you moved on, tomorrow or day after tomorrow, and the best way to carry liquor, anyhow, was inside of you. The patrols returning from their tour of duty hurried to catch up with the progress the others had made; and the men relieving them went out into the dark, crooked streets, pleasantly tanked up.

Bing drank because he had come home, the only successful graduate of his class, and thank God, home meant nothing to him any more. He drank because Karen was so reasonable, because she had been kind to him, and because he knew that this kindness meant precisely nothing. But he drank alone. He had come up to Neustadt with these men. They were probably nice men; only you hadn't much chance to get close to them on the trip, with them cooped up in their vehicles and you in yours. And now he couldn't get close to them. Home came the soldier — they wouldn't understand how he felt; and if he explained it, they'd stare at him as at a two-headed fetus in alcohol. So what! They were the best soldiers in the world, and in a pinch, you could rely on them to the end. And if they wanted to get drunk, they had a right to — and more power to them!

He stuck his head out of the door to let the evening breeze cool it. There was no wind outside. It had become very dark, the moon was behind a silver-fringed cloud; he could see the oddly hunched outline of the city hall, and the street lamp in front of it — curlicued iron, its light bulb switched off. And from farther away, the voices of a couple of men on patrol, out of tune, but good and loud, singing "A Pretty Girl Is Like a Melody." . . .

Something was wrong. Bing didn't know what it was, he couldn't put his finger on it, and there wasn't a sound aside from the singing. He went back into the dining room and spoke to Master Sergeant Ebbett, the ranking noncom. Ebbett looked up from his glass and said, "If there's trouble, we'll hear about it in plenty of time. Why don't you go to bed and sleep it off?"

Ebbett's eyes were small and bloodshot and his look said plainly: Why don't you mind your own business, Bud? So Bing said, "It's too early to turn in. Mind if I take a little walk?"

"Go ahead!" shrugged Ebbett. "Just don't get lost. I ain't going to send anybody tonight to search for you."

"I know this town like my own pocket," said Bing. "I won't get lost." He took his carbine and his flashlight and marched out of the Hotel *Zum Adler,* suddenly sober, but still with the feeling of tenseness. He thought he knew where it came from and how to get rid of it.

He did know the town like his own pocket, even in the dark, and he laughed to himself. He took back alleys and pitch-black passageways that led through houses from one street to another, and he emerged on Breite Strasse, which seemed to have been given its name, Broad Street, as a joke, so narrow it was. He flashed his light to find Number 9, and rang the bell.

There was no answer. He sniffed the night air and waited, chasing off a short wave of disappointment. He looked down the street, along the curving walls of the houses, and knew, suddenly, what he had been missing and had not been able to pin down: the white flags were gone.

He rang again. Glancing upward, he found that Frieda's house didn't show white, either — not even a handkerchief.

Then he heard soft, shuffling steps. The door opened a slit, and then wider; for a moment, yellow light spilled out of Number 9. He stepped hurriedly inside and closed the door behind him.

She was barefoot and had thrown a jacket over her nightgown. She said, *"Ach Gott,* it's young Herr Bing! You scared me." She drew him close, so that he felt her warm body, and led him gently up the stairs. *"Shhh* . . . the children are sleeping. I'm so glad they finally dozed off. What a day it was for them!"

455

"Exciting?"

"You'd be surprised how they know the difference!" she said.

"What difference?"

"*Die Amerikaner,* they say, they give us chocolate. Are the Americans going to be here always?" She pressed Bing's arm. "And this is our good room, 'the *Salon,*' Robert calls it. I let him, he's a good husband, I married well. But what does he know what a real *salon* is like? When he says the word, I must always think of the *salon* your parents had, with a real grand piano and satin chairs. And I had to clean it every day. Your mother was particular."

Bing sat down in the grandfather chair and rested his boots on the footstool. She bent down to stroke his hair; her jacket came open, he looked down her breasts.

"You know how I recognized you?" she whispered. "You still have the mouth and the chin you had as a boy, stubbornlike; you always had to have your way. I think you still always get your way, don't you? . . . My God, how he sits there; Robert never sits in that chair, he saves it for visitors on Sunday."

He wished she'd stop talking about Robert who saved his good furniture for Sundays.

"You used to sit on my lap," she said, "now I could sit on yours. That's only fair, isn't it?"

She didn't wait for a reply. "That's good," she said, "that'll make me warm. Take off that belt, it's hard. What have you got in there? Cartridges? *Ach,* this war! Take it off."

He unhooked his cartridge belt. "Tell me, Frieda — why are all the white flags down?"

He could feel her move away, just a trifle. Then she came closer again.

"That! Oh, that's nothing. I guess people think you can't see them at night, anyhow." She took off her jacket. "This *Ersatz* wool — it scratches my skin. . . ."

Her arms were round and white, and she had smooth shoulders. Her nipples shone dark through the pink fluffiness of the gown. She saw his eyes on them. "They're still good. I didn't feed my children that way. Robert said I should, he's just superstitious, they don't grow any worse if they're fed from the bottle. A woman's got to hold on to what she has."

"Did anyone tell you to take down your white flag?"

"Remember?" Her tone was far-off. "Once you came into my room and you saw me before the mirror. Your eyes were as big as saucers, and I knew what you were thinking. Feel them — are they still the same?"

His hand went to her breast.

"Both hands!" she urged.

"I asked you something!"

She laughed. "I asked *you* something! How are they?"

"Nice and firm!"

"You were such a little boy then! What would your mother have said? I'd have been fired. . . . Kiss them."

He did. She looked down on him as if he were still the little boy, and she felt the soft drawing in her breast and through her body.

He tapped her gently on the back. "Who told you to take down the white flag?"

"*Ach,* this war! Always this war. A woman who works for Bundesen at the wine cellars."

"What did she say?"

"She said it wasn't necessary any more to have that rag out. And I knew for whom she worked, so I took it down."

"Get off," he said, "get off me!"

She put her arms about him and clung to him and kissed him and ran the tip of her tongue over his eyelids and his cheeks and behind his ear lobes.

"Stay," she pleaded. "You must stay. You won't be sorry."

She stopped dead. They both had heard it. The shot. And then a whole volley of shots. And then hobnailed boots running. They stared at each other, white-faced. She picked up her jacket but seemed not to have the strength to cover herself.

Bing grabbed his belt and his carbine and ran down the stairs and out of the house. He must reach Dillon and the men in the hotel. They didn't know the town; he knew every one of its crooked byways. He could lead them, to fight back, or to escape.

He ran through a deserted alley. Over the firing and the shouts, he heard his own steps and his breathing. He cursed and prayed: It couldn't be true, he couldn't be punished that cruelly; but if punishment had to come, let it come on him, not on the others, the innocent drunks.

Into a passage — how dark it was! All windows were closed. The people, the bastards, the traitors, they hid behind their walls, in their beds, waiting for the outcome. The cobblestones were sharp under his feet. He stumbled.

He came into the next street. It wasn't more than two blocks to the hotel, if Dillon and the men were still there. The firing increased in volume.

He wanted to cross the street. Then he heard the hobnailed boots to the right, and the hobnailed boots to the left. He saw the glint of bayonets, and the dull reflections on the German steel helmets. They were blocking the street from both ends. He ducked back into the passageway. He heard their voices, their laughter. They were getting along all right. There seemed to be more men in this one street than Dillon had all together, even figuring that all the patrols had succeeded in getting back to the hotel.

No sense waiting in the passage. He made his way back through it, hoping that the next street would be free. It was. But when he started to run down it, another group of Germans appeared at the corner. They were all over this God-damned town.

There was no other direction for Bing than the alleyway back to Breite Strasse. This he took — no longer running, but stealthily walking, taking advantage of his rubber-soled boots. Around the bend of Breite Strasse, too, were the voices of German soldiers. Bing dashed across, through the still open door of Number 9, and threw the lock into its bolt. Slowly, each step like a rock, he walked upstairs. The carbine trailed in his hand. He hadn't fired a single round — not one.

The woman was still sitting in the big chair. She looked as if she had been weeping. She saw him and came to him.

Bing turned off the light, went to the window, and opened the shutters. He listened to the firing, which grew more and more sporadic. Then a single last shot, and a roar of shouts. The bells of St. Margarethen's began to ring.

He closed the shutters but didn't turn on the light. He had betrayed his Army — Dillon, Troy, Yates, everybody. When they needed him most, he hadn't been there. He hadn't fought the Germans either, though he could have picked off a few, in Breite Strasse or any other street, before they could have got him. He had run. He had run into hiding with his mother's old maid, in the town where he was born and grew up, the most successful graduate of his class.

"You knew it all along, you bitch," he said into the dark. "See this knife? No, you can't see it, but it's in my hand, all right. I'm going to run it through you, if it's the last thing I do."

She whimpered.

He stood, undecided. So, if he killed her — then, what?

She said, her voice childishly high: "I didn't know it. All I knew was about the white flag. I prayed you'd come here tonight. With me, you're safe."

He heard her feet pattering on the linoleum floor. She was quite near him, now, seeking him.

"Come to bed," she whispered.

His fist shot out, blindly. He hit something soft, giving.

There was a short, sharp gasp. Then he heard her whisper, "Hit me. Anything. Anything that makes you feel good. Here I am. . . ."

In city hall, where Troy had inaugurated the short-lived American rule, *Kreisleiter* Morgenstern conducted his purge. He had come back with the garrison of Neustadt, the loyal section of the *Volkssturm,* and an under-strength Battalion of Infantry that had been separated from its Division, had lost its way, and was easily persuaded to turn and give battle to so small an opposition. Morgenstern had no illusions. Perhaps he wouldn't remain in Neustadt forever, but while he was here, he would make the most of it.

"The Americans locked up in jail?"

The garrison commander, a kid of a second lieutenant, grimier than he had a right to be with the battle so short, said eagerly, "All locked up. Ten of them. Six badly wounded. All of them drunk. Swine."

"I want you to leave the dead lying around," said Morgenstern.

"What an example!" said the Lieutenant.

"Now, bring me that black-frocked whoremaster, that little monk!"

Two soldiers shoved in Father Schlemm.

The priest had not gone to bed at all after he had seen the white flags disappear. He had sat up on the stiff-backed chair in his study, meditating. When the soldiers had come to pick him up, he was ready.

"What do you think, Lieutenant?" asked Morgenstern. "A man with a fat neck like that wiggles longer when he hangs from a rope, doesn't he?"

"Takes longer to cut through the upholstery," confirmed the Lieutenant.

"Traitor!" said Morgenstern. "You know what we do with traitors, no doubt?"

Father Schlemm said, "You and your soldiers had gone. If it is treason to save a German town from being destroyed, to save the women and children of many of the men with you — your own wife among them, *Herr Kreisleiter* — innocents all, from being killed by American cannon . . ." He played with the cross that hung from his neck, and repeated what he had told Troy: "The Church is a mother, it prefers preserving to destroying."

Whatever Morgenstern felt about his wife, he could not, publicly, condemn a man for having saved her life.

"You must think we're even more stupid than you are!" he thundered suddenly. "Do you suppose we don't know what went on the last twenty-four hours? How you were closeted with the Americans? What you plotted?"

"Why don't you ask the people who informed you to tell you the whole story!" the priest remonstrated softly. "Ask them! Ask Bundesen! He'll tell you that I tried to have him made *Bürgermeister*."

"Bring in Zippmann!" Morgenstern ordered.

Zippmann was pushed in. He had been beaten up, and his face was swollen and bloody. Father Schlemm looked at him, and a slight shudder ran over his smooth skin.

"Well, *Herr Bürgermeister!*" crowed Morgenstern.

"I — I was forced to accept . . ." Zippmann stammered.

"I spoke the truth!" Father Schlemm was fighting for his life. "The

459

Americans asked whether Bundesen was a Party member. That's why they picked the apothecary."

"String him up!" said Morgenstern.

"Whom?" asked the kid Lieutenant.

Morgenstern protracted the sweetness of the moment. His eyes went from the priest to Zippmann and back, and finally settled on the bundle of misery that was the American-appointed Mayor of Neustadt.

"Him!"

Father Schlemm began to pray, hastily mumbled Latin words. Still praying, he followed the crying and struggling apothecary to the curlicued lamppost before the city hall. And as Zippmann was pulled up, kicking, his thin old neck lengthening, his meager, gray legs, emerging from his pants, Father Schlemm was observed to kneel down, though the cobblestones must have hurt his knees.

Bing heard the key being turned in the house door. He started up. He looked at the woman who sat, meek and subdued, in the big chair, and said, "They won't get me. Not alive, they won't. And you won't be alive, either, to see it."

She listened to the heavy steps on the stairs. Then she began to shake with suppressed laughter. "That's Robert! He's the only one with a key."

"Isn't that tough!" said Bing, gripping his carbine and pushing back the bolt.

Frieda's husband stood in the door, staring into the muzzle of Bing's weapon. But Bing didn't fire. The woman had hurtled herself before the surprised man, protecting him with the same body that Bing, the boy, had admired.

Her words came fast.

"If you shoot, it'll get up everybody, you'll be lost." Then she turned and hugged her husband, who still didn't seem to be able to adjust himself to the new situation, and who was looking dourly at her scanty dress. She took the rifle from his shoulder and threw it into the far corner of the room. Bing picked it up.

"Don't excite yourself, my little Robert dear," she said, pressing her body against his. "You know what trouble you have with your heart if you excite yourself. It's all very simple."

"*Ja*, I can see that!" he said, trying to push Frieda away.

She hung on to him. "First you listen to me!" she said energetically. "Do you think I want murder and bloodshed in this house? A scandal, perhaps? Wake up the children? I'm very happy they're sleeping through all that noise, the shooting on the streets; thank God they're healthy."

"Prostitute!"

The word was not a common one in the man's vocabulary; Bing could hear that.

"The children!" she raised her hand. She was shamelessly showing her body to both men. "Watch your language! You're always so hasty, Robert, and afterwards you're sorry, and you go on your knees and beg my forgiveness. It's only because we have a guest, and because I have some feeling of decency, that I don't make you do it right now. I could! I could make you crawl like a dog and lick my feet . . . !"

Bing believed her. She had a power over this man that had quite obvious roots.

"Guest!" the husband dared to protest, but in a very moderate voice.

"Yes, a guest!" She stepped to Bing and took his hand and fondled it. "I knew him when he was that high!" Her other hand stretched out at the level of her hips. "That high! It's young Herr Bing, the son of the Bings I used to work for and who were so kind to me."

"And a Jew, too — in my house! The blood has been soiled!"

"The blood . . . !" she mocked. "Your mind is nothing but a great big cesspool. Don't you ever come near me . . . !"

The threat made the husband reconsider. "He's my prisoner," he suddenly announced. "I must turn him in."

Bing said, "That's where you're mistaken, mister. I've got your gun, and my own in addition. You're my prisoner." It wasn't much of a prisoner, Bing thought. The warrior husband wore a pair of old riding breeches, a civilian jacket that had been ripped at the sleeve, and an armband marked *Volkssturm*. He was a little shorter than his wife, and looked not too well fed, and kind of down-at-the-heel.

Robert thought awhile and then came up with, "But you can't get away either! The streets are full of our soldiers."

"You're both prisoners!" Frieda cut short the dispute. "Young Herr Bing is going to spend the night here. I'll bring some blankets, and he can sleep on the big chair. It's the best we have," she turned to Bing with a twinkle, "and you're a soldier. Robert's spent the night in the woods, so he should have the bed."

Robert nodded. It was the first break his wife had given him.

"Don't you feel badly, Herr Bing," she added, "I'll make you comfortable, all right. . . ."

The husband didn't like the promise in her voice. He grumbled that he must stay to watch the young Herr Bing.

"Now don't be a mule!" Frieda said. "It was you who said that he couldn't get away. So come to bed, it's an ungodly hour."

"Tomorrow, I'll turn him in!" the husband insisted.

"Tomorrow, we'll see." She dragged him off, but returned shortly with

461

blankets and a pillow. "Let me put him to sleep," she whispered to Bing. "Then I come back and let you know."

Bing looked at his watch. He, too, was tired. But he could see his way, now.

He sat down. He wanted to sleep a little, he would need all his strength for the hike back to the Division, and he wasn't too sure how he would manage to sneak out of town. And when he got back to the Division, how would he explain that, of all the men with Dillon, he, alone, had escaped? And what would he say to Troy and to Yates when he met them, later? And Karen would know; Karen could look right through him. And how was he going to go on living with himself?

He thought of the woman Frieda who had saved him, and his teeth went on edge. If you came right down to it, it was Karen's fault, too. . . . Don't kid yourself — it was you who went to Frieda. You left the others to die. You ran from the Krauts, from men like Robert, men in patched-up jackets who probably don't even know how to handle a rifle. . . . Perhaps it was better to break into the other room and kill this Robert, and the woman, too — and then to go out, to run amuck, to go on killing, killing as many Krauts as you could, until they got you and it was all over.

He stretched himself. It was a comfortable chair, and he wondered why Robert, his host, cuckold, prisoner, and guard, all rolled in one, hadn't objected to his using it. The good Sunday chair . . . He pulled out his knife and began to scratch the veneer and to slash the upholstery.

He was interrupted by Frieda. The door had come open soundlessly. It must have been well-oiled; and he thought, she's probably pulled tricks like this before. He got up and pushed open the shutter. Outside it was graying.

She looked disheveled. "We have a little time," she said, "just a little, for us." The nightgown fell around her feet. She stood there, her breasts pushed forward, her hips wide.

Then she glided into the chair. "What's this?" she asked suddenly. She had touched some of the stuffing that gaped out of the mutilated chair.

She jumped up. Her face became ugly. "That was bad! Why did you do it? And me, having done everything for you . . ." She bent over the chair, her buttocks big and coarse, and tried to push the stuffing back into place.

"It's all ruined!" She was near tears, her face was crude and broad. "All ruined! Go! Leave us alone!"

Bing picked up the German rifle and hung it over his shoulder. Then he took his own carbine and left the house, without looking back at Frieda or her Sunday chair.

The streets were deserted except for a lonely German guard whose foot-steps sounded clearly through the early dawn. From Breite Strasse an alley led to the north end of Neustadt, and through carefully cultivated, fenced-in small gardens into the fields.

Bing reached the fields and felt safer. He tried to stick to hedges and shrubs, and where he had to cross open territory, he ducked and sometimes crawled. He waded the river far north of the bridge, well out of sight of the sentries he was sure the Germans had placed there. Then he came into the woods and kept on going, the sun at his back. He shrank from any strange noise and, at times, even from the small dry twigs breaking under his own feet. He didn't permit himself a minute's rest; he kept his mind constantly sharpened; and he welcomed the pangs of hunger because they, too, made him forget his betrayal.

He had become clear about himself. He had returned home to find that he was like those who had expelled him — a strutting conqueror; overbearing, at one moment, the next a coward hiding behind a woman's skirt, leaving his own men in the lurch. Perhaps he stretched the point. Perhaps he had done nothing that anyone else, under the same circumstances, wouldn't have done. But then, to read betrayal into self-preservation, to feel the compulsion of self-sacrifice for something already lost, was an equally German trait — wherever he turned, he was up against the same thing he thought he had escaped.

Toward noon, he came to the end of the woods. At his feet lay a wide field, green with the wheat that had just begun to sprout, and beyond the field was a small road along which a half-dozen armored cars were prowling.

He ran across the field, waving wildly, shouting unintelligible words. The lead car stopped. He reached it and leaned against it, feeling his legs give under him. A dusty, young, clear-cut face emerged from the turret, a youthful fresh voice asked, "Good God, Sergeant — where do you come from?"

A dry sobbing shook Bing. He had come home, really home.

Word of the massacre at Neustadt was spread from Command Post to Command Post. By the time Bing reached Division, Farrish and Willoughby had made their decision.

Having started the venture to Neustadt and Paula Camp, Farrish had to finish the job — and do it spectacularly. Half-measures would bring down over his ears the sticklers for dotted lines on the map, with whom Corps and Army and Group abounded. He arranged for a couple of squadrons from the Tactical Air Force to punish the town, and prepared to move in in force.

Twice, the medieval cellar of Bundesen Brothers, Wine Merchants of Neustadt, saved the lives of Kellermann and the Professor — once, when the Germans came back; and again, when Farrish delivered his blow.

Some of Dillon's men had smashed the heavy lock on the cellar gate, had gone down and come up with a case of what Herr Bundesen complained was his finest, though it really was one of the cheaper grades. Herr Bundesen possessed no spare lock. So the President of the Chamber of Commerce posted himself at the door to his underground treasure. If he couldn't control the Americans, he could at least keep out his neighbors.

On lonely guard, he heard the German troops come back into Neustadt; he followed with bated breath the course of the one-sided night battle; finally, he thought that it was safe to emerge. He left long enough to head the crowd shouting *Heil!* to the victors. He didn't see the two men in striped suits step out of the shadow of the street and push through the unwatched door, the younger man leading, almost dragging, the older one.

Down in the lowest level of the cellar, in the pitch-dark, in the musty, sour smell of the wine, they cowered — Seckendorff numb, Kellermann determined to sit it out.

"Poor fellows," mumbled the Professor.

"Which poor fellows?"

"The Americans. . . ."

"Outnumbered . . ." said Kellermann. "I still got some of their cigarettes."

"We were always outnumbered," sighed the Professor.

Kellermann said soberly, "They don't know what they're up against. I don't think they'll ever know. They are like tourists. Let's drink."

He took out a bottle and began to tackle the cork with his thumbnail and teeth. The cork gave. "Here!"

They drank. The old wine made their weakened bodies logy. They fell asleep.

They woke up with thunder in their ears. They didn't know whether it was day or night, they only knew that the earth was being shaken by the pounding of giant fists. Thousands of bottles danced on their racks and on one another, adding their shrill jingle to the dull detonations.

The Professor, trembling, reached out for Kellermann. Kellermann took him into his arms; the slight, emaciated body felt almost like a child's. Torn out of the long sleep of exhaustion, feeling the ground move under and above him, uncertain whether he was nightmaring or awake, the old man whimpered, "This is the end! . . ."

"Nonsense," said Kellermann, "we're being bombed." He got up. His feet groped toward the stairs. He saw a flickering light. It came closer. Herr Bundesen, candle in unsteady hand, in terror of his life, was trying to hide in his subcellar.

The wine merchant saw the gaunt figure in concentration-camp stripes.

464

The wavering candlelight fell on the deep hollows, the black scars, the gleaming eyes. Death was coming at him, out of the skies and out of the bowels of the earth. Herr Bundesen screamed. He dropped his candle, turned, and fled.

All was dark. Kellermann listened to the stumbling steps echoing above the jingling of the bottles.

Then he was thrown to the ground. Minutes of resurgent rumbling followed; the house over their heads was coming down. He waded through wine and glass shards. The darkness was filled with heavy dust and acrid smoke.

"Kellermann! Kellermann!" came the Professor's croaking voice.

"I'm here! Let's try to get out!"

They crawled up the stairs to the cellar's upper level. Part of the house had tumbled in. They made their way past blocks of stone that had stood for centuries, past Herr Bundesen's smashed body, to the daylight streaming in through the beams that partially blocked the cellar gate. Above them, the ruins of the house were burning.

Kellermann crawled through an opening between two beams and then pulled out the Professor. For hours, they walked the deserted, almost impassable streets. The few people alive were too much concerned with themselves to notice them. What had survived of the German troops had fled to the hills. The smoke-darkened sky was streaked with the orange glow of the flaming town.

The Professor, finding himself alive, asked expectantly, "What are we going to do now?"

"Go home," Kellermann said simply. "Home to the Ruhr, home to Kremmen. I'm taking you along."

"Yes," said Seckendorff, "that will be fine."

On the market square, they encountered the first troops of Farrish's Division.

The Americans were retaking the town without formality. They didn't halt long. They didn't bother to set up a Government, neither did they worry about electricity and garbage disposal. There was no electricity, and the whole of the ancient town was garbage.

And there was no longer a city hall where a Government could be installed. Of the market square, only the curlicued lamppost had remained undamaged, and Mayor Zippmann, appointed by Troy, still hung there to greet the Americans re-entering Neustadt. He hung there until some MP officer, observing that every vehicle slowed down near the lamppost to give its riders a passing look, ordered him cut down so that traffic might go through unimpeded.

7

Why did Biederkopf, Schreckenreuther's second in command, disregard his superior's orders, and discontinue the machine-gunning of the remaining prisoners of Paula Camp after the Commandant and the five thousand evacués had gone?

Biederkopf himself couldn't give a straight answer to the question when Yates, on whom it fell to interrogate him, asked it.

It wasn't pity for the six thousand human wrecks that were left — about a thousand had been mowed down while Schreckenreuther was still within hearing distance. It wasn't pity because Biederkopf had a blank where an ordinary man might have pity. The crawling, humiliated, starved, squealing skeletons, by the very nature of their systematically induced process of dying, had sunk below what you would rightly call human; and Biederkopf never had considered them quite that. No, it wasn't pity.

Was it that he hoped to gain the good graces of the Americans moving on the Camp? Certainly, this contributed to the decision that evolved in Biederkopf's low, thick skull. On the other hand, he knew that the six thousand prisoners left to him would look less repulsive in the graves that Schreckenreuther's foresight had provided than alive and showing the sore skin on their bones, their bloated bellies, their reeking filth.

What was it, then?

Partly panic. As long as Schreckenreuther was there, he served the faithful assistant as a representative and symbol of the system that allowed the little man to say, I was ordered and don't blame me. If held to task, Biederkopf would still say so — and he did say so to Yates. But somehow, with Schreckenreuther gone, it didn't sound so good.

Partly, it was lethargy that influenced Biederkopf. After the Commandant's departure, the power that emanated from the top of the Governmental structure, that seeped down through Schreckenreuther to Biederkopf and through him to the lowest common SS Guard and trusty, ceased flowing. He didn't feel like carrying through the orders Schreckenreuther had received and transmitted to him; he didn't feel like obliterating the traces. And there was no one to make him do it. He just stopped working. It was that simple.

The remnants of the SS stopped working. They stood around or walked about aimlessly. Occasionally, they would kick a prisoner they stumbled on; but there was no system in it. Only the kitchen and the storage hut with the food supplies were jealously and sharply guarded. Had it not been for the food, the SS would have bolted Camp. A few did anyhow — those who had relatives, or friends near by left without formality.

No sentries stood on the watchtowers, and the barbed wire was no longer charged with electricity. The current supplied from Neustadt had been cut off suddenly for reasons nobody thought about much. Only the general weakness of the prisoners prevented a break.

It was not until the first direct reports of the Americans' approach that Biederkopf bestirred himself. The prisoners, who had been lying in the sun, dozing in the semisleep of exhaustion, starvation, and fever, were shooed back into the huts; the recent dead were dragged along with them. The thousand that had been shot lay still uncovered in their graves — but that was outside the Camp and did not disturb Biederkopf's sense of orderliness.

He had the remaining SS draw up, in platoon formation, before the administration hut, while he himself went to the gate, a Committee of One, opening the Camp to the conquerors.

He was surprised and disgusted to find a dozen or so prisoners already there. They were the strongest of those that had remained in the Camp. They were walking arm in arm, supporting each other. A few had gone beyond the gate. Some were shouting hoarsely, and waving. They were waving at some small vehicles approaching carefully from the distance.

Biederkopf ran and caught up with the prisoners.

"Back!" he shouted.

They laughed at him. Skulls, death heads, with fiery feverish eyes, laughing at him.

He saw, suddenly, with a fear which engulfed him and pushed his stomach into a bottomless pit, his mistake in letting them live. With the American vehicles coming close, the prisoners had changed, become formidable — an enemy. And an enemy he no longer could get rid of because here were the Americans, only a hundred, only fifty yards away.

He had to be there first! That was the only way to save himself. *He* must surrender the Camp — not they, not the striped, implacable enemy.

He spurted forward. He outran them. He waved. He was the first to meet the first American armored car in Paula Camp.

"Ich übergebe —" he shouted. "I surrender —"

The American officer, his face grim, jumped out. Biederkopf saw the dark, threatening eyes, the lips set firmly, the sharp lines that winged from nose to mouth, the determination in every feature. It hit Biederkopf — this wasn't a man you could deal with; this was a man who dealt with you!

"Your pistol!" said Yates. "You're under arrest!"

Speechlessly, Biederkopf watched the officer permit the prisoners to surround him, press his hands, touch his clothes, weep and laugh and slobber over him.

"You're free!" Yates was saying to them. "You're free!"

Troy's men went wild.

Yates saw them go wild and he didn't stop them.

He saw them discover the interior of the huts; the prisoners piled in the bunks — the dead with the living, the corpses all but indistinguishable from those whose chests still fluttered as their lungs tried to pull oxygen out of the pest-ridden, stinking air.

He saw them discover the thousand dead, machine-gunned behind the camp, thrown into the fresh graves, barefoot and obscenely naked, everything about them shriveled except their skulls and their genitalia. And because they were so shriveled, their wounds appeared magnified, and superfluous; they had died a double death.

He saw Troy's men find the concrete waterhole, ten by twenty feet, its slimy fluid fetid with debris, from dead mice to rusty tin cans.

A tall, red-haired corporal pointed to the waterhole. "What's that?" he asked, his Adam's apple moving convulsively.

A prisoner, one of a group that had attached itself to the troops, remembered his school English. "We drink that," he said.

"All of you?"

"We used to be twelve thousand."

Yates saw the American soldiers find the shoes, the whole storehouse of shoes — thousands of them, neatly stacked and paired and tagged, new ones, worn ones, and those torn and patched and torn again.

"Whose are these?"

"How do we know? They're long dead, who wore them."

A mausoleum of shoes.

Yates saw Troy's men come upon the struggling, fighting crowd of prisoners who had burrowed through the fence to the garbage pile next to the kitchen. They were digging in the offal, together with the maggots. He saw them sicken as the prisoners wolfed down rotting peelings and moldy crusts, black stumpy teeth tearing decomposed sinews from bones turned black.

A little private, almost a child, began to sob.

"You cry?" said a prisoner. "We've been eating from the dead. It isn't so bad if you get at them soon enough."

But most of the Americans did not cry. Nor did they vomit. A kind of holy fury came over them. The same men who had gleefully worn the silk hats of the citizens of Neustadt, now banded together to hunt for the SS, to flush them out of the darkness of the huts, from behind the storage hut, from under the roof of the administration building.

They took the SS men's own truncheons and whips and let them have it. The red-haired Corporal beat a tall, good-looking, smooth-faced guard slowly, methodically, until the German's head was pulp. The prisoners crawled close and sat on their bony haunches and nodded their skull-like heads and cheered, hoarsely quavering.

A short, squat SS man came panting down the road between the hutments, his eyes popping — four Americans chasing after him. Yates saw him; he stepped forward and tripped him up. The SS man fell head down, screamed, and slithered on his stomach. He never got up. The four Americans pounced on him. One jumped on his chest. He jumped three times, with all his weight. The German trembled and stretched like a worm put on a hook, and was dead. A second American bent down, sliced off the dead SS man's ring finger and pocketed the heavy ring with the fatal insignia, the two lightning flashes.

Some soldiers discovered a supply of rope. They found themselves five SS men and pummeled them down the road to the gate, and then along the fence to the machine-gun tower. Yates saw one of the Americans climb up the ladder, an end of rope slung over his arm. He laid it over one of the beams, so that both ends dangled down. Yates saw the SS men being hoisted, one after the other. He heard their terrified shrieks. He dug his hands into his pockets and watched.

Later, when he met Karen, he said, "You know, it seems as if we had one common mind, one common reaction. I don't think the men wasted one word over that. And nobody used a bullet."

He pointed at the tower and the black puppets hanging from it.

She paled.

There was a certain fierceness in his voice. "Got to do this job before our civilized inhibitions catch up with us."

"Troy's been asking for you," she said.

"Troy can wait," he answered. "I'm going to take it all in. I never want to forget it!"

Troy had taken over the administration building.

Karen came in and said, with forced casualness, "If you don't do something, Captain, you won't have any SS men left alive. Some ought to be spared for a trial with trimmings."

"I know," he said tiredly, "I'm having them rounded up now. I should have seen to it sooner — but, God! I don't know where to begin. . . ."

"You're doing all right," she said. The comfort she wanted to give didn't quite come off.

"I have no food, no medical supplies, no water, no beds, not even enough lousy DDT to start fumigating these poor guys. I thought I'd seen pretty near everything a man can see in a war. But this . . . !" He shook his head. "What am I to do? My medics tell me there's typhus, typhoid, TB — every conceivable disease. And I sit here, with these dying — I don't know

469

what to call them. Have you a word for them, Miss Wallace? I just know they're continuing to die, right under my hands. I'm having the food distributed that was stored in the Camp, I throw in what I think I can spare from the rations of my own men — and it may be enough for one meal. I've radioed to the General for supplies, for doctors, nurses, medicines — but when will they come? And meanwhile?"

"I understand," she said gently.

"Did you have any idea of what we were getting into?" he asked miserably.

She wanted to smile encouragingly and say: It isn't as terrible as all that. But she couldn't, because it was exactly as terrible as all that. "There've been reports about concentration camps," she said. "Stories in newspapers and magazines, and books."

"I don't read much; and if I'd read them, I don't think I would have believed them. I would have thought it was propaganda."

"Farrish had no right to send you into this with nothing, with bare hands, practically."

"That's no excuse for me!"

For a moment he got away from his self-reproaches and saw the woman in front of him, her face soft with what she felt for him. "You're very kind. You want to make me feel better, I know." His eyes grew thoughtful. He frowned. "It's no good, Miss Wallace. I'm thoroughly fouled-up."

He fell back into what obsessed him. "It was my duty to know my requirements beforehand and to get them. That's a commanding officer's job! I wouldn't dream of going out without ammunition, would I?"

"But you couldn't possibly know!"

"Maybe you're right. I'm not sure of anything, any more, except that I want to get out of here. I want to do some fighting, some clean killing. I want to get the war over with, I want to forget the whole thing!"

She could see him, wanting to forget. In the years ahead, whatever he might be doing, she could see him stop, suddenly, hand covering his eyes, blotting out the picture of the crawling skeletons of Paula, or the memory of the men he had led to battle and had seen fall.

"You must stick it out," she said with a compassion so great that it penetrated the layers of impressions crowding in on him. "You must do all you can; and be convinced you are doing all you can. Believe me, you are. . . . That's your only way."

With quickened responsiveness he reached across the table, knocking aside the stack of documents between them, and gripped her hand. "Thank you," he said. "Thanks."

She let her hand rest in his.

Then her eyes fell on one of the objects he had pushed aside — a book with a strangely designed cover.

470

He saw her stare. He let go of her hand and hastily buried the book beneath the stacked papers.

"What is that?" she asked.

"I didn't want you to see it. I was studying it when you came in. I'm sorry you saw it."

"But what is it?"

"I don't know what's written in the book," he said slowly, "but the binding is made of tattooed human skin."

Then he jumped up and shoved his canteen bottle to her mouth. "Drink this, Karen!" he urged. "Get hold of yourself! Please!"

About thirty SS men, including Biederkopf, survived the rage of the soldiers. On orders of Troy, they were put to work removing the dead. The SS, shivering with fear, dumbfounded and sullen over their sudden fall from power, discovered their sensitivity to the dead and the dangers of disease, and tied handkerchiefs before mouth and nose. The prisoners silently observed the slow work of their former masters.

Looting began. The stronger among the prisoners ransacked the SS barracks. They found weapons, boots, pieces of uniform, delicacies. Troy's men, having had their pick, didn't object. They had their hands full at the storagehouse, trying to distribute the available food equitably. It was being stolen even as they were taking inventory.

Troy was handicapped because he had to deploy the larger part of his men far outside of Paula Camp, to guard it against a possible German surprise attack. To keep order inside of Camp, to hand out the food, to take care of the most urgent medical cases, he had no more than a hundred men. They might have been enough, had he been able to employ the terroristic discipline the Nazis had enforced over the sick and enfeebled. But he had to go easy on them; it was he who had brought them liberty — and very little except liberty.

The more he saw, the heavier he felt the weight of his job. He had not even the means to take care of Dr. Valentin's precious cancer cultures. The American medical officer, a captain, dragged Troy and Yates into the hospital hut. "Have a look at this!" he said and pulled the cover off a woman whose breasts were two big festering wounds. "I've given her an injection. She's going to die."

"My God!" said Troy. "What did they do that for?"

"I suspect they wanted to manufacture cancer," said the Doctor. "Lieutenant Yates, could you try to find out from the other patients?"

A few questions from Yates established the suspicion as fact.

The Medical Captain pulled at his lip. "But that's insane!" he said. Then he turned to Troy. "What are we going to do with the people who did this thing, and with the ones who stood by while it was being done?"

Yates, forcing down an urge to run and hide and give in to the convulsion of his stomach, said acidly, "Captain Troy wants to keep them alive."

"Keep 'em alive?" asked the Doctor. "Well, you're the C.O. But in here I'm the boss, and I decide! Damn it, I wish I could decide. I'm tempted to practice some mercy killing. . . ."

Troy groaned. He alone blocked the riot that was due; he alone stood between the new kind of justice and the condemned — but he was stubborn. He pulled the SS off the burial detail and had them locked up in a hut and called on his most reliable noncom — Sergeant Lester, who had been returned to him from the Base Hospital at Verdun. Lester was to be in charge of the guards in front of the hut. He was to pick three good men for the job.

Lester's face was expressionless. "I'll try, sir," he said.

After a while, he came back to Troy. "You're out of luck, Captain. Everybody refused. They told me to tell you they'll be glad to kill the bastards, kill 'em any way you like. But they won't protect them."

"What did you answer?"

"Nothing," said Lester. "I'm on their side."

"We'll see about that!" said Troy.

It was mutiny, plain and open mutiny. If he wanted to save the SS, he would have to go himself and get the men to guard them.

His heart heavy, his face dark, Troy went with the Sergeant. He got his men into some kind of formation, and said, "Many of you know me for a long time, some of you since Normandy. How do you think I feel?"

There was some muttering.

"I thought we'd come here, throw open the gates, and say to these concentration camp prisoners, Go home! You're free! Well, things didn't turn out that way. Most of them can't walk farther than the gate. And if they could, we can't let them out because they're diseased. So we must keep them here until we get reinforcements and supplies, and we must keep order. I know that some of the prisoners swiped weapons. You will take those weapons away from them. There's going to be no rioting as long as I'm in charge. Now about the SS. Several of them have had accidents."

A few guffaws came from the ranks.

"At ease! I said accidents. If I used any other word for it, I'd have to lock up some of you alongside the SS. I don't want to do that. We're short-handed as is. Now get this: There are going to be no more such accidents. Is that clear?"

The men were silent, but it was the silence of opposition.

"The guys who strung up those bodies at the tower will take them down. There'll be justice, in due time, and by the proper authorities. There'll be no more lynching. We're not Nazis; we're fighting for something better."

He noticed that Karen had come and was listening. He began to feel self-conscious.

"I want three volunteers for that guard detail!" he said abruptly.

Nobody stepped forward.

"All right then!" His face became set, his chin pushed forward. "Sheal! Kosinski! Bartlett! You go with Sergeant Lester! Company — dismissed!"

He about-faced and marched away, angry at himself, angry at Farrish who had condemned him to this task.

Night fell.

Yates interrogated Biederkopf. Biederkopf was puzzled and harried. He saw the gulf between himself and this good-looking, well-knit American whom he would have given a job on his own force, had he been a German. Why was the American so much against him?

Yates asked about the concrete mixer of which he'd heard from the prisoners.

"You have to teach them," Biederkopf said morosely. "Now you Americans have set them free. Look at what they're doing! We Germans are an orderly people. I've only done my duty."

"So you considered yourself a teacher, did you?"

"Yes," said Biederkopf.

Yates said, "In civilian life, I'm a teacher myself."

"Then you understand!" said Biederkopf.

Yates gave up. He escorted Biederkopf back to the hut in which the SS men were held. The Camp was dark, and the road was difficult to follow. Yates had to rely on Biederkopf's sense of direction. The SS officer was co-operative; he clung to Yates, worried that they might lose one another and that he might find himself alone. Yates had the eerie feeling that the ground was somehow alive, that things were crawling or scurrying, avoiding him and Biederkopf, and yet sticking to them.

Sheal, on guard before the jail hut, challenged. Yates made Sheal unlock the door and shove Biederkopf in with the others. He asked himself why he hadn't shot the self-styled pedagogue on the way. Was it because of Biederkopf's attitude of complete trust? A louse in the seam of your underpants also entrusts itself to you, and you kill it. Was it because Troy would have taken the execution as an offense against his authority? Troy need never have known what happened. Or was it that these things cannot be done with premeditation, and that the opportunity for impulsive rage had passed?

Karen and Troy were alone when Yates returned to the administration building. They were sitting in silence, facing one another.

473

Yates sat down, tired. The silence grew deeper. He sensed that some threads were being spun between the two, perhaps without their being conscious of it. He glanced at Karen. He thought what a damned fool he once had been, and how she had slapped his face. The memory was still disagreeable, but he didn't smart under it. She had been right. . . . There had been something between her and Bing; he wondered whether that was all over. He wondered how Bing was doing in Neustadt. People grow away from each other, people change.

"I think I'll turn in," he said and forced a yawn.

"No, please don't," Troy said quickly. More calmly, he added, "I can't sleep, everything about this Camp is like a fever dream. We should raze it to the ground, leave no trace of it."

"We should preserve it," said Yates, "and organize Cook's tours from all over the world, and especially from America."

Troy lit a cigarette. "Maybe you're right. But count me out. I've got enough for the rest of my life with what I've seen and smelled and heard since this morning. Karen's lucky, she can write it out of her system."

"I will!" Karen said passionately. "But people won't believe it."

"When I'm out of here," said Troy, "I won't want to believe it myself. A man can't live with that in the back of his mind. I look at you two, or at any other decent human being, at my own men, and I think life could be all right once we're through with the war. And then I think, How can you tell about anybody? Take any of those Nazis we locked up, put him into a civilian suit, let him loose in New York or Chicago or Denver or Los Angeles — he looks like anybody else. It frightens me."

Yates was suddenly conscious of his warts. "Jesus!" he said, rubbing his fingers. He saw his Campus and the football field behind it, the field covered with huts. He saw himself, a shadow of himself, in striped, baggy uniform, pleading for a scrap of food, trying to drink out of the mudhole, whipped to backbreaking work.

If they'd won the war . . . , he thought — but they hadn't won it.

A shot fell. Then shouts, some angry, some desperate. The quick crackling of dry wood aflame cut through the night.

Troy grabbed his pistol and rushed out. One of the huts was burning, the fire shooting up steeply in the quiet air. Its flames outlined the hut sharply; and faces and struggling arms showed behind the glowing windows. Shrill screams rose over the roar of the fire.

Outside, the glow lighted the milling, swirling, shouting crowd. Troy, followed by Yates and Karen, rammed his way through the concentration camp prisoners, stepping on them where they weren't quick or strong enough to move back.

They're armed, damn it! Troy thought. He rushed in to them, despite

474

the rifles and submachine guns they held pointed against the closed door of the burning hut.

But they didn't budge. Those around him, who could see his determined face, were held by the others pressing in on them from behind.

Troy pushed aside the useless Sheal who, white-faced, stood his post before the flaming hut. "The key, man! The key!"

Sheal finally understood. He fingered through his pockets.

Troy didn't wait. He threw his powerful body against the door, breaking the lock. But the door, though it was smoldering in its upper part, didn't give — the SS from the inside were pounding it against its frame in a vain attempt to smash it open.

"Water! Buckets!" shouted Troy. "For God's sake, Yates, get these guys going!" A few soldiers appeared at the fringe of the crowd. "Get water!" Troy bellowed at them. But whether they couldn't hear their captain, or didn't want to understand him, or were so fascinated by the spectacle that they couldn't tear themselves loose, the soldiers stayed on, mute and immobile.

"You know there's not enough water!" Yates tried to hold back Troy. "And there's no way of getting it up here! . . . Come out!" he shouted, in German, to the trapped SS, "*Kommt heraus!*"

The door, burning fiercely, suddenly gave. In its frame appeared Biederkopf, screaming, his face madly contorted, his bushy hair terribly singed, his uniform burning in places. Others, behind him, were pushing him out.

Biederkopf saw the prisoners, the stripes moving with the flames. He saw the weapons turned at him. With desperate strength, he pressed back the living torches trying from behind to push him into the gray, pajama-clad vengeance.

Then the roof came down and the walls caved, and the stinking pyre burned down.

Troy, his own eyebrows and hair singed, his hands and face blackened, turned from the smoking heap.

"Collect those weapons!" he ordered his men.

The prisoners gave them up willingly enough.

"Sheal!"

Sheal came forward; his mouth was set stubbornly.

Troy rubbed his red-rimmed, smoke-filled eyes. "What happened?"

"I couldn't help it!" said Sheal, "I honestly couldn't. All of a sudden, they were around me and around the hut. . . ." He pointed at the prisoners who were rapidly disappearing into the night.

"Why didn't you call Lester?"

"They weren't threatening me, sir."

"Who fired the shot?"

"I didn't, sir."

"Did they?"

The prisoners had gone.

"No, sir — the shot came out of the hut. Maybe one of the SS had a gun. Maybe they got scared when they saw the prisoners. I would have been scared, sir, plenty, if I'd been an SS man."

"Go on!"

"The shot must have killed a prisoner. They got mad. They didn't do nothing to me. They set fire to the hut. It burned right off. No rain, sir; you know we had no rain."

"It was your God-damned job to guard this hut. To guard those bastards, with your life, if necessary. And you knew it, Sheal!"

Sheal swallowed hard. Then he said, "Maybe you put me in the wrong job, sir. I was in the Bulge. I want to kill Krauts."

Troy didn't answer. He looked at the smoldering remains of the hut, and then at Sheal. "Go to sleep," he said heavily; "there's nothing left here to guard."

8

Toward noon, next day, Farrish arrived.

With him came the correspondents, the press photographers, the censorship officer, the hangers-on of the headquarters. Led by Willoughby, and imbued with his panegyrics on the Great Man's purpose, they swept in behind the striding General.

They swept past Troy and Yates. They swept past the men who had taken the Camp. They stopped to corral such prisoners as had neither time nor energy to get out of their way. With cautious fingers, they touched bony arms and welted skins, expressing their outrage and holding handkerchiefs before their noses.

Troy watched it as long as he could. Then he approached his General. It was difficult to get Farrish's attention, although Troy knew that his salute had been obvious.

"Where are the SS guards kept?" one of the reporters was asking.

Willoughby turned questioningly to Troy.

"They were burned to death last night," Troy said slowly.

Farrish swung toward him. "What!"

"An accident, sir," Troy offered.

"Far too many accidents around you, Captain!" barked Farrish, and then, controlling himself before the press, he added, "I'll have a word with you, later."

The General's tone failed to dismiss Troy. "One thing, sir — the supplies! The food — the medicines — the things we need that I've requested.

476

We need them badly. Right now, sir, people in this camp are dying from hunger!"

Farrish glared at Troy, but Troy held his glance.

Willoughby rushed into action. "General Farrish has made all arrangements to feed the inmates of this camp!" he announced loudly. "Will the cameramen please get ready?" Then, turning to Troy, "If you want to be helpful, get some of those prisoners together so we can shoot pictures. Be on your toes, man! This is a historic moment!"

Troy watched the entourage make for the huts, the General parading at its head. A painful bitterness filled him. So this had been his mission — to clear the road for the press!

Yates came up to him. "Ditched?" he asked. "Take it easy. We're lucky Biederkopf was fried. Otherwise we'd have to watch him pose with Farrish."

Farrish's train was changing its contour. It was grouped about an unhappy lot of prisoners.

Yates heard one of the photographers call, "Give us a little smile, General!"

"The General doesn't like to smile," Willoughby came through. "And this isn't the occasion."

Troy and Yates followed the tourists. Cameras ground, bulbs flashed at every turn. Farrish in front of the open mass grave; Farrish at the entrance of one of the huts, the shaven skulls of the inmates showing through the doorway. Farrish holding Schreckenreuther's punishment book.

"Get a close-up of this one, boys. The tattoos are the thing!"

Farrish watching the scabrous body of a prisoner being fumigated with DDT. Farrish handing out a C-ration can — the supply trucks were just arriving. Farrish at his best, standing at the bedside of one of Dr. Valentin's cancer cases.

Farrish at the microphone: "The liberation of Paula Camp is, perhaps, the crowning achievement of the men in my Division. I am as proud of this as of the many victories to which I led them in the field."

And dancing about the sightseeing group, like a mother hen with her chicks, or a medicine man with his victims, the omnipresent Willoughby.

"Doesn't that guy have any feelings?" Troy asked.

Yates said, "Sure! He can feel, all right! But he can't afford the pause to look and see, and maybe he doesn't want to see. He's just busy!"

"Ghoul!" muttered Troy.

And then it was over. Most of the correspondents hurried back to file their stories; Karen gave hers to Tex Myers for transmission. Those who remained in the Camp ambled around, trying to pick up background stuff, trying to find prisoners of some prominence whose names might have news value in the States, or prisoners with relatives in America, preferably in the areas where their papers were published. Most of the inmates kept clear of them. They found out soon that the newsmen had nothing to do with the dispensing of food. And many prisoners were busy retching what they had hastily swallowed; their shrunken stomachs wouldn't keep down any solids. That took away much of their attraction. Above all, however, the reporters knew that their papers and press services would limit the horror stories; Wheaties sticking in the public's craw were no boon to circulation.

With his customary bluntness, Farrish broke the news of the Neustadt disaster to Troy. He concluded by asking the stunned Captain, "What do you have to say for yourself?"

There was plenty Troy could have said in his defense: His Task Force had been too small to secure a line of communication; once he had pushed on, Lieutenant Dillon was responsible for Neustadt, and Dillon apparently had paid for his mistakes with his own life; both Neustadt and Paula Camp lay outside Farrish's sector, and the push should have been coordinated with the Division whose proper sector it was; finally, after it had been learned that the Nazis were evacuating Paula Camp and killing off the remaining prisoners, no time was left to reconnoiter against the possibility of an odd German unit of superior force happening into Neustadt.

Willoughby was prepared to counter, and if necessary, to squelch all such argument. But he didn't need to exert his legal talents.

To Troy, the killing of Dillon's men in Neustadt was too similar in pattern to the massacre of Fulbright's platoon in the Bulge. And it came on top of his inability to cope with the mess in Paula Camp. He didn't defend himself.

He didn't blame fate, or hard luck — there's more to it when the run of it is constant. He had led his company from the beaches of Normandy to here. He had been all right in the beginning; perhaps the strain of war had begun to tell. There were things he could no longer control; he had grown tired. But that he had let himself reach this point was his own responsibility. A man had to know his limitations when the lives of others depended on him.

Willoughby, standing behind Farrish, could see Troy's face, the pinched mouth, the vacant eyes. He had wanted to bring up the matter of the roasted SS, but he curbed himself.

Farrish was saying, "You can see, Captain, that I have no other alternative."

"Yes, sir."

"You're obviously unable to carry out the functions of command."

"Yes, sir."

Farrish's white hair bristled. "God damn it! Say something besides Yes, sir!"

Farrish stopped for breath. He couldn't afford failures. Failures were part of the conspiracy against Farrish.

Willoughby used the pause. He thought it was abject loyalty that made Troy take it in the neck and cover up for Farrish and, ultimately, for him, the originator of the plan. He said, "There's nothing personal in this, Captain. You were given your chance — and it just didn't work out. . . ."

"My men and officers get their chance!" Farrish picked up. "I'm proud of them. If I haven't selected everyone myself, at least I'm rooting out everyone who doesn't measure up. That's my principle. That's how I've been winning my share of the war."

The General had been winning his share of the war. Troy had been losing his.

"That's all right, sir. I accept my responsibility." Troy's words came with difficulty. "I'll resign my commission. I've been an enlisted man before, I can be one again."

"Leave my decisions up to me, will you, Captain?"

The man took it too hard. But Farrish couldn't get up and say, It's my fault, too. First, because it wasn't his fault; nothing was. Second, because somebody had to stand up and declare: I accept responsibility. Troy had done that. Farrish wasn't vindictive once he had his way.

"Nothing personal in this, you understand!" he echoed Willoughby.

"Yes, sir!"

"Report to G-1 for re-assignment."

"Yes, sir."

Troy left Farrish's trailer.

Inside, Willoughby said, "Too bad, sir. He was a good man. Ran into him, once, at Rambouillet. Reliable line officer. I suppose, the job was just too big for him. . . ."

"Clarence Willoughby!" said Farrish. "You still don't know me. This hurts me more than him. But a man's got to have principles."

Troy walked slowly to the administration hut, to collect his stuff. If he could avoid it, he wouldn't say Good-by to his men — how could he explain himself to them? Better that he just disappeared. The First Sergeant and the Company Clerk would know, so would the officers; he would ask them to mention that Farrish had called him away from the Company. It was the truth, incidentally, even if it wasn't the whole story.

He looked at the Camp he had liberated. He could see some improvement. The dead had been cleared away; the foul, disease-filled straw was being burned. The stench bit his nostrils. Food had been handed out twice;

and men were learning to walk again. He had to be fired before things could really be bettered.

Karen was waiting for him in his room. He had hoped to be alone. She would sense that something was wrong, and he could do without that. She would ask questions, and he knew that he wouldn't give any answers.

But she didn't ask anything. She sat on a hard, straight chair, one of her pants-encased knees braced high by her clasped hands, leaning back and balancing herself on two of the chair's legs.

"I'm leaving," he said abruptly.

"I know," she said.

News, around here, traveled too damned fast for him.

"Willoughby cornered me," she told him. "I got the Neustadt story straight from him, and I had an idea of what was going to happen to you. It was all cut and dried. Very ugly. If I hadn't been around the Army so long, it would burn me up."

She shrugged and smiled.

"Nice of you to put it that way," he said. "Unfortunately, they were right. I was the officer responsible. Farrish was fair enough about it. I lose my command, I'll get another assignment. I've got no complaint."

"Farrish is a jackass," she said. "And Willoughby's vicious."

"That's beside the point, Miss Wallace."

"Karen."

"That's beside the point, Karen," he repeated, dryly.

She let go of her knee and leaned forward. "What is the point, then?"

"Forty-two lives. How much does a life weigh? A million pounds? I don't know. And the men I lost in the Bulge; you never heard of that, did you? Of course not. I never told anyone about it. Yates knows, but Yates can keep his trap shut. Why am I telling you this? Oh yes, because you're nice and kind and generous and you're trying to make it easier for me. Well, it doesn't work. It's still forty-two lives."

He gathered his papers and jammed them into a dispatch case.

"Forty-one," she said, "Sergeant Bing got away."

Troy looked up. "Did he? Good. I like him."

"I like him, too. Very much."

"Do you?"

"Yes, I do."

And as he said nothing, she continued after a while: "When Willoughby told me what happened in Neustadt, I had a great big ache in my heart. If Willoughby hadn't been around, I think I would have cried right then. I could see the boy, those clever eyes, and the honesty in them. I could see him as he was one night in a ruined town in Normandy, with the moon coming through the empty windows, and his head against them. I could see him as he came back from one of his hog-calling jobs — that's what he called them — after the man who was next to him had died."

Troy listened. He wished she would remember him that way, too — that strongly, that plastically, that deeply anchored in her heart. But that was a crazy and unrealistic wish, as crazy as when he sometimes wished that the Bulge hadn't happened to him — and now, Neustadt.

"Why do you tell me this?" he asked gruffly.

"So that you know that I know how it feels to lose men."

"This is different," he said. "You love the man."

She faced him. He was so big and hurt and confused.

"I can tell you how I would have felt had I loved the man. Would you like to know?"

"Cigarette?"

"Thanks." She lit it, and her eyes followed the first puff of smoke.

"A woman who loves a man and loses him, or thinks she's lost him . . . Captain, there would have been no tears, not for a long while. Just a great, heavy emptiness, growing and growing, blanking out your heart. And no way of expressing it — the irrefutable loss, the forever of it."

She was very beautiful, he thought. He had never seen so beautiful a woman.

"Karen!" he said.

"Yes?"

"I'll be all right."

She said softly, "I don't want to have to worry about you."

He came to her and took her hand, hesitantly.

9

FIELD MARSHAL von Klemm-Borowski called it a *Kessel,* the Americans called it Encirclement, or a Ring. Actually, the German word was far more expressive. A Kessel was a caldron in which you sat, which you couldn't get out of, desperately as you tried, and in which you waited for the fire to be lit under you.

That it should happen to him, after he had succeeded in taking most of his troops back over the Rhine, shook Klemm-Borowski's belief in himself to the core. Where had he, the master mathematician, the specialist in logistics, failed to calculate the figures that threw his entire balance sheet into disorder?

As long as the ring was tenuous, he had thrown counterattack after counterattack against it; but he had known he would fail, because he had made a cardinal mistake. Yet, how could he have avoided it? If, in anticipation of the Allied encirclement, he had moved out of the Ruhr and saved what was left of his Army Group, the loss of the industrial region would have sealed the doom of German resistance. And in trying to hold on to the Ruhr area and to defend it, he was bound to be cut off, to fall into the caldron, and to be forced to look on helplessly as the Allies whittled down the island he held, strengthening their ring, drawing it tighter, until they could throttle him.

He knew, too, that his was the last intact German Army Group in the West. With him out of the game, the High Command might try to close the front once more, to fight a delaying battle between Rhine and Elbe — but it was a delaying battle, nothing more.

His final Command Post was in a two-family building, part of a housing project outside of Kremmen. He had chosen the house because it looked so ordinary; neither the enemy's air nor his ground observation could conclude that here the Marshal was directing the last defense of the Ruhr. He didn't have to do much directing. The order was, as usual, to fight to the last man — an order Klemm-Borowski hated to give because it had been repeated so often during this war; it had always indicated defeat; and it never had helped.

He had enough time to deliberate on his defeat and to speculate on the future of his country. He was sure he would not partake in that future; but the defeat taught him certain lessons for the future, to be applied by future German Generals and politicians.

He wrote them out, in his meticulous German script. Then he sent for Pettinger.

Pettinger had lost some of his buoyancy, but was managing to keep himself rigidly positive. Though he knew that retreats and defeats had mounted to the point where it was impossible to accept any more, he could not afford to buckle under. This was a totalitarian war that could be followed only by total victory or total defeat — if it was to be defeat, then let the whole country, Europe, the world, be dragged down in flames. If you cannot rule it, destroy it.

The Field Marshal's tired hand was pointing at the map.

"You see, *Herr Obersturmbannführer,* there is no hope."

"It looks bad," Pettinger confirmed unemotionally. What was the sense of telling the fat, owlish person across the table that, as long as men were left, and the men had guns, there was hope? The Marshal had deteriorated, Pettinger found. He ate heavily; on the table stood the remains of a roast duck.

"I'm not only a mathematician," Klemm-Borowski continued, "I'm also a student of history. Nations don't just perish. There's always a next round. And just as we prepared for the next round in 1918, so must we now."

Pettinger smiled wryly. There could be no next round.

The Marshal pulled a sheaf of papers from under the tray of duck bones. "Here, I've outlined the preparation for it. And I've picked you, Colonel, to see to it that this document gets to the right people and is used in the right way."

"I'm honored."

Klemm-Borowski paused and coughed. Then he asked, "Don't you want to know why I can't handle this matter myself? And what is in these papers? And why I've picked you?"

"Why, sir?"

"I'm an anachronism, Pettinger. With all my fancy figures and supply tables, I still fought a war of the past. All right, you remind me of Operation Buzzard — I liked it, I liked the fun of it, the game of wit. But it was a sideshow. I'm a *Junker,* Pettinger, I'm a relic of the Middle Ages, and I'm going out. And I lost this battle, the last of the war. I'm going to die."

The Marshal looked up. He thought he would find something on Pettinger's face — grief, awe, pity — some sentiment — any sentiment.

But Pettinger's face, handsome in its hard way, remained set.

Klemm-Borowski went on, less flamboyantly. "So I won't be around to see my testament put into effect. Someone else will have to do it."

"Of course," said Pettinger.

The Marshal had trouble recapturing his thread of thought. "Now, I could have selected a man of my own class, my own background; my staff is riddled with them — but they're not much good. Not good for this job," he corrected himself.

Pettinger suddenly thought of Dehn as he had been in the end, broken but still maintaining his diseased arrogance, and wondered in what hole he might be rotting.

"We didn't hang enough of them after the Witzleben revolt," he commented.

Klemm-Borowski, who had known Marshal Witzleben intimately, winced. "They were good men in their way, Pettinger, decent Germans."

"But anachronisms," Pettinger reminded.

"Therefore I chose you," the Marshal said with forced cheerfulness. "I think I've chosen wisely."

"I think you have," Pettinger affirmed. "I will definitely live, barring freak accidents. What about the testament?"

"I skip the personal part; I have little money, and only two spinster cousins on the estate in Pomerania. The important part is political. We must see the mistake we made. I know you're a National-Socialist and you won't like to hear me blame the Führer. But this situation" — he pointed at the map — "calls for open language."

"Go ahead!" Pettinger smiled; it was a boyish smile, quite charming; he hadn't displayed it for a long time, not since Paris. "Don't be intimidated by me, sir."

Who's he to tell me that? The thought crossed the Marshal's mind, but he disregarded it.

"What a folly to let ourselves be led into a two-front war! And I don't mean a two-front war in the ordinary sense, with fighting in the East and in the West simultaneously — we might have been able to manage that. It was really two *wars!* One, the old-fashioned kind — how slight were the differences of opinion between us and the English and the Americans! What difference did a few markets and sources of raw material make? How easily we could have shared Europe! A little less thunder on our part, a little more conciliation — and we could have got along splendidly, for — note this well, Pettinger! — we and Western Europe and America belong in the same orbit; we have the same set-up, the same civilization, the same morals."

"Suppose we have!" Pettinger said. "Suppose the tanks hacking at us fire Western bullets — they're just as deadly."

"Through our own fault!" cried the Marshal. Then he calmed down. "The second war we fought was different. A war against a different world, so strange and alien to us that no compromise was possible. That attack from the East was directed against people like me. But you can fight fire only with fire, fanaticism only with fanaticism, ruthlessness with ruthlessness."

"We weren't ruthless enough?" Pettinger asked bitterly.

"Yes, we were, I think. But we had to fight that other, the stupid war, too. That's what defeated us. We must liquidate the unnecessary war in order to continue the necessary one. And it's people like you who will have to carry on the fight — sometimes openly, with arms; sometimes lying low, waiting your chance, relying on the fact that things are bound to break your way."

Pettinger saw light. Much of the Marshal's confession had struck him as drivel, a defeated man rationalizing his defeat, trying to shove the blame off himself, off his own kind, onto others. He had been on the verge of telling Klemm-Borowski that, if *Götterdämmerung* was at hand, he, Pettinger, and the men like him would go down in an eruption of powder and glory and destruction, leaving the enemy a field of ruins that could not be rebuilt for a century.

But Klemm-Borowski was offering a more immediate possibility that might save you the trouble of going down heroically. Self-destruction was fun only while it lasted; you'd never get around to reading your own obituaries and the accounts in the history books of the future.

"Things will break our way," he paraphrased. "How?"

"The English and Americans will be sorry they ever won this war — they won it for the Soviets! Don't forget, Pettinger, Europe is still the heart of the world, and Germany the heart of Europe. I tell you, right now, in London and Washington, they are asking themselves the question: What kind of Europe, what kind of Germany is this going to be — their kind, that's our kind — or the Russians'? They cannot wipe out civilization's outpost against the East without wiping out themselves. Having destroyed us, they'll have to coddle us and build us up again, because they need our help. And here's where you come in, Pettinger. In the band they will need for their music, they won't give you the first fiddle, immediately; don't expect too much. They'll give you the little triangle to tinker with; you'll make just an occasional sound. But who else can play their tunes? Pretty soon, you'll have to handle the drum, too, and then the horns, and then the cello — and finally, you'll step once more onto the conductor's podium."

Pettinger nodded. "You know a lot about music, sir."

"Yes. I'm a man of culture. That's why I'm not quite up to the modern stuff that's going to be played."

He chuckled. He handed the papers to Pettinger. "Here's the testament. You'll carry it through?"

"Yes, sir."

"Call it Plan Klemm-Borowski. A man wants to live on, somehow. You'll have to work fast. The first step is to open up the entire front in the West."

"What!" Although he had discarded his *Götterdämmerung* conception, Pettinger was not yet ready to hand over everything.

"Sure! Let them come in! Let them go to the Elbe, beyond the Elbe! Let them go to Moscow! And if they don't fall for that, the farther East they go, the more of our kind of Germany will be saved. Every man that gets into British or American captivity is an asset. He'll be able to fight again some other day. Get rid of the highly overestimated and antiquated idea of treason."

Pettinger weighed the proposition once more. The logistics expert was consistent.

Klemm-Borowski pronounced, "We're working for the next round!"

No, he was not quite consistent. "*We*, sir?" asked Pettinger.

The Marshal stared.

"I know you aspire to the true greatness of the man who gives his life for the idea," Pettinger said with a trace of fervor. "What would National-Socialism have been without the martyrs of 1923, the men who fell in front of the *Feldherrnhalle* in Munich?"

The Marshal was disturbed. Having decided to go out of this life, to sacrifice himself for his people and his country, he didn't want to be pushed on the way.

But Pettinger had come to his own conclusions. The miracle had happened, and it had come from the most unexpected source. Klemm-Borowski's ideas had gushed into the vacuum which had been lying behind Pettinger's diehard pose; and he was once more brimming with hopes and speculations. The Marshal's plan was not only feasible, it was the only chance. Pettinger swallowed it, hide and hair, digested it, appropriated it, varied it, adjusted it to several eventualities. The whole question of authorship, which the tottering Marshal stressed, was irrelevant. True, the Germans had a weakness for generals who lost their wars; however, to exploit that weakness required a posthumous publicity campaign which Pettinger was not willing to undertake. The plan could function only if each of its stages had every aspect of anonymous spontaneity.

Pettinger rose. "Your Excellency, you yourself said you must die. The success of your plan rests on your reputation. And your reputation is good only if you're dead."

Klemm-Borowski jumped up. He was so outraged that he sputtered.

"Hold it! Hold it!" Pettinger soothed. He pulled the testament out of his pocket and read aloud its first words: "*I die at the head of my troops to save Germany.*"

"I'll die, Colonel Pettinger, when I'm ready to!"

"Imagine, sir, the sad figure you would cut as a war criminal in an Allied Court! Who, then, will be able to take your last will seriously, to carry out the co-operation with the British and Americans that you recommend — the same British and Americans who're out to hang you?"

"I can't be tried. I only did my duty as an officer in the war."

"And what about Operation Buzzard? An open breach of the Rules of Land Warfare! They'll get you on that."

The Marshal said nothing. He felt caught.

"You haven't got much time!" said Pettinger.

The Marshal said harshly, "I was brought up in the spirit of loyalty, German loyalty. Where the lord went, his yeomen followed."

"I don't have your upbringing, sir," Pettinger conceded, "I've learned loyalty in the Party — not a bad school. It's just because I am loyal that I don't follow you in your death. I was ordered to execute your will."

Klemm-Borowski said tersely, "I have no more to tell you. Good luck and godspeed. Dismissed!"

But Pettinger, much as he wanted to get out of the Ruhr pocket with the ticket on life the Marshal had written for him, made no move to leave. He became formal and said, "Your Excellency — I have a little time. I can always get away. One man who knows the country can slip through easily. You appealed to my loyalty. I'm going to prove it to you. I'm going to stay with you to your end."

"I order you to leave me!" The Marshal said sharply.

Pettinger knew that Klemm-Borowski could call in his aides. "I have your last will, sir!" he warned. "By announcing your intention to commit suicide, you have declared before the world that you're no longer responsible for your actions. I have to stay with you!"

The Marshal settled back in his chair. Something must happen. Perhaps the Americans would come and take him and Pettinger and the testament, the whole mad dream.

Then he got up. He reached for his belt and holster and strapped it around his stomach. He put on his helmet and walked to the door.

Fingers closed over the handle of the door before he could reach for it. "What's that for, Pettinger?"

"Sir, I'm coming along!"

"I'm going into the line, to die at the head of my troops."

"Sir, I will accompany you."

The Marshal turned and went back to his desk. He sat down and stared through Pettinger. Pettinger pulled out a pack of cigarettes. "Care for one?"

Klemm-Borowski didn't move. Pettinger lit his cigarette, holding on to it to suppress the shaking of his nerves.

"They wouldn't let me die," the Marshal said. "My men love me. They would protect me."

"I thought so," Pettinger agreed. "It wasn't a good plan. What are you going to do?"

"Wait. . . ." the Marshal said miserably. "Wait for the Americans to come through. . . ."

"And surrender alive?"

"No." And with a fluttering of his hand, "No, no. . . . In the houses around here I have the Headquarters Company. I'll fight with them, and die with them."

"They won't let you die, either," Pettinger said. "Your men love you. They'll protect you."

The Marshal broke into cackling laughter. "I can't die, Pettinger! Nobody will let me die! Give me back my papers!"

"You have a pistol!" Pettinger said flatly.

"Oh yes, yes! I have a pistol. . . ." Klemm-Borowski's worried face lightened. He pulled the weapon out of its holster, looked at it doubtfully, then he seemed to form a decision, and he toyed with his gun, pointing it at Pettinger.

The cigarette had burned down to Pettinger's fingers. "You could kill me," he said quietly. "Then, what? You'd have to find another man for your paper. You'd have to go through the same procedure again, and you'd still have only the choice between sitting in some prisoner's dock or killing yourself now."

He threw away the stub and stepped on it.

"Give me your pistol!"

The Marshal's hand wavered. He thought of the glory of his country, of the armies he had seen marching through the streets of Paris and Warsaw and Vienna and Prague and Minsk. His hand, holding the pistol, crept over the table toward Pettinger, as if pulled by a compulsion. Then it relaxed, and the pistol dropped on the wood.

Pettinger picked it up casually. He aimed at the Marshal's heart.

The shot brought officers and men into the room. A speechless Colonel faced Pettinger.

Pettinger pulled out Klemm-Borowski's testament. "You know this handwriting?"

"Yes. It's the Marshal's."

"Read it!" ordered Pettinger. "Read it aloud!"

The Colonel swallowed and wet his lips. "*I die — at the head of my troops — to save Germany. With this highest sacrifice — I leave to the nation — the task —* "

"That's enough," said Pettinger, folding the document and putting it back into his pocket. "His Excellency, Field Marshal von Klemm-Borowski, requested that I do him this last favor. You will see that he is buried with full military honors."

The Colonel, still shaking, could only say, "*Jawohl!*"

Pettinger turned to go. He wanted to get away before the Colonel and the others regained sufficient composure to begin asking questions. But the exit had to be made with dignity.

"*Meine Herren,*" he said, "Field Marshal von Klemm-Borowski was a great man. He died so that Germany may live."

"*Jawohl!*" said the Colonel. But Pettinger was already gone.

10

THERE WAS something unreal about the last weeks of the war. For the men who had come all the way from Normandy, it was as if they had been marching through fog for an interminable time, so long that the fog had become the norm. And now the fog was lifting. You could see the land and patches of the sky, trees and roads, and it was so unbelievable — the sharp outlines, the firm earth, the green, fragrant grass. Sometimes you would stop, remember, and think that for the first time in your life you were seeing. What had you used your eyes for until this moment? You remembered the feeling that had been with you always, in Normandy, at Falaise, at Liège, crawling through the Huertgen forest, the icy cold earth of Luxemburg crashing around you in the darkness of the Bulge, the spurt across the iron girders of the Remagen bridge — take the next hill; a thousand more rise beyond it; and at the foot of one of them it will get you. Now, there weren't so many more hills. You could count them on the fingers of your hand. You were approaching the end of the Crusade, and at the end lay a broad, gray, muddy river most people never had heard of — the Elbe. This was one river your Engineers would not have to bridge, one river you would not have to cross under fire, making your way over swaying pontoons. No Heinie soldiers would be dug in on the other side. The Ally would be there who had made the long trek, too. And that would be the end. Hard to imagine. But you must accustom yourself to the idea.

If it was unreal to you, it was even more so to the Germans. They knew it was over, and yet they refused to let the fact penetrate their consciousness. They followed the maxim of an ironic poet they had burned, years ago, and acted out his prophetic joke: *Nothing will happen that you don't like to have happen.* Quixotically, they tried to live up to their Führer's melodramatic, illogical pronouncement that he would fight on even if the hands of the clock showed five minutes past twelve. Their day was over at midnight. They tried to hold back time the inexorable, and the logic of history. They would go into battle, hastily scraped-up reserves, battle groups without organizational unity, their chains of command neither anchored at the bottom nor welded at the top; odd equipment and a ludicrous supply system; maneuvers without strategy; led neither by the idea of victory nor the desperation of defeat, but by an illusion — the illusion that German organization could not break down for the reason that it was German; that the Army still existed because the German Army could not be beaten; that the Harz mountains were the Caucasus and that they could fall back into unlimited *Lebensraum;* and all the while oblivious to reality: they were caught in the constantly narrowing space between hammer and anvil.

In the midst of the fighting, they would suddenly awaken. Befuddled and bewildered, some would give up, expecting to be treated like erring children who had dared into a world too big for them.

Yates, fascinated and at the same time repelled by the mental quirk developed through this mass trauma, interrogated many of them.

A German captain, surrendering a regiment that had hardly the combat strength of a company, said to him, "We were not taught to recognize defeat."

"Do you recognize it now?"

The man thought hard. His face, lined with what he had gone through during the last weeks and days, was working. "No," he said finally. "I just need to close my eyes, and I feel that sitting here before you on an empty gas can, in an American prisoner camp, is a bad dream."

"And the other is the reality?"

"Yes."

Yates said, with ill-concealed exasperation, "Don't you see that your damned dream life is costing real lives — mostly German, but ours, too? What will you tell a mother, one of your own German mothers — her son died to keep up the comforts of your dream world?"

The man winced. "What do you want, *Herr Leutnant!* I'm only a soldier."

"Only a *kleiner Mann,*" said Yates.

"Yes, a little man," said the Captain, astonished that Yates knew the term which he, the German, had employed in the secret of his soul. "I obey orders. But nobody was there to issue an order to stop fighting. So we had to continue."

To the end, the Germans stuck to the contradiction which their particular manic conception resolved: they were only little men, on the one hand; they were greater than anyone else, on the other.

Yates gave up. There was no argument against national schizophrenia. The only argument lay in tanks and guns and planes and men and guts and endurance. Yates's argument had won the war. But the disease remained.

You had to make it easy for the Germans. If there was no one on their side whose orders would rip the German troops out of their dream and rub their noses in the realities of time and the tide of battle, the Americans would have to perform the job.

The loudspeakers came out again. This time they were mounted on armored cars and light tanks; they had to be as mobile and as speedy as the advance of the Armored Divisions, and DeWitt had insisted that his men get the same protection as any other soldier fighting armored warfare. Every available man of the Detachment was put behind a microphone, and sent out to tell the Germans that the time had come to hand over their weapons; to corral them; to direct them to the prisoner collecting points.

Bing was teamed up with Lieutenant Laborde.

Laborde was as fearless as ever, as pinched-faced as ever; but behind his sour visage gleamed the intoxication of success. He kept a little notebook with columns of figures listing the number of prisoners he had taken and with whom he credited himself. He kept a scrupulous accounting, although nobody praised him for his record or was even interested in it. And on days when the take was meager, he would fidget and squirm and force his driver and Bing to go out with him on lone wolf missions.

Had Laborde been able to speak German, he would have dispensed with an announcer. Without one, he was helpless to boost his account. He was glad enough to get Bing, despite his resentment against him. He had never forgotten or forgiven the fact that Bing had witnessed his one defection — that first loudspeaker mission which cost Tolachian's life.

To Bing, it was not a matter of choice. He was ordered, he was assigned. He could have tried to pull strings, he could have talked to Yates, or through Yates, gone to DeWitt. He did neither. One job or another — one brass or another — what did it matter, anyhow?

It mattered to Yates. He sought out Bing shortly after the assignment to Laborde's tank. He was deliberate in making the question a direct one: "How d'you get along with Lieutenant Laborde?"

"I get along, thank you."

A thin, thin layer of sadness, like a spray of fixative on a carbon sketch, seemed to have spread itself over Bing's features. The attitude toward life which Yates had envied him was gone — the attitude that said: Life's my cake, I'm going to eat it, and have it, too, and fling it right in your face if I want to.

Bing meant a lot to him. In retrospect he could see that the very fact of Bing had pushed him forward — the youthful insolence with which Bing had tackled the Fourth of July leaflet, the definition of the whole complex of war aims; the unselfish, enthusiastic, almost gnomish busy-bodyness with which Bing made possible the brief idyl with Thérèse; the plucky matter-of-factness that made it bearable to listen to BBC's broadcast of their obituary — even to laugh at it.

He knew Bing needed help, now, or at least straightening-out, and he had learned that in war this help is an obligation as holy as that of the medic who pulls you, wounded, out of the line. He had denied it to Thorpe, once; he had paid the penalty.

"What's the matter with you, Bing?" His question was almost tender. "Why can't you talk it out? We know one another well enough — you've seen me when I didn't measure up. Something about a woman? Karen?"

Bing shook his head. His mouth was a bitter line; something new on Bing's face.

"Leave me alone, will you, Lieutenant? It's my business, isn't it? And Laborde's all right. I like him. The crazier he gets, the better. Why not!"

"What happened to you? Was it — your homecoming? I was happy to give you your chance in Neustadt. Shouldn't I have done it?"

"Neustadt was all right. Laborde's all right. I'm all right."

"What happened in Neustadt?"

"What happened in Neustadt . . . !" Bing turned away his face. "Nothing! Just a quaint old city — they're a dime a dozen in this part of the world."

Yates picked his next question carefully. "Well — when the Nazis came back — and you were there, outnumbered — you've never talked about it."

"I never talk about it, sure." Bing laughed. "Haven't you done things in this war you'd rather not talk about?"

"You know I have. But then I talked about them — or I did something about them. And I felt better."

"Maybe I don't want to feel better. Maybe I want to go on feeling as I do, doing what I'm doing, living my own dirty little life and getting accustomed to getting along with myself. Maybe I like that. And what kind of guy are you? Always poking your nose into other peoples' business. Missionary! Crusader! Oh, I know all the big words. I was writing them when you were too lazy even to think about them. And get this — I liked you better, then. At least you weren't so God-damned nosy!"

"I'm sorry," said Yates.

He went away, depressed. Why hadn't he been able to help Bing? Had he approached him the wrong way? Bing had put his finger on it: There had been a time when he avoided getting close to people. That hadn't worked, and he had swung to the other extreme. . . . That was probably what Bing was sensing — that was why the boy didn't thaw out.

Yates saw himself — Young Man of Excessive Good Will and Idealistic Prerogative. Disgusting. Stupid, too. That's why he had been no match for Willoughby; that's why he always stood alone when it came to a test — Sir Galahad with a silver bar and a chip on his shoulder.

You had to live among people, not in opposition to them, or aside from them. Yet, he'd felt for Bing. It had gotten him nowhere. Now, he knew why: whatever was troubling Bing was beyond the boy's confidence in him.

I'm no Troy, thought Yates. Troy wouldn't go in for my kind of mental gyrations, and yet Troy has influenced more men than I ever have. You can't be just a sharer of burdens, Yates concluded. You must work with people, join in with people, be one of them, even if you have to trim some of your finery.

Laborde's tank was always in difficulty. It was not a regular component of any of the Combat Commands to which it was attached for his roundups; besides, it was secondhand — a light tank that had been bounced around in combat and that Ordnance had patched up time and again. There was always something needing repair, something missing.

Laborde fought a perpetually losing war with the supply and maintenance men on whom he depended. When his engine stalled or broke down, it was the last to be repaired; when the tank ran short of gas, Bing had to beg or steal a supply; and the tank never had been equipped with the gaily colored signal panels which were now constantly in use.

Only an Army that had absolute air superiority could afford to discard the advantage of camouflage and show brazenly the red, orange, or yellow panels on the tops of its vehicles. The bright patches of color were especially necessary for the tanks. During these last weeks of the war, the American armor far outran the latest information that the Air Force had entered on its maps. Armor was jabbing deep into territory that still was marked as enemy-held. The bitter experience of American columns bombed or strafed by their own planes before the mistake was perceived had taught the need of more definite visible identification than the tanks' white stars allowed.

But the Sergeant at Signal Supply was curiously unable ever to raise a set of color panels for Laborde.

It was, of course, Laborde's way of throwing his weight around. Unfortunately, the weight of a Lieutenant wasn't much, and at the front, with men who had seen several campaigns, it was infinitesimal.

Bing had to make up for it, whether he wanted to or not.

All morning, he had been trying to raise a piece of the orange panel that, according to Signal Operations Instructions, was the identifying color of the day.

Laborde said, "So we'll go out without the panels. I've wasted three hours sitting here, and we haven't done a thing today. Let's go!"

"Let me try once more," said Bing. "Maybe I can swipe them somewhere."

"What! Take them from another vehicle that might need them just as much? There's too much stealing going on all around. We'll take our chances."

"The Sergeant at Signal Supply said I should try at Ordnance," Bing said tiredly. "Take it from one that wouldn't go out today. Just borrow it."

"We have no time," decreed Laborde.

He had his way. Recently, he'd been having his way more often than not. Bing didn't insist, didn't put up a fight, let things slide, because he was too numb to care.

Charlie, the driver, was already in his seat. He was a lanky, close-mouthed man of about thirty, a former garage mechanic from a town in Ohio. He had plastered the available space inside the tank with pin-up girls, and Laborde had raged and made him rip them off. "I don't like lewdness," he had shrilled. "Sex has its place, but not inside my tank."

Charlie had said nothing, but he failed to make the slight repair on Laborde's seat in the right of the turret. Every bump on the road, or in the field, was a painful jolt to Laborde. Laborde didn't object to the pain; it was as much a part of his pattern as his tens of thousands of dizzying spins inside the model cockpit, when he had been a living test tube for how much a human stomach could stand.

Bing put on his tanker's helmet, his earphones, and the throat mike, and climbed into his seat next to Laborde. He could have chosen the empty seat to the right of the driver, but Laborde, fearing that Charlie's silent antagonism and Bing's sullen arrogance would nurture each other, had made plain that he wanted Bing up in the turret.

They were going at a good speed, and the riding was smooth. Bing liked riding inside the tank, especially when the hatches were buttoned up, and the only link to the outside world was the periscope. It gave you a feeling of security, especially after what had happened in Neustadt. Rationally, Bing knew that the thin armor of the light tank protected him, at best, against light infantry weapons, and that a well-aimed German *Panzerfaust* would go right through it — he had seen enough blasted, burned-out tanks to have no illusions about that. But the comfort remained, and he didn't discourage it; it was good and counteracted somewhat the nervous tenseness that Laborde's very presence created.

Laborde liked to keep the turret hatch open, even when small-arms fire threatened. He made a point of despising the little security the tank offered. What was the war if you took no risks? Even the mounting figures in the notebook were only a sublimation. If you looked at them closely, you knew how easy the job really was. Too easy.

Bing watched Charlie impersonally — Charlie's lean, strong hands on the two levers that controlled the direction of the tank, Charlie's foot on the accelerator, caressingly almost, sensitive to each irregularity on the road. The luminated indicators on the instrument board trembled slightly. Charlie grinned, "Fine day!"

His voice sounded tinny through Bing's earphones.

"Yep," said Bing. "Want some gum?"

Laborde was standing up, leaning out of the turret, scanning the road.

"I'm chewing, thanks," said Charlie.

Bing, mindful that every word over the communications system would come to Laborde, tapped Charlie on the shoulder for the wad of gum the driver was pushing around between his big teeth. Charlie passed it back to him. Bing pasted the gum carefully on Laborde's seat.

Then he glanced through the periscope. They had reached a column of tanks that belonged to the Combat Command with which Laborde's team was to work. The tanks were still advancing on the road.

Bing switched on the radio. For a while nothing came — the column moved in silence. Then a definite order was given.

The tanks left the road and dispersed in a straggling line. They slowed down and seemed to be feeling their way toward an objective. The open fields over which they maneuvered were coming to an end; several small patches of wood hove into view of the periscope, and there were some puffs of whitish gray from between the trees whose tops were lacy in Bing's sight. Laborde still hung outside the turret, the upper part of his body unprotected. Charlie buttoned his personal hatch.

He slowed down.

Bing pulled back the bolt of the machine gun and threw it into full load.

"What d'you slow down for?" Laborde's cranky voice came over the earphones.

Charlie, eyes pressed to his periscope, said, "You want us to run ahead of the line?"

Laborde came in, leaving the hatch open. "I'll let you know when I want you to slow down or go off the road."

"The road may be mined," Bing warned.

Laborde again went outside the hatch. Bing could see his boot tapping impatiently.

"Still worried about your life?" sneered Laborde. "I've always brought you back safe and sound, haven't I?"

Bing said nothing. He wasn't worried about his life. He didn't give a damn about his life. Not since Neustadt. But why argue that with Laborde? "A dead loudspeaker tank's no good to anybody," Bing remarked flatly. "And the German mines don't know we have good intentions."

"Safe and sound!" repeated Laborde. "Haven't I? Answer me!"

"Yes, sir," said Bing. "We were lucky."

"Luck! What's luck?" Laborde coughed. "You stake your life, you get it back. No half-measures, no hesitations."

Bing thought that over. Neustadt had been hesitations and half-measures; and the end effect was complete failure, complete cowardice. He could say nothing against Laborde, nothing to make him stop and wait until the line of tanks caught up with them.

Laborde was directing the tank toward the first patch of trees, to the right of the road. Some of the fire that Bing had observed from the distance had come from there. Now, the grove was silent.

Laborde's plan was clear. If he could make the Germans he suspected in the patch of woods come out and surrender before the main bulk of the fighting tanks arrived, he could really chalk up one to his credit. He took his tank fairly close to the trees, a hundred, eighty, sixty yards. Bing momentarily expected the typical, sharp clattering of bullets and shrapnel on the tank's armor. But nothing came.

Laborde ducked inside. He sat down in the chewing gum, closed the hatch over his head, said to Charlie, "Keep cruising slowly in front of those trees!" and to Bing, "All right, start talking!"

Bing grabbed the hand mike that was connected with the loudspeakers mounted to the sides of the turrets.

"Deutsche Soldaten!"

In a way, it was good to speak again. Words were his weapon. In the words which Laborde was unable to understand, he could escape him, be on his own. In these words, also, he could compress, by the very arguments that were to convince them, his hate and contempt for the enemy, and escape his hate and contempt for himself. After the first few words his mind spun thoughts by itself. Somehow, he could listen to his own words as to an echo, a little awed that the words kept rising and that there was such sound within him. He was like a poet spilling out verse, it was the best in him that he gave, and there it was and took form, aside from him and independent of him, and he felt good and strong and purposeful.

He told the Germans in the woods that he had come at the head of a large unit of armor, that the tanks had taken thousands of Germans and that this was the last warning. They could heed it and throw away their weapons and come out of the woods with their hands raised, and nobody would hold it against them. They had fought long enough, a stupid war.

"When you look at it now, when the war is nearly over — what did you fight for? To give a few men, who always exploited Germany, the chance to make additional profits by exploiting Europe. To keep in power a few men who are now packing their jewels and precious possessions and running for their lives from the Russians investing Berlin. Did you fight for yourselves? Where is your gain? Your wives dead or fleeing or hiding in air-raid shelters or already under Allied occupation; your sons and fathers and brothers dead, wounded, in flight, or prisoners; Germany a tiny strip of territory pressed between the Russians in the East and the Allies in the West. What a mistake to make — to think you could rule the world when you couldn't even rule yourselves! Think it over! A man fights when the fighting makes sense. But what sense does your fight have, now that it's over, now that the futility of it bursts in your faces? You should have quit years ago, you should never have started it — but now, now, in these last few minutes, before our tanks come down on you and lay it on and speak the last, irrevocable, iron word — now, act! Save your lives out of which so many years have been wasted, save them so that, perhaps, they'll be good for something in the future! Surrender!"

His head was throbbing. The sweat ran down from under his helmet, down his cheeks; his eyes smarted, and his lips were parched. He reached for his canteen bottle and gulped down the water and spit; the chlorine taste was strong.

There was no sound, only the soft purring of the motor as the tank slowly pushed alongside the woods. Bing wiped his mouth and eyes and peered through the periscope. The trees were close, he believed he could see every needle of the pines, the fresh, sappy buds at the end of the twigs.

They were young trees, mostly, and suddenly he had a longing to get out and lie under them, and feel the giving of the needle-covered earth, and capture the smell of spring in the land.

"Nothing moving," he said.

Laborde pushed open the hatch. He stuck out his head, in the way an unfledged pigeon pokes its scrawny neck over the rim of its nest.

Bing had a suspicion that forced him into uncontrollable laughter. "I think we've been preaching to the trees and the birds," he sputtered. "Wasting the Government's gas and electricity and brains. . . ."

Laborde made a choking sound of anger. "We'll see!" he said threateningly. "We'll see! Driver, into the woods!"

"For Chris'sake!" shouted Bing. "It may be a trap!"

"Left lever!" That was final.

Charlie, the driver, obeyed. He didn't even look through his periscope. He crashed into the young trees. He went straight ahead, his face set. He hated Laborde.

They went through the patch of woodland. They crossed it in not quite two minutes; then there were no more trees, just fields again, and a ravine.

Laborde saw that the woods had been empty. They had talked to nobody, to the thin air, they'd been fighting windmills with windy words. He could see signs of German occupation — discarded equipment, empty shellcases, a crushed helmet. They must have run when they'd seen the tanks. They had not waited for Laborde and his loudspeakers.

Charlie stopped the tank. It was oppressively hot. He opened his hatch. "What we do now, sir?" he asked, his head outside.

Laborde swung himself completely out of the hatch. Bing saw the chewing gum sticking to the seat of his pants. Laborde sat down, leaned his back against the hatch, stretched himself, lit a cigarette, and said moodily, "Wait."

"O.K., sir," said Charlie.

"Wait," said Laborde. "Maybe those tanks will find out in time that there's nobody left to fight them."

Bing stuck his head and shoulders out of the turret, and sniffed the air. From somewhere came the sound of firing.

"We must have picked the wrong patch of woods," Bing said, for Laborde's benefit.

"Could be," said Charlie.

Laborde said nothing. He studiously examined the terrain, the ravine slightly to the right, the sprouting field to the left.

Bing heard a thin drone. Very far up in the sky, a formation of fighter bombers winged east. He thought back to the skies of Normandy. The same blue, the same mood, only now, the war was almost at its end. A whole cycle had passed. Again the sky, and the thin drone.

One of the planes sheared off.

Laborde looked up. "Ours. I should have been in the Air Force. But they wouldn't take me. A man's a man, up there."

The plane seemed to plummet down.

"Perfect dive," remarked Laborde. "Must have seen some Nazis. Watch the fireworks."

Bing thought of the signal panel he had not been able to get. The plane was coming closer every second.

Bing dove into the tank.

"That's us!" he shouted.

Laborde saw it, too. But he didn't jump into the hatch. He remained on top of the tank, standing upright, waving frantically, shouting words that were drowned by the roar of the onrushing plane.

"Get going!" cried Bing. "Into the ravine!"

He thought of closing the hatch, but Laborde was still outside. Then the hail of bullets. Laborde's shadow across the opening of the hatch disintegrated. Parts of him fell into the tank, ludicrous, the chewing gum sticking to the seat of the pants.

The tank jumped forward. Bing fell to his knees.

Down! Down! he felt.

Then the blinding and the crash.

Bing saw the walls of the tank rise, its compartments spilling, a rain of silly items, smoke bombs, screwdrivers. Charlie's head, bloody, his eyes staring, a hole gaping where the throat had been.

Bing felt himself pinioned. A weight and a pain where his legs had been. And the walls of the tank still turning, or was he turning? And the heat, the heat, the yellow smoke. The pain, the terrible pain. Then the smoke and the flame took form. It was a giant, Tony, the giant with the child's heart. If it happens somewhere, it happens to me. They had killed him, and he had been a good man. That's what we've been fighting for. And then it wasn't Tony, but Karen, or perhaps Yates. They came so fast. And the pain. With Frieda, too, the pain. Wipe her out.

Wipe it all out.

II

The clerk in the headquarters of the Combat Command, to whom Yates finally was referred, listened patiently. He was accustomed to such calls.

"It's a week since we had word," said Yates. "Lieutenant Laborde and Sergeant Bing and the driver were to have reported back four days ago."

The clerk, entrenched behind his little field desk, moved his feet. He looked at the Lieutenant and at the Corporal who had come in with him

—a rosy-faced, stumpy fellow whose pale eyes seemed transfixed by the clerk's file case.

"An identical filing system," said Abramovici, "is employed throughout the Army. Provided it is kept right, a clerk is able to check in a minute — "

"Yeah!" said the clerk, "but if these men were attached unassigned?"

"That complicates the matter, but not unreasonably. A system has been devised for such contingencies. Will you let me have a look at your morning reports?"

"No," said the clerk.

They had reached the mysterious mill where the red tape was spun, and Yates was determined to cut through it here and now. "Let's leave your files for a moment. There was only one loudspeaker tank with your Combat Command. If anything happened to it, you'd know without cross-checking."

"We do know," said the clerk.

"Why didn't you speak up right away?"

The clerk pointed his thumb at Abramovici. "He didn't give me a chance, sir!"

"I did!" protested Abramovici. "The importance of the files lies in their value as a source of supplementary — "

"What happened?"

"Dead."

Yates had a sudden, nagging pain at the back of his head; and he thought it isn't true. Some people are so full of life that death will not touch them. There must be an error. All those papers constantly being filled out and circulated and dispatched — how easy it is to make a mistake! Then he thought of his last talk with Bing. . . . It was true. The boy was dead. Something had sapped the joy of life out of him; and his actual death had only harvested what had been germinating in him before. You can only mourn it, you cannot cry out against it.

"Where did they die? How?"

The clerk went to his file case and, under Abramovici's scrutiny, let his hands dig among the papers.

"Everything's in order," he said, after a period of pregnant silence. "I knew we'd notified your unit. Through channels. You know how channels are, these days. The war's going too fast. And a couple of casualties have no priorities. Just routine . . . Here's a copy."

Yates took the sheet of paper. It was a fifth or sixth copy, and the lettering was blurred. Or maybe it was his eyes.

From, To, the usual code names, abbreviations, capital letters. A language he hated, dead and sterile, but perhaps the best way of reducing enormous events to something the human mind can grasp. Arabic One,

Two, Three. Yes, here, the facts: In line of duty — near village of Schoenebrunn — a few figures in brackets, apparently the map co-ordinates — ahead of own lines — by American aircraft — and so on and so forth. . . . A very bad copy.

"May I keep it?"

"Yes," said the clerk, "I've got one for my records."

"Have they been buried?"

With a patent dig at Abramovici, the clerk said, "Your Corporal should be able to tell you what that means — there, the notation at the bottom of the sheet."

Abramovici craned his neck around Yates's arm to read. He said nothing, but his feet seemed to plant themselves more firmly on the ground.

"There's nothing left to be buried," said the clerk. His competitor's silence had made him conscious of the full meaning of his words. "Only the shell of the tank, burned out, and not much of that. . . ."

Yates felt a peculiar weakness; it went all through him, and his thoughts were somehow fuzzy. A verse filtered through his mind. *It is some dream that on the deck you've fallen cold and dead. My Captain does not answer.* . . . His Captain! The boy wasn't anybody's Captain, he lay on no deck, nothing was left of him to lie anywhere. And that he needed another's expression of sorrow to express his own, irked Yates. He said to the clerk, gruffly, "Thanks. Thanks for the dope."

And he motioned Abramovici to leave.

Back in the jeep, he studied his maps.

"Are we going — there?" asked Abramovici.

"It isn't far. Three hours, I guess, if the roads are in any shape." After a time, after Abramovici had started the car, he added, "I really don't know what for. It does nobody any good."

"Maybe we can find something," Abramovici said with forced hopefulness. "His watch or his pen. We could send it home."

"Yes," said Yates, "we could."

Where the winter wheat was not sprouting, the land was fallow. There had been little sowing this spring. The peasants, too, seemed to have been caught by the peculiar national sensation of the Germans in these months of the year 1945 — of being suspended in mid-air, with time standing still, so that even the seasons lost their function.

Only here and there, an old man walking over the fields; or a tired woman, stooping low, glancing up as the jeep rushed by.

Yates and Abramovici passed through the village of Schoenebrunn. It had suffered hardly at all from the advance. A few shellholes in some of the houses, a German 88 abandoned at its town line, chickens crossing

500

the road, suddenly spurting aside with frantic cackling and anxiously spread wings as the jeep came upon them.

And then fields again, and the patches of straggling woods where Bing had spoken his appeal to nobody.

Yates raised his hand, and Abramovici turned the jeep off the road, letting it slowly bounce over the plowed-up, track-rutted field. A tank bulked in the center of the field, its gun still pointed at an enemy long gone, one of its tracks shot off, arching on the ground like a tremendous caterpillar whose head had been smashed by an invisible foot.

"That's not it," said Yates.

"Can't be," confirmed Abramovici. "No loudspeakers."

Yates pulled his map out of the compartment in the dashboard.

"Must be around here."

Abramovici pointed toward the small patch of woods on the right. A straight, freshly broken path lay through it, as if a herd of elephants had tumbled through, crashing the saplings and young pines.

"Let's follow that," suggested Yates.

"No can do." Abramovici stopped and peered down the trail. "Too rough for the jeep."

"Let's go round the woods."

Abramovici nodded. He drove slowly. His face was drawn with apprehension, his eyes had lost some of their vagueness as he searched the terrain in front of him.

Yates pulled a pack of cigarettes out of his breast pocket. The first cigarette didn't want to come out, he tore it and saw the tobacco spill. The second lit badly, it burned along the side, and Yates threw it away and gave up smoking.

They turned left, following the rim of woods.

"They must have come out somewhere," said Yates, just to say something. "Unless they got stuck in the middle of it!"

They turned left again.

"There!" called Yates. He saw the other end of the trail, where the tank had broken out of the trees. "But where did it go?"

Abramovici jammed the brake. The motor stalled. "I almost went down there!" His apologetic laugh froze in his throat. He jumped out of the jeep with an agility he had never shown and half-climbed, half-slid into the ravine.

Yates followed him.

He saw it now, too — the burned-out, smashed shell of Laborde's tank, riddled and seared, the muzzle of its gun bent like the twig of a tree, the loudspeakers mounted next to its turret flattened like tin cans run over by a tractor.

They reached the bottom of the ravine. Yates's hand was bleeding. He didn't notice it.

"Your hand!" said Abramovici.

"What about it? Oh, yes. . . ."

They walked toward the wreck with halting steps, as you might approach an altar.

"There's nothing left in there," Abramovici said in a low voice, to reassure himself, or to give himself a reason for not examining the interior of the tank.

Yates glanced at him. Abramovici stood there, and his whole attitude said: I can go to this point, no further.

Yates thought of many things. They came to him like hasty clouds on a wind-filled morning — Laborde sitting on the table, embracing the bottles, after the air raid on Château Vallères — the squabbling Yugoslavs in the DP Camp of Verdun — Mulsinger and Heberle lined up against their stakes — and now this tank that had turned over, and over, and burned. After all these days, it still seemed to ooze smell — not the smell of death, not the smell of burned rubber and hot metal — a smell all its own, infinitely bitter, like rust and dust and old clothes falling to bits from age. Or, perhaps, it was the shade and the coolness of the ravine in which no breath of air stirred, or the piece of blue sky that reigned above it in immutable harshness, and that would be there for years and years, until corrosion finally ate away the metal, until brush overgrew it and built a green, dense thicket over the shapeless steel coffin.

Yates pushed himself forward.

He used one of the bogey wheels as a step to reach the gash in the turret.

I must do this, he said to himself. I went and saw Thorpe, too. This is worse.

Then he looked.

Rays of light, seeping through the tortured opening of the hatch, through the holes that shrapnel had torn in the light armor, through the seams that had come open in the crash, crisscrossed each other and touched twisted metal, some of it molten and hardened again in odd design. He looked for something resembling human figures. He saw dark clumps that could be anything. Piles of ashes.

Then he let himself glide down.

When he felt ground under his feet, earth, good earth, when he looked up to the sky and saw real light instead of the sickly, ghostlike strands inside the tank, he sat down. He sat down and breathed deeply and felt the reeling of his head come to rest. The vision of a Bing cruelly burned, but still recognizable in shape or feature, the vision from which he had shied and which he had forced himself to face, faded.

502

"Nothing?" asked Abramovici.

"Nothing," said Yates, "thank God."

Then he was silent and stared at the steep walls of the ravine. After a while, he was disturbed by Abramovici's strange murmuring. He looked up.

Abramovici was standing, facing the wrecked hull of the tank, bending, straightening himself, and bending again. From his lips came words that rose and fell with his swaying.

"*Yiskadal veyiskadash shemah rahboh. . . .*"

"What are you doing?" Yates started to say, then stopped. It was a ritual, he knew, although he didn't understand it. He got up, and took off his helmet.

The singsong increased in volume. It seemed to rise from the bottom of the ravine, from the tank with the nothing inside — to swing in the air, to die away only to be taken up once more by the odd little man. It was lulling and sad and comforting.

Abramovici stopped.

He turned to Yates and smiled, a wise, gentle smile.

"For the dead," he said, "a prayer . . ."

Yates and Abramovici drove along in the backwash of the last advance. By the hundreds and thousands, German prisoners were marching along the road to the American rear. To reach American captivity was to them a personal victory, and they marched singing and laughing, not like an Army beaten to the ground, but almost like men who had been liberated. There were few American escorts to these prisoner columns; their own officers led them in straight formations, and the privates carried the officers' baggage, and the officers' boots were shined and their breeches were tailored and trim; and at the road crossings, American MP's obligingly informed them where they could receive their next meal. It was all splendidly organized.

It annoyed Yates. His sense for decorum, of the How and What of behavior, was thrown off gear. And he had just come away from the smashed tank. Paula Camp was still fresh in his mind, the rows of machine-gunned dead in their open graves. Yet here marched these columns of strapping men, defeated, yes — weren't their enemy's armies running at will over their land? — but pointedly showing no concern, expressing by the very way they walked that they had given up their arms because they wanted to and because, for the time being, the only places where they would find food for their voracious bellies, where they could continue a semblance of their organization, were the provisional prisoner enclosures that the Americans had set up.

Yates had the jeep stop at the head of one of the singing, tramping columns. He crooked his index finger twice at the young Major marching in front of it.

The Major gave a strident, *Das Ganze, halt!*

The column stopped, the song stopped, hundreds of curious eyes were directed at the lone jeep whose two dusty occupants looked anything but the victors.

The Major slowly followed Yates's beckoning finger. Yates stared at him until the man remembered; he jerked up his hand to the shield of his cap and saluted. Then the German said, *"Hier ist unser Marschbefehl!"* and pulled out a sheet of paper.

Yates took it and scrutinized it. The orders were correct; they were signed by some lieutenant of a divisional MP company.

Then he handed the orders to Abramovici. "Will you read them aloud and translate them into German for this major?"

"But I know what's in them!" the Major protested. "I can read English!"

"Translate!"

Abramovici, who didn't quite follow Yates's intent, nevertheless came through with precision. Abramovici could breathe life into any official document.

"Louder!" ordered Yates.

Abramovici bawled out his words; the first ten or fifteen ranks of the column heard every one of them.

Abramovici finished reading. The Major, baffled but undaunted, stretched out his hand to receive back his orders.

But Yates held on to the paper. "Does it say anywhere in the orders that you are to sing?" he called out. "Perhaps you have another paper that gives you permission to sing! Do you? Show it to me!"

The Major now was visibly rattled. "Nobody mentioned singing, sir," he admitted. "I gave orders to sing because — "

"Because of what?"

"Because I thought — we felt like singing — it makes marching so much easier. . . ."

"Corporal Abramovici! Explain to the Major where he's going and what situation he finds himself in!"

Abramovici rose in the jeep, stretched himself to his full height, and pulled up his pants.

"You are going into captivity," he trumpeted. "Captivity is the state in which a captured soldier finds himself."

The Major narrowed his glance. He looked from the little speaker to Yates, who sat back, his eyes impersonally evaluating the column.

"Captivity is preferable to death," boomed Abramovici, "but it imposes certain restrictions. The prisoner of war lives in compounds that are enclosed by barbed wires; he won't be able to roam the countryside at will, taking what he pleases and shooting up whom he pleases. That will be only a memory, a nostalgic picture of his past, unattainable under his present circumstances, or at any foreseeable future."

The Major fidgeted. There was suppressed snickering in the ranks.

"To many of you" — Abramovici now turned to the future — "captivity will be a chance to improve yourselves. Up to the rank of corporal, you will work. That will do away with much of the boredom that naturally befalls a man deprived of his liberty. It will also set you on the road to becoming useful members of society, when and if the Allied Governments decide to set you free. Noncommissioned officers will be employed in a supervisory capacity."

Yates observed a German Private First Class at the flank of the fifth row; disappointment visibly crept over the man.

Abramovici faced the young Major. "Officers do not work. The privileges of their rank remain in force."

A kind of muttering went through the ranks. The Major winced, and the other officers, forming the first three ranks of the column, shuffled uncomfortably.

"They may continue to idle away their days. They will have no batmen, they will carry their own baggage and shine their own shoes and wash their own clothes if they want them clean."

A large, stolid-looking soldier, his strong wrists sticking out from too-short sleeves, came up from behind. Wordlessly, he placed two good-sized bags at the Major's feet, saluted stiffly, and returned to his place in the ranks.

"In conclusion," said Abramovici, "let me say that except for those who will die a natural death over the course of the years, you will survive. The mortality rate in American prisoner of war camps is low. Ahead of you is a future not brilliant, maybe, but all the more secure."

He sat down.

"Perfect!" said Yates.

He handed the marching orders back to the Major. "You can go ahead now."

The German pocketed the paper and picked up the bags. There was hate in his eyes. He said hoarsely, "We fought a gentlemen's war. We gave up like gentlemen. We expected to be treated like gentlemen."

Yates said flatly, "I'm afraid you're wrong. You didn't fight a gentlemen's war. You gave up because we forced you to and because you were in terror of the Russians. And you're being treated better than you deserve."

The Major said nothing. He turned on his heel — not as smartly as he wanted to, because his heavy bags impeded him — and shouted, "*Achtung! Vorwärts! Marsch!*"

505

The column passed by Yates. They were treading heavily now, and they were absolutely silent. It was a long column and Yates thought that a word from the Major would have been sufficient to make these men rush the jeep and kill him and Abramovici. But apparently, the idea had never entered the German's head.

And then they came to the Elbe.

They couldn't see the river until they were quite close to it, but they knew they were approaching it. All over the flat fields troops at rest were deployed; tanks and guns stood idle; ack-ack batteries pointed their noses at the sky — but it seemed a mere gesture.

Here, the war was over.

A deep feeling of relief came over Yates. They had made it. The bow-string that had been tensed for so long a time snapped suddenly, and trembled. Life was worth a life again, not the price of a jagged piece of metal.

He put his arm about Abramovici's sturdy shoulders and said, "Look at it! God damn it! It's over and done with! We're through with the job. God, it's beautiful!"

Abramovici nodded and pursed his lips and whistled a dance tune, and it was so out of keeping with his usual sobriety that Yates grinned and then broke into open, uproarious laughter.

"Let's go crazy!" Yates said. "We can afford to go crazy for a day, such a day!"

Abramovici kept on steering the jeep, avoiding the drunks that came swerving on the road, bottles raised high, shouting, their helmets askew.

"It was a good war," said Abramovici. "My father used to say to me, Leopold, he said, a war is absolutely no good unless you get through alive. There's the river, sir — what now?"

The river was a broad, mud-colored band, flowing quietly and imperturbably. Barges were sunk in its shallows, on both shores, and the smoke-stacks and superstructures of tugboats stuck out of the water like warning signposts of a past that Yates wanted to push behind, as far and as fast as he could.

There were objects floating down the river, wreckage of boats and floats, and some bloated bodies, grotesquely round and secure of their course. A group of men on the bridge thrown across were busy clearing the flotsam of war from the bows of the pontoons.

"Over there," Yates directed Abramovici. "Looks like a parking lot."

They got out of their jeep and began to walk toward the water. Yates was aware that his elation was fizzling out fast; a moment ago he had wished he could telephone, or at least cable Ruth, and tell her the great good news — that they had won the war, that it was definitely and for all times over, that he was standing at the shores of the Elbe River, safe and sound and unscratched, that he was going to be home, soon, and that he loved her, deeply, at this great moment of his life, the greatest, the rebirth.

It was she with whom he wanted to share this moment — and the moment was dissolving under his hands. Perhaps he was wearier than he realized. Perhaps the span bridging this moment and that haze-covered morning when his boat edged its way down the Hudson was so vast that he couldn't see he had reached its end. Anyhow, it was easier to say *I'm tired* than to brood about why the day wasn't quite as he had imagined it when he could only dream of it. Perhaps, too, he was not in the right spot. There must be places where you could abandon yourself, or where troops paraded down conquered streets, with flags flying and bayonets gleaming — where victory was victory.

Or, perhaps, the Germans had spoiled it. They had let the war fizzle out. There had been no historic second when the order "Cease Firing!" hurtled along the line, when men came out of their holes and embraced each other. Here, in this sector, the war was over; at other sectors, it continued in its haphazard way.

Or, perhaps, the war was never over.

The guard on the American side of the bridge gave Yates's papers a cursory examination.

"Want to go over there, sir?"

"Yes."

"We want everybody back by 1800. That's orders."

"What's the matter? Trouble?"

"I don't know," said the guard. "They say there have been incidents. The Russians are a pretty tough bunch, you know!"

"Is that so?"

"I hear that, from tomorrow on, all this cross-traffic will be cut out. Only official missions, from then on."

"You mean they're declaring the whole Russian Army off limits?"

"I've been over there!" said the guard. "A pretty tough bunch!"

"You said that already!"

On the other side, two full-bosomed, bemedaled girls in high-necked tunics stood guard, submachine guns strapped over their shoulders. That is, they stood arm in arm with three American soldiers, while a fourth one took a picture of the whole group. One of the girls, a freckled, whitish blonde, flashed Yates a gold-toothed smile. He waved at her, as he and Abramovici passed by. They walked up the long, smooth embankment where Red Army men lay in the grass or strolled about with the measured step of people who have done a long day's work and now have come to the park to enjoy the evening.

But farther on, more and more came up and crowded jubilantly around the two Americans. Their uniforms were threadbare and patched, but their weapons were carefully kept.

Some of the Russians were drunk. One of them, a stout, chesty fellow with Mongolian features and a Circassian hat, pounced on Abramovici and whirled him around and around, until Abramovici squeaked and tore himself away and fled to Yates's side. The soldier in the Circassian hat spread his arms in a gesture: *All this way you have come!* and again: *All this way we have come!* and then he clasped his hands and grinned.

"The Russians," said Abramovici, "are like children."

Yates pointed at the machine pistol of a man just passing. With its drum magazine it looked very effective. "Some children!"

Then he added, "But the joy that's in them! The uninhibited joy!"

The joy was enviable and disturbing at the same time. It was the joy he wanted to feel, the joy that, he was sure, was the moment's due, and of which he seemed incapable.

"What's the matter with us?" he asked, more of himself than of Abramovici. "What do we lack?"

Abramovici felt complete and at ease. All was well, inside and outside of him, and Yates was in one of his queer moods. "Americans," he said, "are a serious, businesslike people. That's why we'll get ahead in the world. Americans don't make a move without purpose. I am proud of being an American, especially when I see the Germans or the Russians or other foreigners."

It wasn't the answer Yates needed. He wasn't even certain of what troubled him. All he knew was that he must have this joy, this release. And this was the day!

They were coming into the town of Torgau. The houses, not too badly destroyed, grew denser along the road. Abramovici stopped to study a Russian and German poster freshly pasted on the wall. "They're quick with posters!" he said.

Yates wasn't interested in posters. He wanted an answer, a person who could give him an answer, and he knew who the person was. He had thought of him when he saw the man in the Circassian hat swing Abramovici. He had thought of him again when they passed the man with the machine pistol.

"Remember Kavalov?" he asked.

"Sure I remember him," Abramovici said disdainfully. The way Yates's mind jumped around! It made Abramovici uncomfortable. "The Russian Navy man. We had him at the mess, in Verdun."

"I wonder whatever became of him. . . ."

"There are millions of Russians," Abramovici said philosophically. "They're like dollar bills. They count only in batches."

"Maybe." Yates's steps became more and more determined. He was heading for what had been the center of Torgau. It was as if he were looking for someone.

"You don't expect to find him here?" Abramovici's worry now became real. Some people, who couldn't take the right care of themselves, cracked under strain; they also cracked if the strain was suddenly removed.

"No, I don't suppose I'll find him. But I wish I could."

"Why? What do you want him for?"

"I don't know — he's a man I once met who seemed sure of his ideas."

"I'm sure of my ideas, too," Abramovici said peevishly, "and mine are of proven value in war and peace times."

"He said he'd get out of the Verdun Camp and get back to his Army and help them fight," Yates insisted. "So it's possible. . . ."

"What's possible?"

"That we'll meet him here."

People, when they got themselves into such a state, must be humored. "All right, Lieutenant," conceded Abramovici, "I hope we meet this Kavalov. But then, what? What's the good of it? The war is over and soon we'll all go home. And if we don't happen to meet him, what's the difference? Let's go back to our side of the river. We've seen enough here — it's just another town that got a shellacking. . . ."

Across the street, a Russian sat in front of a house. Yates could see only the man's back — but the back was familiar. A strong back. Under the drab cloth of the uniform, the dense seed of scars that had been Kavalov's might be hidden. Yates crossed over the rubble to the house. The hair on the back of the man's head was Kavalov's, blond and thick, and the neck had the same strength.

Yates came up behind the Russian.

"Kavalov!" he said, and laid his hand on the man's stiff shoulder strap.

The Russian swung around.

He saw the American. His face broke into a wide grin that took away from the prominence of his forehead and chin. His deep-set eyes lit up. He gripped Yates's hand and shouted, "*Tovarich* American!"

But he wasn't Kavalov.

"Kavalov!" repeated Yates, feeling let-down and foolish.

The Russian shouted something into the house, and a half-dozen other soldiers trooped out and embraced Yates and Abramovici and drew them into their circle.

"Kavalov!" The first Russian pointed at Yates. "*Tovarich* American!" Then he pointed at himself and shouted, "Pavlov!"

The others shouted their names. They seemed to think that anyone unable to understand them must be hard of hearing.

Yates shook his head. He pointed at himself and said, "No! No! *Njet* Kavalov!"

"*Njet* Kavalov!" shouted the soldier Pavlov. "*Nitchevo!*" Then he cocked his head and, critically, looked Yates up and down. "*Tovarich* American?"

Yates nodded reassuringly. Pavlov embraced Yates and kissed his cheeks. Yates got a whiff of garlic and alcohol and good strong sweat.

The Russian waved grandly. From somewhere a bottle appeared. Pavlov forced it into Yates's hands.

Vodka, Yates thought, and he had a careful swig. But the stuff didn't taste as he imagined it would; it tasted like German kümmel. And it was potent. He had another swig.

Warmth ran down his gullet and into his stomach and spread from there through his limbs. He began to feel better. He passed the bottle to Abramovici. The Russians laughed and approved.

Abramovici shook his head violently. He was surrounded by seven big Russians, but he had not won the war to spoil his health. Pavlov came over to Abramovici. He raised the bottle with a significant nod at Yates, shouted, "Kavalov!" and took Abramovici in his arms as a nurse takes a baby, and shoved the neck of the bottle between Abramovici's teeth and poured.

Abramovici spluttered and kicked, and the Russians roared. Gradually he became quiet, his short body resigning itself to the violation, his face red as a brick, and his eyes bloodshot.

Finally, Pavlov let go of him. He held the bottle against the light, his mouth rueful, and then threw the bottle on the rubble, where it crashed and splintered.

"*Nitchevo!*" said Yates.

"*Nitchevo!*" said Pavlov. He gave a yell, and a German appeared, mincing around with busy little steps. Pavlov pointed at the cellar. The German saw Yates and sidled up to him with a torrent of pleading words. He had nothing. He was poor. They had taken everything he had owned. He wanted protection.

Pavlov said a few words to the men with him. They broke the cellar door with a minimum of effort and emerged, their arms bulging with bottles. It was the same brand — kümmel. Pavlov indicated he wanted glasses and chairs. "*Kulturni!*" he explained loudly. For a while, the German was busy setting out chairs and a table and glasses in front of his house and cellar, a street café in the rubble.

Yates felt no compunctions. He wanted the liquor. Abramovici swayed about, babbling happily that victory, unless celebrated in style, was no victory at all.

Pavlov raised his glass.

"Roosevelt!"

"Stalin!"

"Churchill!"

After each name, the glasses were emptied. Yates opened his collar.

"Kavalov!" he toasted, and he felt a lump in his throat, and swallowed the kümmel hastily. He wiped his eyes.

Pavlov rose and swaggered around the table and embraced Yates again. He smelled more of liquor and less of garlic, and Yates liked the smell. Strong men should have a strong smell. He drank.

Pavlov began a rambling speech to which nobody listened. Some of the names sounded familiar to Yates, they seemed to float slowly through the air and touch his ears almost caressingly. "Stalin!" and "Roosevelt!" and "Kavalov!" He wondered whether this Pavlov knew Kavalov, or who he thought Kavalov was, but it didn't make much difference. Kavalov was a symbol of something.

Pavlov sat down. They drank. The mousy German stood around, his unhappy eyes counting the bottles still left.

There was a pause. Yates felt the Russians look at him expectantly. He knew what he had to do. He got up and they clapped their hands, and Pavlov made the German applaud, prodding him a little.

Yates looked around. Abramovici had his head on the table and was snoring softly. Yates saw the Russians, many Russians; he lost count of them. They all looked the same. Dollar bills. No, not dollar bills, Abramovici was a fool without any imagination and feeling for the great things in life. They looked like Kavalov.

"Kavalov!" he began softly. He felt himself sway and held on to the corners of the table. You can't keel over, now. Be *kulturni*.

"Well, Kavalov — what do you say now? I knew you'd be here. I knew I'd meet you, knew it all along. Had to, you know? What do you say about the three little monkeys Ruth gave me, God bless her? No see, no hear, no talk — I've looked around, and I've listened, and I'm going to speak now. It's been a good war, whatever they say. I know it, I know it — but what's the matter with me? Can you tell me? You sit there, in joy, and get drunk, and I'm drunk, too — but sad. Why? I've lost so many people. People I should have loved — Tolachian — and Thorpe — and Bing. All I've got left is Abramovici, and he snores. But how many have you lost? And you've got those scars on your back, and on your wrists where they hung you up. I've done a fairly good job, too, haven't I? I killed Dehn, in a manner of speaking, and I killed Mulsinger and Heberle — you don't know them, and you haven't missed a thing not knowing them, believe me. And I've been inside Paula Camp, and it's cut into my gizzards; I'm a sensitive man, a schoolteacher, don't laugh at me — I've got my scars, too. Of course, you haven't had Willoughby on your neck, so you were lucky. On the whole, I would say, the score was pretty even. Then why don't I feel what you are feeling? Why don't you answer? Can't you answer? The war is over, and from now on it's going to be smooth. Glory, Glory, Hallelujah! You shake your head: It isn't so! All right, humans are humans, they'll always be weak and stupid and at each other's throats. That isn't it, either? You take that for granted! I don't get you — you contradict yourself. On the one hand, you tell me we're not finished — we're only at the beginning of something; on the other, you lose yourself in liquor and belches of joy! You even sing! You've got your limitations, too! You should be glad you got as far as you did, and can sit down now and take it easy. Always driving yourself, driving yourself forward. . . . But you have the joy. Maybe the joy doesn't come from resting and looking back. Maybe it comes with looking ahead, seeing life as a struggle, burning yourself out in it, giving yourself to it. You're a sonofabitch. You force me into this. I didn't want it. I was content. I thought I'd done enough. But all right. We'll go on from here, you, and I. Only give me your joy. Give it to me. I need it. . . ."

Yates raised his glass and shouted, challengingly, "Kavalov!"

The Russians joined the toast. Pavlov came over and embraced Yates. They lost their footing and rolled on the ground, among fragments of glass, empty bottles, and rubble.

The German picked up the one full bottle remaining on the table and made off with it, looking back furtively and pitying himself.

Book Six

KNOW YOUR PLACE

I

THE *Autobahn* leading through the heart of the industrial Ruhr area branched off, and the secondary road, like a descending arrow, pointed to the city of Kremmen.

Yates felt a kind of elation. But the driver was looking boredly ahead, and Abramovici was dozing in the rear of the jeep. Yates ordered the car stopped and got out.

His elation was a sharpening of what he had felt on accepting his new assignment. "Would you like to go to Kremmen?" DeWitt had asked him. "I want you to start a newspaper there for the Germans. Keep close liaison with Military Government. I'm giving you first crack at Kremmen because you know Willoughby and have run across Farrish. That should make it easier."

Yates had understood. "It should," he had said to the Colonel. "Thank you."

And now, he was moving in. He stood at the edge of the hill; his eyes, blinking and teary from the glare of the sun, followed the branch road to the serrated ruins of the city. Kremmen! the Pittsburgh of the Ruhr, the former domain of the Rintelens and now the domain of Farrish and Willoughby. The name "Kremmen" had brought certain images to Yates's mind: a place enveloped in smoke, by day, and roofed by the bloody glow of the furnaces at night. But the city lying bright in the sunlight before him was like a blind man with empty sockets; it took in the sun but showed no signs of recognizing it; and instead of the thick smell of burning coke, the fine particles of the dust of destruction wafted toward him, drying out his nostrils.

He sighed and out of habit rubbed his fingers and then smiled with the renewed surprise and pleasure at finding them smooth, the warts gone, the skin healed. Shrewd, shrewd body, he thought; and laughed at himself. It was so like him to use the disappearance of his bothersome growths as a yardstick for the victory, the relief over having survived, the release from his fears.

He turned and called to Abramovici: "Hey! Wake up! We're almost there!"

Abramovici started. The sun had baked one side of his face, and he massaged his cheek. Then he looked down into the valley.

"That place? What do we want there? If any people are left, they should have enough sense to pack up and move."

Yates settled himself in his seat. "Let's go!" he ordered, and the car shot forward, downhill, into Kremmen.

Kremmen had never been beautiful, but it had had life. Now, rubble rose behind paneless window frames — bricks, slabs of mortar, rusty bathtubs and stoves, and articles nobody could define. Weeds grew on the rubble. The driver made a wrong turn and got stuck in streets nobody had bothered to clear; the craters were filled with stinking, muddy water. Finally, Yates found the cleared route where the litter had been neatly stacked alongside the burned-out, crashed houses. Like tired flies, people picked their way among the debris. The closer the car came to the working class district, the more thorough appeared the job of the Air Force. Yates drew in his breath sharply. He knew that smell, the smell of the hedgerows of Normandy. Under the rubble were still the dead.

"What a punishment!" commented Abramovici.

Then the street grew wider, the small ruins fell back, and the giant blocks of the Rintelen Works hove into sight. Some of these blocks were completely burned out; only the twisted skeletons of the original buildings, filled with the wreckage of the machinery they once had housed, were left standing. But whole blocks seemed virtually intact. On the central plaza, an ironic bomb blast had deposited the steel statue of Maximilian von Rintelen neatly at the foot of his own monument; he sat there, his powerful, bearded head thoughtfully supported by his hand, staring at what remained of his creation.

Plenty had remained, Yates observed. "Punishment . . ." he said to Abramovici. "Fell a little unevenly, didn't it?" And then added, "I wonder what we're going to do with this. . . ."

"Who's we?"

"Our people!" said Yates. The car bounced and he hung on to the windshield. "Damn it! The population is still here! And at least part of the Works."

Abramovici thought for a while. "The Army," he said finally, "assigns each man the job he's best fitted for. We're strictly concerned with re-education. What happens to other things is Colonel Willoughby's business."

Yates looked at Abramovici. Pink-cheeked, stout, and plodding, the little man was right, as always.

Yates's hand, still at the frame of the windshield, tightened. He thought of the empty feeling that had followed victory, the let-down that had left him sitting at headquarters, listless, for weeks. He thought of the men who hadn't lived to see that day — of Bing, and Thorpe, and Tolachian.

"Re-education!" he asked hoarsely. "Toward what?"

"Oh, you'll think of something," said Abramovici.

The car stopped at the former Kremmen Dragoon Barracks, Farrish's new headquarters. Yates looked at the sentry boxes in their fresh olive drab paint, at the insignia of Farrish's Matador Division emblazoned on a big white signboard above the main gate, at the Presidential citations and the long list of battles and victories underneath the insignia.

"I'd better think of something," he said.

Willoughby was bitter. Governing the district of Kremmen wasn't turning out to be the easy and pleasant job he had expected. He told Farrish: "We're supposed to show them our kind of Government, and in four fifths of the city, we have neither water mains, nor gas, nor electricity, nor sewers going; aside from the fact that the troops have taken over the best of the buildings still standing."

"Let the Krauts move together," the General grunted. "You want me to move out of these barracks?"

Willoughby had no answer. Farrish didn't live in the luxurious villa which his rank might very well have afforded him. He stayed with his headquarters troops in a large complex of three-story brick buildings, symmetrical, each a replica of the other, each in itself like a Prussian soldier on parade — the barracks that once had belonged to the Kremmen Dragoons.

The Kremmen Dragoons had been a *Traditions-Regiment.* They and their tradition had been smashed in the Caucasus, but the memory of their flags, their drum and fife corps, their showy parades, lingered on. Farrish was jealous of that memory; he wanted his Matador Division recast in the image of the Kremmen Dragoons — a spit-and-polish outfit even though the inverted leather of his soldiers' boots was hard to shine.

Originally, Willoughby had approved of this practice. It was a nice touch that, even after victory, Farrish remained a soldiers' General, living with his men, supervising the details of their daily life — down to the windows that had to sparkle, the barracks yard that had to be spotlessly policed, the helmet liners that had to be lacquered. Willoughby knew the value of that kind of publicity, within the Army, and back in the States.

But his military ivory tower made Farrish more difficult to deal with when it came to Willoughby's day-by-day tasks. It strained Willoughby's loyalty to the man. Farrish's ambitions began to run counter to what Willoughby was able to deliver; yet Farrish had absolute power over him. Farrish would chuckle over the pasting Kremmen had received in the final stages of the battle for the Ruhr — "The biggest pasting ever, Clarence!" — and wouldn't see that this very pasting prevented Willoughby, his Chief Military Government Officer, from breaking records in peace as Farrish had broken them in war. If Farrish learned that in some German town, less damaged than Kremmen, the streetcars were running, Farrish wanted his streetcars running, too, even if the total trackage was no more than a couple of miles.

"I want order! I want things to get started!" The words, repeated again and again in the General's strident command voice, rang in Willoughby's ears. And faster, Willoughby added to himself, and on a bigger scale than anywhere else. He knew why — hadn't he helped to put the bug in the General's ear? A war reputation was well and good, but back in the States they forgot easily. Farrish had his new future to think of — politics: Senator, Governor, and more. So Willoughby was constantly under pressure, constantly mending his fences with Farrish, constantly inventing little projects that solved nothing basic but, at least, gave the General some special satisfaction.

And Willoughby had his own future to think of.

Every day brought him face to face with this future. His job forced him into close touch with civilian life — even if it was the civilian life of a foreign, conquered country. In the suppliant businessmen, lawyers, officials, whose political and economic security depended so blatantly on his good graces, Willoughby saw a depressing preview of what he, himself, might be in a year's time, when he came back to the States. He toyed with the idea of staying permanently with the Occupation Army — better to be a big fish in a small pond than a minnow in the ocean. But he was sure that ultimately the small pond would dry up — Germany would not be occupied forever. He read the newspapers from the States, the letters from Coster, the senior partner of Coster, Bruille, Reagan and Willoughby, and realized with panic that he should be back in America, in the race for the big reconversion money, for the positions and jobs and clients that determined a man's postwar career. He was stuck, stuck in Kremmen, stuck with his loyalty to Farrish; when his turn came to go back home, he would have to start in the race with a heartbreaking handicap — unless he managed here, from Kremmen, or through Farrish, to create for himself an advantage that would guarantee him a solid jumping-off point on his return. Longingly, he thought of the Delacroix deal. If he had succeeded in tying up Prince Yasha Bereskin with the Amalgamated Steel interests . . . ! But that had been spoiled by Yates.

Willoughby brought to his job all his resources for petty politics, all his ability to compromise, all his charm. But it didn't seem to be enough. He became harried; he was querulous when his decisions were so much as questioned; he was overworked. Supreme Headquarters deluged him with contradictory directives. They demanded de-Nazification and told him to fire the Nazi Party members in his civilian German administration. They demanded a smooth-functioning Government which depended on the very men he was supposed to throw out. They demanded he get the Rintelen Works going — *Steel!* they needled, *Germany needs steel!* — but didn't tell him who was to own and to run the Works.

Eventually, he cleared his desk of papers, orders, and directives, and said, "I am Kremmen!" and turned around quickly to see whether anyone had heard him, in which case he would have added, "Subject to General Farrish's approval."

And then he chose his fourth and final Mayor.

Take a work horse from the plow and harness it in front of a gig. It will feel puzzled, out of place, it won't enjoy the change, and it won't go any faster.

That's how Troy felt after the novelty of his assignment as Public Safety Officer under Willoughby had worn off. Sometimes he asked himself why Willoughby had picked him, of all people. The answer was easy; he only needed to look at Loomis, whom Willoughby had requested from DeWitt and placed in charge of Economics — *Wirtschaft,* the Germans called it. In the town of the giant steel mills, Loomis knew as much of *Wirtschaft* as Troy knew of the police which he headed. And the other failures whom Willoughby had chosen to head the rest of Military Government's departments were no better.

What the hell — I'm a failure, too, Troy concluded; and I should be grateful that Willoughby took me out of the ranks of the unemployed and gave me something to do. He had been grateful. He had thrown himself into his work, had cleaned out the police force, kicked out the President of Police who was a leftover from the Nazi regime, and replaced him by an Inspector pensioned off in 1930 and consequently untainted by Nazism. He had had the uniforms of his new police force dyed blue, and issued shining badges, produced by Loomis according to New York design. The crowning achievement, as far as Willoughby was concerned, was the inspection of the police by Farrish.

If Troy had let it go at that, and pulled along his little gig quietly, and, like Loomis, said Yes to Willoughby at the frequent conferences, he could have lived comfortably and happily. But it wasn't Troy's kind of happiness. Troy was conscientious.

Kremmen, with its half-destroyed houses, its blasted doors and windows, was a thieves' paradise. War and the habits of Nazism had undermined conventional morals; the destruction, starvation, unemployment following in its wake taught and forced the average citizen to take where he could. And then there were the Displaced Persons, and the men and women who had returned from the concentration camps with their grudge against those who had made hay under the Nazis. Curfew meant nothing. How can you find a man slipping through ruins? At night, murder was added to theft.

This much Troy saw: it wasn't a matter to be solved by any police, American or German.

He came to Willoughby. "All right," said Willoughby, "I'll get the General to give you a Battalion. Raid the bastards. Clean them out!"

Troy's big hands were spread helplessly. "Don't you see, Colonel? We've got to give them work! We've got to put them up somewhere, organize community houses, organize food." To him it seemed so simple, logical. Why wasn't it done?

Willoughby grew cool. He pulled forward the fat under his jowls, and his small, worried eyes closed. "You stick to your job, Troy," he said.

Troy knew what was going through Willoughby's mind: Troublemaker! Lost his own command, now he wants to screw up mine.

He retreated. That night he wrote to Karen. He wanted to write her from his full heart; ten times he started and tore up the sheets, each attempt sounding stupid, complaining, petulant. The letter he sent off was a humorous account of uniforms, badges, and small inconsequential incidents. It closed, *Why don't you come here? It'll be fun. Perhaps there's a story in it for you.*

That had been two weeks ago. There had been no answer.

Troy was trudging to another of Willoughby's conferences. It was senseless, tiresome. Willoughby didn't want suggestions, much less opinions. He wanted to hear himself talk, hear the Yesses of his aides, men Troy would never have tolerated in his own company. Willoughby seemed to need perpetual confirmation. Troy didn't understand the man, and it worried him. It worried him as much as did the people from the concentration camps who, still in their tattered uniforms, furtively roamed the streets. Troy had a kind of kinship to them and felt some responsibility for them. He remembered the days of Paula Camp. And there was nobody to whom he could talk about these things.

In the austere conference room — trust Willoughby to rig up something important for himself! — Troy took the seat next to Loomis. Loomis's thinning dark hair was receding noticeably, but the expanding forehead added nothing to his expression. Loomis began to make conversation about everything being just fine. Troy didn't commit himself and was relieved from further embarrassment by Willoughby's opening remarks.

Sarcastically, Willoughby said, "We can't have local Government by SHAEF directive, we've got to have a Mayor. We've had three in as many weeks — a professor, a doctor, and a former newspaperman."

518

Troy knew that, and wondered why Farrish hadn't raised a stink over so many switches in personnel; apparently, the General couldn't distinguish one Kraut from another.

Willoughby continued darkly, "Seems we had tough luck. Each time we install one in office, some bright character from Counter-Intelligence comes around and tells us the guy's been a Nazi. Well, this Mayor is going to stick! Even if he's Hitler in disguise — I can handle him!"

Loomis leaned over to Troy and whispered he knew who the new Mayor was, and that he'd suggested him to Willoughby in the first place. Troy nodded; to him, it was not much of a recommendation.

Willoughby announced, "Fellow I've chosen is Herr Lämmlein, a *Generaldirektor* or Vice President of the Rintelen Works. A businessman — and I know he was never a member of the Nazi Party. Kremmen is a company town, the Rintelen Works ran everything, they were the bread and the butter of the people — "

He stopped and smiled wryly.

"Well, if not the butter, at least the bread. The prominent position that my man holds with Rintelen will give the people confidence in their Government. And he speaks English. Personally, I like businessmen. They're sober and enterprising and know how to organize. Of course, we'll see how he works out before we make it a definite appointment."

Troy had no opinions on businessmen. He believed that Willoughby had chosen carefully before making the announcement. And he suspected that, since Willoughby was transforming his Military Government into a group of diligent Yes-men, he also was building a similar German machine.

"Everybody agreed?" asked Willoughby. "Captain Troy?"

Troy felt Willoughby's heavy glance from under the drooping lids.

"Yes, sir!" he said. "Of course!"

Yates made his way past lines of Germans patiently waiting in the bomb-shaken corridors of the Kremmen *Polizei-Präsidium.* Some of the Germans greeted him effusively, *"Guten Tag, Herr Leutnant!"* Others seemed on the verge of accosting him; but he brushed by. He had made his first call on Willoughby and had learned that Troy was in Kremmen, and he was following the immediate impulse to see the Captain. The babble in the corridor pursued him into Troy's office until he closed the door behind him.

Troy already had a visitor. He and Karen were standing at the window, close to one another, looking out at the landscape of shaggy ruins. They turned quickly, and Troy came forward, his hulking figure dark against the stream of light.

"Yates!" he said. "Boy, it's good to see you! . . . First Karen, then you. And all in the same day!"

"Hello, Karen!" Yates greeted.

Karen came over and shook his hand. For the first time it struck Yates that she didn't belong in any uniform.

"She came in only a few minutes before you," Troy said. "I've been so God-damned lonely. Have you heard? I'm a policeman, now —" He opened the top drawer of his desk and pulled out a handful of his glittering police badges. "Don't they look like New York? Except this is the coat of arms of Kremmen. . . ." He stopped. "I hope you two plan to stay here a while?"

Karen was studying one of the badges, her finger tracing the design. "They are really nice," she said admiringly.

"Tell you what I'll do," said Troy. "I know a jeweler here. I'll order him to make a small one in gold for you — you can wear it as a good-luck piece. You'll accept it, won't you?"

She nodded, "I'd love it."

They're kind of nice, together, Yates thought, and said, "I just dropped in to say Hello. We'll all be seeing one another. I have to make a newspaper for the Krauts of Kremmen."

"Stay for a minute!" Troy urged. He wanted to be alone with Karen but was afraid of it, at the same time.

"I must get to the printing plant," Yates went on evenly. "Abramovici's there all by himself."

"Abramovici?" asked Karen.

"Yes — the little guy whose pants keep slipping. He's my assistant, now. Don't you remember him?"

"Where is Bing?" she said.

"Bing —" said Yates. And he thought: Oh my God, why did this have to come up? "Why don't we sit down!" he suggested.

Troy brought Karen a chair. Yates took her hand; it was cold.

"Bing is dead," he said simply.

She felt numb and dull. A light had gone out that wasn't her light but that had warmed part of her way.

"How did he die?" she said, mechanically fingering Troy's police badge.

Yates told the story, omitting the cruel details. But she had been too close to the war for too long a time not to be able to fill in the touches that gave the picture its tragic depth. And the boy came back to her as he had been; his quick, live eyes; even snatches of what he had said. . . . *That life goes on! That there will be springs, many springs, after we are gone, that girls in light clothes are going to meet young men and that they will hold hands, long after our hands have rotted away — I'm so insatiable, I don't want it to end; what have I had?* That was after he'd seen the white-haired Tolachian killed. Bing had wanted to live.

520

If only I'd known, she thought. He wanted me so much. No, not even if I had known. . . . But how can you tell?

Yates felt for what had been between the woman and the boy, and what was dead, now. "He was with Laborde," he said. "Laborde was like a time bomb; you could hear the ticking, but you didn't know when it would go off. I talked to Bing, tried to ease him away from Laborde. I didn't get anywhere. Bing was apathetic, almost resigned. He had come to the point where hanging on to life didn't matter."

Karen said nothing. The dead man was very real, very alive in her mind; no one could change that. And she didn't want it changed. Yates was trying to reconcile the irrevocable and the incredible for her. It was well meant, but she didn't want it.

"I liked him," said Troy. "I would have taken him into my company any day." Yet, he thought, he'd been jealous of him. He wondered if in some strange, remote way he might have harmed him. "I gave him a pair of my pants once. But he returned them."

She looked at the two men. They were both trying to help her. As if they could. . . . After a while, she said, "I'm glad he got back to Neustadt. He at least had that."

Yates, who had a clearer idea of how Bing had felt after coming home to Neustadt, did not correct her.

2

THE WIDOW Rintelen was a big woman. Everything about her was big — her protuberant eyes, her cheeks, her chin, her flesh that was bloated and swollen. Only her hands and feet were small and ludicrous, and her voice which was also soft and mostly frightened, the result of the years during which Maximilian von Rintelen had held undisputed sway over her life and the lives of most of the people of Kremmen.

In a sense, Maximilian von Rintelen — the ennobling prefix *von* had been given him by the late, unfortunate Kaiser — still ruled his home, through his spirit, which the Widow could feel, sometimes almost physically, or through his portrait that filled the wall panel at the top of the broad, carpeted stairway of the main hall of the manor house. The portrait, done in the manner of Rembrandt, showed him against a dark background, his magnificent white beard sweeping over his wide chest, his close-set, greedy eyes peering into every corner of the house, his sensual lips half-hidden by his mustache. An aura of light from the top corner of the canvas shot across his bald pate and concentrated on his hands. They were long, gnarled, grasping, punishing hands, and the Widow had only to glance at the portrait to recall their touch and the power they had generated.

He was old, seventy or seventy-five — he had been middle-aged when he married her, the young, slender girl — and yet he appeared timeless and it seemed most unnatural that he should ever die; and he had not died the natural way — he had died in harness, one night, when bombs dropped by American planes on the Rintelen Steel Mills caught him in the rubble of his empire.

Where was the man to take his place? There was none. The time for great men had passed.

Dehn, the son-in-law, who had married Pamela — whether for love or money was never quite clear to the Widow because Dehn was so terribly correct and noncommittal, and Pamela never spoke about it — was away in the war. So Lämmlein had taken over: Lämmlein, the shrewd, gray Vice President of the Works, gray eyes, gray skin, gray hair, gray suits. He was good in his way; cultured, a compromiser. But he was not a great man, and the Widow sensed that the empire Maximilian von Rintelen had left her would crumble under her hands.

It was still a big house, palatial, and the Widow worked over it, dragging her bulk from one large room to the other, trying to maintain discipline in the tiled kitchen, over the cook and the maids and the butler and the gardener. But they were foreigners, and they were unmanageable now that Germany was trampled to the ground by the invaders.

With a sigh, the Widow let herself glide into the chair behind the big, modern, glass-topped desk. They were an eyesore, this desk and its chair; they did not fit in with the House or the hall — but they were Maximilian's desk and chair, salvaged from his office after the bombing.

Pamela came down the stairs, the rug swallowing her steps. The Widow felt her daughter's presence and jumped up with surprising quickness, as if she had been caught at some felony.

"Sit there!" said Pamela, her low voice contemptuous. "There's nothing to his chair. It's just a chair."

"I'm nervous. You came upon me so suddenly."

"The chair! The desk! I wish it had all gone to pieces. This whole house! It depresses me. I want it redecorated. I suppose now that the stupid fighting is over we can get it done." Pamela perched on the desk. Her hands left spots on the glass top and the Widow wiped them off.

"It's still *his* house! As long as I live, it's his house!" said the Widow in her high-pitched, fatty tone.

"You know perfectly well that Maxie built this house to keep you busy while he went after his own pleasures."

"Pamela! I don't want you to call your father Maxie!"

Pamela faced the portrait. "Maxie . . . !" she laughed, a gurgling, insinuating laugh, as if the old man were about to step out of his frame and chuck her under the chin.

"Your father was a great man, a wonderful man, an empire builder!"

"I never liked him. What's left of him? What's left of the empire?"

The Widow tore open the middle drawer of the desk, pushing it hard against the blubber of her stomach. "How petty you are! How little you know!" She pulled out a map and threw it on the top of the desk. "See for yourself! Parts of the Kremmen plant are destroyed — but only parts. The foundry could be back in operation within a few weeks! Lämmlein says so himself. And what about the other plants? Mülheim? Gelsenkirchen? Hardly touched! And the mines? You cannot destroy mines."

"So the Americans will take them. Let them. You'll never get away from Maxie's hands. Why don't you bury him and what he left?"

"You never loved *your* husband, Pamela."

"Look at me!" Pamela got off the desk, her hands stroking her hips. "And look at yourself!"

"I am looking at you! Put on some shoes. Close your gown."

"I've got nothing to be ashamed of, thank God!"

The butler came in. He was a square-faced Hollander and he looked as though he might burst out of his predecessor's cutaway.

"Gentleman to see Frau Pamela."

Pamela smiled at him and said, "I guess I'll have to dress. . . ."

The Widow said to the butler, "Cornelius! You still haven't swept up!"

The butler turned as if he hadn't heard her. The Widow buried her head in her hands.

Pettinger entered softly. He wore an ill-fitting, unpressed business suit, and the cuffs of his shirt were frayed and dirt-rimmed. The bones in his sharp face seemed more pronounced, the skin over them tighter; or, perhaps, the shadows were deepened because he needed a shave. Yet, he managed to maintain an appearance. His shoulders were straight as always, and his very carriage emphasized the discrepancy between himself and what he wore.

He looked around. He liked the place, it had quality. It was run down — but what wasn't, these days? He looked at the fat old woman, bowed but regal. With a little propping up, what a front!

He coughed.

The Widow started.

"Frau von Rintelen?"

She wanted to ask who he was, but he didn't give her the chance.

"I won't tell you my name, madame. The less you know, the better for you. Where is your daughter, Pamela?"

"What do you want?" She was frightened.

"I'm a friend of Major Dehn, your son-in-law."

From the stairs, Pamela asked, "What about him?" She came down slowly, imperceptibly pausing on each step. Pettinger lowered his lids, as if she were too much for him to see — and in a sense, she was. A man on the run gets thirsty, very thirsty.

Pamela noticed the reaction. "Where is Major Dehn?"

Pettinger placed his hat and overcoat on a chair. "I don't know," he said. "When I saw him last, at the Rolands-Eck on the shore of the Rhine, he said to me: My friend, if ever you need anything, you must go to the Rintelen house, to Pamela. . . ."

Pamela screwed up her mouth. "And why didn't you stay with my husband?"

Pettinger turned to face both women. "Major Dehn was perhaps my best friend. A little high-strung, but a fine man to work with, and a pleasure to command. I assure you it was a very difficult decision. But some must live on, and others must sacrifice themselves."

Pettinger intended to slide in here on the wings of tragedy. He couldn't tell them how unceremonious the parting had been, and that he still didn't know what had become of Dehn.

"And who decides," asked Pamela, with a vicious lilt, "who is to live and who is to be sacrificed?"

"I do!" said Pettinger.

That crushed the Widow's incipient revolt against the intruder. Whoever he was, he had spoken with the Master's Voice which, like Maximilian von Rintelen's, tolerated no opposition.

He continued, "It is essential that I stay here."

The Widow shook off her trance. "With what right — "

"Madame!" Pettinger interrupted her gently. "I am a German officer. I have important work to do. Your estate, this house, are ideal for me."

"I'm sorry!" the Widow said as authoritatively as her birdlike voice permitted.

Pamela's eyes showed more than a casual interest. "How long are you planning to stay, Herr . . . ?"

"Call me Erich."

". . . Herr Erich?"

"I don't know. I realize what it means to you; so I'll stay no longer — than — " His eyes opened wide and fastened on Pamela's supple throat. "Than absolutely necessary."

The Widow pleaded, "A man like you will be tracked down. And then? Pamela and myself would be arrested; the house would be taken from us, the house and the steel mills and the mines, the heritage my husband left us. . . ."

"If you refuse," he said slowly, "you might as well hand me over to the Americans, madame."

"But the house . . . !" clamored the Widow, cornered.

He smiled. "There isn't a house in all Germany as safe as yours."

The Widow, who was constantly seeing the house crash about her ears, turned her bulk to Pettinger and looked him over, doubtfully.

"A poor man's house," he explained with good humor, "or an ordinary, respectable house — they're no good. They will be searched or looted or taken; their owners will be dispossessed at the whim of any American. Not so with yours. The Americans respect the big things. The name of Rintelen is a big name. It is known in America. The big people over there knew him. The financial pages of their newspapers gave columns to him and his empire — such a man, his widow, his house, will not be touched."

It was something she hadn't thought of. It did her good. She said, "Maximilian von Rintelen would have liked you as a guest, I'm sure. But he was a man who could face anyone. I hope this house is safe. It won't be, if they should find you here."

She was right. But Pettinger had been running since the day he disposed of the Field Marshal, slipping through the net dozens of times, ducking, hiding, one night here, the next night there. He wanted to sleep, bathe, get into decent clothes, find a base for his operations, begin to weave the threads to others like himself.

"Madame," he said, "they can't find me here, unless they happen to look here. But if I should be caught elsewhere — anywhere — you will surely lose the empire that Maximilian von Rintelen built, including your house. It will be taken from you, sooner or later, unless our military defeat is turned into a political victory. There are men to do that. They're now in a desperate spot, these men. If you want to drive me away . . . !" He shrugged.

The Widow shook her heavy head; her every bulge showed her worry. She saw the jeopardy to herself, the house, and the heritage, in whatever she decided to do.

"Take him upstairs, Pamela," she said at last. "Show him a room. . . ." Her voice was that of a little girl who has been pummeled by the boys.

"He can have some of Dehn's clothes," said Pamela.

"Don't!" cried the Widow. She was clinging to everything her own husband, the empire builder, had ever owned. "You don't even know if he is — "

"Dead?" asked Pamela. And repeated, casually, "Is he dead, Herr Erich?"

"There's always hope!" Pettinger said cheerfully. Then he looked at Pamela and saw that she wasn't so eager for this particular hope. His feet felt the softness of the rug on the stairs. After the stones on the roads he had tramped, the rug alone made staying on worth while.

"You wouldn't have a glass of *schnapps?*"

"I shall serve you the drink myself," she promised as she led him into one of the guest rooms upstairs.

Hans Heinrich Lämmlein, Mayor-to-be of Kremmen, drove up to the Rintelen estate in excellent spirits. He liked his sleek, dark limousine which Loomis permitted him to run with American-controlled gasoline. He liked the feeling of purpose and security which had returned to him much sooner than he had dared to hope. He had known this feeling would return the moment he had figured out Captain Loomis and prevailed on him to introduce him to Lieutenant Colonel Willoughby. And Willoughby was his kind of man, despite their difference in appearance and character, despite the gulf between the conqueror and the conquered. What they had in common transcended boundaries, language, tradition, uniforms, and sentries with fixed bayonet.

He greeted the Widow with the respect due the controlling interest in the Rintelen Works, but with that touch of familiarity permissible to the faithful administrator who knew the secrets of the books and the problems of the time. Pulling up his pearl-gray, impeccable tie so that it fit snugly to his stiff, high collar, he announced, "The Americans are easier to get along with than I expected. It makes a difference whether a person is bred in our Western civilization, or not. I've had a spirited exchange of ideas with Lieutenant Colonel Willoughby, the Chief Military Government Officer; and the result is most favorable, most favorable. Madame, I want you to be the first, as it should be, to hear the good news."

"*Ach!*" said the Widow. "What good news can there be these days? Cornelius! . . . I wish these foreigners would learn to obey. I want him to bring us some sherry. But they are getting more difficult instead of better. We've lost the war. One feels it in everything. . . ."

"I'll get you the best servants, Frau von Rintelen. I am going to be the American-appointed, American-backed Mayor of Kremmen!"

The Widow sat bolt upright.

Lämmlein allowed himself a smile. "Think what this means, Madame!"

The Widow could imagine very well what it meant. She saw the bombed-out parts of her husband's creation rise from the ashes, rebuilt by the labor that Lämmlein now could command. She saw the furnaces going, fired by coke that Lämmlein now could requisition. She saw the sherry brought in by obedient butlers whom Lämmlein now could press into service. She could see it all, even to the satisfied, though still grudging face in the portrait; but she hesitated to give her expectation free play. The shock of the last months, of defeat, breakdown and bombings, the frightening presence of the stranger in the house, was not dispelled that swiftly. It seemed so absurd that the power torn from the Rintelens' hands, in battles whose course she had followed in fear, would be turned back to them so lightly, so unceremoniously.

Lämmlein, his gray face expressionless, observed the Widow's swaying emotions which showed plainly on her fat-embedded features. "Naturally, we can't expect something for nothing," he said.

He waited to let the importance of this bit sink in. Her face fell, her mouth snapped tight, her eyes became hostile and said plainly that she wasn't going to give up anything for the aggrandizement and gain of Lämmlein.

"Don't forget," he warned, "without the Americans' support, you own nothing but a questionable title to some half-destroyed properties. The Colonel has consented to come here this afternoon for a private little conference — just the three of us and Frau Pamela."

He studied the Widow. She looked more than ever like a tub, and her black dress, closed tightly around her triple chin, made her grotesque.

"You may want to change your gown, madame," he suggested. "I've taken the liberty of bringing your jewelry from the safe in the air-raid shelter. We want to make an impression."

The safe, a secret known only to the Widow, the dead Maximilian, and Lämmlein, stood deep in the reinforced shelter underneath the destroyed office building of the Rintelen Works in which her husband had found his death. If only he had gone there in time! The shelter had stood up under the tumbling of everything on top of it.

She sighed. She took the shiny metal box from Lämmlein, and, holding it carefully in her small, fat hands, waddled to her husband's desk and put it down gently. She opened the box. The jewels Maximilian had given her glittered against their pale blue velvet cushion. A fortune!

"I think you should wear them," said Lämmlein.

Then he noticed Pamela and the man coming down the stairway. Lämmlein placed himself in front of the jewels.

With a few steps, Pamela was at her mother's side. "Do you want to sell them?" she asked.

The stranger followed her and glanced past Lämmlein at the treasure. He said nothing; but Lämmlein saw him wet his lips.

The Widow snapped closed the lid of the box.

"Herr Erich," said Pamela, "meet Herr Lämmlein."

The two men sniffed at one another. The stranger's face was familiar to Lämmlein, though he couldn't place it.

"Lämmlein," Pettinger repeated thoughtfully, "Lämmlein. . . . You never joined the Party, did you?"

"No, I didn't." Lämmlein's gray face became a tinge grayer. "Herr von Rintelen didn't wish — "

"I remember!" said Pettinger. "There was quite a correspondence on the matter, until the old man up there" — he pointed vaguely at the portrait — "took a hand."

He saw the glint of recognition come into Lämmlein's eyes.

"This is insane!" Lämmlein broke out. "What are you doing here?"

"Frau Pamela and I have agreed that, for the time being, I shall take the place of Major Dehn, who's unaccounted for. I'm wearing his suit, you see! Same size, same everything." He patted Pamela's hand.

Lämmlein flushed with worry and outrage. "There are people in this city who remember Major Dehn!" he spluttered.

"I won't leave the grounds," Pettinger assured him. "You can see I'm not quite myself; I need rest. I will count on you to be one of my — let us say: go-betweens?"

"I will do nothing of the sort!"

Pettinger was part of the Germany that had been a source of pride and profits to Lämmlein. Lämmlein would keep his mouth shut. But that Germany was gone; and he was not going to get himself involved in any underground affairs. He had a wife, four strapping children, and the Rintelen Works.

Lämmlein found his bearings. "You will leave immediately! I'm going to be the Mayor of Kremmen! Germany's future lies in co-operating with the Americans!"

"Who tells you that I want to do anything but co-operate with the Americans?" Pettinger said angrily. "I want to talk to you — alone!"

"Not now — we haven't time. . . ." Lämmlein blinked nervously. "*Herr Oberstleutnant* Willoughby — the Military Governor — he's coming here. Due any moment — "

"That's wonderful!" said Pettinger. "That's why I must talk to you, now!" Holding Lämmlein's arm tightly, he prodded the Mayor-to-be into the library.

Once inside the room, and the door closed, Pettinger relaxed his grip. "Sit down!" he ordered.

But Lämmlein didn't sit down. "The war's been lost, *Herr Obersturmbannführer!*" he pleaded. "All you can do here is spoil what I am trying to build!"

Pettinger pushed him into a chair. "If you want to be the Americans' Mayor — go ahead! Fits in perfectly with what I have in mind. . . ."

In short words, he outlined Field Marshal von Klemm–Borowski's strategy for a German come-back, without so much as a mention of the dead logistics expert's name. He watched Lämmlein's face and noted the changes that came over it, as anxiety gave way to consideration, and finally unqualified acceptance of the idea.

"Play along with them!" Pettinger concluded. "Preserve for us what can be maintained. Because, beaten and defeated, we still hold the balance of power. But we must know where we're going! We must have a perspective! We must have a leadership, an organization that works through all channels — through what Government the occupants permit us, through business, schools, the Church, through demobilized officers and returned prisoners of war. Slowly, playing one occupant against the other, making it difficult for them, rebuilding only what we need, patiently — until *Der Tag* when we'll spring forward, full-grown, and dictate our terms!"

"Whose terms?"

Pettinger left the question open. "Yours — mine. . . ."

They returned to the ladies. Pettinger gulped down a glass of the sherry which Cornelius, the butler, had finally brought, and said to Lämmlein, "Perhaps your friend Willoughby can get us some Scotch whisky?"

"And cigarettes!" Pamela added.

When Willoughby arrived at the manor house, the stage was set for him. In the center of the main hall, on a high-backed thronelike chair, sat the Widow, resplendent in her jewels. Her long gown covered her bulk to the ankles so that only her small feet in their elegant pumps were visible. To her right, half-buried between blankets and pillows, reclined Pettinger in the largest, most comfortable chair in the hall.

"If I'm to be Major Dehn," Pettinger had said as they worked out the details for Willoughby's visit, "I'm going to be right with you. I'm not going to *cacher* myself away and run the risk of being suddenly found or reported by the servants. The best way of being unobtrusive is to be right where everybody can see me."

Lämmlein had fingered his wilting collar. "Men of your age are in the Army," he had said. "Willoughby's bound to ask why you're not in an American prisoner camp, and who released you, and from where, and when, and *Show me your papers*."

"Look at me!" Pettinger had answered. "I'm ill. I'm an invalid. The Russian winters have been too much for me."

Lämmlein had chuckled, and Pamela had propped Pettinger's sinewy body with pillows and tucked him in the chair, making sure that in the process as much of her as possible brushed against him as often as possible.

Willoughby was sitting *vis à vis* the Widow. He saw a certain pathos in the devoted little family — an impressive though worn setting, the draft coming through the shattered window softly moving the hair on the invalid's head. The Old World splendor gave him a feeling of inferiority mixed with condescension. Once he got through here, maybe he'd be able to buy the whole manor house, ship it across, and set it up in the suburbs. That the style was imitation Wilhelm the Second, he didn't know; it was rich.

Willoughby took his time to warm up; with palpable disinterest he inquired after the huge woman's health, and where had Major Dehn served? And where had he been stricken with illness?

Pettinger named a Russian village in the vicinity of Stalingrad that he knew so well.

Willoughby frowned. "Very unwise of you to lose yourself in the unlimited space of Russia. Biting off more than you could chew, underestimating the enemy. But these were always German traits."

Pettinger agreed. But he added, following Klemm-Borowski's testament, "You see it too mechanically, Colonel. One night, we beat back a Russian attack. It was thirty or forty below zero. They remained mowed down in front of our positions. We figured what wasn't killed would freeze to death in half an hour. Four hours later, just before dawn, these same men rose from the frozen ground and attacked. And beat us. I don't know what makes them fight that way. But I know we were your protection against the East!"

His emaciated face showed spots of color. After so many years, Pettinger was still baffled, and furious.

"Now you Americans have beaten us!" he went on and coughed pathetically. "Now you will have to look out for yourselves."

Willoughby stroked his plump thighs. "We out-produce everybody. We'll take on all comers." He laughed.

Lämmlein, who didn't like the political slant of the conversation, whispered something to the Widow. The Widow slowly reached for a bell and rang. A maid entered, carrying tea things.

"How long since you're out of the German Army, Major Dehn?" asked Willoughby.

"A year and a half," said Pettinger. "I wish we had quit then. . . ."

"Not really!" said Willoughby. "The Rintelens must have made a neat pile — the bigger the longer the war lasted."

Lämmlein came to the rescue. "Taxes!" he said. "Nazi regimentation! And look at the destruction. What do we have now?"

The tea was poured into Meissen cups.

Willoughby was still interested in Pettinger. "Before the war, what was your position in the Rintelen Works?"

Again, Lämmlein wanted to jump into the breach. But Pettinger anticipated him.

"Oh, well — formally, I believe I was on the board of directors. I was interested in the fine arts, paintings, sculpture. I traveled — Italy, England, France. You see, Colonel" — his voice became soft — "Pamela's and mine was a marriage of love." He took her hand and fondled it. "Herr von Rintelen, God bless him, always tried to make a businessman of me." He shook his head, smiled, "I used to feel: What good is all that money if you use it just to make more?"

From under his lids, he observed Willoughby. The American seemed satisfied that the male heir was no threat to whatever he intended.

Willoughby reached for his cup. He sipped the *Ersatz* tea and made a wry face. Lämmlein had insisted the vile stuff be served. He was out to achieve precisely the effect the scene was creating. He wanted to demonstrate potential and past performance, and present plight.

The tea made Willoughby speak out bluntly.

"You've lost the war. You know what your people have done in conquered countries; Major Dehn will bear me out. You know we could do the same here."

Neither Pettinger nor Lämmlein commented; Pamela was handing the invalid his cup. Willoughby's gaze stopped at the Widow; it was she, after all, who headed the family corporation.

The Widow chirped, "We are at your mercy." Her English was slow and halting, and her effort gave the impression that she wanted to please the visitor.

"I'm going to make your man, Lämmlein, Mayor of this town. That ought to show you that we don't take advantage of our position."

"More tea?" said the Widow.

"No, thanks."

"A cookie?"

Willoughby tried one. It tasted like straw.

"What's in that?"

The Widow said, "We have little to eat." And as she felt Willoughby's eyes appraise her heft, she blushed, "I'm a sick woman!"

"Sorry," said Willoughby.

"*Ach,*" said the Widow, "you have pinned us to the ground. How will we ever raise ourselves?"

"Well, now —" Willoughby imagined himself pinning the gross figure to the rug of the manor house. Then he looked at the statuesque, too fleshy Pamela, and at the son-in-law who was a playboy. It would be a pushover.

Pettinger nodded lazily. He feigned fatigue. And he thought how dead right he had been in taking refuge in this house. This American businessman in uniform was the best possible guarantee for his safety, the most luxurious cloak for his operations.

Willoughby stretched himself. "Mr. Lämmlein, have you explained to the family the difficulty of the Rintelens' position?"

"I think Frau von Rintelen knows — in general terms. . . ."

"Well, let me make it specific," said Willoughby, stroking forward the flesh under his jowls. "It was a total war. There are people on our side who consider the role that the Rintelens played in the same light as — well — as the activities of Himmler, or Streicher. . . ."

The bracelets on the Widow's colossal arms began to tinkle. "But this is impossible!" she twittered. "We never mixed in politics. What was my husband to do? Refuse the Government's orders? Have his properties confiscated by Goering? Have himself locked up in a concentration camp?"

Pettinger said, "Papa was always so correct!"

"I understand," said Willoughby. "Herr von Rintelen tried to hold on to what he owned — that's why you're now in danger of losing it. How many of our men, would you guess, were killed by Rintelen products?"

"You don't condemn a German soldier for having shot at you!" Lämmlein said. "He was ordered to do it!"

"But we keep him behind barbed wire," Willoughby countered dryly.

Pettinger was quite calm; he saw no threat whatever to his asylum. If there were Americans with that kind of grudge against German industry, they weren't in power — otherwise, the Rintelen Works would have been taken over by them the day their troops took Kremmen.

"If you have come to take me away," the Widow said heroically, "I am ready."

Willoughby listened to her warbling. He had the feeling that it wasn't she talking at all, that a music box was hidden somewhere in that stomach.

"I said I understood your position. I said I'm not prejudiced. I'm going to make Lämmlein the Mayor of Kremmen, provided we can come to an understanding. If we can't, you may lose everything, even this house."

Lämmlein said, "We have been beaten. We will do anything — within reason."

"That's the spirit!" said Willoughby. "Madame?"

"Anything within reason."

Willoughby was satisfied. "The Rintelen Works are owned entirely by the family?"

"Yes," said the Widow, proudly.

"That's bad," said Willoughby.

Both Pettinger and Lämmlein were tense. The men knew that Willoughby was finally coming to the point. Pamela hated him. Her hand gripped Pettinger's, and he answered her pressure.

"Don't you see," said Willoughby, "any German plant, today, is a highly uncertain property. We may consider it as war potential and destroy it — we may use it for reparations. . . . What you need is somebody outside Germany who has some interest!"

"Delacroix!" cried Lämmlein.

Willoughby controlled a slight jump. He had been trying to think of an angle for bringing in Amalgamated decently; but this was much better. He was cool when he asked, "What about Delacroix?"

Lämmlein's eagerness had changed back to dejection. "Old history, unfortunately, as business deals go. As soon as our armies took Paris, Herr von Rintelen went there and saw Prince Yasha Bereskin — you know who he is?"

"I've heard of him," smiled Willoughby.

Pettinger fidgeted under his blankets. Paris, the days of victory and retreat, Yasha and Sourire . . . He suddenly sympathized with the Widow's *Ach, you have pinned us to the ground.*

"And the Prince accepted what Herr von Rintelen offered him," said Lämmlein.

"Blackmail!" said Willoughby.

Lämmlein turned and regarded the dead man's portrait. "Persuasion — shall we call it persuasion?"

"Blackmail!" insisted Willoughby.

"Herr von Rintelen bought back the 20 per cent of his stock which were owned by Delacroix."

"The sale is legally not valid. Won't stand up before any court. I'm saying that as an American and as a lawyer."

"We have the papers!" said Lämmlein.

"Papers!" scorned Willoughby. "Signed with a bayonet at your ribs!"

"Herr von Rintelen used no such crude methods."

"Mr. Lämmlein! It is for everybody's benefit to say that he did."

Pettinger's chest was giving trouble again. "Why not?" he said between coughs. "Let's say he did."

Willoughby sighed. "You Germans lack insight. I always thought so. You have to be pushed to see matters realistically."

Lämmlein nodded. The Widow was getting away cheaply, at that. If the 20 per cent of Rintelen shares were returned to Delacroix, the Widow would keep the remaining 80 at the price of 20. Quite a bargain, considering that the 20 per cent really had cost old Maximilian nothing since he had paid the Prince in Nazi-manipulated francs, just fancy paper.

"Tea?" said the Widow.

"Thanks," said Willoughby. He was having a vision. He saw himself presenting Delacroix's defunct interest in the Rintelen Works to Prince Yasha. In return, Yasha was tying up with Amalgamated Steel. Amalgamated, Delacroix, Rintelen — one combine, with a world to be rebuilt, rebuilt in steel! And it was he, Willoughby, who handed the whole kit and caboodle to CBR & W. After that, perhaps, it would be W & CBR, and the least he would get, on the side, was a seat on the Board of Directors of Amalgamated; neither Old Man Coster nor the steel people were pikers, you had to say that for them.

He rose. "It was a pleasant afternoon, *Herr Bürgermeister.*"

"Thank you, sir," beamed Lämmlein and grasped Willoughby's hand.

Pettinger seemed to have dozed off. The visit had been a tax on his limited strength.

3

KELLERMANN's first instinct was to run.

Herr Bendel, Director of the Welfare Office in Kremmen's city hall, had not exaggerated when he called the place the "Lower Depths." It had once served as barracks for foreign workers shanghaied to slave in the Rintelen Works. The foreigners had been evacuated by the Americans and were housed in something slightly better, the new DP Camps. The barbed-wire fence around the Lower Depths was still there; and the building itself, its top floor laid bare by incendiary bombs, was even more crowded now that it had become the Home for the Political Victims of National Socialism than it had been when the slave workers were quartered in it.

With the bitter weariness of waiting for he knew not what, Kellermann walked aimlessly through the dark, dank rooms; not even the dry, dusty summer heat that came through the paneless windows could drive out the accumulated mold and the stench of thousands of tired, unwashed bodies. The place was like another jail, another camp, except that the guards were missing.

Then why didn't he run? Why didn't they all run? Nobody held them in the Lower Depths! But the liberated inmates of the concentration camps, clothed in the stigma of their past — where were they to go in a shattered land?

Kellermann said to himself that he could do nothing but wait until the Professor came out of the hospital. It had been fortunate that the old man had passed out cold in front of Herr Bendel. Had he keeled over on the street as they trudged through the rubble hoping for a familiar face, he probably would have died there. Who would have helped them — the people shunning them for their striped rags that set them apart, classed them among the victors, turned them into witnesses of a crime of which no one wanted to be reminded? Or the dour straw bosses from whom Kellermann had inquired about work? There was work — more than all the available hands in Kremmen could finish in years. But nothing was being organized. The Americans seemed to wait for the Germans to start; the Germans were waiting for commands from the new authorities and learned only what was *Verboten*. In the little that was being done, they got along without Kellermann.

He thought how right the Professor had been. "*Status quo ante!*" Seckendorff had guffawed. "Under the Nazis, we were the lowest thing in the country. That somebody has stepped on top of the Nazis doesn't mean we have come up!" And the Professor had suggested the Welfare Office. His collapse at the office forced the official touch, forced Bendel to send

534

for an ambulance to take the old man to the Kremmen Emergency Hospital. It was ironic that Bendel should do anyone a good turn. One couldn't call handing out a ration card and a slip entitling one to stay at the Home for the Political Victims of National Socialism a good turn. It was even more ironic to Kellermann that after the long trek up from Neustadt, after the weary weeks in Kremmen, Bendel's should be the only familiar face he had encountered — the same hard eyes peering over the same steel-rimmed spectacles in the same way as they had under the Republic and under the Nazis.

All this made Kellermann realize he was procrastinating. Waiting for the Professor was a lame excuse for doing nothing. And yet he remained in the Lower Depths, reclining in his own and others' dirt, sulking that something was owed him, taking the soup that was handed out once a day from a big, greasy vat.

Sometimes he would dream up magnificent schemes for the salvation of everybody, only to sink back before the impossibility of it. He had simply fallen into a rut, as did everybody who entered here. He saw them come in. He saw the hope that still might linger on their faces vanish like the light of a candle snuffed out under an overturned glass. Some took up stealing because they had nothing and needed everything, which sealed the doors of those citizens who still had doors all the tighter against them. And they stole from each other — a spoon, a tin plate, cigarette butts, an old handkerchief, a pair of torn underpants, anything anybody else owned or acquired.

He did try to stop that kind of thing. It seemed his knack for leadership was gone. Men like Balduin and Hammer-Carl were ruling the roost. Kellermann had run across many such men — the Nazis had made it a point to introduce the criminal element into the concentration camps, and these former procurers and convicted killers had been handy as trusties, supervisors, spies, and stooges. Liberated along with the others, they, too, had drifted into the Lower Depths.

Balduin, complete in patent-leather pumps, faultlessly creased trousers, and the striped prisoner's jacket he wore because of the fear it inspired in the minds and hearts of the citizens of Kremmen, was offering Kellermann a place in the gang. He had been painting a glowing picture of the ease with which they looted and organized holdups, broke into houses and traded their booty on the black market.

"Thanks," said Kellermann. "That wasn't what I was in camp for."

Balduin snorted through his flattened, once broken and badly mended nose. "Scared of the police?"

Kellermann shrugged.

A newcomer, a girl, pretty even in her rags, came into the room. "Is there an empty bunk?"

Balduin lifted her chin and appraised her. Then he turned to Keller-mann and said softly, "Like her?"

Kellermann roused himself from his brooding and looked at her. She was better than average. "Not for you!" he said to Balduin.

The ex-procurer gave the girl a pat on the behind and asked her, "Want to come along with me?"

The girl sized him up.

"No," she said.

"I could force you," Balduin said tentatively.

Kellermann rose from his bunk.

"But it isn't worth it," Balduin conceded. "Got more of your kind than I can use." He moved on to Hammer-Carl whose muscle-bound body lounged in the doorway. "Let's go!" he said.

Kellermann watched them leave. The girl was still there.

"How long were you in?" Kellermann asked the girl. He didn't have to elaborate the *in*. The *in* meant only one thing.

"Two and a half years," she said. "First jail, then Buchenwald."

He gave her a sympathetic glance. In the sordidness of the Lower Depths, despite the dirt on her hands, feet, face, and neck, despite her baglike, loose-fitting dress, there was something fresh, something healthy about her — perhaps because she had joined the community so recently. A red ribbon held her soft hair close to her head and emphasized its dark sheen. Her eyes had a gay light, and when she looked directly at Keller-mann, her brown pupils focused so intently that she seemed slightly cross-eyed. Her skin was tanned — a smooth, live skin, surprising when he thought of her two and a half years in jail and camp.

"What did they get you for?" he asked.

"What for . . . !" she said. "They didn't like my face, I suppose."

"I'm sorry."

"I hate to be questioned. I've been questioned too much in my life, and it never was fun."

She was wiggling her toes. Her feet were well built, and she had good legs and pretty knees and supple thighs — her way of sitting gave him ample opportunity to take it all in.

"My name's Marianne."

"I'm Rudolf Kellermann."

"Are you all alone?" She moved imperceptibly closer.

He sensed it and said, "Yes." After a while, he went on, "That is, I wasn't. There was an old man, but they took him to the hospital. They say he'll get out in three weeks or so."

Marianne thought, He would be the kind who dragged old people around with him. "You should have younger friends," she suggested.

"I was with him in Paula Camp," Kellermann said. "We escaped from there, together. And he's not very practical — an old professor. He was famous, though, in his time. Professor Seckendorff of the University of Munich."

"I know who he is," she said quickly.

Kellermann felt her tenseness. "How do you know?"

She reached into her bosom and took out a soiled clipping. "From the new paper the Americans are publishing. . . ."

Kellermann read it eagerly, and with mixed emotions. It was a letter to the editor, signed by one Dr. Friedrich Gross of the Kremmen Emergency Hospital, who wrote that he once had studied Latin under Seckendorff. *It might interest the editor and the public in general.....* , it started, and gave in detail and mannered style the history of the Professor and his two children up to the time he collapsed in Herr Bendel's office and was carted off to the Hospital, where he was being treated by the undersigned. The letter closed with the statement that men like Professor Seckendorff represented the best in Germany, the true Germany of the poets and philosophers.

Stirred as always when he was reminded of the Professor's story, Kellermann returned the clipping. The girl folded it carefully and slipped it between her breasts. She thought how lucky she was to have found the newspaper and to have read it thoroughly, and that now and here, of all places, she had met the man who could tell her more about Seckendorff. She always had had an instinct for what was good for her; a fine nose, as it were, that picked up the scent of her opportunities. She only needed to follow it; the one time she had disregarded it had led to her arrest and her stay in jail. Sticking her hand into the pocket of a plain-clothes man! Her instinct had told her *No* — but he had looked so well-fed, so well-dressed, so solid and stupid!

"Why did you save that clipping?"

She was so immersed in her thoughts, and in the plan which was swirling through her mind, that Kellermann had to repeat his question.

"What? *Ach ja.* . . ." She decided to hold back just a little.

"Well — why? You can trust me!"

She knew she could trust him. But that wasn't the point.

"Very simple," she said finally. "My name's Seckendorff, too."

She looked at his face. It mirrored surprise, pleasure — then doubt. In all the time he had been with the Professor, as often as the old man had spoken of his children, the existence of a Marianne Seckendorff had never been mentioned.

She pulled out another slip, Bendel's chit assigning her a place in the Lower Depths. There was her name, black on white, countersigned by the Welfare Director: *Marianne Seckendorff*.

"Any relation of the Professor's?"

Her answer came immediately, glibly. "I'm his niece. . . . Poor Hans and Clara. That's when I was arrested, in Munich, in front of the University. They tried to make me talk. They tried to make me admit that I'd helped to hand out the leaflets. But I kept quiet. It was terrible. They beat me. . . . No, they didn't leave any scars," she added hastily. "I don't know what they used, but I thought I would die."

Kellermann, who had gone through that more than once, said considerately, "Don't talk about it. Try to forget it. I know how it is. It comes back, at night. . . ."

"I didn't confess anything!" she said proudly and faced him, her eyes crossing slightly.

And she hadn't confessed. The Secret State Police, questioning the little pickpocket, had touched only cursorily on the name similarity between her and the two student leaders. The arrest of all three, during the same week, in the same neighborhood of the same city, was charged to coincidence. The Gestapo had been satisfied with the fact that Marianne was the daughter of a Heidelberg tinsmith; her trial had been short and correct, and had ended with her commitment to jail.

"It seems to run in your family," said Kellermann, paying her as much of a compliment as he ever did. His natural caution was abating. He was beginning to transfer some of his feelings for the Professor onto her — with an added something, perhaps. The years in Camp had dulled his senses. But now, they were coming back to life. "You deserve better than this," he said gruffly. "We must get out of here — you, me, all of us. Otherwise we'll die in this rot!"

She agreed, certainly. A few hours in the Lower Depths had been enough. This was no place for her.

"You and I," she advanced carefully, "*we* could make it. From the little I've seen of Kremmen, there's enough around for two people who're smart and determined not to get lost. . . ."

He felt the quick stab of disappointment. But once, she had been involved in the students' revolt! However amateurish, however futile the attempt had been, it had required a certain amount of unselfishness and self-renunciation. . . . "It isn't just you and me," he said patiently, "it's all of us. We survived the Camp and the jail and the investigations and the tortures — we're the only ones with clean hands — we have a kind of obligation — we carry the future — do you understand that?"

Marianne understood perfectly. The man was cracked. In a way she pitied him as he sat there, still very much the skeleton, in his dilapidated striped suit. But she was too reasonable a person to allow herself to give in to sentiment, to side with him, to try to save him. She rid herself of her pity, but held on to the compassion that was in her face. She talked to him in a low, soft voice; Kellermann lost his reserve; she was able to pump him about everything concerning the Professor — his background, views, and personal quirks; his children, their ideas, behavior, looks; details of his trial before the People's Court in Munich; his life in Paula, the lessons he gave in Medieval Latin to Dr. Valentin, the Camp's medical officer. The more Kellermann talked about it, the more incensed he became, the more he told her; until, finally, he believed he had brought her back to the road she once must have trod; whereas she had a fairly complete picture of the Professor and his martyred children.

"Do you get now what I mean?" he asked her, his eyes clouded. "Will you help me?"

"Help you? In what?"

He explained his scheme. A great big health resort with large windows and light and sun porches; food and nursing care for the victims of the camps and jails; workshops to train them in new and useful jobs; courses in the processes of democracy and administration; a tailor shop and a shoe store to equip them for the entrance into a new life. "And it's all to be had! It's there for the taking! The rich lived very well during this war. We only need to organize and push it through!"

It wasn't imagination the girl lacked. She could see the big, palatial, sunny place, and she could see herself in it. She looked as if she were staring through the moist, fungus-covered walls of the Lower Depths, her eyes focused narrowly and hard.

Then she said, "I want that. I want that very much. And I'm going to get it. And I'll have it long before you ever do, but not by waiting for the scum in here to pull themselves together. I'm young and I've got all it takes. You're a dreamer, Rudolf Kellermann. Why don't you get wise . . . ?"

Kellermann winced. The Lower Depths crashed back on him. He saw her leave. He didn't even feel sorry.

Yates and Karen had a working agreement. She would help him with the make-up of his new paper, which was being printed on salvaged equipment in the cellar underneath the bombed-out plant of the former Kremmen *Allgemeine Zeitung*. "At Coulter," he had confessed to her, "a mop-haired kid came bicycling by the house every afternoon and threw the paper on the porch. That's all I know about newspapers." He, in turn, would give her all the leads and tips that came to his office for her series on "Life in an American-ruled German Town."

Karen liked to work with him, she liked to discuss things with him, she liked his way with Abramovici. She knew Yates liked her, too, and she half expected him to renew the play for her he had made in Normandy; and she knew she would be disappointed if he did.

She came into the cellar, walked by the softly clicking linotype machines, then through a cubbyhole — a combination morgue and reception room over which Abramovici reigned undisputedly — and entered an even smaller one which served as Yates's editorial suite. He sat bent over some proofs, the yellowish electric light stressing the wrinkles at his eyes which showed how much the war had aged him, and angling shadows so that his fine nose seemed elongated, his cheeks thinned, his chin and forehead jutting. Or was it that he was working too hard?

He pulled up a chair for her. "Business or pleasure?"

"Business."

"Always business, isn't it? All right. . . ." He picked up a copy of his paper's issue of last week and gave her a rough translation of Dr. Gross's letter. "What do you think of it?"

"Nothing for me. Old stuff, the Munich students' revolt. Tex Myers wrote it up for *Collier's*."

"Is that so!" he said. "But what happened to Kellermann?"

"Who is Kellermann?"

"The other fellow. The Professor's side-kick. They both escaped from Paula Camp together. They popped up in Neustadt. They were brought in to Troy and me by Bing — " He stopped. "I'm sorry, Karen."

She said nothing. . . . The small, crooked street in Neustadt, spring sun on cobblestones; herself, the boy; and Bing suddenly stepping forward to the two lonely figures shunned by everybody, to the old man sitting at the curb, and the other man standing tiredly . . . It no longer hurt, except for a dull pain inside her chest.

"Don't be so sensitive," she said abruptly. "Bing brought them to you — then, what?"

"I thought I'd make this Kellermann Mayor of Neustadt. But the local padre opposed it, and we compromised on a druggist who, I hear, was hung by the Nazis when they got back into Neustadt."

"You'd still like to make Kellermann a Mayor?"

Yates's eyes lost their smile. "Willoughby picks *Bürgermeisters* in these parts."

"Where's my story?"

"What became of people like Kellermann? How do they live, now? What jobs do they find? Coming from concentration camps, do they have any influence? What's Herr Lämmlein doing for them? Are we Americans using them? Or what?"

"You've got an idea there," she said slowly; "but I'm not sure it's pretty."

"It should be printed anyhow," he answered dryly.

They heard Abramovici's unmistakable steps. He tramped in, splashed with mud, and announced indignantly, "A newspaper office should not have to be reached by driving through a half-filled crater."

"You could have driven around it. We always do. Did you find out about Kellermann?"

"I will need the afternoon off to clean my field jacket. Tomorrow, I'll compose a request to Lieutenant Colonel Willoughby to have the crater filled. Through channels. You can sign it."

"About Kellermann!" said Yates.

"I had to go to the Welfare Office, too," Abramovici continued. "The big boss there is Herr Bendel. People who hedge in the face of an American noncommissioned officer should be removed. That's what I told him. Tomorrow, I'll write a second request to Lieutenant Colonel Willoughby on Herr Bendel. You can sign it."

"Abramovici is the gadfly of Military Government," Yates remarked to Karen. "Unfortunately, they think it's me." He turned to Abramovici, inquiring a third time about Kellermann.

Abramovici wiped a splash of mud off his round cheek. "He's in some stinking place they call the Lower Depths." He saw that Karen was readying herself. "You don't want to take her there, sir! It's against all principles of hygiene!"

"Come on, Lieutenant!" said Karen.

Miffed, Abramovici asked, "Now, can I have the afternoon off?"

Yates nodded. In the door, he was overtaken by Abramovici. He felt something being pressed into his hand. He looked at it, then grinned. It was a small can of DDT.

To Yates, it was Paula Camp without the SS; it was the Verdun DP Camp without the open sky above the barracks. Here, the horizon was outstretched hands — young ones and old ones, in varying shades of gray; all thin, demanding, pulling at him and Karen. Then, in the semidarkness of the hallway, the faces emerged, and whether they were the faces of children or patriarchs, they were all stamped; and the eyes were voracious, wolfish, and had a hard glint.

He threw his body forward against the ring of faces. Karen thought he was brutal; he was strong and well and they were nothing, wisps, shadows with greedy eyes. The ring gave and became a hungry wave that trailed them, pursued them, babbling, gurgling, always at the point of breaking and disgorging the stinking refuse of the Depths.

Yates and Karen walked fast, without looking back, up the flights, down the halls, through the rooms, up flights again; they didn't talk; there was nothing to say; he gripped Karen's elbow and drove her along. Eventually, they found Kellermann, sitting on his bunk where Marianne had left him. Yates chased everyone else out of the room; the inmates obeyed grudgingly, like whipped mongrels.

"You don't remember me?" Yates said. "We met in Neustadt. I'm glad you got through that all right. What are you doing now?"

Kellermann had got up and was standing listlessly; his ears appeared too large for his shrunken face. "I remember, I remember."

"So you've come to Kremmen," Yates went on, just to say something. He felt Kellermann's unspoken questions: What do you want here? Going slumming? Seeing how low people can sink? Checking up on what you haven't done?

"What are you doing now?" Yates was repeating himself.

Kellermann shrugged and pointed at the room, at the shaky cots with their broken wiring; the filthy, torn blankets; at his roommates' miserable possessions — junk from a junk pile, the discarded discards of a ruined city.

"Are you ill?"

Before Kellermann could answer, the door burst open. A gush of Lower Depths people poured into the room, part of them continuing their rush out through the other door, part of them huddling for protection behind Karen and Yates. On their heels pressed a half-dozen blue-shirted, badge-flashing, club-swinging German police, whose clubs fell limply to their sides at the sight of the two Americans in uniform.

Yates shouted, "God damn you! Stop it! What do you think you are — the SS?"

The policemen, ferocious until a moment ago, reverted to what they really were — undernourished, middle-aged citizens whose power had been taken away in one scoop. Immediately, the crowd behind Yates and Karen came forward and began to threaten the police, continuing their shrill imprecations despite the fact that American MP's were entering the room. The MP's sauntered in leisurely; they had left the dirty work to the Fritzes.

"Who the hell ordered you to terrorize these people?" Yates demanded. "Who's in charge here?"

"I am!" called a voice from the door. Troy pushed past his MP's and the German police. His face was sweated, his collar open, the muscles of his neck bunched.

He saw Karen. He pulled out his handkerchief, wiped his forehead and his angry lips, and said hoarsely, "What are *you* doing here? This is no place for women! Yates, take her out!"

She turned to go, but Yates held her back.

Troy took off his cap and twisted it between his dirt-stained fingers. Having blown his top, he became apologetic. "Oh, for Chris'sakes — we've been chasing two gangsters all through town and into here. Now they've got away. How're we going to find anybody in this hovel with people piled on top of one another and you blocking us!"

"You sure have come a long way since Paula Camp!" Yates observed.

Troy felt Karen's eyes on him. Again, sweat broke out all over him. "What do you want me to do!" he snapped. "They've formed gangs. They steal, and worse. And me, I've got to keep order in this town."

Yates turned to Kellermann. "Who are the gang leaders?"

Kellermann stood silent.

"You're harming your own cause. Who are they? Where can we find them?"

"Sorry," said Kellermann.

"Are you afraid to tell me?"

"No."

"I'd like you to co-operate, Herr Kellermann."

"People steal because they have to," Kellermann said indifferently.

Troy scrutinized him. "Don't I know this guy, Yates? Isn't he your candidate for Mayor of Neustadt?"

"Yes, he is," confirmed Yates.

"And he's in with them, too!" The thought of Neustadt, of the personal debacle he had suffered there, wiped out whatever patience Troy had left. "You pick 'em good, don't you, Yates!"

Karen glanced from Kellermann to Yates to Troy. Troy didn't look back at her. He studied his boots. Then he said, tonelessly, "We might as well leave."

"I'd like to talk some more to Kellermann," said Yates. "Karen and I came here for a story."

Troy chewed his lips. Suddenly, he ordered, "Sergeant! Clear out everybody!" And, turning to Kellermann, "You stay!"

"All right! Let's get going!" bellowed the MP Sergeant. The German police got busy, *Raus! Raus!*

Finally, all was quiet. Yates asked, "How do you like your story, Karen?"

Karen said nothing. She went to Troy and pulled up his tie.

"I'm trying to do the decent thing," Troy grumbled.

"I know," she said.

"If I don't break up these gangs, I'll have the same trouble tomorrow, bigger trouble in a week."

"You can't put Conditions in jail . . ." She wanted to help him.

Yates bristled. "We got these people out of Paula Camp. Maybe that's not the end of it. Maybe we've got to do a little more than that."

"Do — what?" Troy asked bitterly. "Don't you think I'd like to clear out this place and the whole stench and filth that's in it?"

The sureness left Yates. "I don't know," he said deep from his chest. "Everything's cock-eyed!" If Bing were alive! Bing would have had an answer. . . . Almost with vengeance, he turned on Kellermann, "And you, why haven't you come to us? We're trying to find Germans we can trust!"

"The way I look?" asked Kellermann.

They would have thrown him out, Yates knew it. The remnant of a man, shaggy hair, stubbled beard, inflamed eyes, shoes in tatters, the striped pajamas from Paula shredded and mended and torn again.

"Didn't anyone issue you clothing? Shoes?"

"No."

"Haven't you asked for it?"

"Asked whom? — Can you give me a cigarette?"

Yates hastily pulled out his pack. "Here, take them all. I'm sorry. Should have thought of it sooner, really."

"I know what the Captain wants here," said Kellermann. "The police visit us regularly. But what does *she* want?" By a slight motion of his head he pointed at Karen who, silent and observant, seemed to have understood everything.

Yates gave Kellermann a light. "Miss Wallace is from an American newspaper. She wants to find out what happened to you fellows. A story."

Kellermann studied her. "A story? There is no story. Nothing has changed here in Kremmen."

"Maybe the story is that nothing has changed." Yates became conscious that in his split-second answer he had stated the whole case.

Kellermann laughed softly. "I came to the Welfare Office. The same official sat there who refused us dole under the Republic, who denounced us to the Nazis under Hitler. Now he's sending us to live in the Lower Depths."

"Don't you think we'd clean him out if it were brought to our attention?"

"Herr Bendel is there on Mayor Lämmlein's authority. All important officials are."

"What's he saying about Lämmlein?" asked Troy.

Yates gave the gist of the information to Troy and Karen, and inquired, "It's true what he says, isn't it?"

"Sure —" Troy became defensive. "I can't help it if Willoughby —"

"Of course he can't!" Karen said to Yates. "What are you proposing to do for *this* man?"

With forced cheerfulness, Yates began to enumerate to Kellermann a series of charitable offers. Kellermann's watchful eyes became frankly cynical. Yates floundered. "What's the matter with you? Are you so pleased with your present setup —"

Kellermann stopped him. "So maybe you'll get me a suit of clothes and a pair of shoes; that's fine. Maybe you'll try to get me a job working in some American Army kitchen. That's fine, too. That'll make you feel better." He carefully extinguished his cigarette and saved the stub.

It could have been Bing speaking. Angry in his helplessness, Yates asked, "But what *do* you want?"

"You wouldn't understand."

"Give us some credit, Herr Kellermann. I can try to understand."

"You've lost a lot of credit," said Kellermann. "You had all the credit in the world when you came and beat the Nazis. . . . It isn't me at all. It's many people — thousands, tens of thousands — people who would help you to remake this country into something decent. . . . No, Lieutenant, I don't think I'll accept your charity. I'll leave this place when everybody else is getting out of it."

Kellermann was flushed. He had spoken what he had wanted to say for a long time. Then he felt the deflation of his words. He needed a suit, and he needed a job, and all he had done was to repulse the one American who had some confidence in him.

Yates was less shocked than disappointed. Then he thought, The man is just another victim of improvisation. Or was it merely improvisation? Was it, perhaps, something much more serious? Sourly, he explained to Karen and Troy, "Kellermann wants no help for himself. He wants us to solve the whole problem."

"Well, how?" asked Troy. "If he sees any way, I'll try it!"

Yates switched back to German. "What would you want us to do, Herr Kellermann?"

Kellermann was in a dilemma. It was easy to outline a utopian scheme to a girl like Marianne — but dreams were not blueprints. "Take us — take us out of here!" he stammered. "A big house for all — trees — light — rehabilitation — classes — workshops . . ." He saw he had to curb himself, to form coherent sentences. He clasped his hands. "You see — give us one of those estates — the Rintelen estate, for instance. We'll run it all right. But perhaps this is asking too much. Just give us *any* place. Give us a chance to work. We'll work hard. We'll rebuild our lives. . . ."

Yates translated painstakingly, *A big house for all — trees — light — rehabilitation — classes — workshops* . . .

But under the words of Kellermann's dream Yates could hear the sound of another man's words — Willoughby, sitting in a grandfather chair next to the washstand in the dingy room of the Hotel *Goldene Lamm* in Rollingen, speaking his mind, asking for what the American people had sent its armies into Europe.

4

WILLOUGHBY received Karen and Yates in the conference room of Military Government. He was genial and effusive. "The furniture is from Rintelen," he explained. His hand glided along the cream-colored, smooth wood of the oval table. "I've had the walls draped, it makes the room warmer. And it hides the plaster."

In the corner, on a little dais, drooped an American flag. Willoughby gestured toward it. "Present from the General. He wants to have flags in every office, but we don't have enough. I've requisitioned a gross. Meanwhile, this will have to do."

He fell into a giant swivel chair at the head of the table, and pointed to the two smaller chairs on either side. "Sit here, will you? I'm going to ring for the Germans, and then I'll show you how we operate here. It's all very smooth, very civilized; I have them well trained."

He laughed again and laid his pudgy hand on Karen's. "I hear you've been visiting our charitable institutions. Don't think I don't know the seamy side of Kremmen! Give us some time, Miss Wallace, give us some time!"

He expected an answer. But when she merely nodded, he turned to Yates. "That goes for you, too, Lieutenant. I'll be glad to have the road to your printshop fixed, but give me the privilege of selecting my German officials. I'm glad I have some. I can't hand out ration cards in Herr Bendel's place — or would you expect me to do that, too?"

"No," said Yates, "frankly, I wouldn't." He kept a straight face. Abramovici's neatly typed missives must have landed squarely on Willoughby's desk, and since such official correspondence was routed through numerous hands, it must have cost Willoughby some effort to remain civil about it.

"Did Troy talk to you about the Rintelen estate?" Yates inquired casually. Willoughby had to be polite in Karen's presence, so Yates thought he might as well bring that up, too.

Willoughby rubbed his jowls. "As a matter of fact, he did. Do you have any particular interest in it?"

"No," said Yates, "not personally."

Karen observed the two with a tight little smile. She enjoyed a good fight, and this was one, suavely as it was conducted, calm as the voices were kept.

"You took Miss Wallace to that Home for the Political Victims of National Socialism, didn't you?" said Willoughby.

"Yes. Any objection, sir?"

"None whatever! And that's what gave Captain Troy the idea to ask me to use the Rintelen estate for these people?"

"We might have discussed it," said Yates. "Are you going to requisition the estate?"

"I'm giving it serious consideration, Lieutenant!" said Willoughby.

"Can I announce it in the paper?" Yates pulled out the notebook he had acquired since taking over his new job.

"We don't want to do anything premature!" Willoughby said thoughtfully. He looked at his watch. "Ten o'clock sharp," he remarked, and reached for the small silver bell that stood next to the ash tray before him. "Prussian punctuality! It makes a great impression on these Germans."

The bell tinkled. It was still swinging in Willoughby's hand when the wings of the main door parted and the Germans filed in, shepherded by Loomis. They took their stand behind the chairs, Lämmlein at the foot of the table directly opposite Willoughby. They bowed toward Willoughby. At a sign from Loomis, they pushed back the chairs and hurriedly sat down, very constrained, very straight, their faces charged with the dignity of the occasion.

"That's my Chamber of Commerce," Willoughby whispered to Karen. "Solid people, aren't they?"

He placed the bell next to the ash tray. "Good morning, gentlemen!"

"Good morning, *Herr Oberstleutnant!*" they answered, almost in unison.

Yates eyed the faces within the oval. They were ten men, including Lämmlein — all of different backgrounds, trades, ages; yet, there was something uniform about them, in their lack of graciousness, their stiff courtesy. Only the gray man facing Willoughby seemed somewhat at ease, in spite of his bookkeeper's exterior, his stiff collar and narrow-shouldered suit.

"This is Lieutenant Yates, editor of the new Kremmen paper," said Willoughby, "and this is Miss Wallace of the American press. Loomis, will you introduce the Mayor and the directors of the Chamber?"

Loomis got up and rattled off a list of names and the various trades represented. Each man stood up as his name was called, bowed toward Willoughby, and sat down again, breathing a little faster, as if he had surmounted a hurdle.

"What's the order of business?" asked Willoughby.

Mayor Lämmlein pulled an elegant briefcase from the floor and laid it carefully on the table. Then he took a key ring out of his pocket, picked over several keys, meticulously selected the right one, unlocked the briefcase, took out a sheet of paper, and read a list of items, first in English, then in German. The nine directors of the Chamber of Commerce nodded

547

at each item — every one of which Yates found piddling. He leaned over to Willoughby and whispered, "What about the Rintelen Works?"

Willoughby frowned. "Not on the agenda!"

"Oh," said Yates. "When is it coming up?"

"Patience! Patience!" whispered Willoughby.

A bald-headed, pompous man with a gold chain across his vest was reading figures. He represented the Coaldealers' Association of Kremmen; he was bemoaning the fact that the number of licenses would have to be restricted, first, because there was so little coal available, secondly, because the business was crowded anyhow.

Lämmlein translated, and Willoughby murmured approvingly. "Will you ask him, Lämmlein, whether he has worked out a list of people who should get licenses?"

The representative of the Coaldealers' Association had prepared precisely such a list, and he began to read firm names and addresses. When he had finished, he looked questioningly at Lämmlein. Lämmlein looked at Willoughby.

Willoughby, to whose heart one Kremmen coaldealer was as dear as the next, said, "Well, shall we give them the licenses?"

"I think so," said Lämmlein.

"All right," said Willoughby, "next point."

"Question!" said Yates.

"Question?" said Willoughby. He reached for the bell and toyed with it. Then he sighed. "Go ahead. But make it brief. We've got a hell of a long agenda."

"How old is your Coaldealers' Association?" Yates spoke English, he wanted neither Lämmlein nor the man with the gold chain to know that he was able to check on any variance in their statements.

The representative of the Association, after having received the translation of the question, said, "*Fünfzig Jahre,*" and Lämmlein said, "Fifty years."

"You have worked as usual during the last thirteen years?"

"Yes, as usual."

"Does the Association have the same officers now that it had during the last thirteen years?"

The representative of the Association didn't like this harping on the last thirteen years. They were the years under the Nazis. Lämmlein, his face remaining as correct as ever, translated the answer, "There was one change. The secretary of the Association died of angina in 1938."

"The Association, like every other organization, worked according to National Socialist principles?"

"We had to!" said the bald-headed man. His pate had assumed a pinkish hue, and tiny drops of sweat glistened on it.

548

"If you restrict the number of licensed coaldealers, from what viewpoint do you select the licensees?"

The answer, this time, came directly from Lämmlein, "Business stability."

Willoughby cleared his throat. He felt he had permitted enough of this. But Yates didn't take the hint. Yates hammered away, "Business stability — if you restrict competition, if you assure a man's market, and if there's a scarcity of goods, anyone's business is bound to be stable. Don't you think that the same people who ran your Coaldealers' Association and your Chamber of Commerce, under the Nazis, now, by assigning licensees, usurp an even greater power over the lives of the community?"

"The Lieutenant asks us . . ." Lämmlein translated Yates's attack word by word, less out of a desire for thoroughness than out of his need to gain time. The German members of the conference stared at the table in front of them. The coaldealer fished an enormous handkerchief out of his breast pocket and began to blow his nose vigorously. Karen looked studiously noncommittal, but took notes; and Willoughby, secretly cursing Yates, twirled a pencil until its tip broke.

It was Loomis who dispelled the cloud — perhaps because he had not even noticed how heavy and black it was. He said, "Wait a minute — as you see, nothing is done without our approval!"

"*Jawohl!*" confirmed Lämmlein, visibly eased, and hurriedly put Loomis's statement into German. The directors of the Chamber of Commerce looked up, and at each other, mumbling approval. Karen stopped writing; and Willoughby put the broken pencil aside, turned to Yates and asked, suppressing the sarcasm he could have used cheaply, "Satisfied?"

Yates said nothing.

Willoughby continued with the agenda.

They talked about the projected opening of a soap factory and a paper mill, provided sufficient fats and pulp would become available. Willoughby acidly refused permission to a manufacturer who proposed production of wooden toys.

"Luxuries! Toys! We won't allow the use of precious materials and labor for anything of that kind. It won't hurt the children of Germany to know that their fathers lost the war."

The Germans looked duly glum, but since they knew very well that wooden toys didn't influence their real interests one way or another, they didn't bother to contradict him.

Farrish came in during a routine report on the liquidation of the Kremmen Nazi Party bookstore.

Lämmlein heard the commotion at the door and stopped dead. It was the first time he had seen the General, and the thrill he felt almost jerked

549

up his hand, but he remembered in time, and merely stood at respectful attention. The others, too, had risen.

Willoughby, proud, and with just enough restraint to make Farrish feel that he had stepped into a beehive of important activity, reported that he was conducting a conference with the local Chamber of Commerce. Not that he liked the sudden inspection; it would cost him at least an hour of his time. He would have to call another meeting to cover the rest of the agenda which would now go out of the window. And why hadn't Farrish let him know? He could have made some sort of preparation. As it was, everything would have to be done extemporaneously.

"Chamber of Commerce!" said Farrish. "Like back home, huh?"

He roared at his own joke, and everybody, including the Germans who hadn't understood him, snickered obligingly.

Then Farrish fixed his luminous eyes on Karen. "Back with us again, Miss Wallace!" Brushing past the Chamber of Commerce men, he advanced on her and grasped her hand. "How's Willoughby doing? Isn't he a clever boy, the way he handles these Krauts?"

He turned to the others. "Why are you standing? Sit down! Carry on! Just act as if I'm not here. I'm just a kibitzer!"

He roared again and let go of Karen's hand.

"Sit down, everybody!" Willoughby ordered. "Loomis, have chairs brought in for the General's staff!" Carruthers and a number of other officers had been waiting at the open door for Farrish to make up his mind about staying on. Willoughby offered the General his own swivel chair at the head of the table, posted himself next to it, and waited for the staff to enter and be seated.

Then he said, "Perhaps the General would like to address a few remarks to the Germans here who are, in a fashion, the leading citizens of this district? The man down there, sir — yes, the little one in gray — he's the new Mayor. Lämmlein, take a bow! Knows English, too. He'll translate."

"I thought we had a Mayor!"

"He didn't work out," Willoughby explained. "We fired him."

"Fired him?" said Farrish. "Good! That'll show them that in my area nobody's married to an office chair."

He rose. With the flexible tip of his crop, he pushed aside Willoughby's ash tray, the silver bell, and the assorted papers.

He looked at Karen and beamed. "Shall I tell 'em?"

In answer, she poised her pencil. He stroked his bristly hair, contentedly and thoughtfully. He has an audience, and he has the press, thought Yates.

"The Colonel here has asked me to say a few words to you. I might as well. I want you to know what I feel about this occupation business, and what I want you to do. I think you all know who I am and what I've done

550

in the past. Now, we've come here to teach you something about democracy. Democracy, that's the rule of the common man; everybody has equal rights. Is that clear? Are there any questions?"

Lämmlein, translating, came through bravely. There were, of course, no questions.

"Well, we have a hell of a situation here, what with practically the whole city in ruins, and the morale of the people in a sad shape. You can't even drive through the streets without getting the stench of it. We're going to change all that. I have the best Division in the United States Army, and I'm going to have the best occupation area in Germany."

Even stronger nodding followed Lämmlein's translation. The Germans approved of the General's regional patriotism.

"I want the main roads cleared, and I want the streetcars to run. I want you to get back to some kind of normalcy with everybody knowing what he's doing and everybody in his place. Occupation — that's Army rule. In the Army, everybody knows what he's doing and everybody has his place. Is that clear?"

The Germans agreed entirely. They, too, wanted to get back to a setup in which everybody had his place — the Chamber of Commerce men running their businesses, and the other people working for them.

"Now about de-Nazification. I have orders from Supreme Headquarters to clean out every God-damned Nazi. I'm known for carrying through my orders regardless of cost — and this isn't going to cost us a thing!" He interrupted himself, leaned down to Karen, and said, "Well put, huh?" Then he straightened himself, and knocked the handle of his crop on the flat of the table. "We're going to clean the Nazis out of everything! I'm going to have the most de-Nazified area in Germany! That'll give you people a chance to straighten yourselves out with your God, who certainly didn't approve of this Nazi business — and with us, who don't approve of it either."

He paused and glared at his audience, supporting himself by placing the knuckles of his strong fists on the table. The Germans held to discreet attention.

"Well, Willoughby," asked Farrish, "is there anything else you want me to tell these Krauts?"

Willoughby complimented the General on the speech and said he had covered the whole subject, and that his words would have an excellent effect. Perhaps he would like to hear a spokesman of the Germans assure him of their co-operation?

"All right," said Farrish, "if he makes it snappy."

He sat down in Willoughby's swivel chair and began to swing it, his fingers pressed flat against each other.

Lämmlein, to whom Willoughby had left it to carry the ball, was not quite sure of his approach. The General reminded him of the late Maximilian von Rintelen, though the empire builder, of course, had been shrewder. But there was a good likelihood that Farrish was hiding a similar shrewdness behind his blustering. Lämmlein asked himself whether he should mouth a few platitudes and let it go at that; saying nothing, he at least wouldn't offend the all-powerful. On the other hand, it was very possible that Farrish would object to generalities, would expect clear-cut opinions, and would scorn anyone trying to soft-soap him. And if he talked to the point? It might cost him everything, his position, the continued existence of the Rintelen Works.

Lämmlein's gray face paled as he hesitatingly put down the papers he had been holding.

"Sir," he said, "we look up to you not only as a great military hero — having had a few of those in the history of our country, we know them when we see them — not only as to the man who has power over our lives and in whose magnanimity we trust, but also we look upon you as our teacher."

"Quite a mouthful," Yates heard the General say to Karen; but he seemed prepared to swallow it.

"We must be willing to learn," Lämmlein continued seriously. "Seeing the ruins of our beloved city every day, every hour, we say to ourselves that somewhere we have made a tragic mistake."

"You bet!" boomed Farrish.

"Please? . . . Oh. And we are grateful to you, sir, that you have undertaken to help us to overcome this mistake. We, too, want this district to flourish again. We want to make it the first and the best and the most beautiful in all of Germany. Ruined now, but still available to us is everything for this purpose: Not only the streetcars — that we can take care of, sir, in the shortest possible time; not only the roads whose importance for the needs of your Army we more than recognize; but the great industrial potential now lying dormant, which we can resurrect. I anticipate the day when the products of Kremmen — Kremmen steel, Kremmen machines, Kremmen coal — will once more roll from our rebuilt railroad sidings; when food and the other necessaries of life will flow to us in trade with other parts of Germany, yes, the world. And let me say that on that day, not only I, but all the citizens of Kremmen will say a quiet word of thanks to the man whose understanding, whose tolerance, whose co-operation, have made all this possible."

Lämmlein breathed deeply, and his gray, lusterless eyes rested solemnly on Farrish. Farrish, who at first had been doubtful, wished that sometimes, at least, one tenth of such praise would be handed him by his own people. After all, what had he done for those Krauts? He had bullied them.

"We realize we have to eradicate from our midst the criminals who have thrown us into our misery," Lämmlein continued. "Yes, de-Nazification, I say! But we must proceed with caution. I can afford to plead this, for I was never a member of that — that Party."

The word *Party* was pronounced with such contempt that it seemed to fall like a blob of rheum.

"And I suffered for it. But shall we judge a man by a label, or by what he has done? Let him be punished, yes, for his weakness — but let him be put to work rebuilding what his weakness helped to destroy! We cannot get the streetcars running without skilled personnel! We cannot begin to think of taking up production in the Rintelen Works without the managerial talent required! Ultimately, the decision is up to you, sir, you who have the greatness of mind to weigh the importance of every one of us, you who have the interest of the city at heart. I am sure, you will make the right choice."

Farrish was sure, too. Yates saw that the great man was moved, stimulated, and in the mood to be condescending and forgiving. Yates saw that Farrish was about to put his foot in his mouth, and he sympathized with him; Lämmlein had taken the General for a beautiful ride. And Willoughby wasn't protecting Farrish; Willoughby was gloating with the anticipated credit he would get for his well-trained seals.

Farrish said, "Mayor Lämmlein, I want to repeat the words of our Chief, General Eisenhower. *We have come as conquerors, but not as oppressors.* I mean that. I want you to come to me whenever you have any trouble that Willoughby here can't fix. I know a good man when I see one. In our country we have two Parties, and I haven't asked a single one of my officers and men whether he's a Democrat or a Republican. To me, a man is a man, first; whatever else he is, comes after. Is that clear? Any questions?"

Yates had a few. But even if Farrish, pleased with himself, the day, and his job, hadn't strode out, Yates wouldn't have asked them; Farrish's world was beyond reasonable argument. The General was flowing along on a mobile pedestal.

He couldn't even talk to Karen, for Willoughby had claimed her and was telling her how smart these Germans were, but that the problem was easy if you knew how to handle them.

Abramovici was no connoisseur of women. He considered them functionally; he had loved his mother most on the days when she pleased his stomach best. But even he could not entirely close himself to the charms of Marianne Seckendorff. She was dressed simply, and Abramovici could see that her suit was well worn; yet she had managed to make its lines accent her shoulders and slim her firm hips.

She observed the effect she had on Abramovici, and she was satisfied. He kept staring at the soft, full curve of her chin and lips, his mouth slightly open as if frozen in a whistle that never achieved sound.

The suit and her down-at-the-heels shoes were Marianne's entire capital. She had amassed it, at the Lower Depths, through the ex-procurer Balduin, who, for services rendered, had presented her with a stolen radio. She had gone to the black market and had haggled hard and had finally traded the radio for her present get-up. Looking at Abramovici, she knew the effort had been worth it. She expected the little Corporal to proposition her, and she was prepared to fence him off diplomatically — one didn't sweat so hard to get a little runt holding down a chair in some anteroom. She was saved, however, from having to exert her diplomacy by the fact that Abramovici, at last, reminded himself of the alluring females on the Army's VD posters.

So, complete with her clipping of Dr. Gross's letter on the Seckendorff family and the Munich students' revolt, she was ushered in to Yates.

"Well!" said Yates. "I didn't know they grew them in Kremmen like that."

She smiled winningly. "To tell you the truth, Lieutenant, these are the only clothes I own. And I'm not from Kremmen. I'm from Munich."

With a pretty hesitancy, she handed him a slip of paper.

He read the mimeographed document — *Release from Concentration Camp Buchenwald,* signed by a Lieutenant Farquhart, MC, and with her name entered in ink, *Marianne Seckendorff.*

He looked up. "Well — if you're from Munich, what are you doing here, in Kremmen?"

The question didn't sound inviting; but in his face she believed she read a different reaction. "*Ach Gott!*" she sighed, "you Americans! You have a head and a will of your own! I got a ride on an American truck. I said to the soldier who drove it, 'Munich!' and he said, 'O.K.,' and then we drove all night, and in the morning we were in Kremmen. 'O.K., Babe!' he said to me. '*Raus!*'"

Yates didn't ask further details of the night ride. He could imagine what had taken place. "And now you want to go back to Munich, Fräulein Seckendorff?"

She raised her hand in a forlorn little gesture. "It makes no difference where I stay. I have nobody in Munich, no relatives, no friends."

She was entering on dangerous ground. Her eyes grew intent and crossed slightly. "I would like to stay in Kremmen, if I could. Here. . . ."

She took out the clipping, and handed it to him, shyly.

He glanced at it and asked her to sit down. "You aren't related to Professor Seckendorff?"

"He's my uncle."

"Have you been to the hospital? How's he getting along?"

She said sadly, "I've tried. But they didn't let me see him. Rules. Everything is very strict now." She smiled again to assure Yates that she didn't think he was so terribly strict.

"I could probably arrange for you to visit him!"

She murmured that he was so kind! She had every intention of avoiding the old man. She could not afford to have her little white lie come out until she was definitely settled.

"Would you?" she teased.

"Before you go, remind me to give you a note to Dr. Gross," Yates said. Then he shoved aside the papers on his desk and sat back. "Tell me about yourself!" He thought that in this dreary town, this dreary work, he might as well enjoy the flake of beauty and excitement that had drifted in front of his desk.

"What is there to be told? After the Munich affair, the name of Seckendorff was like a curse. . . . I wasn't a student, though. I don't like books. I'll read a hundred pages or so, and then I get bored. I'm from the practical branch of the family."

Yates chuckled.

"But I knew what Hans and Clara Seckendorff were doing. They tried to keep me out of it, they must have feared what was going to happen. I'm stubborn when I make up my mind that something is right. So they let me distribute some of the leaflets, too."

"That was very brave," said Yates.

Her dark eyes brightened. "I was more sensible about it than they were. I wasn't caught with anything incriminating."

Yates scrutinized her. He couldn't come to any conclusion. Until she had claimed that she, too, had participated in the distribution of the students' well-meant but amateurish leaflet, she had been true to type.

"How did the police catch you?"

"Not with the leaflets," she said with a sly pride. "Not with any of the other people who were involved. But they were after the whole family — you know what they did to my uncle."

"Yes. And what did they do to you?"

"I'd rather not talk about it."

Her hands clasped her knee nervously, her skirt was pushed up a couple of inches, and Yates saw the live, warm skin. He didn't think they had done too much to her. She showed no physical traces, and if you disregarded her tawdriness, she seemed well-balanced.

"You can tell me," he said. "I saw Paula Concentration Camp when our troops came in."

Marianne appraised the American. She had come to him because the clipping had been a natural lead to the newspaper office. She had not expected to be tested so soon in the game; but the test had to come some time; and if she established herself now, the thing would be over and done with. If only he weren't such a fish! If only he reacted in some way! She was relying on her body to cover any holes in her story. She had watched many an American soldier transverse in amazingly short time the stage from commanding, *Hello, Fräulein, kommen Sie her!* to that of being the Fräulein's loyal escort and provider. She was counting on that naiveté. But the man she was facing was not naive; though she could sense that her presence had quickened his glands.

"They didn't break any bones. They didn't even scratch my skin. First they tried it with light. Day and night the light in my face till I thought I'd go blind or crazy with headache, and I wished I'd go blind. I didn't confess. Thank God, I had nothing to confess. Hans and Clara had been arrested before me, and they had been caught with the leaflets; so there was nothing I could betray. . . ."

He couldn't concentrate fully. She was the best piece that had come his way for a long time. Yet — he felt he must watch every word. "And then?" he asked kindly.

"They questioned me — one after the other. And then — then — they took me. You mustn't tell anyone, ever — I don't know why I tell you — except you're so understanding, so nice. . . ."

Her hand came over the desk. He looked at it. It was well-formed, slender, supple. For a moment, he was tempted to take it. Then he thought of this hand gripping a prison cot, and slowly, slowly loosening its grip as she gave.

The hand remained alone. The hand withdrew.

"The worst night came in early March. They came into my cell and forced me to undress. Four of them. I thought this was the end. But they didn't touch me. They led me along a corridor into another cell. There stood a big wooden vat, filled with water. Slabs of ice swam on top of it."

"Slabs of ice . . ." he said.

"Do you know," she said plaintively, "that I wasn't sure whether it was ice cold or steaming hot? Of course I saw the ice, but I was unable to think about it. I stood in the vat up to here — " her hand indicated her abdomen. "Up to here, yes."

"Cigarette?"

He thought she needed it. And she did. She was in the grip of her own fancy. In Buchenwald she had seen the woman to whom it had happened, an ugly, elderly person with whom the SS could have had no fun.

He gave her a light.

"It was like knives. Thousands of knives, stabbing, cutting. A terrible, unbearable, exquisite pain."

The *exquisite* registered. He believed the scene, every word of it; it was too detailed to be invented. He could see her naked, in the hands of the four brutes — it was easy to see through her clothes, they seemed cut for it, and she wore them tight. And yet, he sensed the impersonal about it; the strange incongruity: as if the two naked women, the one offering herself to him, now, the other one held in the vat of ice, who matched one another to the small beauty mark underneath her ear, still were not identical.

"And then?" patiently.

"I must have fainted, slipped. I came to in my cell. They had taken away my blanket, the window was open. I was covered with ice. Or it felt like ice. I don't know. Then I was sick, for weeks, in the prison hospital. I thought I would die. But I didn't. Later, they sent me to Buchenwald."

She sat quietly. She had done all she could. It was hard to get started, to plant your foot firmly on the first rung. Afterwards it would be easier.

"But why this special treatment?" Yates asked.

"I have thought about that," she answered.

"And what is your idea?"

She was conscious that, now, the spell of her story was broken. Everything depended on how deeply it had affected the American.

"My feeling is that somebody must have given the order not to mar my body. . . ." And she added, "It isn't marred."

Yates considered this information. All he need do was date her up. It was as simple as that. This is what she had come here for. Offer herself and then have him get her a room and American food and more clothes. It was a straight, businesslike arrangement, and he knew of several like it. And she was pretty enough not to disgrace him.

Except that it was too simple. Too simple and too cheap.

"I'm happy that you're physically all right," he said. "What can I do for you?"

She turned so as to give him an opportunity to study her profile, down to the curve of her breasts. "You're terribly kind. . . ."

Of course he was. Suppose he made it a one-night stand. He had earned it. She was asking for it. No, she was asking for more. And even if the ice vat was only a fever dream, or something with which they had threatened her, even if only half of what she had told him was fact, she had been in Camp Buchenwald and she deserved a better break.

Since he seemed unable to make up his mind, she put it more directly. "I've had a hard time. I want to improve myself. I'm willing to do anything for it."

He knew that.

"With my record, things are very difficult," she said. "The Nazi Government is gone — but . . ."

He knew that, too. The Lämmlein regime made rehabilitation a personal venture. Some set out on this way, like this girl; others refused to take it, like Kellermann. Well, if you followed her approach and accepted the world as it was, you had to make the best of it. But this best wasn't quite good enough for Yates.

"The Americans . . . ," she said hopefully.

"The Americans are your best bet?" He switched languages. "Do you speak English?"

"Yes, a little. I have learned in school."

"Can you type?"

"Type?"

"Yes, type — " he moved his fingers over an imaginary keyboard.

"Yes, oh yes. But not too quick."

"I can't give you a job here," he said, "but I'll give you a letter to Captain Loomis at Military Government. Maybe you'll have better luck with him."

He was fairly sure she would. At MG, they had so many offices into which they could slip a pretty, willing girl. Let her find her sugar-daddy there.

"Thank you," she whispered, "thank you."

As he wrote the letter, he glanced at her, occasionally, over the paper. She had given him up; the radiance had gone out of her, and she looked rather insipid.

Then he gave her the letter, and returned the discharge slip from Buchenwald. She was already at the door when he called her back.

"You forgot something, Marianne!"

Her face was a blank.

"I thought you wanted to visit your uncle in the hospital?" he said.

He was already penning the note to Dr. Gross he had promised her, and he didn't watch her. He didn't have to. He had made up his mind to give Loomis a ring and ask him to have her checked through Counter-Intelligence.

5

LÄMMLEIN was closeted with Willoughby.

"I've been letting you get away with murder!" Willoughby said. "And don't think that I don't know it."

"Murder?" Lämmlein asked innocently.

"That's just an expression. I could have said rape, theft, lies — anything."

"I'm not as bad as that!" smiled Lämmlein.

"That stuff you handed the General!" Willoughby swung in the swivel chair from side to side. "The General was kind enough to say that he would receive you under certain circumstances. I prefer your not taking advantage of this offer."

Lämmlein raised his hands. "But that goes without saying, sir."

"I want absolute co-operation. I don't mind your building your own little machine in Kremmen, as long as I control it. I want no monkey business behind my back."

"No monkey business," Lämmlein assured him. "I know my place."

Willoughby noticed the direct quote from Farrish, and he looked at Lämmlein, trying to fathom what lay behind the gray complexion.

"Of course it is very difficult," Lämmlein said slowly, "to do right by you, sir, if one is continually exposed to all sorts of pressures. We are the vanquished, we have to obey — but what are we to do if we're caught between conflicting interests?"

"What I say, goes!" Willoughby stated sourly. "Who's been pressuring you?"

Lämmlein appeared to squirm in the throes of divided loyalties. "You probably know all about it, sir. I can't imagine he proposed it to me without your approval!"

Willoughby squinted. "Who — proposed — what?"

"Captain Loomis, sir!" Lämmlein threw himself into a rush of apologies.

Willoughby suspected that Lämmlein was trying to split the ranks of Military Government. "So?" he asked. "What about Captain Loomis?"

"It came to me through Herr Tolberer of the Coaldealers' Association," Lämmlein said. "Tolberer thought I knew about it — you heard Tolberer speak at the meeting, sir; he isn't very bright."

"No, he isn't, I suppose. Get to the point."

"Captain Loomis has laid a 10 per cent tax on all business establishments he permits to be licensed."

Willoughby got out of his seat. He stepped to the window.

He had a perfect view of the ruins of Kremmen; the day was clear and sunny. Ruins are deceiving. You look at them from the bird's-eye view, and you think there can be no life. But if you walk through the rubbled streets, you find that people still dwell in the less damaged rooms, that small stores are springing up in cellars and in rear houses accessible only by a climb over debris. The two hundred thousand people left in Kremmen had to trade somewhere, they had to start making some sort of living, had to produce something to sell or exchange. It was such a simple, logical idea, this racket of Loomis's — too simple, too logical, perhaps, for Willoughby to have thought it up himself.

Willoughby turned and caught Lämmlein in an expectant smile.

"Such a tax," Willoughby stated matter-of-factly, "is discretionary with the local Military Government. It helps to curb inflationary tendencies by drawing off surplus cash. You Germans ought to appreciate it — you had a runaway inflation in 1923."

"The payments are to be made to Captain Loomis?" inquired Lämmlein, his smile having vanished completely.

"Yes, of course!" Willoughby seemed a trifle annoyed. "He is accountable to me!"

They called it *Club Matador,* in honor of Farrish and his Division, and to attract the American men and officers on the loose in the ruins of Kremmen. They served wines and liquors, which were pretty good since they came out of stolen stock through the black market, and thin beer that didn't sell too well. The prices were outrageous, even for American pockets; they had to cover not only Loomis's rake-off, but the city taxes and the Reich taxes that went into a reparations fund, and the black market profits, and then some for Herr Weiner, the proprietor, and for the syndicate of which he was the front man and in which Mayor Lämmlein also had a finger.

But the place was jammed.

You entered it through a ruined house and a courtyard infested with a great number of boys who hunted cigarette stubs, or promised to take you to their big sister, or both.

Inside, you were received by a pompous doorman in dark brown uniform with gold epaulettes, and a hat-check girl in short silk panties, bra, and a tiny white apron, and by the laughing sound of many voices, German and American, mixed with the slouching, egging rhythm of boogie-woogie.

The band was narrowed in at one edge of the tiny dance floor. Sometimes a couple, pushed sideways by the mob of dancers, would tumble into the drums; a slight pause would ensue, and then the dancing would start again, hot, liquor-sodden, breast against breast.

Loomis, crowded against Marianne, and she against Willoughby, sat at a corner table, hemmed in by two German couples. The Germans had been constrained at first; but as the whisky softened the Americans, one of the Germans, a pinched-faced, pale, long-haired man who looked like a dope fiend and probably was one, got up enough courage to try to sell Willoughby a Breughel; together with a document guaranteeing its authenticity. He spoke atrocious English. The other German man was fat and kept his hands folded around the stem of his glass. He was staring at Marianne. She wore the new costume she had made Loomis get her. The nunlike severity of its neckline set off the soft oval of her face. Her wide hat, with its frou-frou feathered brim, forced you to look deep into her eyes. She was spectacular. At intervals, the fat German would drop his handkerchief, his fork, or any other handy object. He would bend over

560

groaningly, to peek under the table at her legs, down to the ankle straps and slender, arched heels of her pumps. He could see Willoughby's pudgy hand resting in proprietary caress on her knees and thighs. The fat German didn't mind; it made things more attractive.

Loomis noticed that Marianne inclined more and more toward Willoughby. It roused the fighting male instinct which had reached a new bloom in him during the last days, ever since Marianne, with her letter from Yates, had stepped into his office and into his life. It had been a honeymoon of constant bliss and constant new discoveries; he had had no idea of what the human body could do and feel; led by her tender hand, he had traveled through spheres that made his past life one period of mourning for what he had missed.

He had wanted to shut her off from the world in the room he had requisitioned for her. But she had insisted on putting in her hours at the office. She loved him, she said, but she would not be his kept woman. He had sighed over so much morality, and he had let her have her way — what could he do but let her have it, in everything? He dreaded the moment when someone would discover his treasure.

The moment came when Willoughby dropped into his office and said, "Cute secretary you got yourself! Any more where this came from?" Loomis had behaved in the worst possible way; he had shown his concern and his worry; he had never learned what had been so important that Willoughby had come to see him in his office; and he had had this party at the Club Matador foisted on him.

And she, the whore, had jumped at the chance.

Look at the way they danced! How she clung to Willoughby! As if she'd never been in his own arms — arms that ached for her. And Willoughby! His jowls dripping pleasure, his fingers feeling her back, his hips pushing against her. Loomis had never known pangs of jealousy, this frustration at being unable to do anything. Get up, tear her away from that man, smash his face, and beat her, right, left, all over her smooth body.

They came back to the table, breathless, holding hands. Loomis managed a lop-sided smile.

"The Colonel dances very good," she said, pronouncing Willoughby's rank as *Colonöll* and rolling the R in *very*.

Willoughby drank what was left in his glass and called for more. The fat German, neglecting his partner, mumbled something about his *Schuh* and bent down to tie his laces. The dope fiend started plugging his Breughel.

Loomis decided to do something. He got up. Before the fat German could emerge from his dive, Loomis had him by the scruff of his neck and was shouting at him. The waiter rushed over with two men who looked

561

like bouncers or SS men on parole. Several American officers began to cheer on their buddy. Herr Weiner, the proprietor, edged his sleazy Tuxedo through the crowd and mingled his apologies with Loomis's tirade against God-damned Krauts who were bothering American officers' ladies.

Throughout all this, Marianne sat like a princess caught in her carriage by the begging mob, slightly bored, slightly amused, using her napkin as a Chinese fan.

Willoughby said to her, "Brutes, all of them. You're too good for them."

"You're so understanding," she smiled, "so nice."

"No, I'm not," he said. "I'm a brute at heart, too. But I'm the kind of brute who loves to be tamed. It's a tricky game, but very exciting. Would you like to play it?"

She didn't understand every word. But she understood enough to know that it was a proposition.

Herr Weiner, appreciating the power that Loomis represented, finally settled the affair by having the fat German peeper and the dope fiend who wanted to sell the Breughel thrown out with their women.

"Well!" said Loomis. "Now we have some *Lebensraum*. The nerve! I ordered the table reserved and then they crowd us. Who the hell won the war?"

The music started up again; Willoughby nodded to Marianne, and they wedged themselves in between the dancers. Loomis stared at the empty glasses, the dishes on which the sauce had jelled, the pale pink spots the wine had left on the tablecloth. He thought of Crabtrees, who was home now, a hero with the Purple Heart he had managed to wangle. Loomis thought of the whole war, the trouble it had been to him, how he had been pushed around, always a second fiddle, and how, now, the only fruit of victory he could claim was being grabbed out of his hands.

He got up and walked heavily over to the dance floor, pushed his way through to Willoughby and tapped his shoulder. Willoughby thought Loomis wanted to cut in; he said, "It isn't customary here. This isn't a Red Cross affair."

"I want to talk to you."

"Now?"

"Now."

"Pardon me!" said Willoughby. Carefully, with intimate protectiveness, he led Marianne back to the table.

"Well — what is it about?" Willoughby was annoyed and showed it plainly. He had a good idea what it was about.

Loomis had wanted to appeal to Willoughby's fairness, had wanted to remind him of all the possibilities open to him, and that it was cruel and heartless and below his dignity to deprive a poor man of his one little ewe lamb. But Willoughby's face was set; for all its sallowness and fleshiness, it was harsh, a danger signal.

So Loomis blurted out, "She's my girl, see? I found her, I fixed her up, and I'm going to keep her."

Willoughby's squat finger beat out a tattoo on the tablecloth. "I suspected that was how you felt about it when you raised the rumpus with the Krauts. Don't be a fool, don't get your bowels in an uproar, take it like a gentleman. The town is full of women, and you can have them for a pack of cigarettes."

Loomis got up. "Marianne!" he ordered, "we're leaving!"

Willoughby put his hand on her shoulder. "She likes it here. She will leave when I consider the evening ended. And with me." He spoke quietly, matter-of-factly, as if it were all settled and agreed.

"I won't stand for it!" screamed Loomis.

"What are you going to do about it?"

Loomis forgot where he was and what he was and what he was supposed to represent. He saw only Marianne, smiling, pleased, above the fight. He saw her as she had been, her lips close to his ear, her fingers taunting.

He leaned over the table. His hand went to Willoughby's collar and began to pull.

Willoughby took a spoon and rapped his knuckles. "Sit down!"

The sharp rap hurt Loomis. It brought back a spark of sense.

"I don't want any trouble," said Willoughby. "Not with you or anyone else. But if you want trouble, you can have it. I've been patient about a lot of things. When I pay the bill here, I know I'll be overpaying because you're getting a 10 per cent cut. You're getting a 10 per cent cut out of everything that operates in this town."

Loomis's shoulders slumped.

"I don't mind your soaking the Krauts. But from now on, you'll share, and share alike. From now on, also, you will know your place. Come on, Honey," Willoughby turned to the girl, "let's get back to the floor."

Marianne floated into his arms. She tilted back her head; her sleek black hair shone in the indirect lighting, and her whole face expressed her compliance. She had been able to get most of the dispute; she understood their language better than she spoke it.

Willoughby was not the man to overlook the lessons of his predecessor. He didn't want to have the tables turned on him by some Chicken Colonel or Brigadier General dropping around with the good intention of showing interest in the operations of Military Government and, incidentally, its personnel.

It was easy to convince Marianne that her duties now lay outside the office; her devotion to work, her aversion to being a kept woman, which had so frustrated Loomis, vanished in the course of one arduous night. She wasn't tempting fate. She had been spectacularly lucky to have climbed to the pinnacle in so short a time. It was best to rest awhile on what she had achieved, to enjoy life, to acquire a wardrobe, to pad her body where it needed padding, and to start a small collection of costume jewelry, as well as a modest store of cigarettes, soap, and toilet water.

Willoughby was faced with the problem of employing her usefully. Even if she slept until noon, he did not believe that a girl should spend the balance of her day in idleness. Left to her own devices, she might get ideas about what was good for her. He could give her all she needed and desired, and more. But he knew human nature; he knew the devilish itch that so easily gets under the smoothest, best-cared-for skin and makes you feel that perhaps, just around the corner, something a little better, a little richer, a little spicier is waiting for you.

Neither did he believe that a person's talents, that her very availability, should go to waste. The first night — he had been tired out quickly — she had sat by his side, playing with his fingers, and had given him the story of the ice vat, elaborating on the original which Yates had heard. Willoughby had seen her eyes dilate with horror; he had felt her crawl into his arms, poor scared little thing; he had caressed the flesh that once had been covered with ice — how could she have stood it? You never know the human capacity for bravery and endurance! And he had whispered to her, "It's all over now, Honey. We're here and we'll protect you, and you must forget about it. Do you feel better, now? Do you feel good and warm?" And his chubby hands had wandered over her, on a mission of comfort and rehabilitation.

But he did have a job for her. He created the job. He went out to the Widow and persuaded her that she needed a house companion. He said he was concerned about her being alone so far away from town with only her daughter and the invalid Major Dehn. "I want you three women to be compatible, happy together. And I want to come out here on occasion and enjoy the feeling of home — I've been away from my own so long!" He appealed to the conscience of the Widow; he told her of Marianne's sufferings, of the ice vat. "Every good German should make efforts to atone for that kind of thing, if you know what I mean." But in the end, he had to override the Widow's and Pamela's protests with: "Why do you go out of your way to make things difficult for me and for yourselves? There are many Americans who want me to requisition your whole estate."

"*Requisition?*" the Widow piped.

"Requisition, confiscate, take away." He cupped his hand and led it over

Maximilian von Rintelen's desk in a sweeping motion. "*Phhht* — gone, *kaputt!* Rintelen, manor house, all!"

And on this sunny Sunday morning, no cloud in the peaceful blue sky, he was driving Marianne in his open touring car, beyond the confines of the city, off the main highway, onto a macadam road that ran through mangy fields, past scrubby hills, and into the neatly planted, nurtured forest of young pines that was the Rintelen estate.

"Oh, this is beautiful!"

Light-flecked, its repaired windows gleaming in the sun, the manor house lay before them like an enchanted castle in the woods, its gingerbread towers rising perkily, its great, arched entrance proclaiming the promise of splendor and shaded, snug luxury.

"This is your dream house!" Willoughby announced, stopping the car on the crunching gravel. "Here you will live."

She nestled up to him. "You're so understanding! So nice!" Then another, frightening thought took hold of her. "Oh no! Not alone! Not without you!"

He got out and gallantly offered her his hand.

"I've seen to everything, Honey. You'll have company. The two women who own the joint live here with an invalid. They'll give you their nice apartment and move into the guest rooms, or wherever they want to go. And you'll be very friendly with them and let me know what goes on here. . . . Let me show you the grounds."

He led her around the house, over the soft grass of the lawn, into the park. He showed her the bench in the arbor which had been Hitler's favorite resting place whenever he came to Kremmen and stayed at the Rintelens.

"I'll be out here frequently," he promised. "Or I'll bring you into town for a good time at the Grand Hotel, or at the Club Matador — you won't be bored."

"They may not like me here," Marianne said suddenly.

He took her into his arms and kissed her tenderly. "Don't you worry, Honey. They'll dance when you whistle. And like it."

She laughed and whistled and danced a few steps over the piny ground.

God, she's beautiful! he thought, and he was very happy.

Pettinger, watching them from the curtained window of his upstairs room, thought she was beautiful, too.

6

THE ROT of boredom was fastening itself on Pettinger. The war and his function in it had accustomed him to quick decisions that were put into immediate action. Speed and constant doing had shaped his manner of living and his habits. It made adjustment to his new status of being cooped-up in the luxury of the manor house and in the ever-demanding arms of Pamela an ordeal. The network he was trying to create wove itself, but at snail's pace; and the progress intermittently made was no relief to his restless, fidgeting mind.

Too rarely for Pettinger's limited patience, Lämmlein would bring messages from men contacted after prolonged effort. These fugitives in hiding, who were trying to re-establish connections, to set up groups and organizations, let Pettinger know that they agreed with his plan. They agreed that dissatisfaction was growing rife in the occupied area. But they were not nearly as unanimous when it came to the question of which man's leadership they would accept. They counseled to go slow, to let some grass grow over their tracks; they maintained that nobody among the few left of the old gang could step forward to channelize and crystallize the work; they advised that new people be groomed to serve as fronts, preferably men who had the absolute confidence of the occupying power; they complained that the majority of the population was too concerned with personal problems to do much except grumble. However, they were doing their best in spreading anti-Russian rumors and in working on the American troops through women and other civilian contacts. They were quite successful, since the Germans were bred on hate against the East, and the Americans, averse to anything they had not tried themselves, were naturally suspicious of the Russians.

Pettinger studied every newspaper he could get, English or German. He scoffed at the advance notices of the Nuremberg trial — a sham, he said. He approved of the disputes among the Allies that came in the wake of the San Francisco Conference. Every conflict in the Allied Control Council gave him a dose of hope — but everything was so slow, so damnably slow, and the sameness of the days and the sameness of the nights threw him into long fits of depression and made him rely on the easing warmth of schnapps.

When Pamela informed him that her mother had been forced to open the house to Willoughby's concubine, he was momentarily panicked. Nervously, he listened to her despairing and possessive arguments: he must go and live in the gardener's cottage; he must pass himself off as one of the workmen on the estate — besides, the hedges needed clipping.

Then he came to his senses. "Have the hedges clipped by the Polack," he said curtly. "Willoughby knows I'm your husband and that I'm here. Fine thing to throw me out of your bed and put me into the gardener's cottage!"

He smiled. The conversation ended with his savoring a mischievous idea.

After Willoughby had deposited Marianne and was gone, Pamela rushed to Pettinger's room, agitation, hatred, fear plainly written on her face.

"She's a spy!"

"I know something about spies, my dear," Pettinger replied. "The ones I had to deal with were never that pretty."

"You've seen her already?"

"From a distance."

He felt her sticky, sweated palm as she anxiously touched his hand. "You no longer look anything like a sick man. You'll have to stay in your room, you won't even be able to go out for a walk. She'll see you. The American will be here constantly to visit his floozie. *Ach, Gott!*"

Pensively, he asked, "What kind of person is she? German, of course?"

"Of course. And right out of a concentration camp, though she doesn't look it. With American food and stolen clothes — no wonder."

"They are up and we are down," Pettinger said philosophically. "It'll be a pleasure to have her locked up once more."

"When?" she demanded. "When?"

He had no ready timetable, just a vague promise. "Maybe you're right," he offered finally. "One of these days, I'll have a look at her and decide what we'll do with her."

"I wish she were dead," Pamela said, from the heart.

Pettinger stared at her, frowningly. It occurred to him that she was quite capable of murder.

Marianne didn't insist on taking the Widow's apartment. She had looked it over and had said to the Widow, "I wouldn't think of depriving you of your comfort." She could have made them carry out Willoughby's orders; but she took into consideration the fact that she would have to live with the Rintelen women and that she would have to get along with them — the more modest and unassuming she made herself, the sooner the Widow and Pamela would forgive her; and she ought to tell them that her being billeted here was entirely Willoughby's idea.

"These Americans, you know, madame — they simply go mad if they like you; charming men, in their way, but no conception of other people's rights, of courtesy, of good form."

Also, the Widow's rooms were a museum, a nauseating potpourri of pastels, stuffed little pillows, laces, and bric-à-brac. Marianne couldn't have turned around twice without breaking some of the gypsum world; she preferred moderne. They compromised on the downstairs room that had been Dehn's whenever he couldn't avoid staying at the manor house.

She spent her first night at the house quietly enough, got up late, and made a half-hearted attempt at being the Widow's house companion. She was politely rebuffed; she shrugged off the snub and went for a walk through the grounds.

It was early afternoon when she returned. Quietly, she entered the main hall. Whatever the time of day, inside the hall it seemed to be dusk and the air was heavy. On one of the end tables stood a vase of honeysuckle. She stopped to pluck a spray and put it in her hair. She was feeling good and began to hum a little tune.

The tune broke off. Almost hidden from sight, in the deepest easy chair in the hall, sat Pettinger.

"Pretty tune," he said. "Pretty voice. Surprised to see me?"

She put the honeysuckle back into its vase.

"I'm Pamela's husband."

He was wearing Dehn's light gray slacks and a loose-fitting, broad shouldered smoking jacket. He laid aside the old magazine he had been leafing, rose, and said, "Call me Erich. I suppose I should have come down yesterday to welcome you. I'm ill. I was in bed."

"You don't look ill." Her lips had gone dry; she wetted them furtively.

"I have my good days and bad," he said.

She was glad Willoughby wasn't there to see him. She had begun to like it here; and she knew that Willoughby was too cagy to leave her under the same roof with this strong, handsome, and apparently healthy man.

"I hope you're comfortable?" he asked. "Pamela was against having you here; but I think this house can stand a little livening up. You've been in a concentration camp, I hear? Must have been very bad. These things have been hidden from us so carefully; they're only coming out now. I feel ashamed, really. And we, who've been so proud of our music, our theaters, our cultural achievements! In my little way, I've been supporting the arts. Well, that's over now. No more money, no more arts."

All the while, his eyes were wandering over her.

She was conscious of his eyes, of being probed; but somehow, she didn't mind it. Here was a real gentleman, class, and she had to remind herself that she had long outgrown the pickpocket stage and was, by reason of her American connections, his equal — unless she made a boner.

"The concentration camp wasn't nice," she said.

"Pamela tells me you had some horrible experiences. Ice vat, or so?"

Despite the dusk, she could see the glint in his pupils. Her heart beat loudly.

"They kept me in there," she said, "naked."

568

"Not possible!" he exclaimed. "You must tell me about it sometime, when we've grown to know each other. You were a Communist?"

"Oh my God, no!" She was so frightened that her eyes crossed. If the Rintelens labeled her Communist and passed the word to Willoughby — good-by manor house, good-by clothes, good-by everything.

Pettinger was relieved of his main worry. She obviously spoke the truth. If she wasn't a Communist — and from the moment he saw her he hadn't considered this likely — she could be anything that suited her fancy.

"Sit down!"

She obeyed instantly, meekly.

"Well, then — why the ice vat?"

Only the old answer occurred to her. "Somebody must have ordered that my body should not be marred. And it isn't."

He looked at her legs, her blouse. He compared her firmness to Pamela's sensuous flabbiness. "How fortunate for you!"

"Yes, isn't it?" She wanted to smile invitingly. After all, her luck was holding out. The line that had worked with Yates, with Loomis, and with Willoughby was working with this man, too. He was eager for her, plainly. But she couldn't smile; he made her lose her self-assurance, the security of her status as the conqueror's hanger-on. His informal dress, his easy, conversational tone — everything about him was smooth as a glove and yet disquieting; she'd felt the hard, tapping finger in his questions. She a Communist! Of all things!

He picked up the magazine. She saw him roll it tight. With a twist of his wrist, he began cutting the air with it. It was like a whip or a club, and it held her eyes. It was a familiar gesture.

She shivered. For a moment, she considered running out, back to Kremmen, back to Willoughby. . . . But now he was talking again, in that light manner which somehow laid itself around her and trapped her.

"Well, then, Marianne, why were you really arrested?"

"It was all because of my name," she said, her voice small. "The Seckendorffs were in that Munich students' revolt. I was in Munich at the time. The police picked me up. . . ."

"How stupid!" he said gently. "And you weren't even related to the traitors?"

She did not answer.

"Well, were you?" He laid his hand on her hair. His fingers pressed the back of her head.

"Don't!" she whispered.

"Were you?" His fingers were a vise.

The pain made her float between anxiety and the wish to throw herself at his feet.

"No, I wasn't."

The vise turned into a caress. She felt herself go limp and heard him say, "Everything will be all right, Marianne," and heard herself answer, "Yes, Erich."

That night, he came to her. He locked the door behind him and sat down on her bed. She pulled the covers up to her chin.

After a while, they heard steps in the corridor. Bare feet paced up and down outside the door. Then the steps receded.

"That was Pamela," he said. "I hate possessive women. Don't you ever be jealous of me."

"No," she said. And after a pause, "Pamela will hate me."

"She does anyhow. Women have such intuition. Don't fret. You've got your American Lieutenant Colonel to protect you; and I'm here, too. Give me your hand."

The heat in her bed was stifling; her body burned as though she had fever.

"I'll have to stay here," he laughed, "she'll be waiting up for me all night."

After he had allayed her fever, and when she'd quieted down, he reverted to his subject. "Intuition. I don't claim any. But I'm not an American. So don't give me any of your hokum. You're really a nice girl who started life on the wrong foot. I don't want to know the details. But don't pose as a political martyr in front of me. I don't like martyrs — they're stupid. And political martyrs are the dumbest of them all. You've got lovely skin. Ice vat! I don't mind your getting in right with the Americans. We all have to, one way or another. Maybe, one day I'll ask you to do me a few small favors. How's Willoughby? I mean, as a man?"

In answer, she drew closer to him.

"*Ach*," he said, "sometimes I ask myself how they ever won the war. . . ."

Breakfast was a disagreeable experience. Pamela hardly touched her food. She rapped her spoon against the rim of her cup in a steady tinkle that, she knew, annoyed the others.

The others were just as annoying to her. The Widow was shoveling a great number of crumpets into her mouth and complaining that the egg was too soft. "Two and a half minutes!" she chirped. "All they have to do is look at a watch. But they can't even tell time. Or they don't care to. And it's such trouble getting eggs." Then she shifted her target and asked Pamela what was wrong — had she slept badly? "You could have dressed for breakfast, too," she said, "especially since we have *guests*. . . ."

"Guests!" said Pamela. "They live with us, don't they?"

Marianne looked up, but said nothing. She scooped out her egg daintily, and picked the crumbs off her plate, admiring the design on the Dresden china. Then she drank her coffee and put down the cup hastily. "I can ask the Americans for some real *Bohnen-Kaffee*," she suggested helpfully.

Pamela stared at her. "Don't bother!"

"But they've got it. Why shouldn't they let us have some?"

Pamela breathed faster. "We, at least, have some pride!"

"Have some sugar for your pride," said Pettinger, offering Pamela the bowl.

Pamela groaned. She shoved back her chair and walked out, her crumpled nightgown trailing below her negligee.

Later, she came to Pettinger's room. She knew he would have his story ready; she was determined not to accept it. She wasn't going to share him, especially not with an American's whore.

He saw her face, distraught, paunchy, almost tragic after the night without sleep, and proceeded to break her determination. He humiliated her, forcing her to admit that she had searched for him all through the house; that she had listened at Marianne's door; that she had posted herself before his, ear pressed to it, burning with rage and frustration.

"Why didn't you knock, Pamela? Why didn't you call me? Why didn't you come in?"

"The door was locked."

"I must have locked it out of habit. So many things going through my head, you know how I am. . . ."

"You weren't in your room at all!"

He gave her his hard, masklike smile. "I slept like an angel. I just didn't hear you."

It was a brazen lie. She swayed a little. And then she thought: I wish it were true. Oh God, I wish it were true.

"Erich," she said, "I am the kind of woman who'd rather not have her man at all than not have all of him."

He appeared bored. "Very outmoded, considering the shortage of men in Germany."

She laughed suddenly, a strained laugh. And then, softly, she said, "Erich, kiss me."

He did, perfunctorily.

She stepped back. Her face was livid. Her words came hoarsely, "I don't know who you are. But there are people who'd like to know, who'd like to know that you're here, going about in my husband's clothes, sleeping in his bed. You must go on, you must sleep with me, you must be a perfect husband — "

This slut, this oversexed Brunhilde, claiming him with every ounce of her flesh! And he was tied to her — only through her he could have what he needed: this haven, the tenuous connections built through Lämmlein.

Thin, thin ice.

He smoothed his forehead and gave his eyes a good-natured twinkle. "I thought you were smarter. What do you take me for? She's Willoughby's woman. He brought her here."

"That would be an added attraction — you'd have two people to laugh at: the American and me."

"She's straight from a concentration camp! How could I trust her?"

"Who says you trust her?"

"My dear Pamela — you don't know the girl at all. I have spoken to her."

"I suppose you have," she said pointedly.

He ignored the dig. "She's no good. She got into the concentration camp through some administrative mix-up. She isn't even a relative of the Seckendorffs who were involved in the Munich students' revolt. She's just an unprincipled little opportunist who is trying to get what she can out of the situation into which we all have been thrown. She'd sell me out even faster than you would, my darling, and for less reason."

"So she's putting something over on the Americans. . . ." Pamela said slowly.

He grinned. But not on me! He was pleasantly surprised at his own undiminished capability for sober estimates, and his disregard for them. He saw Pamela's eyes fill.

"What is it now?"

She sniffled, "You're in such terrible danger. . . ."

He was safe, again. "Suppose we continue in our own little family circle, you and I. Suppose you leave the worrying to me and trust in my lucky star. You must believe in it. I do."

When he saw Marianne, after lunch, he let her know that he would come to her as soon as practicable, and that Pamela was duly pacified.

7

DEWITT arrived in Kremmen without fanfare. After depositing his baggage at the Grand Hotel where Military Government and transient officers were billeted, he drove to the Kremmen Dragoon Barracks and found Farrish in his apartment on the top floor of the Administration Building. DeWitt was amazed at its good taste and well-planned comfort.

"Nice, huh?" Farrish greeted him. "I've got a Second Louie around who was in the interior decorating line. Don't like him much, I think he's a swish, but very useful at this kind of thing."

"You seem to enjoy it. . . ."

Farrish tried to take the worried frown off DeWitt's lined face with the news that Germany was the best of all possible lands to be occupied by the best of all possible armies; that Kremmen was the best district in Germany, occupied by the best division; and that Willoughby was the best man for Military Government.

"You were a damned fool to let him get out of your outfit," said Farrish.

DeWitt said, "My loss is your gain."

"Have you seen my streetcars?"

"Of course."

"I find that most of them run empty," said Farrish. "We have miles of trackage cleared through parts of the town where nobody ever goes. Willoughby is doing something about that."

"What?"

"Well, he talks about reopening the Rintelen Works. About city planning. I'm very much interested in that. Don't you see the great chance we have? We can really do things here! If we had one tenth that power in the States! Look at the mess there — strikes! Here, I put my finger on the map, and tomorrow they start clearing up where I had my finger. You see results! For my money, the Krauts aren't so bad. They're willing, they're accustomed to discipline."

"You seem to know a lot about them."

"What is there to know? I know Americans, don't I? Where's the difference? Besides, I get around. Now take Lämmlein, that's the new Mayor Willoughby picked. Went hunting with the two of them the other day. Nothing shows up a man like the way he hunts. There was this buck, beautiful animal. The Kraut fires, misses. Then it's my turn. I got the buck. But that's not why I'm telling you the story. I saw this Mayor of Willoughby's smile when he lost the buck. I like that, I like a good loser. I like sportsmanship. In war and in peace. As long as they know their place. That's true here, that's true in the good old U.S. — isn't it?"

DeWitt stroked his chin. "Well — that depends on who assigns them the places. . . ."

Farrish, startled for a moment, broke into noisy laughter. "Clever! What brings you here, old man?"

"I'm having a look around. I have one of my men publishing a newspaper here. Do you ever see it?"

"Willoughby says it's very helpful. I can't read the crap. But an organized community must have a newspaper. Public opinion, you know; education, morale. I'm in favor of that. . . . They printed a story on me. With pictures. Wait a minute, I must have it around somewhere — Carruthers!"

Carruthers appeared.

"Where's that clipping, Carruthers — the one from the German sheet?"

Carruthers fetched it. DeWitt fished through his pockets, found his eyeglasses, carefully slipped them out of their case, and put them on his broad nose.

Farrish had been waiting impatiently. Now he boomed, "Look! *Farrish, der Panzer-General!* That's the headline. Farrish, the Armored General. I can't read it, except for the names and the dates, all the battles. It's nice to have. You've got a good man on that paper. And the Krauts know with whom they have to deal."

DeWitt decided to have Yates on the carpet for this. The Government's money was not to be spent for personal publicity on any general, especially not Farrish.

"And if you should be replaced tomorrow," DeWitt said slowly, "we'd have to build up another man."

"Why should I be replaced? I'm going to stay here. I like it here. Unless, of course — but this is strictly between us — there's a movement on in my home state — they say they want me to run for the Senate. But I'll take it only if they can guarantee the election. And what's a Senator anyhow? One among ninety-six."

A spark of irony lighted DeWitt's eyes. "I thought you hated politicians."

Farrish tickled the shining calves of his boots with the tip of his crop. Then he bared his teeth. "I'd be the politician to end all politicians. I've got my strategy all lined up. It's like at Avranches. I break through, and then there's no holding me."

"Does Willoughby know?"

"He says if they draft me, it's in the bag. Look at the record I'm piling up here. We've got the streetcars running and water in three quarters of the town and electricity and a brand-new police department. They look like American cops, too. Willoughby's sent a bunch of pictures over and they've been in all the home town papers. Every little bit helps."

"Yes."

"Well — wouldn't you vote for me?"

DeWitt's hand trembled slightly and he rested it on his knee. He was afraid of something. Not of Farrish, not of any one person — he didn't know of what.

"I can't vote for you; I don't live in your state."

"That's right, you don't. Too bad. . . ."

I don't live in Farrish's world, DeWitt thought. He did not argue with Farrish as he had done while the war was on. It seemed that the end of hostilities had frozen Farrish in the attitude in which the General then had found himself; nor had the ensuing passage of time thawed him out. You don't bend ice or mold it, you break it or apply the torch.

DeWitt encountered Willoughby on entering the perpetual semidarkness of the dining room of Kremmen's Grand Hotel. The blasted windows had been boarded up; daylight could only trickle through the holes in the

574

wood or through the seams where the boards did not fit to each other; the few bulbs in the chandelier were unable to penetrate the somber height of the hall.

Yates, already seated at a table at the far end of the dining room, got up, anticipating the Colonel's joining him. But DeWitt stopped at the door and asked Willoughby, "How's Yates working out? Is he helping you at all?"

Willoughby knew that DeWitt would take any derogatory remark coming from him as a point in Yates's favor. "I don't see how I could run the town without his paper. Of course, he's still inclined to be radical, but that's just what we need. Military Government, Colonel, is a heavy work horse, it must get the whip sometimes."

His lips were set in a smile, and his tone was bantering. Since the days of Luxemburg, Willoughby felt self-conscious whenever he thought of DeWitt — as if the old man knew something about him, or could see through him; though what the hell was there to see? In view of Yates's constant sniping, Willoughby was particularly anxious to know the reason for DeWitt's sudden visit.

"I'm expecting to have dinner with Captain Troy and Miss Wallace — you probably know them. If I'd been informed in advance of your arrival, sir, I would have reserved the evening for you. . . ."

"I don't know them — but let's all get together, anyhow!" said DeWitt, and waved Yates over.

Soon after, Troy and Karen arrived.

"The four of us are alumni of Paula Camp," joked Willoughby to the Colonel; but since no one wanted to talk of that experience, the soup was eaten in silence. Finally, Willoughby burst out, "How long do you think you'll stay with us, Colonel?"

DeWitt wiped his lips. "Frankly, I don't know. The General wants to show me around; there ought to be lots to see." He studied the strained expression on Willoughby's face, the deep sacks under his eyes, the shadows under his jowls. The man was working hard, you had to credit him with that; and he wasn't happy.

Yates noted the Colonel's guarded answer. "It's a very interesting town," he said, and, turning to Karen, "isn't it?"

"The General is very proud of the things you've done," DeWitt said to Willoughby.

Willoughby replied with studied affability, "We all work together. Troy has built an excellent police force, and I think that Yates's paper has an appreciable effect on the Germans. . . . All toward the same end."

Yates leaned forward. "I print your handouts faithfully, if that's what you mean."

"They're necessary," said Willoughby.

575

"The one on the *Panzer-General* came from you, too?" DeWitt asked dryly.

"General Farrish liked it very much."

"I know," said DeWitt. "He told me. Told me of your new Mayor, too. Good shot, I understand."

"Lämmlein," said Karen. "Lämmlein organized a Home for the Political Victims of Nazism here in Kremmen. That's where we found some of the men from Paula Camp. They call it the Lower Depths."

Willoughby concentrated on mashing his potato. He tried to think of something to stop this trend of conversation. "Lämmlein," he said. "Funny name. You know what it means? Little lamb!"

"Is he?" asked DeWitt.

"He's a Vice President of the Rintelen Works," said Yates. "Steel. Big stuff. Most of those characters were tied up with the Nazis from top to bottom. But apparently we're lucky. This one wasn't. He was never a member of the Nazi Party — he says."

"You don't have to sneer!" Willoughby said sharply. "We've checked. He's the best man for the job. We've tried practically everybody else. You see, Colonel, Yates's job is easy. He steps into a printing plant and starts his little paper. *We*'ve got to work with *people!*"

He wanted DeWitt to bear down on Yates; but the Colonel cut his roast beef into squares and said nothing.

Yates put aside his fork and knife. "Maximilian von Rintelen was one of Hitler's financiers. He made piles of dough on the tanks and the guns and the shells he furnished the German Army. Captain Troy, you were a line officer — do you believe in rewarding that kind of thing?"

"Leave Troy out of it!" ordered Willoughby. Once more, his tired, worried eyes looked to DeWitt for help. Then he turned on Yates. "Rintelen is dead! I thought we had made an agreement, Yates — I handle Military Government affairs, and you write about them — favorably, if you please!"

"That about outlines your job," said DeWitt.

"I know!" The bitter lines around Yates's lips deepened. "I impose my own censorship! . . . What I see in the Lower Depths I can't print, because it would be a disgrace to the Army. The story that I should print — what we're going to do with the Rintelen Works — I can't get, although that's what the people need to know. It's their livelihood! Are *we* going to run the Works? Will the remaining machinery be dismantled? Destroyed? Rebuilt? All of it? Or only a part? And who's going to own it? The Rintelen family? The Allies? The people?"

The waiter served dessert and coffee. Everybody fell silent. Then Willoughby said with a grating laugh, "You're one for the books, Yates!"

DeWitt put a cherry pit on his spoon. "Well, what *are* you going to do with the Rintelen Works?"

576

Willoughby changed his tone. "I'm glad you'll have the chance to see things for yourself, sir. Stick around for a couple of weeks and you'll find that we're worried about transportation and sewage disposal and rubble removal and where to get half a dozen new policemen and an engineer for the water works and some coal for electricity and roofing for the billets of the troops and — "

It was a long list, and Willoughby emphasized each count.

"Who'll own the Rintelen Works?" he went on, surer of himself than he had been at any time during the dinner. "The very question is out of our reach! We're faced with practical problems. Let somebody in Washington worry about policy. Who are we . . . ?"

Flushed with the conviction of his own words he looked around the table. DeWitt seemed to approve. Karen smiled, but he couldn't make out what kind of smile it was. Troy mumbled something. And Yates . . .

Yates said, "You used to talk differently, Colonel Willoughby. Once you even gave me your very concrete opinions on why the American people sent its armies across the ocean. . . ."

"Why?" said DeWitt.

Willoughby threw his napkin on the table. "Lieutenant Yates — I've suspected it for the longest time — now I know it. You hobnobbed with the Russians as far back as Verdun! Kavalov, or whatever his name was. You're a Communist. You're dangerous. You don't belong in this army — "

"Stop it, Willoughby!" DeWitt put down his cup. His brows were low and straight as a gray furrow. "We don't throw around recriminations like that. A man's entitled to his opinions, even in the Army. And if you don't like Yates's questions, that doesn't make him a Communist or anything like it."

Willoughby rose. "Sir, I am perfectly willing to talk over this matter with you, privately."

"I see nothing that needs any confidential discussion."

"All right." Willoughby nodded slowly. "I see how you feel. Then will you excuse me? I have an appointment."

"Sure! Toddle along! . . . No, don't bother. I'll take care of the check."

Willoughby hesitated, waiting for Troy and Karen to follow him. As they made no move to get up, he went off alone, straightening his shoulders as he wound his way between the tables.

After Willoughby was gone, Karen tried to make small talk. She did not quite succeed, and DeWitt ended the awkward session by asking Yates to come up to his room for a report on the paper.

Troy led Karen to the small bar and ordered French 75's — a new concoction born of the Army's requisitioning of large stocks of German cham-

577

pagne and cognac; the two, mixed, had a good kick. He ushered Karen to one of the little round tables and crammed his huge frame into the narrow chair next to hers. He twirled the stem of his glass. He was in a confusion of emotions, a whole prismatic spectrum of feelings that revolved slowly and blurred each single one; he searched for the one that he could begin on as a lead to the others, so that he could lay all of them, nicely ordered, before her and tell her: This is me and this is how I feel about you and what you mean to me — take it or leave it.

He saw her expectant face, the natural red of her fine full lips penetrating the worn-off layer of lipstick; her boyishly strong, stubborn nose; the velvet texture of the skin on her cheeks; the small, well-formed ear with its pink lobe, half-framed by short, self-willed curls. His heart was in his throat. He silently pleaded with her to help him get started; but she seemed perfectly content to sit with him without saying a word.

He was a dolt, he thought. How he had sat through the dinner without once opening his trap, letting Yates carry the ball for something which he, himself, somehow felt was right! He wasn't good at talk; the right answers occurred to him only long after they should have been given; and with Karen around, his tongue was tied for fear of blundering. He imagined himself putting Willoughby on the spot; that would have made it easy to speak to Karen about everything else. But he wasn't that kind of man. And the more he thought about it, the more he lost courage; and the few moments that were his to declare himself were slipping away.

He had finished his drink. He wasn't accustomed to drinking, never had much taste for it. Occasionally, before going into action, he used to help himself to a swig to get rid of the sagging feeling in his stomach.

The French 75 began to work. He felt heady, and although his heart moved back from his throat to where it belonged, it was pumping violently.

"Karen," he said huskily, "I don't know how long you're going to stay here. I'm awfully mixed up. I'm nobody important. But I've got to ask you this one thing. . . ."

His big fingers moved nervously.

"I hate to ask it. Do you know why? Because if I don't ask it, I won't get an answer. What do I want an answer for? Answers say Yes or No, and there's nothing more to it. The way it is, I can at least nurse along my hopes, and have some moments when I think I feel good. But the doubts are bigger than the hopes, and it's the doubts I can't stand. I have to get clear about it."

Karen had known that this moment would come. This solid man was easy to read through. He had all the qualities you would want in a man to whom you were to stick for the rest of your days. There had been times when she longed to be in his arms. And yet, now, she wanted to escape the finality of an answer.

She was glad that the bar was filling up. Various officers she knew were on the verge of coming over to Troy's table. She made her nods of greeting formal enough to keep them away; but she felt their effect on Troy. He closed up again.

"Waiter!" he called. "Two up!"

The German waiter rushed over nimbly.

Troy raised his glass and, with a forced laugh, said, "What's it going to be, Karen?"

She could not say, I love you. She could not even say, I'm very fond of you. With him, any such statement was commitment. And she could not say, I'm not sure. She was perfectly able to gauge her own feelings, and he knew that.

"I don't want to say Yes or No, now. I want to wait. Do you mind?"

He gulped down his second champagne cocktail. "Yes, I do mind."

She took his hand and held it. It was hot and damp. "Help me," she asked. "Why don't you?"

"I? Don't be silly. And don't try to put a pillow under my behind if I'm due for a fall. I guess I'll survive. Are you still in love with Bing?"

She let go of his hand.

"I'm sorry," he stammered. "I guess I don't know what I'm saying. It's Yates, isn't it? I've got eyes in my head. . . ."

"That's a sophomoric way of dealing with it. Why don't you take my word?"

"You haven't given me any."

"I said I wanted you to wait."

"Karen, I love you."

He closed his eyes as if he were pretending he wasn't there. He was pale and the muscles at his temples moved rapidly.

Some of the men at the bar were turning their heads toward them.

"Two up!" called Troy.

The waiter served them.

"What do you want me to do?" Troy asked, grabbing his third glass.

"Steady, now," she said softly. "Give me time." She finished her cocktail; it had a sharp, tangy taste.

Troy saw Yates. Yates had come in, gone directly to the bar and taken a stool. Troy could hear his conversation with an Air Force major who had been saying how lucky we were that the war had ended before the Germans could get enough of their jet jobs into the air.

"Yates!" Troy called. "Come over here!" He would precipitate something. Anything. Get things straight.

But Karen took the initiative. She smiled as Yates sat down, and said, "Nice going at the dinner table. You certainly earned yourself a medal or —"

"I should have myself crowned with a toilet seat," said Yates. "What do I achieve by telling off Willoughby? All right, it makes me feel easier. . . ." He shrugged.

"It made me feel wonderful!" said Karen.

Troy gave her a sidelong glance. So that was the kind of thing that made her feel wonderful! . . . "Talk! Talk!" he said suddenly. "But nothing's being done."

"You're being bitter," said Karen.

"All right, so I'm being bitter. I've got a right to be bitter. I made a lot of men die so I could liberate Paula Camp — and then what? These people are still in the Lower Depths. I've had to arrest some of them."

Karen asked, "What about the Rintelen estate?"

Troy flushed. "I suggested it to Willoughby. He said to give him time. Everybody wants me to give him time!"

"Willoughby doesn't believe in soaking the rich," Yates mentioned. "He told me the Army didn't come over to Europe to put the great unwashed in power."

"Well, we didn't," said Troy. "And I don't see what that has to do with it."

"*You* want to put the Kremmen unwashed in the Rintelen house — that's one way of soaking the rich," said Karen.

"Think it out, Troy!" challenged Yates. "Logically! First you give the people the estate; next thing you'll hand over the Rintelen Works to them."

"Maybe Willoughby is following policy," said Troy, depressed. "Waiter! Three up!"

The waiter served the French 75's. Troy drank his thirstily, without waiting for Karen or Yates, and waved for a refill.

He heard Yates lecture, "Policy, hell! In the first place, there isn't any; in the second, nobody's clear on it; in the third, who follows it, anyhow?"

"Policy!" said Troy. "Nuts!"

"Policy is what the man on the actual spot does. Maybe, up there, they have something in mind. Maybe it's good, maybe it's bad, maybe they don't know themselves. But by the time it reaches the man on the spot, it's so watered down that it makes no difference anyhow."

"What about Willoughby!" Troy said belligerently.

"Willoughby's the man on the spot. But we're around, too. You see what I mean?"

"I understand only as much as my men could understand." Suddenly, Troy lowered his head. "But they took me away from them. . . ."

"Steady! Steady!" said Karen.

"I've given him time, haven't I?"

"Whom?"

"Willoughby! He should have made up his God-damned mind! And I won't let him forget. I'm going to remind him, that weasel-brained, mealy-mouthed, too-big-for-his-own-pants . . . !"

He almost pushed over the small table getting out of his chair. " 'Scuse me!"

He strode out.

"What's he up to now?" Karen asked, anxiously.

"I have an idea." Yates frowned. "I hope he doesn't get himself into trouble. . . ."

"Run after him and see — " she begged.

Yates shook his head. "He'd just get mad. There are things a man has to settle for himself."

To Karen, the room seemed larger without Troy, empty. She lit a cigarette, but couldn't hide her concern.

"You're pretty keen about him, aren't you?" Yates said.

She felt his dark, serious eyes on her; just a trace of a quizzical smile on his lips.

"Yes," she admitted.

"I'm very happy for you." All Yates's warmth and sincerity were in his deep voice.

"Happy? I don't think anything will come of it."

"Why don't you drop the pretense and get together with him?" Yates said. "If you don't, I'll proposition you, myself — you're almost the only person here with whom I can feel at ease."

"I feel at ease with you, too."

Startled, he laughed. "That's the nicest way I've ever been turned down. You haven't turned Troy down, have you?"

"No . . ."

"Well?"

"I know too much about him. That's what makes me hold back. And he's the first man I've known who's been too reluctant, or self-disciplined, or conservative, or modest, to ask me in so many words to go to bed with him."

"Troy usually goes the whole way."

"Yes. But do *I* want to? Sometimes I think he's kind of lost — always swimming straight for shore, as he sees it. Suppose he doesn't hit land?"

"Well, help him, Karen! If you love him. . . ."

"I could easily lead him. It might even be fun — if he didn't notice what I was doing."

A shadow seemed to glide over her face, leaving some sadness on it.

581

"But maybe I've come to the point where I want to be led? I've been independent for such a long time. . . ."

"I understand." Yates saw her: Observant eyes, a little cynical, perhaps; a pen that scribbled down the thoughts of a great number of people and tailored them for an even greater number.

"I've picked my men almost as I've selected my stories — for what I could get out of them: Stimulation, emotion, chemistry. I've always taken, never given more than I had to, always kept for myself a part of me that was nobody's business."

"And Bing?" Yates asked gently.

Her eyes became moist. "That's all over and he's dead. It hurt."

"You see?"

"No, David Yates, I don't; and neither do you. I've got to have this little reserved corner. Call it what you like — emotional security — self-preservation — it's a fetish with me. The men I've known felt it. It kept them from becoming too serious. That was all right with me; just what I wanted."

"But it won't work with Troy. . . ."

Yates felt her hand on his. "I love him too much," she said. "And it just wouldn't be fair to take a man like that and hang on to your own reservations. But before I give those up, I want to be sure that he's the man to take their place."

Yates patted her hand. "I used to think like that. In the end, it makes you pretty lonely and miserable. When I come home, and if she's still as I remember her, I'll know something about loving my wife."

Karen was silent. She thought of the little girl in Paris who had come to her, searching for Yates.

After a while, Yates said, "During the war, it was different. But now I can close my eyes and see Ruth. Close your eyes. How do you see your man?"

"How? . . . Lots of ways — but most of all as a beaten man, taking his beating well — but accepting it, not fighting back. A woman's got the right to see her man as the God-damned hero he's supposed to be. I want him to fight back — "

"Open your eyes, Karen. What do you think Troy is doing now?"

"Willoughby?" she asked. Then she looked at Yates. He was grinning broadly and finishing up the French 75 in his glass.

Troy caught Willoughby just as he was leaving his room. Willoughby was wearing greens, garrison hat, and all his ribbons. His blouse bulged from the pistol he carried under his armpit. He had never fired it. He had never been close enough to where he would have had to fire it; but he felt safer carrying it around.

"Sir!" Troy was swaying slightly from the effect of his drinks and of the stairs which he had taken three at one step. "Sir, I want to ask you something."

Troy was too big to be brushed out of the doorway.

"Does it have to be now? I've got a date."

"I can see that," said Troy. He lounged against the doorpost and looked down at his stout superior, disliking everything about Willoughby. Troy didn't even own greens. During the fighting, he hadn't needed them; and now he would have felt foolish hiking to the quartermaster store and buying the finery.

"Ask your questions during office hours!" said Willoughby, still blocked by Troy's broad chest.

"Just a little bet I've made." Troy cocked his head ironically.

"You're drunk," said Willoughby. "All right, walk me down the stairs."

Troy about-faced and let Willoughby emerge from his room. Then he put his big arm around Willoughby's shoulder and hoarsely whispered to him, "What about the Rintelen estate? I wanted to stick all those guys from the concentration camps in there — remember, sir?"

"Yes, I remember." Willoughby was on his way to the estate. He should.

"When can I start moving them?"

"I will let you know in time."

"When?"

Willoughby freed himself from Troy's embrace. "Captain, I will not be pressured!"

"All I want is a clear answer," Troy pleaded drunkenly. "Are you requisitioning the property?"

"Who sent you?" Willoughby was outraged. Yates, again. Now that DeWitt was here, Yates figured he could go ahead with his little schemes of making the world a cushiony place for the underdog and of making life unpleasant for Willoughby. And they were using this poor sap as a front.

"Who *sent* me?" Troy's forehead was creased with the effort of thinking.

"That kind of stuff doesn't grow on your own dirt, Troy! Who put you up to it?"

Troy might have taken a simple refusal in his stride; but after the impasse with Karen, this slur was too much for him.

The stairs turned. He blocked Willoughby's way. "Colonel Willoughby — this grew on my dirt all right. It's my business. I liberated Paula Camp. I lost a lot of men doing it. And I want to know what I did it for — so that you and the General could have your pictures taken?"

Willoughby's face went white; even in the shadow of the stairway, the white showed frighteningly. He tried to shove Troy aside.

Troy didn't budge. "I just want an answer, and I want it straight. No

583

excuses, no dilly-dallying, no phony promises. We've been given too much of that stuff, and we've been handing out too much of it. Do I get the Rintelen estate, and when?"

"I'll have you out of MG tomorrow!" Willoughby's voice grated.

"Thank you, sir," Troy said evenly. "That's as good an answer as any."

He let Willoughby pass and followed him slowly. He saw Willoughby walk briskly across the lobby. Nothing makes a dent in him, thought Troy. Nothing.

Then he returned to the bar and sat down, heavily, in the same narrow chair next to Karen's.

"Waiter!" he called. "Three up!" His hand shook.

Karen and Yates saw how disturbed he was. Karen burned to question him, but waited.

He turned away from her. "I feel all right. Feel much better."

"What did you do?" asked Yates.

"I got myself fired. Blew my top. Thank you. It was a swell idea."

Yates felt let-down. He could talk talk talk. And here was a man who did something. And look at him.

"I guess I'll be out of my job tomorrow," Troy said and began to laugh tonelessly. "I don't give a damn. The wonderful thing in the Army is that they can't fire you; they've got to provide a spot for you. And the more you screw up, the less you have to work."

Karen's heart constricted. She had let him go on this errand, and in the shape he was in. And he had jumped into the melee and naturally had come out second-best. What had she wanted him to do? Prove that he could fight? He had proved it a hundred times. And who was she to want him to run his head against stone walls? A stupid bitch who didn't know what she had when she had it, too finicky to take the best her man could offer her because he didn't offer with it an insurance policy for her precious private corner.

"Don't worry!" Troy said. "I'll get this estate out of him if it's the last thing I do. When I was looking at his fat mug, it came to me — why I have to do it. Things have to add up, don't they? A victory is a glorious thing, something men died for — and what we've got isn't glorious. . . ."

Karen wished he would ask her now if she loved him. Now she would tell him.

But he was wrapped up in the new ideas he had found. She could see the labor of his mind on his broad face.

Yates was the only one considering the matter soberly and practically. "What are we going to do about it?" he asked.

Troy came awake to the present. "Do? Nothing! Let it ride!"

"I'd like to take it up with DeWitt. While he's here, we might as well get the Old Man's opinion."

"Oh God, no!" Troy was disgusted. "I've never gone to any brass to have them fix something for me, and I'm not going to start now. The whole thing isn't worth it."

Yates said sharply, "It isn't you, and it isn't your job. Can't you get that into your head? It's the Rintelen estate. It's whether Willoughby is right or I am, and Bing, and a lot of other fellows whose names I don't even know and who believed that they were fighting for something new. . . . If I can print in my paper next week that the Rintelen estate has been handed over to former concentration camp prisoners, it's going to spell something to the Germans — that we mean business with our democracy. The hell with your job."

Without waiting for an answer, Yates went to the house phone and called DeWitt's room. Returning, he said, "The Old Man's still up. Couldn't sleep, I suppose. He wants us to bring a bottle."

They got a bottle of cognac from the waiter and trooped upstairs. De-Witt, in a creased blue dressing gown, sat on the only chair in the dismal room. His eyes were red-rimmed; the straggly gray hair on his chest came through his open shirt.

"Sit on the bed," he invited.

Ceiling and walls had been cracked by the force of an air bomb; they had been patched up but not painted, and the welts of wet plaster looked like a skin disease. The window, half boarded up, permitted the damp night air to blow through.

"Good for my rheumatism," DeWitt joked. "Let's have the drinks."

By now, Troy's head was reeling. He leaned against the bedpost to steady himself and resolved to say nothing; he was afraid his heavy tongue would trap him. Karen felt equal to a fight; Yates was dead sober.

He gave the Colonel the facts. DeWitt listened quietly, now and then sipping his cognac, and smacking his lips.

He felt the expectation of the girl and the two officers as they turned to him, after Yates had finished. He said, "I'm afraid there's nothing I can do."

"You could see the General!" said Karen, more sharply than she had intended.

"With what, Miss Wallace? There's no law that the Army must evict industrialists' widows from their homes. The care of former concentration camp prisoners is strictly a matter for the German authorities. For nationals of Allied countries we could assume jurisdiction. But the people you're talking about are German citizens."

"Sir!" said Yates. "We have an obligation. When we pull out of here, finally, we want to leave behind a country minus the bastards who forced this war, their power smashed. A new kind of country. An American experiment."

"Who's experimenting?" asked DeWitt. "General Farrish?"

There was silence. Troy's head slumped forward, then jerked up again as, startled, he realized he had been dozing. Karen went to the basin and drew a glass of water; she forced it into Troy's hand.

"Don't let him drink it," said DeWitt. "I hear it's polluted. Willoughby's sewerage and Willoughby's water mains mingle too freely."

"Well," said Karen pointedly, "then you know the score."

DeWitt stood up and shuffled through the room in slippered feet. Finally, he turned to Karen. "What is the score? As a soldier, I've had to deal with thousands of men, and as individuals I've found most of them honest, fairly intelligent, co-operative. We even won the war. This country we conquered is our responsibility — granted. But it looks like we can't even take care of people who were beaten and starved for the things that brought us into the war. Or maybe they're not the same things, maybe it was something else. I don't know. The longer I'm in Germany, the less I understand."

Of his three listeners, only Yates conceived the extent of the man's quandary. You couldn't rush him. He wasn't ready. But Karen, Troy's immediate future uppermost in her mind, continued her demands.

Tiredly, DeWitt said, "Give me something to go on! What is it about this Rintelen estate that makes it such a problem? We've taken over many buildings we wanted; a signature is all that's needed. And I know Willoughby! I know he goes out of his way to do his men favors if he can afford them. He would be the first one to tell Troy, 'Take the estate! Set yourself up in it.' But he's not saying it. Why?"

It was the key question. And Yates saw that DeWitt was honestly wanting an answer, but neither he nor Karen could supply it. Troy was dozing off again.

Troy came acutely awake when Karen, discouraged, bade him and Yates a disgruntled good-night. They had come down from DeWitt's room, and Troy, his tongue thick, had said, "Why not make a night of it?"

"Thank you, no. I'll see you tomorrow."

He stared after Karen. "What a woman!" he grumbled. "Too good for me. Oh, damn it." He turned and found himself with Yates. "You still here?"

"Just one nightcap," said Yates. "I sleep badly these days."

"Let's get drunk."

"No."

"Why not?"

"Because it doesn't help."

"Sure does!"

"No," said Yates and took Troy by the arm and led him back to the bar.

586

They had another round of French 75's. The bar was almost deserted now, and the German waiter was intentionally slow.

"What a woman!" said Troy.

"Hell of a nice girl," agreed Yates. "Known her since Normandy."

"Since Normandy . . ." said Troy. "You sonofabitch."

"Why am I a sonofabitch?" Yates said dryly.

"Guy like me runs after her, his tongue hanging out. And I can't get first base. And you know why? Because you're a sonofabitch." He slapped Yates's thigh. "Been carrying on with her all that time? Of course, of course. You've got everything — brains, looks, gift of gab, everything. Me, I'm just a big lug." He flexed his muscles. "Feel that! Feel my arm! All brawn, no brain. No shenanigans. I just get it in the neck, from everybody."

Yates had to laugh, though he felt sorry for Troy. "She slapped my face once, you know?"

"Good for you, Bud. Got too fresh too soon? She isn't that kind of girl. With her, you've got to go slow, slow and easy. The way I do it. Only I don't even get to first base. Because all the bases are taken. There's a guy standing on every damned base, first, second, third, and one banging a home run over the plate. Always the same guy. You, Bud."

Yates didn't reply. At the moment, Troy wasn't capable of digesting any sensible answer. Yates wanted to leave. Sleeping was better than nursing drunks; but he didn't want to give the German waiter, the bartender, the bellboy, the satisfaction of carrying a drunken American to his bed. He would have to stick it out, wait until Troy had spilled the worry, the frustration, the bitterness that were in him.

Yates knew what would come after the self-pity. He was glad that Karen was gone. "Let's get going. You've had your nightcap. Waiter! Check!"

"I pay!"

"All right, you pay."

Troy pulled out a wad of the poison-colored paper that served as Occupation Marks. Yates counted the change and shoved it into Troy's hands. He got Troy to his feet and gingerly led him through the empty lobby to the stairs.

"What floor?"

"Third."

As they neared the second flight, Troy stopped. "Here's where I had the fight with Willoughby. Same identical spot. Told him I liberated that camp. That I lost my men doing it. And for what? So he and Farrish could get their faces into the papers. Oh my Lord God!"

He sat down on the stairs and buried his face in his hands.

Yates let him sit. Troy sat still, abandoning himself to his mourning.

After a while, he raised his face; his cheeks showed the traces of tears. "I guess I didn't behave any too well."

"So what."

"I'll be O.K. now. You don't have to come along."

"Let me help you to bed."

Troy, clinging to the railing, went ahead. Yates took the key from the hook on the doorpost and unlocked Troy's room. It was even less cheerful than DeWitt's. On the bare table stood a white-framed picture of Karen, carefully clipped from one of the newspapers in which her column appeared.

Troy threw himself on the bed. "Thanks, Bud," he said. And after a pause, "I was going to beat you up, you know — on the stairs, where I had the fight with Willoughby."

"Why didn't you?"

"I didn't feel like it, after all."

"It wouldn't have helped you, either."

"I suppose, not. I'm very tired. You can go now."

"Listen, Troy. Get this into your head. I'm out of the race."

"Out of the race. . . ." He repeated it, mechanically. He hadn't understood it.

"There's nothing between Karen and me. You've been chasing shadows. Once, in Normandy, I tried to have an affair with her. Mostly, I think, because it was the beginning of the invasion and because I was afraid. I thought I might as well grab her. Tomorrow, I thought, I could be dead and all the grabbing would be over. Or, perhaps, because she was the only woman around. It's all so long ago, I'm not sure."

"Nothing?" said Troy.

"Nothing."

"You aren't just rocking me to sleep?"

"No."

Troy turned over. His big body curled up. He sighed a little, like a baby that's been fed, then he belched; finally, he mumbled, "Good night."

"Good night."

Softly, Yates closed the door.

8

MARIANNE knelt at the foot end of the bed, its metal fluting dividing her body with its shadows. She smiled at Willoughby and said, "Are you finished, now? You must take me to the manor house."

"Not yet. In a little while."

"I must have sleep, Clarrie!" she pouted.

She had called him Clarrie ever since learning that his first name was Clarence. Willoughby gave her whatever pet names the mood of the hour brought to mind: My Little Bird, My Honey, My Rosebud, My Lamb, My Tigress. He even learned a few German endearments like *Liebling* or *Mädelchen;* he purred them, which made her laugh and say, "*Ach,* what funny man you are, Clarrie!"

"Funny?" he would ask.

She would pat his shoulder and make him roll off; she would look at him and arch her back and be convulsed with laughter.

"What's so funny?"

"*Ach,* you, Clarrie!"

He would go quietly and put on his trousers and sit on his chair and smoke a cigarette. Only his eyes would remain fixed on her hungrily, jealous and beaten at the same time.

At first, he had consoled himself: She's mine and I can do anything I like with her. Even the picture of the ice vat assumed a new reality, with himself as one of the men holding her down. But as she lay there, arching her back, and laughing, she wasn't his at all.

Then the thought: Drop her, get rid of her! had entered his mind, only to bring him the painful realization that he couldn't drop her, that he couldn't get rid of her, at least not until he had conquered her. She was chimerical; you had her in your arms, yes, God damn it, all of her, and you had nothing. She was a succubus, a witch, that taunted you and led you on, a constant promise of happiness never fulfilled — and there was no end to it.

"I must have sleep," Marianne repeated. "The Widow, she is such heavy work."

"Don't you like living at the Rintelen house?"

"Yes, oh yes!" she assured him hastily. "But it is late. . . ."

"All right, let me dress you."

"You're nice, Clarrie," she said, "so understanding."

He grunted.

"My shoes!" Imperiously, she stretched her foot, her toes flexed.

His knees hurt him. The thin, worn rug of the room — even if his was the best room in the Grand Hotel — hardly softened the cold concrete floor.

He buckled the ankle strap, caressing the soft flesh of her instep. She withdrew her foot, stepped back, and he was left kneeling.

"Well?" she picked up her bag. "We still must drive back to the house."

"I'm coming." He rose heavily. The enchantment was over, the rare hour that he allowed himself for his personal happiness and diversion. Sometimes, when he looked at all the other men enjoying the pasha's existence brought to them by victory, and compared it with his own troubled day, he felt the curse of this drive of his. He was tied to his work and his plans and to the obstacles that piled themselves up before him; and wherever he moved, whatever he did, he was ringed in by the same circle.

You thought that, with this girl, you could break it — hell, no. Now he would take her back to the manor house of the Rintelens, the same house, the same property which Troy had demanded from him earlier in the evening. Willoughby was filled with a restless anger against himself. First, his blow-up in front of DeWitt, then the empty threat against Troy. The way to deal with Troy and the crowd hiding behind the man, was, of course, *not* to fire him. That would only lead to more talk, more questions; these rumors traveled up and down the echelons, were blown up, distorted, received damaging significance; an army, sitting on its collective ass, had nothing else to do but gab, gab, gab. No, he wouldn't transfer Troy. He would keep him warm, wrapped up in cotton, until his own hands were free, until the deal between Lämmlein and Prince Yasha was sealed, signed, and delivered. After that, neither the Rintelen estate, nor Troy, nor even Farrish, mattered.

But suppose the pressure on him was increased? Suppose Troy's foolhardy rush against him was only the opener of the campaign? DeWitt was capable of going directly to Farrish. . . . Farrish would laugh those damn fool crusaders out of his headquarters if they came to him with complaints that the Military Governor wasn't handing out estates.

"You think so much," said Marianne, still waiting. "Always you think. It is not good for you. It makes your face funny. We go?"

"Yes, my *Liebling*."

Pettinger slumped in his chair and stared at the book in his hand. Then he felt the fleshy warmth nozzling at the back of his neck. Pamela's breasts. With a curse, he snapped the book closed and threw it on the floor.

Pamela stepped in front of him. "Your nerves — again? They're particularly bad, it seems, on the evenings when that slut goes to Willoughby. . . ."

"Is that so?" he said sarcastically.

All evening he had been fighting the fact that Marianne was out paying reparations to the enemy.

He heard the door slam after Pamela. A sudden suspicion seized him. Where was she going? He went after her, catching up with her in the park, at the bower from which Hitler once had gazed over the lawns, the flower-beds, and the fringes of forest that now stood darkly against the moonlit sky. The five-fingered leaves of the wild vine swayed in the soft breeze. For once, the smell of decay from Kremmen was blotted out by the fragrance of the night.

Pamela moved over on the bench so that he might sit down. The right hour and the right place, he thought, and the wrong woman. Even in the dark of the bower, he saw how ugly and shoddy and played-out she was; it whipped his hankering for the slim, dark-haired Marianne.

In a minute she'll paw me, he thought, and he began to speak hastily of the man who had died so timely a death in the Berlin Chancellery's air-raid shelter, and who — how long ago? — had sat here where Pettinger now was sitting. All his annoyance, at himself, at Hitler who had chosen the dramatic but easy way out, at Pamela, at life, was in his tone.

Pamela withdrew her moist, heavy hand from his. "He, too, had a flair for getting himself invited — "

"If you think I like staying here!" Pettinger parried her dig. "All my — vitality! I'm losing it by dribs and drabs. . . ."

"Well, it's certainly not me who's sapping it!"

Angrily, he tore at a tendril. It was tough and clung to the vine, and he gave it up. "Do you think your constant scenes, your ridiculous jealousy, make it more pleasant for me?"

Hate in her voice, she said, "You like it all right here — as long as *she's* around. . . ."

He made a move to go.

"Stay here!" she said. "I want to talk to you. I rarely get the chance! . . . I've got eyes in my head! Why don't you understand that I know you're in this vile mood because, right now, *she's* being laid by Willoughby?"

True, he thought. He wasn't being any too careful; Pamela, too, had feelings, ideas, desires, damn her.

"I've been watching you," she warned, "you and that strumpet. I've had about enough of it."

Pettinger looked at her, at the yellow glint in her eyes, and shrugged contemptuously and thought: When will she get accustomed to it? I'm due for another tour with her. She's got to have her dose of consolation.

Her voice was tortured. "Please, Erich — just don't let me catch you!"

"What would you do?" he asked, tiredly.

"I could tell the Americans: He isn't Dehn. He isn't my husband. He's a stranger. Ask Lämmlein who he is. Lämmlein knows. . . . They'd arrest you."

It was a pitiful attempt. "They probably would," he admitted, sure that she was bluffing. "They would arrest me and you would lose me for all time. If you chop down the tree, it doesn't bear fruit."

"You've poisoned the fruit!" she cried.

"Don't be absurd, Pamela!" he said and added a half-hearted, "I love you!" and forced himself to kiss her.

The wind had shifted. The heavy odor of Kremmen was noticeable

591

again. Pamela accepted the kiss and thought: Why doesn't he believe me? It's the same shock over and over — like drops of water hitting on end the same spot. How long can a person stand it?

She heard a car turn into the driveway. She felt Pettinger tense.

She clutched his arm. "No, you don't!" she said. "You'll stay here, with me. . . ."

Abramovici led Kellermann and Professor Seckendorff into Yates's cubbyhole office. He was deliberately avoiding physical contact with the two, but especially with Kellermann, who still wore what remained of his striped garb. "You won't need me now, Lieutenant?" he inquired and, following Yates's "No," retreated hastily from the germ-ridden company.

Yates shoved aside the SHAEF ukase he was editing, rose, and warmly shook hands with both men. "Let me look at you, Professor! Well, you still could put some meat on the old bones — they didn't feed you any too well at the hospital, did they? Sit down! Make yourselves comfortable!"

The Professor sat down gingerly, as if he were afraid of hurting the secondhand civilian suit Dr. Gross had given him. Kellermann remained standing.

Yates saw how loosely the suit hung on the old man's body, how cynical the lines in Kellermann's face had become. "How long are you out of the hospital, Professor?" he said with an attempt at cheerfulness. "Have you found a place to live? Or does Kellermann want you to stay at the Lower Depths, too? . . ."

"We don't know, yet," Kellermann said with a touch of sarcasm. "This is the Professor's first day out. I picked him up at the hospital. We came directly to you."

"I'm glad you did that!" Yates had known that Kellermann would come, sometime. The man's gesture of refusing help, in the Lower Depths, had been too grand to last in Willoughby's Kremmen. "You should have dropped by much sooner, Herr Kellermann."

The Professor was clearing his throat.

Yates wanted to make it easy for him. "You know, Professor Seckendorff, I may be able to take care of you! The main thing is that you're well again. As your old Romans put it: *Mens Sana in Corpore Sano!* The mind! The will to live!"

"And insulin," Seckendorff managed to interject.

"Insulin — of course, you need that. I shall speak to some of our Army doctors. But don't worry about anything else. There must be people who still know your academic reputation. Perhaps we can get you a job doing some research, or teaching — or would you like to do an article for my little Kremmen sheet? And as for a place to live, I'll send the Corporal along with you when you go room-hunting. That ought to do it. . . ."

592

Yates turned to Kellermann and said pointedly, "And if you're ready for a job, we can arrange that, too — "

"We have come to make a report," said Kellermann.

The wind went out of Yates's sails. He was unable to do anything about the conditions that forced the two men from Paula Camp to come begging to him, but he had wanted to give them some encouragement. And now, they, too, came to him with a *report*. Reports, denunciations, accusations, were thrown at him all day long, as they were at any American connected with Military Government. Most of these reports were negligible and vicious. The Germans seemed to find a peculiar joy in denouncing one another, in doing what they thought were favors to the authorities. Only Yates didn't like being that kind of authority.

"It's one of my jobs to listen to reports," he said, not bothering to hide his disappointment.

Kellermann began, "There's a girl, Marianne Seckendorff — "

"Marianne Seckendorff? She was here to see me. You mean at the hospital they didn't allow her to visit the Professor — " Yates turned to the old man. "I gave your niece a note to Dr. Gross. I made it clear to him that she was your only relative."

"She is not my niece," said Seckendorff.

"She's not — " Yates looked at the Professor's lined, hurt face and then, beyond him, at the shabby walls of the cubbyhole. A flake of beauty, he thought, somewhat tarnished — but what do you want in this country?

"She isn't his niece," Kellermann repeated; "she isn't related to him at all. I met her at the Lower Depths. She said she handed out leaflets in Munich. She spoke of the Professor's children as if they had been her closest friends. Then she left the Lower Depths and I heard she got herself some job with your Military Government. . . . I thought seeing her might do the Professor some good — so I told him about her. Well — " He stopped, and with a nod at the old man — "You see, she cashed in on his children. . . ."

"I don't even know where they are buried," Seckendorff said tonelessly. "Somewhere, little mounds, nameless. The number painted on the wooden board washing out in the rain and fading in the sun."

"Whether her name is really Seckendorff, we don't know," Kellermann went on. "She isn't the Professor's niece, so it stands to reason that she had nothing to do with the Munich students' revolt." He smiled vindictively. "We thought you might be interested, sir."

I told them at MG to check up! Yates thought. Why hadn't they? . . . But they must have.

"That's a grave charge you're making. *Herr Professor*. Deliberate misinformation to the American occupation authorities is no joke. You're absolutely sure — she couldn't be a distant relative . . . ?"

"Sir, I wish there lived a young one of my blood. I'd take her to my heart, go to the end of the world to find her, make her take the place of the children I lost." The old man's arms opened in an embrace. The empty space between them was painfully expressive.

Yates felt cheap. At the same time, he grew hot under the collar. If Willoughby discovered that one! . . . "What do you want me to do about it?" he broke out. "Announce it in the newspaper?"

Kellermann threw in, "I told the Professor to be big about it! . . . Let the girl have her fun. There's lots of other people whose accounts should be settled before hers."

The dig landed. Yates moved uncomfortably in his chair. He was possibly the first American on whom Marianne had tried her stunt, and he had believed most of it. Her name was probably genuine; he had seen her release papers from Buchenwald — but that was the only point in his favor. If he tried to stop the girl now from whatever she was doing, he would end up as a publicly confessed fool, and Willoughby would certainly make the best use of it.

Nobody was forcing him to do anything. He could forget about the Professor and Kellermann — broken men released from concentration camp. It was a small matter, of no consequence. A small matter, like Thorpe coming to him, back in Normandy. A small matter, the memory of two young people, executed long ago, buried nameless in nameless graves.

He reached for his telephone and dialed Loomis.

"Hello, Captain!" he said after hearing Loomis's nasal twang. "This is Yates, at the paper."

Loomis didn't seem any too pleased.

"Remember that girl I sent you, about a month ago — Marianne Seckendorff?"

He believed he heard Loomis gasp.

"Was she ever checked through by Counter-Intelligence?"

"How do I know?" Loomis came back belligerently. "I put through a request. What more do you want me to do?"

"Any results?"

"Not that I know. Why should they tell me?"

"O.K.! O.K.! . . . Do you know where I can get hold of her?"

For some reason, Loomis became enraged. He began to curse, ending up with, "Go ask Willoughby!"

For a moment, Yates was flabbergasted. Then he said, "Why Willoughby? What's she got to do with him?"

He heard Loomis laugh at the other end of the wire. The laughter was followed by a sneering, "Wouldn't you like to know?" and by something sung in an outrageous falsetto. But the words were clear: "My Heart Belongs to Daddy!"

Softly, Yates replaced the receiver. For a while he sat silent, lost in thought. What woke him was Kellermann's light cough. "Lieutenant, do you still need us?"

"Yes," said Yates with sudden resolution, "I do." Again, he dialed, and when he had established his connection, he said into the phone: "Troy? — Yates. . . . Yes, I'm dandy. Say, I want you to do some fast checking. . . . Top Secret, just between you and me. . . . Dame named Marianne Seckendorff. . . . Supposed to have been gone over by CIC. . . . Find out where she keeps herself and what she means to our mutual friend W. . . . I'll be over at your place in twenty minutes. Can you get going right away? . . . Yes? Wonderful. . . . Roger. Out."

Yates rubbed his hands. He gave instructions to Abramovici to have Seckendorff and Kellermann fed. Then he rushed upstairs and, blinking in the bright daylight, swung himself into his jeep and was off.

Troy's eyes followed Yates. Yates was angrily pacing through the room, his usually composed face working, his hair disheveled from the haste with which he had torn off his cap, his hand sweeping the air as he talked. Troy got a quiet pleasure out of the exasperation of the man who, since they had known one another, had always found the right word at the right time.

Yates wheeled around to face Troy. The lines that led from his sharp nose to the corners of his mouth were deep with disgust. "And I was the one who sent her over to you people!"

"Why?"

"Because I had no job for her — and also because I didn't like her."

Troy reached for a folder which was marked, in big black letters: MARIANNE SECKENDORFF — *Investigation*. He gave Yates a broad grin and said, "You don't want me to enter that, do you?"

"Don't try to be funny," Yates said darkly. "We're a prize bunch of boobies, all of us — and I don't see why you're so damned placid about it."

"How was I to know that your face was going to be red, too?" Troy asked innocently.

"You were supposed to know everything!" Yates came back. "Why wasn't she checked through CIC? She was on your pay roll, wasn't she?"

Troy raised his big hands, expressively. "Brother, I get my requests through channels. I get them from Willoughby. I was never ordered to look into the matter. This is the Army! So don't get excited."

"But you yourself said — "

Troy wiped his broad forehead. "Listen, Yates. You called me half an hour ago." His big hand came down on the folder. "And I started this thing right away. I've been running around ever since. And now we

595

have something to go on. We know from the Civilian Motor Pool that your Marianne — "

"Don't call her my Marianne!"

"All right. We know that Marianne Seckendorff lives out at the Rintelen estate. We know that Willoughby has placed her there. We know that almost every night he either goes out there himself or sends out a driver to pick her up. And we know that she's been making fools out of us — most of all, out of Willoughby. What do you suggest now?"

"You're the Public Safety Officer," Yates said with relish. "You decide."

Troy said, "I'd like to pick her up at that manor house, bring her down here, and let you take her through the paces."

"And what is that going to accomplish?" Yates sat down on the bench at the far wall, designed for German complainants. "She isn't working for MG any more, is she? And since when is political activity against the Nazis standard requirement for the post of Willoughby's bed warmer?"

"It's negligence, to say the least," Troy argued. "Why did he stop the CIC check?"

"Because she's no longer on the pay roll. Because Counter-Intelligence has no jurisdiction over his private *Fräuleins*. That's what he'll say if anyone asks him. *If*."

"We might create a big enough stink for Farrish to hear of it. And Farrish is kind of particular about what goes on in his bailiwick."

Yates got up from his bench. He came close to Troy's desk and looked at the Captain from squinting eyes.

"I don't like your approach. It's petty. It's the way Willoughby would work it if he had somebody on his list and caught the guy in a spot."

"You make me sick!" Troy's face was set. "I've been kicked out of every job where I could feel clean. I'm hanging on to this one by Willoughby's grace. How am I going to defend myself — like a gentleman?"

Yates stopped cold. "Sorry," he said.

"Stop feeling sorry. Let's do something. We can't let the thing roll. It's too good, whatever is in it. Let's ask DeWitt."

Somewhat astonished at Troy's suggestion, Yates admitted, "I've been thinking of that."

"And I'm not running back to Poppa either!" announced Troy, who had caught Yates's tone. "I just think he's a good man!"

"I agree," said Yates. Marianne Seckendorff, the Rintelen estate, Kremmen, it was a setup; wherever you probed, something was wrong. Not completely wrong, mind you, nothing illegal, nothing for which blame could be fixed. Everything was smooth enough on the outside. But perhaps Marianne Seckendorff's little white lie was the fissure that could be spaded to send the bricks tumbling.

Sticking his fist directly into Willoughby's hornet's nest of personal relationships, plans, games, and combinations meant open war. And at some point, he and Troy might run up against Farrish. He needed some backing; at least some moral backing.

Over cocktails, before dinner, he and Troy talked to DeWitt and gave him the whole picture. DeWitt asked many questions. His most important question was: "Do you two boys know what you're letting yourselves in for?"

Yates answered for both of them, "Yes."

The crow's-feet at DeWitt's eyes deepened with his smile. "Then let's have a showdown," he said.

9

IT WAS a red-letter day for Willoughby.

The General, for once, had not bothered him. At the Offices of Military Government, everything had gone as it should, which enabled Willoughby to take off at five and be ready to receive Lämmlein in his room at the Grand Hotel. And Marianne was due to spend the night with him.

The hours had bent themselves to his purposes, one matter promptly following the other — private business after the official, and pleasure after business. On such rare days, all a man needed to do was a little arranging in advance: send out one of MG's civilian drivers to pick up the girl; let Lämmlein know it was high time to come through on his promises.

Lämmlein arrived on the dot. The Mayor was carrying a sepia morocco leather briefcase, stamped with Willoughby's initials in gold.

"The briefcase," said Lämmlein, "is a token of the appreciation the people of Kremmen feel for their Military Governor. The contents, sir, are in the nature of reparations. Frau von Rintelen, the family, and myself are happy to restore to their rightful owner the purloined shares of the Rintelen works, together with all papers pertaining to them. Do you care to go through them?"

"Of course I do!" said Willoughby jovially. "It's a beautiful bag you gave me, but I'd still like to have a look at the cat!"

For a good while, the two men were busy examining documents, counting stiff sheets of special bond paper, jotting down figures, adding, and checking. The slanting rays of the sun cast their last glow over Willoughby's sweating jowls and gave a certain splendor even to Lämmlein's unassuming gray. Then dusk fell. Willoughby heaved a deep sigh, gathered the papers, locked the briefcase, and stowed it away among his long johns in his pack.

Lämmlein rose, empty-handed. "We have fulfilled our obligations," he said pompously, and yet not quite certainly.

"O.K., Lämmlein my boy! You've done well by everybody!"

"I am still Mayor only *pro tem*. . . ."

Willoughby chuckled good-naturedly. "I'll make it definite. I hereby appoint you *Bürgermeister* of Kremmen until there are elections. I expect you know enough about democracy to take care of yourself at the ballot box? . . ."

"Yes, *Herr Oberstleutnant*." Lämmlein gave no sign of going. "I'm honored to serve as long as I'm of help to you and to General Farrish. . . ."

Sticky as a buzz-fly, thought Willoughby. "Well?" He didn't conceal his impatience.

"We'd like something more permanent, sir, something tangible!"

"You want it in writing?"

Lämmlein ceased being the submissive German official. "I am ready to go ahead with production at the Works. I need full power from you. We've given you a lot, sir. The rest belongs to us. Agreed?"

"Tomorrow!" said Willoughby. "Tomorrow everything will be taken care of." And as Lämmlein still hesitated, he took him firmly by the shoulder and ushered him to the door.

The slight beginning of a dispute failed to have effect on Willoughby's good mood. His mind worked overtime as he shaved and dressed for the evening with Marianne. His mind was busy planning his trip to Paris, to Yasha. He would have to reshuffle his appointments. He would have to groom Loomis to take his place during his absence. He would have to get Farrish's permission to take off. None of this presented much of an obstacle.

Willoughby saw prosperity around the corner. He counted the months he would have to stay on in Germany, after his return from Paris. Six months, at most. Then back to CBR & W. The war, after all, had been a good investment. Some people went in for paintings and diamonds, others collected cameras, or sold watches to the Russians, or soap and chocolate and cigarettes to the Germans. Small fry, breaking the law for petty booty. Laws were not made to be broken, laws were made to stay within. He had always maintained that war was like peace; except that in war the stakes were bigger, the opportunities greater, and the decisions you were called upon to make far graver. But aside from that — everything was connections and thinking three moves ahead and using the brains God gave you, in Indiana or in the Ruhr.

And the evening with Marianne lay ahead of him. He'd have dinner for two served in the room.

In the end, Pamela caught him red-handed.

She was on her way to Marianne's room to say that a phone message had come from Willoughby's office; a civilian driver from Military Government would fetch her at seven o'clock. The door was unlocked. Pamela knocked, but didn't wait long and entered. She saw that Marianne had just had time to throw the bedcover over herself and Pettinger.

Pamela, pale and with trembling voice, managed to convey Willoughby's message; then she went out and waited in front of the door, leaning against the wall, trying to quiet her blood that seemed to surge through her in short, irregular waves.

Eventually, Pettinger came out, the healthy tint of satisfaction on his thin cheeks, his shirt open, his jacket and tie thrown casually over his arm.

"Oh, you, Pamela!" he said.

"Yes, I, Pamela," she answered.

And then he laughed, as men do in such a moment — small doses of embarrassment, triumph, and apology in his laugh, but most of it false, false, false.

As if by agreement, they both lowered their voices; neither of them cared to have Marianne listen in.

Pettinger, between his shallow excuses and alibis, kept thinking: How far will she dare to go? And how am I going to keep her from losing her head and giving me away?

"Stop snapping your suspenders!" she hissed.

Guiltily, he dropped his hand. The first thing was to force her into a cooling-off period; afterwards, one would see to what degree she would calm down and could be appeased.

Pamela was trying to curb her own hysterics. She wasn't going to spend herself in words that didn't hurt him. She could see he was afraid that she would betray him.

He followed after her when she walked off, having had her say. For the rest of the afternoon, he didn't let her out of his sight. Repeatedly, he made attempts at conciliation, sometimes in a humorous vein, sometimes sentimentally, once falling back on the old Nazi theory that it was the duty of a superior man to perpetuate the race regardless of outdated ethics.

"Don't tell me you planned to present Willoughby with a bastard," Pamela said to that.

He didn't even accompany Marianne to the car, as he usually did. After dinner, he sat in the hall, glumly turning over the fact that Willoughby knew every person in the house and that Pamela couldn't be made to disappear without his hearing of it.

The Widow, vaguely wondering what had happened but not sufficiently aroused to inquire, kept the radio playing. Pamela pretended to read.

"Where are you going?" Pettinger jumped up as Pamela left her chair.

"To my room, if I may!" she said sarcastically. "I wish to lie down. Do you object?"

"I'm coming with you."

She chose to misunderstand him. "Not tonight," she smiled, and gave him a slight pat on the cheek. "You reek of her."

She locked her door in his face. Over the noise of the radio that came from the hall, Pettinger heard the familiar sounds of her preparation for bed — the water running into the basin, the shoes falling to the floor, the clattering of her toilet articles on her dressing table. He began to feel easier and rejoined the Widow, offering to play her a game of Sixty-Six, which was simple and unexciting and therefore preferred by the old woman. But his ear was strained for any untoward steps inside or outside the house.

Pamela, shoes in hand, went through her bathroom into the empty guest room connecting with it, down the back stairs, through the pantry and the kitchen, and left by the rear exit of the manor house. The car was in the garage; but she was afraid of using it — Pettinger would hear the grating of the heavy doors and the starting of the motor. She ran the full length of the macadam road. The trees on both sides of the road seemed to close in on her. Sometimes she stopped to hear whether she was being pursued. She was afraid he would kill her. It was easy here. And who was to say he did it, with bands of foreigners and soldiers roaming the countryside? He would kill her without asking questions. He would never know that he need have no fear of her — she would not betray *him*. If you chop down the tree, it doesn't bear fruit. But she was going to get rid of the girl. And once the filthy little tramp was moved out of the manor house, back to the dirt and the sewers from where she had come, he would be chained, chained and tied with the bittersweet chains of the house, and the loneliness, and his needs.

Breathlessly, Pamela reached the main highway to Kremmen and caught the streetcar at the end of the line. She stayed on the platform where it was darker. The car was rattling into town. Few people rode it, that near to curfew.

"Where is Military Government?" Pamela asked the conductress.

"*Die Militär-Regierung?*" The conductress, in her worn-out uniform, looked suspiciously at the hefty, sweating woman with her hair and dress awry. "I'll tell you where to get out." And she did, obviously glad to be rid of the passenger.

From the car stop to the Headquarters of Military Government Pamela had to walk several blocks. It was totally dark. She stumbled over rubble still cluttering the side streets, past the broken slabs of concrete, past the bent and rusty girders that were part of her father's Works and her own inheritance.

600

Then she saw the great white sign; the helmeted guard at the gate stepped forward.

"What do you want, *Fräulein?*" The guard was bored and mistook her searching steps for the oblique approach that ended with the exchange of a pack of cigarettes for less lasting pleasures.

"*Herr Oberstleutnant* Willoughby?" she asked. "Where is Lieutenant Colonel Willoughby?"

"Dunno," said the guard. "Left long ago."

"I must find him."

"Tomorrow!"

"Where is he?"

"Aw, *kommen Sie her, Fräulein!*" said the soldier.

She came closer. He was broad-shouldered, round-faced, and he had a gold tooth that reflected faintly the dim light of the nearest streetlamp.

"Tell me where is *Herr Oberstleutnant?*" She smiled at him, promisingly.

Somebody rapped at the door, loudly, insistently. Willoughby jumped up.

"Damn it! What's the matter with that waiter? The moment you're kind to those Krauts, they get insolent. . . ." He opened the door. "Troy! What the hell — "

He recognized Yates behind Troy.

"What do you two want? I'm busy."

"Marianne Seckendorff in this room, sir?" asked Troy.

Yates said, "She's in there all right. We know it from the desk. We'd like to see her, sir."

"What for?"

"To arrest her, sir."

"What!" Willoughby's face showed a choleric mixture of rage and bewilderment.

"Will you please let us get in, sir?"

Troy, looking easily over Willoughby's shoulder, saw Marianne moving through the room. Willoughby continued blocking the door; Troy and Yates were making no move toward retreat. Somebody had to give.

"Come in!" Willoughby said between his teeth. "And you'd better make it a good story. . . ."

Yates sauntered in and began to study Marianne.

Willoughby drew himself up in indignation. "What's it all about?" he snapped. "Which of you two cooked it up?"

Marianne smiled, first at Troy, then at Yates. "Good evening," she said sweetly, "how do you do?"

601

"We're doing fine," said Yates. Then he turned to Willoughby. "Sorry to intrude on your privacy, sir. We'll just take the young lady along, and there'll be no further disturbance."

"I asked you some questions, Lieutenant!"

"We've been ordered to pick up Fräulein Seckendorff," said Yates. "It's an investigation."

"There are only two men who give orders in Kremmen, General Farrish and myself. And I'm ordering you to get out!"

Quietly, Yates said, "We're arresting Miss Seckendorff on verbal orders from Colonel DeWitt."

Willoughby lost some of his front. What were they planning to do? Smear his name? Ridiculous. They hadn't a leg to stand on. It was a trumped-up affair.

"Your Colonel DeWitt is a visitor in this sector. He's not entitled to issue orders!"

Yates smiled to himself. He suddenly thought of Abramovici and how the little man could have thrown the rulebook at Willoughby. Still without raising his voice, Yates said, "I can't argue with you, sir. Colonel DeWitt's orders are good enough for me any day. If you wish to take up the matter of channels with him, I'm sure the Colonel will be glad to discuss it."

Willoughby did one of his fast switches. His face settled in an expression of friendly good-fellowship. He sat down, pushed aside the dishes on the table, pulled out a cigarette, knocked it deliberately against the nail of his thumb until the tobacco settled, and lit it.

"Now tell me, Yates," he said, "what's behind this? Why harp on the girl? What's she done?"

Behind his slow, genial words, his thoughts followed one another rapidly. These guys weren't after the girl, they were after him. They were trying to pin something on him. But what? The Rintelen deal was absolutely aboveboard; besides, only the family and Lämmlein knew of it. But Marianne might know — why on earth did he have to put her out there! So suppose she knew! So what! As Chief of Military Government, it was his duty to restore properties to their rightful owners. . . .

"What's the charge? What has she done?" Willoughby asked again.

"We don't know what she has done," said Yates. "We'd like to find out."

"So you have no charges against her!" Willoughby became a tinge more severe.

"She's a German. We don't need any charges. Suspicion is enough."

Willoughby knew that. And he knew, too, that Yates must have something more to go on than just DeWitt's backing and a hunch. He stamped out his cigarette.

"All right, Lieutenant Yates, I guess two can play at the game just as well as one. *I* am arresting Marianne Seckendorff. She's in my custody. I think that will satisfy Colonel DeWitt, won't it?"

Outgunned, thought Yates, outmaneuvered, outwitted. For a minute, he was able to say nothing, feeling only the disagreeable sensation of Willoughby's ironic eyes on him. All that was left to him and to Troy, whose feet he heard shuffling the floor in embarrassment, was to beat a hasty retreat.

Willoughby nodded and smiled, "Two can play the game, as I said, Lieutenant. . . ."

And then Yates smiled, too. "Colonel DeWitt will appreciate your cooperation, sir. It makes it so much easier for us." His voice changed suddenly. He spoke German. *"Fräulein Seckendorff! Anziehen! Kommen Sie mit!"*

"What! What are you saying?"

"Sir, I told the young lady to put on her hat and come along with us. I have the car downstairs. We'll take her to my office. I've prepared everything for her interrogation there. You're going with us, aren't you, sir? After all, technically she's in *your* custody. . . ."

"Now wait a moment!"

"We have to start work on the case tonight, sir. There are some witnesses whom I can't hold over. So, with your permission — *Kommen Sie, Marianne!*"

Marianne obeyed his sharp commands. The fact that Yates had come — the first American to whom she had given her story — indicated that all she had built up, all she had earned by the shrewd work of her mind and body, was hanging by a thread.

She had been watching every move of Willoughby's. He had been fighting for her, and fighting he wasn't ridiculous at all, he wasn't Clarrie, funny and with sad, hungry eyes — and then he'd somehow lost the fight and gone limp.

Now, with a worried frown, he was bustling after Yates and the other officer, the Captain. Yates was treating her with courtesy, opening doors for her and motioning her to go ahead. She saw him stop at the desk and heard him tell the clerk, "We'll be at the newspaper plant, in case Colonel DeWitt asks for us."

Marianne wondered vaguely why they were going to the newspaper. Then, unnerved, she realized that it was there that her career had begun and she asked herself if it was going to end there, too. Her panic let up during the ride. Comforted by Clarrie's hand on hers, she had time to make up her mind. She had done no wrong, had committed no crime, and the little white lie about her participation in the Munich revolt had harmed nobody. Every German who could, attributed to himself a past of struggle against the Nazis. It was fashionable, it was useful — and she *had* been in jail, she *had* been in a concentration camp, she *had* suffered. Marianne felt quite righteous about it.

She was not taken to the gloomy star chamber she had expected, but to Yates's small office. Marianne began to relax. Yates's opening questions were friendly and pleasant; he asked her name — Marianne Seckendorff; her age — twenty-two; her place of birth — Heidelberg. All of this was safe territory; and Willoughby's encouraging nods diminished her anxiety except for the persistent prickle of the one, salient point: What did Yates really want?

He went back through the years, checked the date of her release from Buchenwald, of her transfer from the Munich city jail to the concentration camp, of her original arrest. She saw Willoughby's mounting boredom; she noticed that Troy was doodling on a pad of paper, sketching little mannikins with oblong faces, oblong noses, and oblong ears, tearing off sheet after sheet, crumpling it, and throwing it into the wastebasket.

"Can you tell me," asked Yates, "what was in those leaflets that you helped to distribute?"

"It was so long ago . . ." She smiled.

"But considering the difficulties involved, the risks you took, you must have wanted to know what the leaflets said?"

He translated the question for Willoughby. Willoughby nodded. Willoughby saw nothing dangerous in the question. She was a nice kid, and she hadn't liked the Nazis, and she'd done something about it; he respected that.

"It was against the Government," she said to Yates. That was a safe enough answer; if people had been killed for the writing and distributing of the leaflet, it must have been very much against the Government.

"Yes," said Yates, with a thin smile, "against the Government. But I'd like you to tell me a bit more about it."

"It's been so long," she repeated, "so long ago. And all the terrible things I've had to go through since then . . . I simply knew that anything Hans and Clara were putting into their leaflets would be the right thing. I read it, of course, but not very thoroughly."

"Tell me about your family," Yates changed his approach.

"What do you want to know?" She was fairly sure now where Yates was leading. They wanted to nail her white lie. If Clarrie were not in the room, she might even admit to it, tell Yates that she exaggerated a little because she was so hard up and needed clothes and food and all the things that the Americans had in such plenty. But with Clarrie around, she would have to stick to her story. She didn't want to hurt him; besides, he was a man who would believe nothing she said, once he had proof that she had lied to him. And there *were* things she wanted to keep from him,

604

things that didn't concern him — the wonderful, hard, exerting, secret hours with Pamela's husband.

"What do I want to know?" said Yates. "Everything. Your father, what was his business?"

Her father had been a tinsmith, going to work every morning in blue overalls, his luncheon carefully wrapped in newspaper. But that wasn't enough for the brother of a Professor. He had to be something better. "He was a roofing contractor," she said.

"How was he related to Professor Seckendorff?"

"He was his brother, naturally." She smiled.

"Older? Younger?"

"The younger brother."

"Marianne — it so happens Professor Seckendorff had no brothers."

Marianne's eyes, crossing slightly, focused on the wall behind Yates. Willoughby inquired hastily what Yates had said.

Yates told him.

Willoughby turned to her, "Marianne — is that true?"

"No."

"You see!" said Willoughby. "What do you intend to prove?"

Troy had stopped doodling. He was taking notes.

"If the Professor had no brother, Marianne, you can't be his niece."

"But I am!" she said. Her voice was at the breaking point. In another minute, she would burst into tears. She fished a handkerchief out of her pocketbook. "Somebody's been lying to you about me! People are so envious. They don't want you to have anything!"

"What? What?" said Willoughby. His heart turned to her.

"Maybe they'll say I've never been in concentration camp? Maybe they'll say I haven't been tortured just because I have no scars? Yes, I have no blemish on my body, they were very careful when they put me into the ice vat. . . . Oh, you Americans, what do you know . . . !"

"What is she saying? For Chris'sake, Yates!"

"She's dishing up that old story of the ice vat," said Yates.

Willoughby rose angrily. "At all other times, Yates, you're a sucker for people who pretend to be victims of the Nazis. Suddenly, because I have chosen to help this particular girl, you get skeptical."

Marianne broke into a wail. She employed what English she knew for Willoughby's benefit. "The Gestapo — they ask me — the same way — the same way . . ."

"This is disgusting!" said Willoughby. "You're supposed to be an officer and a gentleman."

"She's been taking all of us for a ride, including you, Colonel. And I'm going to show it to you! . . . You said it, sir — disgusting!"

"You'd better!"

"Stop sniffling, Marianne — it's bad for your complexion. Now tell me, when did you see your uncle last?"

She blew her nose; she really had been crying — out of fear, out of self-pity, out of anger at having been driven so hard. She powdered her nose.

"Come on! Come on! When was it?"

"In 1942, in Munich. Poor uncle, he was always so worried about Hans and Clara . . ."

Yates pressed a button under his desk. Somewhere outside, a buzzer went off.

Then the old man came in. He blinked, uncertain of what was wanted of him, confused by the people crowding the small room. He saw the back of the girl's head, the fine shadow on her nape; he saw Willoughby, the questioning eyes above their pouches.

"Who's he?" Willoughby was asking.

Marianne turned around. The old man looked nice. She saw how thin he was, and that he needed food and care. His hair was straggly, his thick lips a little bluish, his large teeth showed gaps. She looked at Yates. She became conscious of his expression. He was watching her. Then it struck her — the old man, Yates's waiting. . . .

She jumped up. The old man was in her arms. He was being kissed — he reeked of bad soap and dust and disinfectant. But she kissed him. And she cried, "*Ach,* I'm so happy! So happy! Uncle, my darling!" The rest of her greeting was so fast that even Yates could not follow it.

She was overacting. Yates sensed the false note, but the false note was not enough to use as proof.

What difference did it make that the old man wrenched himself free, pushed her away, and protested, "I'm no uncle of yours! *Herr Leutnant* Yates — what kind of show is this?"

She had weathered the crisis, with even smoother sailing ahead. All she had to do was to carry through her role; and she did it well. Having been pushed away so rudely, her joy of welcome stunted, she complained softly and pitied him — "the poor man, what he must have suffered. . . . He doesn't remember me, not even me. . . ."

Professor Seckendorff guffawed loudly. "I'm perfectly normal, *Fräulein.* I have an excellent memory. I'm run down and old, but not that old."

"Uncle — don't you remember Munich? Don't you remember Hans and Clara?"

The mention of his murdered children by the woman who had appropriated their name, their fate, their memory, goaded the Professor into an outcry. "I won't have you use them! Doesn't anyone have a spark of honor? Herr Yates, how long do you wish to continue this farce?"

Willoughby, despite the exchange of fast-flying German, surmised what had taken place. He was no longer so sure that there weren't loopholes in Marianne's story, but he was sure that Yates's scheme had failed; and he felt a kind of professional pride in the girl for carrying the thing off so splendidly despite Yates's line-up of tricks. She had defended not only herself, but also her Clarrie; she had saved him considerable embarrassment; she had paid back in kind for the humiliation Yates and Troy had piled on her and on him. And he was going to stick to her, whether she was this uncle's niece or not.

"Yates," he said, "don't you think you'd better throw in the towel? This is Professor Seckendorff, isn't it? Well, professors are notorious for their lapses of memory — you're one yourself, you ought to know. And the years he spent in Paula Camp didn't improve him. I understand — it's very sad."

"Marianne," Yates said doggedly, "you're sure that you recognize this man as your uncle?"

"How long do you want to drag it out, Yates?" Willoughby intervened. "Maybe it isn't the Professor's memory, maybe it's something else. You're enough of a psychologist to know what grief and pain and the sense of loss can do to a man. Maybe he wants to monopolize all the suffering for himself and his children. . . ."

The idea was feasible, and Willoughby had clothed it in humane terms. Yates had based everything on the old man's word. He had accepted it at its face value because it agreed with his suspicions, with his purpose, with his resentment against arbitrary power and against Willoughby and all that Willoughby stood for. And Troy had followed his lead. Now, Yates saw the Professor with disillusionment and doubt. He saw a human wreck that had survived by odd chance, starved physically, starved mentally, wrapped up in his own bitterness, kept alive by dreams, illusions, and injections.

That was what he had built on. It was symptomatic, perhaps, of everything he tried to do. For whom was he working? A ruined old man who lived with the dead in the past?

The Professor was turning from one to the other of the men. He even pleaded with Willoughby, "Sir — my children — they died a clean death — their memory, protect their memory. . . ."

"What's he saying?" asked Willoughby. "Why don't you keep these beggars out of it?"

Outside Yates's office, Abramovici, guarding its privacy, had a visitor.

"No!" he said. "*Fräulein,* I can't let you see Colonel Willoughby. He's in conference, a staff conference. In the American Army, we have three classifications, and since the war, four — Restricted, Confidential, Secret, and Top Secret. This is Top Secret. Nothing you may want to tell Colonel Willoughby can possibly have the importance of Top Secret."

"But will he see me afterwards?"

"I don't know. I work for Lieutenant Yates. I can tell you what he is going to do, unless it happens to be classified information."

"Then, please, let me talk to your Lieutenant Yates!"

"He's in the conference, too!"

"Please, *Herr Soldat.* . . ."

Abramovici's pale eyes examined her. She saw his look, and she thought she knew what was in his mind. She came forward and sat on the edge of Abramovici's desk, the flesh of her thighs pressing against her skirt.

"Please . . ."

"The desks in this office," he said, too vaguely to make his point quite clear, "are Government property." He picked up his ruler and jabbed it timidly into her flesh. She laughed.

But she wasn't amused. She had come a long way — over the macadam road, by the rattling streetcar, through rubbled streets, to Military Government; from there, finally, to the Grand Hotel, where the desk clerk had said that Colonel Willoughby was at the newspaper plant. The stagnant water, ankle-deep, in the shell crater in front of the plant, had soaked her shoes and stockings. Wet mud clung to her knees. Her feet hurt; and inside her breast she carried a nagging, burning pain, as if her heart were giving off the acidity common to the stomach after too rich a meal. It had been too rich a meal, in a sense — a dish of dust and dirt with a sauce of hate.

"Tell your Lieutenant it's Pamela Rintelen," she urged. "He knows the name."

"The American Army," said Abramovici, "is not impressed by names. One German means just as little as the other."

"*Jawohl,*" Pamela said acidly.

Then she promised Abramovici money. She promised herself. Abramovici said, "My dear *Fräulein,* this country is being administered without fear or favor. It is a matter of principle. Once a rule is broken, it stops being a rule. I am busy. I've wasted enough time with you, which, properly, belongs to the U.S. Army. Go. Leave. Out. *Raus!*"

Her eyes implored him. But she dared say no more. She followed the imperious waving of his hand, and left.

All was quiet around Abramovici. He began to work. Carefully, he cut the text out of the galley proofs in preparation for pasting up a dummy for the paper's next edition. His scissors worked slower and slower. He frowned. He *was* curious about his late visitor. People were always coming to him with the most urgent air, acting as if the welfare of the American Army depended on their word, their information, their reports. Afterwards it turned out to be nothing, a piddling matter that didn't even require the setting in motion of the tiniest channel.

He noticed that he had cut the wrong way. His deft hands went through the pile of scraps, long ones and short ones. He had made a mess of it, he'd have to do it over again. Angrily, he got up. He'd have to go to the composing room and order the foreman to pull him another set of proofs.

He opened the door. Pamela stood in front of him.

"It's after curfew," he said.

It had been after curfew when she arrived.

"After curfew . . ." he repeated.

"I'm not going to leave, *Herr Soldat,* until I've spoken to Lieutenant Yates or Colonel Willoughby."

"All right, *Fräulein,* come back in!" Abramovici brushed the cut-outs from his desk into the wastebasket. "The basis of Military Intelligence is patience and judgment. Tell me what you have on your mind." His pompousness made everything he said sound official.

"It's about Marianne Seckendorff," she began. "She is not what she pretends to be."

"We know that," he interrupted her. "It is doubtful if you can make a substantial contribution to the facts already in our possession."

The little soldier's firm assertion upset Pamela. "Maybe you don't know everything?" she pleaded.

"Do you wish to make a statement to me, *Fräulein,* or don't you?" Abramovici asked resignedly.

"I do!"

She unfolded her story, studiously avoiding the mention of the other guest in the manor house. Abramovici was taking short-hand notes, now and then glancing at her out of his watery, indistinct eyes. The more she told, the less sure he was that he should hold her in the anteroom. Military Intelligence was patience and judgment. He had displayed his patience. But what about his judgment?

"So, she never was in any ice vat!" said Pamela.

Abramovici put aside his pencil. "Wait here for me!" His voice was strained. "I'll call Lieutenant Yates."

Abramovici opened the door to Yates's office and beckoned urgently. Yates came out. Abramovici saw the vexation and discouragement in Yates's face. Apparently, things weren't going for Yates as they should. Abramovici, who had expected to be called down for the interruption, immediately swelled with importance.

"Lieutenant, I've got Pamela Rintelen here, and I've got a statement that I've pulled out of her!"

He started to read. He sensed Yates's growing excitement, and himself began to tingle with it. By the time he had finished, his cheeks glowing, Abramovici was convinced that by his shrewd work on Pamela he had saved the situation.

Yates reined in his emotions. Coolly, he assayed Pamela. "Would you repeat the whole story? In front of Fräulein Seckendorff?"

Pamela straightened. She was a big woman, and she appeared Wagnerian now, the empire builder's child. She was going to punish the intruder, all the intruders, in this one — the Americans, the man who had usurped her husband's place, and the girl, Marianne. This was her hour, and she was ready for it.

"Would I?" she said. "With pleasure!"

Yates led her into the inner office. Abramovici slipped in after them; he was her discoverer, he wanted to see her perform.

"This is Pamela Rintelen," said Yates.

For one wild moment, Willoughby's jaw dropped. In this single second, everything had changed for him. Pamela knew of the Rintelen deal — was Yates on to that, too? . . . Before he could pick himself up, Yates was driving ahead.

"She has come to give us some additional information pertaining to the case at hand." He turned to Pamela. "Will you tell us all you know? You may speak German, Corporal Abramovici here will translate."

Pamela showed no reaction to Willoughby. She looked at Marianne. Marianne tried to stare back but was unable to make it — the righteousness, the triumph, the cruelty in Pamela's eyes were too much. And she was terrified.

"Fräulein Seckendorff," said Pamela, "was brought to our home by Colonel Willoughby, as a house companion for poor Mother. As if we needed one. She was forced on us. There was something peculiar about her; that was plain to see. I've known people who worked for my father, foreign workers, and they never were the same after two weeks in a camp. *Ach Gott!* That life doesn't leave you sleek and well-groomed and beautiful! But the Colonel told us she had been in the Munich revolt, and in concentration camp, and in an ice vat, all sorts of things, and he believed them all. And neither Mother nor I could contradict him, because we were Germans and we'd been beaten."

"Clarrie!" cried Marianne, "stop her!"

"Go on," said Yates, "nobody's going to stop you."

"But one can't live in the same house with people and expect all one's secrets to hold. Fräulein Seckendorff talked. She even bragged how she had fooled you Americans. She was in no Munich revolt, she never saw a leaflet in her life. She was in jail, and she was in a concentration camp — but there were common, ordinary criminals in those places, too. She can tell you why she was locked up. Ask her! But then she saw that with a political past, she'd have easy riding with you Americans. So she gave herself one, and she took you in, and she had a wonderful time with her new clothes and with her new men. Let her have all that. Let her. . . . But not in our home, not in the house that my father built, not in a German home!"

Marianne's world had burst.

She had managed to fence off the old man, but now, the array against her had grown too solid. She stood alone. The faces around her were alien faces, everybody an enemy. She looked down at her feet and the floor; the floor was far off and her feet were part of something that didn't belong to her. She saw her feet as they had been in the Lower Depths, cracked toenails, dirty, shoeless. You were at the bottom of the ladder, you had nothing, and they wouldn't let you climb up. They had everything. Look at Pamela, meaty and rich! Look at these Americans, well-fed and well-clothed and secure. Even the old Professor had his dead children; they had attended the University, and they hadn't appreciated what they had and had gone out to spoil it for themselves with their stupid leaflets. And because the old man belonged to those who had, he was against her, too.

Try to climb up! Try to become somebody! The moment you put your hands on the ladder's first rung, they stepped on you and beat your fingers until they were bloody and broken and you had to let go.

She listened to the dry voice of the little Corporal translating. Even he was fat. Foreign nasal sounds. They were settling her fate in their own, foreign language.

They were against her, so she was against them. She was against all of them, except perhaps Clarrie, who had been kind and had closed his eyes to what he didn't want to see.

But above all she wanted to destroy the man who had betrayed her, who had loved her only this afternoon, loved her with his hard hands and his hard kisses, who had drawn her secrets from her and had laughed at her and laughingly spilled them to Pamela — to the woman who had the house and the clothes and the food and everything for which you had to give the blood of your life.

"Fräulein Seckendorff," Yates said softly, "have you anything to say?"

He thought she would try to deny Pamela's story. It would take him fifteen minutes, a half hour at most, to break her — cross-examining, alternately using the Professor and Pamela to debunk her defenses.

But Marianne said, "It's all true. I was arrested in Munich because I picked somebody's pocket. I'm not related to Professor Seckendorff. It so happens I have the same name; there are many Seckendorffs in Germany. I read the story of the Munich revolt in your newspaper. I thought it would help me to get a job. I heard the story of the ice vat in Buchenwald. I was sent there after I finished my term in jail. What more do you want to know?"

611

"That's all," said Yates.

He was warm and a little flushed, and was asking himself: What now? Where do we go from here?

Willoughby, who had guessed from Marianne's tone that she had made a confession, excitedly demanded an exact translation from Abramovici.

Abramovici said, "A man who has so many duties must apportion his time, sir. Let me transcribe my notes. Then I'll give you a translation."

"For crying out loud, get on the ball!" said Willoughby.

Yates said, "He's doing what he can, sir."

Marianne reached a conclusion. She was going to take the dagger Pamela plunged into her, and stick it right back, and twist it. If she was to be outcast, Pamela was not going to enjoy the fruits of her victory.

"I haven't finished yet," said Marianne.

"What?" said Yates. "Hold it, Abramovici — get this down. All right, come on, Marianne, make a clean sweep of it."

Marianne said, "You think you have it all, now, and that I'm done for. Well, maybe I am! I was cheap, and I tried to get out of it cheaply. Perhaps you Americans want only to go after the little people. Seems like you do — leaving the Rintelens with what they have! Everybody knows they were Nazis."

Yates decided that the girl was letting off steam against Pamela and the Rintelens. And from her viewpoint, she was right — why should she be hooked and scaled and not the bigger fish? But he didn't want her confession weakened by personal accusations.

"No recriminations, please, Marianne — that won't help you any. Besides, the Rintelens were not Party members. Unfortunately."

"What about that fine son-in-law? What's he doing all day alone in his room, and nobody allowed to go in? What about this Major Dehn?"

Abramovici broke off in the middle of a shorthand flourish.

"Major Dehn!" said Yates. "At the manor house of the estate?"

"Pamela's husband!" Marianne insisted on pronouncing the title her lover had given himself, with scornful satisfaction. "Or perhaps he isn't. He certainly didn't behave that way to me. . . ."

So that had been Dehn's connection with the Rintelens, Yates thought. He had just enough time to shove a chair behind Pamela.

She sat down weakly. What had she done? What *had* she done! In delivering the other woman to judgment, she had also delivered her own man!

Yates was hammering away at Pamela. "Your husband, Major Dehn, is dead!"

"What is this?" asked Willoughby. "What's going on here? What're you saying?"

Nobody paid any attention to him.

Pamela's flaccid face was graying. Her hands went to her temples, she began to gasp and sob.

"Water!" said Yates.

Abramovici ran and returned with a glass full of water. Yates splashed it sharply against Pamela's face, saw it run down her cheeks, her shoulders, the top of her blouse.

"Major Dehn surrendered after we crossed the Rhine. He committed suicide. I saw his body myself."

"A sensitive man," commented Abramovici, "too sensitive for his own good."

"Pamela Rintelen Dehn!" Yates demanded, "who's the man at your house posing as your husband?"

"I don't know," Pamela said miserably.

"What do you mean — you don't know!" For the first time this night, Yates raised his voice. "You live with the man, eat with him, you sleep with him — and you don't know?" He switched to English. "Colonel Willoughby — you've been out at the Rintelen house! Can you give me a description of the man they call Major Dehn?"

Hoarsely, Willoughby said, "What about Major Dehn?"

"He is not Major Dehn! The genuine article was buried in Luxemburg. Have you any idea, sir, who the man might really be?"

Willoughby felt himself go cold all over. "He must be Dehn! He's an invalid!" he sputtered.

Yates pounded, "What does the man look like?"

"Tall, smooth, bony face — "

He was interrupted by Pamela. "I swear I don't know who he is. He came in one day and said he would stay. He looked ill then, I believe he was ill. Lämmlein said we should let him stay."

"Does Lämmlein know him?"

"I think so. . . ."

Lämmlein's name, suddenly injected, drove Willoughby to frenzy. "God damn all of you!" he bellowed. "Why doesn't anyone tell me what's going on here? Abramovici! Translate!" But he didn't wait for Abramovici to leaf back through his pages of notes. He continued to shout, "I tell you I've nothing to do with this!" Then he became conscious of Marianne as the source of his predicament. "I laid the girl, so what! She's double-crossed me, she's double-crossed everybody!"

Marianne sidled up to Willoughby. He pushed her back rudely. "Don't you come to me, now. *Fort! Weg!*" He used some of the little German she had taught him.

Her eyes narrowed. He, too, was abandoning her. His cheeks that he had made her caress hung down disgustingly over his jawbones, the pouches under his eyes made him look like the vicious, fat, impotent, demanding man he was. She had settled with Pamela and Pamela's husband; she might as well close the account.

"*Fort! Weg!*" she mimicked. "I know you wish I'd never come into your life. But when you wanted me, it was *Liebling* this and *Mädelchen* that!"

"Abramovici! Yates! What's she saying?"

Abramovici was taking notes as fast as he could. And Yates was in no mood to interrupt the flow of Marianne's rage.

"Fine people that jump on a girl for trying to get a bed to sleep in and clothes to cover her body! But I know too much about you, Clarrie, *mein Liebling — ich weiss zu viel!*"

Willoughby raised his hand. He was going to strike her.

"Uh-uh!" said Yates. "An officer and a gentleman!"

"The 10 per cent you and Loomis are getting out of every business in Kremmen! I heard you! I heard every word you two said in the Club Matador! *Herr Leutnant*" — she turned to Yates, and he saw the tears in her eyes — "I am nothing, a girl alone, and everybody ganging up on me. . . ."

"It's all right, Marianne — *gut, gut,*" said Yates, "we'll take care of you. . . . Abramovici, you've taken down everything?"

"Yes, sir!" said Abramovici. "A GI typewriter, if kept in good condition, will easily produce six copies."

"Six copies," said Yates, "one of them for Colonel Willoughby. . . . Captain Troy, we'll have to hold the two women overnight — but don't put them in the same cell. I suppose that's all right with you, Colonel? You no longer want Fräulein Seckendorff in your custody?"

"You're a fool, Yates." Willoughby trembled as he offered him a cigarette. "You go out of your way to collect enemies. . . ."

Yates accepted the cigarette.

As the office was being cleared, the Professor touched Yates's elbow. "*Herr Leutnant* — the memory of my children — "

"Oh, yes," said Yates, "Professor Seckendorff. . . . It will be taken care of." He put his arm around the old man's shoulders.

"Thank you," said Seckendorff. "From my heart."

10

THE CRISIS had come. It required careful analysis, a cool head, and the immediate mobilization of all his resources. Willoughby was equal to it.

His outrage against Yates, and the icy despondency he had felt when the investigation turned from Marianne to Pamela to himself, were momentary anxieties. These he quieted before his car had covered much of the distance between the newspaper plant and the Grand Hotel. His mind began to sift the facts that had come pounding in on him in that single evening. He paid grudging respect to the long-range planning that must have gone into Yates's achievement, and listed the strikes against himself:

He had befriended a girl who turned out to be a disreputable interloper. But she had fooled everybody. Of course, he should have had her checked through Counter-Intelligence; they had a point there. He would say the check became unnecessary because the girl gave up her job with MG.

He had accepted at face value the identity of the man using the name of Pamela's dead husband at the Rintelen estate. Why should he have questioned it? The Rintelens were respectable people. Willoughby scoffed. He must get hold of Troy and order him to arrest the unknown at the manor house before Yates could get the jump on him. The arrest would have to be handled with tact and dispatch so that the whole matter would be kept from Farrish. If the man should turn out to be a potentially dangerous character, it would sit badly with the General. Maybe one could say that Marianne had been placed in the manor house to keep an eye on what was going on there — it happened to be the truth, too! That the bitch would go to bed with the man posing as Major Dehn was unforeseeable. Too much trust in the Krauts, on all sides. He would clamp down on the whole nest in the manor house; he had his hands free now that Lämmlein had delivered Yasha's shares of the Rintelen Works.

Lämmlein! Lämmlein was involved, too. Here was the real rub. A man looked like a bank clerk, harmless, officious — went out hunting with the General and let him have the buck. . . . But how could you know what went on inside his head? Pamela said the Mayor could give the real identity of the man at the manor house. . . . Must have been in cahoots with him all along. God damn these Krauts, none of them are any good. And that wasn't all Lämmlein knew. The Mayor was in on the deal with the Rintelen shares and the deal with the 10 per cent tax on all business in Kremmen. The lousy 10 per cent, Willoughby thought, which he had to divvy with Loomis at that, might cost him plenty. It only went to show that you can't meddle with small stuff if you want to be in the Big League.

What anger Willoughby permitted himself, he turned against Loomis; Loomis had pulled him into that 10 per cent rook. Then the anger subsided, and Willoughby asked himself against what and whom, in the final analysis, he had to take measures.

By the time his car reached the Grand Hotel, Willoughby had ready a rough of his plan of action.

He routed Loomis out of bed.

Loomis, his face as crumpled as his pajamas, took some time to come fully awake. Dimly, through the haze of his sleepiness, he perceived that Willoughby was in some kind of difficulty.

"What do you come to me for?" he said with heavy tongue. "First you take my girl, then you mooch in on my business — you've got no friends, nobody. I don't like you. Lemme sleep."

Willoughby shook him, pulled him up.

"Get dressed! And fast!"

"Why?"

"Don't ask dumb questions. I'm in trouble — maybe. But so are you!"

"I'm in no trouble. What's the matter?"

"They know about the 10 per cent deal."

This jerked Loomis into pained wakefulness. He ran about trying to find his shorts; his scrawny legs, their sparse hair bristling, were an added grotesquery.

"Here!" Willoughby picked the shorts up from the floor and threw them to him. "You're a messy slob. Always been one. Here's your shirt. Want me to dress you, too?"

"What'll we do? Who knows about it? Who found out?"

The corners of Willoughby's mouth were screwed in contempt. "Who found out! You gave it away yourself! Talked about it in public, in a public bar, in front of Marianne, didn't you?"

"You started it! You mentioned it first!"

"I don't give a continental who started it. You! I! She came out with it, anyhow. Yates knows it. Troy knows it."

Loomis sat down on his bed, his fly partially open, his shirt unbuttoned. He stared at Willoughby, and through Willoughby, and repeated over and again, "What'll we do? What'll we do?"

"If you can manage to pull yourself together, you get into a car and drive over to Lämmlein's home. I don't care if he's in his pajamas, just bring him here — that's one thing you can do. Troy and Yates have only Marianne's word to go by. That dame turned out to be some pippin! You, of course, believed her — the dumb story of the ice vat. Ridiculous! That she was in the Munich revolt — girl like that! In a Munich beer cellar, maybe! Well, they caught her in her own swill of lies, and she got icky — and here we are."

"What'll we do?"

"I told you! Get Lämmlein! Lämmlein knew of your 10 per cent deal all along. He's got to keep himself and his Chamber of Commerce quiet. I'll hold him responsible. If we go, he goes; that's all there is to it."

"Yes," nodded Loomis, "yes, yes. If you think that's the right thing to do."

"The right thing! The *only* thing!" Willoughby saw no reason for telling Loomis that there were a number of other items about which he wanted Lämmlein kept quiet. Loomis could hardly be trusted with what he already knew. God, the people with whom you had to work!

Willoughby took Loomis's field jacket from the hook and hung it over the Captain's shoulders. "We've only got tonight to straighten out everything. I'll be waiting for you in my room."

He shoved Loomis out of the door, switched off the light, and led him down the corridor. Loomis stumbled down the stairs, he was awake but dazed. Willoughby, gazing after him, shook his worried head. He should never have brought Loomis into Military Government — not into his Detachment, anyhow. Loyalty! Friendship! Perhaps pity. Never mix your emotions with your duties. It always ends up with your having to foot the bill.

Loomis was feeling his way through the dark, dank streets. A slight mist had settled. He cursed; he wiped his windshield, stepped on accelerator and brakes alternately, trying to make the best time and to avoid the sudden, blocked-off shellholes. The roads improved somewhat as he approached the suburbs, but they were darker, too; coal was short, and Lämmlein was saving electricity at night by permitting one street light per block, at most.

Finally, he reached the salmon-pink, undamaged, well-kept villa that was Lämmlein's home. He did not bother to drive up to the curb. He jumped out of the car, ran along the square-cropped mulberry hedge to the big, solid door of the house, searched for, found, and pushed the bell button. He heard no answering steps or voice. He saw no light go on. He was sweating. He isn't home, he thought, the bastard isn't home. What'll we do? What'll we do?

He pulled out his pistol and knocked its butt against the wood panel of the door. The knocking resounded through the night, a hollow drumming, more fury than purpose. Now the lights came up, in Lämmlein's house and in the neighboring houses.

"*Ja, was ist denn? Ja! Ja!*" an anxious woman's voice from the top floor.

"Open up! Where's Mayor Lämmlein?"

"*Ja! Ja!*"

Steps behind the door. The door opened, still on the chain.

"American *Militär!* said Loomis. "Open up! Lämmlein!"

The woman, long, thin, bony, her angular frame ill-concealed in a rich, orange, fringed negligee, took the chain off the door, tremblingly.

"*Was ist denn?*"

Loomis pushed her aside. "Where's Lämmlein?"

She pointed upstairs. Loomis rushed up the stairs, the pistol still in his hand. On the gallery of the top floor, framed in the doorway to his bedroom, enshrouded in a wide, white nightshirt, stood *Bürgermeister* Lämmlein.

"Ah, Captain Loomis!" he said, obviously relieved. "You frightened us.

My poor wife. The knocking was familiar, you know — that's how the Gestapo used to come, at night, always at night. . . ."

"You've got to come along immediately. Colonel Willoughby — "

"Nothing's happened to the Colonel? Come into my room, please. It's cold out here. I'm very sensitive to sudden draft, Captain. It's the bad food, never enough, low caloric value, you know. . . ."

Loomis followed the Mayor into his bedroom. Lämmlein was trying to find his robe in the closet. "*Ach,*" he said, "my wife — she puts my things in order. Then I can never find them. Well, here are the slippers, at least." He opened the small, marble-topped night table.

Loomis watched him put on the slippers, pick up the blue tufted quilt from the bed and wrap himself in it. Lämmlein's slowness drove him quietly crazy.

"I told you Colonel Willoughby's waiting for you, didn't I?"

"But what happened? What happened? Things can't be in such desperate state that we can't wait till I get dressed. . . ."

He was too steeped in recent German history to leave his house at night voluntarily without knowing for what reason.

"What happened!" said Loomis. "Everything's been betrayed. There's an investigation, and you're in it. So are we all. How long will it take you to get ready? God-damned Krauts, so God-damned slow — slow — slow!"

He paced through the room, from the flower-curtained windows to the white door, a friendly, restful room that made him all the more restless.

"*Ach Gott!*" said Lämmlein, "that is terrible."

"Yes, terrible, certainly!" said Loomis. Lämmlein, lethargic, punctilious, was climbing into his long underwear. Loomis wanted to get back to Willoughby; Willoughby was his only crutch. "Why does it take you so long to get dressed!"

Why did it? Lämmlein was mislaying his clothes; his socks of yesterday had been thrown into the laundry, and where were his clean ones? Lämmlein was delaying. He was feverishly trying to shake off Loomis. Ever since Loomis had blubbered his *Everything's been betrayed,* Lämmlein had been busy reducing the momentous announcement to terms that had meaning to him. What could have been betrayed that might injure him? In anything he had done he had been careful to stay within the letter of the many laws and ukases of Military Government and of that part of the German penal code which had been permitted to remain in force. Where he had trespassed, he had seen to it that it was the occupants who forced him to trespass — whether it was the handing over of the Rintelen shares, or the payment of a rakeoff on business. He was just a little man, obeying orders. The only weak point was Pettinger, even though, there too, he had acted only as a little man — but a little man obeying the command of the competing and, for the time being, submerged power. Any investigation of Willoughby and Loomis and himself was bound to lead, at some point, to the Rintelen estate and the Rintelen Works — the one factor likely to implicate him must be obliterated. Now. This night.

Lämmlein searched for and ultimately found his high laced boots. He had not worn them for a long time. The laces were threadbare. He bent down to lace his shoes, and, from his oblique position, observed Loomis. He tore the shoelace. He began to tie a knot. The knot slipped apart. Now, he had to rethread the lace through the eyelets.

"Sonofabitch! God damn you to hell!" Loomis had reached the end of his patience.

"Please?" asked Lämmlein.

"Why aren't you ready?"

"You should have phoned me," said Lämmlein. "I would have been ready when you came. . . ."

Yes, why hadn't he phoned? Why hadn't Willoughby thought of it? You can't think of everything. Or maybe Willoughby was afraid of using the phone.

"You have a car, haven't you?" said Loomis.

"Yes. Don't you remember? You were kind enough — "

"All right. I'll go ahead to the Grand. You take your car and come to the hotel as soon as you've finished dressing."

"Yes, sir," said Lämmlein. "I'll be there presently."

Loomis stormed out.

Lämmlein kicked off his boots and pulled a sensible pair of shoes out of his closet. He listened to Loomis's steps, downstairs through the hall, then, outside, on the gravel. He heard the motor of Loomis's car start up, and the car take off into the night.

He smiled for the fraction of a moment. Then he threw himself into his clothes, called to his rawboned wife that he'd probably be back in a couple of hours, ran to the garage, and backed out the large black limousine, his sleek, speedy official car that used to belong to the *Gauleiter*.

Yates was folding and unfolding the copy of Abramovici's transcript. Despite the hurry in which it had been done, it was as neat as anything Abramovici had ever turned out on the typewriter.

DeWitt reached for it. "Let me have it back, please, before it goes to pieces. What are you so nervous about?"

"It's never happened to me," said Yates, "never before tonight. I see the puzzle, the fragments begin to make sense, some are still missing, but the picture begins to emerge."

"What picture?" asked DeWitt, the motion of his hand indicating that he considered the results before him passable, but not overwhelming. "A pretty girl sneaked into somebody's bed under false pretenses. That's the only thing you've proved. Everything else is hints, conjectures, and statements that are no good unless corroborated."

"Well," said Troy, "it's a little more than that, isn't it? The 10 per cent racket of Loomis and Willoughby — good Lord, and we've come here to teach the Germans democracy!"

"Witness: Marianne Seckendorff — whom you've shown as an irresponsible liar."

"A Nazi hiding out at the Rintelen estate — Willoughby's own hangout, same place we can't pry loose from him."

"How do you know he's a Nazi?"

Yates said, "Well, he isn't Dehn! Dehn is dead!"

"But who is the man? Why hasn't he been picked up?"

Yates shrugged. "Sir, I felt this thing was too involved to go ahead without further orders from you."

"Oh, the old Army game! I've been in the Army too long to like it." DeWitt leaned forward, his hands spread powerfully. "There comes a time when you've got to strike out on your own, if you know what you're after. Do you know? What is it? Willoughby? The man at the manor house? Farrish? Or something bigger than all these men?"

Yates frowned. Running his hand through his hair, he said, "I don't know, sir. Things have been piling in on me tonight, sort of. I haven't had much time to think them out."

"Think them out! Go ahead!"

"I used to have warts. I burned one out — it came back, in the same spot or somewhere else. It's a pattern. Willoughby wouldn't have done what he did unless he thought he was one of many like him, unless he felt he could get away with it. He has certain ideas about why we came to Europe. We're the champions of free enterprise — free to do what is most profitable as long as nobody conks us over the head. I used to feel we had no program. He makes me think we have one. . . ."

Yates had been speaking quietly. He was watching whether DeWitt was going along with him or, at least, accepting his premise.

After a pause, DeWitt said, "You hate too much."

A slight smile was in Yates's eyes. "Learned it in the war, sir. I wouldn't want to forget it again for all the peace and comfort in the world."

"Let's get down to earth!" said DeWitt. "Do you think we have enough — as you put it — to conk those guys over the head?"

Yates remained serious. "I suppose we can have a local success."

"Then what are you waiting for?"

"I'm only a Lieutenant, sir — and at heart, a college instructor. And if, tomorrow, the General orders Hands Off?"

"Tomorrow is a long way off," said DeWitt. "Tomorrow I will see Farrish and some other people. Meanwhile, the night is yours."

He fetched the cognac bottle from his bag, took three small glasses from the table, filled them, and raised his own.

"To what will it be?"

"Home!" said Troy. He thought of Karen.

"The great crusade!" said Yates, wistfully.

DeWitt was very sober.

"The Army!" he said.

It was about one in the morning when Lämmlein arrived at the Rintelens' manor house. He found Pettinger still awake, raking up the fine gray ashes of papers burned in his fireplace.

"So you know already . . . ?" were Lämmlein's first words.

Pettinger pointed at the ashes. "Nothing new in my life!" He put aside the poker. "I hoped you'd come, *Herr Bürgermeister*. I'll need a local guide tonight. Pamela's been gone since eight. The Widow's completely bats —didn't you hear her fluttering?"

"Pamela's gone . . ." said Lämmlein.

He leaned against Pettinger's bed, his mouth open, his eyes popping — a man who's been trying to swallow too big a dumpling. Pamela's absence connected with Loomis's midnight warning. Lämmlein fidgeted. Why should Pamela have denounced him? She knew he was the sole protector of the Rintelens' interests!

Pettinger cried, "*Gott verdammt!* Don't stand there thunderstruck! Do something! You know this town! Where do I go?"

"You had a quarrel?" Lämmlein said tonelessly.

"Yes, of course! She's been grabbing at my Peter every other minute. Who can put up with that, months and months and forever?"

"Where's the girl, Marianne?"

"How do I know? Willoughby sent for her. She usually spends the night with him."

"You've been playing around with her, too?"

Pettinger snorted. "A man needs some relief!"

Lämmlein's hands were searching along his body, he didn't know for what, aimlessly.

"This is worse than I thought," he groaned. His abstinence from Party politics, his cultivation of Willoughby, all the work, all the dirt he'd had to eat—for nothing. Pettinger was the rotten slat that broke and set his scaffolds tumbling.

"You're no good for anything!" Pettinger was saying. "Get hold of yourself."

Lämmlein stared. His prostration turned into rage. "No good!" he screamed. "No good! Perhaps I invented your big ideas! Erich Pettinger, *Obersturmbannführer,* pretending to be the leader of the new Germany, the great politician playing one power against the other — but he can't even keep two women in line or control his own tail!"

For a moment, Pettinger was shocked by the attack from the meek little official.

"It's easy to be important and clever," Lämmlein continued to rail, "when you're in power! Anybody can do it, any postcard painter, any rabble rouser, any bum! But when you have no power — when you've got to be patient and wait and organize and plan — "

Pettinger slapped Lämmlein's face. Under the impact, the *Bürgermeister's* head sprang on its neck. The blow reduced Lämmlein to his proper status and re-established German discipline. The Mayor's face was ashen, except for the spot where Pettinger's hard hand had landed.

"I've killed people for saying less," informed Pettinger. "And just in case you have any notions of turning me over to the Americans and of using my body, neatly packaged, to get back in their good graces, let me throw some light on your position. Who palmed me off on Willoughby as Major Dehn? You did. So we're tied together and we'll hang together if they catch me. . . . I may be in a spot, I may even have gotten myself into it — but you're going to do everything to get me out. Is that understood?"

The extent of the catastrophe caught up with Lämmlein.

"Yes," he said.

"Well, take me somewhere!" ordered Pettinger.

"Where do you want to go?"

"I have no idea."

Lämmlein pleaded, "Willoughby's waiting for me!"

"Let him wait! Find a place in Kremmen. I've got to keep my contacts. We can't allow a thing like this to interfere with history!"

Lämmlein looked at him. History! The man was being driven from his last hiding place, by his own stupidity, and babbled of history! Yet there was something grandiose in Pettinger's attitude. Lämmlein trembled. A postcard painter had led him and his country to the height of their glory. What mattered was not what a man was, nor whether he was cornered — but the vision that was in him.

"I know a place," said Lämmlein: "the old air-raid shelter under Herr von Rintelen's bombed-out office. I'll take you there. You'll stay in it for about a week — then I'll bring you out of town."

Pettinger frowned.

"You'll miss the comforts of home!" confirmed Lämmlein, with a last flicker of insurrection.

Pettinger picked a fluffy, pink blanket from the foot end of his untouched bed.

Lämmlein hurried him, "The place hasn't been used since the war.

Haven't you got a flashlight? I think I have one in the car. Take two blankets. I'll manage to get some food to you. Come on, come on! . . ."

Out of the drawer of his small Victorian desk Pettinger took his Mauser pistol and ammunition. "You can use it as a rifle, too," he showed Lämmlein. "The wooden case serves as a stock, you see?"

Lämmlein glanced at the barrel gleaming in dull blue. "I hope you won't have to use it," he said from the heart. He wanted no shooting match. The only thing that could save his hide, office, and interests was Pettinger's complete, silent disappearance.

Pettinger didn't answer. Blankets over his arm, the cased pistol held in the hollow of his armpit, he walked down the stairs, into the main hall, past the Widow who sat, heavy, behind her husband's desk, shuffling through old ledgers.

Lämmlein, tripping along behind his leader, caught up with him and suggested, "You might take leave of Frau von Rintelen. She's been a very kind host, after all."

Pettinger stopped, turned, and looked. He saw the hulk of flesh, motionless. For a brief second, he glanced upwards at the portrait of the empire builder, Maxie with the grasping hands.

"Come on!" he said.

His pace quickened. By the time he reached the door, he was almost running.

Lämmlein had trouble keeping up with him.

I I

At NINE o'clock sharp, DeWitt drove up before the offices of Military Government, looked at the directory mounted next to the entrance, and walked up to the second floor. He moved down the corridor already filled with German petitioners, until he reached the door with the large, prominently lettered sign, V. Loomis, Capt., QMC, Economic Affairs — *Wirtschaft*.

He walked by the saluting Sergeant who held down the desk at the door, into Loomis's sanctum. Loomis had not yet arrived. DeWitt sat down in the Captain's chair behind the dark, smooth-finished desk. It was just as well that he was here first; let Loomis, after a night which could not have been too restful, have his morning surprise.

The phone rang. DeWitt didn't touch it. He heard the Sergeant outside answer the extension: "No, Colonel Willoughby, the Captain isn't here, yet. Thank you, sir. Yes, sir."

Willoughby was up and around; that was good, too. DeWitt wondered what actually went into the thinking of these people. Probably, nothing

out of the ordinary. It was just that, having won the war, they were setting up a new code for themselves, with many less restrictions than they
would have had at home or during the fighting. No, it couldn't be an entirely new code. Yates was right. Men form their morals and laws on the
basis of previous experiences, habits, customs. The seed of the flowers that
bloomed over here lay back in America. How could he expect these men
to sense, without help, that unlimited power does not mean unlimited
freedom? To some, war had been blood and pain and sorrow; to many
more, a bonanza. Now that no more blood was being shed, the pain let
up, the sorrow receded. Now that Victory offered its favors to everybody,
you were a fool not to take them. Where was his right to blame Loomis?

Loomis opened the door and stopped short as he saw the visitor.

"I've taken your chair," said DeWitt. "Sorry."

"Please keep it," said Loomis. "As long as you're comfortable, sir." He
hung up his hat, blouse, and weapon. He gave as much time to it as he
could. But he couldn't postpone forever the moment when he would have
to turn and face DeWitt.

"Sit down," said DeWitt.

It was odd being asked to sit down in your own office. To Loomis, it
was also an indication of his position — he was already being stripped of
his rights and privileges.

DeWitt saw the puffy, pasty texture of the Captain's face. The man
hadn't slept well, maybe not at all. The shadows under his eyes made them
appear small in their swollen lids.

"I haven't had coffee," said Loomis. "The Sergeant has an electric
heater, liberated, you know? Would you like some coffee?"

"No, thanks," said DeWitt.

With that, the generalities were exhausted. Loomis knew that DeWitt
would now come to the point.

DeWitt did it with particular kindliness. "I don't want to frighten you,
Loomis," he said, "I don't want to shock you into anything. We know that
there's been an ugly business. I mean that 10 per cent rakeoff that you've
been getting."

"It isn't true!" Loomis broke in. *You deny everything,* Willoughby had
said last night to Lämmlein and to him. *No matter how they ask you and
what they promise you, you deny everything. They haven't a shred of
proof.*

DeWitt raised his hand in mild rejection.

"But I swear to you, Colonel. . . ." *You deny everything and let me
worry about the rest.*

"Please, don't swear," said DeWitt.

"It's a vicious rumor, sir. The girl spread it because she wanted to get
even with Willoughby and me."

"Willoughby told you?"

"Yes, sir."

"What else did he tell you?"

"Nothing."

"Nothing?"

That DeWitt didn't threaten or shout, or lay down the law, unnerved Loomis. He bit his nails.

DeWitt thought: They don't even have the courage to stick by what they've done. Where's the great difference between them and the Germans?

"Sir, don't you think we should call in Colonel Willoughby? He'll be glad to confirm. . . ."

"Not yet, Loomis, not yet. I wish to talk first to you because, somehow, I feel that you have extenuating reasons. Will you permit me a few personal questions?"

Loomis nodded.

"What were you in civilian life, Loomis? You had a small radio store, right? You have a wife, right? You made a living?"

"Just about."

"And now your store is closed down?"

"The wife is keeping it open."

"Well, there are no radios to sell."

"No."

"And then you came overseas. You've had men under you, many men. Did you ever have any employees?"

"For a time I had one."

"But over here, as early as Normandy, you had power over more than a hundred people?"

"Yes."

"How did it feel?"

"Good."

"They had to do as you told them. How did that feel?"

"Good."

"There was a man named Tolachian. You ordered him to go out on a mission into the line. He did not return."

Loomis's limbs were lead, cold lead. He was glad he was sitting down. Reluctantly, he said, "But somebody had to go, sir! Somebody had to do the job!"

"You chose *him*. He was in your power. Then you came to Paris. How did that feel?"

"Good," Loomis admitted doubtfully.

"You had a good time. You had power over men and power over supplies — food, gasoline — that were scarce and therefore high in value.

Maybe you did a little business on the side. So many people were on the black market, why shouldn't you be?"

"It's not true, sir!"

"It's so long ago, Loomis. Nobody's going to hang you for it. I've almost forgotten it myself. Except that another man, Thorpe, went to pieces over it. Well, I suppose it couldn't be helped. And you had your power that you had to protect."

"He was cracked before that," said Loomis.

"You came to Luxemburg and the enemy attacked. You still had your power. But it wasn't much good under fire. You didn't want to risk it. You didn't want to risk even that small existence in a radio store, back in America. So you left."

"General Farrish's order," said Loomis. "And Colonel Willoughby sent me." But he didn't sound convincing. The picture DeWitt was drawing began to blot out Loomis's own image of himself. And DeWitt's picture tallied in many points with Loomis's own, except that it was sharper, deeper, with the sure brush that makes some paintings so superior to photographs.

"And finally, Germany. Instead of a few hundred men, you've power over tens of thousands. And you know that it's not going to last forever. Others may want to share your power; and the people you rule, at some time, will come back into their own, and you will go home, back to your radio store. But you won't be the same man in the same store, you've been in the war, you've grown older, and what have you got to show for it? You must make what little time you have, count. So there you are. It's all very understandable, very clear, even forgivable. It takes all sorts of people to make a war, and it's not your fault that you were pushed into your particular place. And if you study it now, after looking into yourself and at what you've done — " DeWitt smiled — "don't you find that most of the time you were pushed, not pushing, that you were forced into what you did, that you acted the way you did because any other choice would have been against your interests?"

"Yes," said Loomis, "that's true. I never wanted it. I was always unhappy if somebody suffered. But if they hadn't, I would have. . . ."

"It's the war, Loomis. It costs casualties. Tolachian, Thorpe, and now you, too, in a sense. But you're lucky. You're going to live. I cannot judge you too severely. Take me. I was your commanding officer. I, too, bear my share of responsibility for these things, and sometimes, I sleep badly. And I'll have a certain say in what's to be done with you. Will you co-operate with me?"

You deny everything, Willoughby had said. Loomis lowered his head. He looked at his knees, at his hands that rested on his knees, and he felt tired. He could never stand another night like the one he'd been through, running to stop one leak while tearing open another; seeking sympathy and help, and finding no one not equally frantic. Perhaps, DeWitt had cajoled him into this conclusion. But he preferred it that way. He wanted to rest.

"Yes," he said, in a thin voice, "I'll co-operate."

DeWitt lit a cigarette. "Let's not call the Sergeant. You can type? All right, here's the typewriter. You sit down here. Paper? Yes, and a copy. What do I want as heading? Well — the date. And then — no, don't call it confession. Just *Statement*. Ready?

"First paragraph: *The undersigned and Lieutenant Colonel Clarence Willoughby.* . . ."

It was hard for DeWitt to have to put Farrish through the wringer. In his way, the General was a magnificent soldier; besides, DeWitt had watched him grow from a Tank Battalion Commander to what he was now: The victor of Avranches and Metz, the liberator of Paula Camp, and the undisputed ruler of the Kremmen Dragoon Barracks.

DeWitt knew there was a blind spot in Farrish. His achievements in battle and the servility of the men with whom he surrounded himself had strapped blinders to the General's eyes so that he kept staring straight ahead, always ahead, with no chance to measure, to see slants, to moderate. In many ways, he was lovable; a big animal that couldn't help smashing things because it was so big; but no one had dared to muzzle and lead it; that was its danger to itself and to the world.

"You know," said Farrish, "there comes a time between one thing a man does and the next, when he likes to rest a while. Catch his breath. I've got everything down pat. It runs itself, almost. I wake up and listen to Reveille, and I know it'll be a well-ordered day, same as yesterday was, and same as tomorrow will be." He nodded to emphasize his words. "System! You've got to have a system! And you've got to have the right people working for you."

"That's exactly how I felt," said DeWitt. "When I came to Kremmen I said to myself: Now you're going to take a little break. Sit back and watch how things work out."

"Guess you earned it, old man."

"But things aren't working out so well."

"Having trouble? Anything I can do?"

"No. It's not me. You're having trouble."

Farrish laughed, his old, powerful, booming laugh. "You don't say! I'm sitting here, right on the spot, watching everything — and I'm having trouble?"

"You ought to have this Mayor of yours arrested," said DeWitt.

"Lämmlein?"

627

"Yes, I think that's his name."

"You've always liked to interfere in other people's affairs. Meddlesome. Maybe it comes with age."

"It's for your own good," said DeWitt, pocketing the slur. "He's making a fool of you. That wouldn't be so terrible. But he's making a fool of the things you were supposed to fight for, and of the things for which you sent thousands of your men to die."

Farrish's voice was grating. "Listen, DeWitt, no one's ever made a fool of me. I stake my reputation on that. I told you I was out hunting with the man; so I know him. I've picked every one of my officers from field grade up. I can judge people."

"Oh yes," said DeWitt, "and your Mayor lost his buck and smiled about it. Maybe he gave it to you?"

Farrish pulled at his chin, furiously. "Lämmlein's done everything Willoughby's ordered him to do. Look at this town! You've had enough time to see it! The streetcars are running, the main roads are cleared, it's got electricity, water, a sewage system, and business is starting up. It's the best God-damned town in Western Germany. I've seen others, believe me. Go out, compare!"

DeWitt said quietly, "And the man who runs the Public Utilities is the one who always did it. And the man at the head of the Welfare Office is the one who headed it under the Nazis. The very people whom you liberated out of Paula Camp live in a hovel that can only be called another concentration camp. And the Rintelen Works are still in the hands of the same Rintelens who furnished the stuff to kill off your men. You haven't brought any changes. You haven't brought any democracy here! What's going on? Who's holding down the lid?"

"Democracy . . . !" boomed Farrish. "You're just hepped on one subject! You want to turn everything upside down! What practical experience do you have? I've sat in on the discussions of the Chamber of Commerce! I know the problems! You think all Germans are bums and you can't trust 'em. But I've got to administer this district with what I have! A man's got to know his place and do what he's told to do! I look after the rest!"

"All right!" DeWitt sighed. "It seems I have to give it to you the hard way."

Farrish snorted.

"General, in your nice clean Dragoon Barracks, in your nice, comfortable apartment, you've been presiding over a nest of corruption that's falling apart right now, under your very eyes that never saw a sign of it. You don't see anything because you're smug as all hell, sitting on top of your victories and forgetting that they're not an end in themselves, but a means to an end. Well, maybe you didn't forget it. But the end that you have in

628

mind: to use them to climb higher, to become Senator or Governor of your State and maybe President of the whole United States — that's not the end that counts."

"Corruption!" croaked Farrish.

"Yes, corruption! You remember Metz? You remember your men who died because your gas was sold on the streets of Paris? Well, that's nothing compared to what's been going on here."

"You'd better back that up with facts!"

Farrish was shaken. Criticism was one thing — but this kind of attack on everything that was sacred to a man, was quite another! Come to think of it, he and DeWitt never had agreed on the things that mattered. He had won his battles in spite of DeWitt's opinions. And since when was it a crime to let yourself be drafted into politics? Politics! . . . And if DeWitt had the facts to back up his charges?

"Come on!" challenged Farrish, his voice strident. "Facts! Facts!"

DeWitt began to recount the course and the results of the investigation of Marianne Seckendorff. He described the confrontation of the girl and the Professor, from Troy's notes, and then, culling from Abramovici's transcript, Pamela's entrance, Marianne's breakdown, the recriminations, the denunciations —

"And there you have it, General. The unknown Nazi at the Rintelen estate, the whole set-up out at the manor house, directly and indirectly protected by Willoughby. Last night, my man Yates and Captain Troy went out to arrest the fellow hiding there — but he was gone. We don't know where he is. But we know who's involved in the 10 per cent racket: Your top MG officers and the man who let you have the buck, and who is in everything, in the administration of Kremmen, in the Chamber of Commerce, and in the Rintelen Works — your Lämmlein, your paragon of a good German."

"Hearsay!" boomed Farrish. He was out of his chair and pacing around DeWitt, as if he could wall him in with his steps, and so dam up the whole story. "Hearsay! A clever yarn. Based on the words of a hysterical, lying, jealous, criminal woman. Makes me laugh! I want facts, not rumors. I'm an American. I want the testimony of Americans, officers!"

"Call Willoughby," said DeWitt.

"I will! I will!" triumphed Farrish. He strode to the door and tore it open, shouting, "Carruthers! Carruthers!"

Carruthers came running.

"Take a car. Drive into town. Pick up Colonel Willoughby at MG. Immediately."

Carruthers twirled his mustache. "Pick up Colonel Willoughby," he repeated. "Immediately. Yes, sir."

Carruthers was gone, and the two men were alone again. DeWitt was depressed though he was coming close to achieving what he had set out to do. He saw how hard Farrish was trying to hold on to himself; the bristling white hair, the ruddy face were the mask behind which the man was fighting his doubts.

Farrish was blustering. "We'll get to the bottom of this in no time. I'll have you eat your words, DeWitt! Yes, sir! It isn't Willoughby, it isn't Lämmlein—" he was hammering at his chest below his ribbons—"it's me, me! I'll resign if it's true! I'm no good for this job if it's true!"

"Don't be so hasty. You've got a very good outfit here, and you're keeping it in good shape. You have your work cut out for you. . . ."

"Work!" jeered Farrish. "Any jerk can tell men to paint white and red bands on their helmets. I'm worth more than that! A hell of a lot more!"

DeWitt said nothing. He waited. Farrish, after a while, got tired of pacing through the room, and sat down. He was still attempting to keep up a front, but the veneer was transparent. He was thinking; he was adjusting himself to the possibility that DeWitt's accusations were true—and what was he going to do now? What were his next moves? Was he going to court-martial Willoughby? And how to replace him? And how to smooth out the whole mess so that Corps and Army and Supreme Headquarters didn't get too upset? And which superiors had to be talked to, how many were his friends? Who would raise a stink? On whom could he count? Things weren't as black as they had seemed. What was one little scandal in one town, when there were dozens of such towns under American occupation, each one, probably, with its own mess and thousands of men's fingers in ten thousand pies? It had been a big war, a hell of a big war. And Kremmen was in all likelihood still the best run town of them all.

He was fairly composed by the time Willoughby was brought in. Carruthers had enjoyed taking Farrish's orders literally and had treated Willoughby as if he were under some kind of arrest.

Willoughby protested Carruthers's action as soon as he had saluted the General. What was this disgusting and outrageous manner of Carruthers? Willoughby said he was conscious of no act on his part requiring it. This was the American Army, and where it stood was American soil, and in America a man was not found guilty until tried.

Farrish cut him short. "What's this I hear about a 10 per cent rakeoff, Willoughby?"

Willoughby, feeling relatively safe behind the fences he had mended last night with Loomis and Lämmlein, looked at the General with sad and amazed eyes. "Sir, I have never given you reason to doubt my loyalty. To me, you're the greatest man in this Army. I've felt that way since Normandy. In the Bulge Battle, I helped to save your life when the Germans of Operation Buzzard came through the line. Why do you doubt me now?"

Farrish became uncertain. And Willoughby was hewing to a line fixed by Farrish's own hopes. The General already visualized himself as a splendid statue and he didn't want it chipped.

"I have my reports," said Farrish, torn and unhappy.

Willoughby smiled mournfully. "Sir," he said to Farrish, "I'd hoped to spare you this. By God, you've got so many more important tasks that I thought it better not to bother you with petty, vicious rumors. Some people, particularly a certain Lieutenant Yates — he puts out the German newspaper in Kremmen — have been backstabbing me for the longest time."

Farrish frowned. He knew how it felt to be stabbed in the back.

"I've tried to be above such things," Willoughby went on. "I've offered my friendship to Yates on several occasions, explaining my viewpoints, requesting him to lay off. But the matter goes deeper. Yates has a bias against the constructive work that you, sir, and I are trying to do in this district. He's only interested in tearing down. He's a radical, a Red!"

Farrish reached for his whip and softly rapped its handle against the edge of his desk. "A Red, huh? So he doesn't like constructive work, huh?"

Willoughby stared meaningfully at DeWitt. "Unfortunately, General, he's found some support from your own friends. I'm sure Colonel DeWitt didn't mean to become a pawn in this conspiracy, but he was a natural for it ever since our difference of opinion on the closing of the Luxemburg radio station."

He waited, expecting DeWitt to break in. As DeWitt said nothing and didn't even look up, Willoughby continued, with less assurance, "You may recall, General, you yourself gave me orders to stop broadcasting during the Bulge and to save the unexpendable equipment of the transmitter. . . . Well, it seems that Yates has compiled and edited various rumors, originating mainly from German women. Sir, if you wish to question me on the basis of that kind of evidence, I stand ready to answer. But I don't think it should be necessary."

Farrish was profoundly uncomfortable. Had he been alone with Willoughby, he would have said to him: All right, go back to your office, you've got work to do.

But DeWitt sat there, like a Shylock.

"There's a man at the Rintelen estate. . . ." said Farrish.

"I know of him, sir. I've given orders for the man's arrest."

Farrish scratched his head with the tip of his whip. "But I know the man escaped!"

"We'll catch him, sir!" Willoughby said confidently.

Farrish coughed. "Well, then. . . ." He looked at DeWitt to see whether he would have to go on.

DeWitt was waiting, still waiting.

Farrish drew breath for a renewed attempt. "The 10 per cent, Willoughby, the 10 per cent!"

Willoughby stiffened. "Not a word of that is true!"

Farrish got up, put his whip next to his fountain pen and pencils, and beamed at DeWitt, "As far as I'm concerned, old man, I trust the word of an American officer more than that of some German trollop."

"You're a liar, Willoughby," said DeWitt.

Willoughby's paunchy face reddened. "I demand an apology!" he shouted. "I demand — General Farrish . . . !"

"Here," said DeWitt, pulling a paper out of his pocket, "I have the word of another American officer — a signed statement by Captain Loomis who, I understand, was involved with you in the whole deal. Let me read it to you, General. *Kremmen, today's date.* First paragraph: *The undersigned and Lieutenant Colonel Clarence Willoughby.* . . ."

It was a lengthy document. It gave the details of the operation, the date starting on which proceeds of the private tax leveled on all Kremmen business, large and small, were split between Loomis and Willoughby, the reasons for the split, the methods of collection, everything.

DeWitt read it through in a monotone. He felt no pleasure, no satisfaction in having felled Willoughby. If anything, he felt worn out, old, disgusted.

As the words followed one another, Willoughby seemed to sway. He grabbed hold of the back of a chair for support. Don't duck now! he thought. Stay put, keep standing, be steady. He saw things as from a great distance, sharply and in miniature. But soon enough his perception registered the General's face, ready to burst, the blue of his eyes effervescent against the lobster color. Willoughby's perception picked up speed. Farrish will shout, he'll rave, and then, what? He can't afford to do much; the more of this gets out, the more ridiculous it'll make him. And I've got the Rintelen shares.

The toneless, tired voice of DeWitt stopped. Willoughby heard Farrish say, "Yes. I see. Oh, yes." Pitiful. The great man had no words, couldn't even shout or threaten.

Then Farrish did shout. It took him some moments to collect the breath for it.

"Get out! Get out of here! Get out of Kremmen!"

"Yes, sir."

The breath was dissipated. The General's tone was thin, reedy. "I could have you court-martialed. But I don't want to dirty my fingers with this!

632

God damn it! I'll have you out of the ETO, out of everything! You report to Base Section, Colonel Willoughby!"

"Yes, sir!"

The way to Le Havre leads through Paris, Willoughby thought. In Paris was Yasha. He'd hand over the Rintelen shares to the Prince. It was a business transaction, legal and above board, and nobody could horn in on that. They imagined they had won — Yates, DeWitt, the whole faction of Crusaders. But they hadn't. They couldn't win. They would never win. He had always been one jump ahead of them, in war and in peace. Yes, sir.

"Out!" said Farrish.

Willoughby saluted smartly.

At the gate to the Barracks of the Kremmen Dragoons, he bummed a ride into town on a rations truck.

"Cigarette?" He offered his pack genially to the driver.

"Yes, sir, thank you, sir," said the man.

12

"PETTINGER," Yates said to Troy, "Erich Pettinger, Lieutenant Colonel of the SS, friend of Prince Yasha Bereskin, organizer of Operation Buzzard, the man who gave orders to have your captured men massacred in the Bulge Battle, the man who planned to have the people of Ensdorf suffocated in their mine — and there Lämmlein gave me the name. And he was so casual about it. . . . It was almost funny. Only I didn't feel funny. I felt my heart jump."

Yates had come directly from the arrest and interrogation of Lämmlein to Troy's room in the Kremmen *Polizei-Präsidium*. His face still showed traces of what had stirred in him when the last piece of the puzzle fell into place; his full, fine lips twitched occasionally, his dark eyes shone, the lines on his forehead refused to smooth out.

"How did you get him to talk?" asked Troy. "Lämmlein must have known what it would mean to him. . . ."

Yates looked at his hands, rubbing his index finger where the wart had been.

"I guess breaking men is a trade like any other. I knew he would crack when I told him that Willoughby was out. *And when the Governor goes, the Mayor goes, too?* he asked me. Then I let him know that General Farrish himself had ordered him arrested. Suddenly he was only a little man, standing alone. That's what did it."

"But the identity of Pettinger — " Troy strapped on his pistol belt. His chin was set. He thought of the soldier Sheal, clinging to him, after emerging from the pile of dead.

633

A feeling of great tiredness crept into Yates, as if the battery had nearly spent itself. "Through Loomis and the Widow, all Lämmlein's moves during last night were clear. I could tell him the time he hid Pettinger — so he told me the place. And once I had the dope on the air-raid shelter with its two exits, there was no point in his holding back Pettinger's name. Lämmlein was licked because he had no idea how little we really knew. And that's the end of it."

"I can't figure you out, Yates." Troy looked at him intently. "To me, this is maybe the biggest moment in the war. Once, in the Bulge, you promised me to help me find the guy who murdered my men — well, you've come through, and it's been a long time, and we've worked hard enough for it. Don't you feel anything?"

"We haven't got him yet," Yates said evasively.

"We'll get him!" Troy rose. "I never was so certain in my whole life. It makes sense. Somewhere, sometime, this war had to add up. . . ."

Yates smiled back, a thin, weary smile. "When that colorless individual said to me: 'Pettinger!' I thought for a moment, *This is it*. But, Troy — what's one man, even if you throw Willoughby into the bargain? It's only a beginning. When I got on the boat and we went down the Hudson and across, I didn't know I'd get into something that goes on and on. . . ."

For a minute, Troy was lost in thought. Then he pulled himself together and said, "Anyhow, let's go fetch the guy."

"Don't you want to call Karen and take her along?"

Troy understood Yates's suggestion. This expedition was his own final rehabilitation. But he declined, for her sake. "It might be a messy business."

They went with a dozen men, enough to cover both entrances to the Rintelen air-raid shelter. They had along the wretched Lämmlein who, in his correct but sweated business suit, looked oddly out of place among the armed and steel-helmeted soldiers.

They drove through the main gate of the Rintelen Works, following a road that had been hacked into the jungle of rust-eaten, gnarled steel, of broken and split concrete. They saw the gangs of workmen cleaning up — Lämmlein had begun in earnest to rebuild the Rintelens' empire. The office building once stood to the right of this road; only its shell was still there: Three walls, the fourth almost entirely collapsed.

The shelter entrance was around the corner, partially hidden by debris — a hole, half the size of a man.

Troy took charge.

"You stay here with five men," he said to Yates. "I'll take the others around and block the other exit of the shelter."

The men tumbled down from the big truck. "You'd better get ready to fire," ordered Troy. "The man in there is armed; I want no casualties."

Then he took off, followed by the half-squad who were to complete the trap. Yates saw Troy and his men weave in and out of the rubble, bobbing up and disappearing again, bobbing up once more, and finally nothing — only the sunlit, empty desert of ruins. He choked down a sigh. It wasn't that he was moved for himself. He had ceded to Troy his own rights to Pettinger. But there was something beautifully fateful in the picture of Troy once more leading soldiers, leading them in this last, personal reckoning — it gripped you and held you and gave you the slight shiver you experienced during Beethoven's Fifth, or a sunset after a thunderstorm.

Then Troy came back, alone.

"Found the place," he reported. "All set."

Yates called Lämmlein from the truck where he had been retained under the driver's guard.

"You'll go in there," he said. "Tell Pettinger that the game is up. Tell him to come out, quietly, without arms. We prefer to settle this matter without bloodshed. But we're prepared to shoot him to bits if he makes any trouble. Tell him that."

Lämmlein shook his head. He was unable to speak. He was unable to move. Yates must see that. Why did he demand the impossible?

"Herr Lämmlein," said Yates, "we won't send in any of our own men. You don't expect us to do that, do you? You put him in there, you get him out."

Lämmlein stared vaguely. He saw in Yates's eyes the same hardness that had overpowered him during the questioning. Oh, he had held his own; to each question he had had an answer proving decisively that someone else was to blame. Except for Pettinger. Pettinger had left him holding the bag. Lämmlein swallowed. And so he had confessed, had given away everything, had given away himself.

He heard Troy say evenly, "Get going! I'd hate to have to make you get going."

All right, all right — he was going. Slowly, tortuously, Lämmlein walked toward and into the dark, yawning hole.

Outside, they waited. The sun was broiling. The soldiers, their rifles pointed in the direction of the shelter, seemed to waver in the shimmering, dry, dust-saturated air. A faint, musky smell of decay was rising from the ground.

Yates and Troy were listening. But no sound came from the shelter. Pettinger must be hiding deep inside; it must be taking Lämmlein some time to reach the man in the cave.

"You don't think he fooled us?" said Troy. "Perhaps there's a third exit, and the two gents have skipped and are laughing their heads off?"

"No," said Yates, "I had the layout checked."

"Perhaps Pettinger is keeping Lämmlein down there, as a hostage or something?"

635

"He'd make a hell of a mistake," said Yates. "He'd overestimate considerably the value Lämmlein has to us. And he must know that we'll push in there some time or other. . . ."

"Perhaps Pettinger's gone long ago; Lämmlein can't find him, and the damned fool is so afraid of us that he doesn't dare to come up? . . ."

The crack of a shot. It seemed far off, and it was followed by a low rumbling.

The soldiers tensed.

Then a face appeared at the entrance, deathly pale, a gaping, distorted mouth. Lämmlein was able to pull himself out before he collapsed.

"Medic!" cried Troy.

Blood was trickling from Lämmlein's abdomen, he was writhing in pain, bubbling foam stood on his lips, his eyes were turned up, only their yellowish whites stared blindly.

"Give him a shot!" said Troy.

The medic was cutting open the sleeve of Lämmlein's suit. He jabbed in the needle. Lämmlein began to breathe more regularly. He was trying to form words, now; Yates put his ear close to the thin, colorless lips.

"Can't — control his — tail. . . ." Followed by angry, painful coughing. Maybe Lämmlein was laughing at something, but what it was, Yates couldn't make out. "Come out — shoot, go ahead — shoot — can't control — nothing. . . ."

"He's no help," said Yates. "Can't you stop the bleeding, Corporal?"

"No, sir."

"You'd better get an ambulance," said Troy.

The medic left.

"What'll we do now?" Troy seemed angry, or disappointed, or both.

Yates got up. "Two men!" he called. And, turning to Troy, he said quietly, "I'll go in. It'll be a pleasure to shoot it out."

Two men had come up to them and placed themselves close to Yates.

"Let me handle this," said Troy. "I told you I won't have any casualties. Not this time. He isn't worth any one of you getting so much as a scratch on the knee!" He stared at the dark hole of the shelter's entrance.

Yates followed his eyes; and he suddenly thought of the people of Ensdorf.

Finally, Troy seemed to have made up his mind. He waved to the driver, and the man ambled over. "Do you still happen to have your breaching charges?"

"Breaching charges . . . ?" the driver said; then the slow light of understanding went over his face. They had issued him the stuff in Normandy, four bags with eighteen half-pound blocks of TNT in each, to be used to blast the way for his truck through the hedgerows. He had almost forgotten about them, since TNT was all right as long as no cap was inside it; forgotten, the bags had rested in a corner under his seat all this time.

"Shall I bring them over, sir?" he asked.

"I wish you would."

The driver went to his truck and returned, a bag under each arm, the caps and fuses in his pocket. Troy placed one of the bags on the top step leading down to the shelter. He slipped the fuse into the cap. The driver pulled a pair of pliers out of his pocket. Troy crimped the cap to the fuse, then he inserted the cap into the well of the center block of the breaching charge.

"There!" he said, measuring off about three feet of the fuse, cutting it, and handing the end to Yates. "That'll do. What time do you have, Yates —exactly?"

Yates said it was 1618.

"Sixteen eighteen," said Troy, adjusting his watch. "Give me fifteen minutes on the dot. Then you light the fuse. You've got a minute and a half to make it back to the truck." He smiled. "Good enough?"

"Good enough," said Yates, taking the fuse from Troy.

Troy picked up the second bag of TNT, and began his climb to the shelter's other exit. Yates waited. The ambulance came. Lämmlein, unconscious, was lifted on a stretcher and taken away. The minutes dragged. You have too much time for your thoughts in such minutes. Thoughts of the man who'd be shut in down there, and who would have to wait, too, an interminably longer time, feeling the hunger he had brought to other people; the maddening thirst; the hopeless cold; the cold of hopelessness; the stifling, immovable air growing thicker; the body weakening; sleep, long hours of sleep with dreams that would sit on his chest and clamp on his heart till he awoke clammy with sweat; until he fell into the last, terrible sleep. Or he would go mad with fear and desperation and not know. And how long would it take him to realize and believe that this was the end, that the tunnel, blocked on both sides, was sealed forever?

Anyhow, thought Yates, the man was lucky. He had a gun. He could end it fast. But he wouldn't. Because he would hope, and hope. . . .

Time, also, for Yates to think about himself. This thing he would do, this simple lighting of a match, was like a black double line ending an account. You could look at the balance. There was much written in red, and much he would wish to blot out, never tell anyone, not even Ruth. This thing he was going to do, he would not be able to tell, back at home — they would stare at him: What was he? Still one of theirs, teaching advanced German B, drinking tea with them in the social room, making conversation with Archer Lytell, the Head of the Department?

No, he would tell Ruth. If any person on earth, she would understand him. All he had done from the day he had touched ground in Normandy, he had done for her, too — unwillingly, grudgingly, reluctantly, still he had done it, for her and for himself, both. He longed to tell her about it — about the lighting of this match, about everything, from the beginning. It was too much to keep locked inside; it would drive him crazy if it remained locked up; it had to be put into words, it had to be said. What good is what you have learned if only you know of it?

He looked at his watch. It was time.

He ordered the men away. He struck the match, cupped it in his hand, held it to the fuse, and, for a moment, watched the fire eat its way. Then, with deliberate slowness, he turned and walked to the truck.

The seconds . . .

Then the crash and the rumbling and the dust. And the answering crash from Troy's end.

It was done.

13

"HEAVE-HO!"

"Heave-ho!"

They were hoisting the Widow on the old truck.

It was a last resort. At first they had set up a ladder for her to climb. She had put her small feet on the bottom rung, and then despairingly stepped onto the ground again. She had stood there, a great, trembling hulk, her head low, her eyes downcast. And now three soldiers struggled to lift her, while two, on the truck, held on to her arms and pulled. The truck was of the wood-burning kind, with the burner mounted on the rear; and it wasn't just the feat of hoisting the Widow — she had to be squeezed past the burner as well.

She did not struggle. She stared vacantly at the two soldiers straining above her. Without her being conscious of it, tears ran down the mounds that were her cheeks and lost themselves in the tier of folds that was her chin. The soldiers weren't hurting her; something more than her body was in pain. Everything she had lived for, the whole meaning of her life, lay back across the green lawn, behind the hushed, watching crowd, inside the House that Maximilian von Rintelen had built for her, and which she was losing, irreclaimably and finally, with each hoist and pull. The birdlike cries fluttering in her throat died there.

At last she was on the truck. The soldiers helped her into the chair behind the desk that had been her husband's. Her huge arms fell on the flat top, and her useless hands curled over its edges as if she were trying to make it one with her flesh and bulk.

Karen, who with Troy was watching the procedure, felt the tragedy of the old woman. The Widow was no longer the glittering tub who represented what Troy and Yates had been fighting. She was derobed of her splendor, a mountain of despair. Involuntarily, Karen started for the truck.

Pamela's outbreak of obscenities stopped her and throttled whatever she wanted to say. Pamela, now being forced to get on the truck, was screaming her curses broadside — at the Americans; at the people from the Lower Depths helping to load the personal belongings permitted her mother and herself; at the slyly leering Cornelius who was returning to Holland and who had come to say good-by; at the world; at the day she was born; at the day Pettinger had come into the manor house.

She saw Karen step forward. "Bitch!" she shrilled.

Troy made a move toward the truck. But he stopped. Without a word, he and Karen understood one another. To talk to the Widow was meaningless — as meaningless as Pamela's obscenities, as meaningless as the two gross women being carted off into anonymity.

"Where will they go?" Karen asked.

Troy shrugged.

The truck began to move. The outlines of the two women became blurred by the thick smoke of the burner. Silence followed the departure. It lasted until the truck was out of sight. Then the crowd broke up. The former inmates of the Lower Depths streamed into the manor house, in an orgy of seizure.

Troy led Karen past the empty stables and garages, past the cottages of the help, each cottage a complete house with kitchen and every other facility.

"We haven't much time," Karen said with a tender regret. "Farrish is here, tassels and all. . . ."

"Oh, we've got a few minutes!" Troy was both happy and grave, and his voice was husky as he told Karen, "Look at all this! And what we're going to do with it! We're going to put the people in the manor house and the cottages, and we'll convert the stables and garages into living quarters and workshops. If necessary, we'll set up some Quonset huts on the lawns."

He spoke like a builder, a sensible American seeing a job to be done, a job that interested him. Karen pressed his hand.

"When I go back to America," he went on, "I want to settle down. I'm going to build me a house. I'm going to settle down and live and forget."

"You won't be able to forget."

"No. I guess I won't. But I'm going to build that house. I can work hard, Karen. You don't know how hard I can work if I see what it's for and that something comes of it."

She looked at the garden, the woods in the distance, the rolling land, the horizon fringed with the smokestacks of Kremmen. She looked at the manor house, which was like a fortress he had taken. And she looked up at the man next to her, his quiet, strong, waiting face. She thought of the war and how it had ended. And she thought that the time had come when life would be bearable only alongside such a man.

"Will you live with me?" he asked calmly.

"Yes."

"You and I, together?"

"Yes."

"You're sure, Karen? This is for keeps — "

In answer, she turned to him. His kiss was harsh and tight-lipped, and she felt his hard chin.

"Darling," she whispered, "*this* is how you do it. . . ."

Then he took her back to the manor house, his steps unhurried and firm. It was to Karen as if he carried her.

It had been decided that Professor Seckendorff would speak for the people from the Lower Depths, and that Abramovici would translate the salient parts of his speech for the American military authorities present in the hall of the manor house.

That a broken old man with no future of his own should take over in the name of the future, held a sad symbolism for DeWitt. He could feel the dignity that lay in the slow-spoken words which he did not understand; he sensed the passion, born from suffering, which penetrated them; but it was the dark red fire of dying embers. DeWitt looked around, from Kellermann, who had escorted the Professor to the foot of the stairs and waited there, to the huddled mass of hollow-cheeked men and women who, by the grace of the Americans and a quirk of fate, had become the owners of the estate. Their awe was probably a token of their fear of the Americans rather than of the speaker's effect on them. Were they thinking that they had rotted in concentration camps or suffered the humiliation of the Lower Depths so that others could have the life in the manor house? Hardly, thought DeWitt. If contrasts grow too big, they lose their significance; the dirt farmer doesn't hate the bank, he hates the sheriff who forecloses on him.

Abramovici's blaring voice broke the mood. The words, now denied the emotion the Professor had given them, fell stridently, with each thought taking on the lusterless reality of fact.

"This House is a community experiment," Abramovici said, "much as the concentration camp was one. We survived concentration camp because we helped one another, because we worked with, and not against, one another."

Abramovici paused. DeWitt saw the little man scanning his notes in order to pick the next points. The Colonel wished he had understood the Professor.

"What else did we learn in concentration camp? We learned that the enemy does not necessarily come from across any front lines or any borders. What do we want, what have we always wanted? A country in which men and women can live free of fear, secure in their lives, their ideas, and the fruits of their work. In Germany, the enemy of the kind of life we want has suffered a defeat; but he has not been crushed—"

DeWitt's eyes wandered back to the people from the Lower Depths. Their enemy had been Germans, like themselves.

"That enemy is not limited by borders," Abramovici trumpeted, "Germany's or any other country's. Let us consider this House as a school that will turn out fighters against that enemy, wherever he hides. . . ."

Suddenly, DeWitt was conscious of the impatient tapping of Farrish's boot. He saw Abramovici fold up his papers and, flushed and happy, return to the American ranks. Then Farrish walked up the stairs with deliberate tread. He took his stand next to the flag that was mounted where Maximilian von Rintelen's portrait had hung. He looked down at his audience — the Americans to one side, the bedraggled Germans crowded on the other. His hands fumbled; he missed his whip.

"I've had my eyes on this estate for the longest time," Farrish said. "I thought, This is just the place we need for you people. I've always been one to look out for the interests of the common man. Not that I'm a man of theories and great ideas. I don't know the first thing about them. I'm just a soldier. But I see what has to be done and I go ahead and do it. That's how I won my battles. That's how we won the war. So I went ahead and got you this house. But remember, it is American property. Wherever we stand, there's America, the greatest country on earth, and we stand for no nonsense. What the Professor here has said is well and good, and I approve of it. I've always approved of noble sentiments. But with all of that, a person's got to know his place. . . ."

DeWitt glanced at Yates. He motioned his head slightly, toward the door. The two tiptoed out as Farrish continued.

"Couldn't stand it," said DeWitt.

They sat down on a stone bench close to the entrance of the manor house.

"I'm sure he saw us go out," said Yates.

DeWitt shrugged. "I'm going back to the States, anyhow. I've asked to be retired. Just the right, ripe age. And the war has been won, after a fashion."

"There's still so much to do," Yates said. Out of the corner of his eye, he observed the Colonel. DeWitt looked old.

"I know there's a lot to be done," agreed DeWitt, "but now, you'll be able to handle it without me, I guess. You and Troy and anyone here with some integrity, some honesty and purpose."

Yates considered that. He knew the Old Man was right. He was able to be on his own and could deal with what came his way. He had graduated.

"You see," DeWitt went on, "when the Willoughby question came up, Farrish promised to quit if I proved that he was making a mess of it. And we proved it to him. He didn't have the guts to come through. Great, big Farrish! He didn't have the guts to admit that he was wrong and not the man for building the world we fought for. I said to him, 'General, there just isn't enough room here for the both of us.' He laughed. You know how he laughs; I used to like it, used to think it was a good, strong man's laugh — but it isn't. And when he stopped laughing, he said, 'All right, old man, then *you* go.' So I'm going. . . ."

Yates said, "You're sure, sir, that you're doing the right thing?"

DeWitt picked up a pebble and threw it away.

"No," he said, "the trouble is I'm not sure at all. However, it doesn't make much difference where you are, these days. Good man, your Professor! While Abramovici told us what he'd said, I kept thinking: If that enemy ever won out in our country, I'd end up in a concentration camp, too."

"I'd be proud to meet you there, again," said Yates.

The ceremony seemed to have ended. The General was coming out of the manor house. He looked at DeWitt and Yates, sitting on their bench. His mouth set in an angry line, but he said nothing.